MARKETING CHANNELS

Prentice-Hall International Series in Management

ATHOS, COFFEY, and RAYNOLDS	*Behavior in Organizations: A Multidimensional View, 2nd ed.*
BALLOU	*Business Logistics Management*
BAUMOL	*Economic Theory and Operations Analysis, 4th ed.*
BOLCH and HUANG	*Multivariate Statistical Methods for Business and Economics*
BOOT	*Mathematical Reasoning in Economics and Management Science: Twelve Topics*
CHURCHMAN	*Prediction and Optimal Decision: Philosophical Issues of a Science of Values*
COHEN and CYERT	*Theory of the Firm: Resource Allocation in a Market Economy, 2nd ed.*
CULLMAN and KNUDSON	*Management Problems in International Environments*
CYERT and MARCH	*A Behavioral Theory of the Firm*
FABRYCKY and TORGERSEN	*Operations Economy: Industrial Applications of Operations Research*
GREEN and TULL	*Research for Marketing Decisions, 3rd ed.*
HADLEY and WHITIN	*Analysis of Inventory Systems*
HOLT, MODIGLIANI, MUTH, and SIMON	*Planning Production, Inventories, and Work Force*
KAUFMANN	*Methods and Models of Operations Research*
KEEGAN	*Multinational Marketing Management*
MANTEL	*Cases in Managerial Decisions*

MARKETING CHANNELS

LOUIS W. STERN

A. Montgomery Ward Professor of Marketing
Northwestern University

ADEL I. EL-ANSARY

Professor of Marketing and Business Administration
The George Washington University

Prentice-Hall, Inc., Englewood Cliffs, New Jersey 07632

Library of Congress Cataloging in Publication Data

STERN, LOUIS W. (date)
   Marketing channels.

   (Prentice-Hall series in international management)
   Includes bibliographical references and index.
   1. Marketing channels. I. El-Ansary, Adel I.,
joint author. II. Title.
HF5415.125.S76   658.8'4   76-23417
ISBN 0-13-557124-3

10 9 8 7 6 5 4

Printed in the United States of America

Prentice-Hall International, Inc., *London*
Prentice-Hall of Australia Pty. Limited, *Sydney*
Prentice-Hall of Canada, Ltd., *Toronto*
Prentice-Hall of India Private Limited, *New Delhi*
Prentice-Hall of Japan, Inc., *Tokyo*
Prentice-Hall of Southeast Asia Pte. Ltd., *Singapore*
Whitehall Books Limited, *Wellington, New Zealand*

CONTENTS

PREFACE

Of all the various elements of the marketing mix that are employed in facilitating the exchange of goods and services, perhaps the most unique to the study of marketing are the organization and design of effective and efficient channels of distribution. Discussions of pricing have their antecedents in the field of economics. Understanding promotion and persuasion demands a strong foundation in psychology and sociology. Discussions of product policy have been generated from a combination of findings from fields as diverse as engineering, economics, and the behavioral sciences. But in order to find any comprehensive statements of theory and practice with regard to marketing channels, one must generally turn to the marketing literature. This is not to say that individuals from other fields have not made significant contributions to an understanding of channels. Certainly, institutional economists, operations management scholars, geographers, and even some political scientists have explored interactions among various levels of distribution and problems that are unique to the distribution function. But concentrated attention to the interrelationships among the organizations (e.g., producers and middlemen) that are involved in moving products and services from their points of origin to their points of consumption has emanated, almost solely, from the work of marketing scholars and practitioners.

In light of this originality, it is highly surprising, indeed, that so few individuals have directed their attention to synthesizing the various writings on marketing channels over the years in the form of a textbook for use in classrooms or for reference in practice. Perhaps one of the primary reasons for this void is the fact that no overall cohesive and appealing analytical framework has been developed which has spurred the introduction of such a text. Although several important frameworks based on classical economic models or on game theory have been formulated, none seems to have provided the impetus for a comprehensive statement of channel practice and management. Unfortunately, because of their limiting assumptions, many of the analytical models presently available fail to capture the exciting behavioral dynamics of the marketplace and thus are less rooted in reality than they otherwise might be.

Clearly, there exists both a practical and a scientific need for a better illumination of the behavioral dimensions of the distribution process. Although there can be no doubt that economic incentives provide the major motivation for many of the organizations engaged in the process, there is also no doubt that the way in which the wide variety of distributive relationships are forged and maintained is a key determinant in accomplishing the task of making goods and services available for consumption. A series of complex social interactions is critical to the success of any one organization in its efforts to serve its clients better. Because of the complexity and significance of these interactions, marketing channels—that is, the networks of institutions involved in the distributive process—can be analyzed more completely when they are viewed as social systems. Placing the emphasis exclusively on the economic incentives inherent and manipulated in them is myopic. This understanding is particularly important when attention is turned to the channels for nonprofit and publicly financed services.

This text concentrates on providing a full and deep treatment of the *political, social,* and *economic relationships* among the various institutions and agencies comprising marketing channels. In doing so, it focuses on the variety of means available for securing effective management in the distribution of goods and services. The text underscores the need for *interorganization management* through the use of approaches, frameworks, and perspectives that have been developed and investigated in such fields as political science and international relations, sociology, psychology, organizational behavior, and economics. Understanding the management of channel relationships is the center of the analysis, and the marketing channel, as a whole, is viewed as the relevant unit of competition. The approach adopted is systems-managerial.

Furthermore, this text is both descriptive and prescriptive. That is, there are descriptions of what takes place within channels and how channels are organized as well as discussions concerning how channels should be organized. Because the emphasis is on the development of effective methods of inter-organization management within *commercial channels* of distribution (i.e., *the set of institutions and agencies, exclusive of ultimate consumers or end-users, that is responsible for making goods and services available for consumption*), a normative theme is present throughout. While descriptive material is necessary in order for the reader to develop an appropriate perspective of the opportunities and constraints provided by situational and environmental factors, the text has a more grandiose goal than merely describing present practice. The hope is that the interorganizational framework also provides a blueprint for even more efficient and effective channel organization—especially from a managerial perspective—than currently exists, as well as an exciting, intellectually challenging analytical approach to distribution questions.

In fact, it would not be exaggerating too much to say that a great deal of the existing literature dealing with distributive institutions, such as retailing and wholesaling establishments, could be classified as nonanalytical, anecdotal, overly descriptive, or downright boring. One of the major purposes of this text is to place the analysis of marketing channels back in the mainstream of marketing studies. Due to the lack of intellectual challenge provided by much of the existing literature, there has been a dramatic shifting away, in the academic world especially, from institutionally oriented studies to studies dealing with consumer behavior, mathematical modeling of decision making, or social marketing. However, no matter what the orientation of the marketing scholar, there is absolutely no doubt that distributive institutions are vital in the marketing process. Therefore, the need is clear: undergraduate and graduate students and marketing scholars must have a fresh, insightful, stimulating, and useful approach in order to awaken more interest in finding solutions to distributive problems that are critical to all of marketing. And practitioners must have broader models than the economic ones with which they have been dealing if they are going to cope adequately with the challenge of the 1980's and beyond. Perhaps for these reasons, more than any others, this text was written.

The text contains fourteen chapters. The first chapter, "Marketing Channels as Interorganization Systems," provides a broad overview of the framework adopted for organizing channels. It briefly introduces the reader to the relevant behavioral dimensions involved in interorganization management as well as the marketing flows that are inherent in the distribution process. Chapters 2 and 3 basically describe the structure, competition, and dominant management modes within retailing and wholesaling, while Chapter 4 provides an overview of the management of physical distribution activities by channel members. In Chapter 4, considerable discussion is devoted to the determination of customer service standards and inventory policies, as well as to an examination of the various warehousing and transportation alternatives available to channel members. In some cases, where readers have had an adequate background, it may be possible either to skim Chapters 2 through 4 or to read them selectively. The chapters have, however, been included in the text so that those readers without such a background can acquire the needed knowledge relatively easily. It should be noted, though, that Chapters 2 and 4 are quite lengthy. *The reader is advised not to attempt to cover either chapter in one sitting.* There are logical breakpoints found halfway through each, i.e., page 59 in Chapter 2 and page 178 in Chapter 4.

Chapter 5, "Channel Structure and Institutional Change," explores theories that describe why channels have emerged and take the shape that they do as well as why specific institutions within channel systems have altered over time. Chapter 6 is devoted to an assessment of the performance of channels and the institutions comprising them. It incorporates both a broad, societal viewpoint and a managerial or "micro" viewpoint.

Chapters 2 through 6, then, provide the basic background and description needed for understanding the working of channels. In Chapter 7, the focus turns to the opportunities for interorganization management. In fact, Chapter 7 represents an elaboration of the perspective introduced in Chapter 1. It deals with the need for role specification, the use of power, conflict management, channel leadership, and effective communication within channels. Chapter 8 describes the legal constraints on interorganization management, generally, and, in particular, the limitations on the use of social and economic power in channel systems.

Chapters 9 and 10 focus on how the principles of interorganization management have or might be implemented. Chapter 9 deals with the setting of various policies within channels, while Chapter 10 discusses and describes vertical marketing systems of all types—administered, contractual, and corporate. In Chapter 11, attention is turned to the question of channel leadership and a discussion of which institutions are likely to be in the best position to allocate resources within channels.

Given the need for effective communications within channel systems, as established in Chapters 7, 9, and 10 in particular, considerable attention is devoted to this topic in Chapter 12, which examines communications problems and the development of information systems. Chapter 13 provides a description of the marketing channels in international markets. Chapter 14 is devoted to a discussion of the marketing channels for the variety of services provided by profit-oriented, nonprofit, and publicly financed organizations.

ACKNOWLEDGMENTS

There are three sets of individuals who have deeply influenced the structure and content of this book. Although there is some overlap in the sets, one group has operated primarily in support and encouragement of the first author of this book, another has aided the second author, and the third has been important to both authors.

The first author is deeply indebted to his colleagues at Northwestern University and his former colleagues at The Ohio State University for their stimulation and interest. Most particularly, he is thankful and appreciative for the contributions made to the development of the approach taken throughout much of this book by a number of doctoral students over the years. Brian Sternthal, C. Samuel Craig, Larry Rosenberg, Jay Brown, Lynn Gill, Frederick Beier, Robert Schulz, Ernest Cadotte, David Hunger, Mahmoud Triki, Neil Maddox, Fuat Firat, Alice Tybout, Robert Spekman, Jack Kasulis, Reinhard Angelmar, Richard Bagozzi, and Robert Tamilia were, along with the second author, instrumental in the effort to formulate an interorganizational perspective relative to marketing channels. The efforts of two Northwestern Ph.D. students—Ruby Roy Dholakia and Lynn W. Phillips—had an incalculably high effect on the manuscript as it progressed towards completion. In fact, Lynn Phillips played a major role in the revising of a number of chapters in the book. Patricia Simmie's proofreading of the galleys was also very helpful. And the patience, thoroughness, and speed of Marion Davis, Jane Marks, and Sabra Van Cleef in typing the manuscript were significant factors in its preparation. Thanks also go to Richard Kilmer, Ted Skoglund, Michael Weston, and the late LeRoy Timon for their strong belief in the need for interorganization management in marketing. All of these people, and many more, are owed a great deal for their contributions. Deep and affectionate appreciation go to his family and especially to his mother for their support as well as their continuous and unwavering advocacy.

The second author acknowledges the valuable feedback provided by his undergraduate and graduate students at Louisiana State University who read early drafts of the text as a part of their assignments in channel courses and seminars offered throughout 1972-1975. He is particularly appreciative of the comments supplied by Robert Robicheaux and Joseph Abramson, and the capable research assistance of Andy Dimerdjian, Mustafa Razian, Deborah Babin and Abramson and is grateful to Gloria Armistead for her expert typing assistance. He acknowledges, with deep gratitude, the support of his wife, Nawal, who provided encouragement, typed some of the early drafts, and sacrificed many vacations along the way. His sons, Waleed and Tarik, deserve special mention. Waleed's timely interruptions often brought with them needed diversions, while Tarik occasionally destroyed some pages, which forced some new writing and fresher thoughts.

Finally, both authors owe a great deal to such scholars as Wroe Alderson, Louis P. Bucklin, James L. Heskett, Stanley Hollander, Philip Kotler, Bert C. McCammon, and a host of other luminaries in the field of marketing on whose work they have heavily relied throughout this text.

MARKETING CHANNELS

ONE

MARKETING CHANNELS AS INTERORGANIZATION SYSTEMS

When a consumer walks into a local furniture store to purchase a new sofa, armchair, or bedroom suite, it is unlikely that he or she has been fore-warned, prior to his/her visit, that delivery on the furniture will take an average of ten weeks and, in not atypical cases, as much as four to five months. If the consumer were to seek out a reason as to why this lengthy waiting time exists, the response would be very predictable. Depending upon to whom in the marketing channel the question was directed, the answer would likely entail placing the blame for delayed delivery on the "other parties" involved in the product's distribution. In actuality, the answer is relatively complex, and at its core are systemic issues relating to the ineffective interorganization management of the distribution channels for household furniture.[1] Specifically, furniture manufacturers face strained production capability due to (1) increases in demand that are not accurately projected, (2) long lead times (two to six months) needed to obtain uphol-stery materials from fabric mills, and (3) labor shortages in North Carolina and Virginia, where many of the major furniture production centers are lo-cated. On the other hand, the traditional furniture retailer believes that the manufacturer is giving preferential treatment to the large furniture "ware-house" dealers, such as Levitz and Wickes, and therefore indirectly is dis-criminating against his customers. Differences in treatment would not be

---

[1] Stanley H. Slom, "Need Some Furniture? Better Plan Sitting on the Floor Awhile," *Wall Street Jour-nal*, Vol. 50, No. 87 (November 2, 1972), p. 1.

unjustified, however, because the traditional furniture retailer has generally shied away from assuming any risk or financial burden associated with holding inventory. Rather, he places orders with the manufacturers when he has an order in hand from his customer.

The scenario in the furniture industry is reenacted countless times in different settings every day. Distribution channels for the delivery of such essentials as health services, automobiles, food, governmental services (e.g., garbage collection, mass transit), and financial services (e.g., mortgage loans) are often managed ineffectively and inefficiently, a situation resulting in not only an enormous loss of resources but in a disgruntled and disaffected consumer who seemingly is caught up and put upon by forces which he/she cannot control. The solution lies, it appears, not only in adopting consumer-oriented objectives and programs but in managing the systems responsible for the delivery of the objectives and programs in a more satisfactory manner.

The need for effective distribution systems management is especially crucial as economies move into periods of stunted growth. As new market opportunities decrease for many industries, numerous companies shift their marketing strategies away from expanding total market demand and toward building market share within their existing markets.[2] Such a situation forces, in turn, a reassessment of many corporate functions, particularly distribution. Although marketing strategies and tactics have traditionally been developed by management on the basis of a study of ultimate consumer or end-user needs, environmental contingencies are likely to compel deeper attention to distribution problems. For example, it has been predicted that, in periods of low economic growth, there is likely to be "a shift away from what the consumer wants and more critical emphasis on establishing a relationship with the jobber, wholesaler, and retailer . . . Instead of asking what kind of toothbrushes the consumer wants, one must go to Kresge, Sears, and the drug stores and find out what kind of packaging, display cases, delivery, pay terms, and buying incentives they need."[3]

The area of analysis that is most directly pertinent to finding solutions to these and other types of marketing channel problems is called the *management of interorganization relations in marketing channels*. This area of study is basically concerned with *the process of achieving availability* for consumption rather than with merely the process of consumption. Specifically, interorganization management seeks to improve overall distribution system performance through more effective management of the relations among the

---

[2]"Marketing When the Growth Slows," *Business Week* (April 14, 1975), pp. 44-50.
[3]*Ibid.*, p. 48.

organizations responsible for the delivery of a particular product or service to its predetermined points of consumption.

The directing and controlling of interorganization relations within a marketing channel are complex tasks. As a prerequisite, they require an in-depth understanding of the nature of marketing channels themselves, including their general purpose and composition as well as the specific functions, flows, and interdependencies that are ongoing between the various participants in the channels. In this chapter, we will begin to examine these aspects of marketing channels by viewing the channels as *interorganizational systems—that is, as sets of interdependent organizations that, by an exchange of outputs, are involved in the process of making a product or service available for consumption.* Taking this approach to the study of marketing channels offers a significant advantage in that it provides a comprehensive framework for analyzing both the process and practices underlying the skillful management of distribution activities.

DISTRIBUTION AND THE "COMPLETE" PRODUCT

The subject of *marketing channels and interorganization management focuses basically on delivery.* It is only through distribution that public and private goods[4] can be made available for consumption. Producers of such goods (including manufacturers of industrial and consumer goods, legislators framing laws, educational administrators conceiving new means for achieving quality education, and insurance companies developing unique health insurance coverage, among many others) are individually capable of generating only form or structural utility for their "products." They can organize their production capabilities in such a way that the products that they have developed can, in fact, be seen, analyzed, debated, and, by a select few perhaps, digested. But the actual large-scale delivery of the products to the consuming public demands different types of efforts which create time, place, and possession utilities. In other words, the consumer cannot obtain a finished product unless the product is transported to where he[5] can gain access to it, stored until he is ready for it, and eventually exchanged for money or other goods or services so that he can gain possession of it. In fact,

---

[4]The term "goods" is being used in its broadest sense to encompass all things of value. For an enlightening discussion of the distinction between public and private goods (broadly defined), see Mancur Olson, Jr., *The Logic of Collective Action* (Cambridge, Mass.: Harvard University Press, 1965).

[5]We of course acknowledge the equal status of the female. However, we continue to use the traditional "he" to avoid unwieldy construction.

the four types of utility (form, time, place, and possession) are inseparable; there can be no "complete" product without incorporating all four into any given object, idea, or service.

COMPOSITION OF DISTRIBUTION CHANNELS

A marketing or distribution channel, as previously noted, is an interorganization system comprised of a set of interdependent institutions and agencies involved with the task of moving anything of value from its point of conception, extraction, or production to points of consumption. As an example, some of the institutions and agencies involved in the distribution of air conditioning equipment are portrayed in Fig. 1-1. Included in Fig. 1-1 are the business firms that are primarily responsible for the flow of title of the merchandise from manufacturer to end (industrial or residential) user. Although excluded from Fig. 1-1 are the numerous agencies and institutions that *facilitate* the passage of title and the physical movement of the goods, such as common carriers, financial institutions, advertising agencies, and the like, they, too, are members of the interorganization distribution system for this particular product.

The Relevant Number of Channels

Even though it is incomplete, Fig. 1-1 permits at least a beginning conceptualization of the various channels of distribution for air conditioning equipment. Thus, depicted in Fig. 1-1 are *nine* different channels of distribution for such equipment.

Any time a new institution or agency is added to or eliminated from a given channel, it is important to treat the new configuration as a new and different entity, because the problems in managing relations within the channel become distinctly different. For example, when a manufacturer decides to employ manufacturers' agents rather than use his own company-employed sales force to interact with dealers, he is confronted with a new set of interorganizational relations that involve motivating, directing, and controlling a set of independent businessmen who divide their promotional efforts among many manufacturers' products as well as his own. There are, therefore, different managerial problems involved in dealing with agents as opposed to company-employed salesmen, with distributors as opposed to

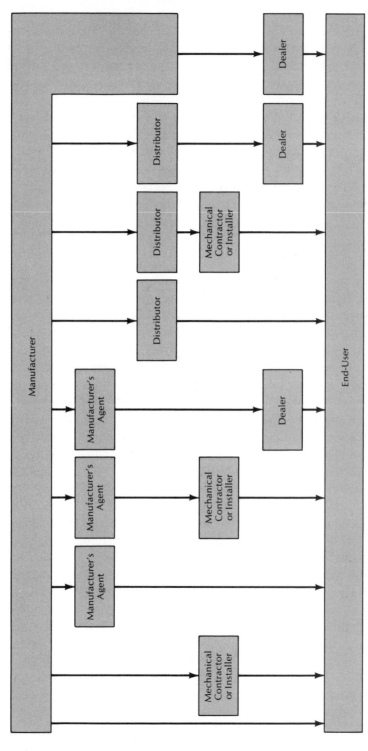

FIGURE 1-1 Marketing Channels for Air Conditioning Equipment

5

sales branches, and with independently owned retail outlets as opposed to vertically integrated retail and wholesale establishments.[6]

This principle is meaningful for the interorganizational management of any kind of distribution system. Thus, hospitals will confront different problems in organizing, planning, and controlling their output when they join health maintenance organizations as opposed to dealing with individually owned and managed clinics and physicians' offices. Politicians must adopt different styles and approaches when they interact with (and attempt to control) existing political organizations (e.g., the Republican National Committee) as opposed to organizations comprised of their own self-selected workers (e.g., the Committee for the Re-election of the President).

Channels as Competitive Units

In addition, implied in Fig. 1–1 is the notion that competition is not simply defined by horizontal relationships. That is, economic battles involving distributors versus distributors and dealers versus dealers will not, in the long run, determine the ultimate victors in the marketplace. Rather, the relevant unit of competition is an entire distribution system comprised of the entire network of interrelated institutions and agencies. For example, in the passenger tire industry, Firestone's system of distributors and dealers is in competition with Goodyear's entire system, and the long-term standing of either company will depend in large measure on how well each company manages the relations among the institutions and agencies involved in the distribution task so as best to satisfy the needs of the end-users of tires. This concept holds even though distributors in any given geographical area handle the product lines of more than one manufacturer. The way that the individual manufacturers coordinate their activities with the various distributors and vice versa will determine the viability of one type of channel alignment versus other channel alignments made up of different institutions and agencies handling similar or substitutable merchandise.

Returning to the example of the air conditioning equipment industry, we can underscore the above point. General Electric has vertically integrated the wholesaling operation for its equipment by purchasing or establishing wholly owned distribution points throughout the United States. Carrier Air Conditioning Company basically relies on independent wholesale distributors, while other manufacturers have developed systems which are variations on

[6]It should be noted carefully, however, that not all channels are manufacturer-dominated. Interorganization management may also be undertaken by middlemen, as indicated throughout this book and as discussed explicitly in Chapter 11.

these two basic approaches. In the competitive struggle between General Electric and Carrier, crucial determinants of success will be, for General Electric, its *intra*organizational abilities, whereas Carrier will have to rely more heavily on *inter*organizational management. The situation is, however, complicated by the fact that neither company restricts itself to simply one mode of distribution; therefore, each must develop separate sets of skills to deal with the various channels employed in moving its products from production to consumption.

CHANNEL MEMBER COORDINATION
VERSUS CHANNEL MEMBER SUBOPTIMIZATION

If, within a given distribution system, an institution or agency does not see fit to coordinate effectively and efficiently with other members of the same network, but rather to pursue its own goals in an independent, self-serving manner, it is possible to predict the eventual demise of the channel alignment of which it is a part as a strong competitive force. Ideally, then, a channel member should attempt to coordinate his objectives, plans, and programs with other members in such a way that the performance of the total distribution system to which he belongs is enhanced. However, it has been argued by some students of distribution that such integrated action up and down a marketing channel is actually a rarity, that channel participants are not concerned with all the transactions that occur between each of the various links in the channel, and that middlemen, in particular, are most concerned about the dealings that take place with those channel members immediately adjacent to them from whom they buy and to whom they sell.[7] In this sense, channel intermediaries are not, in fact, functioning as enlisted member components of a distribution system, but rather are acting individually as *independent markets*, with each one choosing those products and suppliers that best help him serve the target groups for whom he acts as a purchasing agent. From this perspective, the middleman's method of operations, the functions he performs, the clients he serves, and the objectives, policies, and programs he adopts are the result of his own independently made decisions.

This notion of each channel intermediary acting as an independent market must be qualified and analyzed with regard to total channel performance. Although an "independent" orientation on the part of any channel member may indeed be operational at times, it is put into effect only at the

[7]Philip McVey, "Are Channels of Distribution What the Textbooks Say?" *Journal of Marketing*, Vol. 24 (January, 1961), pp. 61–65.

risk of sacrificing the levels of coordination necessary for overall channel effectiveness, efficiency, growth, and long-run survival. Thus, a high degree of independent, suboptimizing behavior on the part of individual channel participants serves as a detriment to the viability of the total interorganization network. The problem for actors within any distribution network is, therefore, to cooperate in developing an interorganization system that will minimize suboptimization to the extent that a high degree of channel coordination is still attainable.

CHANNEL MANAGEMENT: COORDINATING, DIRECTING, AND CONTROLLING SUPERORGANIZATIONS

As an aid in the implementation of objectives, plans, and programs that will generate competitively viable distribution systems, it is useful, from a managerial/analytical perspective, to think of marketing channels as *superorganizations*.[8] The term "superorganization" implies that channels have characteristics of all complex organizations, even though channels are comprised of collectivities (business firms, day care centers, welfare agencies, and the like) rather than individuals. We usually think of people being organized into task-oriented groups, not necessarily large units such as business enterprises. However, complex organizations are most typically described in terms of their human factors rather than their physical factors. When the terms "business," "organization," "institution," "agency," "firm," and "channel member" are used in the context of a distribution channel network, the reference is to the collective management of the entity and not to its physical facilities, machinery, etc.[9]

An Organization's Characteristics

It is possible to compare the relevant dimensions of an organization as specified in the organization theory literature with those of extant distribu-

[8] Initial development of this concept may be found in Louis W. Stern and J. L. Heskett, "Conflict Management in Interorganization Relations: A Conceptual Framework," in Louis W. Stern (ed.), *Distribution Channels: Behavioral Dimensions* (Boston: Houghton Mifflin Company, 1969), pp. 288–305. See, also, Louis W. Stern, "The Interorganization Management of Distribution Channels: Prerequisites and Prescriptions," in George Fisk (ed.), *New Essays in Marketing Theory* (Boston: Allyn and Bacon, Inc., 1971), pp. 301–314.

[9] C. Glenn Walters, *Marketing Channels* (New York: The Ronald Press Company, 1974), pp. 15–16.

tion channels generally. Following Weick's summary,[10] an organization can be operationally defined in terms of the following characteristics:

> A cooperative relationship among its members
> Collective goal(s)
> Differentiation of function among its members
> A highly formalized unit with explicit rules and policies
> Structural complexity
> Interdependency among its members relative to task performance
> Communication among its members
> Criteria for evaluating the communication
> A stable and explicit hierarchical structure
> Integration through strictly defined subordination

Thus within any given distribution channel network, there exists a *cooperative relationship;* otherwise, the network could not exist. There is, however, no assumption made here as to the extent or effectiveness of the cooperation that exists; obviously, cooperation varies widely, and some channel situations are more chaotic and atomistic in this respect than others. For example, many fast-food franchise systems have engendered a high degree of cooperation between franchisor and franchisee (e.g., Kentucky Fried Chicken, McDonald's), while others have witnessed franchisee revolts within the system (e.g., Chicken Delight).

It is also possible to argue that *collective goals* operate within distribution channel networks, even though the goals themselves may not be explicitly noted or constantly accepted. Certainly, the desire to serve the ultimate consumer in a satisfactory manner seems to pervade distribution systems, although there are frequent occasions when one might question whether such a goal is being pursued adequately. In addition, channels represent a grandiose *division of labor* among the institutions and agencies comprising them. For example, Alderson has uniquely described this process of *functional differentiation* in his discussion of wholesaling:

> Wholesaling is a manifestation of sorting as an essential marketing process. Goods are received from numerous suppliers and delivered to numerous customers. The essence of the operation is to transform the diversified supplies received into outgoing assortments on their way to customers. The justification for an independent wholesaling operation rests largely on the ratio of advantage growing out of this intermediate sorting.[11]

[10] Karl E. Weick, "Laboratory Experimentation with Organizations," in James G. March (ed.), *Handbook of Organizations* (Chicago: Rand McNally, 1965), pp. 194-260.

[11] Wroe Alderson, "Factors Governing the Development of Marketing Channels," in Bruce Mallen (ed.), *The Marketing Channel* (New York: John Wiley & Sons, Inc., 1967), p. 39.

Similar descriptions could be framed for each and every institution within any channel network.

There would be no channels of distribution without transactional routines among members, and for a transaction to be routinized, it must happen according to *explicit rules.*[12] Channel members must understand the rules. Performance rests on the belief that one channel member will behave as another expects him to. Although channels are not often as "formalized" as typical complex organizations, they approach such formalization by the adoption of rules. In fact, within any channel system, positions and duties are generally fairly well ordered and defined. Relationships are also institutionalized. Channels are not simply ad hoc assemblages, but are among the more enduring forms of socioeconomic organization in our society. Explicit rules and policies regarding delivery, billing, order size, standardization, customer care, and the like are the vehicles that permit routinization and the formation of what Alderson has termed "organized behavior systems."[13]

Incorporation of a Chain of Command

It is not necessary to document the self-evident notion that channels are *structurally complex* or that *communication* (and criteria for evaluating it) exists among their memberships. It is, however, possible to note that many channels are different from complex organizations in that formal chains of command are often lacking within them. Thus, if "a stable and explicit hierarchical structure" and "integration through strictly defined subordination" are required in the formation or identification of a super-organization, surrogates for such a structure or subordination must be located in order to implement interorganization management. Although it is reasonably clear that chains of command exist within vertically integrated systems (e.g., within General Electric's distributor network for air conditioning equipment or among the clinics comprising the Kaiser health maintenance organization in California) and within some franchised systems, such authority networks are not immediately self-evident in the majority of extant distribution channels (e.g., within the furniture, food, and steel industries). Therefore, if the dictates of organization theory are followed, it would seem essential, from a normative perspective, to build into interorganization systems an *informal* system of authority, at the very least. In

[12]*Ibid.*

[13]Wroe Alderson, *Dynamic Marketing Behavior* (Homewood, Ill.: Richard D. Irwin, Inc., 1965), pp. 37 and 43–45.

order to organize the resources of distribution channels, it may be necessary to uncover or develop loci of power, or power centers, within the system. Such a requirement is explored in detail in Chapter 7.

THE SIGNIFICANCE OF INTERDEPENDENCY: CHANNELS AS SYSTEMS

Perhaps most important to an implementation of interorganization management is an understanding that channels consist of *interdependent* institutions and agencies; in other words, that there is interdependency among their members relative to task performance. A channel can be viewed as a system because of this interdependency—it is a set of *interrelated* and *interdependent* components engaged in producing an output. A distribution channel is comprised of two major subsystems or sectors: *commercial* and *consumer*. The commercial subsystem (to which major attention is given in this book) includes a set of vertically aligned marketing institutions and agencies, such as manufacturers, wholesalers, and retailers. The consumer (industrial and household) subsystem is incorporated in the *task environment* of the commercial channel, a notion that is developed more fully later on. Each commercial channel member is dependent on other institutions for achieving its goal(s). For example, a producer (manufacturer, physician, welfare agency) is dependent on others (retailers, hospitals, day care centers) in getting his product to the consumer and, thereby, in gaining its objectives (profits, improved health care, a reduction in the welfare rolls).

Perhaps the most glaring example of the recognition of this interdependency in recent years was the effort expended by the Credit Committee of the Toy Manufacturers Association to save Toys R Us. This major retailer of toys was threatened with bankruptcy because of the weak financial condition of its parent company, Interstate Stores, Inc. The TMA Credit Committee worked directly with banks in devising a plan that not only kept Toys R Us healthy but also prevented toy manufacturers, in the aggregate, from losing $80 million in sales. The decision of the banks to grant credit to Toys R Us was, to a large extent, based on the fact that six of the largest toy manufacturers were willing to extend credit to Toys R Us on their own.[14] Clearly, the six manufacturers and the members of the TMA Credit Committee realized the importance of adopting an interorganizational perspective in the marketing channel for toys.

[14]"How the TMA Saves Toys R Us," *Toys* (May, 1975), pp. 45–47.

A Network of Systems

The distribution channel has boundaries, as all systems do. These include geographic (market area), economic (capability to handle a certain volume of goods or services), and human (capability to interact) boundaries. Furthermore, a channel, like other systems, is part of a larger system which provides it with inputs and which imposes restrictions on its operation. A channel exists as part of a distribution structure that encompasses other channels. The distribution structure is a subsystem of the national environment, which is a subsystem of the international environment. Both the national and international environments encompass physical, economic, social, cultural, and political subsystems that influence the development of and impose constraints on the focal channel system. The configuration of systems is portrayed in Fig. 1–2. The impact of these environments on individual channel members and on channel organization and design is discussed throughout later chapters.

Again, it is important to underscore that the core of the systems concept is the interdependency that exists among the components. Such interdependency is apparent in any channel system—even in a channel in which the consumer is not being adequately served, such as in the furniture example given at the outset of this chapter. In fact, an input-output relationship exists between each member and every other member of the channel—the output of the manufacturer is the input of the wholesaler and so on. The channel is a system of systems; dependency among its members is pervasive, not only with respect to one another but also with respect to all other systems of which they are a part.

Conflict: An Output of Dependency

Although dependency is essential in order to divide labor effectively and achieve the work of the channel, it is also productive in other respects. Thus, one might argue that any time there is a dependency relationship, there are present the seeds of conflict. This fact is true whether one is talking about the dependency relationship in a household (e.g., between mother and child), in international affairs (e.g., between the United States and Israel), or in distribution channels. Conflicts can and do take place within distribution channels over how much inventory should be carried by various members, who has the right to represent a particular product within a given territory, whether prices are being maintained at "reasonable" levels, why

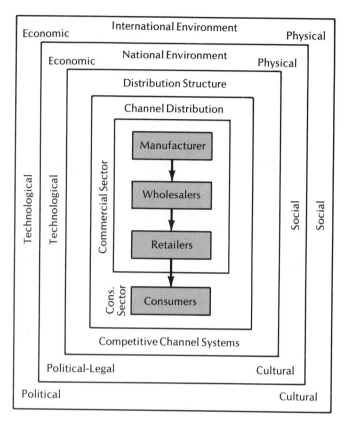

FIGURE 1-2   The Channel as a Processing Subsystem within
the Environment

distributors and dealers are sometimes bypassed via direct selling, and the like.

Generally, conflict is thought to be dysfunctional and, therefore, is often defined as behavior designed to destroy, injure, thwart, or control another party in an interdependent relationship.[15] However, such a view is too negatively oriented, because it is clear that the existence of conflict is frequently highly functional—without it, systems might become passive, noninnovative, and eventually nonviable. Thus, even though conflict is opponent-centered behavior,[16] the conflict bred by the dependency rela-

---

[15]Raymond W. Mack and Richard C. Snyder, "The Analysis of Social Conflict—Toward an Overview and Synthesis," *Journal of Conflict Resolution*, Vol. 1 (June, 1957), pp. 212-248.

[16]Although conflict can be viewed as opponent-centered behavior, competition is behavior that is

tionship is not all "bad." What one must seek to avoid is *pathological conflict*, or, colloquially, moves that are malign for the parties involved and for the entire system itself.[17]

In international relations, wars may be viewed as a pathological conflict—in the process of engaging in behavior designed to thwart another country, the aggressor also kills off its own young men and women. In distribution channel relations, examples of pathological moves are less vivid but nonetheless are easily defined. Thus, when retail druggists were pressing manufacturers to maintain retail prices on their brands through the policing of Fair Trade laws, Lever Brothers found it difficult to control the pricing behavior of "pine board" (cut rate) drug stores relative to Pepsodent, the best-selling brand of toothpaste at the time. In retaliation, the druggists removed the brand from their shelves, thereby forcing consumers to request packages each time they wanted to replenish their household supplies.[18] Surely this was a pathological move in a conflict situation, for in the process of "hurting" Lever Brothers, the druggists hurt themselves by foregoing sales volume and by inconveniencing their customers. The entire system suffered as the result of the boycott. Similar situations are found when a supplier slows up deliveries if a reseller is slow with his payments or does not follow some kind of policy dictate of the supplier. Such actions do not get at the cause of the conflict between the parties and therefore cannot offer viable long-run solutions to it. Instead, they often make matters worse rather than better—the pathology escalates.

A central task in interorganization management is to seek ways to manage conflict. In other words, it is essential that ways be found to keep conflict from becoming dysfunctional and to harness the energies in conflict situations to produce innovative resolutions.

ROLE SPECIFICATION IN CHANNELS

When units are interdependent, they are interdependent with respect to something that all of the units wish to achieve but that cannot be achieved through the efforts of one unit in the system on its own without the expen-

---

object-centered, and cooperation involves joint-striving. For a discussion of each type of behavior, see Louis W. Stern, "Antitrust Implications of a Sociological Interpretation of Competition, Conflict, and Cooperation in the Marketplace," *The Antitrust Bulletin*, Vol. 16 (Fall, 1971), pp. 509–530.

[17] Kenneth E. Boulding, "The Economics of Human Conflict," in Elton B. McNeil (ed.), *The Nature of Human Conflict* (Englewood Cliffs, N.J.: Prentice-Hall, Inc., 1965), pp. 174–175.

[18] Joseph C. Palamountain, Jr., *The Politics of Distribution* (Cambridge, Mass.: Harvard University Press, 1955).

diture of a tremendous amount of resources, as when vertical integration takes place. Therefore, in a system in which parties must cooperate in order to achieve an end, it is imperative, for the effective functioning of that system, that the role which each party will assume within the system be understood and clearly defined. In fact, within a channel of distribution, channel members should, again in a normative sense, come to some agreement on the "domain" of each; domain agreement or consensus refers to a mutual understanding regarding the population to be served, the territory to be covered, and the functions or activities to be performed by each component of the system.[19]

In the absence of "domain consensus" within a system, one can expect a good deal of dysfunctional conflict. After appropriate market segments have been isolated for attack and market targets have been established, a first step in effective interorganization management is the specification of role relationships—or the rights and obligations of each of the component members of the system. To accomplish this, it is useful to employ the notion of marketing functions or, in channel terms, marketing flows. These are the activities or tasks that must be participated in if the system is going to survive and, it is to be hoped, flourish. The more carefully managed the flows are, the more viable the system will be.

Marketing Flows in Channels

A flow is similar to a function, but the term "flow" is somewhat more descriptive of movement. Since the heterogeneity of supply and demand constitutes obstacles to efficient exchange, such problems as physical movement, matching assortments, and stimulation become part of the inherent structure for designing the channel system.[20] Figure 1–3 depicts eight universal flows. Physical possession, ownership, and promotion are typically forward flows from producer to consumer. Each of these moves "down" the distribution channel—a manufacturer promotes his product to a wholesaler, who in turn promotes it to a retailer, and so on. The negotiation, financing, and risking flows move in both directions, whereas ordering and payment are backward flows.

It is interesting and useful to note that any time inventories are held by one member of the channel system, a financing operation is underway. Thus, when a wholesaler takes title and assumes physical possession of a portion of

[19] James D. Thompson, *Organizations in Action* (New York: McGraw-Hill Book Company, 1967), p. 26.

[20] Ronald Michman, *Marketing Channels* (Columbus, Ohio: Grid, Inc., 1974), p. 6.

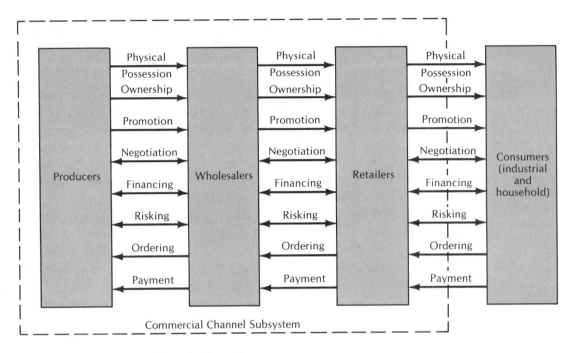

FIGURE 1-3   Marketing Flows in Channels

SOURCE: Adapted from R. S. Vaile, E. T. Grether, and R. Cox, *Marketing in the American Economy* (New York: The Ronald Press, 1952), p. 113.

the output of a manufacturer, the wholesaler is financing the manufacturer. Such a notion is made clear when one examines the carrying costs of inventory. The largest component of carrying cost is the cost of the capital tied up when inventories are held in a dormant state. (Other carrying costs are obsolescence, depreciation, pilferage, breakage, storage, insurance, and taxes.) The reason for the significance of capital costs is relatively obvious—if money were not tied up in inventory, a firm would be able to invest those funds elsewhere. In effect, capital costs are opportunity costs of holding inventory. Thus, when one member of a channel has been "freed" from holding inventory—when his inventories have been exchanged for cash—he may reinvest these funds. In the furniture industry, traditional furniture retailers operating on a sold-order basis choose not to participate in the backward financing flow. On the other hand, "warehouse" furniture retailers do participate in this flow directly and thereby receive benefits from manufacturers in the form of lower prices and preferential treatment.

Many other examples of the backward flow of financing can be found, beyond those associated with the holding of inventory. Thus, when a department store buyer commits himself to purchasing a large volume of a particular fashion good prior to the mass production and shipment of the item, the commitment may be factored and the funds used by the garment manufacturer to finance his production process. Prepayment for merchandise is also another example of the backward financing flow.

The forward flow of financing is even more common. General Motors Acceptance Corporation is a specific institution established by the manufacturer to finance not only ultimate consumers of its automobiles but also inventories held by dealers. In fact, all terms of sale, with the exception of cash on delivery and prepayment, may be viewed as elements of the forward flow of financing.

Channel Specialization

All of the flows (like marketing functions) are indispensable—at least one institution or agency within the system must assume responsibility for each of them if the channel is to operate at all. But it is not necessary that every institution participate in the furtherance of all of the flows. In fact, it is for this reason that the channel of distribution is an example of a division of labor on a macro scale. Certain institutions and agencies specialize in one or more of the flows, as is indicated in Fig. 1–4. The use of these and other intermediaries largely boils down to their superior efficiency in the performance of basic marketing tasks and functions. Marketing intermediaries, through their experience, their specialization, their contacts, and their scale, offer other channel members more than they can usually achieve on their own.[21]

Compensation Basis for Channel Members

From an interorganization management perspective, the extent to which any given institution and agency within the channel participates in the various flows should determine the compensation received by that unit for its role in the total channel system. It is this notion that allows a more complete picture of the consumer's role in the system. The more the commercial channel subsystem expects the consumer (industrial or household) to assume an active role within the system, the greater should be the consumer's compensation. Thus, when the present system of food supermarkets replaced the

---

[21]Philip Kotler, *Marketing Management*, 3rd ed. (Englewood Cliffs, N.J.: Prentice-Hall, Inc., 1976), p. 279.

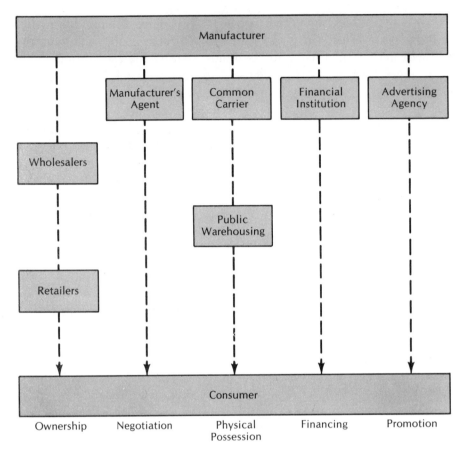

FIGURE 1-4   Channel Institutions Particular to Selected Marketing Flows

previous system of food distribution through small, neighborhood stores, the consumer was called upon to engage more fully and participate more deeply in facilitating the flows. In order to be efficient shoppers, housewives are now required, by the present system, to allocate more resources during any one shopping trip than they did in the past, to make selections without in-store assistance, to transport themselves and the food they buy longer distances, and to store more merchandise and thereby hold larger inventories. While there has been a concomitant reduction in housewives' participation in the negotiation flow (due to the development of brand-name merchandise and the existence of a one-price system), there can be little doubt that the effort which they are required to expend to make the system work is considerable. Compensation for the consumer's participation must follow; such compensation is found in the lower prices paid for food under the present system than under the previous one, inflation aside.

In addition, in the short-term future, it is likely that the need for recycling is going to place the consumer in a unique role within the distribution channel, as discussed in Chapter 14. In the recycling case, the flows in which the consumer will be participating may be more similar to those assumed by manufacturers, because the consumer is, in reality, the "producer" of the recyclable item.[22] Clearly, a new compensation scheme will have to be developed to accompany the change in flow participation; the effectiveness of such a scheme may be the critical variable in the success or failure of recycling (and the concomitant antipollution) efforts.

The notion of compensation for participation is, of course, directly relevant to activities in the commercial channel subsystem. It would seem obvious that channel members should be paid only for what they actually do within the system. However, such is not always the case. For example, in many lines of trade, standard trade discounts have been established based on the position (e.g., wholesaler, retailer, carrier) that an institution occupies within the system. Although these discounts are frequently called "functional" discounts, they are often based not on what flows a specific institution is performing and its coverage of these flows but rather on trade tradition. For example, one manufacturer has been known to grant large discounts to his distributors on the basis of the warehousing (physical possession) functions they perform. In a recent analysis of distributors' financial positions, it was found that they were earning returns on their investments of 50 to 100 percent. While middlemen are entitled to earn satisfactory returns, the amounts generated by these distributors were inordinate and indicated that the distributors were "coasting" quite comfortably on the high level of market demand for the product of the channel. Upon further investigation, it was found that undue compensation was being granted for the warehousing operations of the distributors because the manufacturer was, in actuality, consigning much of the component inventory needed for the installation of the product to public warehouses located near the distributors. The manufacturer was also assuming a large portion of the expense associated with the leasing of the space in the warehouses. The conclusion was apparent—the manufacturer had been overcompensating the distributors for their rather minimal participation in the flows of physical possession, ownership, and financing.

---

[22]William G. Zikmund and William J. Stanton, "Recycling Solid Wastes: A Channels-of-Distribution Problem," *Journal of Marketing*, Vol. 35 (July, 1971), p. 35.

The Channel Audit

It is clear from this not atypical illustration that role relationships had not been delineated in an effective and meaningful way from the outset and that the domains of both the manufacturer and the distributors were overlapping. What is needed in such situations is an *audit* of the flows in the channel in order to determine the extent of participation of the members in each. An audit of this nature will not only permit an adjustment of the compensation structure within the channel, but should also lead to the elimination of cost duplication and thereby result in the lowering of prices to end-users.

The beginning point of a channel audit may involve the construction of a matrix of system relationships. Such a matrix describes the channel, permitting precise comparisons of the operations of the various channel components as well as comparisons of one channel system with others. In such a matrix, the institutions and agencies included in any given channel can be portrayed as components of the system. Important elements of the task environment (i.e., the portion of the environment upon which the system depends) can also be shown. Thus, by employing a matrix, it is possible to represent the structure of various relationships within the channel system and between system components and the task environment.

A complete matrix would encompass all firms in the channel. However, a channel might contain 500 firms, which would require 250,000 cells—a matrix too complex to portray here. Thus, levels within the channel rather than individual firms are presented in Fig. 1–5. Likewise, it is not feasible to include all components of the task environment, since the components are too numerous and not always identifiable. Nevertheless, the important components can be easily recognized and are portrayed here, also.

The system matrix in Fig. 1–5 uses the commercial channel for a manufacturer's new automobiles as a relatively uncomplicated example.[23] The channel consists of the manufacturer, his dealers, an advertising agency, and an independent sales finance company that finances both dealers' purchases from the manufacturer and consumers' purchases from dealers. Competitors' channels and consumers represent the most important elements of the task environment. In the history of new car distribution, additional and important task environment elements, among others, have been the

---

[23] For an application of the system matrix to the pharmaceutical industry, see Mickey C. Smith, Kenneth B. Roberts, and Darego Maclayton, "The Pharmaceutical Industry I: Distribution Channels and Relationships," *MM&M Journal* (January, 1976), pp. 32-34.

		Commercial Channel				Task Environment			
		Mfr.	Dlr.	Sfc.	Ad. Ag.	Cons.	F.T.C.	N.A.D.A.	Competitors' Channels
		1	2	3	4	5	6	7	
Manufacturer	1		A B C D F	F D	C D		D	D	
Dealer	2	D G F		D H F		A B C D F	D	D	
Sales Finance Company	3	D E F H	D E F H			D E F	D	D	D E F H
Advertising Agency	4	D				C			D
Consumer	5		D G F	D F H					D F G H
Federal Trade Commission	6	D	D					D	D
Nat'l. Auto. Dlrs. Assn.	7	D	D				D		D
Competitors' Channels				D F H	C D	A B C D E F	D	D	

Flow: Direction: Code:
            Mfr.   Cons.

Flow	Direction	Code
Ownership	⟶	A
Phys. Poss.	⟶	B
Promotion	⟶	C
Negotiation	⟷	D
Financing	⟷	E
Risking	⟷	F
Ordering	⟵	G
Payment	⟵	H

FIGURE 1-5   Matrix Analysis of Marketing Flows in a Marketing Channel for Automobiles: A Manufacturer's Perspective

SOURCE: Adapted from Louis W. Stern and Jay W. Brown, "Distribution Channels: A Social Systems Approach," in *Distribution Channels: Behavioral Dimensions*, ed. Louis W. Stern (Boston: Houghton Mifflin Company, 1969), p. 10.

Federal Trade Commission and the dealer trade organization, the National Automobile Dealers Association (NADA).

The meaning of each cell can be demonstrated by cell (row 1, column 2). This cell shows the nature of the relationship between the manufacturer and the dealer when the manufacturer initiates the interaction. The manufacturer promotes cars to dealers (C), negotiates the terms of sales (D), passes the automobile and its title to dealers (A and B), and, at the same time, accepts certain business risks (F) in his relationship with dealers. The backward flows for the dealer-manufacturer relationship are contained in cell (2, 1). The dealers order from the manufacturer (G), negotiate the terms of sales (D), and accept risk (F). All other cells are analyzed in the same way. The relationships involving the NADA and the FTC are not marketing flow relationships. Since these relationships have been characterized by bargaining, the marketing flow "negotiation" has been used to typify the nature of relationships involving these organizations. Thus, the matrix, as a starting point for an audit of channel relationships and roles, depicts the variety of channel interactions. These include *intra*organizational interactions (within a channel member's firm, e.g., cell 1, 1), *inter*organizational interactions (between channel members, e.g., cell 1, 2), and extrachannel or environmental interactions (between the channel members and the task environment elements, e.g., cell 1, 6).

Reallocating Channel Tasks

The flows are, to some extent, capable of being shifted among the agencies and institutions comprising a channel. This holds true for any distribution channel, whether it be for automobiles, air conditioners, health services, or governmental programs. If it is found that one channel member cannot perform an activity as efficiently and effectively as another, then it is detrimental to the output of the channel not to reallocate the activity. This reallocation process is the primary task of interorganization management. For example, in many industries, cooperative advertising allowances are granted to retailers in order to encourage the retailers to advertise given products in local media. Unfortunately, much of this cooperative advertising money is wasted, from the point of view of the institutions granting it, because the retailers' advertisements are frequently poorly conceived and executed. It may be highly preferable for this aspect of the flow of promotion to be absorbed by another channel member within the system which might be more adept at developing a consumer franchise for the products in question. If this is the case, the gross margin of the retailer receiving the allowance may be reduced as funds are reallocated within the system. It is, therefore, essential that, over the long run, the reallocation process result in greater retail sales volume, higher merchandise turnover, and thus a greater return on investment.

Obviously, such reallocation processes often meet with resistance. Shifting activities is not an easy task, and data have to be marshalled in order to convince affected agencies of the merit of the shifts. In actuality, such shifts involve the judicious use of power and the employment of conflict management strategies. Nevertheless, the construction of viable distribution systems depends on this shiftability concept.

SUMMARY

A marketing channel may be defined as an interorganizational system made up of a set of interdependent institutions and agencies involved with the task of moving things of value (ideas, products, services) from points of conception, extraction, or production to points of consumption. Its primary focus is on availability—delivering valuable objects to points at which they may be easily examined, evaluated, and consumed. Marketing channels should be considered as the relevant units of competition; the viability of any given organization depends greatly on how well it interacts and coordinates its efforts with other organizations which purvey its ideas, products, or services.

To a significant extent, marketing channels may be thought of in terms of superorganizations, because they possess many of the attributes of complex organizations. Thus, any given channel can be characterized as including a cooperative relationship among its members, collective goals, differentiation of function among its members, explicit rules and policies, structural complexity, communication, and interdependency among its members relative to task performance. Channels often differ from complex organizations in that they do not always incorporate a stable and explicit hierarchical structure. In order to implement interorganization management within a channel without such a chain of command, it is necessary to seek informal sources of authority based on the social and economic power of its various members.

Because channels are comprised of sets of interdependent institutions and agencies involved in producing an output (e.g., consumer satisfaction), they can be viewed as socioeconomic systems. The dependency relationships that exist within such systems breed conflict that must be managed if the system is to remain viable. However, conflict can be functional as well as dysfunctional; it is, therefore, the task of interorganization management to harness the conflict that arises and to aid in preventing pathological moves as a reaction to conflict situations.

A crucial element in interorganization management in marketing is the specification of roles to be performed throughout any given channel system. Such role specification involves outlining the relevant domains of each member; that is, the population to be served, the territory covered, and the functions or activities to be performed. Certain flows—physical possession, ownership, promotion, negotiation, financing, risking, ordering, and payment—must be incorporated if the channel is to operate at all. The allocation of participation in the flows will determine the roles of the various members in the system. Compensation for each member should be based on its degree of participation in the flows. For on-going distribution channels, the setting of compensation levels will depend, to a large extent, on an evaluation of performance based on a channel audit. In addition, efforts to achieve greater effectiveness will depend, in large measure, on shifting the flows between various channel members.

In order to provide the basis for effective interorganization management of distribution systems, it is imperative that one understand the structure, orientations, and management practices of each of the several key levels within these systems. The next several chapters deal with the major components of channel systems. Examination is undertaken of the history, evolution, structure, and management of retailing, wholesaling, and logistical institutions.

DISCUSSION QUESTIONS

1. What are some alternative approaches to the study of distribution channels beside an interorganization systems approach? What are the different concepts, consequences, and orientations for channel management that might flow from these different approaches? Which offers the most comprehensive framework for the study and practice of channel management?

2. Why, in your opinion, is the interorganization management of distribution channels an important aspect of a firm's marketing strategy?

3. In a low-growth economy, many strategists are emphasizing "demand management" rather than "demand stimulation." How might this affect a firm's marketing mix, particularly as it relates to distribution? If there is a continued deemphasis of demand stimulation in the future, will the role of interorganization management in marketing become more or less important as an influence on overall corporate performance?

4. Peter F. Drucker, a well-known management scholar, recently described the distribution function as the "economy's dark continent," implying that this aspect of organizational activity has long been ignored as a potential area for strategic development. Why, do you feel, was there such neglect for so long a period of time?

5. Consider these examples of contemporary marketing channels:
   Avon's distribution system delivering cosmetics direct from manufacturer to consumer through a sales force of 400,000 saleswomen.

Levitz' warehouse-showroom method of furniture distribution, which stocks large quantities of furniture delivered to each warehouse-showroom at considerable savings, thus enabling Levitz to pass lower prices on to the consumer.

Hanes Corporation's consignment marketing channel for its L'eggs pantyhose, wherein the retailer takes no title for the goods, makes no financial investment, and performs no delivery service or display maintenance, but receives only a certain percentage of the pantyhose sales for his allocation of space to the L'eggs display.

(a) Select one of the above channels and speculate who the other channel participants are and to what extent each member participates in the eight universal marketing flows.

(b) How might these flows be shifted either among the members now in the channel or to different agencies or institutions not presently included in the system? What do you think would be the implications of such shifts?

(c) Within each of these distribution systems, specify what the consumer's role is from a flow-absorption perspective. How, in turn, does this affect the consumer's level of "compensation"?

6. Almost every American, at one time or another, interacts with the distribution system for automobiles. Unfamiliar to most, however, is the industry's notoriety for the amount of conflict often generated between its channel participants, causing, in fact, one leading manufacturing company to hire a retired Supreme Court Justice to arbitrate any disputes it has with its dealers.

Within the context of the automobile distribution system, offer hypothetical or actual examples of functional, dysfunctional, and pathological conflict. State your reasons for thinking that your examples typify each of these conflict behaviors.

7. "A marketing channel is a group of firms which constitute a loose coalition engaged in exploiting joint opportunity in the market." Write a normative analysis of this statement from a total channel performance perspective, being sure to include the concepts of "domain consensus," "channel coordination," and "superorganization."

8. Do you think an interorganization management approach is useful and applicable to all types of distribution channel systems? Which types of distribution channels would seemingly need it the most? Which would find it the least applicable?

9. Should advertising agencies and financial institutions be considered as channel members? Why? Why not?

10. Prepare a systems matrix for a candy manufacturer who distributes through rack jobbers to supermarkets.

11. Is it more useful, from a managerial perspective, to think of consumers (end-users) as members of a channel or as elements in the task environment to the channel? Can consumers be "manipulated" and/or incorporated by interorganization management?

TWO

RETAILING: STRUCTURE, COMPETITION, AND MANAGEMENT

This chapter deals with the structure of and competition in retail markets as well as with the management problems and practices of retailing institutions. Its purpose is to provide a reasonably clear picture of the level of distribution called retail trade, so that, when relationships between distribution levels are examined later in this book, it will be possible for the reader to bring to the discussion and analysis an understanding of the particular orientation of retailers and thus add substance to the complexities encountered in developing interorganization management policies in channel systems where retailers play a crucial role.

THE STRUCTURE OF RETAILING

Retailing deals with the activities involved in selling goods and services to ultimate consumers. Thus, a retail sale is one in which the buyer is an ultimate consumer, as opposed to a business or institutional purchaser. In contrast to purchases for resale or for business, industrial, or institutional use, the buying motive for a retail sale is always personal or family satisfaction stemming from the final consumption of the item being purchased.[1]

---

[1] Theodore N. Beckman, William R. Davidson, and W. Wayne Talarzyk, *Marketing*, 9th ed. (New York: Ronald Press Co., 1973), p. 234.

While the commonly accepted conduits of retailing are stores, the mail, house-to-house salesmen, and automatic vending machines, it is logical to include under the retailing rubric all "outlets" that seek to serve ultimate consumers. These would include service establishments such as motels and hotels, as shown in Table 2-1. Under the broadened concept of marketing, such "outlets" as hospitals, day-care centers, churches, and perhaps even public schools might also be included. These latter institutions, as well as banks and financial institutions (the "retailers" of money), have been omitted from Table 2-1 for a simple reason—it is difficult to quantify their output in terms of dollar sales volume.

TABLE 2-1 Retail Sales of Store, Nonstore, and Service Institutions

Store Retailing	*1963* *(billions of dollars)*	*1972[a]* *(billions of dollars)*
Food stores	$57.1	$95.0
Automobile dealers	45.4	88.6
Department stores	20.5	46.6
Eating and drinking places	18.4	33.9
Gasoline service stations	17.8	31.0
Apparel stores	14.0	22.0
Lumber and building materials stores	14.6	20.1
Drug stores	8.5	14.5
Furniture and home furnishing stores	10.9	21.3
Liquor stores	5.2	9.2
Nonstore Retailing		
House-to-house selling	2.4	4.0
Mail order or catalog retailing	2.4	5.0
Vending machines	1.5	6.9
Services		
Hotels, motels, tourist courts, camps	5.1	8.5
Personal services (laundry, dry cleaning, beauty shops, barber shops, photographic, shoe repair, funeral, alteration, etc.)	9.2	13.0
Automobile repair and other automotive services	5.4	12.3
Miscellaneous repair services (electrical, watch, jewelry, furniture, etc.)	6.7	11.9
Amusement, recreation services, motion pictures (dance halls, theatrical presentations, bowling, billiards, commercial sports, etc.)	3.0	6.2

[a]Unadjusted

SOURCES: U.S. Census of Business: *Retail Trade*, Vol. 1, pp. 8-9, 1967; *Selected Services: Special Report*, pp. 1-6, 1963; *Survey of Current Business*, March 1974, pp. 5-12; and *Monthly Selected Services Receipts*, March 1973, p. 3.

Of the various categories of retailing institutions listed in Table 2–1, store retailing is by far the most significant, accounting for 85 percent of total retail sales volume. Within the store retailing category, food stores obtain the greatest share, accounting for 25 percent of total retail sales in 1972, as shown in Table 2–2. If one adds eating and drinking place receipts to the food store sales, then food-oriented purchases would consume over one-third of retail expenditures, giving some notion of the emphasis Americans place on certain types of oral activities. The automotive group (auto

TABLE 2–2   Trends in the Share of Establishments and Sales—Total and by Groups

| | 1963 | | | | 1972[a] | | | |
| | Establishments | | Sales | | Establishments | | Sales | |
	Number (thousands)	Percent	$ (billions)	Percent	Number (thousands)	Percent	$ (billions)	Percent
Retail stores	1628	62%	212	86%	1751	—	388	85%
Nonstore retail	80	3	6	3	162	—	16	4
Service	914	35	29	11	NA[b]	—	52	11
	2622	100%	247	100%	NA	—	466	100%
Retail Stores—By Merchandise Groups								
Food stores		23%		27%		18%		25%
Automobile dealers		7		21		8		23
Department stores		1		10		5		12
Eating and drinking places		24		9		24		9
Gasoline service stations		15		8		15		8
Apparel stores		9		7		9		6
Lumber and building material stores		7		7		6		5
Drug stores		4		4		4		4
Furniture and home furnishing stores		7		5		8		6
Liquor stores		3		2		3		2
		100%		100%		100%		100%
Nonstore Retail By Type								
House-to-house selling		83%		38%		87%		25%
Mail order or catalog retailing		5		38		5		31
Vending machines		12		24		8		43
		100%		100%		100%		100%

TABLE 2-2 continued

| | 1963 | | | | 1972[a] | | | |
| | Establishments | | Sales | | Establishments | | Sales | |
	Number (thousands)	Percent	$ (billions)	Percent	Number (thousands)	Percent	$ (billions)	Percent
Service Stores by Type of Service								
Hotels, motels, tourist courts, camps		9%		17%		NA[b]		16%
Personal services (laundry, dry cleaning, beauty shops, photographic, shoe repair, funeral, alteration, etc.)		49		31		NA		25
Automobile repair and other automotive services		15		18		NA		24
Miscellaneous repair services (electrical, watch, jewelry, furniture, etc.)		16		11		NA		12
Amusement, recreation services, motion pictures (dance halls, theatrical presentations, bowling, billiards, commercial sports, etc.)		10		23		NA		23
		100%		100%				100%

[a]Unadjusted and estimated (based on preliminary 1972 Census data).
[b]NA = not available.

SOURCES: U.S. Census of Business: *Retail Trade*, Vol. 1, pp. 8-9, 1967; *Selected Services: Special Report*, pp. 1-6, 1963; *Survey of Current Business*, March 1974, pp. 5-12; and *Monthly Selected Services Receipts*, March 1973, p. 3.

dealers, gas stations) transacted about 31 percent of all sales, while department stores accounted for approximately 12 percent.[2]

Retail stores constitute approximately two-fifths of all nonfarm establishments in the United States. Interestingly, though, the total *number* of

[2]It is important to note that there are significant problems in using and analyzing Census of Business data in order to portray movements and shifts over time. As Dalrymple and Thompson point out, merchandise groupings are not necessarily descriptive of the type of merchandise sold, due, in large part, to the existence of scrambled merchandising. Three religious goods stores studied by Dalrymple and Thompson reported sales of packaged alcoholic beverages, cigars, cigarettes, curtains, draperies, hardware, footwear, furniture, and major appliances. In addition, there are changes in Census classifications from one enumeration to another, as well as reclassifications of establishments to reflect changes in the character of their operations. Also, each merchandise group encompasses several components, and changes in one or several of these are masked by the aggregation process. Thus, the category "food

retail stores has changed insignificantly since the Great Depression in 1929.[3] Within the various so-called merchandise groups listed under the heading "Store Retailing" in Table 2-1, there have, however, been varying patterns. The number of food stores has declined, the number of gas stations has increased, and the number of drug stores has remained relatively stable over the last 25 years.[4] On the other hand, the number of stores in the apparel, furniture, and general merchandise groups (department, variety, and general merchandise stores) has fluctuated over time; this fluctuation may be accounted for by the fact that such stores are directly competitive and that their fortunes ebb and flow as consumer preferences shift from one to the other and back again.[5]

To a significant extent, however, statistics do not reveal the underlying dynamics of the exciting developments that have occurred over the past century. There has been a veritable revolution in retailing, even though small shopkeepers are still local "landmarks" in every community. Briefly recounted below are some of the more important events in the revolution.[6]

The Revolution in Retailing

The structure of retailing has been significantly affected by the emergence of new institutions as well as by the evolution of existing ones. In particular, the major developments seem to have been related to institutional types known as department stores, chain stores, supermarkets, planned shopping centers, discount houses, and various forms of nonstore retailing.

---

stores" includes grocery stores, meat markets, fish markets, fruit and vegetable markets, and candy, nut, and confectionery stores. Within the "food store" category, only grocery stores have fared remarkably well over time. Finally, the Census defines a retail establishment as one that makes at least 51 percent of its sales to retail customers. Under such a system, up to 49 percent of a store's sales could be misclassified. Although such misclassification might not affect drug store sales significantly, since most sales are made to the consumer in such outlets, they might have an important effect on sales of lumber yards. See Douglas J. Dalrymple and Donald L. Thompson, *Retailing: An Economic View* (New York: The Free Press, 1969), p. 17.

[3] See *ibid.*, pp. 13–15, for a discussion of trends.

[4] The stability in the number of drug stores is, according to a number of observers, directly related to the entry restrictions erected by trade associations of pharmacies and pharmacists through their influence on state pharmacy boards. See *ibid.*, p. 13; Leonard W. Weiss, *Case Studies in American Industry* (New York: John Wiley & Sons, Inc., 1967); and Joseph C. Palamountain, Jr., *The Politics of Distribution* (Cambridge, Mass: Harvard University Press, 1955).

[5] Dalrymple and Thompson, *op. cit.*, p. 15. This shifting is explained by the "accordian theory of retail development." See Stanley C. Hollander, "Notes on the Retail Accordian," *Journal of Retailing*, Vol. 42 (Summer 1966), p. 29, and Chapter 5 of this text.

[6] The following discussion of the historical developments in retailing is largely based in Louis P. Bucklin's careful study entitled, *Competition and Evolution in the Distributive Trades* (Englewood Cliffs, N.J.: Prentice-Hall, Inc., 1972).

The basic characteristics of each of these types, among others, are enumerated in Exhibit 2-1, while some of the major historical developments in retailing have been capsulized in Exhibit 2-2.

The Emergence of Department Stores.   In the 1700's and early 1800's, the dominant force in retailing was the full-line general store. However, the growth of American cities changed this dramatically. As cities grew, downtown pedestrian traffic grew, and, as a result, local merchants were faced with a high level of demand to satisfy. Since ownership and managership were not yet divorced, the entrepreneur-manager reacted to expanded demand by increasing his volume while, at the same time, narrowing his product line in order to keep the business small enough to control. However, by narrowing the lines they carried, these merchants were also limiting their total absolute sales and profits. As a reaction, some entrepreneurs eventually began adding to their lines. Finally, during the first half of the 1800's, the idea of delegating managerial responsibility for merchandise groups developed.[7] In addition to this managerial advancement, certain cultural, social, and technological forces were also operating which set the stage for the birth of the department store. Women began spending more, both in terms of dollars and as a percentage of family expenditure. The invention of the sewing machine allowed for the rapid development of the ready-to-wear industry. Merchants began paying more attention to price as a promotional instrument, and increased literacy and broader newspaper circulation made large-scale advertising possible. In addition, public transportation designed to bring people to downtown areas was developing.[8]

The first department stores, such as A. T. Stewart, Marshall Field & Co., and Jordan Marsh Co., were often started in conjunction with a wholesaling operation. There was, therefore, direct contact between the department store and the manufacturer. This type of integration allowed the early department stores to choose between alternative strategies. They could maintain high prices and use their higher gross margin position to provide better services, or they could choose to reduce prices and pass some of their savings on to the consumer.

Department stores following both alternatives proved successful (see Exhibit 2-2). In the 1870's, for example, A. T. Stewart was averaging sales of $60,000 per day.[9] Macy's, in the 1870's, was selling between $1 and $2 million per year. Marshall Field, in 1882, had an annual sales volume of $4

---

[7]*Ibid.*, p. 55.

[8]*Ibid.*, pp. 56-57.

[9]*Ibid.*

EXHIBIT 2-1   Characteristics of Selected Major Retailing Institutions and Forms of Organization

Department Stores are retail organizations that (1) sell a wide variety of merchandise, including piece goods, home furnishings, and furniture; (2) are organized by departments; (3) have large sales; (4) sell mainly to women; (5) are located typically in downtown shopping districts or in newer shopping centers; (6) frequently establish branch operations; and (7) usually offer a large amount of "free" service.

Specialty Stores retail a broad selection of a restricted class of goods. While there are departmentalized specialty stores of considerable size (e.g., Filene's and I. Magnin), the term "specialty store" is most commonly applied to small and medium-sized establishments or boutiques handling limited lines of soft (clothing, linens, etc.) or hard (kitchen utensils, appliances, etc.) goods.

Chain Store Systems are characterized by: (1) central ownership or control; (2) central management; (3) similarity of stores; and (4) two or more units. (Recent Census classification has expanded the number of stores comprising a chain to eleven or more.) Buying power combined with managerial efficiencies characterize effective chain store system operations.

Supermarkets are generally low-margin, high-turnover retail organizations. In the food industry, a supermarket can be defined as a large, departmentalized retail establishment offering a relatively broad and complete stock of dry groceries, fresh meat, perishable produce, and dairy products, supplemented by a variety of convenience, nonfood merchandise and operated on a self-serve basis.

Planned Shopping Centers are integrated developments, under single ownership, with coordinated and complete shopping facilities, and with adequate parking space. The stores in the centers are leased to various retailers. Frequently, the stores in the centers engage in joint advertising, promotional, and public relations programs.

Discount Houses are retail establishments which generally have the following features: (1) a broad merchandise assortment, including both soft and hard goods; (2) price as the main sales appeal; (3) relatively low operating cost ratios; (4) relatively inexpensive buildings, equipment, and fixtures; (5) an emphasis on self-service operations; (6) limited customer services; (7) emphasis on rapid turnover of merchandise; (8) large stores and parking areas; (9) carnival-like atmospheres; and (10) frequent use of leased departments.

Nonstore Retailers are typified by three general types of organizations.

1. *Automatic merchandisers* utilize vending machines. The assortment offered is limited to stable products of low unit value and certain other convenience goods. Costs of operations are usually high due to the use of expensive machines that require considerable stocking time and repair labor. Thus, both prices and margins are typically high.

EXHIBIT 2-1 continued

2. *Mail order houses* are establishments that receive their orders by mail and make their sales (deliveries) by mail, parcel post, express, truck, or freight. Retail mail order houses are of three main types: the department store merchandise house (Alden's, Montgomery Ward, Sears, Roebuck, and Spiegel); the smaller general merchandise firm which carries lines that are far less broad than would be found in a department store; and the specialty house (e.g., Franklin Mint Corporation). Generally, installment credit is used extensively and other commonly offered services include telephone ordering, convenient pickup depots, catalog stores, strong guarantees, and liberal return policies. Prices are supposedly lower than at conventional retailers' outlets, although postal and delivery charges tend to bring their prices closer to those existing elsewhere.

3. *House-to-house selling* is typified by organizations, such as Avon and Stanley Home Products, that engage in direct sales to ultimate consumers in the latter's homes. Demonstration and return after trial are among the various services offered by house-to-house sellers, while cash, rather than credit, is the usual mode of transaction. In general, overhead costs are relatively low for these operations, with the major expense items being travel costs and salesperson turnover.

SOURCE: Many of the definitions and descriptions provided above can be found in greater detail in James M. Carman and Kenneth P. Uhl, *Phillips and Duncan's Marketing: Principles and Methods,* 7th ed. (Homewood, Ill.: Richard D. Irwin, 1973), pp. 175–225.

million. By the end of the century, Macy's annual sales were $8 million and Marshall Field's were $20 million.[10] The department stores, then, showed substantial growth in their early years.

However, the growth of department stores did not stop at the turn of the century. In 1899, department store sales were estimated to be $161 million, or 1.6 percent of total retail sales. By 1929, these figures had risen to $4.3 billion, or 8.9 percent of all retail sales. Between 1929 and 1954, however, the department store declined in relative importance, accounting for only 6.2 percent of retail sales in 1954. By 1967, they had regained their former position, accounting for 10.4 percent of total retail sales.[11]

Part of the department store's decline in the 1929–1954 period was due to innovative competition, especially from chains and discounters. Another, perhaps more important, factor was the department store's ties to the central business districts in the nation's cities. The health of the depart-

[10] *Ibid.,* p. 59.
[11] *Ibid.,* pp. 59–60.

EXHIBIT 2–2   Selected Historical Vignettes in Retailing Development

General Store Type/ Specific Store	Historical Background
Department Stores	
A. T. Stewart's	Located in New York City, A. T. Stewart's was the first department store. Opening its doors in 1863, Stewart's occupied a five-story building and was run by one general superintendent and nineteen assistants.
Stern Brothers	Stern Brothers of New York was one of the earliest of the prestige-type department stores. It followed a high-service strategy, catering to high-fashion markets. Although the store had high prices, it offered its customers strong product guarantees, delivery service, luxurious atmosphere, and credit.
R. H. Macy	Macy's chose to pass savings on to the consumer and, as a result, developed a low-price image. It did, in fact, sell its merchandise at low prices, using extensive advertising to announce its low-price approach. Unlike other department stores, Macy's prices were fixed in that they were not subject to negotiation. While it offered a strong product guarantee, it did not grant credit.
Chain Stores	
A & P	A & P is generally considered the first chain store in the United States. It began as a very small operation, when in 1859, George F. Gilman and George Hartford opened a tea shop in New York. By 1865, they had expanded their operation to 25 stores selling tea and groceries. Also, they had adopted the name Great Atlantic and Pacific Tea Company, or, as they are known today, A & P. By 1880, the 25-store operation had expanded to a 100-store chain, and by 1900, this number had doubled.
	Prior to 1912, the A & P chain had been able to generate cost savings primarily because of its backward integration into wholesaling. Then, in 1912, the A & P organization began opening what it called economy stores. Credit and delivery were eliminated. These economy stores were small, one-man, low-margin, high-turnover, cash-and-carry operations. They were tremendously

EXHIBIT 2–2 continued

General Store Type/ Specific Store	*Historical Background*
	successful. Thirteen years after their introduction by A & P, the A & P organization had grown to 14,034 stores representing a growth rate of 44 percent per year.
F. W. Woolworth Co.	In 1879, the first Woolworth store went into operation. It was a major innovation, not only because it signified the chain store's movement into the notions and houseware fields, but also because it was the first variety store to come into existence. By 1928, when 89 percent of all variety stores were owned by chains, Woolworth owned 33 percent of the stores, and its outlets accounted for 35 percent of total variety store sales volume.
Supermarkets	
Piggly Wiggly	The forerunners of the supermarkets were the Piggly Wiggly food stores introduced around 1920 by Clarence Saunders. These stores introduced the idea of self-service, but were unable to employ it as an operating advantage because of the small sizes of the stores. Like its future counterparts, Piggly Wigglys had both customer turnstiles and checkout counters.
The Big Bear Market	Going into operation in 1932, this store, located in Elizabeth, New Jersey, was one of the first supermarkets in the U.S. Housed in an old automobile plant, it displayed its groceries and produce in the cartons they came in. Its attraction was obviously not atmosphere, but price, and customers reportedly traveled as much as 100 miles to avail themselves of the store's low prices. The operation existed on a margin of 10 percent, as opposed to the traditional margin of 30 percent. However, the payoff proved worthwhile, with Big Bear achieving previously unheard of annual sales of $3 million.
Discount Houses	
E. J. Korvette Co.	The beginnings of the modern discount house operation were initiated in the late 1940's, when E. J. Korvette Company went into business, selling primarily electrical

EXHIBIT 2-2 continued

General Store Type/ Specific Store	Historical Background
	appliances. Also, Korvette is acknowledged to be the first concern to realize that low-margin, low-service, high-turnover techniques could be used to sell a wide variety of both soft and hard goods (e.g., clothing and appliances). In 1954, Korvette opened its first broad-line discount department store, and by 1962, it had 17 such stores, selling merchandise at prices that were 10 to 30 percent below the prevailing level.
Catalog Retailers	
Sears, Roebuck & Co.	Although Sears later blended its operations into a chain effort, its initial beginnings were as a mail-order house. Richard Sears, in fact, began his mail-order career as a railroad-station agent by offering watches for sale through his fellow agents. The profitability of this venture prompted Sears to quit his job with the railroad, and take his operation to the public. He found a partner in A. C. Roebuck, and they began to deal directly with the masses through newspaper advertising. Their sales and product assortment expanded steadily, until in 1891 the company had garnered more than $100,000 worth of annual business. However, by 1900, this figure had risen to almost $11 million, and by 1908, to $50 million.

SOURCE: Adapted from Louis P. Bucklin, *Competiton and Evolution in the Distributive Trades* (Englewood Cliffs, N.J.: Prentice-Hall, Inc., 1972).

ment store has traditionally been directly linked with the health of the central business district, which is where these operations began. It was precisely because of this relationship that the invention and widespread use of the automobile dealt such a severe blow to the department store.

Although department store operators were not quick to realize it, the automobile was to greatly alter the course of their institution's development. General Robert E. Wood, president of Sears, Roebuck, aptly surmised the automobile's impact when, reflecting on the situation in 1938, he wrote:

... the automobile has revolutionized American business, yet the great body of retailers were long oblivious to its eventual effect on retailing. With a larger and larger proportion of the population possessing autos, the problems of parking space, traffic congestion, and resulting inconvenience to downtown shoppers became more and more serious. The automobile made shopping mobile, and this mobility now created an opportunity for the outlying store, which with lower land values could give parking space; with lower overhead, rents, and taxes could lower operating costs, and could—with its larger clientele created by the automobile—offer effective competition for the downtown store.

I look for this movement of decentralization to continue. Not only the wealthy, the well-to-do and the middle class will move out of the congested areas of the cities, but a great deal of working people ... Existing department stores in the central area will continue to exist, but their relative importance may decline.[12]

Combined with a deterioration of public transportation services, the outward movement to the suburbs made possible by the automobile was clearly a major factor behind Wood's accurate predictions.

During the mid-1970's, department stores made a major resurgence.[13] The traditional department stores began an aggressive expansion into new geographic territories and continued their expansion into regional shopping centers. In addition, they developed "spin-off" operations (for example, Dayton-Hudson now has erected discount hard good centers, home entertainment centers, and jewelry specialty shops). The merchandising strategy inside the traditional department store has also changed with the development of departmentalized specialty shops. All of these factors, combined with increasingly sophisticated buying and inventory management, have brought about a considerable growth in the department store segment of general merchandising, particularly for firms like Dayton-Hudson, Bloomingdale's, Neiman-Marcus, and Marshall Field & Company.[14]

The Development of Chain Stores. The major retailing institution to arise in the 1920's was the chain store organization. The chains were a logical competitive response to the growth of department stores in that chains, through their economic advantages, offered lower prices and more conven-

---

[12]See "Chains Were Active in War Effort," in the series "50 Years of U.S. Retailing," *Chain Store Age—Executive Edition* (March, 1975), p. 18.

[13]See Douglas J. Tigert, "The Changing Structure of Retailing in Europe and North America: Challenges and Opportunities," University of Toronto Retailing and Institutional Research Program Working Paper No. 75–02 (January, 1974), p. 7.

[14]For example, see George Lazarus, "An Upbeat Field's Makes Magic on Magnificent Mile," *Chicago Tribune*, Section 2, March 21, 1976, p. 7; and Frederick C. Klein, "Chicago Thoroughfare Emerges as a Mecca for Wealthy Shoppers," *Wall Street Journal*, March 3, 1976, p. 1.

ient locations. By 1925, some 50,000 chain grocery stores had already been established, Walgreen's and Liggett's were rapidly expanding in the drug store field, and Woolworth's had captured a large share of the variety store business (see Exhibit 2-2). But it was not until 1925 that the chain concept was widely adopted by general merchandise retailers. For example, during 1925, J. C. Penney added 100 stores to its emerging chain organization, pushing its total number of outlets to 676. Also in this year, the most significant development was the entry of the leading mail order houses into the chain store field. Following the lead of Montgomery Ward and Sears, Roebuck, practically all of the important catalog operations decided to augment their mail order sales by opening retail outlets.[15]

By 1929, chain stores had become a major force in the United States economy. Eleven percent of all retail outlets were affiliated with a chain, and 22 percent of all retail sales were made by chains. In fact, in apparel, chains had gained 28 percent of retail sales. J. C. Penney had now grown to over 1000 stores; alone, it accounted for 4 percent of all clothing store sales. And, of course, chains dominated the food industry with 32 percent of all retail food sales.[16]

The growth of the chains during the twentieth century has followed a very interesting pattern (see Table 2-3). Until 1930, chains were expanding tremendously by opening new units. Between 1930 and 1950, the growth in the number of chain-owned units was slight (except in the food industry, where it showed a significant reduction), but growth in sales volume was substantial. Since 1950, there has been strong growth in both outlets and sales.

The 1930-1950 slowdown was the result of a number of impinging environmental factors: (1) During this period, many food, drug, variety, and other chains were shifting to supermarket or self-service operations. To accomplish this shift, they were closing several small stores and replacing them with one large store. (2) There was a need to consolidate after the hectic growth rate experienced in the 1920's. New organizational structures were needed, managerial problems had to be solved, and a pool of management talent had to be developed. (3) The Depression of the 1930's caused a shortage of funds for use in expansion. Since consumers had little to spend, there was little to be gained from expansion. (4) World War II created shortages of manpower and building material as well as restrictions on nonmilitary construction.[17]

---

[15]"50 Years of U.S. Retailing," No. 1, *op. cit.*, p. 14.

[16]Bucklin, *op. cit.*, pp. 61-62.

[17]Godfrey M. Lebhar, *Chain Stores in America 1859-1962*, 3rd ed. (New York: Chain Store Publishing Co., 1963), p. 31.

TABLE 2-3 Growth of Chain Stores for Selected Types of Retail Stores

	Establishments (percent)				Sales (percent)			
	1948	1958	1963	1967	1948	1958	1963	1967
Food Stores								
Single units	92	91	87	85	62	51	46	42
2–10 units	3	3	3	4	7	9	9	10
11+ units	5	6	9	11	31	40	44	48
Department Stores								
Single units	32	20	15	11	37	14	8	6
2–10 units	13	15	17	15	21	24	22	15
11+ units	55	65	68	74	43	62	70	79
Drug Stores								
Single units	89	87	84	83	73	71	67	61
2–10 units	6	8	9	8	9	11	12	10
11+ units	5	5	7	9	18	18	21	29
Variety Stores								
Single units	57	55	49	51	14	16	16	17
2–10 units	11	11	11	6	6	6	4	4
11+ units	32	34	40	43	80	78	80	79

SOURCE: U.S. Census of Business—various years.

The post-1950 growth (in number of stores) was undoubtedly greatly stimulated by the move to the suburbs and the growth of shopping centers. Proportionately, total retail sales accounted for by chains (defined as having two or more units) increased from 30.1 percent in 1954 to 36.6 percent in 1963. Comparable figures, using an 11-unit breakpoint, are 19.9 and 25.5 percent, respectively. By 1971, the 11-or-more-unit figure had risen to 30.7 percent.[18] In 1971, chains accounted for 87 percent of department store sales, 77 percent of variety store sales, 52 percent of food store sales, 42 percent of shoe store sales, 34 percent of drug store sales, and 31 percent of tire, battery, and accessory store sales.[19]

The economic advantages of the chain store may be traced to four sources: bargaining power, wholesale function efficiencies, multiple-store

[18] Roger A. Dickinson, *Retail Management* (Belmont, Calif.: Wadsworth Publishing Company, 1974), p. 10.

[19] *Ibid.*

efficiencies, and larger retail store size.[20] Bargaining power efficiencies are developed through the chains' relationships with suppliers; because of the quantity of their purchases, they are able to receive superior prices, service, and managerial attention to their merchandising needs. The wholesale function efficiencies mainly stem from their ability to participate more fully and effectively in marketing flows that were, at one time, the sole responsibility of independent wholesale middlemen. Economies in multiple-store operation are, as Bucklin points out, derived primarily from savings in marketing strategies applicable to many outlets. These savings can accrue from investigation of potential retail store outlets, design of facilities, optimal methods of display, type and depth of product line, promotion, development of staff services for personnel, accounting, lower costs of securing capital and better capital availability, first choice of leases on preferred sites, and lower rental costs.[21]

Despite the rapid growth of chains, there is, however, a significant trade-off involved in the development of chain-type operations:

> The routinization of activities of the large chain, which originally produced the chain's economic advantage, inhibits the flexibility of action. In part this is an organizational problem. In part it is a capital shortage that makes it impossible for older chains to expand as well as to modernize existing stores faced with a high rate of obsolescence.[22]

These are the primary reasons for the decline of A & P during the years since World War II. Chain organizations will undoubtedly be called upon to trade off more and more routinization and standardization for local organizational flexibility. To some extent, this trade-off explains the growth in franchising in recent years, because franchising, as will be seen in Chapter 10, represents a strong and viable alternative to corporate ownership of facilities and thus, to some extent, corporate rigidity.

The Development of the Supermarket.   The supermarket entered the structure of retailing as an institutional form in the late 1920's and early 1930's (see Exhibit 2-2). It introduced several of the modern-day principles of mass merchandising, such as customer self-service and scrambled merchandising. The supermarket's approach to retail distribution, much as it is today, was to serve the public's needs for food and household maintenance items by

[20]Bucklin, *op. cit.*, p. 95.
[21]*Ibid.*, p. 98.
[22]*Ibid.*, pp. 99–100.

providing a comprehensive assortment of these products at a single store via efficient, low-cost methods of distribution.

A number of environmental forces were at work to cause the supermarket to evolve when it did:

1. It developed during the Depression, when people were extremely price-conscious.

2. The automobile was in common use by then, thus reducing the need for small, neighborhood groceries by making distance a less important factor in shopping decisions.

3. Advances in refrigeration technology made it possible to store perishables with a high degree of certainty that the temperature would be as desired (as opposed to the uncertainty when perishables had to be stored in ice-cooled boxes).

4. The need for clerks was greatly reduced by manufacturers' extensive use of advertising to presell their products and brands.

5. Food products were becoming available in consumer-size packages (cans and boxes) rather than distributor-size containers (barrels and crates).[23]

6. Economic conditions made it possible for operators to get large buildings at low rental charges as well as large quantities of merchandise at very low prices from distressed sources.[24]

The initial success of supermarkets was no less spectacular than that of any other emerging institution. As many supermarkets adopted chain forms of organization, they, too, enjoyed the tremendous growth experiences that other chains encountered. Supermarkets rapidly became the primary institutional factor in the nation's retail food distribution system.

During the period 1956–1971, overall retail food distribution continued to undergo a process of simultaneous expansion and consolidation.[25] While the sales of food stores increased in volume 120 percent during this period, the number of food outlets declined by 34 percent. The inroads that supermarkets made into food retailing is evidenced by the fact that by 1971 they accounted for 77 percent of all grocery store sales. In addition, chains were still gaining market share from independently run operations; in 1971, corporate chains accounted for 45 percent of all grocery sales. Accompanying the expansion of this period, however, was a severe decline in profits for supermarkets. For example, operating profit for all food chains dropped 53

[23] Bucklin, *op. cit.*, p. 86.

[24] Beckman, Davidson, and Talarzyk, *op. cit.*, p. 269.

[25] Walter J. Salmon, Robert D. Buzzell, and Stanton G. Cort, "The Super Store—Strategic Implications for the Seventies," report prepared by the Marketing Science Institute with the support of *Family Center*, 1972, p. 8.

percent between 1956 and 1971 from 1.97 percent of sales to 0.92 percent. Average return on net worth also dropped, declining by 38 percent from 14.4 percent in 1956 to 8.9 percent in 1971.[26]

While recent data compiled by the Federal Trade Commission show that return on net worth for large supermarket chains increased to 10 percent by 1974,[27] it is evident that supermarkets have saturated their markets and, as a result, have induced some destructive price wars. In addition, they have become increasingly vulnerable to powerful new competitors, such as fast food restaurants, volume feeding organizations, and convenience food stores. Although supermarkets have adopted counter strategies to battle their decline in operating profit, including distribution cost reduction programs, product line diversifications, and differentiations of their food offering, they have been unable to achieve, in the aggregate, a net profit to sales ratio of greater than 1 percent.[28]

The Emergence of the Planned Shopping Center. In the post-World War II years, billions of dollars were devoted to constructing new highways, and new trading areas subsequently developed at the points of intersection of these heavily traveled arteries. Much of this development was unplanned. But the road-building, along with rapid economic and population growth, gave impetus to planned suburban and regional shopping centers.

At first, chain-store organizations were content merely to observe the growth of these planned shopping centers rather than participate in their development. In 1955, for example, only 6 percent of all chain stores had locations in such centers, but this was soon to change. By 1960, there were over 4500 shopping centers in the United States, and their rising popularity caused a scramble for the most desirable locations by chains and nonchains alike.[29]

Planned shopping centers are especially attractive to large retailers because of their ability to draw customers from relatively great distances. For example, when it was developed in 1956, Old Orchard Shopping Center in Skokie, Illinois (a suburb of Chicago) was intended to draw customers from the entire North Shore of Chicago, or a *radius* of about 10 miles. The prototype of the planned regional shopping center was built in 1950 near Seattle. By 1957, there were 36 regional centers, and by 1965, this number had grown to 469. The growth of the planned regional shopping centers was,

[26] *Ibid.*, p. 19.

[27] See "FTC Staff Report on Food Chains is Published," *Federal Trade Commission News*, July 11, 1975.

[28] See, for example, "Can Jonathan Scott Save A & P?" *Business Week*, May 19, 1975, pp. 128–136.

[29] "Centers, Chains Boomed as Nation Went Suburban," in "50 Years of Retailing," No. 6, *op. cit.*, p. 9.

more than any other factor, the most important development resulting in the revitalization of the department store. In fact, one shopping center authority defines a regional center not by the shifting criterion of its regional draw but by two factors: It must have 750,000 sq ft or more of leasable retail space, *and* it must have two or more major department stores.[30] Because the key to the success of a regional shopping center is the inclusion of a department store as an "anchor," each new center contains at least one (either a branch of a local store or a large chain such as Sears). Thus, the growth of these centers in the suburbs brought the department store to the people.

However, after years of unprecedented growth, the shopping center industry has been slowing down, with little hope of enjoying a quick recovery.[31] Stricter zoning laws, Environmental Protection Agency (EPA) regulations, escalating land value, capital and construction costs, over-stored markets, slower population growth, and less abundant energy sources are among the factors contributing to the industry's problems. As more and more regional centers were built, the maximum draw, or primary trading area, fell to three or four miles by the late 1960's. Although population growth counterbalanced the decline in trading areas for a while, predictions for the future growth of these centers (and especially the new "super-regionals") are not bright. In fact, there is considerable vacant space available in the newer centers.[32] Some developers have speculated that increases in the number of neighborhood and multiuse centers (such as The Citadel in Colorado Springs) will be witnessed,[33] while others are foretelling an emphasis on improving, modernizing, and expanding existing centers, rather than on building new ones.[34] Some shopping center owners have begun pruning unproductive shops from their centers, creating excitement by organizing spectator activities within the centers (such as tennis matches and orchestra concerts), and attempting to reposition their centers to serve the youth market.[35]

The Emergence of the Discount House. The emergence of the discount house as a major retailing institution was largely a phenomenon of the 1950's. Although some units were in operation as early as the 1930's, dis-

---

[30] See statements of Ross Cambell, a research specialist on shopping centers, in Donald M. Schwartz, "End of Era? Shopping Centers," *Chicago Sun-Times*, Real Estate Section, September 14, 1975, p. 15.

[31] See, for example, "Shopping Centers: What's Ahead?" *Chain Store Age—Executive Edition* (May, 1975), p. 23 and Schwartz, *op. cit.*

[32] See Schwartz, *op. cit.*

[33] "Is the Big Regional Dead?" *Chain Store Age—Executive Edition* (May, 1975), p. 25.

[34] Jerry C. Davis, "Need a Cure for All Ills? Try a Shopping Center," *Chicago Sun-Times*, Real Estate Section, September 14, 1975, p. 16.

[35] *Ibid.*

count houses underwent major expansion and growth following World War II, when they began to merchandise nationally advertised hard goods (e.g., electric appliances) at considerable markdowns compared to more conventional outlets (see Exhibits 2-1 and 2-2).

The spectacular growth of discount houses has been attributed to at least three other factors: (1) They located in the suburbs, which were underretailed at the time. (2) More blue-collar workers were moving to the suburbs. Department stores, even in the suburban shopping centers, were aimed at white-collar markets, thus enabling the discounters to fill a void in the market. (3) The spending habits of the working class were becoming more closely in line with those of the middle class. That is, blue-collar workers were becoming more prudent in how they spent their income (which was rising), and therefore were seeking the type of goods being sold by the discounters.[36] By 1967, discount house sales had increased to an estimated $17 billion or 39 percent of all general merchandise groups of stores (department, variety, and general).

Of all the organizational forms of discounting operations, the discount department store has experienced the most explosive growth during the 1950's and 1960's, led by such outlets as Dayton-Hudson's Target stores, Woolworth's Woolco stores, Kresge's K-Mart stores, and Federated's Gold Circle stores. However, some retail analysts, such as the A. C. Nielsen Company, have suggested that the discount department store, and discount houses in general, are entering a slow-growth phase because of demonstrated recent declines in sales. In fact, a number of retailing analysts have predicted a significant decline for discount department stores due to overexpansion, lack of professional management, poor accounting and control systems, new types of retailing competition, declining inventory turnover ratios, and rising wages and other expenses as a percent of sales.[37] Buttressing these predictions are the results of a survey conducted by Dupont which found, among other things, that:

> ... discounters rate poorly in such areas as employee helpfulness, variety of merchandise, and selection of items. . . . Consumers dislike most of the promotional tactics that discount stores have traditionally used, including "limited quantity" sales, which are regarded as come-ons, coupons in store advertising, and rain checks for out-of-stock merchandise.[38]

[36]Charles E. Silberman, "The Revolutionists of Retailing," *Fortune*, April, 1962, pp. 256–258.

[37]These factors are documented by Tigert, *op. cit.*, pp. 25-34. See also Robert F. Hartley, *Marketing Mistakes* (Columbus, Ohio: Grid, Inc., 1976), pp. 31–56.

[38]"Where Shoppers Buy General Merchandise in Competitive Areas and What Prompts Their Decision," *Home Furnishings Daily*, May 22, 1973.

Quality of merchandise was the factor which the surveyed consumers said they liked least about discount stores. Thus, it appears that many of the features of present-day discount houses may be antagonizing consumers. Discount store operators might do well to consider repositioning themselves in their markets if these trends continue.[39]

The Growth of Nonstore Retailing.   The use of automatic vending to retail a wide variety of convenience goods has also grown remarkably over the past two decades. In 1954, sales of the vending machine industry were about $660 million, but soared to better than $2 billion in 1967, making the industry the fastest-growing retail segment.[40]

Particularly interesting, though, in the nonstore retailing sector is the boom that seems to be taking place in mail-order shopping.[41] According to a tabulation by the Maxwell Sroge Company, Inc., a specialist in mail-order business planning and advertising, 1974 industry sales were $14.4 billion, amounting to about 14 percent of all general merchandise sales and 3.5 percent of total retail sales.[42] Buying by mail or telephone accounts for about 20 percent of Sears, Roebuck's sales and 14 percent of Montgomery Ward's. The major reasons for the growth seem to be that (1) more women are working and have less time to shop in stores; (2) shoppers are retreating from crime-plagued urban shopping areas; (3) gasoline is less plentiful and more costly; (4) sales assistance is less available in stores due to the desire of traditional retailers to cut costs.[43]

Surprisingly, at least half of the nation's largest 50 corporations have mail order divisions. The Xerox Corporation offers children's books; Avon Products, Inc., has women's apparel; W. R. Grace & Co. has cheese; American Airlines, luggage; General Foods Corporation, needlework kits; and General Mills, Inc., sport shirts. Among the multiplicity of products and services that can be purchased by mail, the leading sellers are insurance, magazine subscriptions, phonograph records, foods, and books.[44]

Department and specialty stores recognized the sales potential of mail and telephone ordering only belatedly. Now, however, such retailers as Neiman-Marcus, Saks Fifth Avenue, Bloomingdale's, and Bergdorf Goodman

---

[39] See Tigert, *op. cit.*, pp. 37–43.

[40] Bucklin, *op. cit.*, p. 91.

[41] See Rita Reif, "Mail Order: Old Road to New Sales," *New York Times*, Section 3, August 24, 1975, p. 1.

[42] *Ibid.*

[43] *Ibid.*

[44] *Ibid.*, p. 4.

have entered the field and are clearly attempting to appeal to upper middle class and above buying segments by offering higher-priced, sometimes exotic merchandise. Apparently, though, the largest percentage of shoppers from the catalogs distributed by these stores are relatively young people. According to one industry authority, "The generation that made the *Whole Earth Catalog* an international best seller has taught retailers a lesson."[45]

Finally, although house-to-house selling has declined in relative importance over the past several decades, there appears to be a slight resurgence in its popularity. This method of direct sale is used for a wide variety of items, including vacuum cleaners, radios, television sets, furniture, cosmetics, cooking utensils, and brushes. According to Carman and Uhl, there seem to be three main influences directly related to competition which have encouraged some manufacturers in recent years to turn to door-to-door selling:

> First, the rise in competition in many consumer goods markets has necessitated different approaches to the consumer, including such a "hard sell" technique as house-to-house selling. Second, inability to match the tremendous advertising expenditures of major competitors has led some firms to turn to direct selling at the consumer's door. Finally, the fact that some firms have done very well using direct-selling organizations has encouraged others.[46]

Even though over 77,000 establishments are engaged, in one form or another, in house-to-house selling, this sector of retail trade has not been as strong a participant in the retailing revolution as other forms of organization have been.

Institutional Life Cycles

In the preceding discussion of the retailing revolution, it was repeatedly noted that institutions which experienced a remarkably high rate of growth eventually were faced with new competitive, socioeconomic, managerial, and technological forces that presented obstacles to their continued growth. In point of fact, all retail institutions—just like the products they distribute—pass through an identifiable life cycle consisting of four states: *early growth*, *accelerated development*, *maturity*, and *decline*.[47] The nature and shape of this life cycle are depicted in Fig. 2–1.

As indicated in Fig. 2–1, new retail institutions generate high rates of

---

[45] *Ibid.*, p. 5.

[46] James M. Carman and Kenneth P. Uhl, *Phillips and Duncan's Marketing, Principles and Methods*, 7th ed. (Homewood, Ill.: Richard D. Irwin, Inc., 1973), p. 188.

[47] See Bert C. McCammon, Jr., "The Future of Catalog Showrooms: Growth and Its Challenges to Management," Marketing Science Institute Working Paper, April 1973, pp. 1–3.

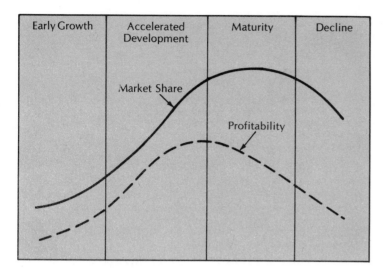

FIGURE 2-1   The Institutional Life Cycle in Retailing

SOURCE: Bert C. McCammon, Jr., "The Future of Catalog Showrooms: Growth and Its Challenges to Management," Marketing Science Institute Working Paper, April, 1973, p. 2.

growth and attractive profitability ratios during their initial stages of development. Illustrative of institutions that achieved extraordinary results during their formative years are the department store in the late 1800's, the supermarket in the 1930's, and the discount department store in the late 1950's and early 1960's. However, as retail institutions mature, they are increasingly confronted by new forms of competition and forced to compete in overstored or saturated markets.[48] As a result, price competition for these institutions intensifies, accompanied by declines in market share and profitability. Ultimately, mature institutions enter the decline stage of their life cycle, wherein they invariably become disadvantaged participants in the marketplace.[49] Thus, from this perspective, department stores, variety stores, and supermarkets are already mature and/or declining retail institutions. That is, they represent methods of doing business that no longer regularly produce high rates of growth or rates of return on investment.[50]

More important, however, for managers is the knowledge that institutional life cycles within retailing have accelerated over the years. For example, McCammon has estimated that the time to reach maturity has declined from approximately 100 years, in the case of department stores, to approx-

[48]Several additional theories of institutional change are explored in Chapter 5 of this text.

[49]McCammon, *op. cit.*, pp. 2-3.

[50]*Ibid.*, p. 3.

TABLE 2-4   Illustration of the Accelerating Pace
of Institutional Life Cycles

Retail Institution	Early Growth	Maturity	Approximate Time Required To Reach Maturity
Department stores	Mid-1860's	Mid-1960's	100 years
Variety stores	Early 1900's	Early 1960's	60 years
Supermarkets	Mid-1930's	Mid-1960's	30 years
Discount department stores	Mid-1950's	Mid-1970's	20 years
Fast food service outlets	Early 1960's	Mid-1970's	15 years
Home improvement centers	Mid-1960's	Late 1970's	15 years
Furniture warehouse showrooms	Late 1960's	Late 1970's	10 years
Catalog showrooms	Late 1960's	Late 1970's	10 years

SOURCE: Bert C. McCammon, Jr., "The Future of Catalog Showrooms: Growth and Its Challenges to Management," Marketing Science Institute Working Paper, April, 1973, p. 3.

imately 10 years, in the case of catalog showrooms (see Table 2–4). Implicit in McCammon's analysis is the point that those contemporary institutions that are now in their initial stages of development will soon be faced with problems and challenges that confront department stores and supermarkets today. Therefore, it is necessary to examine the emerging institutional trends in retailing at the present point in time in order to be able to predict where the opportunities seem to lie in the not-too-distant future.

Emerging Institutional Trends

On the basis of observations of the past and present retailing scene, it is possible to predict, in a conjectural fashion, that low-cost, merchandise-intensive approaches to retail distribution will probably dominate institutional patterns in the decade ahead. This is likely to be true even though there appears to be an increased polarity in retail trade; that is, high-fashion, specialized boutiques, such as those found in Toronto's Yorkville section and in San Francisco's Ghirardelli Square, may continue to exist alongside or within short distances of large mass merchandising operations. In addition, although there is strong evidence of an increase in stores specializing in limited lines of merchandise (e.g., Radio Shack, Soda Shoppes of California, Fairway Auto Mall in Tulsa),[51] trends toward inventory diversification or scrambled merchandising show no signs of abatement.[52]

[51]See "Specialty Store Trend Gaining in the Marketplace," Advertising Age, August 4, 1975, p. 4. See, also, Tigert, op. cit., p. 9.

[52]See Bert C. McCammon, Jr., "Future Shock and the Practice of Management," a paper presented at

The mass merchandising movement can be thought of as involving at least two separate technologies. *First*, it adopts and adapts the *supermarket* method of distribution to an expanding number of commodity lines. Contemporary examples of this approach include the super drug store, the home improvement center, and the family center, also known as the "superstore."[53] Specifically, all of these organizational forms depend on self-service, single-plant economies of scale, sophisticated inventory control, central checkout configurations, and volume pricing in order to appeal to price- and value-conscious consumers. For example, *super drug stores*, such as those operated by the Skaggs Companies, Inc. and Long's, offer a broad assortment of health and beauty aids, cosmetics, housewares, jewelry, party goods, sporting goods, hardware, and related merchandise. As evidence of the extent of their merchandise diversification, only a very small percentage of their total volume typically results from their sales of prescription drugs. *Home improvement centers* (e.g., Republic Lumber, Wickes, Handy Man, and Daylin's) basically appeal to the do-it-yourself market, and most offer broad and deep assortments of building materials, hardware, garden supplies, paint, power tools, and other "self-service" products. *Family centers* or *superstores* focus on serving the consumer's needs for all types of routine purchases or convenience items, mainly through allocating a substantial portion (often 50 percent) of their floor space to general merchandise and notions (e.g., hosiery, underwear, and school supplies).[54] Many supermarket chains, such as A & P, view this type of operation as a logical response to the problems confronting them.[55] Running a minimum of 30,000 sq ft in size and handling 15,000 or more food and nonfood items, superstores do more than $100,000 a week in sales, compared to the $20,000 weekly figure that the traditional 10,000 to 15,000 sq ft (7000- to 9000-item) supermarket averages. By the mid-1970's, superstores comprised approximately 8 percent of the food industry's 200,000 stores and accounted for nearly 20 percent of its sales. Furthermore, some estimate that by 1980, superstores will contribute half of all grocery sales.[56]

The *second* major technology encompassed by the mass merchandising movement is the application of *warehouse* operating principles at the retail level.[57] At the present time, at least three variations on this warehouse retailing theme are discernible, namely, catalog warehouses, home furnishing

---

the Fifth Annual Attitude Research Conference of the American Marketing Association, Madrid, Spain, 1973, pp. 8–13.

[53]*Ibid.*, p. 14.

[54]See Salmon, Buzzell, and Cort, *op. cit.*, p. 3.

[55]"Can Jonathan Scott Save A & P?" *op. cit.*, p. 134.

[56]*Ibid.*

[57]McCammon, "Future Shock . . .," *op. cit.*, p. 14.

warehouses, and general merchandise warehouses.[58] *Catalog warehouses* or *showrooms*, such as those operated by Service Merchandise and H. J. Wilson, generally issue two catalogs a year, one in the fall and another in the spring, and attempt to underprice more conventional retailers by 15 to 25 percent on nationally branded merchandise. By buying on a direct basis and utilizing few employees in their operations, catalog showrooms considerably reduce the labor costs of the overall distribution process. *Furniture warehouse showrooms*, such as those operated by Levitz and Wickes, combine supermarket methods with the warehouse approach.[59] Large displays are available for consumer browsing, and purchases may be made on a "take-with" or "delivery-for-a-fee" basis. Enormous inventories are maintained in a warehouse connected to the showroom, so that the consumer can obtain merchandise on the spot at low prices.[60] Finally, *general merchandise warehouses*, or hypermarkets, typically employ massive warehouses of over 100,000 sq ft devoted to both food and a variety of hard and soft goods lines, including apparel, major appliances, furniture, and housewares. The hypermarket was originally developed in western Europe;[61] the first one in the United States, Meijer's Thrifty Acres located near Detroit, features a 245,000-sq-ft store, bins and metal racks for food as high as 12 ft, and a sophisticated central checkout and materials handling system.[62] As a result of their operating economies, hypermarkets can usually underprice competitors by as much as 15 to 20 percent.

Emerging Environmental Trends

If retailers are successfully to program their operations for future high-yield performance and if manufacturers, wholesalers, and other marketing channel members are going to play significant roles in working with retailers to make the distribution of their products and services more effective and efficient, it is necessary that all parties to the process recognize emerging opportunities and impending constraints by performing environmental analyses. A penetrating analysis of this kind has been conducted by Bert C.

---

[58]McCammon, "The Future of Catalog Showrooms . . .," *op. cit.*, p. 7.

[59]For an overview of this type of retail warehousing operation, see Susan B. Miller, "Furniture Warehouses That Sell to Public Spring Up and Do Well Across the Land," *Wall Street Journal*, May 30, 1972, p. 26.

[60]The reader should contrast this approach to furniture retailing with the one described at the outset of Chapter 1.

[61]See Chapter 13 of this text.

[62]"America's First Hypermarket," *Chain Store Age—Executive Edition* (March, 1975), pp. 25–26.

McCammon, who has been an astute observer of the trends in retailing for several decades.[63]

McCammon has reported on three emerging environmental developments relative to consumption markets which hold broad strategic implications for all marketing channel members. The first development he has isolated is the growing *institutionalization* of the consumption process, which he explains as follows:

> To an increasing extent, organizations rather than individuals are making final buying decisions. For example, 19.6 percent of all automobiles manufactured are *fleet* vehicles, 42.6 percent of all carpet produced goes into *contract* markets, and over 40.0 percent of all life insurance in force is in the form of group policies. Similarly, career apparel or uniform sales to employers and rental organizations are expanding *twice* as rapidly as the total ready-to-wear market, and the furniture and equipment rental business has already become a $1.0 billion industry, with a projected rate of growth of 15.0 percent a year during the decade ahead.[64]

Consequently, the need to examine *organizations* as potential target markets has taken on added significance.

A second environmental development pointed out by McCammon is the notion that consumption markets are becoming increasingly segmented, largely as a result of rising consumer affluence. Because consumers are searching for the precise combination of values to satisfy their more discriminating requirements, *market positioning* and *multiplex distribution* have become significant management issues.[65] Relative to the first issue, distributive organizations may find it necessary to program their entire operations in such a way that they appeal to specific market segments. Prime examples of successful proponents of this strategy in retailing include McDonald's, Radio Shack, and Pier I, all of which project a distinct image that contrasts sharply with the often bland images projected by conventional retailers.[66] These new types of specialty stores are usually small (7,000–15,000 square feet) but are committed to breadth and depth in one or two product lines aimed at achieving "classification dominance" in those lines. According to Tigert, the fastest growth has come with the advent of the major shopping center—these store types make up 60 to 70 percent of the stores in each center.[67]

---

[63]See McCammon, "Future Shock . . .," *op. cit.*, p. 5.

[64]*Ibid.*, p. 12.

[65]*Ibid.*, p. 13.

[66]*Ibid.* See also John H. Holmes, "Profitable Positioning for Retailers," *Journal of the Academy of Marketing Science*, Vol. 1 (January, 1975), pp. 332-339.

[67]Tigert, *op. cit.*, p. 9.

With regard to the issue of multiplex distribution, McCammon has observed:

> Multiplex distribution is a logical extension of market positioning. Throughout the 1970's, firms will increasingly operate *multiple* types of outlets to serve *multiple* market segments, because this is a proven technique for maintaining *competitive dominance* in an era of fragmented demand. Dayton Hudson, an early proponent of the free form concept, currently operates conventional department stores, discount department stores, ready-to-wear boutiques, pants shops, cosmetic salons, book stores, jewelry stores, catalog showrooms, automotive service centers, and warehouse outlets. In short, the company has embarked on an eclectic expansion program on the assumption that this is a logical response to market segmentation.[68]

The third environmental development isolated by McCammon is that a growing number of consumers perceive themselves as either *economic* or *convenience* shoppers.[69] As a result, the mass merchandising movement, because of its value orientation, is a logical response to the economic shopper. At the same time, the rapidly expanding convenience goods-oriented superstores and the increased variety of specialty operations[70] are well suited to serve the convenience markets. Thus, as indicated earlier, it is apparent that the structure of retailing will likely remain polarized, with second-generation mass merchandisers *and* specialty stores attaining a major portion of the growth and profitability in retailing.[71] In fact, as Tigert has observed, most of the new retailing organizations are making inroads into the market of traditional outlets carrying the same product lines on the basis of one of two major strategies or both:

1. *Larger stores* with the consequent economies of scale including warehouse technology, professional management, lower wage costs, cheaper construction and store fixturing, and strong supplier relationships;

2. *A commitment to "classification dominance"* through specialization in one or a few product lines, offering consumers a major improvement in quantity and quality of selection for that product class.[72]

---

[68] McCammon, "Future Shock . . .," *op. cit.*, p. 13.

[69] *Ibid.*, p. 14.

[70] See "Specialty Store Trend Gaining in Marketplace," *Advertising Age.*, *op. cit.*

[71] McCammon, "Future Shock . . .," *op. cit.*, p. 14. Some analysts contend that "super" specialty stores (e.g., Athlete's Foot, Child World, County Seat, Crate & Barrel, The Gap, and Calculators, Inc.) could be the wave of the future, because they blend the advantages of product specialization with the economies of chain-store operation. See Albert D. Bates and Bert C. McCammon, Jr., "Reseller Strategies and the Financial Performance of the Firm," a paper presented to the Structure, Strategy, and Performance Conference, Indiana University Graduate School of Business, November 1975, p. 19.

[72] Tigert, *op. cit.*, p. 12.

Consequences of the Retailing Revolution

Clearly, changes as profound as the ones outlined briefly on the preceding pages have significantly affected the overall structure of retailing in the United States. Interestingly, however, the number of retail establishments has remained remarkably stable since 1929 according to Census data, demonstrating the fact that aggregate statistics merely hide the turbulence within the retailing field. During the same time period, demand for retail offerings has grown, in constant dollars, more than three and one-half times. Given the stability in numbers and the growth in sales, we see that it is obvious that the size of the average retail store has increased significantly, in terms of sales volume generated. With the development of department, discount, and chain stores and the emergence of supermarket merchandising, it should be no surprise to learn that the average sales per store have risen substantially, from a low of $16,000 in 1933 to $221,500 in 1972. Finally, the structure of retailing institutions is becoming increasingly top-heavy. In 1967, retail establishments with annual sales volumes in excess of $1 million accounted for 44.4 percent of all retail sales, even though they represented only 3.0 percent of all establishments. Establishments with annual sales of $49,000 or less accounted for only 5.2 percent of all retail sales, but made up 48.5 percent of the store population. (See Table 2–5 for selected statistical data relevant to the revolution.)

ELEMENTS OF COMPETITION IN RETAILING

Despite the important changes in the size distribution of retail *establishments* or stores, there has not been as significant an increase in the size distribution of retail *firms*. For example, 87 percent of retail establishments in the United States are operated by firms that have only one store in the same general kind of business.[73] Although there are some enormous firms engaged in retailing, they are seldom large enough to dominate their fields. In 1956, *Fortune*'s annual survey of the largest retail firms showed that sales of the top 35 retailers amounted to 12.4 percent of all retail volume; this percentage had risen to only 17.4 by 1969.

Table 2–6 shows the 1963 and 1972 sales of the four and eight largest firms in the two merchandise groupings where giant retailers are most prom-

---

[73]Delbert J. Duncan, Charles F. Phillips, and Stanley C. Hollander, *Modern Retailing Mangement*, 8th ed. (Homewood, Ill.: Richard D. Irwin, Inc., 1972), p. 6.

TABLE 2-5 Consequences of the Revolution in Retailing

	Establishments (percent of total)			Sales (percent of total)		
	1948	1963	1967	1948	1963	1967
A. Unit of Operations						
Single units	90.8	87.1	87.5	70.3	63.4	60.2
Multiple units	9.2	12.9	12.5	29.7	36.6	39.8
2–10 units	4.6	6.3	5.0	11.1	11.1	10.5
11–25 units	0.9	1.0	1.0	2.0	3.1	3.6
26–100 units	1.2	1.5	1.7	3.3	6.7	7.0
100+ units	2.5	4.1	4.7	12.3	15.8	18.6
B. Distribution of Retail Establishments by Annual Sales (operated all year)						
$1 million and more	0.7	2.4	3.0	20.8	38.4	44.4
$500,000–999,000	1.4	2.8	3.3	12.0	15.6	12.9
$100,000–499,000	14.4	23.7	25.9	34.8	31.3	29.5
$50,000–99,000	18.5	21.5	19.3	15.9	10.0	7.6
$10,000–49,000	47.3	38.3	35.3	15.4	6.9	5.2
Less than $10,000	17.7	11.3	13.2	1.1	0.1	0.4

	1948	1963	1967	1972
C. Average Sales Per Store	$73,747	$143,000	$176,000	$221,500

SOURCE: U.S. Census of Business.

inent and compares them with total sales for the whole country. The billions of sales of the four largest corporate food chains amounted to 19 percent of total retail food sales in both years, while the four largest general-merchandise stores did about 32 percent of the business in which they sell. Such figures, however, often overstate the extent of concentration in retailing, for consumers frequently choose among a large variety of different types of stores (general merchandise; variety; discount; drug; tires, batteries, and accessories; etc.) in their purchasing of any given item. The categories of stores, then, seem more to reflect Census convenience than they do consumer shopping habits and significant cross-elasticities. Even ignoring this weakness of the data, Weiss has determined that, except for variety stores, no branch of retailing was any more concentrated on a national scale in 1963 than the textile industry, which, historically, has been viewed as a highly atomistic industry.[74]

[74]Weiss, op. cit., p. 210.

TABLE 2–6 Sales and Market Shares of the Four and Eight Largest Firms in the Retailing of General Merchandise and Food, 1963 and 1972

	1963 Sales (billions)		1972 Sales (billions)	
Stores Retailing General Merchandise				
Largest Four				
Sears, Roebuck	$ 5.1		$11.0	
J. C. Penney	1.8		5.5	
S. S. Kresge	—		3.9	
Marcor (Montgomery Ward)	1.5		3.4	
F. W. Woolworth	1.2		—	
Total, largest four	$ 9.6		$23.8	
Four-firm share of all general merchandise sales		32.1%		31.7%
Next Largest Four				
F. W. Woolworth	—		3.1	
Federated Department Stores	0.9		2.7	
W. T. Grant	0.7		1.6	
Allied Stores	0.8		1.5	
May Department Stores	0.7		—	
Total, next largest four	$ 3.1		$ 8.9	
Next-largest-four share of all general merchandise sales		10.6%		11.9%
Eight-firm share of all general merchandise sales		42.7%		43.6%
Stores Retailing Food[a]				
Largest Four				
A & P	$ 5.2		$ 6.4	
Safeway	2.6		6.1	
Kroger	2.1		3.8	
Jewel Companies[b]	—		2.0	
Acme Markets	1.1		—	
Total, largest four	$11.0		$18.3	
Four-firm share of all food stores sales		19.3%		19.3%
Next Largest Four				
Lucky Stores	—		2.0	
Food Fair Stores	1.0		2.0	
Acme Markets	—		1.9	
Winn-Dixie Stores	.8		1.8	
National Tea	1.1		—	
Jewel Tea	.7		—	
Total, next largest four	$ 3.6		$ 7.7	
Next largest four share of all food sales		6.4%		8.1%
Eight-firm share of all food sales		25.7%		27.4%

[a]Includes only corporate food chains; excludes wholesaler-sponsored voluntary chains and retailer-sponsored cooperative chains.
[b]Includes Jewel's general merchandise stores.

SOURCE: *Fortune*, July, 1964 and July, 1973; and U.S. Census of Business and *Survey of Current Business*.

However, the markets in which retailers compete are local rather than national, because consumers rarely travel beyond twenty miles to secure wanted goods. The best information on concentration in local retail markets is for food distribution. In 218 major metropolitan areas in the country, the top four food retailers, including both corporate and cooperative chains, held, on the average, 50 percent of the market in 1964. This was up from 45 percent in 1954.[75] The four-firm concentration ratio ranged from 23 percent in Fresno, California to over 70 percent in Great Falls, Montana. Generally, the ratio tends to be lower in larger cities. This tendency is found in certain other lines of retail trade as well,[76] indicating that competition is likely to be stiffer and prices lower in large metropolitan areas, because more firms are vying for a smaller share of the urban consumer's dollar. Nevertheless, there is enough evidence to support the contention that concentration is reasonably high on the local level.[77] The emergence of chains and the growth in establishment size has no doubt been directly related to this situation. However, the checks on increased local concentration are more abundant in retailing than in many other lines of trade. Increased consumer mobility, the trend to scrambled merchandising, and, as we shall see, the relatively low cost of entry into retailing have served to maintain a competitive atmosphere in most localities. Unfortunately, those localities that are most in need of more competition, such as ghetto areas in major metropolitan areas, do not seem to incorporate many of these checks.[78]

Data indicate that entry barriers are not insurmountable in retailing. Minimal capital requirements for a retail establishment vary widely, however, due, as Bucklin points out, to differences in the acquisition cost of land, construction charges, the quality of the facilities and fixtures, the proportion that lending institutions (or landlords) will provide, and the precise size of outlet required to compete successfully.[79] Construction costs range from $10 to $30 per square foot. Internal decorations and fixtures for chain units averaged $270,000 in 1969.[80] A rough notion of capital requirement for various chain units is provided in Table 2-7.

---

[75]National Commission on Food Marketing, *Organization and Competition in Food Retailing*, Technical Study No. 7 (Washington, D.C.: U.S. Government Printing Office, 1966), pp. 42–53.

[76]Bucklin, *op. cit.*, pp. 126–130.

[77]*Ibid.*, pp. 125–126.

[78]See Frederick D. Sturdivant, "Distribution in American Society: Some Questions of Efficiency and Relevance," in Louis P. Bucklin (ed.), *Vertical Marketing Systems* (Glenview, Ill.: Scott, Foresman and Co., 1970), pp. 94–115, and Frederick D. Sturdivant (ed.), *The Ghetto Marketplace* (New York: Free Press, 1969).

[79]Bucklin, *Competition and Evolution . . .,op. cit.*, p. 143.

[80]*Ibid.*, p. 143.

TABLE 2-7   Capital Requirements for Chain Stores Built in 1969

Type of Store	Cost Per Establishment (dollars)	Average Size in Square Feet	Cost Per Square Foot (dollars)
Department	1,980,000	83,239	24
Discount	1,049,184	59,018	18
Supermarket	512,642	20,412	25
Variety	495,350	19,206	26
Drug	182,129	10,800	17

SOURCE: Louis P. Bucklin, *Competition and Evolution in the Distributive Trades* (Englewood Cliffs, N.J.: Prentice-Hall, Inc., 1972), Table 4-13, p. 144.

Of more significance as an entry barrier is the increasing role of the planned shopping center. Shopping center managers have consistently elected to choose large chains for their tenants whenever possible, due to financial (loan-attracting) and marketing (traffic-attracting) considerations.[81] For example, in a study of five centers in Louisville, Kentucky, independent retailers accounted for only 42 percent of the establishments, and more importantly, these small firms were allocated less than 20 percent of the building area space.[82] Also, the rents they pay are usually higher than those charged the major chains. The small, independent ladies' wear firm may pay a rent of 7.2 percent of sales, whereas the national department store may be charged only 2.8 percent.[83] In light of predictions that shopping centers will account for close to 45 percent of all retail trade by 1980,[84] the shopping center organizer-entrepreneur will no doubt continue to play a significant gatekeeper role in determining the future characteristics of both the structure of and competition in retailing, despite the fact that the growth in the shopping center segment of retailing has slowed considerably, as pointed out earlier.

More precise statements about the nature of competition in retailing are bound to be riddled with exceptions because of the diversity of retail establishments, firms, and markets. It is, however, possible to make some broad generalizations. McCammon, for example, has suggested that the forms of

[81] *Ibid.*, p. 144.

[82] John R. Foster, "The Effect of Shopping Center Financing on the Opportunity for Occupancy by Independent Retailers," *Southern Journal of Business* (April, 1967), p. 26.

[83] Urban Land Institute, *The Dollars and Cents of Shopping Centers, 1966* (Washington, D.C.: 1966), p. 184.

[84] Bucklin, *Competition and Evolution . . ., op. cit.*, p. 109.

TABLE 2-8   Competition in the Retailing Sector

Type of Competition	Scope of Competition	Corporate Illustrations
Intratype competition	Competition between the *same* type of outlets	Thrifty vs. Walgreen
Intertype competition	Competition between *different* types of outlets	Kroger vs. K-Mart
Systems competition	Competition between *different* types of vertically integrated systems, including voluntary groups, co-operative groups, franchise networks, and corporate chains	A & P vs. IGA
Free-form competition	Competition between free-form cor-porations, each of which operates multiple types of outlets to serve multiple market segments	Daylin vs. Interco

SOURCE: Bert C. McCammon, Jr., "Future Shock and the Practice of Management," a paper presented at the Fifth Annual Attitude Research Conference of the American Marketing Association, Madrid, Spain, 1973, p. 8.

competition portrayed in Table 2-8 are regularly encountered in the retail sector. However, as pointed out previously, many of the larger companies (e.g., Dayton-Hudson, J. C. Penney) are seeking to achieve differential advantages in multiple competitive environments; therefore, the categories of competitive behavior isolated in Table 2-8 are not mutually exclusive. It does appear likely, though, that *intertype* competition will steadily intensify in the future, largely as a result of the emerging numbers of mass merchandisers who are adopting a scrambled merchandising philosophy.

Beyond this, at least two further generalizations can be made regarding competition at the retail level. First, even though economic concentration in retailing has been increasing, due to the myriad of forces already discussed, and though entry barriers are present in some segments of retail trade, price competition is relatively strong, especially when compared to the extent of such competition among the numerous oligopolistic industries in the manufacturing sector.[85] The opportunity for loss-leader selling, differences in product-line width (assortments), private brand policies, and spatial locations as well as cost factors, changes in wholesale prices, and consumer ignorance all combine to induce vigorous price competition on the retail

[85] See Louis W. Stern and John R. Grabner, Jr., *Competition in the Marketplace* (Glenview, Ill.: Scott, Foresman and Co., 1970) and U.S. Department of Commerce Bureau of Census, *Concentration Ratios in Manufacturing Industry, 1963*, Parts I and II (Washington, D.C.: U.S. Government Printing Office, 1967).

level.[86] Retail advertising seems to aggravate this situation. As Weiss has observed about retail advertisements:

> ... they are usually local in character and are therefore done on a small enough scale that most ... groups of efficient size can afford them. Moreover, they clearly make the individual store's demand curve more elastic. Department store sales and supermarket specials only become profitable for the seller if he can advertise them. And the presence of the Sears' catalogue and the food ads put a severe limit on the ability of local retailers to set high prices. By improving market information, advertising has brought retailing much closer to pure competition.[87]

Second, the main competitive weapons, other than price, that retailers tend to use to differentiate themselves from one another are variations in (1) the services offered to consumers (e.g., credit, shopping atmosphere, parking facilities, hours, shopping assistance, etc.), (2) the assortments of merchandise made available (broad, deep, high quality, etc.), and (3) location. It is by alterations in and the effective management of these elements of the retailing marketing mix that Sears differentiates itself from Marshall Field and that the 7-11 convenience food stores differentiate themselves from Safeway supermarkets.

THE MANAGEMENT
OF RETAILING INSTITUTIONS

In the light of the competitive nature of retail trade, the securing of a differential advantage over a retail rival is often an ephemeral matter, and thus effective management is essential in order to permit retention of small advantages for the maximum period of time. That retail management, especially among small firms, is not very effective is a fact clearly reflected in the high bankruptcy rates and amount of ownership turnover of stores among retailers; two out of five new small retail stores go out of business during the first five years of operation.[88]

An understanding of the basic policy decisions of concern to retailers is important for a variety of reasons. First, it permits insight into the specifics of competitive conduct in retailing. Second, it provides information on how

---

[86] See Bob K. Holdren, *The Structure of a Retail Market and the Market Behavior of Retail Units* (Englewood Cliffs, N.J.: Prentice-Hall, Inc., 1960), for a detailed account of these factors in the food industry.

[87] Weiss, *op. cit.*, p. 231.

[88] See Duncan, Phillips, and Hollander, *op. cit.*, p. 60, for a discussion of failure rates among small retailers.

retailers survive and, for a number of successful firms, how they grow. Third, it furnishes a perspective of retailing that is required for effective *inter*organization management. That is, the *intra*organizational decisions that retailers make directly affect *inter*organizational relations, or relations between marketing channel members. For example, if a retailer insists on maintaining minimal inventories, he will force his suppliers to assume heavy inventory carrying costs. If he pursues a heavy and frequent markdown policy, some suppliers may not wish to deal with him because of their desire to maintain a certain price-quality image among consumers. Existing and potential channel members should comprehend which variables retailers study when choosing locations, arranging store layouts, determining merchandise assortments, establishing inventory levels, and the like so that the policies that they set are congruent with retailers' perspectives and requirements.

Retailing management can be defined as the planning, organizing, staffing, directing, coordinating, and controlling of the different facets of a retailing operation. The fundamental task of retailing management is to *develop* and *implement* a *retailing strategy*. Designing retailing strategy involves five basic steps.

1. Segmenting the market for the type of product or service offering.
2. Identifying competitive organizations that handle this class of products and assessing their merchandising strengths and differential advantages.
3. Assessing the resources of the organization in light of the competitive environment.
4. Defining the specific market target in terms of focal market segment or segments.
5. Developing the retailing mix that represents a plan for the allocation of available resources among alternative uses in a coordinated manner to maximize the total impact generated to influence the customers in the defined market target.

Policy decision areas of the retailing mix are shown in Fig. 2–2. They include location, hours, facilities, organizational structure and strength, merchandise planning and control, pricing, buying, promotion and services, and expense management. Emphasized in Fig. 2-2 are several retailing management tenets:

1. The mix should be designed to reach specific market targets (thus, market target is the core of the diagram).
2. The main mix element is merchandising.
3. The elements of the mix should be coordinated in design and implementation to reach the market target (shown by two-directional arrows).

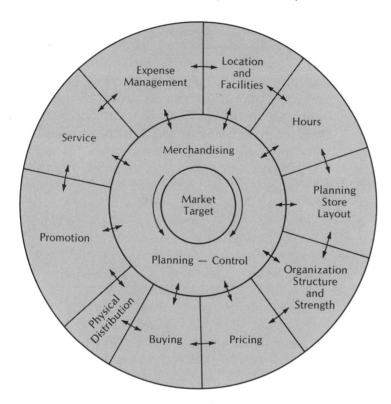

FIGURE 2-2   Policy Decision Areas of the Retailing Mix

The balance of this chapter deals briefly with two elements of the retailing mix that pose special problems for retail decision makers—location and merchandise management. Policy formulation regarding these elements demands precise knowledge not generally available outside retail markets. In other words, marketing managers, irrespective of type of firm served—manufacturer, wholesaler, or retailer—have or can acquire broad knowledge of the principles of promotion and display. But questions of store location and merchandise management are unique to retailing and demand particular attention. Other policy decisions, such as those having to do with store hours and customer services, are of somewhat lesser importance than the central issues of location and assortments, and therefore, will not be discussed here.[89]

[89] For a discussion of these topics, see William R. Davidson and Alton F. Doody, *Retailing Management*, 3rd ed. (New York: Ronald Press Co., 1966); Duncan, Phillips, and Hollander, *op. cit.*; Ronald R. Gist, *Retailing: Concepts and Decisions* (New York: John Wiley & Sons, Inc., 1968); or David J. Rachman, *Retail Strategy and Structure* (Englewood Cliffs, N.J.: Prentice-Hall, Inc., 1969).

Location Decisions

The selection of retail store locations is a critical factor in influencing customer patronage. For example, Nystrom in his classic work, *The Economics of Retailing*, written in 1919, noted that "in no branch of business is location more important than in retailing."[90] In fact, the observation holds true whether the focus is on the retailing of goods *or* the retailing of services by profit-oriented, nonprofit, or publicly financed organizations.[91] Since Nystrom's time, the battle for superior retail sites has intensified, because choice real estate has become increasingly scarce. In fact, due in part to this scarcity, large retailing organizations have, in recent years, begun acquiring or leasing store space left vacant by others rather than building new facilities. The number of vacant stores has increased as retailers, particularly discounters, have been forced to abandon branches in retrenchment programs; these stores have provided an opportunity for other retailers to secure locations that otherwise would not have been available.[92]

Another factor making the decision on location extremely difficult is the fact that the selection of a specific site can no longer be easily amended by the abandonment of the location after several years. Retailers who leave vacant stores for others to occupy pay a large price, because it is likely that their leases were for 15, 20, and even 30 years as opposed to the 10-year leases that were common some years ago. An error in site selection can be very costly, indeed.

Retail store location decisions include the acquisition of sites for planned or expanded facilities as well as the discontinuance or relocation of an ongoing operation. In turn, each of these decisions may be viewed from an *interregional* or *intraregional* perspective. Interregional analysis involves evaluating the market potential of cities, states, or other large land masses,[93] while intraregional analysis involves evaluating the potential of specific locations or sites within a predefined region.

Table 2-9 presents a taxonomy matrix of the various decision sets faced

---

[90]Paul Nystrom, *The Economics of Retailing* (New York: Ronald Press, 1919), p. 168.

[91]The importance of location decisions relative to the marketing of services is detailed in Chapter 14.

[92]See Roger B. May, "Expansion-Minded Retailers Take Over Stores Left Vacant by Recession Victims," *Wall Street Journal*, August 5, 1975, p. 32; and "The Struggle To Rent All Those Empty Stores," *Business Week*, February 9, 1975, pp. 28-29.

[93]Examples of interregional analyses include Louis P. Bucklin, *Shopping Patterns in an Urban Area* (Berkeley, California: Institute of Business and Economic Research, 1966); J. B. Schneider, "Retail Competition Patterns in a Metropolitan Area," *Journal of Retailing*, Vol. 45 (Winter, 1969-1970), pp. 67-74; Donald L. Thompson, "Consumer Convenience and Retail Area Structure," *Journal of Marketing Research*, Vol. 4 (February, 1967), pp. 37-44; and William Applebaum, "Guidelines for Store Location Strategy Study," *Journal of Marketing*, Vol. 30 (October, 1966), pp. 42-45.

TABLE 2-9 A Taxonomy of Evaluation Problems Faced by Retail Location Analysts

Type of Evaluation	Type of Location Decision		
	First Time Acquisition Decision	Multi-outlet Expansion Decision	Facility Abandonment Decision
Interregional analysis	Cell 1	Cell 2	Cell 3
Intraregional analysis	Cell 4	Cell 5	Cell 6

by retail location analysts. The types of location research characterized by cells 1, 2, and 3 are important for those firms that must determine which markets they should enter or abandon, but they are not relevant for deciding upon the location of specific retail stores. Cells 4, 5, and 6 pertain to the latter problem. Generally speaking, major department stores, chain organizations, shopping center developers, and large-scale vertically integrated systems conduct the types of location analyses demanded in all six cells.[94] Smaller retailers, such as local entrepreneurs and intra-urban multi-outlet organizations, concern themselves primarily with the evaluative tasks called for in cells 4, 5, and 6.

In the following discussion, emphasis is placed solely on the analytical tasks required in selecting a specific site (cells 4 and 5), because this location problem most frequently faces all retailers, irrespective of size, and has immediate consequences for individual store performance.

As a general rule, the selection of a specific site is customer-oriented rather than supplier-oriented. Once the general region of operation has been decided upon, site selection involves two basic steps: (1) delineating the relevant trading area and (2) picking a location within the trading area.

Trading Area Measurement and Evaluation. A trading area is the area surrounding an existing or proposed location from which a retailer draws or expects to draw the vast majority of his customers. As indicated previously, retailing is a localized activity, and the bulk of any establishment's sales may be traced to persons within the immediately surrounding area. Basically, the extent of a trading area is determined by two factors: (1) the nature of the product(s) or service(s) being offered, including price, availability from other

[94]See, for example, "Site Selection by Computer Model," *Chain Store Age—Executive Edition*, Vol. 47 (September, 1971), pp. E77-E81.

sources, and the extent to which the merchandise or service reflects the user's taste; and (2) the consumer's perception of the shopping task or attitude toward the buying process. (Some consumers consider shopping a pleasure, while others see it as a chore. Obviously, the greater the number in the former category, the larger the trading area is likely to be.)

In operational terms, a *trading area* can be defined from a buyer's, seller's, and/or sales volume standpoint.

> From a *buyer's standpoint*, a trading area is the region inside which the buyer may reasonably expect to find goods and services at competitive and prevailing prices.
>
> From a *seller's standpoint*, a trading area is a district whose size is usually determined by boundaries within which it is economical in terms of volume and cost for a marketing unit or group to sell and/or deliver a good or service.
>
> From a *sales volume standpoint*, a trading area is the area surrounding the community from which a retailer secures approximately 90 percent of his sales of a representative group of commodities. Sometimes the trading area is classified in terms of primary and secondary areas. The primary area includes 75 percent of the customers, and the secondary area includes 15 percent. The remaining 10 percent represents the fringe or tertiary trading area.

Trading area determination is a complex process, since an area's size is a function of the individual store character and mode of operation as well as the cluster or grouping of stores surrounding the individual store. For example, if the store sells unique and exclusive merchandise, its trading area definitely becomes larger. A case in point is Neiman Marcus in Dallas; because of its novel assortments, its trading area encompasses cities well outside Dallas' limits. Furthermore, because Neiman Marcus uses mail order extensively for some items during Christmas, its trading area is considerably broader than other department stores.[95] In fact, with the increased popularity of mail-order selling and, concomitantly, in-home purchasing, trading areas for a wide variety of organizations have increased markedly in recent years.[96]

Dalrymple and Thompson have observed that trading areas result from the collective responses persons make in balancing the attractiveness of near and distant retail outlets against the cost, time, and energy that must be spent in overcoming distance.[97] Studies have shown that style and fashion goods produce significantly greater consumer travel and search activity than

---

[95]For an interesting discussion and empirical investigation concerning the problems and assumptions involved in estimating the economic potential for retail establishments, see Joseph B. Mason and Charles T. More, "Traditional Assumptions in Trading Area and Economic Potential Studies: A Dissenting View," *Land Economics*, Vol. 46 (May, 1970), pp. 199-201.

[96]See Reif, *op. cit.*

[97]Dalrymple and Thompson, *op. cit.*, p. 98.

low-value, bulky items such as lumber, or convenience items such as food.[98] For existing stores and shopping centers, the geographic extent of trading areas can be established through the use of automobile license checks, charge account records, mail-order lists, check clearings, automobile traffic flow, and newspaper circulation. For example, Sears uses an optical scanner to read customer addresses off credit records; the addresses are then plotted by the computer on maps. An analysis of the customer's demographic characteristics can be obtained from these same records in order to develop a profile of each store's trading area within the Sears organization.

Selecting a Specific Site.   Once potential trading areas are defined, a description of several specifically proposed sites within each is developed with respect to such factors as accessibility and traffic flow, extent of trading area, population and its distribution, income, economic stability, and competition.[99] Evidence that can be used as a first approximation of the value of of a site includes: (1) consumer preference for an existing store or cluster of stores, and (2) natural or man-made barriers to the free movement of customers in the direction of the proposed site. Even though retail location analysis is still a field characterized by its experts as an art rather than a science,[100] it is possible to go well beyond this first approximation in assessing a potential site. For example, Victory Markets, a chain comprised of over 90 supermarkets operating out of Norwich, N.Y., uses a computerized evaluation model to predict the weekly retail sales of a potential site. The predictions generated by Victory have been within 2 percent of the actual sales generated.[101]

Over the years, a number of attempts have been made to bring more rigorous approaches to retail site selection problem solving, including the development of checklist methods,[102] analog methods,[103] gravity models,[104]

---

[98]*Ibid.*

[99]See Saul B. Cohen and William Applebaum, "Evaluating Store Sites and Determining Store Rents," *Economic Geography*, Vol. 36 (January, 1960), pp. 1-35.

[100]See William Applebaum, "Methods for Determining Store Trade Areas, Market Penetration and Potential Sales," *Journal of Marketing Research*, Vol. 3 (May, 1966), pp. 127-141.

[101]"Site Selection by Computer Model," *op. cit.*, p. E77. For another example of computerized site selection, see the approach that the Rayco Company has employed with considerable success in "Can a Computer Tell You Where to Locate Stores?" *Chain Store Age—Executive Edition* (December, 1964), p. E28.

[102]See, for example, Kotler's modification of the traditional check-list approach in Philip Kotler, *Marketing Management: Analysis, Planning and Control*, 2nd ed. (Englewood Cliffs, N.J.: Prentice-Hall, Inc., 1972), pp. 617-619.

[103]See William Applebaum, "The Analog Method for Estimating Potential Store Sales," in Curt Kornblau (ed.), *Guide to Store Location Research with Emphasis on Supermarkets* (Reading: Mass.: Addison Wesley, 1968), pp. 232-243.

[104]See, for example, David L. Huff, "Ecological Characteristics of Consumer Behavior," *Papers and Proceedings of the Regional Science Association*, Vol. 7 (1961), pp. 19-21; "Defining and Estimating

environmental models,[105] regression analysis,[106] sectogram techniques,[107] and microanalytic modeling.[108] A brief descriptive summary of each of these methods is provided in Exhibit 2-3. Most of these methods are, however, plagued with theoretical, operational, or practical difficulties[109] such that retailers must either supplement them with qualitative judgments or resort to rule-of-thumb practices in their selection of a specific site.

Perhaps the most operational and directly useful approach to store location analysis to date has been Applebaum's analog technique. The steps involved in this technique can be paraphrased as follows:[110]

Step 1. Draw four concentric circles on a map in quarter-mile increments around the proposed store location.

Step 2. Determine, usually from U.S. Census data and other government reports, the population of each of the circular zones.

Step 3. Repeat the first two steps for all similar existing stores in the trading area. That is, if the new store will be a supermarket, then the procedure must include all probable competing supermarkets, including those owned by the organization locating the new store, if it is a chain operation.

Step 4. Compute the average drawing power for each circular zone or ring about each similar existing store. (Drawing power is determined by the customer-spotting technique. This technique requires that customers of the existing stores be interviewed, and that the data gathered be processed and "spotted" or located on maps in order to delineate trade areas and market penetration. Applebaum has developed detailed procedures for conducting spotting studies and for determining the number of customers to be spotted.)

---

a Trading Area," *Journal of Marketing*, Vol. 28 (July, 1964), pp. 34–38; and "A Probabilistic Analysis of Consumer Spatial Behavior," in William S. Decker (ed.), *Emerging Concepts in Marketing* (Chicago: American Marketing Association, 1963), pp. 443–461. Huff's gravitation model appears to be the most widely quoted site selection approach in marketing textbooks. Unfortunately, the model suffers from severe operational and practical difficulties. For a discussion of these difficulties, see David B. MacKay, *Consumer Movement and Store Location Analysis*, unpublished Ph.D. dissertation, Northwestern University, pp. 40–43.

[105] See William R. Kinney, Jr., "Separating Environmental Factor Effects for Location and Facility Decisions," *Journal of Retailing*, Vol. 48 (Spring, 1972), pp. 67–75.

[106] See, for example, G. I. Heald, "Application of the Automatic Interaction Detector (AID) Programme and Multiple Regression Technique to the Assessment of Store Performance and Site Selection," *Operations Research Quarterly*, Vol. 23 (December, 1972), pp. 445–457.

[107] See Schneider, *op. cit.*

[108] See David B. MacKay, "A Microanalytic Approach to Store Location Analysis," *Journal of Marketing Research*, Vol. 9 (May, 1972), pp. 134–140.

[109] For a summary of the difficulties associated with many of these methods and models, see MacKay, *Consumer Movement . . ., op. cit.*, pp. 29–67. Also, see Willard R. Bishop, Jr., *An Application of the Intra-Urban Gravity Model to Store Location Research*, unpublished Ph.D. dissertation, Cornell University, 1969.

[110] Applebaum, "The Analog Method . . .," *op. cit.*

EXHIBIT 2-3 Several Quantitative Approaches to Retail Store Location Analysis

Type of Technique/ Approach	Technique/Approach Description
Checklist methods	Lists all factors that must be considered in site selection. Factors are given subjective weights by the retailer, and each potential site is rated on each factor. Numerical ratings result for each site on each factor and factor rankings for each site are then combined to yield an overall evaluation for each location.
Analog models	Sales or volume projections of new stores are based directly on the sales or volume estimates of existing stores.
Gravity models	Sales of proposed retail development are estimated on the basis of a potential site's size and its spatial relationship to the market it serves.
Environmental models	The performance of a retail outlet is described as the sum of the effects of various quantifiable location and facility factors (such as local population characteristics—income, ages, occupational class—competition, nature and condition of outlet facilities), and the effect of managerial actions. A linear statistical model scans the proposed locations and computes the expected contributions of all facility combinations of these locations.
Regression analysis	Annual store sales are predicted on the basis of a set of independent variables that record the demographic and physical characteristics of stores and their neighborhoods.
Sectogram techniques	The spatial relationship between a set of retail facilities and the consumers who utilize them is analyzed on a metropolis-wide basis. Determines how well the spatial pattern of retail outlets and population are matched, identifying those underserved areas as high potential locations.
Microanalytic modeling	Recognizes the multistop facet of shopping behavior. Evaluates potential retail locations using a spatial model defined by means of discriminant analysis and Monte Carlo simulation.

Step 5. For all similar existing stores, compute the average per capita sales for each circular zone or ring.

Step 6. For each zone or ring, multiply the following:

| Average estimated drawing power of the analog (or existing) stores | $\times$ | Average estimated per capita sales of the analog stores | $\times$ | Population in each ring around the proposed store |

The result for each ring is added to obtain the estimated weekly sales of the proposed store site.

Step 7. For a multi-outlet (chain) operation, estimate the effect of the proposed store on existing sister stores by subtracting an arbitrary amount of the profits of existing stores from the trading area of the proposed store.[111]

It should be noted that in Applebaum's method, the individual characteristics of the trading area around the proposed store are accounted for by subjectively adjusting the average per capita sales estimate computed from a knowledge of the sales of existing stores. If management's objective is to choose the best from among several proposed locations, this method can be used to determine the most profitable site. It is not, however, suitable for the more difficult task of deciding upon the best location when a complete enumeration of potential sites does not exist.

Irrespective of the approach taken in the store-location decision process, the retailer's qualitative judgment must enter into the final analysis. This is so because of the great many variables, such as those included in Fig. 2–3, which affect the utility of a location beyond those employed by Applebaum and others in their models or techniques. It would be essential to evaluate factors related to the nature and strength of competition, the socioeconomic pattern of the area, trading area growth potential, the availability of the site, and the existence of facilitating agencies (e.g., mass transit) before a decision is made.[112] For example, in many cases, retailers evaluate current demand and ignore future demand, even though the economic growth potential of an area is critical. In fact, the location decision is a dynamic one because of shifts in population concentration and the continuous development of the structure of retailing, as illustrated in Fig. 2–4.

Despite the multitude of important issues that should be considered when selecting a specific site, many retailers, particularly the smaller operations, choose their locations on an *ad hoc* basis without the benefit of an

---

[111] For an application of basically the same procedure as described in Steps 1 through 7, see "Superior Markets, Inc.," a case prepared by William Applebaum (ICH 10M12 RD 1827).

[112] Robert F. Zaloudek, "Practical Location Analysis in New Market Areas," *Stores*, Vol. 53 (November, 1971), pp. 15, 40–41.

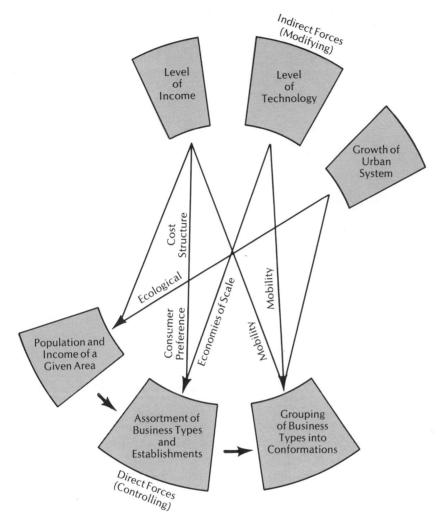

FIGURE 2-3   Forces Leading to Change in the Retail Pattern

SOURCE: James Simmons, *The Changing Pattern of Retail Location* (Chicago: University of Chicago, Department of Geography, Research Paper No. 92, 1964), p. 155.

overall plan of potential site evaluation. Although the smaller retailer's chances of success would be much greater if he assembled and evaluated all pertinent information, he is constrained by the fact that he has neither the manpower nor the financial or the managerial capabilities to conduct a systematic review of cities, suburban areas, or even shopping centers. This problem represents an opportunity for other channel members (particularly wholesalers) who wish to engage in interorganization management. While

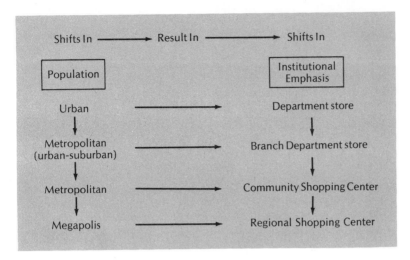

Shifts In ⟶ Result In ⟶ Shifts In

Population		Institutional Emphasis
Urban	⟶	Department store
↓		↓
Metropolitan (urban-suburban)	⟶	Branch Department store
↓		↓
Metropolitan	⟶	Community Shopping Center
↓		↓
Megapolis	⟶	Regional Shopping Center

FIGURE 2-4 Dynamics of Retail Location

the retail location decision is just one element in the design of marketing channel systems, it is, in fact, the most visible and, indeed, one of the more crucial contributors to the profit potential of at least one channel component, the retailer. Because of the interdependent nature of the channel, both reseller and supplier would gain if the retailer was able to obtain more sophisticated locational assistance from his suppliers. This notion is illustrated in Fig. 2–5 where, as indicated, manufacturers and wholesalers provide certain pertinent on-hand information and assistance (at little cost to them) and serve their own ends as well.

Merchandise Management

Merchandise management involves all the activities directly involved in planning, organizing, and controlling the selection, buying, price-setting, promotional, and selling policies of the retail firm's merchandise and service offerings. Regardless of size, the success of the firm depends on the primacy of the merchandising division as the income-producing segment of the operation. The basic objective of merchandise management is to achieve a well-balanced stock, because such a stock will permit the retailer to meet customer demands satisfactorily, improve profits, provide buying information, and optimize investment in inventory.[113]

[113]Duncan, Phillips, and Hollander, *op. cit.*, pp. 303–304. See also Daniel J. Sweeney, "Improving the Profitability of Retail Merchandising Decisions," *Journal of Marketing*, Vol. 37 (January, 1973), pp. 60–68.

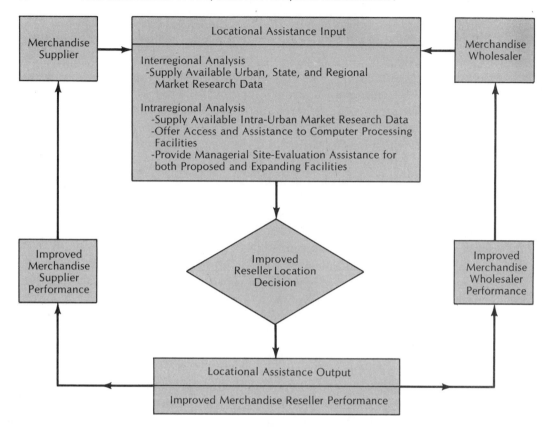

FIGURE 2-5 Causal Sequence of an Improved Retail Location Decision from an Interorganizational Perspective

Merchandise planning and control start first with decisions about merchandise variety and assortment. Variety decisions involve determination of the generically different kinds of goods to be carried or services to be offered. For example, a department store carries a wide variety of merchandise ranging from men's clothing and women's fashions to sports equipment and appliances. A financial institution can offer checking and savings accounts, loans, and safe deposit services or can limit its offerings. On the other hand, assortment decisions involve determination of the range of choice (e.g., brands, styles or models, colors, sizes, prices) offered to the customer within a variety classification. The more carefully and wisely decisions on variety and assortment are made, the more likely the retailer is to achieve a satisfactory rate of stockturn.

The rate of "stockturn" (stock turnover) is the number of times during a given period in which the average amount of stock on hand is sold and is most commonly determined by dividing the average inventory at cost into the cost of the merchandise sold.[114] To achieve a high rate of stockturn, retailers frequently attempt to limit their investment in inventory which, in turn, reduces storage space as well as such expenses as interest, taxes, and insurance on merchandise. "Fresher" merchandise will be on hand, thereby generating more sales. Thus, a rapid stockturn can lead to greater returns on invested capital.[115]

While retailing firms with the highest rates of turnover tend to realize the greatest profit-to-sales ratios,[116] significant problems may be encountered by adopting high turnover goals. For example, higher sales volume can be generated through lower margins which, in turn, reduce profitability; lower inventory levels may result in lost sales due to out-of-stock conditions; purchasing in small quantities may result in additional ordering (clerical) costs and the loss of quantity discounts; and greater expense may be involved in receiving, checking, and marking merchandise. Merchandise budget planning provides the means by which the appropriate balance can be achieved between retail stock and sales volume. For purposes of comparison, aggregate productivity ratios for selected types of retail stores are provided in Table 2-10.

Merchandise Budgeting.   The merchandise budget plan is a forecast of specified merchandise-related activities for a definite period of time. Although the usual period covered is one season of six months, in practice this period is often broken down into monthly or even shorter periods. Merchandise budgeting requires the retail decision maker to make forecasts and plans relative to five basic variables: sales, stock levels, reductions, purchases, and gross margin and operating profit. Each of these variables will be addressed briefly below.[117]

Planned Sales and Stock Levels   The *first step* in budget determination is the preparation of the *sales forecast* for the season and for each month in the season for which the budget is being prepared. The *second step* involves the determination of the *beginning of the month* (B.O.M.) *inventory* (stock on hand), which necessitates specification of a desired rate of stockturn for

[114]It is also computed by dividing average inventory at retail into the net sales figure or by dividing average inventory in physical units into sales in physical units.

[115]Duncan, Phillips, and Hollander, *op. cit.*, p. 324.

[116]*Ibid.*, pp. 326–327.

[117]It should be noted that all of the variables have been treated more fully elsewhere should the reader desire more detail. See Davison and Doody, *op. cit.*, and Duncan, Phillips, and Hollander, *op. cit.*

TABLE 2-10 Aggregate Productivity Ratios for Selected Types of Retail Stores

Productivity Ratios	1963				1967			
	Department Stores	Discount Dept. Stores[a]	Variety Stores	Drug Stores[b]	Department Stores	Discount Dept. Stores	Variety Stores	Drug Stores[c]
Sales per square foot (dollars)	72.00	49.87	36.02	75.18	74.00	57.89	35.72	86.16
Sales per employee (dollars)	21,155	49,695	14,536	23,522	27,542	49,540	18,950	26,711
Annual rate of inventory turnover (dollars)	3.41	N.A.	5.5	3.6[c]	3.48	N.A.	5.4	3.7[c]
Net sales to inventory (times)	5.7	6.04	5.4[d]	5.5	5.8	5.47	5.9[d]	5.6
Gross margin per dollar invested in inventory (dollars)	2.03	1.52	N.A.	2.07[c]	2.25	1.37	N.A.	2.10[c]
Net profit (after taxes) to net sales (percent)	2.29	1.68	2.4[d]	2.9	2.59	2.14	2.7[d]	3.4

[a] All data for 1964, except sales per employee (1965).
[b] Includes data on independent drug stores only, unless otherwise noted.
[c] Includes data for all drug stores, including chains.
[d] Includes data for the 10 leading variety chains only.

SOURCE: Bert C. McCammon, Jr. and Albert D. Bates, The Changing Structure and Economics of Retailing (Columbus, Ohio: Management Horizons, Inc., undated).

each month of the season. If, for example, the desired stock-sales ratio for the month of June is 4 and forecasted (planned) sales during June are $10,000, then the planned B.O.M. stock would be $40,000.[118] It is also important, for budgeting purposes, to calculate the stock available at the end of the month (E.O.M. stock). This figure is identical to the B.O.M. stock for the following month. Thus, May's E.O.M. stock is, if the above example is used, $40,000 (or June's B.O.M. stock).

Planned Reductions The *third step* in budget preparation is *reduction planning*, which involves accounting for markdowns, shortages, and employee discounts. Reduction planning is critical because any amount of reductions has exactly the same effect on the value of stock as an equal amount of sales. Markdowns vary from month to month, depending upon special and sales events. In addition, shortages are becoming an increasing problem to retailers, amounting to $16 billion in the aggregate during 1970. Shortages result from shoplighting, employee pilferage, miscounting, and pricing and checkout mistakes. Generally, merchandise managers can rely on past data in forecasting both shortages and employee discounts.

Planned Purchases When figures for sales, opening (B.O.M.) and closing (E.O.M.) stocks, and reductions have been forecasted, the *fourth step*, the *planning of purchases* in dollars, becomes merely a mechanical mathematical operation. Thus, planned purchases are equal to planned stock at the end of the month (E.O.M.) + planned sales + planned reductions – stock at the beginning of the month (B.O.M.). Suppose, for example, that the planned E.O.M. stock for June was $67,500[119] and that reductions for June were forecast to be $2500. Then,

Planned E.O.M. stock (June 30)	$67,500
Planned sales (June 1–June 30)	10,000
Planned reductions	2,500
Total	$80,000
Less	
Planned B.O.M. stock (June 1)	40,000
Planned purchases	$40,000

The planned purchases figure is, however, based on *retail prices*. To determine the financial resources needed to acquire the merchandise, it is

[118]There are numerous variations used to determine B.O.M. stock. See Duncan, Phillips, and Hollander, *op. cit.*, p. 342.

[119]Derived from a desired stock-sales ratio for July of 4.5 and projected sales for July of $15,000. Remember, June's E.O.M. is the same as July's B.O.M.

necessary to determine planned purchases at *cost*. The difference between planned purchases at retail and at cost represents the initial markup goal for the merchandise in question. This goal is established by determining the amount of operating expenses that are necessary in order to achieve the forecasted sales volume, as well as the profits desired from the specific operation, and combining this information with the data on reductions. Thus,

$$\text{Initial markup goal} = \frac{\text{Expenses} + \text{Profit} + \text{Reductions}}{\text{Net sales} + \text{Reductions}}$$

A term frequently used in retailing is "open-to-buy." It refers to the amount, in terms of retail prices or at cost, which a buyer is open to receive into stock during a certain period on the basis of the plans formulated.[120] Thus, planned purchases and "open-to-buy" may be synonymous in instances where forecasts coincide with actual results. However, adjustments in inventories, fluctuations in sales volume, unplanned markdowns, and goods ordered but not received all serve to complicate the determination of the amount that a buyer may spend.[121]

Planned Gross Margin and Operating Profit   The *gross margin* is the initial markup adjusted for price changes, stock shortages, and other reductions. The difference between gross margin and expenses required to generate sales will yield either a contribution to profit or a *net operating profit* (before taxes) depending, of course, on the sophistication of a retailer's accounting system and the narrowness of his merchandise budgeting.[122]

Buying.   As an integral part of merchandise planning, the buying function is a crucial variable affecting retail store performance. A large amount of chain store buying (e.g., for Sears, Ward's, Penney's, Kroger, Safeway, A & P, and Woolworth) is done centrally, while much of retail buying within major department store chains (e.g., Federated, May Co., and Allied) is decentralized in order to maintain flexibility and adaptability relative to local market conditions. The majority of retailers, particularly for soft goods, retain the services of buying offices or maintain a resident buyer in central markets such as New York, Chicago, Dallas, San Francisco, and sometimes abroad. The general function of the buying office or resident buyer is to provide continuous information about market conditions and merchandise trends within

---

[120]Duncan, Phillips, and Hollander, *op. cit.*, p. 345.

[121]*Ibid.*

[122]See the appendix to this chapter for a glossary of retail buying and pricing terms.

these markets, establish initial contacts with sources of supply, and gather samples in preparation for selection decisions by headquarters or specific stores.

Perhaps the most important element of buying, however, from the standpoint of store performance, is the evaluation and selection of supply resources. This decision has far-reaching effects beyond merely the determination of what goods are to be sold. It also contributes to the type of image the store will convey, the type of customers it will attract, and, accordingly, the relative profitability of the outlet. From an interorganizational perspective, the retail buying decision also carries considerable significance, because it determines which sources of supply will be allowed to reach their ultimate markets via particular retail outlets. The ability to obtain local distribution is clearly a critical factor in the success of both new and established products and services. Thus, a knowledge of the decision processes employed by retail buyers is imperative if other channel members marketing to and serving retailing institutions are going to develop effective promotional strategies aimed at influencing the retailer's selection of merchandise.

Uncovering the determinants of a retail buyer's selection is, however, no simple task. Buying by organizations, including retailers, is, as Webster and Wind point out:

> . . . a complex process (rather than a single, instantaneous act) and involves many persons, multiple goals, and potentially conflicting decision criteria. It often takes place over an extended period of time, requires information from many sources and encompasses many interorganizational relationships.[123]

Webster's and Wind's model of organizational buying behavior is presented in Fig. 2–6.[124] Implicit in the model is the notion that buyers often have authority for managing their firm's contacts with other organizations, and thus perform a "gatekeeper" function. Although the buyer's authority for selection of suppliers may be seriously constrained by decisions at earlier stages of the selection process (e.g., by division managers, in the case of large retailing organizations), the buyer is, in most cases, the final decision-maker.[125]

Although a macro model of organizational buying behavior, such as Webster and Wind's, offers a framework by which potential suppliers may set broad marketing policies aimed at influencing the retail buyer's selection

[123]Frederick E. Webster, Jr. and Yoram Wind, "A General Model for Understanding Organizational Buying Behavior," *Journal of Marketing*, Vol. 36 (April, 1972), pp. 13–14.

[124]For a full explanation of the model, see Frederick E. Webster, Jr. and Yoram Wind, *Organizational Buying Behavior* (Englewood Cliffs, N.J.: Prentice-Hall, Inc., 1972).

[125]Webster and Wind, "A General Model . . .," p. 18.

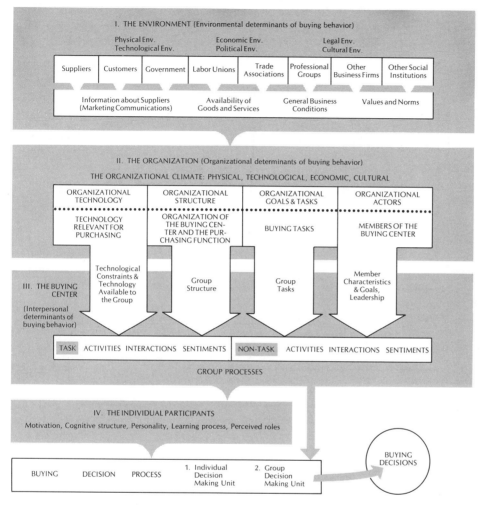

FIGURE 2-6   A Model of Organizational Buying Behavior

SOURCE: Reprinted from "A General Model for Understanding Organizational Buying Behavior," by Frederick E. Webster, Jr., and Yoram Wind, *Journal of Marketing*, Vol. 36 (April, 1972), p. 15; published by the American Marketing Association.

process, its usefulness for more refined analysis is limited by its failure to include the micro-judgmental strategies that the buyer employs when evaluating competing product lines. That is, such a model does not incorporate the evaluative procedures that a retail buyer goes through when processing information about competing brand alternatives. For example, Fig. 2-7 represents a logical flow model of a retail ordering procedure for appliances developed from interviews with the buyer, observations of his current deci-

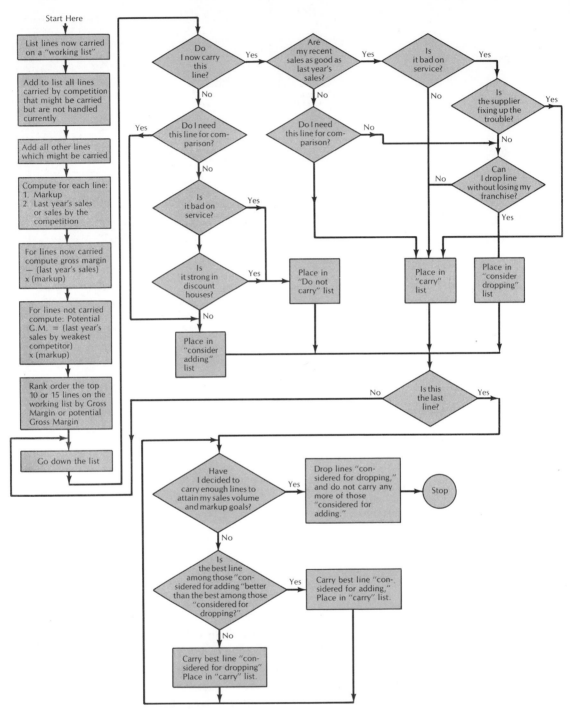

FIGURE 2-7 Logical Flow Model Depicting How a Buyer for a Retailing Organization Decides Which Appliance Supplier's Lines to Carry

SOURCE: Reprinted from "Logical Flow Models for Marketing Analysis," by William F. Massy and Jim D. Savvas, *Journal of Marketing*, Vol. 28 (January, 1964), p. 35; published by the American Marketing Association.

sions, and analysis of written purchasing records.[126] Clearly, as Fig. 2-7 indicates, the selection of an appropriate supplier demands an assessment of a number of complex variables.

The evaluative procedures employed by retail buyers can be classified as particular types of decision rules or *choice strategies*,[127] the nature of which can hold significant implications for those manufacturers or wholesalers desiring to achieve local distribution for their products or services. Once the likely choice strategy employed by a retail buyer is known, the prospective supplier may accept the particular decision rule as a given fact and adjust his promotional efforts to accommodate it, or he can try persuading the buyer to use another rule or choice strategy more favorable to the selection of his product.

The actual choice strategy that the retail buyer uses is a direct result of the type of decision problem he faces when making his merchandise selection.[128] Because the buyer must generally select merchandise from among a number of competing brand alternatives, all of which can be described in terms of their various attributes, the situation confronting the buyer can be accurately described as a *multiple-attribute decision problem.*[129] In general, the evaluation of individual brands and their respective sources of supply involves the rating of alternative sources along some or all of the following ten product attributes or performance parameters:[130]

Demonstrated consumer demand (or projected demand, if a new product)

Projected gross margin

Expected volume

---

[126]For another example, see R. M. Cyert, J. G. March, and C. G. Moore, "A Model of Retail Ordering and Pricing by a Department Store," in Ronald E. Frank, Alfred A. Kuehn, and William F. Massy (eds.), *Quantitative Techniques in Marketing Analysis* (Homewood, Ill.: Richard D. Irwin, Inc., 1962), pp. 502–522.

[127]Development of the choice strategy concept is found in Peter Wright, "Consumer Choice Strategies: Simplifying vs. Optimizing," *Journal of Marketing Research*, Vol. 7 (February, 1975), pp. 60–67.

[128]The authors wish to acknowledge the significant contribution of Lynn W. Phillips to the development of the following discussion.

[129]For an overview of this type of decision problem see Kenneth R. MacCrimmon, "An Overview of Multiple Objective Decision Making," in J. L. Cochrane and M. Zeleny (eds.), *Multiple Criteria Decision Making* (Columbia, S.C.: University of South Carolina Press, 1973), pp. 18–44.

[130]This list is not necessarily in order of importance. Furthermore, the number of attributes considered by the buyer obviously varies from situation to situation. Doyle and Weinberg, for example, in a study of supermarket buyers' decisions, found that buyers examined only eight dimensions, while Montgomery, in a recent study in the same context, reports that 18 different factors were taken into consideration. See Peter Doyle and Charles B. Weinberg, "Effective New Product Decisions for

Merchandise suitability

Prices and terms

Service level offered

Manufacturer reputation

Quality of the brand

Promotional assistance

Vendor's distribution policy (national, regional, or local; exclusive, selective or intensive)

The choice strategy, then, is the method by which the retail buyer evaluates each multiattribute brand alternative and discriminates it from the others available in order to arrive at a merchandise selection.

There are numerous choice strategies that a buyer might adopt.[131] To illustrate its application, consider the situation of a retail buyer choosing among potential suppliers of wristwatches. The buyer employing a *linear additive* choice strategy would, first, assign subjective weights to each attribute dimension listed above according to the evaluative importance he places on each. For example, in the case of wristwatches, manufacturer's reputation and demonstrated consumer demand might, by some retailers, be deemed more important than a factor such as promotional assistance. Second, the buyer would judge each available alternative according to the extent to which it seemingly possessed each of the attribute dimensions. One brand, for example, might be perceived as being of higher quality than the other brands under consideration. After assessing each alternative relative to each attribute dimension, the retail buyer would then combine each of these unidimensional judgments according to a simple linear rule. This rule would dictate the selection of the supply source offering the highest "global utility index" via a process similar to the one depicted in Table 2–11. In the wrist-

---

Supermarkets," *Operations Research Quarterly*, Vol. 24 (March, 1973), pp. 45-54, and David B. Montgomery, "New Product Distribution—An Analysis of Supermarket Buyer Decision," *Journal of Marketing Research*, Vol. 12 (November, 1975), pp. 255-264.

[131] All choice strategies may be carried out overtly, such as via pencil and paper calculation, or cognitively. In fact, most investigations of choice strategy paradigms involve an examination of how well they approximate actual cognitive processes. Although the retail buyer could use either approach, his evaluations of potential suppliers often are done quickly and judgmentally because of the workload he faces. See, for example, Doyle and Weinbert, *op. cit.*, p. 51. One possible strategy is a *linear additive* method of evaluation. For a review of the additive choice model, see William L. Wilkie and Edgar A. Pessemier, "Issues in Marketing's Use of Multi-Attribute Attitude Models," *Journal of Marketing Research*, Vol. 10 (November, 1973), pp. 428-441. Empirical evidence indicating that retail buyers may cognitively use a linear additive method of evaluation has been marshalled by Roger M. Heller, Michael J. Kearney, and Bruce J. Mehaffey in "Modeling Supermarket Product Selection," *Journal of Marketing Research*, Vol. 10 (February, 1973), pp. 34-37.

TABLE 2-11 Hypothetical Application of a Linear Additive Choice Strategy for Choosing Among Alternative Brands of Wristwatches

Attribute Dimensions Taken into Consideration	Evaluative Importance of the Attribute Dimensions to the Retail Buyer (A)	Judgments about Individual Brands of Wristwatches Across All Attribute Dimensions			
		Brand 1 (B_1)	Brand 2 (B_2)	Brand 3 (B_3)	Brand 4 (B_4)
Demonstrated consumer demand (or projected demand, if a new product)	0.9	0.5	0.9	0.4	0.8
Projected gross margin	0.8	0.6	0.6	0.4	0.6
Expected volume	0.7	0.6	0.7	0.3	0.7
Merchandise suitability	0.6	0.5	0.4	0.4	0.4
Prices and terms	0.5	0.5	0.4	0.6	0.5
Service level offered	0.5	0.5	0.3	0.4	0.5
Manufacturer reputation	0.6	0.5	0.6	0.3	0.8
Quality of the brand	0.7	0.6	0.5	0.3	0.8
Promotional assistance	0.3	0.5	0.4	0.5	0.5
Vendor's distribution policy	0.4	0.5	0.3	0.4	0.7
Global utility index for each alternative $$U = \sum_{i=1}^{n} A_i B_{ij}$$		3.22	3.32	2.33	3.90

where
  U = overall judged utility of a brand alternative
  A_i = numerical weight assigned to the ith dimension
  B_{ij} = a numerical value for the jth brand alternative on the ith dimension

watch example, the buyer would choose Brand 4 because of its superior overall evaluation.

On the other hand, the retail buyer might use a *conjunctive* choice strategy in making his selection, and if he did, the results could be different from those arrived at through application of the linear strategy.[132] Using a conjunctive model, the buyer would establish minimum cutoff values for

[132] Both Wright and Russ offer extended discussions of the nonlinear models presented here. See Peter Wright, "The Simplifying Consumer: Perspectives on Information Processing Strategies," a paper presented at the American Marketing Association Doctoral Consortium, Michigan State University, August, 1973, and Frederick Russ, "Consumer Evaluation of Alternative Product Models," *Combined Proceedings of the 1971 Spring and Fall Conferences* (Chicago: American Marketing Association, 1972), pp. 664–668.

each attribute dimension and then compare competing brands against these values. If any of the brands were rated below the cutoff value on any of the attributes, it would be rejected as a choice possibility. For example, in Table 2–11, if the retail buyer established a minimum cutoff value of *0.5* for each of the ten dimensions, Brand 1 would be selected as the best choice, because it is the only brand that meets or surpasses the established cutoff on each attribute.

Another approach that the retail buyer might use is a *lexicographic* choice strategy. Here, the buyer first orders the different attribute dimensions according to importance. Then the buyer compares all the alternative sources of supply on the single most important dimension. If one brand offers a noticeably better outcome on that dimension, it is selected. If, however, a number of alternative brands qualify so that the buyer still cannot discriminate among the various available choices, he then drops down to the second most important attribute dimension and repeats the procedure. This one-dimension-at-a-time process is followed until a choice is identified. In the wristwatch example depicted in Table 2–11, Brand 2 would now be selected, since it is perceived as surpassing all of the other alternatives on the most important dimension—"demonstrated consumer demand."

There are other choice strategies available to the retail buyer. These, as well as those already mentioned above, are summarized in Exhibit 2–4. Not presented are the "hybrid" or modified versions that some of these strategies may take on.[133] For example, since it is possible for several alternatives to exceed all established cutoff values when a conjunctive strategy is used, a further discrimination procedure may be necessary to identify a final choice for the retail buyer. One such mode of discrimination is to combine the conjunctive strategy with a satisficing "first choice rule," whereby the brand chosen is the first one that meets all standards. Another mode of discrimination would be a multistage use of strategies, whereby the retail buyer might employ a conjunctive scheme to narrow the number of brand alternatives and then apply a lexicographic or linear strategy as an aid in making the final choice.

As mentioned earlier, the type of choice strategy the retail buyer uses in judging brand alternatives has significant implications for the planning of marketing efforts on the part of suppliers seeking to serve the buyer. For example, if the buyer is using a lexicographic strategy in his evaluation of a certain product class, a supplier would do best by focusing his promotional efforts on affecting the buyer's beliefs pertaining to what the buyer perceives as the product's most important attribute dimension, because the

---

[133]See Hillel Einhorn, "The Use of Nonlinear, Noncompensatory Models in Decision Making," *Psychological Bulletin*, Vol. 73 (1970), pp. 221-230.

EXHIBIT 2-4   Possible Choice Strategies a Retail Buyer May Employ When Selecting Sources of Supply

General Class of Choice Strategy Model	Specific Strategies	Strategy Description
LINEAR MODELS	Linear additive	Evaluative weights are assigned to each attribute dimension according to its perceived importance. Each supplier/brand alternative then receives a rating on each attribute dimension. These are combined linearly to form an overall judgment for each supplier/brand alternative that can be used as a comparison basis in making the final selection.
	Linear averaging	Same as linear additive, except that the evaluative weights must sum to one to connote a dependency among the attribute dimensions.[a]
LEXICOGRAPHIC MODELS	Regular lexicography	All supplier/brand alternatives are compared on the single most important dimension. If one surpasses all others on that dimension, it is selected. If not, the process continues along the other dimensions until the supplier(s)/brand(s) is (are) selected.
	Lexicographic semiorder	Same as regular lexicography, except that, even though a supplier/brand alternative surpasses other alternatives on the single most important dimension, if the difference is not a significant one, the comparison continues along the other dimensions until the supplier(s)/brand(s) is (are) selected.
MULTIPLE CUT-OFF MODELS	Conjunctive	All suppliers/brands are compared against some minimum cutoff on each attribute dimension. Those supplier/brand alternatives possessing *below*-cutoff features on any dimension are rejected.
	Disjunctive	Same as conjunctive, except that any supplier/brand alternative possessing an *above*-cutoff feature on any single dimension is accepted.

supplier's brand will be chosen if it surpasses all other alternatives on this dimension. However, such an approach may not prove effective if the buyer is, instead, employing a conjunctive decision rule. Convincing the buyer that a supplier's brand is outstanding on one attribute dimension will not be sufficient if the brand falls below standards set for the other dimensions considered. When a linear additive choice strategy is used, marketing efforts could be directed by a supplier at increasing his brand's rating on any attribute dimension, because, in light of the additive nature of the choice process, the increase would affect, in a positive way, the overall evaluation of the brand. In Fig. 2-8, an interorganizational promotional strategy model for influencing decisions concerning retail brand selection is presented. Its purpose is to outline the steps that a manufacturer or wholesaler should

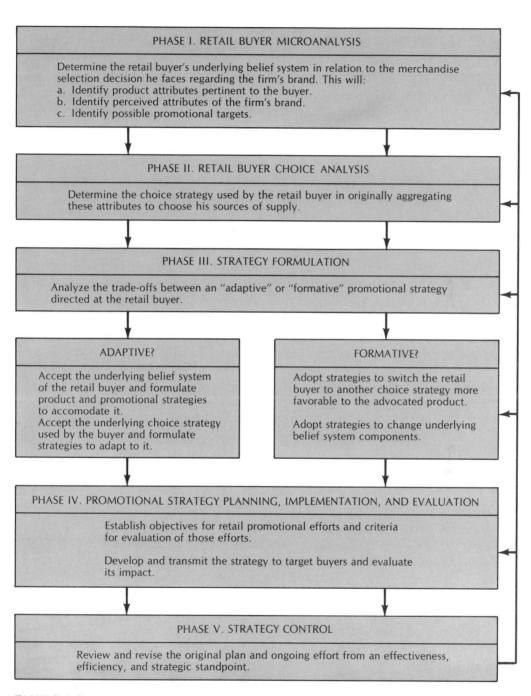

FIGURE 2-8 An Interorganizational Promotional Strategy Model Based on Multiattribute Choice Theory

take if he is concerned about obtaining distribution for his brands in a particular retailing firm.[134]

Inventory Control.   Another integral part of the whole planning process in retailing as well as in wholesaling is inventory control. Inventory information forms the backbone of the feedback system regarding budget implementation. Simply, the retail decision maker needs to know what and how many units are ordered, received, sold, and available on display, in stockrooms, and in warehouses. Two basic types of information systems—commonly referred to as *dollar control* and *unit control*—have been developed. Dollar control is exercised in terms of the amount of money at retail prices invested in merchandise, whereas unit control is usually accomplished in terms of individual items or pieces of merchandise.[135]

Details of the mechanics of inventory control systems are presented at length elsewhere,[136] and, therefore, will not be discussed here. It should be pointed out, though, that the different systems are used for different purposes. Dollar inventory control is essential for the preparation of financial statements and periodic merchandising reports to monitor merchandising plans. One of the most important applications of dollar inventory control is the calculation of a buyer's "open-to-buy" position. On the other hand, unit inventory control is required for day-to-day operating decisions; it provides information on amounts of merchandise on hand and when and what to order to meet customer demand for the merchandising period. Because unit control is performed on an item-by-item basis, the decision maker can follow the turnover and age condition of the merchandise. Unit control guides modification of merchandising and stock plans by highlighting popular items for increased ordering and slow-selling items for special promotions.

One significant development in dollar control of inventory is classification merchandising based upon classifications of related types of merchandise within departments. The Controllers Congress of the National Retail Merchants Association has formulated a Standard Merchandise Classification system, which seeks to provide a common nomenclature or universal language of comprehensive research guidelines that will serve both retail and manufacturing industries as the foundation and basic structure of future merchandising information.[137] A similar system—called the Universal Product Code—has been developed for use in food retailing.[138] As Duncan,

---

[134]For a discussion of the various data gathering and analysis techniques applicable to this problem, see Wright, "The Simplifying Consumer . . .," *op. cit.*

[135]Duncan, Phillips, and Hollander, *op. cit.*, p. 106.

[136]*Ibid.*, pp. 306–330; Davidson and Doody, *op. cit.*, pp. 323–426.

[137]Duncan, Phillips, and Hollander, *op. cit.*, p. 308.

[138]See Chapter 12 for a description of the Universal Product Code and its potential impact.

Phillips, and Hollander point out, the Standard Merchandise Classification is

> ... a coding and numbering system in which all types of merchandise have unvarying identification in all stores, regardless of type, size, or geographic (or within the store) location, or whether the stores keep records manually or on a computer. Tied into a vendor-punched ticket—i.e., machine readable premarking—the codification into nine major areas of consumer demand from fashions to food and into numerous subclassifications is visualized as a universal language understandable to retailers and manufacturers alike.... SMC tells the store in dollars how much business it does in each classification and subclassification, how much inventory it needs to do that business, where to allocate promotional emphasis.[139]

Although adoption of this revolutionary system has been slow, mainly because of the reluctance of retailers to change from individual systems used for many years and the costs involved in the changeover, the implications of widespread adoption are profound from the perspective of interorganization management, as is shown in later chapters. In effect, full adoption will permit the development of interorganizational data systems and, thus, channelwide inventory and financial management.

In fact, both unit and dollar controls are essential to keep stocks adjusted to customer demand, and interorganization data can be forthcoming from one or the other, or both. For example, Kroger Company, a large food chain, has developed a Product Movement Index based on its computerized unit control system.

> The Index furnishes grocery manufacturers with weekly data on shipments of branded goods from Kroger warehouses to its 1,300 stores in 20 states. Through the data supplied, manufacturers learn their weekly sales in Kroger stores, the sales of competing brands, their share of the total market, and the prices paid by consumers.[140]

It should be noted, however, that not only are different inventory control systems used for different purposes, but they are also used for different types of products as well. For example, after studying thousands of items offered for sale at over 200 department stores, IBM Corporation developed separate inventory systems for what it classified as "staple" and "fashion" goods.[141] Examples of merchandise lines falling into the two categories are listed in Exhibit 2-5. Fashion merchandise has a short selling life with limited opportunities to reorder successful styles. Because such items are

---

[139]Duncan, Phillips, and Hollander, *op. cit.*, p. 308.

[140]*Ibid.*, pp. 317-318.

[141]See *Retail IMPACT—Inventory Management Program and Control Techniques Application Description*, 6th ed. (White Plains, N.Y.: IBM Corporation Technical Publications Department, 1970), pp. 1-4.

EXHIBIT 2-5 Examples of Staple and Fashion Merchandise as Classified by IBM's Retail IMPACT

Primarily Staple Items

Automotive supplies
Bedding
Blankets
Books
Boy Scouts' apparel
Boys' wear
Cameras
Candy
Children's shoes
Children's underwear
Corsets and bras
Cosmetics
Domestics
Draperies
Drugs
Fine jewelry and watches
Garden
Gifts
Handkerchiefs
Hardware, paint
Housewares
Infants' wear
Juvenile furniture
Lamps
Linens
Lingerie

Luggage
Men's furnishings
Men's hats
Men's hosiery
Men's shirts
Men's shoes
Men's sportswear
Men's underwear
Needlework
Notions
Pictures
Radio-TV
Rugs
Scatter rugs
Sheets
Silverware
Small electrical appliances
Sporting goods
Stationery
Tots and toddlers
Towels
Toys
Uniforms
Wallpaper
Women's gloves
Women's hosiery

Primarily Fashion Items

Active sportswear
Bridal shop
Budget dresses
Costume jewelry
Daytime dresses
Girls' wear
Junior dresses
Loungewear
Maternity
Misses' coats and suits
Misses' dresses
Misses' sportswear
Men's clothing

Robes
Skirts
Sweaters
Teen wear
Women's bags
Women's blouses
Women's coats and suits
Women's dresses
Women's millinery
Women's shoes
Women's sportswear
Women's umbrellas

SOURCE: Retail IMPACT—Inventory Management Program and Control Techniques Application Description, 6th ed. (White Plains, N.Y.: IBM Technical Publications Department, 1970), p. 3.

EXHIBIT 2–6　Major Criteria Used for Defining the Difference Between Staple Items and Fashion Items

1. Future demand

Future demand for new, untried fashion items is almost always unpredictable. The demand can range from full customer acceptance to complete rejection. Future demand for established staple items usually follows certain statistical patterns, which can be forecasted by appropriate techniques.

2. Style or item life

The life of almost all fashion items is relatively short. Specific items constantly compete with new introductions for customer acceptance. It is not uncommon for an item's life to be much shorter than a season. The life of many staple items, especially the so-called "basic items," is relatively long, and may extend up to several years.

3. Style obsolescence and markdowns

Since the very nature of fashion implies continual change, item changes are very frequent. This is exemplified by female ready-to-wear apparel and other outer accessories. Staple item changes are less frequent. Quite often technical innovations constitute one of the major causes for staple item changes.

Fashion items are highly obsolescent. At the end of its season, an item's value is substantially reduced. Carryover from one season to the next is virtually nonexistent. Consequently, markdowns, sometimes even to a level below cost, are common. Staple items, with the exception of end-of-season (items carried only during one season—for example, winter jackets), are carried year round, and because of the infrequent style changes and relatively long lives, the markdowns experienced are much lower.

4. Reorders

Because of the short selling life, fashion items usually have very limited opportunities for reorder. Also, manufacturers usually commit production schedules fairly early in the season. As a result, the items reordered by the retailer during the season are not always available. For staple items, reordering is almost always possible because the items are shipped from the vendor's stock, and are continually being manufactured. Because of the long selling life, many reorders are possible during the life of an item.

5. Lead time considerations

Lead time for staple items, excluding overseas shipments and special orders, is relatively short, because the items are shipped directly from the resource's stock as

EXHIBIT 2–6 continued

explained in (4). Lead time for fashion items is relatively long for the initial order (preseason order), and short for reorders (in-season reorders).

6. Sales-inventory relationship

IBM's analysis of the behavior of thousands of fashion items indicates that for a particular item there is a direct relationship between sales for a week and the beginning inventory on the floor available for the customer's selection for that week. The relationship suggests that, within certain limits, sales are proportional to inventory. A similar analysis for staple items indicates that such a relationship does not generally exist for the majority of items.

7. Level of decision making

The routine day-to-day decision-making process for reordering staple merchandise should be at the stockkeeping unit level. At each review, the question of which stockkeeping units should be reordered—and in what quantities—must be answered. This is true because the decision to continue the style has been made on a long-range basis.

In fashion, the major routine decision to be made is whether to continue (reorder) the style. For the few styles that are to be reordered, the next level of decision making is necessary: Which SKU's within the style should be reordered and in what quantities?

SOURCE: Retail IMPACT—Inventory Management Program and Control Techniques Application Description, 6th Ed. (White Plains, N.Y.: IBM Technical Publications Department, 1970), pp. 2–3.

sold primarily by display, slow-moving items must be eliminated promptly to make room for items that sell quickly. Thus, a system is needed to supplement the buyer's judgment in determining whether to reorder, mark down, or return certain items. On the other hand, staple merchandise is far more adaptable to fully automatic control. Because of its more constant consumer demand characteristics, sophisticated forecasting techniques may be used as a foundation upon which to build a comprehensive inventory management system. In order to determine which goods should be subject to which type of inventory management procedure, IBM developed the criteria for classification found in Exhibit 2–6.

SUMMARY AND CONCLUSION

Retailing involves the direct sale of goods and services to ultimate household consumers. The overwhelming majority of retail sales is consummated in stores or retail establishments as opposed to other conduits, such as the mail, house-to-house selling, or automatic vending machines. Aggregate statistics regarding retail trade tend to mask the revolutionary changes that have taken place in the structure of retailing since the turn of the century. The emergence of department stores, chain store systems, supermarkets, planned shopping centers, and discount houses as well as the growth of automatic merchandising and mail-order selling has dramatically altered the way in which the business of retailing is conducted. To a significant extent, many of these institutional forms have been subject to life cycles and thus have witnessed periods of early growth, accelerated development, maturity, and, in some cases, decline. In fact, there is evidence which indicates that the life cycles of retailing institutions are becoming considerably shorter, making the structure of retailing even more volatile.

In light of the trends which have been established, it appears that an increasing proportion of retail trade in the near future will be garnered by low-cost, merchandise-intensive approaches to distribution. Specifically, the application of supermarket and warehousing principles to the marketing of general merchandise is likely to have a profound effect on the structure of retailing over the next decade. In addition, emerging environmental trends, such as the growing institutionalization of the consumption process, the increased segmentation of consumer markets, and the strong emphasis on the part of consumers on economy and convenience, will accentuate the trend toward massive merchandising, despite the fact that large numbers of specialty stores will continue to exist.

Even though these formidable trends are present, retailing still remains heavily populated by establishments of relatively small size. In addition, economic concentration in retailing is low (compared with the level of concentration found in many manufacturing industries), enterprise differentiation advantages are often short-lived, and entry barriers are slight (again, compared with other industries). Thus, competition—in terms of prices, securing locations, type and content of advertising, assortments and services provided to customers, and the like—is intense. The need to employ effective management practices is essential for survival, not to mention growth.

Elements of the retail marketing management mix must be combined in such a way as to secure even temporary differential advantages, given the nature of retail competition. Two crucial determinants of success in this regard are location and merchandise management decisions. Location decisions involve delineating a trading area and selecting a specific site within the area. Key dimensions of merchandise management are merchandise budgeting, buying, and inventory control. An understanding of the various choice strategies employed by retail buyers in the selection of supply sources leads to more effective interorganizational relations between manufacturers, wholesalers, and retailers. Furthermore, maintaining appropriate inventory (stock) balances is critical in distribution; if appropriate levels are not achieved, especially via careful merchandise management at the retail level, profits will not be forthcoming and eventual demise can be predicted with certainty.

While it is likely that new retailing institutions will continue to emerge and that existing institutions will continue to evolve during the remainder of the twentieth century, there is considerable room for innovative management within the present institutional mix. As Bucklin observes:

> There are substantial frontiers yet to be conquered in tying together the wholesale and retail sectors of the business, improving logistics and inventory control.[142]

In the next two chapters, attention is focused on the wholesaling institutions comprising channels and on the management of logistical or physical distribution activities. Following a discussion of those areas, attention is then focused on explaining the emergence of channel systems, understanding institutional change, and assessing the performance of existing institutions and channel systems. Thereafter, the main topic for discussion is the effective interorganization management of channel systems, which is viewed as the means by which the "frontiers" will be "conquered."

DISCUSSION QUESTIONS

1. Paul Valery, a famous author, at one time remarked:
   "Once destiny was an honest game of cards which followed certain conventions, with a limited number of cards and values. Now the player realizes in amazement that the hand of his future contains cards never seen before and that the rules of the game are modified by each play."
   Relate Valery's statement to the problems facing high-level retail executives today.

---

[142]Bucklin, *Competition and Evolution . . .* , *op cit.,* p. 168.

2. One author has described the revolution in retailing as a process of "creative destruction," because of the many new institutions that have appeared in this industry over the years. If, as McCammon suggests, institutional life cycles have shortened to approximately 10 years, what types of institutional forms do you predict will arise in the 1990's to "creatively destroy" the institutions that are emerging as powers in retail trade today (e.g., warehouse technologies and organizations, and extensions of the supermarket concept)?

State fully the reasons behind your answer, including also what impinging environmental factors you believe will help to bring about these changes.

3. After answering question 2, assume now that you are a high-level retail executive for a major chain of supermarkets. Given your assumptions about the future, what strategies would you initiate to adapt your organization to the impending environment?

If you were a manufacturer of household consumer durables, what action would you take relative to future retail distribution outlets for your products, considering again your assumptions about the environment?

4. In your opinion, what kind of competition exists in retailing—perfect, monopolistically competitive (atomistic), oligopolistic, or monopolistic? Explain in full, using a variety of different lines of retail trade to illustrate your response.

5. With the growing trend to scrambled merchandising, and the proliferation of "me, too" retail establishments, existing differences between competing outlets are often perceived as superficial by the consumer with the result that a firm's advertising and promotion may often be attributed to a competitor. Consequently, many analysts believe that store positioning will become the most important retail marketing strategy of the 1980's.

Describe what you believe to be the various positioning strategies of:
(a) B. F. Goodrich.
(b) Burger King.
(c) Meijer's Thrifty Acres (hypermarket).
(d) Cadillac.
Enumerate both the advantages and disadvantages that seem to be associated with each of these strategies.

6. Assume that you are planning on establishing a major department store operation with several nearby branch locations somewhere in the United States. Outline the general steps you would undertake in conducting both an *inter-* and *intraregional* location analysis for your store. Included in your outline should be a list of all the factors (e.g., population, buyer power, etc.) that you would take into consideration for each type of analysis.

What types of locational assistance might you seek from manufacturers and wholesalers whose products you planned to carry?

7. Why is an understanding of the retail buying process important from an *interorganizational* perspective? If, through market research, a manufacturer determined that a retail buyer was using a linear choice model in making his merchandise selection, what general promotional tactics might he employ to help insure his product's selection? How would this differ if the retail buyer was instead using:

(a) A conjunctive model?

(b) A lexicographic model?

(c) A disjunctive model?

On an *a priori* basis, what situational factors might prompt the retail buyer to use one choice model instead of another? *(Hint:* Consider for example, such situational factors as *perceived risk attached to the buyer's decision* and *amount of time available to make the decision.)*

8. What is meant by merchandising variety and assortment? What are the dimensions of assortment? What purposes does the merchandising budget serve?

9. As the retailing environment becomes more and more turbulent, which of the following policy decision areas—location, merchandise selection, or inventory control—do you believe becomes more important, as well as more difficult for the retailer? Offer at least *three* compelling reasons in support of your position.

Appendix

A Glossary of Pricing and Buying Terms Commonly Used by Retailers

Original Retail. The first price at which the merchandise is offered for sale.

Sales Retail. The final selling price.

Merchandise Cost. The billed cost of merchandise less any applicable trade or quantity discounts plus in-bound transportation costs, if paid by the buyer. Cash discounts are not deducted to arrive at merchandise cost. Usually, they are either deducted from "aggregate cost of goods sold" at the end of an accounting period or added to net operating profits. If cash discounts are added to net operating profit, the amount added is treated as financial income with no effect on gross margins.

Markup. The difference between merchandise cost and the retail price.

Initial Markup or Markon. The difference between merchandise cost and the original retail value.

Maintained Markup or Margin. The difference between the *gross* cost of goods sold and net sales.

Gross Margin of Profit. Gross margin of profit is the dollar difference between the *total* cost of goods sold and net sales.

Total Cost.

Total cost of goods sold = Gross cost of goods sold + Workroom costs − Cash discounts

Markdown. Markdown is a reduction in the original or the previous retail price on merchandise. *Markdown percentage* refers to the ratio of the dollar markdown during a period to the net sales for the same period.

Off-Retail. Designates specific reductions off the original retail price.

Retailers can express markup in terms of retail price or cost. Large retailers and progressive small retailers express markups in terms of retail for several reasons. First, other operating ratios are expressed in terms of percentage net sales. Second, net sales figures are available more frequently than cost figures. Finally, most trade statistics are expressed in terms of sales.

Markup on retail can be converted to cost base by using the following formula:

$$\text{Markup \% on cost} = \frac{\text{Markup \% on retail}}{100\% - \text{Markup \% on retail}}$$

On the other hand,

$$\text{Markup \% on retail} = \frac{\text{Markup \% on cost}}{100\% + \text{Markup \% on cost}}$$

F.O.B. The seller places the merchandise "free on board" the carrier at the point of shipment or other predesignated place. The buyer assumes title to the merchandise and pays all freight charges from this point.

Delivered Sale. The seller pays all freight charges to the buyer's destination and retains title to the goods until they are received by the buyer.

Freight Allowances. F.O.B. terms can be used with freight allowances to transfer the title to the buyer at the point of shipping, while the seller absorbs transportation cost. The seller ships F.O.B. and the buyer deducts freight costs from his invoice payment.

Trade Discount. Vendors usually quote a list price and offer a trade discount to provide the purchaser a reasonable margin to cover his operating expenses and provide for net profit margin. Trade discounts are sometimes labeled as functional discounts. They are usually quoted in a series of percentages, such as list price less 33% –15% –5%, for different channel intermediaries. Therefore, if a list price of $100 is assumed, the discount applies as follows for different channel members:

List price	$100.00	
Less 33%	33.00	retailer
	$ 67.00	
Less 15%	10.05	wholesaler
	56.95	
Less 5%	2.85	manufacturer's representative
	$ 54.10	

Quantity Discounts. Vendors offer two types of quantity discounts, noncumulative and cumulative discounts. While noncumulative discounts are offered on volume of each order, cumulative discounts are offered on total volume for a specified period. Quantity discounts are offered to encourage volume buying and, legally, they should not exceed production and distribution cost savings to the seller owing to volume buying.

Seasonal Discounts. Seasonal discounts are offered to buyers of seasonal products who place their orders in advance of the season's buying period. This enables the manufacturer to use his equipment more efficiently by spreading production throughout the year.

Cash Discounts. Vendors selling on credit offer a cash discount for payment within a specified period of time. The cash discount is usually expressed in the following format: 2/10, net 30. This means that the seller extends credit for 30 days. If payment is made within 10 days, a 2 percent discount is offered to the buyer. The 2 percent interest rate for 10 days is equivalent to 36 percent effective interest rate per year. Therefore, the passing up of cash discounts can be very costly. Some middlemen who operate on slim margins simply cannot realize a profit on a merchandise shipment unless they take advantage of the cash discount. Channel intermediaries usually maintain a line of credit at low interest rates to use to pay their bills within the cash discount period.

Cash Dating.   Cash datings include C.O.D. (cash on delivery), C.W.O. (cash with order), R.O.G. (receipt of goods), S.D.-B.L. (sight-draft–bill of lading). S.D.-B.L. means that a sight-draft is attached to the bill of lading and must be honored before the buyer takes possession of the shipment.

Future Dating.   Future datings include:

(1) Ordinary dating such as "2/10, net 30."

(2) End of month dating such as "2/10, net 30, E.O.M.," where the cash discount and the net credit periods begin on the first day of the following month rather than the invoice date.

(3) Proximo dating such as "2 percent, 10th proximo, net 60" specifies a date in the following month on which payment must be made in order to take the cash discount.

(4) Extra dating such as "2/10–30 days extra" means that the buyer has 70 days from the invoice date to pay his bill and benefit from the discounts.

(5) Advance or season dating such as "2/10, net 30 as of May 1" means that the discount and net periods are calculated from May 1. Sometimes extra dating is accompanied with anticipation allowance. For example, if the buyer is quoted "2/10, 60 days extra," and he pays in 10 days or 60 days ahead, an additional discount is made available to the buyer.

THREE

WHOLESALING: STRUCTURE, COMPETITION, AND MANAGEMENT

Approximately 98 percent of the total output of United States farms, factories, mines, quarries, oil wells, forests, fisheries, and hunting and trapping is marketed at wholesale. Broadly defined, a wholesale transaction is one in which the purchaser does not buy for his own private or personal use or that of his family but is actuated by a profit or business motive in making the purchase.[1] Obviously, such a broad definition would force consideration here of every form of marketing at every level in a channel other than the purchasing behavior of ultimate household consumers. Our intention in this chapter is not to provide a global view of marketing practices, but to take a brief look at some of the structural and managerial dimensions of wholesale trade—defined quite narrowly to encompass only the operations of specialized wholesaling institutions and establishments engaged primarily in domestic marketing. About 50 percent of the total output marketed "at wholesale" passes through such institutions and establishments. In addition, the focus in this chapter is largely on so-called "merchant" wholesalers—independently owned firms which purchase goods from suppliers for their own account, operate one or more warehouses in which they receive and take title to goods, store them, and later reship them.[2] By assuming such a narrow focus,

[1] Theodore N. Beckman, Nathanael H. Engle, and Robert D. Buzzell, *Wholesaling*, 3rd ed. (New York: The Ronald Press Co., 1959), p. 26.

[2] Richard S. Lopata, "Faster Pace in Wholesaling," *Harvard Business Review*, Vol. 47 (July–August, 1969), p. 131.

it will be possible to become more fully exposed to and examine more thoroughly those channel members normally referred to as "wholesalers," so that when attention is turned to interorganizational management approaches in later chapters, account may be taken of the unique contributions, characteristics, and orientations of these institutions in forming the most beneficial systemwide strategies for the channel.

RATIONALE FOR THE EMERGENCE OF MODERN WHOLESALERS

The wholesaler's functions are shaped by the vast economic task of coordinating production and consumption or, in Alderson's words, of matching heterogeneous demands for assortments at various levels within distribution.[3] Thus, wholesalers aid in bridging the time and space gap between periods and places in which goods are produced and those in which they are consumed or used. In fact, the modern-day functions performed by wholesalers have emerged as a result of:

1. The development of diversified, large-scale mass production in factories located at a distance from the areas of principal use of the output.

2. An increase in the volume and proportion of production made prior to, rather than for, the specified order of users.

3. A corresponding increase in the number of levels of intermediate-user consumption between the production of basic raw materials at the beginning of the channel and the areas of final use at the end of the channel.

4. The increasing need for adaptations of products to the needs of intermediate and final users in terms of quantities, shapes, packages, and other elements of assortments, as well as in pricing arrangements.

5. Continuing increases in both the quantities and varieties of goods and services.[4]

The sorting process of wholesalers is the key to their economic viability. It frequently happens that the quantities in which goods are produced or the characteristics with which they are endowed by nature do not match either the quantities in which they are demanded or the characteristics de-

---

[3] Wroe Alderson, "Factors Governing the Development of Marketing Channels," in William G. Moller, Jr. and David L. Wilemon (eds.), *Marketing Channels: A Systems Viewpoint* (Homewood, Illinois: Richard D. Irwin, Inc., 1971), p. 20.

[4] David A. Revzan, *Wholesaling in Marketing Organization* (New York: John Wiley and Sons, Inc., 1961), pp. 10-11.

sired by those who use or consume them. Hundreds of dungarees are produced at a single cutting, but they are ultimately sold one at a time. These circumstances are multiplied many times throughout our economic system in a variety of different forms that place myriad demands on the sorting process. Thus, as Hill points out, the process may involve sorting by kinds, as when products of different type, grade, and quality are collected and separated into groups of the same type, grade, and quality (as in the case of food for high-class restaurants), or it may take the opposite form of bringing together products of different kind, grade, and quality (as in the case of building materials sold through lumber yards to building contractors as well as ultimate consumers).[5] Sorting may be purely physical in nature (when large lots are accumulated from numerous small suppliers by grain elevators) or may simply involve breaking bulk (i.e., reducing large quantities to small ones).

As will be shown in Chapter 5, channel intermediaries (e.g., wholesalers and retailers) essentially solve the problem of the discrepancy between the various types of assortments of goods and services that are required by industrial and household consumers *and* the assortments that are available directly from individual producers. In other words, manufacturers usually produce a large quantity of a limited number of products, whereas consumers purchase only a few items of a large number of diverse products. Middlemen reduce this *discrepancy of assortments*, thereby enabling consumers to avoid dealing directly with individual manufacturers in order to satisfy their needs.

Wholesalers have been under increasing pressure, however, to prove and improve their economic viability because of several forces threatening their standing in distribution. The three most significant of these forces are, according to Bucklin, (1) the decline of the role and importance of wholesalers in importing and exporting; (2) the fact that manufacturers have expanded the scale of their factories, broadened their product lines, and integrated forward into distribution; and (3) the growth of chain stores.[6] These pressures started building during the late nineteenth century and have not abated since that time. In addition, the wholesaler's unique position in the middle of channels subjects him to the impact of the constant changes and innovations in the whole marketplace.

> Technological advances, product line proliferation, changing retail structures, and social adjustments are only a few of the real problems that complicate the wholesaler's life. Each improved product passing through the wholesale level generates a

---

[5]Richard M. Hill, *Wholesaling Management* (Homewood, Illinois: Richard D. Irwin, Inc., 1963), p. 5.

[6]Louis P. Bucklin, *Competition and Evolution in the Distributive Trades* (Englewood Cliffs, N.J.: Prentice-Hall, Inc., 1972), p. 203.

new demand for investments in warehouse space, market analysis, and sales training, and for myriad adjustments in the wholesaler's information systems. Each
major retailing shift designed to satisfy customer needs obliges him to adjust his
selling patterns, to review his customer service levels, to study product assortments,
and to revise his strategies.[7]

The structure of wholesaling must, therefore, be adaptable and capable of
parrying or absorbing these changes.

THE STRUCTURE OF WHOLESALING

Wholesaling may be characterized as an industry in which the degree of
specialization has constantly increased as a response to the waves of change
mentioned above. In fact, as depicted in Fig. 3-1 as well as in the appendix
to this chapter, the amount of institutional variety in wholesaling is tremendous, and, to some extent, overwhelming. Such a variety offers buyers
and sellers many channel choices, as dictated by such considerations as size,
market segmentation, financial strength, services offered, and chosen method
of operation. It also makes possible a high degree of marketing flow or functional shiftability, whereby all wholesaling functions or a small part thereof
may be shifted from one type of agency to another.

In an effort to provide some semblance of order and analysis to what
must appear to the onlooker as a chaotic structure, academic scholars,
merchants, and the U.S. Bureau of the Census have divided all of the various
wholesaling institutions and establishments into the five major types[8] shown
in Tables 3-1 and 3-2. Several salient facts can be gleaned about wholesaling
in general and about specific types in particular directly from the tables or
from computations based on the data contained in them. First, the volume
of wholesale trade in *constant dollars* was more than three times as large in
1972 as in 1948.[9] Second, merchant wholesalers continue to hold the largest
share of wholesale trade, but the share taken by manufacturers' sales branches
and offices has increased rapidly over the past two and a half decades, sig-
nifying the impact of forward integration of wholesaling functions by
manufacturers. Also, the tendency of large retailers to buy directly from
manufacturers had similar effects. An examination of the percentage distribution of wholesaler sales by type of customer (see Table 3-3) supports

---

[7]Lopata, *op. cit.*, p. 131.

[8]Definitions of the various types of wholesalers can be found in the appendix to this chapter.

[9]Nationally, aggregate sales by wholesalers are larger than sales by retailers because of the large product flow to industrial markets that does not pass through the retail trade *and* because some products
are sold two or more times by wholesale institutions.

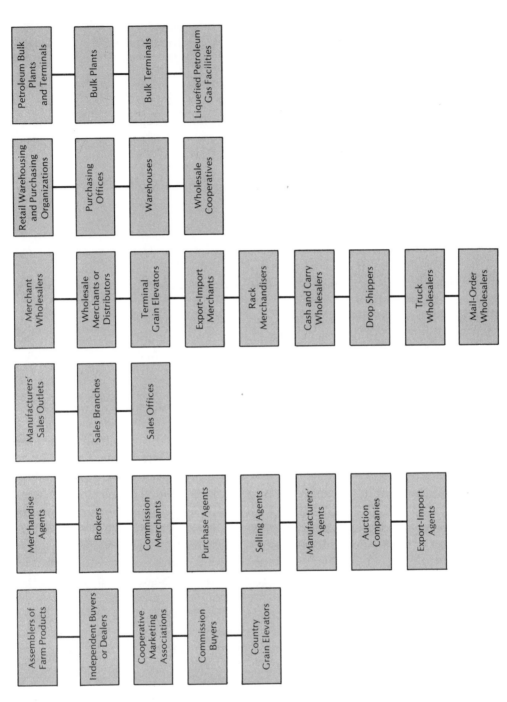

FIGURE 3-1 The Wholesaling Structure—Types of Wholesale Middlemen

SOURCE: Reprinted from Richard M. Hill, *Wholesaling Management* (Homewood, Ill.: Richard D. Irwin, Inc., 1963), p. 25.

TABLE 3-1   Annual Sales of Major Types of Wholesalers, 1929 through 1972

	(in billions of dollars)				
	1929	1948	1963	1967	1972[a]
Merchant-wholesalers	$28.2	$ 76.6	$157.4	$206.1	$353.9
Manufacturer sales branches					
and offices	16.2	50.7	116.4	157.1	255.7
Sales branches	NA[b]	28.5	54.8	67.2	124.5
Sales offices	NA[b]	22.2	61.6	89.9	131.2
Petroleum bulk stations	2.4	10.5	21.5	24.8	33.3
Agents and brokers	14.5	32.9	53.3	61.3	85.6
Assemblers	4.1	9.9	9.8	10.2	NA[b]
Total	$65.4	$180.6	$358.4	$459.5	$728.5

[a] Authors' estimates based on preliminary 1972 Census data.
[b] NA = not available

SOURCE: U.S. Census of Business: *Wholesale Trade, Summary Statistics,* various years.

such a conclusion. Wholesaling to retailers experienced a significant decline from 46.9 percent in 1948 to 37.2 percent in 1974.

Third, there has been a substantial rise in the number of wholesale establishments; between 1948 and 1972, the number of such places of business increased by over 50 percent. It should be recalled from Chapter 2 that, roughly over the same time period, the number of retail establishments remained relatively constant while retail sales grew at a rate comparable to that for wholesaling. Thus, logically extrapolated, this means that the differential in size between the typical wholesale and retail establishment has been continually declining. If size can be taken as an indicator of vertical market power, such a change may have vast implications for channel leadership. However, despite any of the trends apparent in the data, wholesaling, like retailing, is predominately an industry of small businesses—70 percent of all wholesale establishments have no more than seven employees, and the average establishment had only 12 employees in 1967.

Because of their obvious importance in the wholesaling structure, some additional developments within merchant wholesaling and among manufacturers' sales branches and offices are mentioned below.

Merchant Wholesalers

The "merchant wholesalers" category listed in Tables 3-1 and 3-2 includes such service wholesalers as wholesale merchants and distributors, importers, exporters, rack merchandisers, and terminal grain elevators, as well

TABLE 3-2 Trends in the Share of Wholesaling Establishments and Sales[a]

	Establishments (number)				Sales (billions of dollars)			
	1948	1963	1967	1972[b]	1948	1963	1967	1972[b]
Total	216,099	308,177	311,464	369,711	$180.6	$358.4	$459.5	$728.5
	(percentage of total)				(percentage of total)			
Merchant-wholesalers	59.7%	67.8%	68.4%	73.4%	42.4%	43.9%	44.8%	48.6%
Manufacturer sales branches and offices	11.0	9.4	9.9	11.9	28.1	32.5	34.2	35.2
Sales branches	7.3	5.3	5.4	8.4	15.8	15.3	14.6	17.2
Sales offices	3.7	4.1	4.5	3.5	12.3	17.2	19.6	18.0
Petroleum bulk stations	13.1	10.0	9.7	6.3	5.8	6.0	5.4	4.6
Agents and brokers	8.4	8.2	8.5	8.4	18.2	14.9	13.3	10.4
Assemblers	7.8	4.6	3.6	NA[c]	5.5	2.6	2.2	NA[c]

[a] Some of the percentages do not add up to 100% due to rounding or absent data.
[b] Authors' estimates based on preliminary 1972 Census data.
[c] NA = not available

SOURCE: U.S. Census of Business: Wholesale Trade, various years.

TABLE 3-3   Wholesaler Sales by Type of Customer

Type of Customer	1948	1963	1974
Retailers	46.9%	40.8%	37.2%
Industrial, commercial, and government users	31.8	37.6	40.7
Other wholesalers	13.7	14.5	15.0
Consumers and farmers	1.6	1.2	1.3
Foreign buyers	6.0	5.9	5.8
	100.0%	100.0%	100.0%

SOURCE: Bert C. McCammon, Jr. and James W. Kenderine, "Mainstream Developments in Wholesaling," a paper presented at the 1975 Conference of the Southwestern Marketing Association, p. 3.

as a group of limited-function wholesalers like cash-and-carry establishments, drop shippers who do not handle the goods in which they deal, and so-called wagon or truck distributors who combine selling and delivery in one operation. As indicated earlier, merchant wholesalers take title to the goods in which they deal (whether they handle them or not) and operate independently from suppliers on the one hand and from retailers and other customers on the other.

The sales of merchant wholesalers have increased significantly over the time period covered in Tables 3-1 and 3-2, although the growth in their sales has lagged slightly behind, on the average, the growth in GNP (gross national product). In addition, the proportion of merchant wholesaler establishments increased rather dramatically over the time period relative to the increase in the number of establishments of other wholesaler types. However, while overall growth—in sales and establishments—has been strongly positive, the success of merchant wholesalers has varied widely from the standpoint of individual product class groupings. For example, grocery wholesalers have grown more rapidly in recent years because of the strengthening of voluntary and cooperative organizations within food retailing, an interorganizational development to which we return in detail in later chapters. Tobacco jobbers have grown at a slower rate, probably because many of them were absorbed into wholesale grocery operations and because of the increase in direct-vending operations as well as the health controversy surrounding smoking. On the other hand, dry goods and apparel wholesalers have grown at a rapid rate in recent years due, to a significant extent, to the broadened opportunities in lower-cost imported items.[10] (Sales of selected nondurable and durable goods by merchant wholesale groups are shown in Table 3-4 and Fig. 3-2).[11]

[10]Lopata, op. cit., p. 133.

[11]Besides product class groupings, wholesalers can also be broken down into customer categories. Thus, there is one broad class of wholesalers who sell to retailers such diverse commodities as food,

TABLE 3-4   Sales of Selected Durable and Nondurable Goods
by U.S. Merchant Wholesale Groups

	(billions of dollars)			
	1954	1963	1968	1972
Nondurables	$43.2	$61.6	$86.6	$112.8
Groceries and related products	22.2	30.9	44.1	58.0
Beer, wine, distilled alcoholic beverages	5.7	8.2	11.1	15.0
Drugs, chemicals, allied products	3.4	6.0	8.8	11.7
Tobacco, tobacco products	3.2	4.7	5.6	6.9
Dry goods, apparel	5.7	7.1	10.3	13.0
Paper, paper products	3.0	4.7	6.7	8.2
Durables	$39.9	$67.7	$98.0	$136.1
Auto equipment, motor vehicles	4.0	10.5	16.7	27.0
Electrical goods	6.3	10.2	15.0	19.1
Furniture, home furnishings	2.1	3.6	4.9	6.3
Hardware, plumbing and heating supplies	4.9	7.2	9.8	13.5
Lumber, construction materials	6.6	9.2	10.4	15.8
Machinery, equipment and supplies	9.4	17.2	25.5	35.1
Metals, minerals	4.2	6.4	11.0	14.1
Scrap, waste materials	2.4	3.4	4.7	5.2

SOURCE: U.S. Census of Business: *Wholesale Trade* and *Monthly Wholesale Trade Report*, December 1973.

In addition, some merchant wholesalers have found considerable success by restricting their activities to a limited range of products within a product grouping. In groceries, drugs, hardware, and jewelry, specialty wholesalers have been able to aid retail chains in expanding their product lines in directions unfamiliar to chain buyers and merchandisers (e.g., nonfood items in grocery stores).[12]

Manufacturers' Sales Branches and Offices

Branches are captive wholesaling operations owned and operated by a manufacturer. Branch operations are common, for example, in electrical supplies (e.g., Westinghouse Electric Supply Company) and in plumbing

---

drugs, tobacco, hardware, dry goods, and appliances. Another class sells such items as food, paper products, medical goods and supplies, and so on, to restaurants and institutions. A third class sells building materials to builders and contractors. A fourth class sells manufacturing supplies such as tools, chemicals, abrasives, and so on, to manufacturers. In the complex automotive parts aftermarket, there are even warehouse distributors who sell only to other jobbers. However, growth generalities are difficult to make here because of the diversity of products included within each class.

[12]See Louis W. Stern, "Self-Sufficiency: A Fixation Among Large Corporate Supermarket Chains?" *Journal of Retailing*, Vol. 42 (Spring, 1966), pp. 18–25 ff. and Bucklin, *op. cit.*, pp. 233–235.

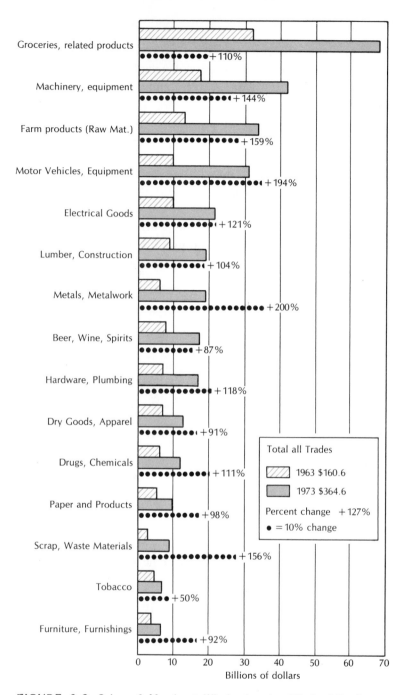

FIGURE 3-2 Sales of Merchant Wholesalers by Kind of Business: 1963 and 1973

SOURCE: U.S. Census of Business, *Wholesale Trade* and *Monthly Wholesale Trade Report*, December, 1974.

(e.g., Crane Supply Company and Arnstan-American Standard). Captive branch operations are also employed heavily by truck manufacturers, full-line farm equipment manufacturers, and large producers of major appliances.[13]

Manufacturers' sales branches are of two types: those that carry inventories and those that do not. The greatest growth has been among the latter type. To a major extent, this development reflects the declining need for local wholesale inventories; manufacturers find that they require salesmen in the field but can often ship directly to their customers.[14] Irrespective of type, manufacturers' sales branches account for slightly more industrial goods sales volume than do merchant-wholesalers, according to Bucklin's data.[15] For industrial goods marketing, the quantities involved and the need for technical expertise seem to favor the sales branch over the merchant wholesaler.

It is, however, important to note that a fourth of the business done by the branches and sales offices is in sales to other wholesale establishments rather than to customers of merchant wholesalers.[16] In fact, almost 56 percent of the merchant wholesaler's industrial goods volume was obtained from another wholesale institution in 1963, according to Bucklin's estimates,[17] and it is very likely that a vast majority of shipments came to these wholesalers from manufacturers' branches. Double wholesaling is even more important for consumer goods, although the channels for industrial and consumer goods are becoming more similar over the years in this respect.[18]

Agents and Brokers

Finally with regard to the overall structure of wholesaling, the relative decline of agents and brokers shown in Table 3–2 masks the increase in the relative importance of manufacturers' agents within this segment. Table 3–5 indicates this shift. These firms have emerged as the major bright spot in

---

[13] Lopata, *op. cit.*, p. 131.

[14] However, as Bucklin points out, the data on manufacturers' sales branches without stocks do not fully disclose the extent to which the manufacturers may be employing other inventory depots not located directly at the sales office. One regional warehouse, for example, may serve several sales offices. Alternatively, the manufacturer may be employing public warehouse facilities—particularly in small territories—rather than constructing his own. Bucklin, *op. cit.*, p. 214.

[15] *Ibid.*, p. 217.

[16] Theodore N. Beckman, "Changes in Wholesaling Structure and Performance," in Moller and Wilemon, *op. cit.*, p. 126.

[17] Bucklin, *op. cit.*, p. 218.

[18] *Ibid.*, p. 219.

TABLE 3-5   Sales by Agent Wholesalers—1939 and 1967 (in millions of dollars)

Type of Operation	1939		1967	
	Volume of Trade	Percentage of Total	Volume of Trade	Percentage of Total
Merchandise brokers	3,391	30.3	14,030	22.9
Commission merchants	2,748	24.5	14,068	22.9
Selling agents	1,742	15.5	6,890	11.2
Manufacturers' agents	1,397	12.5	15,260	24.9
Export and import agents	915	8.2	5,162	8.4
Purchasing agents, resident buyers	575	5.1	1,147	1.9
Auction companies	434	3.9	4,792	7.8
Total	11,201	100.0	61,347	100.0

SOURCE: Census of Business, Wholesale Trade, 1939 and 1967, Bureau of the Census (Washington, D.C.: Government Printing Office).

agent wholesaling and operate very much like salesmen in the field, except that they carry a narrow line of products from a few suppliers related in terms of the needs of their customers.[19] Nevertheless, manufacturers in a few industries have tended to move away from reliance on any type of agent wholesaling organization because they view such wholesalers as not being service-oriented, controllable, innovative, efficient, or reliable.[20]

ECONOMIC CONCENTRATION IN WHOLESALING

Between 1958 and 1963, there was a seven percent increase in the number of merchant wholesaler establishments with less than $1 million in annual sales, a 27 percent increase in establishments with $1 million to $5 million in sales, and a 41 percent increase in establishments with sales in excess of $5 million a year. Still, of some 209,000 establishments owned by 185,000 merchant wholesalers in 1968, only about 1400 were generating over $10 million in annual sales.[21] By 1974, wholesaler establishments with annual sales over $10 million accounted for 38 percent of total wholesaler sales, up

[19] See the appendix at the end of this chapter for a description of the activities of various agent middlemen.

[20] James R. Moore and Kendall A. Adams, "Functional Wholesaler Sales: Trends and Analysis," *1975 Combined Proceedings*, ed. by Edward M. Mazze (Chicago: American Marketing Association, 1976), pp. 403–404.

[21] Lopata, *op. cit.*, p. 137.

from 14 percent in 1948.[22] In general, however, economic concentration in wholesaling is very low, especially on the national level.

> The largest ten wholesaling operations in 1969 held only 3.2 percent of the total business done by wholesalers nationally. Because of the conglomerate nature of many of these firms (e.g., Foremost-McKesson, American Hospital Supply Corporation), the real figure is probably closer to 2 percent. Hence, we find that despite the reduced number of wholesalers, as compared to retailers, the former industry is less concentrated than the latter. The extent of concentration is so slight as to be meaningless.[23]

On a product line or a local geographic basis, wholesaling is a relatively more concentrated industry than retailing. Thus, 13 firms (including Graybar Electric Company) control 30.4 percent of the business done by electrical supply wholesalers; six firms (including American Hospital Supply Corporation) share 19.6 percent of the business done by wholesalers of hospital supplies; 19 firms (including Joseph P. Ryerson & Sons, Inc.) account for 18 percent of the business done by metal service centers.[24] Bucklin's analysis has shown that in one large geographic area (California), the typical number of wholesalers directly operating within all but the very largest metropolitan area is relatively small.[25]

One factor accounting for the extent of concentration is the existence of multiunit or chain operations within wholesaling. While wholesaling is still very largely an industry comprised of single-unit firms, multiestablishment wholesale firms accounted for 47.3 percent of all sales and over 25 percent of all establishments in 1974.[26] In a study of 14 product subsectors, Bucklin has shown that the share of chain operations ranges from a low of 28.1 percent in dry goods to a high of 81.4 percent in petroleum bulk stations and terminals.[27] Furthermore, branch operating wholesalers, who represent about seven percent of all merchant wholesalers, accounted for approximately 36 percent of total merchant wholesaler volume in 1963.[28] It should be noted, however, that most branches in wholesaling are operated in small groups compared to the extremely large systems found in retailing.

[22]Bert C. McCammon, Jr., and James W. Kenderine, "Mainstream Developments in Wholesaling," a paper presented at the 1975 Conference of the Southwestern Marketing Association, p. 5.

[23]Bucklin, *op. cit.*, pp. 243–244.

[24]*Ibid.*, p. 244.

[25]*Ibid.*, p. 245.

[26]McCammon and Kenderine, *op. cit.*, p. 5.

[27]*Ibid.*, p. 258. For documentation relative to leading industrial distribution chains, see "The Chain of Events in Industrial Distribution," *Marketing News*, January 30, 1976, p. 7.

[28]Lopata, *op. cit.*, p. 137.

COMPETITION IN WHOLESALING

Given the extent of economic concentration in certain product lines as well as within geographic areas, one would expect to find a high degree of mutually recognized interdependence in the pricing behavior of wholesaling firms. Economic theorists would predict that competition in such situations would be of a nonprice nature, given the similarity of prices that is evidenced when there are only a few competitors in a market. Coupling the findings on concentration with knowledge that trade association activity of a collusive nature has been found to exist within certain segments of wholesale trade,[29] one can predict that prices would be stable and profits high, again using the classical economist's model.

However, competition, especially in larger market areas, is intense, from the perspective of both price and service. Several factors account for this. First, as in retailing, product line assortments are generally very broad, making price identity among competitors very difficult to maintain within wholesale trade. Second, wholesalers face economically significant retailing, industrial, and business buying organizations, and such organizations are capable of playing wholesalers off against one another as well as threatening to purchase directly from manufacturers if prices are not set to their satisfaction. Although the balance of power can swing in the wholesaler's favor from time to time (as when large wholesaling organizations deal with small retailing firms), any deviance in pricing behavior from that afforded to other channels comprised of organizations purchasing direct from suppliers will rapidly place the wholesaler's channel in a weakened competitive position. In other words, by using his power relative to small retailers and industrial buyers for self-aggrandizement purposes, the wholesaler may be hurting himself in the long run by crippling his customers.

Third, because wholesalers generally deal in large lot size orders, the opportunity for intermarket penetration is high. In wholesaling, market size is generally determined by transport costs, the bulk of the product, and the value of the product relative to freight charges.[30] The market size is not limited by the extent to which customers will travel to buy goods, as it is in retailing. Thus, enterprising wholesalers can find markets stretched by their willingness to meet or beat prices existing in locations quite distant from

[29] Bucklin, *op. cit.*, pp 245-248.
[30] *Ibid.*, p. 266.

their normal trading areas. The efficiency of their operations will, to a large extent, determine just how far their market outreach can extend.

Fourth, entry is relatively easy.

> Although the cost of constructing a new warehouse might range upwards of $10 million for the plant alone, entry into some separate product-line category could be effected at substantially lower fees. The specialist might compete on some basis other than price (such as faster delivery and unusually deep stocks), but his presence nevertheless brings competitive pressure upon the general-line wholesaler, leaving little room to extract higher than warranted margins.[31]

Finally, the most important factor breeding a high degree of competition in wholesale trade was hinted at in Chapter 2—the continual evolution of new distributive patterns (so-called intertype competition, such as that engendered by retail chain stores, cooperatives, and vertical integration) which narrow the security of the established sellers and bring powerful pressures to bear on wholesale markets. In fact, like large retailers, certain wholesalers are striving to achieve a differential advantage in *multiple* competitive environments.

> Consider, for example, the competitive milieu of Stratton & Terstegge, a large hardware wholesaler in Louisville. At the present time, the company sells to independent retailers, sponsors a voluntary group program, and operates its own stores. In these multiple capacities, it competes against conventional wholesalers (Belknap), cash and carry wholesalers (Atlas), specialty wholesalers (Garcia), corporate chains (Wickes), voluntary groups (Western Auto), cooperative groups (Cotter), free form corporations (Interco), and others. Given the complexity of its competitive environment, it is not surprising to observe that Stratton & Terstegge generates a relatively modest rate of return on net worth.[32]

In the light of these five factors, combined with effective action on the part of antitrust enforcement agencies against collusive trade association activities, profits in wholesaling in a number of industries reflect a high degree of competitive activity when compared to those in manufacturing (see Table 3–6).

---

[31] *Ibid.*, pp. 269-270.

[32] Bert C. McCammon, Jr., "Future Shock and the Practice of Management," a paper presented at the Fifth Annual Attitude Research Conference of the American Marketing Association, Madrid, Spain, 1973, p. 9. For a comprehensive discussion of the performance of large wholesaling concerns, see Bert C. McCammon, Jr., and James M. Kenderine, "High Performance Wholesaling," *Hardlines Wholesaling*, Vol. 9 (September, 1975), pp. 17-57.

TABLE 3-6   Profits of Selected U.S. Merchant-Wholesalers and Manufacturers, 1967 and 1972

| | Net Profit on Tangible Net Worth[a] | | | |
| | Merchant Wholesalers | | Manufacturers | |
	1967	1972	1967	1972
Durable Goods:				
Auto parts and accessories	6.85%	10.89%	11.05%	11.53%
Electric parts and supplies	8.65	10.26[b]	14.83	9.37[c]
Furniture and home furnishings	8.90	8.42	7.87[d]	10.62
Hardware	3.87	7.02	9.51[e]	10.62
Plumbing and heating supplies	6.23	7.76	8.41	10.65
Lumber and building materials	6.73	11.00	7.55[f]	11.73
Metals and minerals	8.33	8.44	9.23[g]	9.39
Nondurable Goods:				
Groceries	6.42%	7.77%	11.25%[h]	10.32%
Wines and liquors	7.40	8.56[i]	7.48[j]	4.97
Drugs and drug sundries	6.50	8.75	10.38	12.76
Chemical and allied products	7.43	10.71	8.35[k]	8.24
Apparel and accessories	6.72	5.69	7.83	7.56[l]
Paper	6.92	7.00	8.50	6.27

[a]Median percentages, after taxes.
[b]Electrical apparatus and equipment.
[c]Electric lighting and wiring equipment.
[d]Wood and upholstered household furniture.
[e]Cutlery, hand tools, and general hardware.
[f]Average of concrete, gypsum, plastic products and lumber.
[g]Iron and steel foundries.
[h]Canned, preserved fruits, vegetables, and seafood.
[i]Beer, wine, and alcoholic beverages.
[j]Malt liquors.
[k]Average of agricultural and industrial chemicals.
[l]Average of women's and misses' dresses, children's and infants' outerwear, women's and misses' suits and coats, and women's and children's underwear and nightwear.

SOURCE: Dun & Bradstreet Inc., *Key Business Ratios in 125 Industries*, 1967 and 1972.

As is discussed below, the basic elements important to marketing and, thus, competition on the wholesaling level of distribution are not vastly different from those found in retailing. One would expect a similarity, given the competitive characteristics of the markets and the fact that the wholesaler's prime function is, like a retailer's, to maintain appropriate assortments for his customers as well as to provide services permitting his customers to utilize his products effectively and efficiently.

THE MANAGEMENT
OF WHOLESALING INSTITUTIONS

Understanding how wholesalers serve their suppliers and their customers provides insight into the managerial variables employed in securing differential advantages within wholesale trade.

Serving Suppliers

As indicated earlier, wholesalers are involved, either by virtue of title change or physical possession or negotiation, with nearly half of the shipments made within the country. In 1963, wholesaler volume in the consumer-goods sector accounted for 66 percent of all consumer-goods shipments; for industrial goods, the comparable figure was 43 percent.[33] In the latter category, about which less has been written than the former, significant merchant and agent wholesaling operations are found in the following industries:

Industrial chemicals and explosives

Office furniture

Coarse paper

Stationery and office supplies

Trucks and tractors

Electrical wiring supplies

Electrical apparatus and equipment

Plumbing and heating equipment

Lumber and construction materials

Metals and metal products

Scrap and waste materials

In general, the manufacturers of supplies seem to lean heavily on merchant wholesalers (industrial distributors). Highly technical products, such as chemicals and electrical apparatus, and bulky materials, such as metals, are

[33]Bucklin, *op. cit.*, pp. 208-209.

marketed largely through manufacturers' branches.[34] One might expect all machinery to be sold direct or through branches, but construction and metal-working machinery are exceptions. Manufacturers of the latter tend to rely heavily on distributors because of their engineering orientation. Given this orientation, the manufacturers prefer to turn troublesome marketing problems over to distribution specialists.[35] Similarly, Lopata has observed that:

> Manufacturers, preoccupied with return on investment, prefer to allocate scarce resources to research and production rather than to distribution, which they know has historically delivered a much lower return. Manufacturers frequently view entry into wholesaling as an added burden on their already beleaguered management teams. Finally, and more tangibly, there remains the fear of some manufacturers that the federal government may attack their expansion into distribution operations.[36]

From an operational perspective, suppliers of both industrial and consumer goods may rely on wholesalers for several key reasons.[37]

1. Wholesalers have continuity in and intimacy with local markets. Being close to customers, they are in positions to take initial steps in the sale of any product, namely, identifying prospective users and determining the extent of their needs.

2. Wholesalers make possible local availability of stocks and thereby relieve suppliers of small-order business, which the latter can seldom conduct on a profitable basis. Also, they tend to have an acute understanding of the costs of holding and handling inventory in which they have made major commitments.

3. Within their territories, wholesalers can provide suppliers with a sales force that is in close touch with the needs of customers and prospects. Also, by virtue of the fact that a wholesaler represents a number of suppliers, he can often cover a given territory at a lower cost than could the manufacturer's own salesmen.

4. As already indicated in the discussion in Chapter 1, wholesalers perform financial services for suppliers by providing volume cash markets through which they can recover capital that would otherwise be invested in inventories.

In addition to employing merchant wholesalers extensively, at least 80 percent of companies making industrial goods at some time or other sell

---

[34] Richard M. Hill, Ralph S. Alexander, and James S. Cross, *Industrial Marketing*, 4th ed. (Homewood, Illinois: Richard D. Irwin, Inc., 1975), p. 253.

[35] *Ibid*.

[36] Lopata, *op. cit.*, pp. 132–133.

[37] Many of these same points have been made in more detail by Richard M. Hill, *op. cit.*, pp. 10–14. See also Frederick E. Webster, Jr., "The Changing Role of the Industrial Distributor," *Marketing Science Institute Report No. 75-121* (December, 1975).

through manufacturer's or sales agents, and at least 50 percent of them regularly use multiple-line agents in their marketing programs.[38] Agents can be extremely useful to manufacturers, because the cost of employing them is often lower than that which might be incurred through alternative channels. Agents also tend to be valuable in developing markets for products new to a manufacturer's line, and they can frequently provide a better quality of sales service than the industrial distributor, who often carries in excess of 30,000 items made by hundreds of manufacturers. However, the use of agent middlemen poses, from the manufacturer's perspective, problems of control, lack of flexibility in competitive bidding situations, expense when volume is considerable, divided loyalty, and the burdens of direct shipment, as well as the fact that agents are generally not strong in technical service (e.g., installation or maintenance).[39]

Sales branch distribution, on the other hand, provides manufacturers with well-trained technical specialists, maintenance of strategically located stocks of parts, repair facilities and mechanics, and delivery service, as well as the added sales promotion and information advantages received by having one's own sales force in the field.[40] The obvious disadvantage of establishing a sales branch (with or without stocks) is that a branch

> ... creates its own overhead costs, loads the company with an entirely new set of personnel obligations that may be difficult to diminish when costs must be cut, engenders a need for plant and equipment not otherwise required, and adds tremendously to the work of supervision and management, and to the staff required to carry it on.[41]

From the point of view of the manufacturer, the several salient factors shown in Exhibit 3-1 must be evaluated in determining the type of wholesaling establishment to use; these factors must always be conditioned by the nature of the ultimate market for the goods in question.

Serving Retailers

Manufacturers are generally self-centered and myopic. Their interest is to encourage retailers to promote and sell their own lines of products. On the other hand, wholesalers have a strong vested interest in building up their

[38]Ralph S. Alexander, James S. Cross, and Richard M. Hill, *Industrial Marketing*, 3rd ed. (Homewood, Illinois: Richard D. Irwin, Inc., 1967), p. 238.

[39]*Ibid.*, pp. 243–245.

[40]Hill, Alexander, and Cross, *op. cit.*, pp. 253–254. See also Louis W. Stern and J. L. Heskett, "Grass Roots Market Research," *Harvard Business Review*, Vol. 43 (March–April, 1965), pp. 83–96.

[41]Hill, Alexander, and Cross, *op. cit.*, p. 254.

EXHIBIT 3–1   Criteria of Choice in the Decision of What Type of Wholesaling Establishment to Use— Point of View of the Manufacturer

1. Evaluation of sales efforts of wholesale agency
   a. Extent and activity of sales force of wholesale agency.
   b. Does sales force *sell*, or does it just take orders?
   c. Extent to which manufacturer must supplement wholesaler's sales efforts with own promotion, salesmen, and/or detail men.
   d. Number of lines handled by wholesale agency.
      (1) Does agency handle too many lines to give sufficient attention to manufacturer's line?
         (a) Use of heavy advertising, good margins, realistic pricing to stimulate attention on part of wholesaler.
         (b) Preference, sometimes, for more attention to individual line by use of specialty or limited-line wholesalers.
      (2) Does agency handle competing lines?
         (a) Use of sales or manufacturers' agents sometimes indicated.
         (b) May necessitate creation of exclusive distributorships.
2. Evaluation of relationship of wholesaling agency to channel of distribution for the product.
   a. Type of agency that can give widest distribution and assurance of sufficient retail outlets for line.
   b. When particular types of retail outlets are desired, what types of wholesaling agency can best handle them?
   c. Quality and continuity of relationships maintained between wholesaling and retailing agency.
   d. Degree to which wholesaling agency cooperates in promotion, pricing, financing, and other marketing activities.
   e. Willingness of wholesaling agency to maintain continuous relationships with manufacturer.

SOURCE: Department of Marketing, University of Pennsylvania, Wharton School of Finance and Commerce.

retail customers as merchants, since it is quite likely that, particularly in the case of smaller retail establishments, an individual wholesaler would be able to supply a large part of the retailer's requirements for merchandise. It is in the wholesaler's self-interest to spend considerable effort and resources training, stimulating, and aiding retailers to become better managers. Therefore, wholesalers become directly involved in retail merchandise management. In this respect, the benefits to the retailer derived from relying on wholesalers may be described as follows:[42]

1. Wholesalers can give their retail customers a great deal of direct selling aid in the form of price concessions on featured items, point-of-sale material, and cooperative advertising.

2. Wholesalers often can provide expert assistance in planning store layout, building design, and material specifications.

3. Wholesalers generally offer retailers guidance and counsel in public relations, housekeeping and accounting methods, administrative procedures, and the like.

In the toy industry, for instance, many retailers prefer to make some or all of their total annual toy purchases from wholesalers rather than from manufacturers, because, as one retail executive has indicated:

1. In many instances reorders are filled more quickly.

2. Wholesalers guarantee the sale (any items which are not sold can be returned for full credit).

3. Defective products are replaced promptly.

4. The wholesaler extends long-term credit.

5. The percentage of mark-up by working through a wholesaler is more than offset by decreased inventory costs and improved service.[43]

Obviously, the foremost advantage for many retailers in relying on wholesalers is the fact that the latter buy in large quantities, break bulk to suit the convenience of their customers, and then pass along the savings effected both in cost and transportation, compared, of course, to the costs of obtaining merchandise directly in small lots from distant points. Thus, by using wholesalers, independent retailers can avoid diluting the energies of their often overtaxed executive staffs. Furthermore, these retailers obtain access through wholesalers to a large group of products of small manufacturers that might not otherwise be available to them. Even in the case of large establishments in certain product lines, reliance on wholesalers allows conversion of dead-weight store space, formerly devoted to merchandise storage, into profit-making selling or customer service space.[44] For example,

---

[42]See Hill, *op. cit.*, pp. 16–21 for more explanation and details.

[43]Richard N. Cardozo and James E. Haefner, "Note on the Toy Industry" (Boston, Mass.: Intercollegiate Case Clearing House, No. ICH 14 M 60, 1970), p. 9.

[44]Paul L. Courtney, "The Wholesaler as a Link in the Distribution Channel," in Moller and Wilemon, *op. cit.*, p. 178.

while chains can buy at the same price as a rack jobber, the latter's hold on the market comes from knowing precisely what to buy and minimizing the handling and inventory costs of nonfood products.

Some of the significant criteria used in evaluating, from the perspective of the retailer, whether and what type of wholesaler to "employ" are listed in Exhibit 3-2. As in the case of the manufacturer or supplier, these criteria are conditioned by the nature of the products that the retailer carries and the market he serves.

Serving the Business User

As mentioned previously, merchant wholesaler sales are divided about equally between retailers and business or industrial users. While many of the advantages to the business user from relying on wholesalers are exactly the same as those mentioned above relative to retailers, there are some additional factors which are briefly discussed here.

The short "lead" time on deliveries made available through wholesalers are especially important to industrial users. Flexibility in production scheduling can generally be achieved if production planners know that speedy local deliveries can be forthcoming. This factor is why industrial distributors, perhaps more than most types of wholesale firms, are plagued by the problem of small orders. One steel warehouse reported that 31.7 percent of the orders it received averaged $7.50 per order, created 32 percent of its administration cost, and contributed only 6 percent to its total sales.[45] Before we hastily recommend that such distributors reassess the value of providing such business, it should be remembered that by refusing to handle small orders or by making them expensive to the buyer, the distributor destroys several of the chief reasons for his existence.

In addition, many types of wholesalers provide unique forms of technical assistance that are relatively costly to duplicate elsewhere, except in situations where a buyer can purchase in very large quantities. For example, many steel warehouses and wholesalers of other fabricated metals have facilities for cutting and shaping metal stock to dimensions desired by the customer. Machine tool and accessories wholesalers often have specialists on their staffs who are available to help customers with technical problems pertaining to the use of tools and parts. Indeed, it is not unusual to find such technically trained persons as metallurgists, chemists, draftsmen, and mechanical and civil engineers employed by wholesalers to assist customers with

---

[45] Alexander, Cross, and Hill, *op. cit.*, p. 231.

**EXHIBIT 3-2   Criteria of Choice in the Decision of What Type
of Wholesaling Establishment to Use—
Point of View of the Retailer**

1. Lines

    a. Does wholesaling agency supply all or most of the lines needed by the retailer?

    b. Does wholesaling agency supply all or most of the brands required by the retailer for each of his lines?

    c. Does the wholesaling agency stock an assortment of varieties, styles, sizes, and colors sufficient to meet retailer's needs?

2. Services

    a. Can wholesaling agency assure a continuous and regular supply of merchandise without excessive out-of-stocks or backorders?

    b. Extent of aid given to retailer by wholesaling agency (e.g., promotion, pricing, inventory maintenance, etc.)?

    c. Extension of credit by wholesaling agency?

    d. Delivery by wholesaling agency?

    e. Do types of agencies used result in too frequent and time-consuming calls by salesmen?

    f. Help given by salesmen?

    g. Does wholesale agency's cost structure permit selling price to retailer such as to allow retailer sufficient margins?

SOURCE: Department of Marketing, University of Pennsylvania, Wharton School of Finance and Commerce.

the problems involved in proper selection and use of products.[46] Even managerial assistance is being increasingly provided to business users by wholesalers. Thus,

> An electronics distributor in Ann Arbor analyzed the stockkeeping methods of one of his industrial customers and recommended revised delivery schedules, prearranged items, packs suitable for assembly line use, and standardized item identification. The customer was able to reduce the possession costs on his stock by 15% of its value.[47]

[46]Hill, *op. cit.*, pp. 22-23.

[47]Lopata, *op. cit.*, p. 140.

Indeed, business users and retailers alike must be concerned with the overall or *ultimate cost* of the goods that they purchase, handle, and store— not merely with the price at which such goods are obtained. When adequate accounting is made, it can often be found that the *ultimate cost* of dealing with wholesalers is less than the ultimate cost of dealing directly with manufacturers, even though the quantity discounts made available by the latter are not generally available when using wholesalers as suppliers. Thus, even in the case of industrial goods needed in the assembly of a given product (e.g., electronic tubes for radios), it may be less costly to place the burden of handling, possessing, ordering, and storing the goods on a wholesaler versus having to order in very large lots directly from the manufacturer, especially if the goods will have to be held a considerable period of time before they enter the production process. This *ultimate cost concept* can be applied to justifying the use of wholesalers in situations where they might not otherwise appear to be economical.[48]

Recognition of the ultimate cost concept by both wholesalers and their customers has led to a phenomenon called "systems selling." As defined by Hannaford,

> Systems selling is a broad, inclusive term that may be used to describe any form of cooperative contracting relationship between an industrial distributor and his customer for the ordering and distribution of low-value, repetitively used items for maintenance, repair, or operating (MRO) purposes, or for use in manufacturing original equipment.[49]

The various forms of systems selling[50] are, in actuality, purchasing systems when viewed from the customer's perspective. A procedure links a distributor and his customer together through a contractual understanding which simplifies, streamlines, and creates new efficiencies in the customer's MRO purchasing/acquisition/retention cycle. As explained by Hannaford:

> ... purchasing systems make use of the distributor's special capabilities: his warehousing and inventory management expertise, his vast market knowledge, and his special ability to offer a multitude of customer services such as delivery, credit, provision of control data, engineering expertise, and so on. These capabilities are directed at the small order or nuisance order problems of customers: the hundreds

[48] The term "ultimate cost concept" was introduced to the authors by Richard S. Lopata and Richard E. Peterson, Principals, SAM Associates, Inc., Chicago, Illinois.

[49] William J. Hannaford, *Systems Selling to Industrial Markets: Concepts and Strategies* (Washington, D.C.: Distribution Research and Education Foundation, 1975), p. 3.

[50] Systems selling includes blanket ordering, blanket contracts, national contracts, contract buying, stockless purchasing, systems purchasing, and systems contracting.

of small orders issued annually for low-value, repetitively used MRO or OEM items, the accompanying paperwork burden, the wastefulness of spending 80 percent of a buyer's time purchasing items that account for but 20 percent of the purchasing dollar, cumbersome ordering procedures, and costly storage problems involving waste, pilferage, and the like.[51]

For example, one form of systems selling is "blanket ordering." Blanket orders involve contracts between a distributor and his customer, usually negotiated on a low-bid basis for a fixed period of time. Once a contract is drawn up, customer departments needing materials issue releases against the contract. Another form, called "systems contracting," is a considerable extension of blanket ordering in that the distributor is called upon to supply more functions for the customer and can cover a wider scope of products.[52]

Wholesaling Marketing Management

Although it has been generally admitted by a number of observers of wholesale trade that wholesalers have been slow to pick up and adopt modern business methods and attitudes, there are strong indications that wholesalers are becoming increasingly more sophisticated.[53] Some of the benefits gained through the adoption of more sophisticated managerial techniques and practices on the part of selected wholesalers are portrayed in Tables 3–7 and 3–8. As highlighted above, successful wholesaling is based on the service satisfactions of proximity, broad product assortments, and rapid response to the needs of local retailers, contractors, manufacturers, hospitals, and other customers. What is demanded in wholesaling, then, is the kind of merchandise management found in certain segments of retailing. As Hill points out, merchandising management must involve the wholesaler in fundamental questions of policy.

[51]Hannaford, *op. cit.*, p. 4.

[52]The various forms of systems selling are described in detail in footnote 50.

[53]Lopata, *op. cit.*, p. 130. Evidence of the increased managerial sophistication of certain wholesalers is seen in their development of voluntary group programs (see Chapter 10), their moves toward inventory diversification, particularly in the hardware, building materials, and grocery fields (examples are Hughes, a Florida-based wholesaler, which has evolved into a full-line distributor of electrical, industrial, plumbing, and utility supplies, and Rykoff, which has emerged as a full-line supplier in the food service field from its original role as an institutional food distributor), their integration into retailing (e.g., Malone & Hyde and Nash Finch), their diversification into other wholesaling areas (e.g., Bluefield Supply, Premier Industrial, and J. M. Tull), and their integration into manufacturing (e.g., Bristol Products, Superscope, W. W. Grainger, Earle M. Jorgensen, and Pioneer Standard Electronics). For further discussion, see Albert D. Bates and Bert C. McCammon, Jr., "Reseller Strategies and the Financial Performance of the Firm," a paper presented at the Structure, Strategy, and Performance Conference, Indiana University Graduate School of Business, November, 1975, pp. 21–25. See also "Industrial Distributors," *Forbes*, February 17, 1976, pp. 44–47.

TABLE 3-7   Benefits Derived by Selected Wholesalers by Developing Management Information Systems

| | Results Achieved with | |
Performance Measurement	Conventional Data Processing System	Management Information System
Inventory service level	84.6%	89.6%
Gross margin/net sales	17.3%	20.6%
Average inventory (number of weeks supply)	14.8	13.0
Gross margin/average inventory	73.6%	103.9%
Contribution margin/average inventory	49.6%	79.9%

SOURCE: Management Horizons Data Systems, as reported in Bert C. McCammon, Jr. and James W. Kenderine, "Mainstream Developments in Wholesaling," a paper presented at the 1975 Conference of the Southwestern Marketing Association, p. 7.

TABLE 3-8   Benefits Derived by Selected Wholesalers by Adopting Improved Management Practices

Management Practice	Number of Order Lines per Manhour
Minimum order policy	9.3
No minimum order policy	8.8
Out-of-stocks deleted before orders are picked	13.1
Out-of-stocks deleted after orders are picked	8.2
Item location shown on order or pick ticket	9.3
Item location not shown on order or pick ticket	8.6
Picking sequence specified on order or pick ticket	9.4
Picking sequence not specified on order or pick ticket	8.7

SOURCE: Hardware Institute for Research and Development, as reported in Bert C. McCammon, Jr. and James W. Kenderine, "Mainstream Developments in Wholesaling," a paper presented at the 1975 Conference of the Southern Marketing Association, p. 7.

The general class of products to be carried (groceries, mill supplies, drugs, machine tools), the width of the assortment needed (general line or specialities), and the nature of the marketing operation (full service or limited service) will be largely determined by the definition of the market. It also follows that decisions pertaining to private brands, exclusive franchise, and the type of cooperative arrangements to be encouraged must be made on the same basis. Even such questions as the organization of buying, the selection of suppliers, and the control of inventory hinge upon the characteristics of the wholesaler's market and the variations which are present in these characteristics.[54]

The elements of the retailing marketing mix specified in Chapter 2 are, to a large extent, directly pertinent to wholesaling marketing management, even though there are obvious nuances that make the managerial jobs somewhat distinct. For example, store hours and site selection are not as crucial in wholesaling as they are in retailing. Also, the nature of the promotional process is different in the two sectors. Emphasis in wholesaling has been placed on personal selling, often by "outside" sales personnel and in-house telephone salesmen, whereas emphasis is placed on self-service and "inside" selling-floor sales personnel by retailing establishments. Media advertising plays a much more significant role in retailing than in wholesaling. Instead of relying on media advertising, most of the larger wholesale firms publish and distribute catalogs to their customers. Some of these are enormous volumes and rather costly. For example, one large laboratory chemical house distributes 85,000 copies of its 1000-page book, in which 15,000 items are listed and described. Sometimes a listing in a wholesaler's catalog brings added benefits, besides awareness and/or exposure, as Lopata points out:

> The David Wexler Company of Chicago is a well-known merchant of musical merchandise. A relatively unknown item gains prestige and an aura of special value just by being listed in its catalog—witness the fact that customers have testified "If an item is found in the Wexler catalog, it must be good."[55]

In addition to catalogs, many distributors maintain showrooms that can be visited by customers and from which buyers can be served in the handling of small orders for which immediate delivery is desired. Many business users, for example, look upon the distributor as a sort of retail store conveniently located where emergency requirements can be procured.

Beyond differences in promotion efforts, there are other differences in management approach. First, organizational arrangements tend to vary between retailing and wholesaling. In contrast to the organization structure depicted in Fig. 3–3, retailing operations tend to be a bit more decentralized and departmentalized. Second, delivery is a much more important feature in wholesaling operations than it is in retailing. While certain retailers, such as department, appliance, and furniture stores, still maintain delivery policies, the function assumes minimal relative importance compared to its significance in wholesaling.

[54]Hill, *op. cit.*, p. 6.

[55]Lopata, *op. cit.*, p. 140.

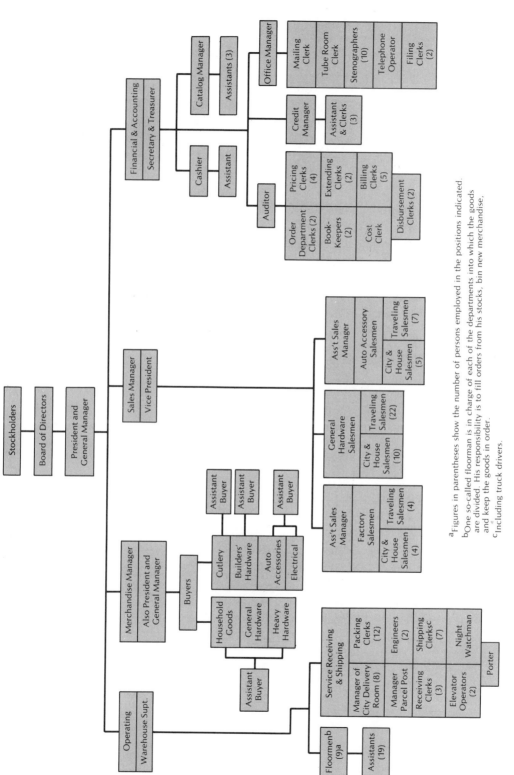

FIGURE 3-3 Organization Chart of a Wholesale Hardware House

SOURCE: Reprinted from Theodore N. Beckman, Nathanael H. Engle, and Robert D. Buzzell, *Wholesaling*, 3rd ed. (New York: The Ronald Press, 1959), p. 351.

[a]Figures in parentheses show the number of persons employed in the positions indicated.
[b]One so-called floorman is in charge of each of the departments into which the goods are divided. His responsibility is to fill orders from his stocks, bin new merchandise, and keep the goods in order.
[c]Including truck drivers.

The two areas where retailing and merchant wholesaling are most similar is the stress that must be laid in both sectors on merchandise management and inventory control. For both, appropriate and adequate assortments are key determinants of success. For example, in the industrial marketing field, the general mill wholesale supply house is reported to carry between 15,000 and 20,000 items in as many as 650 product lines, such as bolts, nuts, belting, bearings, valves, fittings, cutting tools, hand tools, portable power tools, and some metal rods, bars, and tubing. An electric supply firm handles some 60,000 electrical items made by between 200 and 300 manufacturers. Some specialty houses are reported to carry from 30,000 and 50,000 items or more.

The techniques employable for wholesaling merchandise management and inventory control are strongly similar to those in retailing. While specific techniques and approaches to inventory management and control are discussed in Chapter 4, a few observations are made below about problems faced by wholesalers in managing their inventories.

Problems in Inventory Management

A former executive director of the National Association of Wholesaler-Distributors has observed that wholesalers have been prone to think too much in terms of return on sales, gross margins, and net margins instead of return on investment, which is a more enlightened measure of business operating efficiency.[56] In wholesaling as well as in retailing, achieving a reasonably high inventory turnover rate is one of the prime prerequisites to obtaining an adequate rate of return on invested capital. Higher profits on investment are gained both through the effect that a high turnover rate has on operating expenses (as turnover increases, the costs of possession—interest on capital invested in inventory, insurance, property taxes, and warehousing space—decline) *and* on the amount of capital invested in inventory. However, various surveys and trade conferences suggest that the merchant wholesaler's major problem is inventory control and management.[57] One might expect this, since inventory comprises a major portion of a wholesaler's assets, as indicated in Tables 3-9 and 3-10. The latter table portrays the percentage distribution of balance sheet data for ten large, successful wholesaling firms, while the former presents a composite picture of assets for a broad sample of wholesaling corporations.[58] Such a heavy investment in inventory is made

---

[56]Courtney, *op. cit.*, pp. 180-181.

[57]Lopata, *op. cit.*, p. 138.

[58]It should be noted that the management of accounts receivable is also a major problem area for wholesalers. In fact, as McCammon points out, "improved asset management is virtually synonymous

TABLE 3–9 Composition of Assets for Wholesaling Corporations, 1970

Assets	Percent
Current assets	
Cash or its equivalent	7.0%
Accounts receivable	33.0
Inventory	29.5
All other	3.2
Total	72.7%
Fixed assets	
Plant equipment	14.6%
Investments	9.9
All other	2.8
Total	27.3%
Total assets	100.0%

SOURCE: Bert C. McCammon, Jr., "The Changing Economics of Wholesaling: A Strategic Analysis," in *Proceedings of the 1974 Annual Conference of the Southern Marketing Association*, ed. Barnett A. Greenberg (Atlanta: Georgia State University, 1975), p. 92.

necessary by the large number of items that wholesalers must carry in order to serve the needs of their trade. Compounding the problem is the fact that suppliers are generating enormous quantities of new products. For example, in 1974, the automotive distributor carried about 70,000 identifiable items, as compared with 40,000 ten years previously. Furthermore, many of the items that wholesalers must carry are slow-moving articles that are required infrequently but, when needed, are vital to the operations of the wholesaler's customer.

Some of the wholesaler's reactions to his inventory problems have been (1) to demand that suppliers reduce the size and variety of the lines they offer; (2) to select only popular items from among a supplier's line (called, by the trade, "cherry picking"); or (3) to select items and set stock levels according to item demand and item movement.[59] In the last case, wholesalers are dropping many slow-moving and/or low-revenue-producing supply items from their assortments while placing stronger sales efforts behind higher-priced product lines with larger dollar volumes. Concomitantly, these wholesalers are retraining salesmen as equipment demonstrators and discouraging them from merely taking small orders.

(in wholesaling) with improved accounts receivable *and* inventory management." See Bert C. McCammon, Jr., "The Changing Economics of Wholesaling: A Strategic Analysis," a paper presented at the 1974 Annual Conference of the Southern Marketing Association, p. 5. (Parentheses and emphasis supplied.)

[59] Lopata, *op. cit.*, p. 138.

TABLE 3-10 Sales, Profits, and Percentage Distribution of Balance Sheet Data for Ten Large, Successful Wholesaling Companies

Financial Data	Fleming Companies, Inc. (1973)	Malone & Hyde, Inc. (1974)	Super Valu Stores, Inc. (1974)	Genuine Parts Co. (1974)	Pickwick International Inc. (1974)	Lawson Products, Inc. (1974)	Sysco Corp. (1974)	Golden State Foods Corp. (1974)	W. W. Grainer, Inc. (1973)	Taylor Rental Corp. (1973)
Net sales (millions of dollars)	$971.5	$718.6	$1447.7	$501.2	$193.3	$23.1	$457.0	$103.7	$255.9	$19.9
Net profits (millions of dollars)	$ 7.6	$ 9.1	$ 9.1	$ 20.3	$ 9.0	$ 2.3	$ 6.4	$ 1.1	$ 17.7	$ 1.0
Net profits/net worth	15.0%	16.2%	16.0%	16.7%	16.6%	25.0%	15.2%	18.8%	20.4%	18.1%
Net profits/total assets	7.5%	8.2%	5.2%	11.5%	7.5%	18.9%	6.8%	6.6%	13.5%	6.1%
Current assets										
Cash	5.7%	8.0%	2.9%	6.3%	7.1%	15.0%	4.3%	6.3%	2.1%	4.9%
Accounts receivable	22.3	21.4	18.6	24.5	28.0	33.1	30.9	23.6	19.3	44.5
Inventory	52.6	47.2	55.3	49.9	50.7	35.6	44.5	19.1	50.2	24.2
All other	1.7	1.2	2.7	1.0	.7	2.6	.5	2.4	.2	1.5
Total	82.3%	77.8%	79.5%	81.7%	86.5%	86.3%	80.2%	51.4%	71.8%	75.1%
Fixed assets	17.7	22.2	20.5	18.3	13.5	13.7	19.8	48.6	28.2	24.9
Total current and fixed assets	100.0%	100.0%	100.0%	100.0%	100.0%	100.0%	100.0%	100.0%	100.0%	100.0%
Current liabilities										
Accounts payable	37.3%	34.5%	34.6%	24.8%	28.3%	7.1%	23.9%	29.6%	16.9%	11.1%
Notes payable	1.5	.5	—	1.1	3.8	—	16.7	12.2	.4	1.1
All other	2.4	2.5	8.0	3.3	7.8	17.0	6.5	7.4	4.0	3.1
Total	41.2%	37.5%	42.6%	29.2%	39.9%	24.1%	47.1%	49.2%	21.3%	15.3%
Long-term liabilities	8.9	11.9	25.2	2.1	15.1	—	8.1	15.8	12.7	51.0
Net worth	49.9	50.6	32.2	68.7	45.0	75.9	44.8	35.0	66.0	38.7
Total liabilities and net worth	100.0%	100.0%	100.0%	100.0%	100.0%	100.0%	100.0%	100.0%	100.0%	100.0%

SOURCE: Bert C. McCammon, Jr. and James W. Kenderine, "Mainstream Developments in Wholesaling," a paper presented at the 1975 Conference of the Southwestern Marketing Association, pp. 8–17.

SUMMARY

The significance of the wholesaler's role in a channel of distribution is defined by the efficiency of his sorting function whereby he helps match the heterogeneous output of suppliers on the one hand with the diverse needs of retailers, industrial, and business users on the other. There have been increased pressures on wholesalers to prove their economic viability in this respect. Evidence of their ability to maintain such viability through adaptation to changing conditions is seen in the structural variety of wholesaling and the fact that there has been considerable growth in the volume of trade produced by wholesale establishments.

While the size of wholesale establishments is not growing as rapidly as the size of those in retailing, both wholesaling and retailing are still industries of small businesses. Although the overall growth rate has remained relatively high among merchant wholesalers, it has not kept pace with that for manufacturers' sales branches and sales offices, which now account for slightly over 35 percent of wholesale trade. In fact, sales branches have a slightly larger market share of wholesale trade in industrial goods than do merchant wholesalers.

Wholesaling can be classified as an industry having very low economic concentration when viewed on a national basis. However, limited data indicate relatively high concentration in local market areas and on a product-line basis. To some degree, the extent of concentration is due to the existence of multiunit or chain operations. Despite relatively heavy market concentration, price, competition is intense. This is so because price leadership is difficult to institute due to the large number of items carried by wholesalers and because large buying organizations can play off one wholesaler against another. Furthermore, intermarket penetration is possible due to large lot purchasing, entry is relatively easy, and new distributive patterns have emerged and generated a high degree of intertype competition for wholesalers.

Many suppliers use wholesalers to reach their customers because they prefer to turn troublesome, supposedly lower-return distribution activities over to specialists. The benefits available to suppliers (manufacturers, growers, etc.) from wholesalers are continuity in and intimacy with local markets, local availability of stocks, coverage of small-order business, lower costs because wholesalers can spread overhead over many suppliers' products, and relief from the burden of holding inventory.

Often wholesalers' perceived self-interests are more directly involved with the well-being of retailers than those of manufacturers; therefore, it is logical to assume that wholesalers would develop approaches to assure the survival of retailers. Many wholesalers do, in fact, offer retailers direct selling aid, expert assistance in all aspects of retail operations, local and speedy delivery, relief from inventory burdens, quick adjustments, credit extension, and, in some cases, guaranteed sales. Business users can receive many of the same benefits, which may be especially important when it comes to production scheduling and technical assistance.

There is a wide overlap between the fundamentals of retailing and wholesaling merchandise and marketing management. Differences do exist, however. Wholesalers place heavy stress on the use of catalogs, "outside" salesmen, showrooms, and delivery services as well as the abovementioned technical assistance programs. There is, however, a strong similarity in the emphasis placed on merchandise management and inventory control. In both sectors, the management of assortments is crucial to success. Adequate and reasonable inventory turnover rates lead to appropriate returns on investment. Therefore, effective inventory management is essential.

It is important to reemphasize, in any discussion of wholesaling, that a wholesaling agency can be eliminated from a channel of distribution as an entity, but some other institution must be willing to perform the tasks formerly done by the agency. Elimination of a wholesaler is valid from a societal point of view only if the tasks performed by the wholesaling agency can be either partially eliminated or performed more efficiently by some other institution. In fact, elimination of the agency often means only that some other institution takes over the same tasks.

Changes are, however, continuously taking place within wholesale trade, many of which have a strong interorganizational overtone and are addressed in succeeding chapters. For example, Lopata has observed that:

> It is possible to identify some commodity wholesalers who will pass from the scene. Others will swiftly shift to new commodities. Some will build regional or national networks of warehouses along single commodity lines, as have the paper merchants, electrical supply companies, and automotive parts distributors. Others will form tighter wholesale-retail franchised groups, such as Super Valu, Ace Hardware, Butler Brothers, and Western Auto. Still others will become multicommodity super-marketing systems, with all the accoutrements of sophisticated marketing technology. As a matter of fact, such wholesalers as these already exist; a prime example is Foremost-McKesson, whose sales of over $1 billion in 1967 included the wholesaling of drugs, grocery products, liquor, and health and beauty aids.[60]

[60] *Ibid.*, pp. 134-135.

DISCUSSION QUESTIONS

1. Distinguish between a "wholesale sale" and a "retail sale" (e.g., sales at wholesale versus sales at retail).

2. Consider the following statement:
> "A wholesaling operation can be eliminated as an entity, but someone must perform the wholesaling tasks and absorb the costs formerly done by the agency, if it is assumed that the wholesaling tasks are necessary."

Take a position on this statement, pro or con, and offer support for your reasoning.

3. Why do manufacturers appear to have a "keener desire to participate more actively in the wholesaling process" as evidenced by the rapid growth of manufacturer sales branches and sales offices?

4. Debate the pros and cons of forward vertical integration, particularly of wholesaling functions.

5. Prescribe what a wholesaler needs to do over the next ten years in order to remain a viable entity. Should he stand pat or make changes? What changes? (Pick specific industries, such as steel, groceries, hardware, drugs, electronics.)

6. Discuss why the predictions of the classical economist's model fail to adequately describe the nature of competition in the wholesale trade.

7. Would you say that inventory control is a more *or* less important policy decision for wholesalers than it is for retailers? How might inventory management and control problems and approaches differ between wholesalers and retailers?

8. Wholesaling is often thought of as being a less than glamorous intermediary venture when compared to other channel intermediary operations, such as retailing. In your opinion, which of these two would be the most difficult to manage—a wholesaling or a retailing operation? Which would seem to have the best chance, on the average, of achieving a high ROI (return on investment) today?

Which line of trade would you say has had to face more challenges to its survival in the last 50 years?

Appendix
Agency Structures in Wholesaling

Wholesaling agencies, their functions, and the marketing flows. *Note:* All of the agencies described below are "pure" types; in real life we often find agencies which are composites of several of these types.

A. *Merchant wholesalers.* Merchants whose principal business is buying goods in "job lots" and reselling them for a profit to customers who (1) resell the goods again to someone else, or (2) consume the goods in the course of operating a profit-making enterprise. The compensation of a merchant wholesaler is a *profit* that is made *on the sale of the goods.*

1. *Full-function or service wholesalers.* The "traditional" wholesalers who perform all or most of the marketing functions normally associated with wholesaling. Participate directly in all or most of the flows of marketing. Particularly useful in broad retail lines such as groceries and drugs.

   a. *Physical possession flow.*
      (1) Take possession of the goods.
      (2) Maintain storage facilities.
      (3) Maintain stocks of goods sufficient in both variety and quantity to supply customers on regular basis.
      (4) Deliver goods to customer.

   b. *Ownership flow.* Take legal title (ownership) from supplier, pass it on to customer when sale is made.

   c. *Promotion.* May participate in manufacturer's advertising allowances; may print catalogs for trade; may advertise to trade; maintain sales force.

   d. *Negotiation.* Make contact and negotiate over prices, quality, quantity, terms of sale, etc., with *both* supplier and customer.

   e. *Financing.* Extend credit to customers (thereby financing the customer's inventory.) Help to finance manufacturer to extent that wholesaler relieves manufacturer of burden of carrying large stocks of finished goods.

   f. *Risking.* By taking ownership assume all risks of failure to sell goods and of

Source: Department of Marketing, University of Pennsylvania, Wharton School of Finance and Commerce.

changes in the prices of the goods. Risk assumption may be offset by manufacturer's willingness to accept returns and/or guarantee price.

g. *Ordering.* In effect, flow of ordering moves from retailer to manufacturer. In
reality, anticipate needs of retailers and order from manufacturer in advance of
actual sale to retailer (see "risking").

h. *Payment.* Accept payment for goods from customers; pass payment minus
expenses and profit to supplier. May pay supplier *before* making collection
from customer (another form of risk).

2. *Limited-function wholesalers.* Wholesalers who do not perform all of the marketing functions, either by eliminating them entirely or passing them on to someone
else. Some limited-function wholesalers *participate* in all of the marketing flows,
but their *degree* of participation in any one flow may be considerably less than that
of the service wholesaler.

a. *Drop-shipper (desk jobber).* A wholesale merchant who passes on the order of
his customer with instructions to the manufacturer to ship directly to a location
specified by the customer. Maintains no warehouse or inventory, *does not come
in physical possession* of the goods. Much contact with his customers by telephone, hence may have no sales force and may be much less active in promotional flow. Particularly useful in bulky goods and where merchandise typically
moves in carlot quantities. (Sometimes called a "carlot wholesaler.")

b. *Cash-carry wholesalers.*
   (1) *Financing.* Do not finance customers because of no-credit policy.
   (2) *Physical possession flow.* Same position in this flow as the service whole-
       saler with exception that customer assumes burden of delivery.
   (3) *Promotion.* Operation, by its nature, is a cost-cutting one. Dealing often in
       small orders with small retailers, therefore less likely to have an outside sales
       force.

c. *Wagon jobbing (truck jobbing).*
   (1) *Wagon jobbers (self-employed merchants).*
       (a) Little capital, often extend no credit to customers.
       (b) May own goods, but often gets them on consignment from supplier.
       (c) Often maintain no warehouse, buy on hand-to-mouth basis.
   (2) *Driver-salesmen (not really wholesalers).* Takes goods on consignment or
       salary rather than profit.
   (3) Used with perishables and semi-perishables; sometimes with auto parts,
       cigars and cigarettes, candy, sundries.

d. *Rack jobbers.* Important in variety and specialty lines, especially in supermarkets. Maintain racks stocked with merchandise at the retailer's location.
   (1) *Ownership and risk.* Heavy assumption of risk, since the *jobber keeps* title
       and the *retailer is billed only for goods sold from the rack.*
   (2) *Finance.* Rack jobbers assume the sole financial burden for the goods, fi-
       nance customer's inventory by maintaining ownership. Retailer's only invest-
       ment is in the space allotted to the rack.
   (3) *Promotion.* Deal widely in highly advertised, branded, well-known, often-

fair-traded goods. Have to do little promotion on the goods, which are "self-selling" through display. (*Note:* Use of the well-known brands partially offsets the risks of ownership).

3. *Other types of wholesale operations, often of a special-purpose nature.*

  a. *Converters.*

    (1) *Ownership.* Purchase cloth from textile mills; process, dye, or print it on contract basis for garment manufacturers.

    (2) *Physical possession.* Cloth frequently finished in outside plants; converter may never touch it.

    (3) *Finance.* Converter may take entire output of textile mill; may extend heavy credit to garment manufacturers.

    (4) *Risking.* Ownership risk assumed by converter heavy because of fluid changes in popularity of patterns and colors; risk also strong when financing small garment manufacturers (high bankruptcy rate).

    (5) *Ordering.* Highly anticipatory of needs of garment makers.

  b. *Franchise wholesalers.* Retailers affiliate with existing wholesaler, who gives them right (franchise) to use certain name or store-front design. Most *voluntary chains* operate under franchises from wholesalers.

    (1) *Promotion.* Wholesaler may furnish advertising material for affiliates, may aid retailers in display and point-of-sale promotion.

    (2) Often operate on a *cost-plus* basis.

    (3) Often use *preprinted order forms*; outside sales force may give service more of an advisory nature to retailers.

    (4) May furnish accounting service for retailers.

    (5) Participation in marketing flows very similar to service wholesaler, except that *more services* are often provided to affiliates.

B. *Retailer-owner cooperative wholesalers. (DO NOT CONFUSE WITH THE CONSUMER'S COOPERATIVE)*

1. Independent *retailers* form an association, which buys or builds wholesale warehouse facilities which they own cooperatively. The *wholesale* operation is thus not a profit-making institution, but exists only as an arm of the associated retailers. *As a unit*, however, it participates in many of the marketing flows.

  a. *Ownership.* As a legal entity, the cooperative takes title to the merchandise. Legal responsibilities will depend on the form of organization.

  b. *Physical possession.* Cooperative performs all acts of possession, and physical handling of goods.

  c. *Promotion.* Cooperative advertising is executed by the staff of the organization for the membership. Sales force for *selling* purposes often eliminated; outside staff members may render aid to member stores in display, point-of-sale promotion, etc.

  d. *Negotiation.* The cooperative negotiates (on behalf of its membership) with suppliers. Cooperative organization usually set up so that members are supplied on *cost-plus* basis. (Landed or invoice cost plus estimated allowable expenses).

    e. *Financing.* May carry members' accounts on credit basis, but does not really finance members, since it is the *member's* capital which finances the cooperative.

    f. *Risking.* The cooperative, as a unit, may lose money on inventories, but the risk (and profits or losses) are shared by the membership.

    g. *Ordering.* The cooperative is, in effect, passing on the orders of the membership to suppliers. Often use *preprinted order forms.*

    h. *Flow of payment.* Normal-membership, through organization to suppliers.

C. Other agencies involved in wholesaling. *Functional middlemen*, specializing in performance of one or more specific marketing tasks, especially those concerned with *negotiation.* As a rule, participate in only a *few* of the flows. *Not merchants*: their compensation is in the form of a commission or fee for a service rendered, NOT a profit on the sale of goods.

    1. *Brokers.* Agents who specialize in buying or selling goods for a principal. Usually have neither title to, nor possession of, the merchandise.

        a. *Ownership and physical possession.* Through making a sale, they *facilitate* changes in ownership and possession. They do not participate directly in these flows.

        b. *Promotion.* May advertise in trade journals, have salesmen to call on trade. Broker, himself, may be a salesman.

        c. *Negotiation.* Negotiate with customers on price, quantity, quality, terms of sale, etc., within limitations of authority granted by principal. Results of negotiation *binding* on principal so long as broker does not exceed authority given him.

        d. *Financing.* Brokers seldom give or receive credit. Financial arrangements between principal and customer.

        e. *Risking.* Brokers never own goods, take no risk on them, do not figure in the flow of risk *on the goods.* (Naturally, they take their own risks in choosing whom to represent, etc.)

        f. *Ordering.* Customer orders from principal, through broker.

        g. *Payment.* Payment for goods usually goes from their customers to the suppliers. They *may* (but not always) collect from customer and deduct their commission.

        h. With free-lance brokers, each sale is a separate and distinct transaction; may frequently change principals whom they represent.

    2. *Manufacturers' agents.* Functional middlemen who sell part of the output of manufacturers on an extended contract basis.

        a. Difference from brokers.

            (1) Represent limited number of principals, whom they represent regularly.

            (2) Usually represent several, noncompeting lines from different manufacturers.

            (3) Territory definite and limited.

            (4) Prices, terms of sale, etc., set by principal.

b. Involvement in marketing flows similar to broker, except:
(1) May be more active in promotional aspects of selling (e.g., having outside salesmen) than broker.
(2) Will often sell in smaller lots than broker.
3. *Selling (or sales) agents.*
a. Difference from brokers and manufacturers' agents.
(1) Normally handle entire output of the principal (thus, in effect, becomes sales force of manufacturer).
(2) Usually given more complete authority over prices, terms of sale, territory, etc.
(3) May use manufacturers' agents or brokers in places where they maintain no office.
(4) May have quite an extensive sales force and promotional program.
4. *Commission merchants.* (Sometimes called "factors.") Agents who receive goods on consignment for sale on a commission basis.
a. Maintain a warehouse, involved in physical handling of goods, thus participate in the flow of *physical possession.*
b. *Ownership.* Receive goods on consignment basis, have no title.
c. *Promotion.* May maintain full sales force, print catalogs, have sales offices in various cities, advertise in trade magazines.
d. *Negotiation.* Have full power to negotiate price, terms of sale, etc., with customer.
e. *Financing.* May extend credit to customers, often assuming the risk of making collections as *del credere* agent.
(1) *Factoring.* Commission merchants finance their principals. often by *discounting accounts receivable* from buyers.
f. *Risking.* May assume risk of collecting accounts in factoring; may be responsible for payment to principal prior to collection of discounted account receivable.
g. *Ordering.* May order entire output of manufacturer on consignment in anticipation of orders from customers.
h. *Payment.* May collect from customers, forward payment to principal after deduction of expenses and commission.

D. Classification of wholesaling by breadth of line.
1. *General- or full-line wholesalers.*
a. Carry a general or full line of *nearly all* the items of merchandise needed by the type of retailing establishment to which they cater; (e.g., a full-line grocery wholesaler will stock practically everything, with certain exceptions such as meats) that a grocery retailer stocks.
b. Lines, typically, will be numerous. May not always have too much depth or specialized selection within all lines, however.
2. *Limited-line wholesalers.*
a. Stocks are limited to one or a few (usually fairly broad) lines. For example, a

canned goods wholesaler limits his line to canned goods only (in contrast to a general grocery wholesaler).

b. Usually has a more complete assortment within any one line than does the general-line wholesaler.

3. *Specialty-line wholesalers.*

a. Limits stocks to a narrowly defined, specialized line of goods. For example, a jobber who carries only such food delicacies as anchovy paste, pâté-de-foie gras, caviar, etc., is a specialty wholesaler.

b. Generally, specialty wholesalers carry a very wide assortment of a line designed to meet some specialized requirements on the part of their customers.

FOUR

PHYSICAL DISTRIBUTION BY CHANNEL MEMBERS

The efficient and effective management of the physical possession flow by key distributive institutions is critical to the profitability of each and, as later chapters show, is a primary determinant in the success or failure of individual marketing channels. The term "physical distribution" is the one most commonly applied to describe, generically, the task of sustaining a physical flow of materials and products from their points of extraction or production to their points of final consumption.[1] The importance of this area of marketing is highlighted by the fact that the average manufacturer spends approximately 13 percent of each sales dollar on activities associated with physical distribution.[2] In specific industries, the figure is even higher. For example, among primary metals, chemical, and petroleum companies, physical distribution (PD) costs amount to 25 percent of sales while in food manufacturing and in mining, the figure ranges from 30 to over 60 percent.[3]

[1] While various authors make distinctions between the terms "physical distribution," "physical supply," and "business logistics," such distinctions will not be discussed here. For alternative definitions, see John F. Magee, *Industrial Logistics* (New York: McGraw-Hill Book Co., 1968), p. 2; Ronald H. Ballou, *Business Logistics Management* (Englewood Cliffs, N.J.: Prentice-Hall, Inc., 1973), pp. 7–8; James L. Heskett, Nicholas A. Glaskowsky, Jr., and Robert M. Ivie, *Business Logistics*, 2nd ed. (New York: The Ronald Press Co., 1973), pp. 8–10; Donald J. Bowersox, *Logistical Management* (New York: MacMillan Publishing Co., Inc., 1974), pp. 1–2.

[2] Stephen B. Oresman and Charles D. Scudder, "A Remedy for Maldistribution," *Business Horizons*, Vol. 19 (June 1974), p. 61.

[3] Charles A. Taff, *Management of Traffic and Physical Distribution*, 4th ed. (Homewood, Ill.: Richard D. Irwin, Inc., 1967), p. 7.

Although comparable figures are unavailable, the costs associated with the flow of physical possession incurred by merchant wholesalers and retailers are undoubtedly higher than those incurred by most manufacturers, because such a vast proportion of the assets of these middlemen are, as we indicated in the previous chapters, devoted to maintaining sizable inventories. Any improvements that can be made in PD activities can mean greater economic efficiency, better customer service, lower-priced goods and services, and enhanced profitability for the various institutions and agencies comprising marketing channels.

This chapter provides an overview of the management of physical distribution systems from the perspective of channel members. Concern here is on how commercial channel members should view the opportunities made available to them by the various institutions responsible for movement (i.e., transportation modes) and storage (i.e., warehousing facilities). Emphasis is also placed on understanding how inventories can be effectively and efficiently managed by channel members. Attention is first focused on the underlying rationale that should guide the management of any PD system—the so-called *physical distribution concept*. Next, examination is made of four critical decision areas that are important in implementing the PD concept: (1) the determination of *customer service standards*, (2) the establishment of appropriate *warehousing* facilities, (3) the setting of *inventory* management and control procedures, and (4) the selection of *transportation* modes. Finally, attention is turned to overall PD system management, or the effective melding of the various decision areas into a meaningful whole.

THE PHYSICAL DISTRIBUTION CONCEPT

In a renowned study completed over twenty years ago, it was found that, for a number of companies, 10 to 20 percent of the products carried in inventory accounted for nearly 80 percent of the companies' sales and that half of the products accounted for less than 4 percent of sales.[4] In fact, the bottom half of the product lines were found to impose a vastly disproportionate amount of expense and investment on the various companies' distribution systems because of the costs associated with carrying these more slowly selling items in inventory. Such costs can be highly significant,

[4]Howard T. Lewis, James W. Culliton, and Jack D. Steele, *The Role of Air Freight in Physical Distribution* (Boston: Division of Research, Harvard University Graduate School of Business Administration, 1956). See also John F. Magee, "The Logistics of Distribution," *Harvard Business Review,* Vol. 38 (July–August 1960), pp. 89-101.

TABLE 4-1   Breakdown of Inventory Carrying Costs as a Percentage
of the Annual Average Value of Inventory on Hand

Storage facilities	0.25%
Insurance	0.25
Taxes	0.50
Transportation	0.50
Handling and distribution	2.50
	4.0%
Depreciation	5.0
Interest	6.0
Obsolescence	10.0
Total	25.0%

SOURCE: Adapted from L. P. Alford and John R. Bangs (eds.), *Production Handbook* (New York: The Ronald Press Co., 1955), pp. 396–397.

amounting to 25 percent of the average value of inventory on hand, as shown in Table 4-1. The researchers argued, based on their findings, that the firms would be better off if they were to *reduce* the amount of inventory of these products being held in *each* of their *regional* warehouses and consolidate much of the remaining inventory in central warehouses. The companies' salesmen protested, saying that *customer service* would decline because of the longer rail or truck transit times associated with the more distant warehouses. To meet this objection, a system was established whereby salesmen could, upon receiving an order for one of the more slowly selling products, telephone the central warehouse, which would then use air freight services to provide overnight delivery to their customers. Thus, by consolidation of products and increased use of air freight, customer service was maintained while total distribution costs (especially inventory holding costs) were drastically reduced.[5]

Emerging from this study was the basic rationale behind the PD concept, which can be described as a *cost-service* orientation, backed by an integrated physical distribution network, that is aimed at *minimizing* the costs of distribution at a *given level* of *customer service*. Three main components of the PD concept are (1) a total cost perspective, (2) the understanding of relevant trade-offs among costs, and (3) the notion of zero suboptimization, each of which is outlined briefly below.

Total cost perspective. PD management must examine the *total* costs of distribution, including both "visible" and "hidden" costs.[6] *Visible* costs include those

[5]Lewis, et al., *op. cit.*, p. 155.

[6]*Ibid.*, pp. 64–65. See also Oresman and Scudder, *op. cit.*, p. 63.

operating costs associated with warehousing, transportation, and handling, all of which are relatively easy to identify and measure. Visible costs also include other indirect costs associated with inventory investment, property taxes, and inventory obsolescence and storage, all of which are *not* easily measured and are rarely identified as distribution-related expenses. *Hidden* costs consist of lost profit opportunities due to failure to ship the product on time, cancelled orders, and customer dissatisfaction. While never appearing on a profit and loss statement, these costs also have a significant impact on corporate profit performance.

Costs tradeoffs. Even though certain costs may increase while others are purposively reduced, the end result, under the PD concept, is that total distribution cost will, it is to be hoped, decline. For example, in the previous example, increases in transportation costs via the use of air freight were more than offset by decreases in inventory carrying costs.

Zero suboptimization. When one distribution function is optimized, the result will likely be an impairment of the performance of other distribution functions. For example, if a traffic manager attempts to optimize the performance of his own department by accumulating merchandise in order to use high-bulk/low-cost modes of transport, he will adversely affect the ability of the inventory manager to keep inventory carrying costs down to a reasonable level.

In order to implement the PD concept, management must coordinate and integrate the different and typically disparate activity areas shown in Fig. 4-1.[7] As mentioned above, concentration in this chapter is on decision areas dealing with customer service standards, warehousing, inventory, and transportation. This is because a discussion of these areas is more generalizable to various types of channel members than, say, is a discussion of material handling or industrial packaging techniques. More important, however, the four areas selected for emphasis represent the most strategic, as well as the most cost-significant, elements in physical distribution for most channel members.

CUSTOMER SERVICE STANDARDS

Although it is repeated throughout this text, it must be continually emphasized that the process of policy and strategy formulation in marketing starts with a determination of customer needs and desires. This

---

[7]Discussions of integration and coordination problems and approaches are found in Raymond LeKashman and John F. Stolle, "The Total Cost Approach to Distribution," *Business Horizons*, Vol. 8 (Winter 1965), pp. 34–46; George G. Smith, "Knowing Your P.D. Costs," *Distribution Age*, January, 1966, pp. 21–27; John F. Stolle, "How to Manage Physical Distribution," *Harvard Business Review*, Vol. 45 (July–August 1967), pp. 93–100; Charles A. Taff, *op. cit.*, pp. 6 and 14; and Grant Davis and Stephen W. Brown, *Logistics Management* (Lexington, Mass.: D. C. Heath and Co., 1974), pp. 25–44.

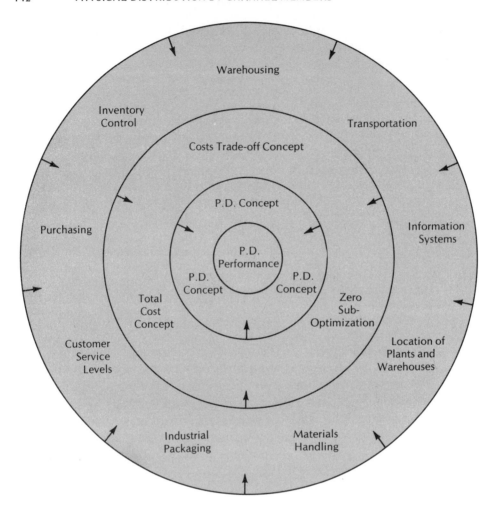

FIGURE 4-1   The Dynamics of the Physical Distribution System

"adage" applies with equal force to the setting of physical distribution policies. In fact, certain studies indicate that a number of purchasing managers consider physical distribution service and performance second only to product quality as a factor in their selection decisions.[8]

The key PD service factors that industrial buyers (e.g., manufacturers, middlemen, and industrial consumers) consider as important are, roughly in order of their popularity, as follows:

[8]See Bernard Klass, "What Factors Affect Industrial Buying Decisions," *Industrial Marketing*, May, 1961, pp. 33-35 and Harvey H. Shycon and Christopher R. Sprague, "Put a Price Tag on Your Customer Servicing Levels," *Harvard Business Review*, Vol. 53 (July–August, 1975), pp. 71-78.

1. Time from order receipt to order shipment.

2. Order size and assortment constraints.

3. Percentage of items out-of-stock.

4. Percentage of customer orders filled accurately.

5. Percentage of customer orders filled within x days from receipt of order.

6. Percentage of customer orders filled.

7. Percentage of customer orders that arrive in good condition.

8. Time from order placement to order delivery (*order cycle time*).

9. Ease and flexibility of order placement.[9]

The critical question confronting the distribution manager is which of these customer service elements are of major importance to his clientele. Answering this question is not an easy task, for empirical evidence suggests that the importance given to each of these various elements varies according to different product/market and purchasing contexts.[10] For example, for some retail buyers, faster average order cycle time (i.e., shorter elapsed time from order placement to order delivery) is not as important as a less variable order cycle. These buyers would accept longer delivery times if the variability of order cycle times were reduced or if price concessions were offered. This situation does not hold, however, for retailers of drug sundries; the latter place a greater emphasis on actual delivery speed.

In order to arrive at an appropriate customer service standard, it is useful to approach the problem systematically. A schematic overview for analyzing this type of problem is shown in Fig. 4–2. It summarizes a physical distribution service (PDS) decision model which involves six steps:

1. Define important PDS elements.

2. Determine customers' viewpoints.

3. Design a competitive PDS package.

4. Develop a promotional program to "sell" PDS.

[9]Heskett, et al., *op. cit.*, pp. 250–251. For additional lists, see P. Ronald Stephenson and Ronald P. Willett, "Selling with Physical Distribution Service," *Business Horizons*, Vol. 11 (December, 1968), pp. 75–85 and William M. Hutchinson and John F. Stolle, "How to Manage Customer Service," *Harvard Business Review*, Vol. 46 (November–December, 1968), pp. 85–96.

[10]For examples of such variability, see James L. Heskett, "Predictive Value of Classroom Simulation," in William S. Decker (ed.), *Emerging Concepts in Marketing* (Chicago: American Marketing Association, 1963), pp. 101–115; Ronald P. Willett and P. Ronald Stephenson, "Determinants of Buyer Response to Physical Distribution Services," *Journal of Marketing Research*, Vol. 6 (August, 1969), pp. 279–283; and Hutchinson and Stolle, *op. cit.*, pp. 33–37.

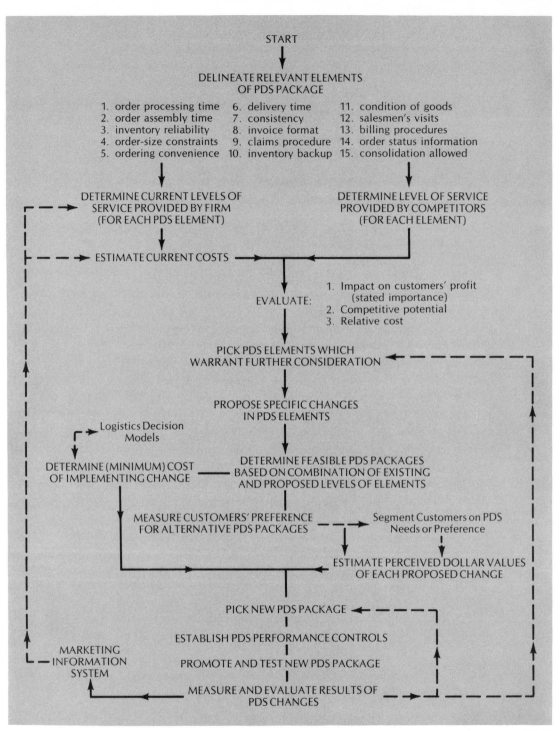

FIGURE 4-2 Schematic Overview of the Management Process for Physical Distribution Service (PDS)

SOURCE: William D. Perreault, Jr. and Frederick A. Russ, "Physical Distribution Service: A Neglected Aspect of Marketing Management," p. 40, *MSU Business Topics,* Summer 1974. Reprinted by permission of the publisher, Division of Research, Graduate School of Business Administration, Michigan State University.

5. Market test the PDS package and promotional program.

6. Establish performance controls.[11]

Of all these tasks, the first three are the most important for the setting of customer service standards.[12] Carrying out this part of the analysis requires the generation of pertinent information through PDS market research. Perreault and Russ suggest a four-phase approach for obtaining the needed information and using it to develop competitive standards.[13]

Phase One: Identify Current PDS Levels and Their Costs. This phase involves an examination of in-house cost data and the informal questioning of salesmen and clients.

Phase Two: Identify PDS Levels for Further Study. According to Perreault and Russ:

> Three criteria are used to identify PDS areas/elements where change has the greatest potential impact for the firm: the *stated importance* of each element to customers (obtained through informal questioning or a formal survey), the *competitive potential* of changes in each element (determined by questioning the firm's distribution specialists about the difficulty that competitors will face in detecting and copying the changes), and the *relative costs* of making changes in the level of service for a particular element of the PDS package.[14]

For example, this part of the analysis might suggest to the manufacturer or middleman that he focus his efforts on changing customer service standards through improvements in order cycle time for rush orders, a reduction in order cycle time variability for regular orders, and a simplification of order placement methods.

Phase Three: Identify Feasible Service Packages. Once the important elements of PDS are established, the next step is to specify possible changes in these elements and identify the costs associated with alternative changes. Certain changes may affect costs that are "visible" in nature; the least cost

---

[11] William D. Perreault, Jr., and Frederick A. Russ, "Physical Distribution Service: A Neglected Aspect of Marketing Management," *MSU Business Topics*, Vol. 22 (Summer, 1974), pp. 37-45. See also Hutchinson and Stolle, *op. cit.*; John F. Gustafson and Raymond Ricard, "How to Determine Levels of Required Customer Service," *Transportation and Distribution Management*, Vol. 14 (May-June, 1964), pp. 34-37.

[12] The necessary tools and techniques for implementing the last three steps can be found in James L. Heskett, "Controlling Customer Logistics Service," *International Journal of Physical Distribution*, Vol. 1 (June, 1971), pp. 140-145.

[13] Perreault and Russ, *op. cit.*, pp. 42-44.

[14] *Ibid.*, p. 42.

solution associated with such changes can then be estimated by existing logistics decision models.[15] For example, PDS research may suggest that the firm's present in-stock service level of 95 percent (indicating that, when a customer wants a product, it is immediately available 95 percent of the time) should be increased to 96 percent. However, it is a well-known distribution axiom that the inventory required to render varying levels of service will increase (as will its cost) at an accelerating rate as the desired service level is raised. For example, raising the service level to 96 percent from 95 percent requires 6 percent more safety stock, and raising the service level to 99 percent from 98 percent demands 14 percent more safety stock.[16]

In addition, certain changes in the PDS package may also encompass costs of the "hidden" variety referred to earlier, and thus may be more difficult to estimate. For example, even when a service level is raised to 96 percent, the fact still remains that the product or service will be unavailable 4 percent of the time. Whether or not this is significant depends upon such factors as the degree of brand loyalty on the part of the firm's ultimate customers, the degree of purchaser (e.g., middleman) sensitivity to PD service failures, the relative effectiveness of competitors' service levels, and so on. In fact, an examination of such "hidden" factors might suggest that an increase in service level is unwarranted. It may be the case that the firm's *ultimate* consumers would not consider switching brands even when they are confronted by temporary out-of-stock conditions. Indeed, one study showed that as many as 50 percent of U.S. household consumers, depending on the product and market, could not be sold a substitute brand when "their" brand was missing from the shelf and that as many as 25 percent refused even a different size or color of their own brand.[17] However, for certain frequently purchased convenience goods items that command less brand loyalty, as well as for many industrial goods, the stockout factor is likely to be a costly one and therefore must be taken into account when the range of feasible PDS packages is narrowed.

Phase Four: Collect and Analyze PDS Customer Preference Data. The impact that the various changes in the PDS service package can have on profits is a function not only of the costs of the changes to the firm but also of the

---

[15]For excellent reviews of a variety of logistics decision models geared toward analyzing the cost effects of these types of changes in the "PDS package," see Ronald H. Ballou, *op. cit.* and Stanley F. Stasch, *Systems Analysis for Marketing Planning and Control* (Glenview, Ill.: Scott, Foresman and Co., 1972).

[16]Shycon and Sprague, *op. cit.*, p. 75.

[17]"The Out-of-Stock Study," *Progressive Grocer*, November, 1968, pp. 5–17.

perceived dollar value of the changes to potential or actual purchasers. Implicitly, it is a question of trade-offs, in that the firm's customers must evaluate how much a change in PDS is worth in terms of the increased price of increased patronage. Determination of the implicit trade-offs made by the firm's customers requires that they provide a simple preference evaluation of the alternative PDS packages. This can be done by presenting purchasing managers with selected pairs of alternative PDS packages and asking them for an estimate of what proportion of their patronage they would allocate to each member of the pair if they represented the only two alternatives.[18] The preference data obtained in this manner may then be analyzed in such a way as to provide scale estimates of the value of different PDS packages to the firm's customers or estimates of the effect that each particular level of PDS has on the overall preference process.[19] In turn, these estimates may be interpreted as "trade-off" values, as perceived by the firm's customers, for changes in the PDS package. As Perreault and Russ note:

> The dollar trade-off values estimated in this fashion provide the marketing manager with an index of which changes the customer considers to be important, and more specifically whether the additional revenue (due to the possibility of increased prices or increased demand) exceeds the additional costs incurred by the higher service level. The result of this type of analysis is the pinpointing of the' PDS package(s), among all those considered, whose cost increases can best be justified by the potential incremental revenues from its target market.[20]

Once the "best" PDS package is identified, distribution management can plan to reinforce or adjust existing customer service standards so that physical distribution service may become a competitive selling weapon for the company. It may very well be the case that the most competitive PDS package is one which offers a lower level of service accompanied by a lower price. Once this "optimal" package is decided upon, management can then undertake a selection of the appropriate warehousing, inventory, and transportation policies that will assure the proper implementation of the desired customer service standards.

---

[18]It seems that purchasing agents are indeed willing to provide such judgmental data. See Perreault and Russ, *op. cit.*, p. 43.

[19]Two scaling procedures have been applied to this problem area: conjoint scaling and a multifactor variation of Thurstone's model for comparative judgment. See Perreault and Russ, *op. cit.* For a discussion of conjoint measurement in a marketing context, see Paul E. Green and Vithala R. Rao, "Conjoint Measurement for Quantifying Judgmental Data," *Journal of Marketing Research*, Vol. 8 (August, 1971), pp. 355–365. For a discussion of multifactor generalizations of Thurstone's law of comparative judgment, see R. Darrell Bock and Lyle V. Jones, *The Measurement and Prediction of Judgment and Choice* (San Francisco: Holden-Day, 1968), pp. 187–211.

[20]Perreault and Russ, *op. cit.*, pp. 43–44.

WAREHOUSING

Warehousing represents perhaps the first vital link in the logistics system for carrying out the customer service standards established by the firm. Because efficient production requires that manufacturing operations be conducted as continuously as possible at relatively few locations, warehouses maintained by middlemen or by the manufacturers themselves are needed to accommodate finished-goods inventories. In turn, these warehouses can be strategically located in or near centers of demand in order to facilitate customer service. Furthermore, because it is not possible to perfectly synchronize production with market demand, the inventories held at warehouses act as buffers to variations between production and sales.

There are two basic types of warehouse facilities available to channel members. These are *private* facilities, either owned or leased by the firm, and *public* facilities, in which space is rented by the firm. From a managerial perspective, this distinction is significant because the firm has full control over its owned or leased facilities. On the other hand, public and leased warehousing facilities can be distinguished from owned facilities by the substantial amount of capital investment that the latter require. Figure 4–3 shows the major factors to be considered in evaluating warehouse ownership alternatives.

In general, *private* warehousing is desirable when a firm needs flexibility in the design of warehouse facilities, wishes to maintain control over the operation of its warehouses, has special storage and handling requirements, and has a relatively constant, high volume of goods moving through these facilities into large metropolitan areas.[21] In contrast, *public* warehousing is desirable for those firms that wish to free themselves from the problems of private operation and thereby obtain professional warehouse management. Public warehousing also permits great flexibility in the location of a firm's inventory, which is desirable if the firm is selling in areas of uncertain, limited, or seasonal market demand. Flexibility in warehouse location is also preferable in regions where rate relationships between different transport modes are subject to significant change. Finally, public warehouses assist firms in obtaining lower freight rates by consolidating the small shipments of various clients into carload lots as well as by receiving pooled car shipments from companies at car- or truck-load rates and then distributing the

---

[21]Heskett, et al., *op. cit.*, pp. 607-608.

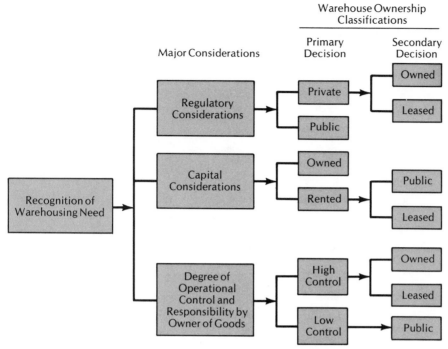

FIGURE 4-3   Major Considerations in Evaluating Warehouse Ownership Alternatives

SOURCE: James L. Heskett, Nicholas A. Glaskowsky, Jr., and Robert M. Ivie, *Business Logistics: Physical Distribution and Materials Management*, 2nd ed. (New York: The Ronald Press, 1973), p. 62.

contents of these shipments to different clients located in its service area.[22] Table 4-2 summarizes and compares many of the basic trade-offs that are involved in choosing between public and private warehousing arrangements.

Several important factors and developments are worthy of note in both public and private warehousing. First, in contrast to private warehouses that are custom designed, *public* warehouses are relatively limited in scope. In fact, they can be classified into six functional categories, following the *Census of Business:*

Household goods warehousing and storage

General warehousing and storage

Refrigerated warehousing

[22]Taff, *op. cit.,* p. 145.

TABLE 4-2   Decision Variables in Choosing among Types of Warehouses

	Types of Warehousing Arrangements		
	Private		
Decision Variables	Owned	Leased	Public
1. Fixed investment	Very high	Moderate, depends on the lease's terms	No fixed investment is involved
2. Unit cost	High, if volume is low	High, if volume is low	Low, since facilities are on "for hire as needed" and fixed costs are widely distributed among users
3. Control	High	High	Low managerial control
4. Adequacy to product line	Highly adequate	Moderately adequate	May not be convenient
5. Flexibility	Low	Low	High; termination of usage can be easily arranged

Food lockers

Farm products warehousing and storage

Other special warehousing and storage

Even with its more narrow scope, the public warehousing industry has been experiencing a steady rate of growth. As of 1975, the industry operated some 15,000 facilities (as compared with approximately 9500 in 1967) and was building new units at the rate of 13 percent annually.[23] Limited data suggest that this trend is especially dominant among household goods and general warehousing operations. One reason for the increased use of public warehousing is the ability of such organizations to provide services to companies with varied distribution needs. For example, Balanced Foods, Inc., a small health food supplier, shifted much of its participation in the physical possession flow to General Warehouse Corporation when it was undertaking a large expansion during the late 1960's. By doing so, it was able to realize multiple benefits, including a greater amount of warehouse space allocated to its products, the use of expensive high-efficiency equipment that the firm itself could not have afforded, a reduction in distribution costs by 15 percent, and a reduction in order cycle time to 24 hours. In turn, these multiple benefits permitted the company to concentrate heavily on its other market-

[23]See Walter F. Friedman, "Physical Distribution: The Concept of Shared Services," *Harvard Business Review*, Vol. 53 (March–April, 1975), p. 26.

ing operations, with the result that its sales volume grew from $3 million to $11 million in five years.[24]

Large companies are also making increased use of public warehouses for a variety of reasons. Mead Johnson & Company has always relied predominantly on public warehousing because of its space flexibility; Tonka Corporation finds public warehousing useful because its space needs fluctuate widely due to the seasonality of the toy business; Alcoa has turned to public warehouses in some areas to speed up its deliveries to customers; Kresge uses public warehouses for a month or two before each of its new store openings to ensure that initial inventories are on hand when needed; Owens-Corning Fiberglas Corporation and Johns-Mansville Corporation have begun to use public warehouses to supplement their own network of private warehouses.[25]

Second, developments in engineering, data processing, and management control, as well as improved interorganizational relations with other warehousemen, have transformed both the image and the task of public warehousing beyond its traditional scope.[26] For example, certain public warehousemen have begun to band together into national associations in an effort to improve and expand the services they offer. One corporate illustration is Distribution America, a network of 12 independent warehouses from coast to coast, which utilizes a computer system to provide an array of shipping and inventory information for its customers.[27] Along similar lines, certain public warehousing operations are beginning to offer a *total* distribution service package on a national scale. One example is USCO Services, the distribution subsidiary of Uniroyal, which developed as a separate entity when Uniroyal reorganized its warehousing operations. Starting as an in-house service with 28 existing warehouses and Uniroyal's sophisticated computer arrangement, USCO entered public warehousing. The company soon began to offer a wide range of services in order to utilize its organization more fully and to bring down distribution costs for Uniroyal as well as for its other clients.[28] Other warehousing operations employing similar strategies include Gulf-Atlantic Warehouse Company, Trammell Crow Distribution Corporation, Consolidated Services, and National Distribution Services (NDS), an independent subsidiary of Eastern Air Lines, Inc. Characteristic to all these large public

[24] *Ibid.*

[25] *Ibid.*

[26] For a discussion of these trends, see "Meeting Those Distribution Needs," *Handling and Shipping*, July, 1975, pp. 37-41.

[27] *Ibid.*, p. 38; Friedman, *op. cit.*, p. 29.

[28] *Ibid.*

warehousing operations is a broad range of services offered, including inventory management; all physical handling and storage of goods; all transportation (including consolidation of shipments and local delivery to client's customers); all paper work such as purchase orders, invoices, and freight bills; and computer and management systems capabilities that can develop efficient distribution programs for clients.[29]

Third, a major development in *private* warehousing is the emergence of *distribution centers*. Distribution centers are distinguished from *conventional* private warehousing operations by the fact that such centers are major centralized warehousing operations that:

Serve regional markets.

Process and regroup products into customized orders.

Maintain a full line of products for customer distribution.

Consolidate large shipments from different production points.

Frequently employ a computer and various materials-handling equipment and may be highly automated rather than labor intensive.

Are large and single-storied, rather than multi-storied.[30]

Clearly, most of these criteria can be met by the more modern public warehousing facilities mentioned above. However, technologically sophisticated public operations are still few in number, and the preponderance of "distribution centers" in operation today are owned or leased for private corporate use.[31] Moreover, there is one other distinguishing characteristic of distribution centers that clearly separates them from the vast majority of public warehousing operations: distribution centers are primarily established for the movement of goods, rather than their storage.[32] As one marketing executive observed regarding his company's distribution center,

Our terminal is in constant motion. At no time is merchandise warehoused here . . . we're strictly a distribution terminal.[33]

[29]Friedman, *op. cit.*, pp. 29 and 36.

[30]See Kenneth Marshall and John Miller, "Where Are the Distribution Centers Going?" *Handling and Shipping*, November 1965, p. 38; and Marjorie Person and Diane Mitchell, "Distribution Centers: The Fort Wayne Experience," *Business Horizons*, Vol. 19 (August, 1975), pp. 89-95.

[31]In fact, one study carried out in Fort Wayne, Indiana, which is one of the U.S. havens for the location of distribution centers, found that 96.2 percent of all distribution centers in the area (26) were owned or leased, with 65.4 percent being company owned and 30.8 percent being leased. See Person and Mitchell, *op. cit.*, p. 92.

[32]Marshall and Miller, *op. cit.*; Person and Mitchell, *op. cit.*

[33]"Meeting Those Distribution Center Needs," *Handling and Shipping*, July, 1975, p. 37.

Thus, the rationale underlying the development of distribution centers is to maintain the company's product in a constant and efficient flow from the moment it leaves production until the day it arrives at its destination.

Many of the world's foremost corporations now operate distribution centers as an integral part of their physical distribution systems. For example, IBM's "World Trade Distribution Center" (WTDC) is one of the largest and most sophisticated of its kind in the world. From its location in New York, the WTDC uses a complex communications network to control the annual movement of more than 23 million pounds of equipment, parts, and supplies.[34] Similarly, Levi Strauss, Inc., operates a huge distribution center in Little Rock, Arkansas, responsible for the rapid movement of its 48,000 product line items from its ten U.S. manufacturing plants to distributors in 70 foreign lands and more than 17,000 stores domestically.[35] Further, from a single distribution center covering 28 acres and more than 1¼ million square feet, the Anchor Hocking Corporation ships 1¼ million pounds of housewares products daily, one of the highest tonnage-shipped-per-day figures in the United States.[36]

Fourth, many other firms employing private warehousing operations have also begun to rethink the economics of storage, and to search for ways to boost productivity and save time and money in their distribution pipelines. Probably the single most important development has been the widespread application of computer technology to private warehousing operations. Linked with equipment and lines for rapid transmission of data, the computer, has, in fact, become the key element in virtually all distribution center operations. Computers are being used to provide extremely rapid service to customers by determining the availability of items required, issuing the proper order-filling, furnishing shipping and billing documentation, maintaining inventory control records, and in some instances providing an automated order-picking function.

Despite the heavy investment often required for a computer and its accompanying support facilities, cost savings have been generated by numerous firms through an updating of their private storage distribution systems and equipment. One example is Marcor (formerly Montgomery Ward), which achieved significant cost savings in its distribution center operations by utilizing computerization and automated handling.[37] Marcor's savings stemmed

[34] Janet Bosworth Dower, "How IBM Distributes—Worldwide," *Distribution Worldwide*, October, 1973, pp. 51–54, 58–60.

[35] Jim Dixon, "Streamlining Storage and Distribution," *Distribution Worldwide*, May, 1975, p. 32.

[36] *Ibid.*, pp. 28–29.

[37] See "Customer Service Sparks Total Distribution Overhaul," *Handling and Shipping*, May, 1968, pp. 55–58.

from a 60 percent reduction in the number of distribution centers operated, reduced labor costs for order processing, reduction in the number of special orders, modern handling equipment, and the central storage of slow-moving items coupled with air freight for rapid delivery.[38] It seems certain that this trend toward reevaluation and redesign of private warehousing facilities will continue, especially in the light of the increase in income-tax depreciation allowances for capital outlays, which should further encourage firms to search for more productive equipment. In turn, the result for private warehousing is a movement toward increasing sophistication and change.

Determining the Number and Location of Warehousing Facilities

Whether a channel member chooses to employ public or private warehousing operations in his physical distribution system, questions still remain as to how many warehouses should be established and where they should be located. The determination of the number of warehouses to be used is directly dependent upon the customer service levels established by the firm. A channel member faced with high customer service requirements will often establish a series of warehouses. Care must be taken, however, that the number of warehouses employed to ensure customer service is not so great as to raise costs inordinately for other PD functions (e.g., inventory management, traffic, etc.). For example, as shown in Fig. 4-4, the number of locations a firm establishes has a cost relationship to several other logistical variables. Thus, the *total costs* associated with the number of warehouses employed must be taken into account. Although the least-cost solution to this problem is unique for each firm because of differences in customer service standards, inventory carrying costs, and so on, the total cost related to the logistical network can be generalized in a manner similar to that shown in Fig. 4-5. The low point on the total *transportation* cost curve in Fig. 4-5 is at a configuration of eight locations. However, total cost related to average *inventory* commitment clearly increases with each additional location. Thus, once the cost trade-offs have been accounted for, the lowest *total* cost for the overall logistical structure is shown in Fig. 4-5 to be a network consisting of six locations.

The location of warehouse facilities will also have a significant impact on the competitive thrust of an organization and, concomitantly, of an entire marketing channel. Just as the number of warehouses established directly affects the ability of the organization and channel to serve its cus-

---

[38]*Ibid.*

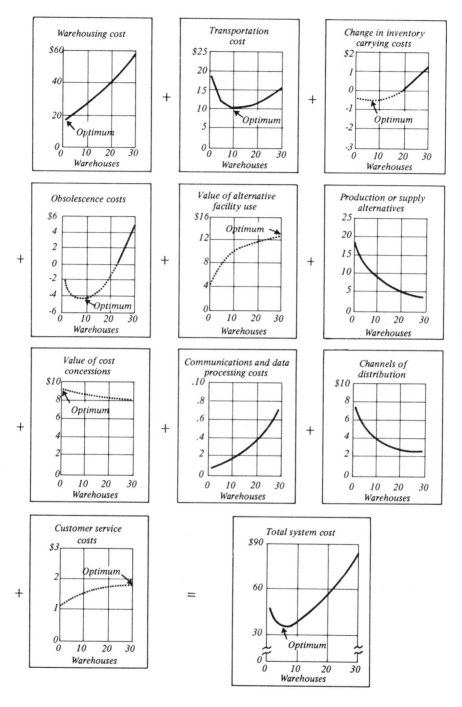

FIGURE 4-4 Ten Cost Categories as a Function of the Number of Warehouse Locations

SOURCE: Raymond LeKashman and John F. Stolle, "The Total Cost Approach to Distribution," *Business Horizons*, Vol. 8 (Winter, 1965), p. 39.

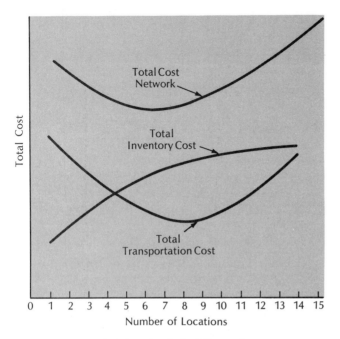

FIGURE 4-5   Total Cost Logistical Network

SOURCE: Reprinted from *Logistical Management* by Donald J.
Bowersox, p. 325. © 1974 by the Macmillan Publishing Co., Inc.

tomers and, at the same time, keep logistical costs in line, so too does the
selection of appropriate warehouse locations. A number of warehousing
facility location models and solution techniques have been developed over
the past two decades which have been important in aiding management to
make better decisions. Brief summaries of some of the more prominent
models and techniques have been included in the appendix to this chapter.
Critical to each are estimates of sales lost because of customer distance from
warehouses, the cost of operating warehouses, and transportation cost (both
inbound and outbound).

INVENTORY MANAGEMENT AND CONTROL

If it were not for the presence of and need for inventories, there would
be no purpose served in discussing warehousing decisions. In fact, although
the decisions involving ownership, type, and location of warehouses are
obviously important, solutions to problems associated with inventory management and control are crucial to the viability of all commercial channel
members, irrespective of the warehousing decisions arrived at. This observa-

tion is particularly salient in periods of slow economic growth. In fact, given the economic conditions of the middle and late 1970's, some top-level executives are beginning to disparage personnel in middle management positions who regularly show large annual sales increases in their divisions but smaller gains in profits, while continually needing more cash from their parent companies. According to these executives, such middle-level managers frequently accept marginally profitable business to build sales volume. To support higher sales volumes and the still larger sales they see ahead, growth-oriented managers often build heavy inventories and plow money freely into plant and equipment. They do not strive for quick payment on receivables, because they do not want to risk irritating customers and losing sales. The problems this behavior creates are evident in the following example.

> A division's sales may rise a healthy 25 percent, say, to $20 million from $16 million the year before. Operating profit may go up 10 percent to $1.1 million from $1 million, which doesn't look too bad. But inventories may rise to $8 million from $6 million, and receivables may rise to $4 million from $2.5 million. A new plant addition to accommodate the added volume may increase facilities investment to $7 million from $5 million. In that instance, operating profit drops to 5.8 percent of total capital employed from 7.4 percent, and it drops at a time when the company is paying 10 percent for money. And the division needs $4.4 million of new cash from headquarters, instead of making a contribution to the corporate treasury.[39]

Thus, the increased emphasis by top corporate executives on achieving adequate returns on investment and on assets as opposed to sales growth during periods of shortages, reduced demand, and high interest rates means that inventory management and control will assume even greater importance in the future than it has in the past.

In general, inventory control theory deals with the determination of optimal procedures for procuring stocks of commodities to meet future demand. The decision concerning when and how much to order is a matter of balancing a number of conflicting cost functions. The objective is to minimize total inventory costs subject to demand and service constraints. The primary cost functions that must be balanced are those associated with holding inventory, ordering inventory, and risking stockouts. Figure 4–6 shows the trade-offs among the relevant cost functions and their respective components. Because the fundamental purpose of any inventory control system is to tell a firm (1) how much to reorder, (2) when to reorder, and (3) how to control stockouts at the lowest cost, the discussion below focuses directly on these three key problem areas.

---

[39]The example and preceding information can be found in Ralph E. Winter, "More Firms Slow Drive for Growth, Bid to Lift Return on Investment," *Wall Street Journal*, December 16, 1975, pp. 1 and 16.

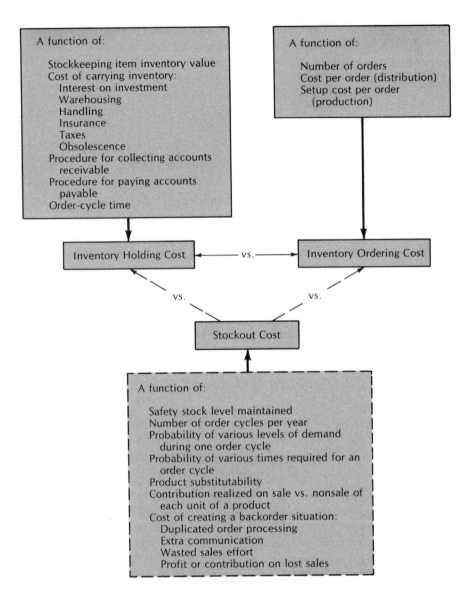

FIGURE 4-6   Trade-offs Typically Found in Managing and Controlling Inventory
Levels

SOURCE: James L. Heskett, Nicholas A. Glaskowsky, Jr., and Robert M. Ivie, *Business Logistics*, 2nd ed. (New York: The Ronald Press, 1973), p. 313.

How Much To Reorder

The quantity to order can be arrived at using an "economic lot size" or "economic order quantity" (EOQ) formula. One of the oldest and most widely accepted economic lot size formulas is stated as follows:

$$Q^* = \sqrt{\frac{2DS}{IC}}$$

where Q^* = the order quantity in units[40]
D = annual demand in units
S = the order processing cost (cost per order in dollars)
I = annual inventory carrying cost as a percentage of C
C = value of a unit held in inventory (unit price in dollars)

As an illustration, consider an inventory control problem having the following specifications for a particular item:[41]

D = 50 units per week, or 50 × 52 = 2600 units per year
I = 10 percent (e.g., this might be derived as shown in footnote 42)
S = \$10
C = \$5

---

[40] The optimum Q is found by the first derivative of $TC(Q)$, i.e., the total cost equation for an annual period, setting the derivative equal to zero, and solving for Q. Thus,

$$TC(Q) = \frac{D}{Q}S + IC\frac{Q}{2}$$

Taking the derivative and setting it equal to zero, we obtain

$$\frac{dTC(Q)}{dQ} = \frac{-DS}{Q^2} + \frac{IC}{2} = 0$$

Solving for Q gives

$$Q^* = \sqrt{\frac{2DS}{IC}}$$

[41] This example is drawn from Ballou, *op. cit.*, p. 292.

[42]

Interest on investment	4.0%
Obsolescence	3.0
Storage, transportation and handling	0.8
Insurance, taxes	0.2
Depreciation	2.0
	10.0%

The optimun order quantity according to the EOQ formula would be

$$Q^* = \sqrt{\frac{2(2600)(10)}{(0.10)(5)}}$$

$$= \quad 322 \text{ units}$$

Although this classical EOQ formula is straightforward and used widely by many manufacturers and merchant wholesalers, it is likely to be of little help to retailers in carrying out their ordering policies. In fact, after devoting a considerable amount of time and resources to studying the possible application of the classical EOQ formula to a variety of inventory problems, IBM Corporation recommended that the formula should not be used by retailers. The reason for this recommendation was that some of the assumptions underlying the formula were not tenable in retailing situations. The questionable assumptions are listed below along with the reasons that they are not applicable to retailing.[43]

1. *Demand is known, constant, and continuous.* Demand in retail is usually not known. It is rarely constant and is seasonal for most types of merchandise. In fact, order quantities are used to build up or reduce inventory in anticipation of varying seasonal demand. Also, demand is not continuous, because of the existence of such merchandise as end-of-season (that is, merchandise carried only during one season, such as winter or summer jackets).

2. *The only costs significant to reordering decisions are inventory carrying and ordering costs.* Frequently, in managing the inventory of a whole department or classification, other factors, not considered by the classical EOQ equation, become very important. The problem of being out of stock is probably the most important single consideration. Furthermore, the costs for individual stockkeeping units (SKU's)[44] are not as significant for the total department as overall inventory and ordering strategies. The EOQ equation certainly does not include all the costs relevant to retail management objectives.

3. *The marginal cost of an additional order or an additional SKU is fixed, and the marginal cost of carrying an additional unit in inventory is fixed.* Marginal costs are synonymous with variable or incremental costs. In other words, marginal costs are the out-of-pocket costs of an additional order or an additional unit in inventory. These costs are different from fixed, indirect, or overhead costs incurred regardless of ordering strategy.

[43] *Retail IMPACT—Inventory Management Program and Control Techniques Application Description*, 6th ed. (White Plains, N.Y.: IBM Technical Publications Department, March 1970), pp. 71–72.

[44] An SKU is a *stockkeeping unit*. It is the lowest level of identification of merchandise. SKU's are usually defined by department, store, vendor, style, color, size, and location.

The most serious problem in applying the classical EOQ equation is the problem of determining costs. In practice the actual ordering costs are not fixed as required by the classical EOQ equation. Inventory carrying cost can vary, for example, with management's changing estimates of the cost of capital. Both inventory carrying cost and ordering cost, when applied to retail situations, include elements of fixed and variable costs that would be very difficult to separate.

The determination of cost elements has been a problem since the classical EOQ equation was first developed, and many attempts have been made to solve the problem. Quite often the costs used are not representative of the real costs involved. Many of the cost elements in actual use are based on estimates involving management decisions, and are "correct" so long as there is full agreement on the decisions made. In many cases the cost estimates are reduced to subjective assessments because of the excessive, time-consuming studies involved.

4. *The whole order quantity arrives at one time.* Frequently, in retail shipments, such an assumption does not hold true. For many reasons, partial shipments do occur, and serious consideration should be given to them. Retail shipments, like many other activities in a department store, are complicated by the highs and lows of volume from month to month, week to week, and day to day. The order quantities should be sufficiently flexible to permit satisfactory adjustment to partial shipments when they occur.

5. *Transaction sizes are small relative to order quantity.* For two reasons, transaction sizes for some staple merchandise are actually large relative to their order quantity. The first reason is the batching of transactions (usually representing sales for one or two weeks) because of data-handling problems and the convenience that batch processing offers. The second reason involves the retail demand process as reflected in customer buying patterns for slow and medium sellers. Customers frequently buy multiple units for many types of merchandise such as shirts, underwear, women's hosiery, etc.

6. *There are no overriding restrictions in order-quantity size.* The classical EOQ formulation does not include any restrictions on the size of the order quantity. For a fixed review time system, the order quantity should be as large as the expected sales during a review time. The order quantity should be at least one pack size in order to be acceptable to the vendor. In many cases, the order quantity cannot be greater than a specified maximum, such as three months' supply or a year's supply. The EOQ equation does not include any of these constraints, and, therefore, it is frequently impractical to apply the results derived from the formula directly.

Consequently, a different order quantity technique has been developed which offers a better solution for retail inventory problems.[45] This approach,

_____
[45] *Ibid.*, p. 73.

called the modified EOQ, attempts to remove the largest stumbling block—the problem of determining costs. The classical approach explained above attempts to identify and quantify all the "true" costs related to inventory carrying and reordering. The modified approach, however, treats the costs in the EOQ formula as control "knobs." These control knobs are made available to management and are to be used primarily for selecting management policies, such as the amount of investment in total inventory and overall ordering workload. In other words, the classical "costs," transposed now to modern control "knobs," should be viewed merely as one of the policy variables in the inventory management system. Turning the control "knobs" to the "left" or "right" makes it possible to vary the balance between inventory investment, on the one hand, and the number of orders, on the other, thus allowing management to examine many alternate strategies.[46] This approach also implies that costs should not be considered fixed and definite. Management can manipulate the modified EOQ equation in order to get the results that will match goals. Furthermore, management can now view inventories as a total investment, not as an investment in an individual inventory unit.

The derivation of the modified EOQ begins by spelling out the component parts of the classical EOQ formula, as follows:

Economic order quantity in units =

$$\sqrt{\frac{2 \times (\text{cost per order in dollars}) \times \text{Annual sales in units}}{\text{Inventory carrying rate per year in percent} \times \text{Unit price in dollars}}}$$

This equation can be further broken down into:

$$\sqrt{\frac{2 \times (\text{Cost per order in dollars})}{\text{Inventory carrying rate per year in percent}}} \times \sqrt{\frac{\text{Annual sales in units}}{\text{Unit price in dollars}}}$$

Now, let the expression under the first square root equal K, and rewrite the EOQ formula somewhat differently to obtain the modified EOQ equation:

$$\text{Modified economic order quantity in units} = K \sqrt{\frac{\text{Annual sales in units}}{\text{Unit price in dollars}}}$$

The K factor is the management control "knob" referred to above. Varying

[46] *Ibid.*

the K factor changes the order quantity and, consequently, the number of orders in a year.[47]

When To Reorder[48]

In order to determine when to reorder, it is first necessary to know the projected demand or *sales forecast* (derived from a standard forecasting technique) as well as the *delivery lead time* and the *length of the review period*. *Delivery lead time* is usually expressed as the number of days to receive stock in available inventory after the inventory replenishment signal has been given. The main components of lead time are order processing time, order picking and handling time, transit time, and unloading and stocking time. On the other hand, the *length of the review period* is usually expressed as the number of days between forecasts, or the number of days between possible reorder decisions. A good approximation of the length of the review period can sometimes be obtained from the basic EOQ model. If the economic order quantity is Q^*, then the number of orders that should be placed in a year's time is given by dividing projected demand for the year by Q^*. Dividing the number of orders that should be placed in a year into the number of weeks or days in a year will tell how frequently the stock level should be reviewed. Thus, using the data from the previous EOQ example, and letting N^* stand for the optimum order interval, we estimate that the stock level should be reviewed every 6.45 weeks:

$$N^* = \frac{D}{Q^*} = \frac{2600}{322} = 8.07 \text{ orders per year}$$

$$\frac{52 \text{ weeks}}{8.07 \text{ orders per year}} = 6.45 \text{ weeks}$$

In retailing, the review period is often very short (e.g., a week), not because of economic order quantity considerations but rather because sales of many items sold at retail are highly seasonal and fluctuate continuously over time, thus necessitating frequent review. In wholesaling and manufacturing, the

[47]*Ibid.* Two of the many excellent sources that describe EOQ formulae for almost any application are Fred Hanssman, *Operations Research and Inventory Control* (New York: John Wiley & Sons, Inc., 1962) and John F. Magee, *Production Planning and Inventory Control* (New York: McGraw-Hill Book Co., Inc., 1958).

[48]The following discussion draws heavily from two sources: Edward W. Smykay and Allan D. Dale, "Inventory Control: What Price Service? Part 1," *Handling and Shipping*, July, 1966, pp. 48–51; and *Retail IMPACT—Inventory Management Program and Control Techniques Application Description*, 6th ed. (White Plains, N.Y.: IBM Technical Publications Department, March, 1970).

length of the review period is typically longer and frequently coincides more closely with estimates derived from EOQ considerations, although the period's length varies widely, depending on the characteristics of the product category under concern.

To compute a reorder point, the projected demand of a product during the review period is added to the projected demand for the product during the delivery lead time. The result is then compared to the quantity of the product available in inventory. The reorder point is reached when the overall projected demand (sales forecast) is greater than the amount available in inventory. For example, assume that a retailer has a review period of seven days, a lead time of ten days, and an available inventory of 110 units.[49] Assume, also, that the sales forecast for the next 17 days is 102 units. The projected average daily sales for the 17-day period is, therefore, 6 units (102/17). Because the next review period is seven days away, it can be estimated that 42 units will be sold in that time, leaving 68 units (110 – 42) in available inventory. If the retailer waits until the next review period to reorder, the order will arrive when available inventory is down to 8 units {68 (units in stock at the end of the next review period) *less* [6 (average daily sales forecast) *times* 10 (lead time)]}.

Suppose, however, that the forecast showed that expected sales during the next 17 days were 119 units. If the retailer waited until the next review point to place an inventory replenishment order, he would be out of stock the day before the new stock arrives. Selling seven units a day (119/17), he would need 49 units to cover the period until the next review point. This would leave him with only 61 units (110 – 49) to cover the ten-day lead time during which he will need 70 units in stock.

Thus, the decision rules for deciding whether to reorder an item held in inventory are the following:

1. If net on hand (available inventory) is greater than the sales forecast, take no action.

2. If net on hand (available inventory) is less than the sales forecast, place reorder.[50]

Forecasting

In determining how much to reorder and when to reorder, the sales forecast is the most critical variable affecting the final outcome. In fact, the short-term sales forecast is the heart of any system designed to solve these

[49] This example is drawn from Smykay and Dale, *op. cit.*, pp. 49–50.
[50] *Ibid.*

problems. For any channel member, the type of forecasting method to be used depends upon the type of demand pattern his customers exhibit.

In general, customer demand patterns can be categorized as (a) regular and highly predictable, (b) irregular but mathematically consistent, and (c) irregular and unpredictable.[51] Regular and highly predictable demand does not require a sophisticated sales forecast system. Type (b) demand (irregular but mathematically consistent) requires statistical forecasting, whereas type (c) demand requires the greatest degree of sophistication in designing an inventory control system.

For most types of customer demand patterns, a short-term computer forecast is the most efficient and most consistent way of obtaining future sales projections. It assumes that the historical sales patterns of a product can be used to predict its future sales, and therefore relies upon such historical data-based forecasting methods as moving averages, weighted moving averages, regression, and exponential smoothing. Although the application of such historical data-based techniques is less reliable for type (c) demand patterns, this problem can be alleviated somewhat by reducing the forecasting interval considerably—say, to one week—which enhances the reliability of the data, and, hence, improves prediction.

Exponential smoothing is the most popular of these common statistical forecasting techniques. It is an algebraic method of varying the weight (or importance) that is placed on past demand data. In other words, the older the data, the less weight is put on them, or , alternatively stated, the weights placed on data decline exponentially as the age of the data increases. In order to use exponential smoothing in forecasting, the weights and the mathematical model to be used must first be determined.

Tables 4–3 through 4–5 show a simple average (unweighted) forecast compared to two exponentially smoothed models, all using the same data. Table 4–3 shows that a simple average (unweighted) forecast always results in substantial overstock/understock, with an average in this example of 56.25.

In Table 4-4, however, a weight of 90 percent is placed on the most recent period's demand. This weighting factor is generally represented by the Greek letter α (alpha) and can vary between 0 and 1 (or between 0 and 100 percent). Here all older data are weighted by 10 percent. To forecast for the next period, multiply the latest period's demand by 0.9 (= α). Then multiply the forecast of this period's demand by 0.1 (= 1 − α), and add the two results together. For example, to compute demand for Period 4:

$$\alpha \times \text{Period 3 demand} = 0.9 \times 195 = 175.5$$
$$(1 - \alpha) \times \text{Period 3 forecast} = 0.1 \times 262 = 26.2$$
$$175.5 + 262 = 201.7$$

[51] *Ibid.,* p. 48.

TABLE 4-3   Forecasting with a Simple Unweighted Average

Period	Demand	Forecast (stock)	Overstock (+) Understock (−)
1	280	280	0
2	260	280	+20
3	195	280	+85
4	180	280	+100
5	260	280	+20
6	385	280	−105
7	400	280	−120
8	280	280	0
Total	2240	2240	450
Average	280	280	56.25

Decision rule: stock to average demand
Result: average inventory = 280
                   average overstock/understock = 56.25

SOURCE: Edward W. Symkay and Allan D. Dale, "Inventory Control: What Price Service? Part 1," Handling and Shipping, July, 1966, p. 50.

Thus, 201.7 units is the forecast for Period 4.

As shown in Table 4-4, this method is not much better than the simple average forecast. Average inventories decline slightly from 280 to 278 units, but the overstock/understock figure (58.25) is worse than that achieved via the simple average forecast (56.25).

Table 4-5 demonstrates the use of a different exponential smoothing equation. This particular model places a weight of 180 percent ($2 \times 90\%$) on the latest period's demand, and a weight of minus 80 percent ($180\% - 100\%$) on all older data. This forecasting method is the same as in the last example, except that the weighted forecast is subtracted rather than added. Again, using Period 4 as an example, we have

$$2\alpha \times \text{Period 3 demand} - 1.8 \times 195 = 351.0$$
$$(2\alpha - 1) \times \text{Period 3 forecast} = 0.8 \times 244 = 195.2$$
$$351.0 - 195.2 = 155.8$$

Thus, 155.8 units is the forecast for Period 4 demand.

The results obtained in Table 4-5 are considerably better than those in Tables 4-3 and 4-4. Although average inventory increased slightly to 284.6 units, average overstock/understock fell to 44.9 units.

Obviously, the selection of the proper weighting factor, or alpha, is

TABLE 4–4   Exponential Smoothing, I

Period	Demand	Forecast (stock)	Overstock (+) Understock (−)
1	280	280	0
2	260	280	+20
3	195	262	+67
4	180	202	+22
5	260	182	−78
6	385	252	−133
7	400	371	−29
8	280	397	+117
Total	2240	2226	466
Average	280	278.25	58.25

Decision: stock to forecast
Result: average inventory = 278.25
       average overstock/understock = 58.25

Model: Forecast = α (new demand) + $(1 - \alpha)$ (old forecast)
      Weight (α) = 0.9

SOURCE: Edward W. Symkay and Allan D. Dale, "Inventory Control: What Price Service? Part 1," *Handling and Shipping*, July, 1966, p. 50.

TABLE 4–5   Exponential Smoothing, II

Period	Demand	Forecast (stock)	Overstock (+) Understock (−)
1	280	280	0
2	260	280	+20
3	195	244	+49
4	180	156	−24
5	260	199	−61
6	385	309	−76
7	400	446	+46
8	280	363	+83
Total	2240	2277	359
Average	280	284.6	44.9

Decision: stock to forecast
Result: average inventory = 284.6
       average overstock/understock = 44.9

Model: 2α (new demand) − $(2\alpha - 1)$ (old forecast)
      Weight (α) = 0.9

SOURCE: Edward W. Symkay and Allan D. Dale, "Inventory Control: What Price Service? Part 1," *Handling and Shipping*, July, 1966, p. 50.

extremely important. In Table 4–5, any weighting factor other than 0.9 will reduce the accuracy of the forecast. The only way to determine the best model and weighting factor for minimizing forecast errors is to test all feasible alternatives. This is best done by using a computer. As discussed in Chapter 12, IBM has developed a computer program library system that classifies demand patterns in terms of various forecasting models, and then recommends whichever model yields the minimum forecast error.[52]

Although exponential smoothing models such as those discussed above are frequently used by manufacturers and wholesalers, they cannot adequately handle the marked seasonal patterns that exist in the demand for retail merchandise. IBM's Retail IMPACT system, however, employs a forecasting technique called "adaptive forecasting" which incorporates mathematical functions describing retail patterns of demand.[53] In IBM's IMPACT system, six types of forecasting models, each representing a different underlying demand process, are available for use in adaptive forecasting: a *constant model*, a *trend model*, a *seasonal model*, an *end-of-season model*, and a *trend-seasonal model*. The basic nature of each model is described briefly below.[54]

Constant Model. A constant model is used to forecast a demand pattern characterized by an essentially stable level of volume with random fluctuations or noise. The model represents demand as centering around an average value, with variations (noise) which may be attributed to random causes and which exhibit no discernible pattern over time. The fact that sales are below (or above) average for one month does not permit any specific inference about sales in coming months. The mathematical representation can be a single term that represents the average. Figure 4–7 shows the monthly sales for a "constant demand" item along with a constant demand model.

Trend Model. The trend model represents a demand pattern that consistently increases or decreases over time, with the increase or decrease of sufficient magnitude to be recognizable through the noise. The mathematical representation is composed of two terms, one of which is an average representing the historical sales of the item, while the other represents the direction (up or down) and magnitude of the trend. These elements, in combination with

[52]*Wholesale IMPACT—Advanced Principles and Implementation Reference Manual*, 2nd ed. (White Plains, N.Y.: IBM Technical Publications Department, May, 1969).

[53]*Retail IMPACT . . . op. cit.*, pp. 43-57.

[54]It is beyond the scope of this book to examine the internal mathematics of each of these models. For a brief, but not comprehensive, description of the mathematics involved in these forecasting processes, see *Retail IMPACT, op. cit.*, pp. 55-57.

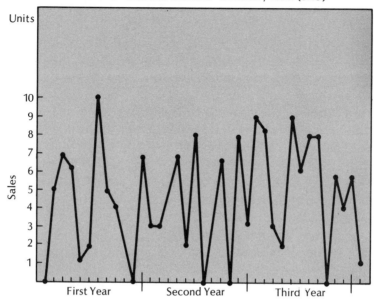

Sales of a "Constant Demand" Inventory Item (SKU)

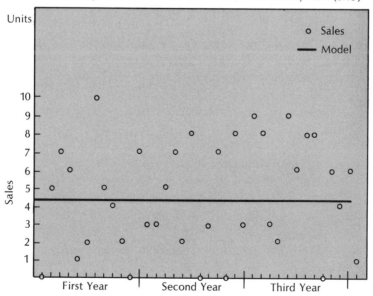

Forecasting Model of a "Constant Demand" Inventory Item (SKU)

FIGURE 4-7 Demand Pattern and Appropriate Forecasting Model
for a Hypothetical "Constant Demand" Inventory Item
(SKU)

SOURCE: Reprinted by permission from *Retail IMPACT—Inventory Management Program and Control Techniques Application*, 6th ed. (White Plains,
N.Y.: IBM Technical Publications Department, March 1970), pp. 37 and 44.
©1970 by International Business Machines Corporation.

others such as forecast error and an allowance for the possible development of seasonality, are used to project the model into the future for forecasting purposes. The sales of a typical "down-trending" inventory item (SKU) and a corresponding trend model are shown in Fig. 4–8.

Seasonal Model. The seasonal model represents a demand pattern that is characterized by high and low periods that recur as a function of time. These seasonal or cyclic patterns occur at about the same time during each year as a result of external conditions (school opening) or internal factors (January "white sales"). Because of the fact that such seasonal processes are a predominant factor in retailing, special mathematical functions must be used to seek out and describe the underlying demand patterns. The mathematical functions (sines and cosines) incorporated in this adaptive forecasting model are actual patterns themselves, as opposed to simple points, percentages, or comparisons of this year to last year. These functions are combined and superimposed in many ways to form the best approximation of the true demand process. Figure 4–9 shows a typical sales pattern and corresponding forecast model associated with a seasonal inventory item.

End-of-season and Trend-seasonal Models. The end-of-season model is used to forecast demand for merchandise that is taken off the shelves for a major part of each year so that there are no sales during that time. The trend-seasonal model is used for the same purpose as the seasonal model, but is formulated somewhat differently. Both the end-of-season and trend-seasonal models are determined by combinations of the seasonal technique described above. Examples of end-of-season and trend-seasonal models are shown in Fig. 4–10.

Low-volume, Lumpy-demand Models. These models are used for merchandise that sells at a very low rate and displays very erratic patterns of behavior. In fact, the behavior of individual low-volume and medium-volume inventory items is usually such that no well-defined seasonal pattern can be established. However, if taken at a group level (e.g., a particular style within a store or end sizes within a style, etc.), a seasonal demand pattern may be detected. Thus, by grouping low- and medium-volume inventory items, and thereby making the seasonal demand pattern more pronounced, the adaptive forecasting technique is able to make effective use of its seasonal models.

In general, the IBM Retail IMPACT adaptive forecasting program searches for and develops the appropriate models to best describe the underlying demand process at the retail level. Further, each model may carry additional elements that automatically adapt to changes in the pattern as these changes become significant and discernible to the system.

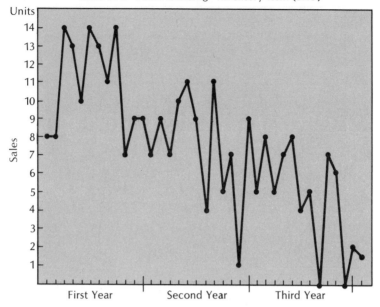

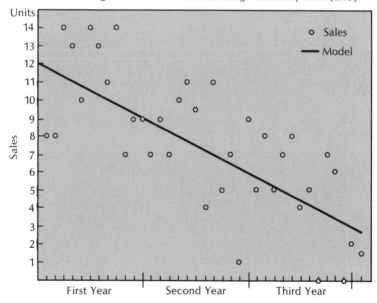

FIGURE 4–8 Demand Pattern and Appropriate Forecasting Model for a Hypothetical "Down-trending" Inventory Item (SKU)

SOURCE: Reprinted by permission from *Retail IMPACT—Inventory Management Program and Control Techniques Application*, 6th ed. (White Plains, N.Y.: IBM Technical Publications Department, March 1970), pp. 37 and 45. © 1970 by International Business Machines Corporation.

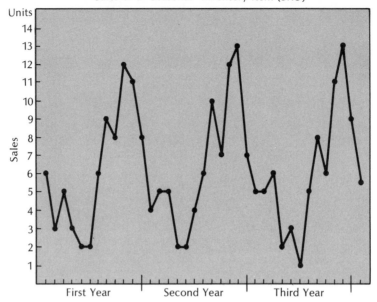

Sales of a "Seasonal" Inventory Item (SKU)

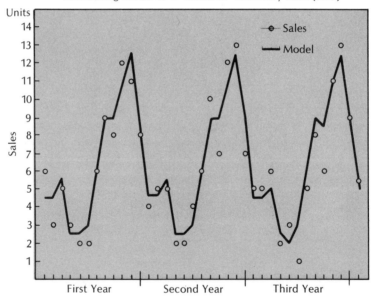

Forecasting Model of a "Seasonal" Inventory Item (SKU)

FIGURE 4-9 Demand Pattern and Appropriate Forecasting Model
for a Hypothetical "Seasonal" Inventory Item (SKU)

SOURCE: Reprinted by permission from *Retail IMPACT—Inventory Management and Control Techniques Application*, 6th ed. (White Plains, N.Y.:
IBM Technical Publications Department, March 1970) pages 38 and 46. ©
1970 by International Business Machines Corporation.

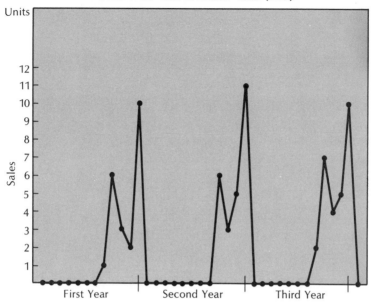

Sales of an "End-of-season" Item (SKU)

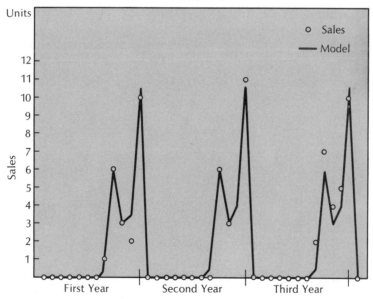

Forecasting Model of an "End-of-Season"
Item (SKU)

FIGURE 4-10(a) Demand Pattern and Appropriate Forecasting
Model for Hypothetical "End-of-Season" Inventory Items (SKUs)

SOURCE: Reprinted by permission from *Retail IMPACT—Inventory Management and Control Techniques Application*, 6th ed. (White Plains, N.Y.:
IBM Technical Publications Department, March 1970), pp. 38 and 46, ©
1970 by International Business Machines Corporation.

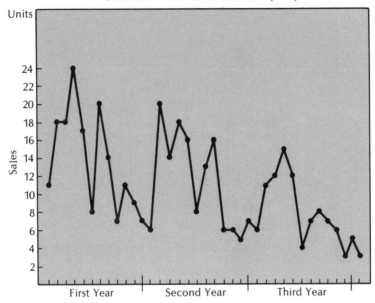

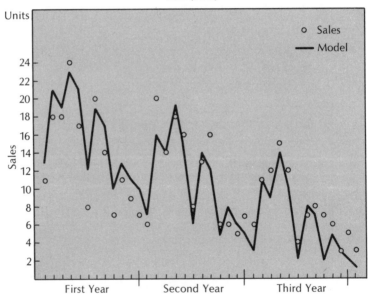

FIGURE 4-10(b) Demand Pattern and Appropriate Forecasting Model for Hypothetical "Trend-Seasonal" Inventory Items

SOURCE: Reprinted by permission from *Retail IMPACT—Inventory Management and Control Techniques Application*, 6th ed. (White Plains, N.Y.: IBM Technical Publications Department, March 1970), pp. 38 and 46. © 1970 by International Business Machines Corporation.

Controlling Stockouts

Up to this point in the discussion of inventory control techniques, attention has been focused on the maintenance of "base stocks." If sales forecasting were perfectly accurate, carrying only base stock in inventory would always provide "perfect" inventories; the problem of stockouts would never occur. This fortunate (but unlikely) state is depicted in Fig. 4–11. If, however, it is known in advance that each forecast will have some error in it (as it almost surely will), then action must be taken to ensure that this error does not seriously weaken customer service.

Ideally, a firm would never have a stockout, but maintaining a 100 percent service level is usually prohibitively costly. In order to minimize stockouts at a reasonable cost to the firm, it is necessary to predict the likely forecasting error. The term used for this prediction is the *standard error of*

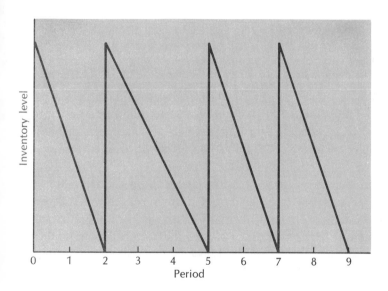

Average inventory is equal to the order quantity divided by two. This is so because inventory levels at the beginning of a cycle are equal to the order quantity, and are exactly zero the end of the cycle:

$$\left(\frac{\text{Order quantity} + 0}{2} = \frac{\text{Order quantity}}{2}\right)$$

FIGURE 4-11   Inventory Level with No Sales Forecast Errors

SOURCE: Edward W. Symkay and Allan D. Dale, "Inventory Control: What Price Service? Part 1," *Handling and Shipping,* July, 1966, p. 51.

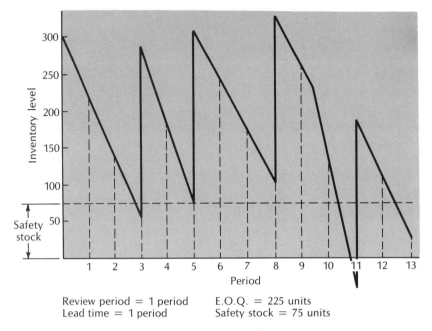

Review period = 1 period   E.O.Q. = 225 units
Lead time = 1 period   Safety stock = 75 units

FIGURE 4-12 Inventory Level with Sales Forecast Errors

SOURCE: Edward W. Symkay and Allan D. Dale, "Inventory Control: What Price Service? Part 1," *Handling and Shipping,* July, 1966, p. 51.

the estimate (S.E.). The standard error is employed to determine how much extra "safety" stock is needed to cushion against customer demand larger than the sales forecast. Figure 4-12 depicts the effect of forecast errors and the insurance, or cushioning, that safety stocks provide.

If it is assumed that sales forecast errors are random and normally distributed, it is possible to set average stockouts at any level desired.[55] If forecast errors are, in fact, random and normally distributed, then adding one S.E. to the average inventory will reduce stockouts from 50 to 16 percent, giving an in-stock frequency of 84 percent. However, additional safety stocks yield diminishing returns in improved customer service levels. For example, adding two S.E. of safety stock to average inventory reduces average stockouts to 2.3 percent, while the third S.E. reduces stockouts to 0.3 percent. Furthermore, adding one S.E. increases inventory in-stock frequency by 34 percent, while the second S.E. brings an 11 percent improvement. By adding

[55] The following discussion draws heavily on Edward W. Smykay and Allan D. Dale, "Inventory Control: What Price Service? Part 2," *Handling and Shipping,* August, 1966, pp. 60–63.

a third S.E., a less than 2 percent improvement is achieved. Table 4–6 illustrates many of these trade-offs by showing how a hypothetical problem concerning the control of stockouts is solved.

It is important to note that, for inventory control purposes, safety stocks should not be counted with base stocks. When reorder points are computed, for example, the required safety stocks should be subtracted from available inventory before it is compared to the forecast, because safety stocks are only insurance against forecast errors. If they are counted as available inventory, the result is a low forecast that will, in turn, lead to a stockout.

To compute average inventory for decision-making purposes, simply divide base stock by two, and then add safety stocks. This is done because safety stocks are assumed to be the same at the beginning and end of a cycle.

As indicated earlier, every channel member must determine, through PDS research, the customer service level best suited to it by balancing the cost of holding additional safety stock versus the costs of stockouts. The example and graph in Fig. 4–13 show one method of finding the service

TABLE 4–6 Hypothetical Problem Dealing with the Control of Stockouts

Order Cycle	Forecast (stock)	Actual	$(Actual\text{-}Fcst)^2$
1	311	280	961
2	273	260	169
3	191	195	16
4	225	180	2,025
5	300	260	1,600
6	411	385	676
7	306	400	8,836
8	220	280	3,600
	2237	2240	17,883

$$S.E. = \frac{17,883}{8} = 47.3$$

$$\text{Average inventory} \; \frac{2237}{8} = 279.6^a$$

[a]If this firm were willing to endure stockouts for about 50 percent of its order cycles, it could hold an average inventory of 279.6 units. To increase customer service levels to 84 percent, average inventory would have to be increased to 326.9 units (279.6 + 47.3). To increase customer service levels to 97.7 or 99.7 percent would take an increase in average inventory to 374.2 units and 421.5 units. In this example, a 17 percent increase in average inventory brought a 34 percent increase in customer service levels. The second and third 17 percent increments brought only 14 and 2 percent increases in customer service levels.

SOURCE: Edward W. Symkay and Allan D. Dale, "Inventory Control: What Price Service?, Part 2," Handling and Shipping, August, 1966, p. 60.

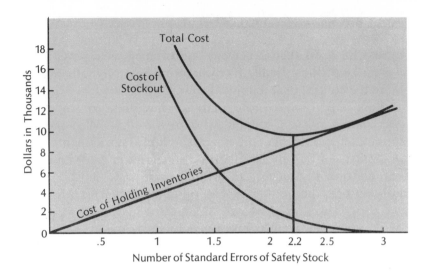

Cost of holding safety stocks and cost of stock outs. Lowest point on total cost curve will show the number of standard errors of safety stock that will minimize costs. Here, 2.2 S.E., or $8800 of safety stock yield the lowest total cost. This quantity will give a customer service level of 98.6% and cost $9200 a year. Carrying any other quantity of safety stock would increase total costs.

Assume: average number of orders per year is 1000.
  Average order size = $2000
  Profit margin = 15%
  Expected return on investment = 10%/yr.
  Average sales per customer = $4000/yr.
  Order cycle = 1 month
  Inventory holding cost = 20% of inventory value
Customer reaction to stock out:
1. Back order
  Results in a one-month delay in receipt of $2000. Cost of stockout is given by lost earnings on $2000 for 1/12 of one year. Cost of stockout = $2000 x 0.10 x 1/12 = $16.67

2. Cancel order
  Results in loss of profit on $2000 in sales.
  Cost = $2000 x 0.15 = $300

3. Switch to new vendor
  Results in loss of all future profits. Cost is computed by discounting all future profits by 10%.
$$\text{Cost} = \frac{\$4000 \times 0.15}{0.10} = \$6000$$

Assume that one standard error of safety stock is $20,000 of inventory. At a holding cost of 20%, each S.E. costs $4000 per year.

Assume that 90% of customers will back order, 9% will cancel, and 1% will switch suppliers.

The average cost of a stockout is   16.67 x 0.90 = $15.00
                                                          300.00 x 0.09 =   27.00
                                                    6000.00 x 0.01 =   60.00
                                                          Average cost $102.00

FIGURE 4-13   Determination of Minimum-cost Service Levels

SOURCE: Edward W. Symkay and Allan D. Dale, "Inventory Control: What Price Service? Part 2," *Handling and Shipping,* August, 1966, p. 62.

level that will minimize costs, if different customers' reactions to a stock-out have already been determined.

In summary, the sequence of events that should be employed by a channel member in instituting an inventory control system include the following twelve steps, which are also shown in flow chart form in Fig. 4–14.

1. Establish customer service level.

2. Establish lead and review times.

3. Gather demand history.

4. Test alternatives to determine best forecasting model.

5. Gather pertinent inventory cost information.

6. Compute EOQ.

7. Forecast demand over review period plus lead time.

8. Forecast safety stock requirement.

9. Deduct required safety stock from on-hand inventory.

10. If net on-hand inventory is greater than forecast, take no action and go to next item.

11. If net on-hand inventory is less than forecast, place reorder.

12. If net on-hand inventory is negative, expedite reorder.[56]

TRANSPORTATION MODES

Inadequate transportation service and uncertain transit times can cause a company to hold several days' more inventory than PD plans call for. These problems, in turn, add to the cost of carrying inventory and reduce the number of times that capital in inventory can be turned over during the year, not to mention the undesirable effects they have in terms of poor customer service and missed product promotions. Consequently, the selection of appropriate transportation modes and the maintenance of a concerted effort by PD management to ensure efficient and reliable transportation are both prerequisites to accomplishing distribution objectives. Therefore, in this section, attention is given to describing various transportation modes and the functions that they can perform for various channel members in facilitating the movement of products.[57]

[56]Adapted from Smykay and Dale, "Inventory Control: . . . Part 2," op. cit., p. 62.

[57]The reader should also see Chapter 12 for a discussion of some interesting communication systems that are used by channel members to improve the transportation service they receive.

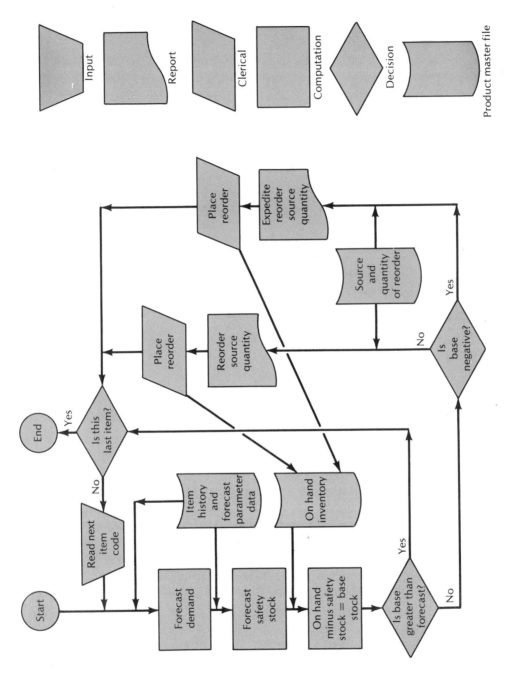

FIGURE 4-14 A Model of an Inventory Control System

SOURCE: Edward W. Symkay and Allan D. Dale, "Inventory Control: What Price Service? Part 2," *Handling and Shipping,* August, 1966, p. 63.

180

TABLE 4-7   Trends in Freight Movement, 1950–1974 (billions of ton-miles)

Year	Total	Cargo Airline		Railroads		Inland Waterways		Motor Carriers		Pipelines	
		No.	%	No.	%	No.	%	No.	%	No.	%
1950	1,094.240	0.240	0.02	628	57.39	163	14.90	173	15.81	129	11.79
1955	1,298.379	0.379	0.03	655	50.45	217	16.71	223	17.18	203	15.63
1960	1,342.724	0.724	0.05	595	44.31	220	16.38	298	22.19	229	17.05
1963	1,446.027	1.027	0.07	622	43.01	234	16.18	336	23.24	253	17.50
1964	1,558.287	1.287	0.08	667	42.80	251	16.11	371	23.81	268	17.20
1965	1,627.730	1.730	0.11	698	42.88	262	16.10	360	22.12	306	18.80
1967	1,745.351	2.351	0.13	719	41.20	274	15.70	389	22.29	361	20.68
1968	1,825.805	2.805	0.15	744	40.75	291	15.94	396	21.69	392	21.47
1969	1,886.246	3.246	0.17	768	40.72	300	15.90	404	21.42	411	21.79
1970	1,937.000	5.000	0.26	771	39.80	318	16.42	412	21.27	431	22.25
1971	1,829.100	5.100	0.28	740	40.46	210	11.48	430	23.51	444	24.27
1972	1,912.500	5.500	0.29	778	40.68	222	11.61	450	23.53	457	23.90
1973[a]	2,013.200	6.200	0.31	830	41.23	234	11.62	472	23.45	471	23.40
1974[a]	2,081.900	6.900	0.33	855	41.07	245	11.77	490	23.54	485	23.30
Percentage change 1950–1974	90.26	2775.00		36.15		50.31		183.24		275.97	

[a]Estimated by Bureau of Competitive Assessment and Business Policy (BCABP).

SOURCE: Association of American Railroads, Air Transport Association of America, American Trucking Associations, Association of OIL Pipe Lines, American Waterway Operators, National Air Carrier Association, Interstate Commerce Commission, Transportation Association of America, BCABP, and the authors' calculations.

In the United States, the bulk of freight movement is handled by five basic modes of transportation—rail, truck, waterways, air, and pipeline—and is facilitated by various transportation agencies—freight forwarders, parcel post, air express, and shippers' associations. Economical arrangements are often created through the interaction of these carriers and agencies with the result being a coordinated system of transportation.

As shown in Table 4-7 and Fig. 4-15, the market shares of the five basic transport modes have shifted dramatically over time. However, as indicated by these figures, the *railroad* is still the dominant mode, even though its share in total ton-mileage dropped from 57.4 percent in 1950 to 41.1 percent in 1974. Despite the decline in the railroad's share in total ton-mileage, it is still considered the major long-haul mover of bulk commodities, such as coal and grain. Furthermore, it offers important services to shippers, such as expedited handling to guarantee arrival within a certain number of hours, stop-off privileges, pickup and delivery, and diversion and reconsignment, which enhance its attractiveness as a mover of a large number of products.

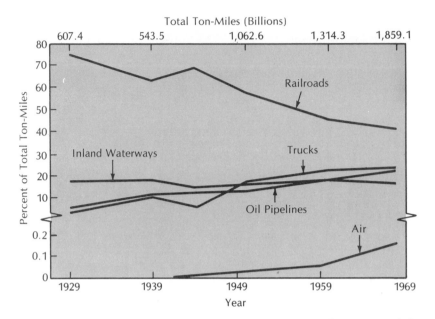

FIGURE 4-15   Forty-year Trends in Usage by Mode as a Percentage of the
Total Intercity Ton-miles Shipped

SOURCE: Interstate Commerce Commission, American Trucking Association, and
Transportation Association of America.

On the other hand, *motor carriers* have some inherent advantages over
the railroad, including door-to-door service as well as frequency and availability of service. Trucking is, however, a relatively short-range transportation service which is less capable than rail of handling all types of freight,
chiefly because of highway safety restrictions on the dimensions of shipments and their weight. For less-than-truckload (LTL) shipments, though,
trucking generally offers more rapid and dependable service than the railroad. In fact, motor carriers handle approximately 80 percent of the country's "small" (500 pounds or less) shipments.[58] Small shipments account
for 70 percent of motor carriers' total business. Partly as a result of their
willingness to handle small shipment traffic, their ton-mileage has increased
183 percent over the past two decades, as indicated in Table 4-7.

Air transportation is being considered by increasing numbers of shippers
for regular service, despite its high rate charges. Over the past two decades,
the air transport industry has developed and defined a basic operating system

[58] Friedman, *op. cit.*, p. 25. See also James C. Johnson, "An Analysis of the 'Small Shipments' Problem with Particular Attention to its Ramifications on a Firm's Logistical System," *ICC Practitioners
Journal*, Vol. 44 (July–August, 1972), pp. 646–664.

that has been able to increase its total cargo movement 2775 percent. Nevertheless, the airlines moved only 0.33 percent of the total freight in 1974, which is still a very small percentage when compared to other modes of transportation, such as the motor carriers or the railroad. The inherent advantage of air transportation is its unmatched origin-destination speed. However, this speed is not directly comparable with other modes of transportation, because it does not include pickup and delivery times as well as ground handling time. Therefore, a well-managed and coordinated truck-rail operation often can match the schedules of the air transport system.

Historically, *water* transportation was the earliest domestic means for moving cargo in large volumes. It has played a vital role in the economic history of the United States. But water transportation is comparatively slow, less dependable, and limited to bulk cargo service along waterways systems. On the other hand, water transport has competitively lower cost. Although its rate of increase in ton-mileage over the last two decades has been higher than that of the railroads, the water transportation system has the lowest (after air transport) share in the total freight moved in the United States. This can be ascribed to a number of problems that have faced the water carriers in the form of restrictions on automation on the waterfront, wage increases, and selective rate cutting by competing modes of transportation.

Finally, *pipeline* carriers have significantly increased their share of total transportation ton-miles during the period from 1950 to 1974. The rate of increase in ton-mileage was about 275 percent. The increase in the number and capacity of the pipelines is due mainly to the increasing need for economic volume movement systems for fluids and solids in hydraulic suspension. Nevertheless, pipeline transportation provides a very limited range of services and capability because of the physical limitations on the products that can be moved by the pipelines. However, pipeline transportation is the most dependable service of all transportation modes and has lower rates of loss and damage to the product.

In actuality, the major market share shifts evidenced in the transportation industry are primarily the result of the increasing economic viability of certain modes in comparison with others. The basis of this economic viability is new technology. Some of the more recent technological changes taking place within each of the mode categories are described in Exhibit 4–1.

Legal Forms of Transport

Four legal forms of transport currently exist as alternatives for shippers: common carriers, contract carriers, exempt carriage, and private transportation. Freight brokers are sometimes considered as an additional legal form.

EXHIBIT 4-1   Technological Changes in Transportation

Railroads. Carriers will continue to build bigger freight cars of all types, and to use a growing proportion of them in single-commodity unit trains for one-way shuttle-type service. Automation in classification yards and computerized freight car control will increase car utilization sharply. The growth of TOFC (trailer-on-flat-car) service will continue, spurred by use of special high-speed TOFC trains between major points. Expanding foreign trade will stimulate the growth of COFC (container-on-flat-car) movements.

Trucks. The number of states permitting use of double-bottom trucks (one tractor and two trailers) is expected to continue growing. More economical engines, including turbines, will be placed in service. Transport demands emanating from a steady stream of new industrial products will stimulate the building of specialized trucks. Many of them will have automated self-loading/unloading capability, especially for rapid handling of flowable solid and liquid bulk commodities. The number of automated terminals will expand.

Air. The biggest change taking place in air freight is the entry of progressively larger subsonic jets. The giant jets due soon will be serviced by new, fully automated cargo terminals. Freight will be handled on pallets and in containers for rapid loading and unloading. New supersonic planes flying at 1200 to 2100 mph will speed up the movement of mail, express, and package freight between many distant points, but supersonics will not soon affect movements of general freight.

Water Carriers. Domestic barge lines will continue to build bigger barges for use in even larger and longer integrated tows. Self-loading/unloading bulk carriers on the Great Lakes and open seas will become jumbo size. Conventional lift-on/off general cargo ships will be replaced by the rapidly growing fleet of container and roll-on/off ships. They will be serviced by highly automated terminals at select points. Huge ships carrying barges will connect inland United States and European ports.

Pipelines. Oil pipelines are becoming more automated and larger in diameter, to hold down costs. Computerized scheduling is helping to expand the variety and number of batches of liquids that can be moved through a pipeline at the same time. A new market for movement and sale of liquid fertilizers may be tapped. More pipelines are being built to haul coal and other bulk commodities that can be crushed and moved with water or other liquids in slurry form. Extensive tests on pipelining solids, such as chemicals in capsules, may bring about a new form of freight transport.

SOURCE: Adapted from Frank A. Smith, "Changes Ahead in Transport Technology," in Hale C. Bartlett (ed.), *Readings in Physical Distribution*, 3rd ed. (Danville, Ill.: Interstate Printers & Publishers, 1972), pp. 339–340.

However, brokers merely "match" freight with carriers without assuming ownership or the risks of operating transport equipment.

Common Carriers. Common carriers are the most regulated for-hire transport agencies. They are required to charge similar rates for similar services, and to publish and make available to the public all rates charged for their services. A common carrier is any transportation firm that makes its services available to all shippers and accepts responsibility for carrying goods any time, any place, on a fee basis. Therefore, a basic characteristic of common carriers is that their services are offered to all potential shippers without discrimination.

Contract Carriers. In contrast with common carriers, contract carriers are those firms who make themselves available for business on a selective basis. They service a limited number of shippers and carry a restricted number of commodities as specified by their operating permits.

Although contract carriers are required to publish the actual rates that they charge shippers, they may charge different rates to different customers for the same service. Operation permits issued to contract carriers are less restrictive than those issued to common carriers. They do specify routes to be utilized and commodities to be transported, however.

Exempt Carriage. The third legal form of transportation embraces a wide variety of transportation activities that are exempt from direct regulation, thus the name "exempt" carriers. Exemptions are usually given on three bases:[59] (1) Geographic area, such as those defined by the Interstate Commerce Commission (ICC) around the periphery of certain cities mainly because of the administrative difficulties of keeping track of the operations of the numerous small, local cartage operators and small delivery trucks. (2) Exempt commodities, under which carriages of "unprocessed" products of agriculture and fishing are largely exempt from economic regulations. Exempt commodities, therefore, are moved at prices lower than those of regulated forms, especially common carriers. (3) Exempt associations, such as agricultural cooperatives and the shippers' associations described later.

Private Transportation. Carried on as an activity incidental to the primary purpose of a business, private transportation refers to the "common ownership of goods transported and the lease or ownership of the equipment in

[59]Donald J. Bowersox, Edward W. Smykay, and Bernard J. LaLonde, *Physical Distribution Management*, rev. ed. (New York: The Macmillan Company, 1968), p. 128.

which they are moved."[60] Private transportation activities fall outside the economic regulation of the ICC. Although nonregulated intercity highway transport accounted for most of the revenue-generating activity in the trucking industry in 1970, its share of the total fell from 60 percent to 50 percent between 1960 and 1970.[61] Where volume of shipment is high, private transportation may prove to be an attractive alternative for users who hope to gain better operating performance, availability, and lower cost. Even when the volume is low, some companies are forced to own or contract for transportation to meet their special transportation requirements not commonly available through the purchase of common carrier services.

Transportation Agencies

Transportation agencies offer transportation services to shippers by handling small shipments and consolidating them into vehicle load quantities. They do not own any line haul equipment.

Freight Forwarders. Freight forwarders are considered to be common carriers of freight and, as such, have similar rights and obligations. However, they utilize the services of other common carriers for the long-distance shipments. Their major function is the consolidation of small shipments into large ones, thereby offsetting the differential between LTL and TL (truckload) rates and LCL and CL (carload) rates, respectively. Freight forwarders achieved a 2.1 percent share of total regulated carrier freight, or more than $591 million in revenue in 1969; that over half of this amount was realized by only three forwarders indicates a high rate of economic concentration in the industry.[62]

Parcel Post. Parcel post services are offered by the United States Post Office. They are designed for small shipments and can be used by nearly everyone. The parcel post uses all air and surface line-haul carriers except pipeline. The rates for air parcel post are usually higher than the surface rates. Parcel post shipments approximated 2.1 million tons in 1969 and totalled nearly $704 million in revenues for a 2.4 percent share of the business done by regulated carriers.[63]

[60]Heskett, et al., *op. cit.*, p. 96.
[61]*Ibid.*, p. 662.
[62]*Ibid.*, p. 105.
[63]*Ibid.*

Shippers' Associations. Shippers' associations are cooperative organizations operating on a nonprofit basis to take advantage of consolidation economies. They perform the same functions as freight forwarders. Although no statistics are available regarding the volume of business done by the shippers' associations, it is believed that their importance has increased over the last decade.[64]

Coordinated (Intermodal) Systems

The idea of coordinating the services of two or more transportation modes can be traced to the early 1920's. However, renewed interest in coordinated systems has grown in recent years. Coordinated systems are those operations which offer point-to-point through-movement by means of two or more modes of transportation on a regularly scheduled basis.[65] There are at least seven possible combinations among the rail, water, air, and truck transportation modes. In addition, there are pipeline connections with other modes that are in common use among oil transportation companies.

Examples of coordinated service combinations are listed below.

1. *Piggyback services* are a combination of truck and rail services. This combination is also known as trailer-on-flat-car (TOFC) service. It refers to transporting truck trailers on railroad flat cars over longer distances than trucks normally haul.[66] The cost is usually less than a truck trailer might incur over the road for the same traveled distance. The result of such a coordinated system is the extension of the trucking industry's range of operation.

   The TOFC service is offered under different plans to provide operating flexibility to shippers. Plan I calls for common carrier truckers to place their trailers on railroad-owned flat cars. Plan II is similar to Plan I except that the trailers are also owned by the railroads. Shippers deal only with railroads that provide a door-to-door service. Plan III calls for shippers to place their own trailers on rail owned flat cars and be charged a flat rate: Under Plan IV shippers provide both the trailer or container *and* the rail cars on which they are placed. The railroad charges a distance fee for the use of its pulling power. Finally, Plan V is based on a joint rate quoted by two or more carriers for truck-rail-truck service.

---

[64]*Ibid.*

[65]*Ibid.*, p. 97.

[66]In a truck-rail combination service, it is possible to haul only the container or box in which the freight is packaged, thus saving the dead weight of the understructure and wheels. Such a service is called COFC, or container-on-flatcar. It has also been used in water-truck combinations. See Ronald H. Ballou, *Business Logistics Management* (Englewood Cliffs: Prentice-Hall, Inc., 1973), pp. 148–149.

The plan allows for the extension of the territory of each carrier into that served by the other.

2. *Fishyback* is a coordinated truck and water service that includes the combination of truck movement with water movement on inland waterways as well as on coastal and intercoastal routes.

3. *Rail-water* is also called "train-ship" coordinated service.

4. *Truck-air* consists of the cooperation of air carriers with a number of trucking firms. The service is widely available throughout the United States.

5. The pipeline combinations include *truck-pipe*, *water-pipe*, and *rail-pipe*. Almost all of these services exist in the United States, although they may not be available for all shippers because of the special operating characteristics of pipelines.

SYSTEMS MANAGEMENT

The complexity of the physical distribution function implies that the different activity areas discussed above must be managed as an integrated whole. A vital link that permits effective planning and control of the activities involved in the flow of physical possession is information. Therefore, the design of a Logistics Information System (LIS) is a critical and continuous process that secures the proper implementation and functioning of the system. Figure 4–16 shows the necessary steps in the development of a LIS, and Fig. 4–17 enumerates the basic areas of cost information usually needed by physical distribution managers in making a LIS operational.

In manufacturing firms, the logistics information systems that are developed should include, ideally, data on the following components.

1. Production planning and scheduling

2. Purchasing

3. Traffic (raw materials and finished goods)

4. Raw materials and supplies warehousing

5. Material handling

6. Finished goods warehousing

7. Inventory control

8. Protective packaging

9. Order processing

10. Billing

11. Location of plant and warehousing facilities

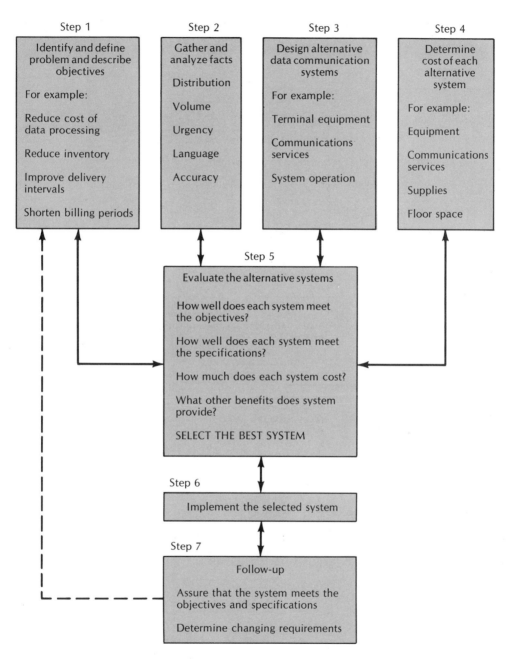

FIGURE 4-16 Basic Steps Involved in Establishing a Logistics Information System (LIS)

SOURCE: Edgar C. Gentle, Jr., *Data Communications in Business* (New York: Copyright, American Telephone and Telegraph Company, 1965), p. 79.

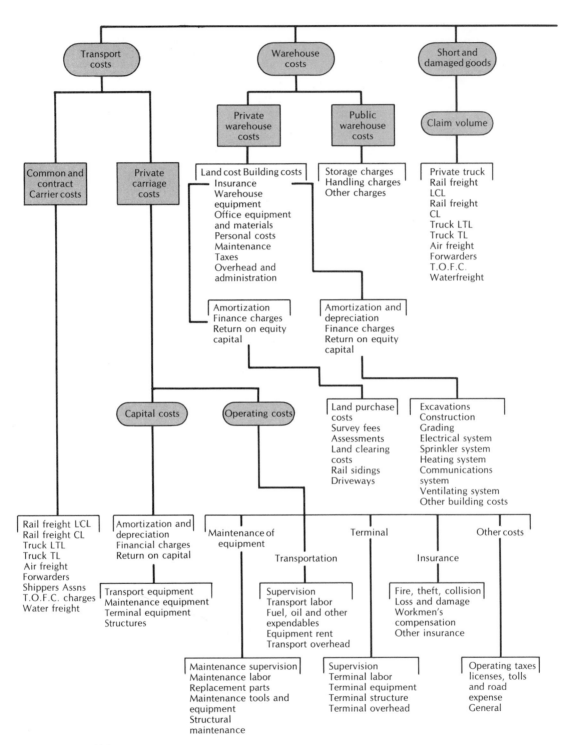

Transport costs

Warehouse costs

Short and damaged goods

Private warehouse costs

Public warehouse costs

Claim volume

Common and contract Carrier costs

Private carriage costs

Land cost Building costs
Insurance
Warehouse equipment
Office equipment and materials
Personal costs
Maintenance
Taxes
Overhead and administration

Storage charges
Handling charges
Other charges

Private truck
Rail freight LCL
Rail freight CL
Truck LTL
Truck TL
Air freight
Forwarders
T.O.F.C.
Waterfreight

Amortization
Finance charges
Return on equity capital

Amortization and depreciation
Finance charges
Return on equity capital

Capital costs

Operating costs

Land purchase costs
Survey fees
Assessments
Land clearing costs
Rail sidings
Driveways

Excavations
Construction
Grading
Electrical system
Sprinkler system
Heating system
Communications system
Ventilating system
Other building costs

Rail freight LCL
Rail freight CL
Truck LTL
Truck TL
Air freight
Forwarders
Shippers Assns
T.O.F.C. charges
Water freight

Amortization and depreciation
Financial charges
Return on capital

Maintenance of equipment

Terminal

Other costs

Transportation

Insurance

Transport equipment
Maintenance equipment
Terminal equipment
Structures

Supervision
Transport labor
Fuel, oil and other expendables
Equipment rent
Transport overhead

Fire, theft, collision
Loss and damage
Workmen's compensation
Other insurance

Maintenance supervision
Maintenance labor
Replacement parts
Maintenance tools and equipment
Structural maintenance

Supervision
Terminal labor
Terminal equipment
Terminal structure
Terminal overhead

Operating taxes licenses, tolls and road expense
General

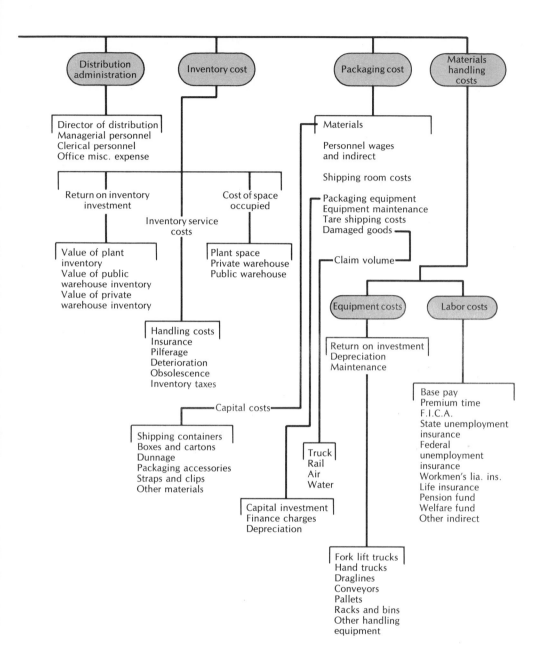

FIGURE 4–17   Cost Information Needed To Operationalize a Logistics System (LIS)

SOURCE: William B. Saunders, "Designing a Distribution System," *Distribution Age* (January, 1965), pp. 32–36.

Generally, the only components that are, in fact, integrated into manufacturers' systems are purchasing, location, inventory control, packaging and handling, and traffic or transportation. On the other hand, the components that should be included in a retailer's system include:

1. Purchasing (store supplies other than merchandising)
2. Receiving
3. Marking
4. Stock rooms
5. Work rooms (alterations)
6. Warehouses
7. Traffic (merchandise supplies and delivery service)
8. Packing and pickup
9. Customer service

Once the appropriate data have been supplied by the logistics information system (LIS), a variety of mathematical techniques are available that can aid the distribution manager in analyzing the information and solving systemwide logistical problems. One of the most popular PD systems management techniques is *simulation*. Via simulation, a manager can construct mathematical models of each of the major PD activity areas and their interrelations. Then, by manipulating these models, he can draw conclusions as to appropriate policies and strategies.[67] Simulation permits distribution management to change one or two variables and know that the resulting changes in the system's operation as a whole are due to that manipulation alone. Great savings can be achieved from the use of simulation, because alterations can be made and tested without disturbing the actual system. Moreover, with the speed of computers, changes whose impact might require years to determine can be assessed very quickly.

One of the best-known simulations of a physical distribution system was developed for the H. J. Heinz Company[68] and was later applied to the

[67]John Dearden, *Computers in Business Management* (Homewood, Ill.: Richard D. Irwin, Inc., 1966), p. 234. For a discussion of the ways of constructing simulation models, see James R. Emshoff and Roger L. Sisson, *Design and Use of Computer Simulation* (New York: Macmillan Publishing Co., Inc., 1970).

[68]Harvey N. Shycon and Richard B. Maffei, "Simulation—Tool for Better Distribution," *Harvard Business Review*, Vol. 39 (November–December, 1960), pp. 65–75. Also, see the appendix to this chapter. A more recent simulation is reported in Edward W. Smykay, "Anatomy of a Ready-Made PD Simulation Program," *Handling and Shipping*, February, 1968, pp. 62-64; April, 1968, pp. 76–77; and July, 1968, pp. 55-57.

distribution problems of the Nestlé Company. The simulation provided answers to basic warehouse location questions (e.g., number, location, allocation of demand to warehouses, etc.) by manipulating cost data associated with a variety of physical distribution system variables. The major distribution elements included in the Heinz Company simulation are shown in Exhibit 4-2.

The Problem of "Maldistribution"

Despite the availability of sophisticated techniques such as simulation, many channel members are not effective in managing the physical possession flow. In fact, research shows that companies with comparatively high distribution costs frequently provide *poorer* service than some of their competitors who have lower distribution costs, even though they are supplying essentially the same products to identical markets.[69] This problem—termed "maldistribution"—occurs repeatedly in companies of varying sizes across a wide variety of industries and is estimated to cost, in the aggregate, as much as $10 billion annually.[70]

One of the major reasons for the significance of this problem seems to be a lack of top management support and effort in integrating the different areas required for effective PD systems management.[71] Another major reason is the seemingly overabundance of "technique"- or "equipment"-oriented approaches to solving distribution problems as opposed to a truly integrated "systems management" approach. Although specific problems—such as inaccurate sales forecasts, losses from inventory stockouts, inadequate inventory information, and the like—can be "remedied" through the use of sophisticated models, the changes required to implement the remedies often create new unexpected problems that are not accounted for by the models and which generally outweigh any improvements achieved. Thus, in practice, the more popular distribution techniques should be viewed only as aids in solving the complex problems frequently encountered. What is required is a method of organizing and performing the complex interdisciplinary analysis needed to avoid maldistribution. The case study in Exhibit 4-3 illustrates how this can be done.

Exhibit 4-4 lists four signs of maldistribution. If any of these signs appears, a channel member should undertake a careful study of his PD system.

[69]Oresman and Scudder, *op. cit.*, p. 63.

[70]*Ibid.*

[71]See Robert P. Neuschel, "Corporate Level PD: Creative or Reactive," *Distribution Worldwide*, December, 1971, pp. 21-25.

EXHIBIT 4-2   Physical Distribution Elements Included
in the Heinz Simulation

1. The customers
The characteristics of the customers that affect distribution costs are
a. Customer location
b. Annual volume of demand
c. The types of products purchased. Different products fall into various commodity classifications and will, therefore, call for different freight rates. When there are regional variations in product mix, an average rate for all products will not do.
d. The distribution of the size of orders. Different size shipments call for different freight rates.
2. Warehouses
The characteristics of the warehouses that affect costs are
a. Fixed investment in company-owned warehouses. Some companies prefer public warehousing, implying a relatively small fixed investment.
b. Fixed annual operation and administrative costs.
c. Variable costs of storing, handling, stock rotation, and data processing.
3. Factories
The location of the factories and the products available at each factory are the elements that most affect distribution costs. Certain warehousing and handling charges at the factory may be properly attributable to distribution costs, but insofar as these costs are largely independent of the warehouse configuration, they may be excluded from the analysis.
4. Transportation costs
The freight costs of moving a product from factory to warehouse are termed "transportation" costs. These depend on the location of the factory and warehouse involved, the size of the shipment, and the commodity classification of the product.
5. Delivery costs
The costs of moving the product from warehouse to customer, termed "delivery" costs, depend upon the size of shipment, the location of the warehouse and customer, and the commodity classification of the product.

SOURCE: Martin L. Gerson and Richard B. Maffei, "Technical Characteristics of Distribution Simulators," Management Science, Vol. 10 (October, 1963), pp. 62–69.

EXHIBIT 4-3   A Case Study Example of Effective Systems Management in Physical Distribution

A large manufacturer of consumer goods was faced with escalating inventories and declining customer service. Over a three-year period, sales had leveled after a decade of explosive growth, yet inventories had continued to climb an additional 30 percent. Customer service had deteriorated over this same period from the traditional 99 percent to less than 96 percent; customer complaints were at an all-time high; and salesmen's morale was seriously affected by the service problem.

Company management had previously made several piecemeal attempts to solve this problem. A linear programming computer model had been developed which had indicated that two more warehouses were needed, an on-line inventory control system had been designed and installed, and various organization changes had been made to focus attention on service and inventories. None of these efforts perceptibly slowed the increase in inventories or decline in customer service. As a result, top management decided that a more innovative approach was required.

The first step taken was to frame the basic question, "How much inventory should we have to provide a competitive level of service, and how can we assure that we achieve that level of service?" With this definition of the scope of the undertaking, a project team was formed consisting of four members: the manager responsible for customer service and warehousing, a line manufacturing manager responsible for production scheduling, a manufacturing systems specialist, and the manager of production and inventory control. This task force was assigned full time to the project, assisted by outside consultants, and made responsible to a steering committee of top management.

The newly organized task force spent its first three months collecting and analyzing operating data and interviewing other company managers to accurately define the problem. Over the three-month data collection and analysis phase, a large number of projects were carried out. In most cases, they were performed by team members themselves, and the tendency to write a computer program to do the work was actively resisted. Most of the work was done with calculators and slide rules.

The following projects are representative of those carried out in the data collection and analysis phase of the project:

A statistical analysis of warehouse shipments by line item measured warehouse variability of demand. The results of this analysis were in turn used to calculate the theoretical inventories required to give 99 percent service. This calculation showed that warehouse inventories were 50 percent higher than required in total, but significantly too low on a handful of products.

A detailed analysis of customer service was based on a sample of invoices and back-orders. Although a service problem was clearly recognized, the company had no

EXHIBIT 4-3 continued

way of measuring the extent of the problem quantitatively. The results of this analysis showed that over a three-year period, service had declined from 99 percent to less than 96 percent. In dollar terms, backorders had risen from an average of $10,000 to more than $500,000.

Manufacturing inventory replenishment was based on the policy of maintaining safety stocks of at least two months' sales. A comparison of actual stock levels with forecasts showed a variance of from one-half to six months instead of the expected two months. This discrepancy prompted further examination which revealed that there were at least two different forecasts for each item—one prepared by the sales and marketing department and another prepared by manufacturing.

An analysis of manufacturing schedules showed that in the company's peak summer months only 20 percent of orders were made on time and that the principal component of lead times was waiting time rather than working time.

At the conclusion of the data collection and analysis phase, a number of major problems were identified:

Inconsistent and inaccurate sales forecasts. In addition to the sales and manufacturing forecasts, a third distribution forecast was also uncovered.

Inappropriate inventory levels. The two-month safety stocks policy led to insufficient protection on some items and excesses on others.

Demand on the field warehouses was much more regular and predictable than demand on the plant after the warehouses had translated customer demand into reorders.

The replenishment policy concentrated on freight costs and ignored inventory and storage costs, and, as a result, overall costs were increased $100,000 annually.

Capacity was severely overloaded during peak months. The scheduling system did not load by manufacturing departments, and lead times were excessive because the scheduling system allowed for large queues of work before each operation.

Of particular significance in this step was the team's concentration on analysis rather than on techniques. The effort was concentrated on causes rather than on determining if various proposed approaches were desirable. Further, since the managers got into the details themselves, they were forced to discard preconceived notions and thus became aware of preconceptions on the part of others, including top management. Finally, as they all worked together in the same room on various points of the same problem, they developed a strong feeling for the interrelationships among their various functions.

Once the key problem areas had been sharply defined, the specialists on and supporting the team could go to work designing solutions. To correct the problem of multiple inaccurate forecasts, the marketing team member and an operations

EXHIBIT 4-3 continued

research specialist developed a sales forecasting system. This system used computerized linear regression techniques to develop a statistical sales forecast, which was then modified by the responsible product manager. The modified forecast was divided by the computer into forecasts for each warehouse to be used in the distribution system and then reassembled by plant to be used in the manufacturing inventory control system.

The manufacturing and inventory control members of the team developed a statistical safety stock system based on the forecast to cover each item in each warehouse. A similar safety stock was calculated for the central warehouses and used in overall inventory control to take advantage of the fact that the variability of demand at the plants would be less than the sum of variability at the warehouses. The problem of lumpy demands from the warehouses was approached by reducing lot sizes of shipments to conform more closely to actual sales demand and by scheduling regular shipments so that freight costs would not increase.

To test the validity of these system design changes, a computer simulation model was constructed to prove that the various elements were truly integrated and that the predicted inventory and service levels were achievable. It was only at this fairly advanced step that emphasis changed to techniques and systems design. Operations research and inventory control techniques were used but only as methods for treating clearly identified problems, not as overall solutions.

The work of the task force did not stop with the development of the solution to the distribution inventory and service problem. Previous analysis had shown that the manufacturing systems could not support even the smoothed demand from the warehouses at certain periods of the year. A new manufacturing and planning system was designed to shorten lead times and to plan capacity on an overall basis so that inventory could be built during slack periods in anticipation of peak demand.

It is obviously essential that manufacturing and distribution work from the same information, but in this step the concept of integrated operations was carried further to raise the question of whether the manufacturing operations could provide the product after they had the proper information. If this last step had not been considered and a new capacity planning and scheduling system designed, much of the previous work would have been for naught.

The changes recommended by the task force were implemented over a period of about one year. The work during the implementation included programming and testing of new computer systems, training of users, and parallel testing of new systems along with old. The impact of the changes was dramatic. Inventories were reduced by 15 percent or almost $8 million. Back orders were reduced from a peak of $500,000 to a more normal level of $10,000 to $20,000. Customer complaints dropped substantially, and operating costs were reduced by more than $300,000 per year, excluding the savings from reduced inventories and improved service.

SOURCE: Stephen B. Oresman and Charles D. Scudder, "A Remedy for Maldistribution," *Business Horizons,* Vol. 19 (June, 1974), pp. 66 and 69.

EXHIBIT 4–4   Signs of Maldistribution

① *INVENTORIES THAT TURN SLOWLY.* Distribution inventories should turn between six and twelve times per year in most companies except in unusual product situations; distribution inventories that turn less than six times per year are a frequent sign of control problems.

② *POOR CUSTOMER SERVICE.* Inventory investment equal to about two months of sales should provide about 99 percent service. Investment of about half this amount should provide about 90 percent service. Failure to achieve these levels of results can mean that the inventory is in the wrong products, the wrong location, or both.

③ *INTERWAREHOUSE SHIPMENTS.* Because stock transfers require double handling, distribution managers rarely transship except in emergencies. A significant amount of interwarehouse transfers is a sign of a system in continual trouble.

④ *PREMIUM FREIGHT CHARGES.* A distribution system that relies on premium freight is in trouble for the same reasons. Cost savings are usually significant when the problem is corrected.

SOURCE: Stephen B. Oresman and Charles D. Scudder, "A Remedy for Maldistribution," *Business Horizons*, Vol. 19 (June, 1974), p. 72.

Furthermore, management may also be wise to undertake an evaluation of PD activities whenever there is a noteworthy change in corporate strategy or structure. The checklist provided in Exhibit 4–5 is a useful starting point for determining when an evaluation is worthwhile.

SUMMARY AND CONCLUSIONS

Physical distribution management is a critical factor in the effective and efficient marketing of all products. However, the costs of activities associated with the flow of physical possession are surprisingly high—so high, in fact, that efforts must be expended to reduce them if distributive firms are to reach their profit goals, particularly during economic periods when sales are growing at very slow rates. Underlying effective and efficient physical distribution management is the physical distribution (PD) concept. This concept takes a cost-service orientation that is aimed at minimizing the costs of

EXHIBIT 4–5   Checklist Method for Determining Whether or Not a Distribution Evaluation Is Worthwhile

When Is an Evaluation Worthwhile?

✓ When the company makes a significant change in its marketing strategy (for example, going direct versus selling to wholesalers).

✓ When the size of the company changes significantly.

✓ When new businesses or products are added to the distribution system.

✓ When the company's geographic mix of shipments changes appreciably.

✓ When five to ten years have passed since the last evaluation.

✓ When any of the four signs of maldistribution shown in Exhibit 4–4 appear.

SOURCE: Stephen B. Oresman and Charles D. Scudder, "A Remedy for Maldistribution," *Business Horizons*, Vol. 19 (June, 1974), p. 72.

distribution at a given level of customer service. The tenets in the concept can be achieved only through a coordinated systemwide physical distribution network.

Developing a PD system should begin with a determination of customer service standards. Arriving at an appropriate customer service standard may involve applying a physical distribution service (PDS) decision model which concentrates on the formulation of PDS packages that are congruent with customers' perceived needs for PD services. Once an optimal PDS package is decided upon, management can then undertake a selection of the warehousing, inventory, and transportation policies that will assure the proper implementation of the desired customer service standards.

The two basic categories of warehouses available to channel members are private facilities, which are either owned or leased by the firm, and public facilities, in which space is rented by the firm. The choice between the two often involves trade-offs between managerial control on the one hand and capital investment on the other. Use of public warehouses appears to be growing rapidly, because the public warehousing industry is becoming more sophisticated in the scope and performance of a wide variety of distributive services. For firms having private warehouses, the development of distribution centers has emerged as a major service factor in physical distribution management. Clearly, the widespread application of data processing technology has significantly increased the ability of warehousing operations of all types to meet the needs of the firms they serve. Determining the number and location of warehouses is a problem the manager faces, irrespective of the private versus public decision. A total cost approach is required, because the solution demands trade-offs among all physical distribution costs and especially those costs associated with warehouse operation, transportation, inventory, and lost sales resulting from slow service.

Inventory management and control will always play a vital role in the operation of firms directly involved in distribution; however, its significance is even more salient in periods of shortages, slow economic growth, and high interest rates. Inventory control encompasses decisions over how much and when to order as well as how much inventory to keep in stock. The objective of inventory control is to minimize total inventory cost subject to demand and service constraints. In order to determine when to reorder, it is first necessary to know projected demand, delivery lead times, and the length of review periods. The reorder point is reached when the overall projected demand (including demand during the lead time) is greater than the amount available in inventory. The decision on how much to order is primarily a function of demand, the order processing cost, and inventory carrying cost.

Critical to decisions on when and how much to order is an accurate sales forecast. The forecasting model used depends on whether customer demand can be categorized as regular and highly predictable, irregular but mathematically consistent, or irregular and unpredictable. Exponential smoothing models are frequently used by manufacturers and wholesalers, because the demand facing them is generally not highly volatile. Retailers, though, often face fluctuating or, at the least, highly seasonal demand patterns. Therefore, adaptive forecasting is needed to cope with the latter's inventory problems. Furthermore, given the fact that sales forecasts are subject to error, controls must be established so that these errors do not lead to a reduction in customer service standards. In order to minimize stockouts at a reasonable cost to the firm, it is necessary to utilize a standard error of the estimate so that appropriate levels of safety stock can be established.

Problems in transporting merchandise can create difficulties in maintaining proper inventory levels and can impair customer service. Therefore, selection of suitable transportation modes is an integral part of developing a sound PD system. To a large extent, rail, highway, water, air, and pipeline networks each have elements of comparative advantage for different shippers and receivers. However, it appears that highway and air transport are becoming more important, even though rail is still the major means of freight movement in the United States. Increasingly, though, combinations of the various modes are being used. Aided by various transportation agencies, such as freight forwarders, the existing transportation system in the United States presents channel members with a myriad of reasonably efficient transport choices.

A key component in the development of coordinated PD systems is information relative to each of the PD activity areas. To assure the continuous supply of relevant data, managers should design a logistical information system. Once an appropriate information system is functioning, mathematical techniques, such as simulation, can be applied to aid in solving system-wide logistical problems. Even with sophisticated techniques, however, "maldistribution" is still common in many industries. Approaches must, therefore, be developed in which evaluations of PD systems will be made as soon as indications of "maldistribution" appear.

The information on physical distribution management provided in this chapter combined with the discussion of retailing and wholesaling in Chapters 2 and 3 form the background necessary to begin an exploration of why marketing channels have emerged as well as an examination of theories explaining the changes that have taken place within them over time. The next chapter is, therefore, devoted to these subjects.

DISCUSSION QUESTIONS

1. What is systems analysis and why is it so useful an approach for managing physical distribution activities?

2. The physical distribution manager has been called "a manager of trade-offs." Explain what this means.

3. Suppose that a firm currently offers the following elements of PDS at the indicated levels and has decided to evaluate how customers view the proposed changes in these levels.

Service Area	Service Level	
	Current	Proposed
Average order cycle time (OCT)—rush orders	72 hours	48 hours
OCT variability—regular orders	+3 days	+1 day
Order placement methods	phone call to salesmen	call to plant via incoming WATTS line
Price ($/unit)	$49	$50

a. How many feasible PDS packages are there to be considered?
b. How can the most appropriate combination be systematically determined?
c. In this example, other PDS elements are explicitly or implicitly held constant.

Add two additional service areas to the example above and suggest hypothetical "current" and "proposed" service levels. Then, develop two PDS packages incorporating the new and "old" areas and discuss which package is likely to be more appealing to you if you were a buyer for a grocery store chain responsible for canned goods purchases. What assumptions did you make in arriving at your answer?

4. Compare and contrast private ownership of storage space with rented storage space with reference to:
   a. The services that can be obtained with each.
   b. The cost of storage.
   c. The degree of administrative control.
   d. The flexibility for meeting future uncertainties.

5. Assume that you are employed by a retailing firm. What are the trade-offs involved in obtaining delivery in three to four days of a given item from a wholesaler versus delivery in three to four weeks from the manufacturer?

6. The following estimates are made about a certain inventory item:
   Demand: 100 units per week
   Inventory carrying cost: 20 percent
   Order costs: $20 per order
   Item value: $20
   Lead time: 1.5 weeks
Determine the order quantity and reorder point. What would you need to know in order to calculate appropriate levels of safety stocks for the above example?

7. Suppose you are given the following data:

Period	Demand	Forecast (stock)	Overstock/ Understock
1	520	520	0
2	500		
3	470		
4	620		

   a. Compute forecasts for periods 2, 3, and 4 using (1) a simple unweighted average; (2) exponential smoothing where weight $(\alpha) = 0.8$.
   b. Compute the average over-/understock.
   c. Explain which forecasting method is superior and why.

8. Contrast the following in terms of speed, reliability, availability, and cost of service.
   a. Truck and rail
   b. Rail and inland water
   c. Piggyback and truck
   d. Piggyback and rail
   e. Company-owned trucking with common carrier trucking
   f. Air and truck

9. Since transportation is so largely a regulated industry, there is little to be gained by a shipper having experts on his staff in the fields of traffic and transportation. To what extent do you agree with this statement?

10. In what ways may the computer be applied to the process of physical distribution? How may the computer be used to help solve the problems of "maldistribution"?

Appendix

Warehouse Location Models and Solutions

The following is a brief discussion of the most widely quoted warehouse location models.

SIMPLE SINGLE LOCATION MODELS

Arithmetic models for locating storage facilities were among the early approaches to the location problem. The method is based on averaging transportation costs within a predetermined market area, either on a point-to-point basis or through the use of a grid-coordinate. In general, the method used is based on cartesian coordinate and analytic geometry.

Simple single-location models are designed to fit generalized location problems that require equating inbound and outbound transportation costs. The generalized solution is a weighted average of the distance of each demand center from the warehouse with demand volumes taken as weights. A mathematical formulation of the model may take the following form. Let

D_i be the demand volume at market i,
(X_i, Y_i) be the cartesian coordinates of demand (supply) center i,
(X, Y) be the cartesian coordinates of the warehouse to be located,
C be the unit delivery cost expressed as a linear function of distance.

The objective is to locate a warehousing point that minimizes total delivery costs. Or

Minimize

$$TC = C \sum_i D_i \sqrt{(X_i - X)^2 + (Y_i - Y)^2}$$

The coordinates of the warehouse, X and Y, can be found by successive approximation solution technique.[1] However, the single-location models have a number of drawbacks.

[1] Ronald H. Ballou, *Business Logistics Management* (Englewood Cliffs, N.J.: Prentice-Hall, Inc., 1973), p. 233; William R. King, *Quantitative Analysis for Marketing Management* (New York: McGraw-Hill Book Company, 1967), pp. 539-40.

First, the models give an optimal solution only when a perfect symmetry exists in the arrangement of markets and points of supply. Besides, they are based on the unrealistic assumptions that there is a linear relationship between transportation cost and distance and that the revenue generated by a distribution system is independent of the warehouse location.

The latter assumption was relaxed by Bowersox, who introduced the effects of delivery time on revenue generated by the system.[2] However, a more sophisticated approach was developed by Ballou[3] based on a modified version of Mossman and Morton's locational model.[4] The following is a brief discussion of the model.

Mossman and Morton developed a locational model based on two economic factors: elasticity of demand to service, as measured in terms of delivery time, and transportation costs. They were related as follows:

$$TC = \sum_{i=1}^{i=n} Q_{oi}^{-\alpha_i t_i / t_{oi}} [d_i f_i + d^1 f^1]$$

where

TC = the total cost of warehousing system.

Q_{oi} = the quantity demanded in market i with delivery time = 0.

t_i = delivery time in market i for the warehouse being located and is a function of the distance from the warehouse to market i and the speed of the transportation mode used:

$$t_i = \frac{[(X - X_i)^2 + (Y - Y_i)^2]^{1/2}}{V_i}$$

where V_i is the speed of vehicle i

t_{oi} = the competition delivery time in market i.

α_i = a proportionality factor for specific market area and product mix.

d_i = the distance from warehouse to market i; it is determined as:

$$[(X - X_i)^2 + (Y - Y_i)^2]^{1/2}$$

d^1 = the distance from plant (source) location to warehouse.

[2] Donald J. Bowersox, "An Analytical Approach to Warehouse Location," *Handling and Shipping* (February, 1962), pp. 17–20.

[3] Ronald Ballou, *op. cit.*, pp. 235–236.

[4] Frank H. Mossman and Newton Morton, *Logistics of Distribution Systems* (Boston: Allyn and Bacon, Inc., 1965), pp. 245–56.

f_i = the transportation rate from warehouse to market i.

f^1 = the transportation rate from manufacturing point (source) to the warehouse.

The model can be expressed in terms of maximum profit location instead of least total cost by adding the price variable. The idea is to establish a revenue function from which net locational profit can be obtained by subtracting locational costs. The objective, therefore, is to choose the location that maximizes net revenue. Or

maximize

$$\pi = \sum_{i=1}^{n} Q_{oi}{}^{-\alpha_i t_i/t_{oi}} [P_i - d_i f_i - d^1 f^1]^{\dagger}$$

where P_i = the selling price in market i. Again, the values of X, Y, the cartesian coordinates of the warehouse location, can be found by successive approximation technique.

MULTIPLE LOCATION MODELS

Single warehouse location models can be extended to provide for more than one warehouse when the location of the first is known and fixed. However, a direct extension of the single-location model to the case of locating multiple facilities has been developed by Ballou[5] in the following manner.

Given m number of warehouses to be located and n number of supply and demand points, then by letting V_{ij} be the volume flowing from plant i to warehouse j (or from warehouse i to demand location j), R_{ij} be the respective transportation rate per unit of distance, and $X_i Y_i$ be the cartesian coordinate of the supply and demand points, the total cost function to be minimized can be expressed as:

$$TC = \sum_{j=i}^{m} \sum_{i=1}^{n} V_{ij} R_{ij} K [(\bar{X}_j - X_i)^2 + (\bar{Y}_j - Y_i)^2]^{1/2}$$

where K is a constant to convert coordinate-based distances to miles, and $\bar{X}_j$, $\bar{Y}_j$, are the location coordinates for the warehouses, which are respectively equal to:

$$\bar{X}_j^{k+1} = \frac{\displaystyle\sum_{i=1}^{n} V_{ij} R_{ij} X_i/D_{ij}^k}{\displaystyle\sum_{i=1}^{n} V_{ij} R_{ij}/D_{ij}^k} \qquad j = 1, 2, \ldots, m$$

---

†This is a slightly different formulation of the model that assumes one plant supplying i markets.

[5] Ronald Ballou, *op. cit.*, pp. 239-242.

and

$$\bar{Y}_j^{k+1} = \frac{\displaystyle\sum_{i=1}^{n} V_{ij}R_{ij}\,Y_i/D_{ij}^k}{\displaystyle\sum_{i=1}^{n} V_{ij}R_{ij}/D_{ij}^k}$$

where

$$D_{ij} = [(\bar{X}_j - X_i)^2 + (\bar{Y}_j - Y_i)^2]^{1/2}$$

The superscript k is the iteration number. Since the method gives the best location for a given prespecified number of warehouses and supply and demand locations, and since the number of warehouses provided may not be optimal, the solution procedure must be repeated for alternate numbers of warehouses and supply-demand locations.[6] Yet such extension of the single-location models is limited in scope and application, because it requires a predefinition of the territories to be served from each warehouse location. Besides, the method may not yield the optimum set of warehouse locations, since the effect of cost nonlinearities was not considered.

Although the model presented above was extended later by Leon Cooper[7] to accommodate the cost nonlinearity effect, Cooper's model will not be discussed here. Instead, more powerful optimizing techniques for locating multiple warehouses will be presented. It should be noted, however, that since most of those models require a high-speed computer to provide for their solutions, only the basic formulation of the models will be presented.

Bowman-Stewart Model

The basic objective underlying the Bowman-Stewart formulation of the multiple-facility location problem[8] is that of determining the optimum area to be served by a distribution warehouse and consequently the number of warehouses needed. The concept is to find the optimum area that minimizes the cost per dollar's worth of goods distributed through the warehouse. It is assumed that warehousing and handling costs vary inversely with volume, that delivery costs vary directly with the square root of the area served, and that other costs are fixed with respect to volume and areas. The treatment of delivery costs is based on the geometric principle that radius and diameter vary directly

[6] *Ibid.*, p. 240.

[7] Leon Cooper, "An Extension of the Generalized Weber Problem," *Journal of Regional Science*, Vol. 8, No. 2 (1968), pp. 181–197.

[8] Edward H. Bowman and John B. Stewart, "A Model for Scale of Operations," *Journal of Marketing*, Vol. 20 (January 1956), pp. 242–247.

with the square root of the area of a circle. The mathematical expression of the model is as follows:

$$C = a + \frac{b}{V} + c\sqrt{A}$$

where

C = cost per dollar's worth of goods distributed (a measure of efficiency).

V = the volume of goods in dollars handled by the warehouse per unit time.

A = the area in square miles served by the warehouse.

a = the cost per dollar's worth of goods distributed independent of volume and area.

b = a "fixed" cost for the warehouse per unit of time.

c = the cost of the delivery, which varies with the square root of the area.

Bowman and Stewart used the method of least squares multiple regression to estimate the model's parameters, a, b, and c. Next, by letting k be a sales density index expressed in terms of dollar volume per square mile $(k = V/a)$, the cost-minimizing area A was found by direct mathematical manipulation to be $A = (2b/ck)^{2/3}$. Once A, the area served by the warehouse, is found, the distant customer location that can be served from a given warehouse is determined by the formula for the radius of a circle, $r = (A/\pi)^{1/2}$. James Heskett and others[9] have noted that the Bowman-Stewart formulation could be amended to include considerations of customer service by introducing different hypothetical levels of transportation costs. For example, high values for transportation costs could be used in areas where customer service is extremely important.

Napolitan's Model

The objectives of the model constructed by Napolitan[10] were to determine the number of branch warehouses, their locations, and the area that should be served by each branch warehouse. The mathematical statement of the model was:

$$f(x) = C_1 X_1 + C_2 X_2 + C_3 X_3 + C_4 X_4$$

where

$f(x)$ = total costs under consideration.

---

[9] James L. Heskett, Nicholas A. Glaskowsky, Jr., and Robert M. Ivie, *Business Logistics*, 2nd ed. (New York: The Ronald Press Co., 1973), p. 429.

[10] Arthur W. Napolitan, "Determining Optimum Distribution Points for Economical Warehousing and Transportation," *Managing the Materials Functions*, American Management Association, Report 35, 1959, pp. 76–82.

$C_1 X_1$ = the cost attributable to sales lost because of distance from branches (customer service).

$C_2 X_2$ = the cost of operating branches (branch model).

$C_3 X_3$ = transportation costs from central warehouse(s) to branches (inbound transportation).

$C_4 X_4$ = transportation costs from branches to customers (outbound transportation).

Each cost factor was determined on the basis of the company's past experience. The total cost function was then minimized through the use of combinatorial programming techniques, so that the optimum solution might be found.

Mathematical Programming

Linear Programming. Linear programming is a mathematical technique for obtaining the optimal solution to problems that can be put in a particular structural form. Two crucial technological and economic assumptions underlie the mathematical formulation of linear programming models: divisibility and additivity.

The method of linear programming has been applied to a variety of problems, of which one of the most notable is the so-called transportation problem. Because of its applicability to warehouse location problems, the transportation model of linear programming will be discussed below.

a. The Transportation Method

A typical statement of the problem is that given m supply sources (warehouses or plants) and n demand sources (warehouses or customers), how can the demand at each demand center be satisfied at minimum total transportation cost?

A mathematical formulation of the problem can take the following form:

minimize

$$\sum_{i=1}^{m} \sum_{j=1}^{n} C_{ij} X_{ij}$$

subject to

$$\sum_{j=1}^{n} X_{ij} = S_i \quad i = 1, 2, \ldots, m \text{ (supply)}$$

$$\sum_{i=1}^{m} X_{ij} = D_j \quad j = 1, 2, \ldots, n \text{ (demand)}$$

$$\sum_{i=1}^{m} S_i = \sum_{j=1}^{n} D_j$$

and

$$X_{ij} \geqslant 0 \text{ for all } i \text{ and } j$$

Here X_{ij} is the quantity shipped from warehouse or supply center i to demand center j; C_{ij} is the unit transportation rate between i and j. The solution to the problem as formulated above can be sought by applying the simplex algorithm. The method can be repeatedly applied to a set of m possible warehouse locations at a time, until the optimal number and locations of the distribution warehouses are found. The solution method, which is usually represented in a tabular form, can be found in any standard textbook on linear programming.

A major advantage of the technique presented above is that, once a model is constructed, it provides the framework for the systematic evaluation of the distribution costs associated with alternative sets of warehouse sites. On the other hand, one can question the applicability of linear programming techniques to real-life problems. The size and nonlinearities involved in many problems are such that application of the method as presented is not currently feasible. The basic sources of nonlinearities generally encountered are the fixed costs of warehouse operation and the nonlinear variable warehousing and delivery costs.[11]

Heskett, et al.[12] have considered three basic approaches for dealing with the problem of nonlinearity. "First, cost curves have been examined to determine whether they approximate linearity over certain segments. . . . Second, nonlinear programming techniques have been developed which attempt to describe nonlinear cost functions by specially fitted equation. . . . Third, attempts have been made to modify the effects of linear programming by combining its use with nonlinear problem elements." An example of the third approach is that of Baumol and Wolfe formulation of the warehouse location problem. Their model will be discussed below.

b. The Baumol-Wolfe Model [13]

The model presented by Baumol and Wolfe was designed to find an optimum set of warehouse locations from a finite alternative set of warehouse sites. The objective was to

---

[11]Alfred A. Kuehn and Michael J. Hamburger, "A Heuristic Program for Locating Warehouses," *Management Science* (July 1963), p. 103.

[12]Heskett, et al., *op. cit.*, p. 439.

[13]William J. Baumol and Philip Wolfe, "A Warehouse Location Problem," *Operations Research* (March–April, 1958), pp. 252–263.

minimize the total shipping costs from m factories to q retail locations via n warehouses. The model was:

minimize

$$\Sigma_{i,j,k} \; C_{ijk} \, (X_{ijk})$$

subject to

$$\Sigma_{i,k} \, X_{ijk} = Q_i$$
$$\Sigma_{i,k} \, A_{ijk} \, (X_{ijk}) \leqslant R_j$$
$$\Sigma_{i,j} \, X_{ijk} = S_k$$

and

$$X_{ijk} \geqslant 0 \text{ for all } i, j, \text{ and } k$$

where

X_{ijk} = the quantity shipped from factory i $(i = 1, 2, \ldots, m)$ via warehouse j $(j = 1, 2, \ldots, n)$, to retailer location k $(k = 1, 2, \ldots, q)$.

$C_{ijk} \, (X_{ijk})$ = the cost of shipping the quantity X_{ijk} including the relevant inventory cost.

Q_i = the quantity shipped from plant i.

R_j = the capacity of warehouse j.

S_k = the quantity demanded at destination k.

$A_{ijk} \, (X_{ij}k)$ = the amount of inventory that will be held as a result of the flow X_{ijk}.

    Baumol and Wolfe handled the nonlinearities in the system by altering the cost objective function to be approximated by the nonlinear expression:

$$\Sigma_{i,j,k} \, K_{ijk} \, X_{ijk} + \Sigma_j W_j \, (\Sigma_{i,k} \, X_{ijk})^q + \Sigma_j V_j r_j \quad\quad (0 < q < i)$$

where K_{ijk} is the cost of transportation and handling per unit of X_{ijk}, W_j is the cost of storage per unit per period, $r_j = 1$ if $\Sigma_{i,k} X_{ijk} > 0$, and $r_j = 0$ otherwise, Σr_j is the number of warehouses used, and V is the administrative cost to the renting firm per warehouse employed. Baumol and Wolfe noted that their cost function is a "concave" one, and that no optimum values of the variables can be found by standard computational methods. However, the authors have used an iterative or recursive type of computation to find a local optimum in the sense that no individual unit of product can be shipped by an alternate route without increasing total distribution costs. The iterative procedure used by the authors requires the solution of an ordinary transportation problem at each stage.

In a later article, Kuehn and Hamburger[14] have pointed out that the Baumol and Wolfe formulation did not include effects of delay in delivery times on customer demand and dealt only with one product or a composite fixed mix of products. The authors have also criticized the linear programming technique proposed by Baumol and Wolfe on the grounds that it leads to the use of more warehouses than is necessary, which increases the cost of logistics significantly.

In the same context, Heskett, et al.,[15] have proposed that "if an added weighting were to be introduced to warehouse-to-customer transportation costs in order to reflect opportunity costs associated with the effect of shipping delays on customer demand, it is likely that much of the claimed bias would be eliminated."

Dynamic Programming. The warehouse location models presented above, as well as the majority of the more sophisticated models developed over the last two decades, are of a static nature in the sense that they have failed to consider the effect of changes in the market conditions over time. Although changes can periodically be introduced to locational strategies, they are usually highly expensive. An alternative way of infusing a time dimension into locational strategies is to formulate present decisions in such a way as to take into consideration various alternative policies and actions, and to aim at minimizing total distribution costs over the entire planning horizon. This concept was emphasized by Kotler,[16] who stated that a "physical distribution system must be designed not for maximum economy for the present so much as maximum flexibility for the future, even if present costs must be a little higher in order to gain this flexibility. The system must be planned with an awareness of future company product and marketing strategy."

To account for this factor, Ronald Ballou[17] has recently applied dynamic programming techniques to the problem of locating and relocating warehousing systems. His model was based on Mossman and Morton's static model for locating terminals as discussed earlier in this appendix. Ballou's model is discussed below.

The method of dynamic programming is a mathematical technique designed to solve decision problems. The technique is formalized by referring to stages, states, optimal decision rules, and optimal policies. The method of solution is to divide the total problem into a number of subproblems in such a way that an optimal policy can be found. Such policy "has the property that whatever the initial state and initial decision are, the remaining decisions must constitute an optimal policy with regard to the state resulting from the first decision."[18]

[14] Kuehn and Hamburger, *op. cit.*, pp. 104-105.

[15] Heskett, et al., *op. cit.*, p. 443.

[16] Philip Kotler, *Marketing Decision Making: A Model Building Approach* (New York: Holt, Rinehart, and Winston, 1971), p. 605.

[17] Ronald Ballou, "Dynamic Warehouse Location Analysis," *Journal of Marketing Research*, Vol. 5 (August, 1968), pp. 271-276.

[18] R. E. Bellman, *Dynamic Programming* (Princeton: Princeton University Press, 1957), p. 83.

Ballou's dynamic formulation of the warehouse location problem was based on a modified version of Mossman-Morton's model presented earlier, namely:

$$\pi = \sum_{i=1}^{n} Q_{oi}^{-\alpha_i t_i/t_{oi}} [P_i^{-d_i f_i - d^1 f^1}]$$

(All variables are as defined above.) If the levels of the various variables included in the model can be forecast over a relatively longer period of time for a number of *selected* warehouse locations, the result will be as those depicted in Table 4A-1.

Table 4A-1 shows the discounted expected profits for five selected possible locations over a period of five years. (The profit values have been discounted at 20 percent to facilitate comparison over time.)

Given this information, an optimal physical distribution strategy can be designed to yield maximum cumulative profit over the planning horizon.

To determine the optimal location and relocation decision over the planning period, let us assume that there is a penalty cost of relocating a warehouse operation of $100,000 (discounted at 20 percent per year). The following algorithm can be useful in finding optimal solution:

1. Subtract each entry in each column from the highest valued entry in that column.

The resulting matrix will be the opportunity cost matrix in the sense that it shows the profit loss resulted from not being at the profit-maximizing location.

2. Find the net gain or loss of moving to the optimal location at the beginning of each period. Relocate warehousing operation if profitable.

In this step each opportunity cost associated with not being in the optimal location is compared with the cost of relocating to the location at the beginning of each period.

TABLE 4A-1   Projected Discounted Profits for Each Location in Each Year of Planning Period

Warehouse Location Alternative	Year from Present				
	1	2	3	4	5
1	194,600	356,100	623,200	671,100	1,336,000
2	176,500	372,000	743,400	750,000	1,398,200
3	172,300	344,700	836,400	862,200	1,457,600
4	166,700	337,600	756,100	973,300	1,486,600
5	159,400	303,400	715,500	892,800	1,526,000

SOURCE: Ronald Ballou, "Dynamic Warehouse Location Analysis," *Journal of Marketing Research*, Vol. 5 (August, 1968), p. 274.

TABLE 4A-2   Location-relocation Plan for Five-year Planning Period

Warehouse Location Alternative	Year from Present				
	1	2	3	4	5
Relocation Cost	100,000	83,333	69,444	57,870	48,225
1	$0S_1$	$15,900S_1$	$213,200R_3$	$302,200R_4$	$190,000R_5$
2	$18,100S_2$	$0S_2$	$93,000R_3$	$223,300R_4$	$127,800R_5$
3	$22,300S_3$	$27,300S_3$	$0S_3$	$111,100R_4$	$68,400R_5$
4	$27,900S_4$	$34,400S_4$	$80,300R_3$	$0S_4$	$39,400S_4$
5	$35,200S_5$	$68,600S_5$	$120,900R_3$	$80,500R_4$	$0S_5$

3. Start at the last period and move backward to find the optimal location and relocation strategy. Calculate maximum cumulative profit.

Applying the above algorithm to the matrix shown in Table 4A-1, we can construct Table 4A-2.

In Table 4A-2 the symbols S_n and R_n mean "stay at location n" and "relocate to location n," respectively. These strategies were determined as follows: Assume that we start period 1 at location 3. Is it profitable to move to location 1 (the one with maximum profit associated with zero opportunity cost)? The decision to relocate depends on how much profit we are foregoing by locating at location 3 and how much it costs us to relocate to location 1. This can be computed as follows:

$$\text{Opportunity cost of } 3 - \text{Relocation cost}$$

or

$$\$22,300 - \$100,000 = -\$77,700$$

and this means that we should stay at location 3.

Decisions concerning each location are summarized in Table 4A-3. This table shows that the optimal strategy is to locate at location 3 during the first three years and then to relocate to location 4 in years four and five. The maximum cumulative profit will then be

$$\$172,300 + \$344,700 + \$836,400 + \$973,300 + \$1,486,600 - \$57,870 = \$3,755,430$$

Simulation Models: The General Approach

Simulation is essentially a numerical technique that involves setting up a model of a real situation and then performing experiments on the model. The value of simulation techniques in the design of warehouse networks has been advanced by Shycon and

TABLE 4A-3 Decisions Related to Alternative Locations

Warehouse Location Alternative	Year from Present				
	1	2	3	4	5
1	S_1	S_1	R_3	R_4	R_5
2	S_2	S_2	R_3	R_4	R_5
3	S_3	S_3	S_3	R_4	R_5
4	S_4	S_4	R_3	S_4	S_4
5	S_5	S_5	R_3	R_4	S_5

Maffei.[19] Their approach requires that management or a consultant specify the warehouse systems to be evaluated. Therefore, unlike algorithmic location models described above, simulation models require the analyst to supply the locational patterns to be evaluated. The model itself does not seek an overall optimum solution, since the optimum pattern of locations may not be among the supplied patterns.

As was the case with all the techniques presented above, the value of a simulation model in solving warehouse location problems depends upon how realistic the model is and how much time it requires in computation.

Perhaps one of the best-known simulations of a physical distribution system was developed by Harvey Shycon and Richard Maffei for the H. J. Heinz Company.[20] The major distribution cost elements included in the simulation were:

1. Customers' characteristics in terms of customer location, annual demand volume, types of products purchased, and the distribution of the size of orders.

2. Warehousing costs.

3. Location of manufacturing facilities and the kinds of products available at each location.

4. Transportation costs from factories to various warehouses.[21]

The simulation provided answers to the basic warehouse location questions concerning the number, location, and allocation of demand to warehouses. It could handle up to 4000 customers, 40 warehouses, and 10 to 15 factories.

[19] Harvey N. Shycon and Richard B. Maffei, "Simulation—Tool for Better Distribution," *Harvard Business Review*, Vol. 39 (November–December, 1960), pp. 65–75.

[20] *Ibid.*

[21] Martin L. Gerson and Richard B. Maffei, "Technical Characteristics of Distribution Simulators," *Management Science*, Vol. 10 (October, 1963), pp. 62–69.

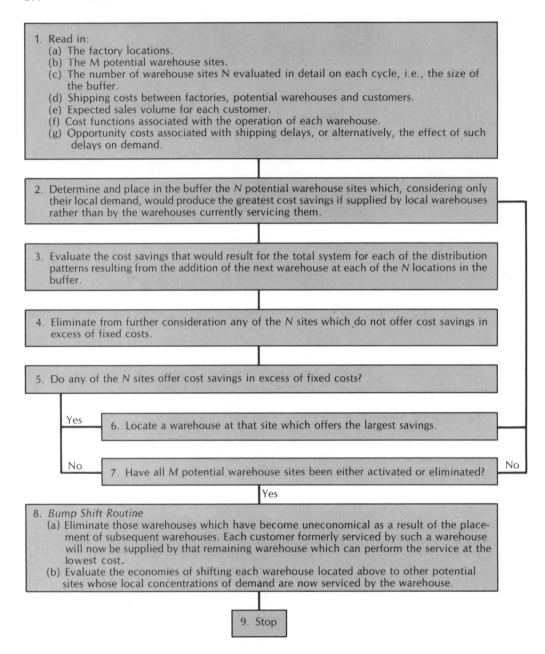

FIGURE 4A-1   Informational Inputs in a Heuristic Program for Locating Warehouses

SOURCE: Alfred A. Kuehn and Michael J. Hamburger, "A Heuristic Program for Locating Warehouses," *Management Science*, Vol. 9 (July, 1963), pp. 643-666.

Heuristic Models

Hinkle and Kuehn have defined the term *heuristic* as "a shortcut process of rea-soning that searches for a satisfactory, rather than an optimal solution."[22] Heuristic programming, therefore, is an approach to problem solving in which the emphasis is on working toward optimum solution procedures rather than optimum solutions.[23]

Kuehn-Hamburger Model. In their approach to the problem of warehouse location, Kuehn and Hamburger have proposed a heuristic program that permits fast screening and evaluation of alternative types of warehouses, transportation systems, and warehouse lo-cation. Three important heuristics were introduced in the program, which are

1. Locations with the greatest promise are those at or near concentrations of de-mand.

2. Near-optimum warehousing systems can be developed if at each stage the ware-house offering the greatest cost savings is added.

3. Only a small subset of all possible warehouse locations needs to be evaluated to determine which warehouse should be added.[24]

The flow diagram explaining information inputs and analytical procedures pro-grammed into the computer is shown in Fig. 4A-1.

[22]Charles L. Hinkle and Alfred A. Kuehn, "Heuristic Models: Mapping the Maze for Management," *California Management Review*, Vol. 10, No. 1 (Fall, 1967), p. 59.

[23]Alfred A. Kuehn and Michael J. Hamburger, "A Heuristic Program for Locating Warehouses," *Man-agement Science*, Vol. 9 (July 1963), pp. 643–666. For an extension of this model, see E. F. Feldman, A. Lehrer, and T. L. Ray, "Warehouse Location Under Continuous Economies of Scale," *Management Science*, Vol. 12 (May 1966), pp. 670–684.

[24]*Ibid.*, p. 645.

FIVE

CHANNEL STRUCTURE
AND
INSTITUTIONAL CHANGE

In the immediately preceding three chapters, the structure and competitive activities of retailing, wholesaling, and logistical institutions have been described. However, the discussion in those chapters was rarely couched in a channel systems context. Rather, focus was on the specific institutional types as opposed to the general task environment in which each type operates. Having a deeper knowledge of the individual components of channel systems is a necessary first step to commencing interorganizational analysis. We are now ready to explore, from a macro perspective, why *channels* of distribution have *emerged*. Once we understand the rationale for the existence of channels, it will then be possible to explain how the various institutions and agencies comprising them are related. In other words, we can attempt to isolate the factors that determine the *structure* of channels. In addition, we can also try to learn why certain seemingly noneconomic channels persist over time.

After providing some explanation for the emergence of channel systems, the structure of channels, and, in some cases, the survivability of supposedly inefficient systems, we can then examine why specific institutions within these systems have altered over time. Although it was shown in the preceding three chapters that the distribution process has undergone certain significant changes over time, no attempt was made to generalize about these movements or to explain them in the context of theories of institutional change. However, such an explanation is highly desirable, especially since the past is often prologue for the future. It is not at all unlikely that certain elements of distributive history will repeat themselves; therefore, it is important to abstract from what has been in order to predict what is probable.

Once an understanding is accomplished relative to the above-mentioned topics, it will then be possible to assess the work of channels, which is the subject of the next chapter.

THE EMERGENCE OF MARKETING CHANNELS

In order to provide an appropriate base for analyzing interorganizational relations in detail, it is important to understand at the outset the underlying reasons for the emergence of channel systems. Here, emphasis is placed on the economic rationale for the existence of channels, because economic reasons are the foremost determinants of commercial structures. Later, it is possible to introduce other determinants, including key technological, political, and social factors, and to examine how these factors influence the makeup or structure of channel systems.

The emergence of channels can be explained in terms of four logically related steps in an economic process, as follows:[1]

1. Intermediaries arise in the process of exchange because they can increase the efficiency of the process.
2. Channel intermediaries arise to adjust the discrepancy of assortments through the performance of the sorting processes.
3. Marketing agencies hang together in channel arrangements to provide for the routinization of transactions.
4. Also, channels exist to facilitate the searching process as well as the sorting process.

Each of these steps is examined below.

The Rationale for Intermediaries

In primitive cultures, most household needs are *produced* within the household. However, at an early stage in the development of economic activities, *exchange* replaced production as a means of satisfying individual needs.

---

[1]The following discussion is based on Wroe Alderson, "Factors Governing the Development of Marketing Channels," in R. M. Clewett (ed.), *Marketing Channels for Manufactured Products* (Homewood, Ill.: Richard D. Irwin, Inc., 1954), pp. 5-22.

The development of exchange is facilitated when there is a surplus in production over current household requirements and when this surplus cannot be held for future consumption because of either the perishable nature of the products or the lack of storage facilities. Thus, if numerous households are able to effect small surpluses of different products, a basis for exchange is developed.

Alderson and Martin have formulated the following law of exchange, which specifies the conditions under which an exchange will take place:[2]

> Given that x is an element of the assortment A_1 and y is an element of the assortment A_2, x is exchangeable for y if, and only if, these three conditions hold:
>
> (a) x is different from y.
> (b) The potency of the assortment A_1 is increased by dropping x and adding y.
> (c) The potency of the assortment A_2 is increased by adding x and dropping y.

These conditions of exchange are more easily met when production becomes specialized and the assortment of goods is broadened. As households find their needs satisfied by an increased quantity and variety of goods, the mechanism of exchange increases in importance.

However, as the importance of exchange increases, so does the difficulty in maintaining *mutual* interactions between *all* households. For example, a small village of only five specialized households would require 10 transactions to carry out *decentralized* exchanges (i.e., exchanges at each production point). This can be shown by calculating the number of necessary transactions for this particular exchange system by using the formula

$$\frac{n(n-1)}{2}$$

where n is the number of producers, each of which specializes in the production of one product. In order to reduce the complexity of this exchange system and thus facilitate transactions, intermediaries appear in the process. Through the operation of a central market, one dealer can considerably reduce the number of transactions. In the preceding example, only five transactions would be required to carry out a *centralized* exchange since, in a

---

[2]Wroe Alderson and Miles W. Martin, "Toward a Formal Theory of Transactions and Transvections," in Bruce E. Mallen (ed.), *The Marketing Channel: A Conceptual Viewpoint* (New York: John Wiley & Sons, Inc., 1967), pp. 50-51.

central market system operated by one dealer, the number of necessary transactions is equal to *n*. This conception of decentralized versus centralized exchange is illustrated in Fig. 5–1.

Implicit in the above example is the notion that a decentralized system of exchange is less efficient than a centralized network employing intermediaries. More specifically, the relative advantage can be demonstrated by de-

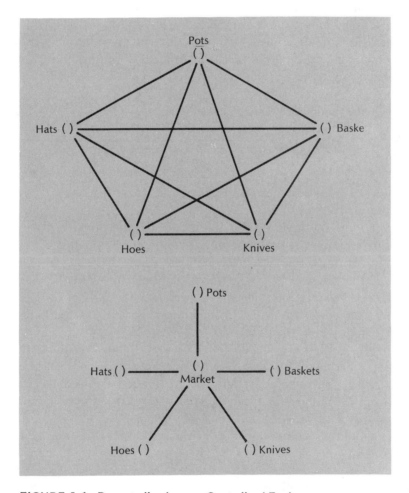

FIGURE 5-1   Decentralized versus Centralized Exchange

SOURCE: Wroe Alderson, "Factors Governing the Development of Marketing Channels," in *Marketing Channels for Manufactured Products,* ed. Richard M. Clewett (Homewood, Ill.: Richard D. Irwin, Win., 1954), p. 7.

termining the *ratio of intermediary advantage*, which is expressed by the formula

$$\frac{n-1}{2}$$

where, again, n is the number of specialized producers. Therefore, in our example of five households, the ratio of advantage of the centralized exchange through one intermediary is 2.

Furthermore, the advantage of an intermediary becomes more evident as the number of specialized producers increases. For example, if we have 50 specialized producers,

$$\text{Number of decentralized transactions} = \frac{n(n-1)}{2} = \frac{50(50-1)}{2} = 1225$$

$$\text{Ratio of intermediary advantage} = \frac{n-1}{2} = \frac{50-1}{2} = 24.5$$

Thus, as the number of producers increased from five to 50, the ratio of intermediary advantage increased from 2 to 24.5.

The same rationale can be applied to direct selling from manufacturers to retailers relative to selling through wholesalers. Figure 5–2 shows that, given four manufacturers and ten retailers who buy goods from each manufacturer, the number of contact lines amounts to 40. If the manufacturers sell to these retailers through one wholesaler, the number of necessary contacts is reduced to 14. The ratio of intermediary advantage here is approximately 3. However, the number of necessary contacts increases dramatically as more wholesalers are added. For example, if the four manufacturers in the example above used two wholesalers, the number of contacts rises from 14 to 28, and if four wholesalers are used, the number of contacts will be 56. Thus, employing more and more intermediaries is subject to diminishing returns simply from a *contactual* efficiency perspective.

It should also be noted that, in this simple illustration, the cost of any two contact lines of transaction, i.e., manufacturer-wholesaler, wholesaler-retailer, manufacturer-retailer, is assumed to be the same. Also, it is assumed that whenever more than one wholesaler is employed by a manufacturer, each retailer will avail himself of the services of each of these wholesalers. Obviously, accounting must be made for differences between direct and indirect communication costs, in the effectiveness and efficiency of the institutions involved in the transaction, and in the quality of the contact between the various channel members.

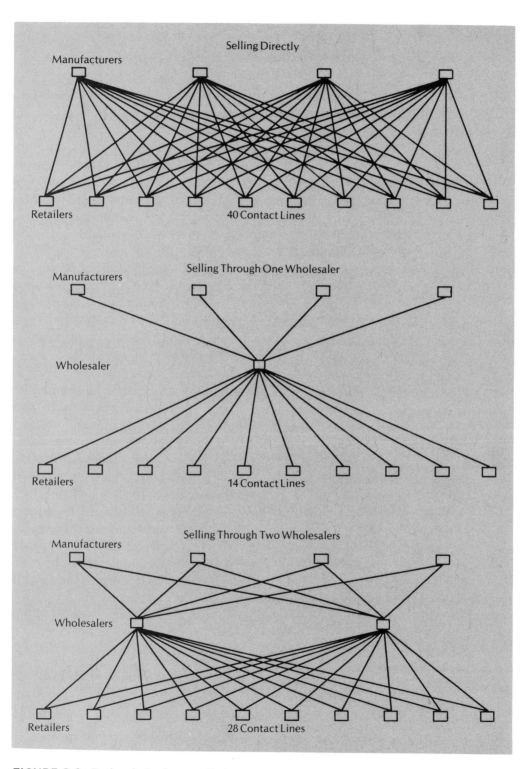

FIGURE 5-2 Rationale for Intermediaries

The Discrepancy of Assortment and Sorting

In addition to increasing the efficiency of transactions, intermediaries smooth the flow of goods and services by creating possession, place, and time utilities. These utilities enhance the potency of the consumer's assortment. One aspect of this "smoothing" process requires that intermediaries engage in the performance of a "sorting" function. This procedure is necessary in order to bridge the *discrepancy* between the assortment of goods and services generated by the producer and the assortment demanded by the consumer. The discrepancy results from the fact that manufacturers typically produce a large quantity of a limited variety of goods, whereas consumers usually desire only a limited quantity of a wide variety of goods.

Categorically, discrepancies in the market exist in terms of space, time, perception, ownership, and valuation.[3] *Spatial* separation is created by the distance between producers and consumers. Increases in specialization and mass production require wider and larger markets, thus making exchange on a local basis insufficient. As a result, regional, national, and international markets must be found for the increasing variety and quantity of goods. *Temporal* discrepancy is created by the lack of synchronism between the production and consumption of goods, yet this discrepancy must be bridged in order for supplies to be available at times when they are demanded. There is always a *perceptual* separation between producers and consumers in a market, because consumers do not know about supply sources and producers do not know where consumers are. In this sense, perception refers to both ignorance and inertia; the separation can, therefore, be closed through the dissemination of information and the use of persuasion. Even when fully informed and motivated makers and users of goods and services are brought together, no exchange is completed until the separation of *ownership* is closed, that is, until the title of ownership is conveyed. Allied to this separation of ownership is the discrepancy of *values* placed upon the good or service by producer and consumer. Intermediaries provide a means for adjusting value to meet the needs of both suppliers and consumers.

The sorting function performed by intermediaries includes the following activities:

1. *Sorting out.* Breaking down a heterogeneous supply into separate stocks which are relatively homogeneous. (Sorting out is typified by the grading of agricultural products.)

[3]W. McInnes, "A Conceptual Approach to Marketing," in Reavis S. Cox, Wroe Alderson, and Stanley Shapiro (eds.), *Theory in Marketing*, 2nd Series (Homewood, Ill.: Richard D. Irwin, Inc., 1964), p. 59.

2. *Accumulation.* Bringing similar stocks together into a larger homogeneous supply.

3. *Allocation.* Breaking a homogeneous supply down into smaller and smaller lots. (Allocating at the wholesale level is referred to as "breaking bulk." Goods received in carloads are sold in case lots. A buyer of case lots in turn sells individual units. The allocation processes generally coincide with geographical dispersal and successive changes in ownership.)

4. *Assorting.* Building up the assortment of products for use in association with each other. (Wholesalers build assortments of goods for retailers, and retailers build assortments for their customers.)[4]

While sorting out and accumulation predominate in the marketing of agricultural and extractive products, allocation and sorting predominate in the marketing of finished manufactured goods. It should be noted that the discrepancy of assortment induces specialization in the exchange process, and the need for such specialization may impede the vertical integration of marketing agencies. For example, a manufacturer of a limited line of hardware items could open his own retail outlets only if he were willing to accumulate the wide variety of items generally sold through those outlets. In general, hardware wholesalers can perform such services more efficiently than can individual manufacturers.

Routinization

Each transaction involves valuation of and payment for goods and services. The buyer and seller must agree to the amount, mode, and timing of payment. The cost of distribution can be minimized if the transactions are routinized; otherwise, every transaction would be subject to bargaining with a concomitant loss of efficiency.

Moreover, routinization facilitates the development of the exchange system. It leads to standardization of goods and services whose performance characteristics can be easily compared and assessed. It encourages production of items that are more highly valued. In fact, exchange relationships between buyers and sellers are standardized so that lot size, frequency of delivery and payment, and communication are routinized. Because of routinization, a sequence of marketing agencies is able to hang together in a

---

[4]Other authors have described the "sorting" processes alternatively as "concentration, equalization, and dispersion" and "collecting, sorting, and dispersing." See Rayburn D. Tousley, Eugene Clark, and Fred E. Clark, *Principles of Marketing* (New York: The Macmillan Company, 1962), pp. 7 and 8; and Roland S. Vaile, E. T. Grether, and Reavis Cox, *Marketing in the American Economy* (New York: The Ronald Press Co., 1952), pp. 134–150, respectively.

channel arrangement. Without routinization activities, marketing channels cannot exist.

Searching

Buyers and sellers are engaged in a double search process in the marketplace. The process of search involves uncertainty, since producers are not certain of consumers' needs and consumers are not certain that they will be able to find what they are looking for. If the search is successful, it leads to the completion of the sorting processes of allocation and assorting. Marketing channels facilitate the process of searching as when, for example, wholesale and retail institutions are organized by separate lines of trade.

CHANNEL STRUCTURE

Although the basic economic rationale for the emergence of channels can be understood in terms of the need for exchange and exchange efficiency, minimization of assortment discrepancies, routinization, and the facilitation of search procedures, such a rationale provides little information as to why channels, such as the one for air conditioning equipment depicted in Chapter 1, are structured one way or another to satisfy this need. A few of the wide variety of possible alternative institutional arrangements are shown in Figs. 5-3 and 5-4. The structure of the channels used by a manufacturer of electrical wire and cable is portrayed in Fig. 5-5. It should be noted, however, that a limitation of all three figures is the omission of logistical institutions and the numerous agencies that facilitate the marketing flows, such as advertising firms and commercial lending institutions.

To explain the key elements determining how channels are structured, Bucklin has developed a rather elaborate theory, the rudiments of which are outlined briefly here.[5] In essence, Bucklin argues that the separation of production from consumption, because of the economic rules of specialization, necessitates the performance of the various marketing functions or flows. These are operationally expressed through a series of service outputs. Industrial or household consumers can provide these service outputs themselves,

---

[5] Louis P. Bucklin, *A Theory of Distribution Channel Structure* (Berkeley, California: IBER Special Publications, 1966). Much of the paraphrasing of Bucklin's model has been drawn from Michael Etgar, *An Empirical Analysis of the Motivations for the Development of Centrally Coordinated Vertical Marketing Systems: The Case of the Property and Casualty Insurance Industry*, an unpublished Ph.D. dissertation, The University of California at Berkeley, 1974, pp. 95–97.

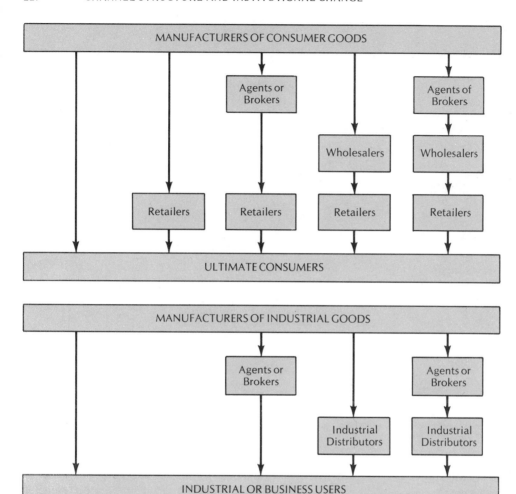

FIGURE 5-3   Alternative Channel Arrangements or Structures

SOURCE: Theodore N. Beckman, William R. Davidson, and W. Wayne Talarzyk, *Marketing*, 9th ed. (New York: The Ronald Press, 1973), p. 209.

or they can buy them from commercial channel members. Consequently, marketing channels that provide higher levels of service outputs reduce consumers' search, waiting time, storage, and other costs by lessening their involvement with the actual accomplishment of these necessary activities. Other things being equal (especially price), consumers will prefer to deal with a marketing channel that provides a higher level of service outputs.

Bucklin has specified four service outputs: (1) spatial convenience (or market decentralization), (2) lot size, (3) waiting or delivery time, and (4)

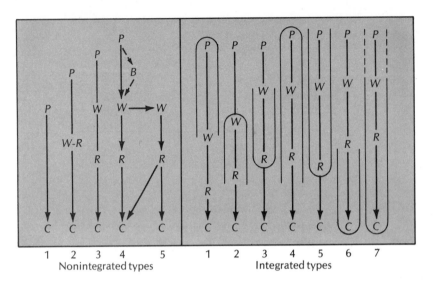

P—Producer.	Nos. 1 and 4—Producer-owned or controlled.
R—Retailer.	No. 2—Wholesaler-owned or controlled.
B—Broker or selling agent.	Nos. 3 and 5—Retailer-owned or controlled.
W—Wholesaler.	Nos. 6 and 7—Consumer-owned and operated.
C—Consumer.	

FIGURE 5-4 Progression from Simple to Complex Channels for Ultimate
Consumers' goods

SOURCE: David A. Revzan, *Wholesaling in Marketing Organizations* (New York: John
Wiley & Sons, Inc., 1961), p. 115. Reprinted by permission of the author.

product variety (or assortment breadth).[6] Spatial convenience provided by
market decentralization of wholesale and/or retail outlets increases consumers' satisfaction by reducing transportation requirements and search
costs. Similarly, the number of units to be purchased at each transaction can
obviously affect the industrial or household consumer's welfare. When the

[6]Bucklin, *op. cit.*, pp. 7-10 and Louis P. Bucklin, *Competition and Evolution in the Distributive
Trades* (Englewood Cliffs, N.J.: Prentice-Hall, Inc., 1972), pp. 18-31. Clearly, the list of service outputs provided to consumers by a channel can be expanded to include provision of credit, maintenance
of product quality, availability of information, stability of supply, availability of personal service and
attention, and risk reduction, among others. For exposition purposes, however, the discussion here is
limited to the four major service outputs suggested by Bucklin in the monograph and book listed
above. For further elaboration on this subject, see Louis P. Bucklin and James M. Carman, "Vertical
Market Structure Theory and the Health Care Delivery System," in Jagdish N. Sheth and Peter L.
Wright (eds.), *Marketing Analysis for Societal Problems* (Urbana, Ill.: University of Illinois Bureau of
Economic and Business Research, 1974), pp. 7-21; Lee E. Preston and Norman R. Collins, *Studies in a
Simulated Market* (Berkeley, California: University of California Institute of Business and Economic
Research, 1966); and Christina Fulop, *Competition for Consumers* (London: Allen and Unwin, Ltd.,
1964), Chapter 2.

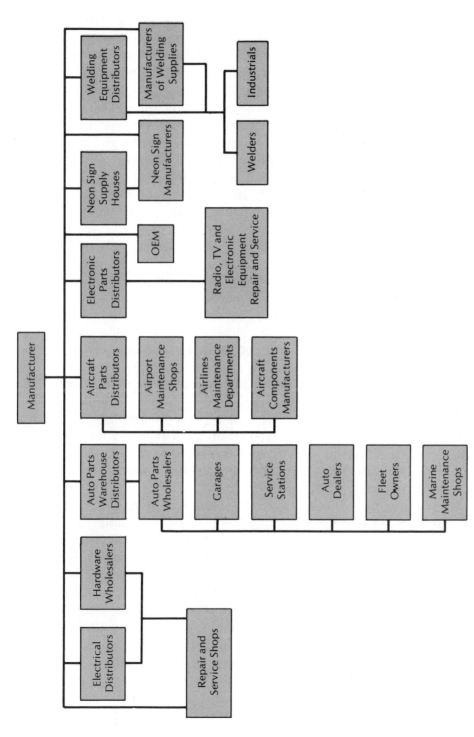

FIGURE 5-5 Channels of Distribution of a Manufacturer of Electrical Wire and Cable

SOURCE: Edwin H. Lewis, *Marketing Electrical Apparatus and Supplies* (New York: McGraw-Hill Book Company, 1961), p. 215.

marketing channel system allows consumers to buy in small units, purchases may move directly into the consumption process. If, however, consumers must purchase in larger lots, some disparity between purchasing and consumption patterns will emerge, burdening consumers with product storage and maintenance costs. Consequently, if price is assumed to be equal, the smaller the lot size allowed by a channel, the higher the channel's output.

The output of waiting time is defined by Bucklin as the period that the consumer must wait after ordering until he receives his goods. Again, the longer the waiting time, the more inconvenient it is for the consumer, who is required to plan his/her consumption far in advance and often pay for it well before actual consumption. Finally, the wider the breadth of assortment—the greater the product variety—available to the consumer, the higher the output of the marketing channel.

These service outputs are achieved through the performance of the marketing functions or flows, as enumerated in Chapter 1. Various channel institutions pool their resources and produce outputs for consumers by allocating their resources in specific ways. The decisions on the amount of output to be delivered by channel members are obviously directly influenced by the amount of service desired by consumers. The result of the interaction between channel member decisions and consumer requirements is a channel structure or arrangement that is capable of satisfying the needs of both groups (see Fig. 5–6). Under reasonably competitive conditions and low barriers to entry, the channel structure that evolves over the long run should, according to Bucklin, be comprised of a group of institutions so well adjusted to its task and environment that no other type of arrangement could create greater returns (e.g., profits or other goals) or more consumer satisfaction per dollar of product cost.[7] This arrangement is what Bucklin has called the "normative channel structure."

The more service outputs are required by consumers, the more likely it is that intermediaries will be included in the channel structure. Thus, if consumers wish to purchase in small lot sizes, then there are likely to be numerous middlemen performing sorting operations between mass producers and the final user level. If waiting time is to be reduced, then decentralization of outlets must follow, and, therefore, more middlemen will be included in the channel structure. The same type of reasoning can be applied to all of the service outputs. However, as service outputs increase, costs will undoubtedly increase, and these higher costs will tend to be reflected in higher prices to consumers. Consumers are usually faced with the choice of dealing with channel structures in which few service outputs are provided but where

---

[7] Bucklin, *A Theory of Distribution Channel Structure, op. cit.*, p. 5.

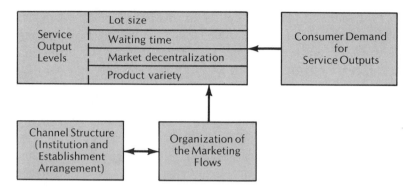

FIGURE 5-6   The Determination of Service Output Levels

prices are relatively low or with those structures where both service outputs and prices are high. As was pointed out in Chapter 1, the more the consumer or end-user participates in the marketing flows, the greater the costs he/she incurs (in terms of search, physical possession, financing, and the like), and, therefore, the more he should be compensated for his efforts. In cases where channel service outputs are low, consumers are supposedly compensated for their additional efforts through the lower relative prices which are provided by such channel structures.

On the other hand, commercial channel members face some difficult choices as well. It is possible to argue that the lower the level of service outputs provided, the greater are the economies of scale that can be achieved by channel members, and vice versa. The final structure that emerges is, therefore, a function of the desire of channel members to achieve scale economies relative to each of the marketing flows and the demand of consumers for service outputs of varying kinds. An optimal structure is one that minimizes the total costs of the system (both commercial and consumer) by the appropriate adjustment of the level of the service outputs.[8] Within a channel, members can attempt to shift the degree of participation relative to each flow in order to provide the greatest possible service output at the lowest possible cost. But such shifting calls for a tremendous amount of coordination and cooperation. This is one reason why the interorganization management of channel systems is so critical.

The way in which channels are structured is, to a significant extent, determined by where inventories should best be held in order to provide appropriate service levels, fulfill the required sorting processes, and still deliver an adequate return to channel members. To explain the process involved in the

[8]Bucklin and Carman, *op. cit.*, p. 12.

determination of inventory locations, Bucklin, using Alderson's original scheme,[9] developed the principle of *postponement-speculation*.[10] According to Bucklin, efficiency in marketing channels is promoted by the postponement of changes in (a) the form and identity of a product to the latest possible point in the marketing process and (b) inventory location to the latest possible point in time. Risk and uncertainty costs increase as the product becomes more differentiated. Postponement promotes efficiency by moving differentiation nearer to the time of purchase when demand is more certain, thus reducing risk and uncertainty costs. Also, the cost of physical distribution of goods is reduced by sorting products in large lots and in relatively undifferentiated states.

Postponement is a tool used by a channel member to shift the risk of owning goods to another channel member. For example:

Manufacturers postpone by refusing to produce except upon the receipt of orders.

Middlemen buy from sellers who offer faster delivery, thus shifting inventories backward (backward postponement).

Consumers postpone by buying from retail outlets where goods are available directly from the store shelf. Also, the shopping process can be viewed as a postponement process.

Speculation is the opposite of postponement. The speculation concept holds that "changes in form, and the movement of goods to forward inventories, should be made at the earliest possible time in the marketing process in order to reduce the costs of the marketing system."[11] Thus risk is shifted to or assumed by a channel institution rather than shifted away from it. Speculation makes possible cost reductions through (a) economies of large scale production, which are the result of changing form at the earliest point; (b) the elimination of frequent orders, which increase the costs of order processing and transportation; and (c) the reduction of stockouts and their attendant cost of consumer dissatisfaction and possible subsequent brand switching.

The character of variables involved in the postponement-speculation theory are shown in Fig. 5–7. The vertical axis represents the average cost of

[9]Wroe Alderson, "Marketing Efficiency and the Principle of Postponement," *Cost and Profit Outlook*, Vol. 3 (September, 1950).

[10]Louis P. Bucklin, "Postponement, Speculation and the Structure of Distribution Channels," in Mallen, *op. cit.*, pp. 67–74.

[11]*Ibid.*, p. 68.

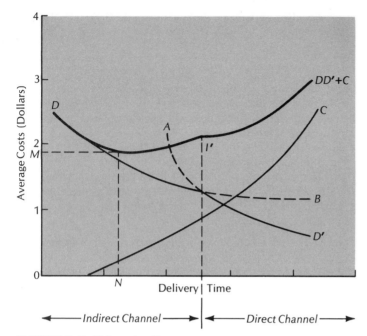

FIGURE 5-7 Using the Postponement-speculation Concept to Determine Channel Structure

SOURCE: Reprinted from Louis P. Bucklin and Leslie Halpert, "Exploring Channels of Distribution for Cement with the Principle of Postponement-Speculation," in *Marketing and Economic Development*, ed. Peter D. Bennett (Chicago: American Marketing Association, 1965), p. 698.

performing some function, or set of functions, for one unit of any given commodity. The horizontal axis measures the time required to deliver the commodity to the buyer after an order has been placed. If these two elements are taken together, the coordinates measure the cost of certain marketing functions or flows performed in a channel with respect to delivery time.

Three basic sets of flows are shown in Fig. 5-7. The curve labelled *C* represents the costs incurred by the buyer in holding an inventory. The curve *AD'* shows the costs of those flows necessary to supply the buyer directly from a manufacturing point some specified distance away. Curve *DB* reveals the costs incurred by flows utilized to ship the commodity from this same production point through a speculative inventory (e.g., a stocking intermediary, such as a sales branch or merchant wholesaler) to the buyer.

The postponement-speculation theory holds that channel structure is determined by the interrelationships of the three sets of curves, C, AD', and DB, as follows:

1. The minimal cost of supplying the buyer for every possible delivery time is derived from curves AD' and DB. As may be seen in Fig. 5-7, especially fast delivery service can be provided only by the indirect channel (i.e., by using a stocking intermediary). However, at some delivery time, I', the cost of serving the consumer directly from the producer will intersect and fall below the cost of indirect shipment. The minimal costs derived from both curves are designated DD'. From the perspective of channel cost, it will be cheaper to service the buyer from a speculative inventory if delivery times shorter than I' are demanded. If the consumer is willing to accept delivery times longer than I', then direct shipment will be the least expensive.

2. The minimal *total* cost curve for the channel with respect to delivery time is derived by summing the cost of moving goods to the buyer, DD', and the buyer's costs of holding inventory, C. The curve is represented in Fig. 5-7 by $DD' + C$. Total channel costs initially fall as delivery time lengthens, because increased buyer expenses are more than made up for by savings in other parts of the channel. Gradually, however, the savings from these sources diminish and buyer costs begin to rise more rapidly. A minimal cost point is reached and expenses for the channel rise thereafter. *Channel structure is controlled by the location of this minimum point.* If, as in the present case, it falls to the left of I', then goods would be expected to flow through the speculative inventory (i.e., an intermediary). If, on the other hand, the savings of the buyer from postponement had not been as great as those depicted, the minimum point would have fallen to the right of I' and shipments would be made directly from producer to the consumer.[12]

In the situation portrayed in Fig. 5-7, the costs of postponement are minimized by the use of a speculative inventory, because the minimal cost point M falls to the left of I'. If, however, the risk costs to the customer had been less, or the general cost of holding inventories at the customer's home (or warehouse, as the case may be) had been lower, then C would be farther to the right. Point M would also shift to the right. With a sufficient reduction in consumer cost, M would appear to the right of I', indicating that direct shipment in the channel would be the means to minimize postponement cost.

[12]Louis P. Bucklin and Leslie Halpert, "Exploring Channels of Distribution for Cement with the Principle of Postponement-Speculation," in Peter D. Bennett (ed.), *Marketing and Economic Development* (Chicago: American Marketing Association, 1965), p. 699. It should be noted that the type of cost behavior discussed above and depicted in Fig. 5-7 excludes from consideration any potential savings from sorting in the channel. Such savings, derived from the possibility of economies in large-scale transport to the speculative inventory point, are, as mentioned in the preceding section, a fundamental characteristic of channels and must be introduced into the analysis before a final structure can be determined.

The theory of postponement-speculation provides a useful basis for understanding channel structure. It is possible to assert that speculative inventories create the opportunity for new institutions to hold title in the channel. The existence of speculative inventories leads to the use of indirect channels; the economic need to have such inventories opens the door to middlemen to demonstrate whether they are capable of reducing the cost of inventory risk-taking (that is, the costs associated with participating in the flows of physical possession and ownership). On the other hand, nonspeculative inventories create an opportunity for different types of institutions in the channel. The latter are freight forwarders, drop shippers, and agent middlemen who do not take title to merchandise but who, in the absence of speculative inventories, facilitate the use of more direct channels of distribution.

It is also possible to apply the principle of postponement-speculation to an understanding of the differences between household and industrial buying. Much household buying is generally fragmented, involves small lots, and is undertaken frequently, especially with regard to convenience and some shopping goods. The costs of holding large inventories on the parts of households tend to be relatively high. Thus, longer and more indirect channels often exist for convenience goods. Speculation is an important determinant of the channel structure for such goods, because there are more points in the channel where inventory may be held. In industrial purchasing, however, the opposite factors generally operate, and thus the presence of nonspeculative inventories has led to the development of a different type of institutional arrangement, where there are more direct, shorter channels.

Beyond consideration of physical possession, ownership, and risk-taking, it is possible to expand the analysis supplied by Bucklin to other flows associated with marketing channels. In fact, each marketing flow may be thought to have a differently shaped cost curve, which may include increasing, decreasing, or constant returns. Thus, savings can be affected if the activities or flows subject to increasing returns are performed at a higher output level. A firm with limited resources in a competitive industry will normally delegate these increasing return activities to enterprises that specialize in them. Through such delegation (or shifting of the flows), the firm is able, as Stigler observes,[13] to lower its average and marginal costs and thereby to improve its competitive position. In essence, specialized channel intermediaries provide external economies to firms employing them. Eventually, however, reintegration of the delegated flows may be warranted as a firm's output

---

[13] George J. Stigler, "The Division of Labor Is Limited by the Extent of the Market," *Journal of Political Economy*, Vol. 59 (June, 1951), pp. 185–193.

expands or as technology changes, because the firm may then find itself capable of performing them at an optimum scale.[14]

Such a pattern of vertical disintegration followed by vertical reintegration can be observed in the case of small manufacturers who rely heavily on agent middlemen to represent them in the market and on specialized storage, transportation, and financing institutions to perform the respective functions in their channels. As these small manufacturers expand, they tend to develop their own sales forces, perform their own storage, transportation, and financing, and thus dispense with the services of agent middlemen and other specialized institutions. Similar analyses can be applied to wholesalers and retailers. For example, Sears started as a mail-order retailer and expanded horizontally. As its operations grew larger and larger, Sears integrated backward in terms of operating its own warehousing and other wholesaling facilities and then in terms of owning or controlling manufacturing facilities. Thus, when a firm's output and its market are limited, it will likely find itself shifting flows onto others in its channel, if it can, in fact, convince others to accept responsibility for these flows.[15] As market size expands, it becomes increasingly economical to vertically integrate, which is a pattern of behavior fully evident among the largest manufacturing and distributive organizations.[16]

It is important to note that there may be considerable problems associated with shifting flows or, as Mallen has put it, "spinning off" functions.[17] It may be exceedingly difficult to separate the joint costs associated with the performance of many marketing flows (e.g., physical possession and ownership). Furthermore, most companies deal with multiple products and services for which costs are shared. There is also a time horizon involved as well as a host of noneconomic considerations. Nevertheless, the concept of shifting flows is a viable one; like so many management decisions, it demands appropriate accounting procedures to be implemented correctly.

---

[14]Control as well as economic considerations are crucial here. In fact, control may override economics in many situations. This factor is discussed in detail in later chapters.

[15]This is not always a foregone conclusion. Very small firms often find it difficult to secure needed services from agents, advertising agencies, and financial institutions, for example, and therefore, must integrate these flows, even though it would be more economical to pass them along to someone else.

[16]For a useful analytical perspective on this issue, see Stanley F. Stasch, *A Method of Dynamically Analyzing the Stability of the Economic Structure of Channels of Distribution*, an unpublished Ph.D. dissertation, School of Business, Northwestern University, 1964.

[17]Bruce E. Mallen, "Functional Spin-Off: A Key to Anticipating Change in Distribution Structure," *Journal of Marketing*, Vol. 37 (July, 1973), pp. 18–25. Also see William P. Dommermuth and R. Clifton Andersen, "Distribution Systems—Firms, Functions and Efficiencies," *MSU Business Topics*, Vol. 17 (Spring, 1969), pp. 51–56.

Additional Factors Determining Channel Structure

Added to these economics-oriented explanations about why channels take on certain structural properties must be considerations of technological, cultural, physical, social, and political factors.[18] For example, the emergence of the supermarket in the structure of food distribution was contingent upon the availability of technologies such as the mass media and mass communications, the cash register, packaging and refrigeration, and the automobile. However, the introduction of the supermarket in developing countries is impeded by cultural variables, such as the high rates of illiteracy, the habit of tasting food products before buying, and the delegation of buying to maids and domestic help. The employment of vending and dollar change machines provides another example of technological and cultural determinism relative to the distribution structure of candy, snack foods, beverages, and other items. Thus, in affluent societies with convenience-oriented cultures, consumers are willing to pay the extra cost associated with buying from vending machines. And the advent and continuous development of electronic data processing systems have enabled manufacturers and middlemen accurately to assess their distribution costs and redesign their respective channels.

Geography, size of market area, location of production centers, and concentration of population, among other physical factors, also play important roles in determining the structure of channels. Distribution channels tend to be longer (i.e., include more intermediaries) when production is concentrated and population and markets are sparse. Furthermore, we find that urban areas are served by a wide variety of retail outlets, including department stores, discount houses, and supermarkets, while rural areas may be served solely by a general store.

In addition, local, state, and federal laws can influence channel structure in both direct and indirect ways. There are laws that prohibit territorial restrictions in distribution, pricing discrimination, full-line forcing, and unfair sales practices. There are also laws that protect channel members from the competition of larger, more efficient rivals or that penalize "bigness" in distribution. And there are licensing boards that screen entrants to particular

---

[18] For example, Preston believes that channel structure is a function of population density and cluster, per capita income, geographic setting and resource endowment, volume and variety of goods, and managerial capabilities. See Lee E. Preston, "Marketing Organization and Economic Development: Structure, Products, and Management," in Louis P. Bucklin (ed.), *Vertical Marketing Systems* (Glenview, Ill.: Scott, Foresman and Co., 1970), pp. 116–133.

channels. All of these political factors are addressed in Chapter 8, which deals with the legal environment of channels.

Social and behavioral variables can also influence the makeup of a channel. For example, Galbraith has advanced the concept of countervailing power as a tentative explanation of channel structure and practices.[19] His theory emphasizes that: (a) private economic power is held in check by the countervailing power of those who are subject to it; (b) economic power begets countervailing power; (c) countervailing power is a self-generating force that complements competition as a regulatory force in the economy; and (d) countervailing power can take many forms, the most important of which is threatened or actual vertical integration. Manifestations of the effect of countervailing power on distribution channel structure are provided by the following examples:

The emergence of the mass retailer to countervail the power of large manufacturers.

Vertical integration by mass retailers, such as Sears' and Montgomery Ward's ownership of manufacturing facilities.

The utilization of private brands by chain retailers to countervail the power of large manufacturers with popular national brands.

The emergence of voluntary and retailer cooperative chains to countervail the power of the large corporate chains.

Trade association activities by small retailers (pharmacies, independent service stations, and independent grocery stores) in an attempt to countervail the power of chains and manufacturers.

Admittedly, more could be said about each of the various factors mentioned above; it is to be hoped that the reader will be able to develop additional examples of their influence on the structure of channels with which he is familiar. The main point, however, to be remembered here is that explanations of channel structure in terms of economic variables alone are obviously insufficient, even though such economic models provide an appropriate starting point for understanding why specific structures emerge. The necessity for going beyond economic variables is made especially clear when one attempts to find an answer to the questions: why do uneconomic channel structures persist over time? In other words, why do not all channels gravitate to or obtain the normative structure specified by Bucklin? The answer comes from examining a myriad of social, cultural, and political as well as economic

---

[19]John K. Galbraith, *American Capitalism*, rev. ed (Boston: Houghton Mifflin Co., 1956), pp. 110-114, 117–123.

variables. As McCammon points out, uneconomic channels may persist for the following reasons:[20]

1. *Reseller solidarity*. Channel participants organize and function as groups that tend to support traditional trade practices and long-established institutional relationships. Trade association actions, attempts by independent retailers to outlaw chain stores, and department store operators' efforts to block discount store operations attest to the role of reseller solidarity in determining channel structure.

2. *Entrepreneurial values*. Large resellers are growth-oriented, tend to adopt economic criteria for decision-making purposes, and use new profitable technologies. On the contrary, small resellers have limited expectations, tend to maintain the status quo, view their demand curve as relatively fixed, and resist growth beyond their limited growth expectations.

3. *Organizational rigidity*. Firms respond incrementally to innovations because of organizational rigidities. Thus, the process of change takes a long time.

4. *The firm's channel position*. Kriesberg grouped channel intermediaries into insiders, who are members of the dominant channel; strivers, who want to become members of the channel; complementors, who perform functions complementary to functions performed by insiders; and transients, who take advantage of temporary opportunities and are not interested in becoming members.[21] While transients usually disrupt the status quo by engaging in deviant competitive behavior, insiders, strivers, and complementors are more interested in maintaining the status quo. Thus, firms completely outside the channel are most likely to introduce basic enduring innovations in the channel structure.

5. *Market segmentation*. New institutions do not appeal to all market segments. Traditional institutions seem to have loyal segments that they appeal to. Thus, these institutions are not compelled to change.

Indeed, to have a goal of moving towards a "normative channel structure," the assumptions of low barriers to entry and competitive conditions must be met. In many of the above examples, entry is purposively inhibited through group action, product differentiation, industrial norms, and the like. In addition, the concept of a normative channel structure is long-run in nature; in a dynamic environment, such a structure cannot be reached at any one point in time. Change must always take place according to an assessment of future requirements, and thus there will always be a gap between the

[20] Bert C. McCammon, Jr., "Alternative Explanations of Institutional Change and Change Evolution," in William G. Moller, Jr. and David L. Wilemon (eds.), *Marketing Channels* (Homewood, Ill.: Richard D. Irwin, Inc., 1971), pp. 136–141.

[21] Louis Kriesberg, "Occupational Controls Among Steel Distributors," in Louis W. Stern (ed.), *Distribution Channels: Behavioral Dimensions* (Boston: Houghton Mifflin Co., 1969), pp. 50–60.

actual and ideal. In fact, it is probably best to adopt an evolutionary view of structure, because what exists always seems to be a compromise between past structure, present requirements, and predictions about the future.

INSTITUTIONAL CHANGE

In order better to understand the evolutionary nature of channel structure, it is important to comprehend how the various institutions that make up a channel system undergo changes over time. By understanding the basic forces underlying institutional change, it should be possible to predict the future advancements and developments in distribution, and, thereby, design channel systems that are more viable over the long term. To aid this understanding, several plausible theories have been formulated which describe the process of institutional change. In this section, a few of the most popular ones are briefly explored.

Cycle Theories

Cycle theories of institutional change rest on the premise that:

> If a rhythm of change is evident in some phenomena and if the rhythmic nature of that change can be measured, then (a) factors underlying the change may be identified and (b) the future direction of the cycle can be anticipated or predicted.[22]

Such cycles may be either *partial* or *complete*. The former describe the rise and fall of an institution, while the latter describe the resurgence of an institution as well as its rise and fall. Figure 5–8 illustrates both partial and full cycles.

Perhaps the best-known partial-cycle theory is the *wheel theory*,[23] which is most often thought of in connection with retailing. According to this theory, a new and innovative institution will appear, generally as a low-status, low-margin, low-price operation, to take advantage of a competitive weakness in an established institution. This new institution gains acceptance and attracts emulators. Then, in order to differentiate itself from its emu-

---

[22]Ronald R. Gist, *Marketing and Society* (New York: Holt, Rinehart and Winston, Inc., 1971), p. 364.

[23]Malcolm P. McNair, "Significant Trends and Developments in the Postwar Period," in A. B. Smith (ed.), *Competitive Distribution in a Free High-level Economy and Its Implications for the University* (Pittsburgh, Pa.: University of Pittsburgh Press, 1958), pp. 17–18.

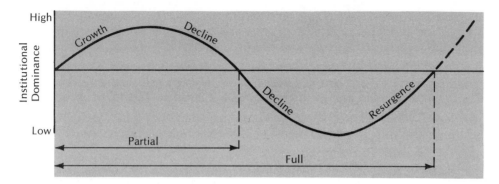

FIGURE 5-8 Partial and Full Cycles

lators, it begins to trade up by acquiring elaborate facilities, increasing services, and thus widening its margin. Eventually, this institution matures as a high-cost, high-margin operation and thus becomes vulnerable to new types of competitive units that emerge in the distribution structure. These new types, in turn, go through the same pattern. Traditional examples in support of the wheel theory include: (a) the emergence of the department store, as a new competitor to small specialty retailers, which became, in turn, vulnerable to discount store competition, and (b) the emergence of the chain grocery store, as a competitor to the corner grocery store, which became vulnerable to supermarket competition.

The wheel pictures an institution as evolving from a low-price, low-margin, efficient operation to a high-price, high-margin, inefficient one. Generally, two forces are central in accounting for this evolution: (1) *The growth in consumer (real) income.* Such growth has generated a need for periodic adjustments in the methods used to serve the more affluent consumer. Very often the method of adjustment used takes the form of additional services. This, of course, raises the operating expenses of the institution. The institution then compensates by increasing its margin. (2) *The comfort of success.* That is, success breeds conservatism and a hesitancy to take risks. Lethargy and dysfunctional bureaucracy set in, raising the expense structure. This, of course, drives the margin up.

A variety of explanations for the wheel theory have been advanced, some of which are listed below.[24] Obviously, these explanations deal directly with retailing, since the theory was developed to describe the evolution of retailing institutions.

[24]Stanley C. Hollander, "The Wheel of Retailing," *Journal of Marketing*, Vol. 24 (July, 1960), pp. 37-38.

1. *Retail personalities.* The aggressive, cost-conscious entrepreneurs who start the new institution relax their vigilance and control over cost as they acquire age and wealth. (This explanation is, of course, similar to the second central force mentioned above.)

2. *Conservative and apathetic management.* Management becomes organization-oriented rather than customer-oriented and therefore blind to the opportunities of a new market situation.

3. *Misguidance.* Retailers are lured by store equipment and supply promotions into superfluously modernizing their stores.

4. *Imperfect competition.* Retailers avoid price competition because of resale price maintenance and the fear of retaliation. Retailers resort instead to the selection of prime locations, elaborate facilities, full assortment and added services to differentiate their product and gain a differential advantage. As the retailer adds services, consumer expectations are raised. Thus, it becomes difficult for the retailer to reduce his services. On the contrary, he is forced to add new services as he loses his differential advantage when other retailers match his original set of services.

5. *Incremental management decisions.* Management decision-making becomes geared to slight modifications of existing operating patterns because of the uncertainty inherent in large-scale changes.

6. *Established institutions have history.* Thus, they tend to be committed and rigid. The innovator has no history and is not committed to any operational patterns. Therefore, innovators are flexible.

7. *Secular trends.* As some market segments become wealthier, they demand more services; therefore, institutions move along the wheel to provide for consumers' needs. Meanwhile, because of the uneven income distribution, some opportunities remain for the new low-service, low-margin institution.

Hollander and other scholars have questioned the validity of the wheel theory on several grounds.[25] First, they argue that the observed high average storewide margins are the result of the added high-markup lines rather than increased margins on original lines. Thus, scrambled merchandising may have created illusory impressions about the wheel phenomenon. Second, they insist that changes in retail margins cannot be judged adequately because of the lack of valid historical information and adequate Bureau of Census retail classification. Finally, these scholars have pointed out that some retailing institutions have not conformed to the wheel pattern. For example, vending machines started as a high-cost, high-margin, and high-convenience type of retailing. Also, suburban shopping centers displayed resistance to the entry of low-margin aggressive outlets.

Nevertheless, even with its drawbacks, the wheel theory provides a

[25] For a review, see Hollander, *op. cit.*, pp. 37–42.

powerful and fascinating descriptive model to apply to institutional change in distribution. To date, it has received the widest attention and the strongest support of any of the available theories attempting to explain such change.

An example of a full cycle theory is provided by the so-called *accordian theory* of retail development, which postulates that American marketing institutions have oscillated between extremes in terms of width of product line.[26] As Hollander has pointed out:

> Domination by general-line, wide-assortment retailers alternates with domination by specialized, narrow-line merchants. Neither the pattern's universality nor its existence can be proved definitely (since there are no valid historical statistics on merchandise assortment), but many astute students of retailing have discerned these rhythmic oscillations.[27]

For example, as depicted in Fig. 5–9, the wide-line general store was followed, in history, by the limited-line specialty shop, which was followed, in turn, by the introduction of the department store with its wide line of merchandise. Additional evidence for the accordian theory is supplied by the fact that the number of establishments in the apparel, furniture, and general merchandise categories of retail trade has shown a tendency to fluctuate over time. As Dalrymple and Thompson assert:

> The reported fluctuations in numbers of stores are consistent with a theory of cyclic redistribution of patronage among these three merchandise groups on the basis of changes in consumer preferences for specialty versus broad merchandising.[28]

Similar changes, in terms of width of line, have taken place within merchant wholesaling over time. The theory does not, however, seem to be directly applicable to logistical institutions, although there have been some cyclical changes in warehousing practices.

Dialectic Processes

It is also possible to view institutional change as a dialectic process in where there is a thesis, or established institutional form, an antithesis, or innovative institutional form, and a synthesis, or a new form drawing from the

---

[26] Stanley C. Hollander, "Notes on the Retail Accordion Theory," *Journal of Retailing*, Vol. 42 (Summer, 1966), pp. 29–40.

[27] *Ibid.*, p. 29.

[28] Douglas J. Dalrymple and Donald L. Thompson, *Retailing: An Economic View* (New York: The Free Press, 1969), p. 15.

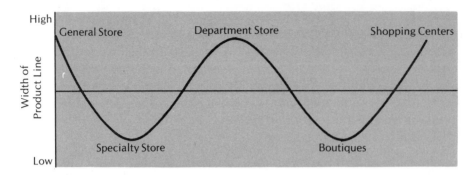

FIGURE 5–9 Full Cycle: The Accordian Theory

other two.[29] For example, the department store, characterized by high margins, low turnover, full service, and a downtown location, could represent a thesis. The antithesis could be represented by the discount house, which is characterized by low margins, high turnover, low service level, and a suburban location. The competition between these two institutions has resulted in the development of general merchandise retailers with average margins, average turnover, a moderate service level, and a suburban location. In wholesaling, the general-line, full-function merchant wholesaler provides a thesis, the cash-and-carry wholesaler represents the antithesis, and the limited-line full-function specialty wholesaler can be viewed as the result of the interaction between the two. A similar analogy can be found in physical distribution, with general merchandise warehouses, limited-service depots, and localized, fast-service distribution centers being used as thesis, antithesis, and synthesis, respectively.

Vacuum Theories

In addition, it is likely that innovative institutions come into being when there is a void in the institutional coverage of the market.[30] The dynamics of such movements as well as the identification of voids can be explained by using Regan's *simplex-multiplex-omniplex* classification scheme[31] and Alderson's *core-fringe* concept.[32] According to Regan's theory, retail de-

[29]Gist, *op. cit.*, pp. 370–372.

[30]*Ibid.*

[31]William J. Regan, "The States of Retail Development," in Cox, Alderson, and Shapiro (eds.), *op. cit.*, pp. 139–153.

[32]Wroe Alderson, *Marketing Behavior and Executive Action* (Homewood, Ill.: Richard D. Irwin, Inc., 1957), p. 56.

velopment can be broken into three stages, which represent various levels of complexity in the product cost-service cost mix offered by the firm. Product cost is used as an estimate of product quality, while service cost is used as an estimate of the level of service provided. The most primitive stage of retail development is the simplex stage. Here the firm offers one level of product quality and a corresponding level of service. Thus, a firm would offer high quality-high service, average quality-average service, or low quality-low service. In order to attract new customers, and thus increase sales and profits, retail firms next expand into multiplex trading. This can be accomplished in several ways. The level of product quality may be held constant while the firm offers more than one level of service. For example, the firm may sell average quality products and provide the purchaser the choice of a low service level or an average service level. Similarly, the firm may hold the service level constant and offer the consumer alternative levels of product quality. The final stage of retail development is the omniplex stage. This stage exists when all possible quality-service combinations are offered. Like the multiplex stage, this stage is reached as the firm increases its offerings in an attempt to expand its market.

On the other hand, Alderson explains the process of void-filling in terms of thrusts made by both established and nonestablished firms. In his core-fringe concept, he postulates that, once a firm gains a market niche for itself, the niche provides a haven for the firm during periods of trouble. Thus, if a firm fails in an attempt to diversify its operations, it can fall back on its market niche for support while it regroups and develops a new strategy. When the firm is being attacked by competitors, its niche assumes the same sort of protective function. Such a concept is useful in predicting the market behavior of conglomerchants,[33] such as J. C. Penney, Sears, Dayton-Hudson, the Jewel Company, and McKesson-Foremost, as they seek to move into areas (such as discounting, lumber stores, restaurants, and general services) unfamiliar to them, i.e., beyond their market niches. The niche's core is, according to Alderson's theory, that part of the environment that is best suited to the operations of the firm. The fringe elements of the niche provide some resistance to attack, thus insulating the core. However, because of their basic strategic commitments to their particular market niches, such firms become vulnerable to innovative strategic thrusts of other firms seeking to penetrate the fringe and eventually the core. The commitments on the part of established firms to specific ways of doing business permit voids to develop in the market and thus create opportunities for new firms to fill these voids.

---

[33]Rollie Tillman, "Rise of the Conglomerchant," *Harvard Business Review*, Vol. 49 (November-December, 1971), pp. 44-51.

The Crisis-change Model

Perhaps the potentially most useful model for both describing and predicting institutional change is the crisis-change model, which isolates four distinct phases through which organizational systems pass as they adapt to crisis situations.[34] According to this theory, adaptation begins with an initial period of "shock," is followed by a period of "defensive retreat," then by "acknowledgment," and finally, by a process of "adaption and change."

The Shock Phase. An organization is considered to be in crisis when any factor critical to the viability of the total system of which it is a part is threatened. The "shock" phase occurs when members of a channel become aware of a threat to the survival or to the objectives of the system, such as when a new type of competing retailing institution emerges. At this point, individual survival is the paramount objective of each member of the total system, which, in turn, leads to a fragmentation of intergroup (intrachannel) relations. The primary focus is, therefore, placed upon the threat, and day-to-day operations become irrelevant. It is during this stage that the established system loses ground to its new competitor as the individual members contemplate *noncompetitive means* of destroying the source of crisis. An illustrative example is the emergence of the chain grocery store and the threat it posed to the independent grocer. When chains first developed, independents spent their efforts predicting the former's eventual demise; their energies were absorbed in developing rationalizations for the "short-term" predicament.

The Defensive Retreat Phase. This stage is marked by the established system mobilizing its forces by imposing controls designed to reduce the threat. These controls do not provide a resolution of the crisis, but merely a means of postponing a confrontation, possibly on another plane. Thus, during the period of the emergence of the chain store, the "defensive retreat" phase was marked by lobbying for legislation to curtail chain store activities. The small grocer realized that he could not compete in the marketplace with the chain and, therefore, felt that he had to eliminate or weaken the chains by subjecting them to crippling controls. Collectively, the small grocers carried out this objective by seeking legislation that would restrict the activities of the newer, more progressive, and more efficient organization and, thereby, curtail its

---

[34]Stephen L. Fink, Joel Beak, Kenneth Taddeo, "Organizational Crisis and Change," *Journal of Applied Behavioral Science*, Vol. 7 (January-February, 1971), pp. 15-37.

effectiveness. The result in the grocery trade was the passage of chain store taxes and the Robinson-Patman Act. Although the threatened system survives during this phase, such defensive actions eventually become self-defeating, because they are not consistent with the goals and objectives of long-term organizational growth.

The Acknowledgment Phase. During the acknowledgment phase, the individuals in the threatened system engage in a process of self-examination and interpersonal confrontation. It is here that the individual members of the system search for new and better ways of communication, ways which ultimately lead to a genuine understanding and a sharing of information. Leadership and decision-making now become open to a wider range of influences, which are given fair consideration. Problems are explored and are not assumed to be manageable by some simple formula. As a result, solutions become more attuned to the nature of the problems. During the "acknowledgment" phase, the established system comes to doubt the validity of its own traditions and begins to experiment with some new alternatives, but in a rather cautious manner. As some structural changes are tried out, the system becomes less and less dependent upon its past history and more in touch with current developments. It begins to discover ways of using structure to facilitate the functions it must perform, rather than attempting to fit functions into preestablished structures. In the previous example, the independent grocer finally came to the realization that he would have to innovate in order to survive. The result of the crisis was the birth of the Independent Grocers Alliance (IGA) and other wholesaler- and retailer-sponsored cooperatives. Overall, then, characteristic of the acknowledgment phase is an increasing excitement about the discovery of something new and better as well as a certainty that it is undesirable, if not impossible, to return to the former patterns of operation.

The Adaption and Change (Growth) Phase. The processes that characterize the period of "adaption and change" reflect effective coping, and they sharply contrast with those that characterize the "defensive retreat." The "adaption and change" phase represents a renewal of the growth process. In this sense it is not really a phase but a rebirth of an ongoing state of development. By the time the system has reached this phase, it has, to a large degree, disposed of dysfunctional behavior in that the subsystems are working interdependently, and each institution complements the total system. It is here that cooperatives like IGA begin to mature and prosper, not only with respect to isolated functions, such as quantity purchases, but throughout the entire realm of the business.

It would appear that the "adaption and change" phase would terminate the cycle, but in reality it triggers the "shock" phase for the system that posed the original threat, for now that system is in crisis. For example, when the chain stores realized the power wielded by the cooperative associations, they were forced to evolve to an "adaption and change" phase, which led to another shock phase for the cooperatives (see Fig. 5-10). The cycle then continues on as a chain of actions and reactions, with progress and efficiency being the result as long as cost-effective technology is available.

Clearly, institutional change is the product of a vast number of forces and circumstances. Besides more generalized environmental and situational developments, such as increased consumer affluence, population decentralization, improved transportation facilities, and the like, there are important influences brought about by the relationships and linkages among firms that induce change, as discussed earlier. All of these forces must be included in an analysis of institutional change and of the simultaneous alterations in channel structures which such change induces if management is to develop an adequate picture of the likely shape of the future of distribution.

SUMMARY AND CONCLUSION

In this chapter, theories describing the emergence of marketing channels, the structure of channels, and institutional change have been explored. These theories provide an appropriate framework for assessing the work of channels, which is the subject of the next chapter.

The emergence of marketing channels can be explained in terms of a series of logically related steps in an economic process. Intermediaries increase the efficiency of exchange and arise to adjust the discrepancy of assortments through sorting processes (sorting out, accumulation, allocation, and assorting). Channel arrangements provide for the routinization of transactions and facilitate the searching process of both buyers and sellers.

Channels are structured so as to provide outputs (lot size, waiting or delivery time, market decentralization, and product variety) to consumers at minimal cost. The extant structure is influenced by consumers when they select combinations of service outputs that minimize their total costs. In theory, extant structure gravitates to a normative structure under competitive circumstances via functional (flow) substitutability and shiftability. A normative structure is one in which no other alignment of firms or functions could create greater benefits to commercial channel members or more consumer satisfaction per dollar of product cost.

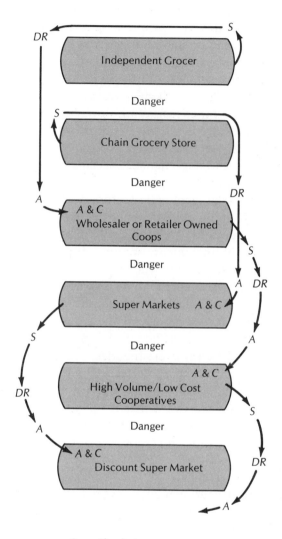

S = Shock stage
DR = Defensive retreat stage
A = Acknowledge stage
A & C = Adaptation and change stage

FIGURE 5-10 The Crisis-change Model: Independent Grocer and Chain Store Example

A specific channel structure may be determined by calculating the trade-offs between risk assumption, economies of scale, and customer service. The postponement-speculation principle weighs the cost of postponing changes in form, time, place, and possession utilities against the cost of adding such utilities early in the marketing process. The greater the savings generated by making changes early, the greater the likelihood that inventory-holding intermediaries will be used in a channel system. It is also possible to expand the tradeoff analysis to other marketing flows beyond physical possession, ownership, and risk-taking. If a flow is subject to increasing returns, a firm with low output is likely to undertake a process of vertical disintegration with respect to it by employing channel specialists but will reintegrate the flow when output increases.

Concentration on economic factors in channel structuring is, however, too restrictive from an analytical perspective. It is necessary to expand the analysis by incorporating technological, cultural, physical, social, and political factors. Only by such incorporation is it possible to explain, for example, why seemingly uneconomic (nonnormative) channels persist over time.

Even though there appear to be powerful forces that buttress the status quo, significant developments have occurred in distribution over the past century. The basic forces underlying these developments can be explained by exploring theories of institutional change. Thus, institutional change has been characterized by (a) cycle theories, (b) dialectic processes, (c) vacuum theories, and (d) a crisis-change model. The wheel theory is the most famous of the distribution cycle theories and postulates that institutions evolve from low-price, low-margin, efficient operations to high-price, high-margin, inefficient ones. As institutions mature, they become increasingly vulnerable to new, low-price, low-margin competitors. On the other hand, the accordian theory, a full-cycle theory, can be used to explain the rise, fall, and resurgence of institutional types.

Explaining institutional change as a dialectic process involves isolating a thesis, an antithesis, and a synthesis. Innovative institutions can also be depicted as filling voids in the coverage of a market. Here, Regan's simplex-multiplex-omniplex classification scheme and Alderson's core-fringe concept are helpful. The former deals with differing levels of complexity in the product cost-service cost mix offered by the firm, while the latter explains how institutions estimate the vulnerability of established market niches as they diversify and innovate.

In addition, institutional change can be viewed as a series of responses to a crisis situation. The four phases of the crisis-change model—shock, defensive retreat, acknowledgment, and adaption and change—depict how a threatened system will, in reacting to a crisis, first develop rationalizations and controls and then engage in formulating new approaches and effective coping.

DISCUSSION QUESTIONS

1. Are "sorting" and "searching" marketing flows?

2. According to Alderson, "the number of intervening marketing agencies tends to go up as distance increases." Distance, in his conception, is measured in terms of "the time and cost involved in communication and transportation." What factors, then, would tend to increase (or decrease) distance?

3. What does Alderson mean when he says that a product is viewed by a consumer as possibly increasing the "potency of his assortment?" Does this concept have any inherent managerial usefulness?

4. What is meant by the phrase "discrepancy of assortments?" What value does it have in explaining the factors governing the development of distribution channels?

5. Is routinization a restriction on economic freedom in marketing channels? How are the concepts of routinization and search interrelated?

6. Explain the tradeoffs between the number of available product alternatives *and* search and information costs; between spatial convenience *and* seller costs. Apply your answer to the health care delivery system and to the distribution channel for stainless steel.

7. Bucklin and Carman state that "An optimal structure is one which minimizes the total cost (both commercial and consumer) of the system by the appropriate adjustment of the level of . . . service outputs." Can you apply this statement to each of the marketing flows?

8. In what way does Adam Smith's tenet—"the division of labor is limited by the extent of the market"—relate to channel structure?

9. Is it likely that vertical disintegration is typical in growing industries while vertical integration is typical in declining industries?

10. Develop at least three examples of situations in which transient firms or organizations have disrupted the status quo in channels of distribution.

11. McCammon has argued that "large firms can overcome their tendency to maintain the status quo by underwriting *elite* activities." What do you think he means?

SIX

ASSESSING THE PERFORMANCE OF CHANNEL INSTITUTIONS AND STRUCTURES

The variety of institutions that form the primary components of channels and the factors that influence the way in which they link up with one another to comprise channel structures have been examined, described, and explored in Chapters 2, 3, 4, and 5. It is useful now to assess, from a historical perspective, the performance of the institutions and the channel structures in which they have been housed, prior to analyzing how various channels should be managed. In this respect, a performance assessment can be made from both a macro-, or societal-perspective and a micro-, or business-oriented perspective. In some cases, the perspectives overlap, and the macro view provides insights into operational features of individual enterprises. In other cases, there is a divergence between macro- and microperformance; such a divergence frequently requires governmental action to narrow it. Here, the performance of distribution channels and institutions is evaluated in terms of (1) system output; (2) costs, efficiency, and profitability; (3) equity.

SYSTEM OUTPUT

As indicated in earlier chapters, the marketing flows (physical possession, ownership, promotion, negotiation, financing, risking, ordering, and payment) are organized by institutions and agencies making up commercial channels of distribution in such a way as to provide goods and services in desired quantities (lot size) when needed (delivery time). These goods and services are made available at a number of different locations (market decentralization) at which they are displayed and generally combined with complementary and substitutable items (assortment breadth) in accordance with marketplace demand. Therefore, the "output" of a given commercial channel of distribution may be conceptualized as lot size, delivery time, market decentralization, and assortment breadth.[1]

In Chapter 1, it was observed that household consumers and industrial and business users are key actors in distribution channels because they participate directly in the marketing flows. However, the lower their degree of participation in the flows, the more work must be done by commercial channel members in providing the "output," and thus the higher will be the final price of goods and services. This rationale explains why the prices charged to ultimate consumers are greater for goods and services that are delivered rapidly in small quantities and which are easily accessible from nearby outlets displaying broad assortments than the prices charged when large quantities, slow delivery, and limited assortments are provided from relatively few outlets. If consumers were willing to increase the amount of search and selection time they devote to the purchase of the former items and thus absorb part of the marketing task, prices could probably be reduced.

Unfortunately, there are no quantitative measures available that provide an insight into aggregate performance regarding system output, beyond global estimates of the dollar and physical amount of goods and services passing through the distribution system.[2] Qualitatively, though, it is possible to point to a number of historical changes.

First, as mentioned in the chapter on retailing institutions, there has been a significant increase in the size of the average retail transaction over time.[3] Consumers are, therefore, buying in larger lots, requiring less marketing flow participation and "output" from commercial channel systems in this respect. The increase in transaction size permits retailers to buy in larger lots, which, in turn, reduces the need for wholesaler services. In turn, these developments permit lower distributive costs, since commercial channel service outputs are reduced, and thus lower prices to consumers are possible.

---

[1]This model and discussion of system output draws heavily from Louis P. Bucklin, "Marketing Channels and Structures: A Macro View," in Boris W. Becker and Helmut Becker (eds.), *American Marketing Association Combined Conference Proceedings* (Chicago, Ill.: American Marketing Association, 1973), pp. 32–35.

[2]See the Chapters on retailing and wholesaling in this text for relevant statistics on the volume of goods and services passing through the distribution system.

[3]David Schwartzman, *The Decline of Service in Retail Trade* (Pullman, Washington: Washington State University, Bureau of Economic and Business Research, 1971).

Similarly, the development of the automobile and improved road networks has, as Bucklin observes, reduced the need for highly decentralized retail systems for *convenience* goods.[4] Offsetting this, however, has been an increase in decentralization for *shopping* items with the emergence of the planned regional shopping center.

Second, there has been no obvious reduction in the willingness of either ultimate household consumers or industrial and business users to accept longer delivery times for the products they desire to buy. Shortages of raw materials may alter this somewhat; in the future, users may have to wait longer in order to be assured of appropriate supplies.[5] The willingness of consumers to postpone and ration purchases of products in short supply (e.g., petroleum), or to accept longer delivery times, will be rewarded, not by lower prices, but merely by being able to secure and consume the scarce commodities.

On the other hand, rising affluence has increased the range of products household consumers would like to buy at a single stop, raising the requirement for broader store assortments and increased speculative inventories within channel systems. Commercial channel "output" has had to rise here; the increase in store size, for example, has been caused by the expanding number of items being stocked.[6] There are, however, serious problems associated with the increase in available assortments relative to desirable levels of consumer choice. If one considers the number of brands to be an element of assortment, then it is possible that there is "overchoice" in the marketplace. In a study of this problem, Settle and Golden surveyed household consumers on their choice perceptions; ideal and perceived assortment size were compared to the actual choices available at the retail level.[7] It was found that actual choices were greater than perceived and ideal choices. This overabundance of brands can lead to inefficiencies in the use of resources and higher prices to consumers. Furthermore, consumers are becoming increasingly confused as to which brands and package sizes of various products represent the "best buys," from a purely economical perspective. This confusion was demonstrated by Friedman in an experiment on consumer choice in which 33 young married women were asked to select the most economical (largest quantity for the price) package for 20 different categories of typically pur-

[4] Bucklin, *op. cit.*, p. 33.

[5] See Philip Kotler, "Marketing During Periods of Shortage," *Journal of Marketing*, Vol. 38 (July, 1974), pp. 20–29.

[6] Bucklin, *op. cit.*, p. 33.

[7] R. B. Settle and L. L. Golden, "Consumer Perceptions: Overchoice in the Marketplace," in Scott Ward and Peter Wright (eds.), *4th Annual Conference Proceedings* (Association for Consumer Research, 1973), pp. 29–37.

chased products on sale at a selected supermarket.[8] Among other findings, Friedman reported that the sampled consumers were, on the average, unable to select the most economical package 43 percent of the time. Thus, even though assortment breadth is generally a desirable output of commercial channel operations,[9] there may be threshholds above which more choice becomes dysfunctional or wasteful.

The broader assortments required on the retail level have, to a significant extent, been responsible for the continued growth and survival of wholesalers and have offset, at least partially, the negative effect on the use of wholesalers caused by the increase in retail transaction size. Specialized wholesalers, such as rack merchandisers, who carry broad assortments of limited lines, have, as pointed out in Chapter 3, been especially successful in supplying food stores with nontraditional items (e.g., phonograph records, magazines, and health and beauty aids).[10] In the industrial goods sector, there has also been an increase in demand for wholesaler services, especially because of the growth in sales of items for which wholesaler support has long been relied upon by suppliers and customers, such as machinery, equipment, and supplies. Offsetting this somewhat has been the tendency to move away from "double wholesaling" in the industrial sector as more and more suppliers find themselves capable of absorbing promotional flows for their products. The latter change has had the greatest negative impact on agent middlemen.[11]

If hard evidence is scant for assessing commercial channel "output" (viewed in terms of lot size, waiting or delivery time, market decentralization, and product assortment), it is virtually nonexistent for assessing how well the heterogeneous production capacity of an industry is fitted by the sorting processes to the heterogeneity of consumer tastes and incomes.[12] There have, however, been some data gathered on this subject relative to disadvantaged consumers to which we refer later in this chapter.

---

[8] Monroe Peter Friedman, "Consumer Confusion in the Selection of Supermarket Products," *Journal of Applied Psychology*, Vol. 50 (December, 1966), pp. 529-534.

[9] For example, Buzzell feels that "most businessmen *and* most academicians would agree that the performance of an industry or company is higher, other things being equal, to the degree that it provides *choice* to customers and to the degree that it manifests *flexibility* in altering its offerings response to changes in demand." Robert D. Buzzell, "Marketing and Economic Performance: Meaning and Measurement," in Fred C. Allvine (ed.), *Public Policy and Marketing Practices* (Chicago, Ill.: American Marketing Association, 1973), pp. 154-155.

[10] The increase in commercial channel output relative to such items comes at a cost to the consumer, however, in the form of higher prices.

[11] Bucklin, *op. cit.*, pp. 33-34.

[12] A channel audit, as specified in Chapter 1, might provide a means for criticizing channel performance along these output dimensions. The end result should produce insights for social as well as business policy.

COST, EFFICIENCY, AND PROFITS

The focus here, as in the previous section, is on the performance of wholesalers and retailers. From a distribution cost standpoint, these institutions account for only a portion of total marketing charges that are incurred in bringing a product from its origin to ultimate consumption. Although their share is the dominant one, accounting for perhaps as much as 75 percent of the total,[13] other institutions (manufacturers, facilitating agencies, and consumers themselves) also contribute significantly to total marketing expenditures.

From a macroperspective, it is obvious to even the most casual onlooker that the cost of distribution in industrialized societies is relatively high. In such societies, progressions in economic development and consumer affluence are accompanied by a shift toward the sales of luxury-type goods, some of which carry extremely heavy marketing costs. The evolution of industrial goods markets also adds new marketing costs to the system, concomitant with economic growth.[14]

Suspicions about the relatively high cost of distribution have been confirmed by the statistics developed in a number of studies on the subject. For example, in a thorough investigation two decades ago, Harold Barger noted that the combined gross margins of retailers and wholesalers were 37.4 percent.[15] Wholesalers' gross margins were 7.7 percent, while retailers' were 29.7 percent.[16] More recent studies on distributive costs have focused on "value added" rather than gross margins. The former excludes from gross margins the costs middlemen pay for services rendered by institutions in other sectors of the economy, such as their expenditures for fuel, electric energy, and transportation. Thus, what remains in the distributive sector are the middleman's own costs, the charges on his capital, his expenditure on

---

[13]Louis P. Bucklin, *Competition and Evolution in the Distributive Trades* (Englewood Cliffs, New Jersey: Prentice-Hall, Inc., 1972), p. 296.

[14]For a thorough analysis of the productivity and performance of retailing and wholesaling in the United Kingdom, see T. S. Ward, *The Distribution of Consumer Goods: Structure and Performance* (London: Cambridge University Press, 1973).

[15]Harold Barger, *Distribution's Place in the American Economy since 1869* (Princeton, New Jersey: Princeton University Press, 1955), p. 60. Gross margin is always stated in terms of sales; the combined figure for retailers and wholesalers as a proportion of cost of goods sold would run over 50 percent.

[16]Stanley C. Hollander has provided some appropriate warnings about interpreting cost figures such as these in "Measuring the Cost and Value of Marketing" in William G. Moller, Jr. and David L.Wilemon (eds.), *Marketing Channels: A Systems Viewpoint* (Homewood, Ill.: Richard D. Irwin, Inc., 1971), pp. 373-383.

labor, and his profits. "Value added" may constitute as much as 70 to 85 percent of the distributive gross margin.[17]

From a theoretical perspective, "value added" supposedly indicates the unique contribution of middlemen to the final dollar value of products or services yielded by their managerial skills in combining labor, capital, and land in various ways.[18] For the 1964–1965 time period, the value added by wholesalers and retailers combined was approximately 23 percent; for the retail sector alone, it was about 14½ percent and for wholesaling, it was 8½ percent.[19] Since 1949, the percentages have been quite stable.

In a recent and highly innovative study, Bucklin computed the value added in the performance of marketing activities in six sectors of the U.S. economy—transportation, retailing, wholesaling, manufacturing, minerals, and advertising.[20] Although his findings are tentative and subject to error because of the way in which the data were derived, they provide some interesting comparisons, as shown in Table 6-1. Thus, in 1967, the value added in the marketing of commodities by the six sectors totaled $163.5 billion. Approximately 72 percent of the total was contributed by retailing and wholesaling, while another 14 percent was contributed by the logistical institutions comprising the transportation sector. The large share accumulated by the former two sectors indicates that any advances in their performance and productivity will have a marked effect on performance and productivity in marketing generally.

Within the agricultural and manufacturing sectors of the U.S. economy, increases in costs have been offset, to a significant extent, by increases in productivity as farmers, processors, and industrial firms have turned to innova-

---

[17] Bucklin, *Competition and Evolution . . . , op. cit.,* p. 298.

[18] The concept of "value added" is truly meaningful only if there is sufficient competition in a market. Otherwise, prices in that market include monopoly or oligopoly profits that are of doubtful "value" to consumers. This weakness in the concept prompted Sturdivant to observe that "the emergence of the value added concept doubtless retarded objective and critical analysis of socially significant questions related to distribution. With . . . a prevailing attitude that marketing costs must equal value or else goods and services would not be purchased, it is little wonder that consumer behavior emerged as the dominant area of interest for marketing scholars." Frederick D. Sturdivant, "Distribution in American Society: Some Questions of Efficiency and Relevance," in Louis P. Bucklin (ed.), *Vertical Marketing Systems* (Glenview, Ill.: Scott, Foresman and Co., 1970), p. 98.

[19] Bucklin, *Competition and Evolution . . . , op. cit.,* p. 300. While Bucklin's computations were called, in his study, distributive trade-cost ratios, they are very similar in nature to value-added computations. Furthermore, Bucklin's findings are similar to those presented in a thorough study by Reavis Cox, Charles S. Goodman, and Thomas C. Fichandler entitled *Distribution in a High-Level Economy* (Englewood Cliffs, N.J.: Prentice-Hall, Inc., 1965).

[20] Louis P. Bucklin, "A Synthetic Index of Marketing Productivity," a paper presented to the 58th International Marketing Conference of the American Marketing Association, Chicago, Illinois, April 14-17, 1975, pp. 4-8.

TABLE 6-1   Value Added in Marketing of Commodities in Six Sectors of the Economy, 1948, 1958, 1963, and 1967

Sector	Millions of Dollars 1948	%	Millions of Dollars 1958	%	Millions of Dollars 1963	%	Millions of Dollars 1967	%
Transportation	$11,560	19.7	$16,070	16.1	$ 17,582	14.3	$ 23,110	14.1
Retailing	26,440	45.1	44,419	44.5	55,708	45.3	75,214	46.0
Wholesaling	12,949	22.1	24,587	24.7	32,740	26.6	43,051	26.3
Manufacturing	6,934	11.8	13,709	13.7	15,227	12.4	20,103	12.3
Minerals	270	0.5	397	0.4	412	0.3	477	0.3
Advertising	439	0.7	685	0.7	1,185	1.0	1,594	1.0
Total	58,592	100.0	99,867	100.0	122,854	100.0	163,549	100.0

SOURCE: Louis P. Bucklin, "A Synthetic Index of Marketing Productivity," a paper presented to the 58th International Marketing Conference of the American Marketing Association, April 14–17, 1975 in Chicago, Illinois, p. 7.

tive technology in employing more expensive and scarcer inputs. Although we have noted in earlier chapters some important changes in retailing and wholesaling operations over the past half century, there has not been an increase in productivity similar to that found in agriculture and manufacturing. In fact, in recent years, wholesaling and retailing performance, relative to productivity, can be characterized, in the aggregate, as downright sluggish. For example, as shown in Table 6–2, between 1968 and 1972, output per man-hour in distribution rose much less rapidly than in other sectors of the economy. The explanation for this lies in the fact that retailing and wholesaling tend to be labor-intensive industries;[21] they have, therefore, traditionally experienced greater productivity problems than the more capital-intensive industries and, as a result, have been major sources of inflation.[22] The consequences of this lagging productivity are highly negative from a microperspective as well, as McCammon and Hammer point out:

> Lagging productivity at some point in time results in lagging wages. Lagging wages, in turn, eventually result in the recruitment of marginal personnel, which further

[21] The proportion of the labor force engaged in service activities in the United States increased from about a quarter in 1870 to 40 percent in 1929 to 55 percent in 1965. The distributive trades (retailing and wholesaling) account for over one-third of employment in services. See Victor R. Fuchs, *The Service Economy* (New York: Columbia University Press for the National Bureau of Economic Research, 1968), pp. 19, 24, and 30.

[22] "Expanding Service Economy," *Quarterly Review of Economic Prospects* (February, 1973), pp. 12–13.

TABLE 6-2   Average Annual Increase in Real Output per Man-hour (1968–1972)

Economic Sector	Percent Increase
Agriculture	4.5%
Mining	3.9
Manufacturing	2.3
Wholesaling	1.7
Retailing	0.8
Total economy	1.9%

SOURCE: Bert C. McCammon, Jr. and William L. Hammer, "A Frame of Reference for Improving Productivity in Distribution," *Atlanta Economic Review*, Vol. 24 (September–October, 1974), p. 10.

depresses productivity. The ultimate consequences of this iterative process is a stagnant and depressed industry.[23]

Nevertheless, there have been some improvements over time in the position of distributive trades relative to production. Between 1929 and 1965, output per person employed in the distributive trades increased at the rate of 1.6 percent per year compared to 2.7 percent for production. However, for 1947–1965, a period of very rapid structural change for trade, the rate of gain was 2.7 percent for distribution compared to 3.5 percent for production.[24] Interestingly, Bucklin has shown that between 1948 and 1965, output per man grew annually at a rate of 3.9 percent for wholesaling as compared to 2.0 percent for retailing.[25] As pointed out above, the major factors behind improvements in retail productivity appear to be increases in transaction size and reductions in the level of service provided per transaction.[26] The faster growth of productivity in wholesaling was likely due, in large part, to the major changes that occurred in the retail structure (e.g., the development of chains, supermarketing, discount operations, and various forms of retailing warehouse operations).

Despite the secular improvement in the relative standing of wholesalers and retailers in terms of output per man-hour since 1948, the more recent figures shown in Table 6–2 are not very comforting.[27] In fact, as a result of

[23]Bert C. McCammon, Jr. and William L. Hammer, "A Frame of Reference for Improving Productivity in Distribution," *Atlanta Economic Review* (September–October, 1974), p. 10.

[24]Fuchs, *op. cit.*

[25]Bucklin, "Marketing Channels and Structures . . . ," *op. cit.*, p. 29.

[26]Schwartzman, *op. cit.*

[27]It is important to note that productivity measures, in and of themselves, yield little information on the adequacy of the services provided. Indeed, as Bucklin has observed, high levels of produc-

TABLE 6-3   Average Annual Increase in Unit Labor Costs (1968-1972)

Economic Sector	Percentage Increase
Manufacturing	3.0%
Wholesaling	5.1%
Retailing	6.2%

SOURCE: Bert C. McCammon, Jr. and William L. Hammer, "A Frame of Reference for Improving Productivity in Distribution," *Atlanta Economic Review*, Vol. 24 (September–October, 1974), p. 10.

lagging productivity and rising wages, retailing and wholesaling companies experienced sharp increases in their unit labor costs between 1968 and 1972 (see Table 6-3). This pattern of rising unit labor costs had a significant impact on profit margins. Internal Revenue Service data indicate that retail profit margins declined from 1.4 percent of sales in 1968 to 1.0 percent in 1972. Wholesale profit margins fell from 1.2 percent to 1.0 percent of sales during the same period.[28]

Performance Evaluation Using the Strategic Profit Model

The strategic profit model has been developed by managerial accountants to evaluate and diagnose cost, efficiency, and profitability problems such as those that confront retailers and wholesalers. Because of the importance of such a model in formulating effective interorganizational strategies (as shown in later chapters) as well as in assessing performance in distribution, it is explained in some detail below.

The strategic profit model (SPM) is portrayed in Fig. 6-1. The SPM is basically a product of the insights into financial management generated by the DuPont Company. DuPont was one of the first to explore, in detail, the interrelationship of various financial ratios. In its planning activities, it de-

---

tivity may be an indication that the system is working poorly. For example, a recent review of wholesaling in Russia noted that sales per square meter of warehouse space were sharply higher than those in the United States. It was hypothesized that because such space was in short supply, rapid turnover was necessary. Sacrificed were "the kind and variety of services to which U.S. manufacturers and retailers are accustomed ...." Bucklin, "Marketing Channels and Structures..." *op. cit.*, p. 30. The information on wholesaling in Russia is from Roger Skurski, "Wholesaling of Consumer Goods in the USSR," *The Quarterly Review of Economics and Business*, Vol. 12 (Spring, 1972), pp. 53–69.

[28] McCammon and Hammer, *op. cit.*, p. 10.

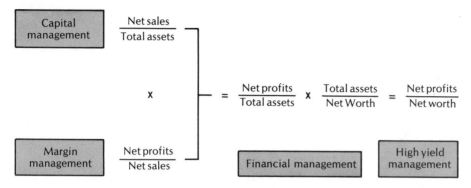

FIGURE 6-1   The Strategic Profit Model (SPM)

SOURCE: Bert C. McCammon, Jr., "Perspectives for Distribution Programming." From *Vertical Marketing Systems,* edited by Louis P. Bucklin. © 1970 by Scott, Foresman and Company. Reprinted by permission of the publisher.

veloped and used DuPont charts (see Fig. 6–2) which illustrated the fact that, for example, asset turnover and net profit as a percentage of sales are related, since the elements contained in them lead to net profits on assets.[29]

The SPM involves multiplying a company's profit margin by its rate of asset turnover and its leverage ratio to derive its rate of return on net worth. Let us look briefly at each of the components of the model.

Net Profits/Net Sales (Profit Margin).   The relationship of reported net profit to sales indicates a management's ability to recover the cost of merchandise or services, the expenses of operating the business (including depreciation) and the cost of borrowed funds from revenues generated during a given time period, as well as their adeptness in leaving a margin of reasonable compensation to the owners for providing their capital at a risk. The ratio of net profit to sales essentially expresses the cost/price effectiveness of the operation.[30]

Although the net profit margin shows how well the firm performs given a particular level of sales, it does not show how well the firm uses the resources at its command.[31] The amount of net profit may be entirely satisfactory from the point of view of the sales volume; however, the sales volume

---

[29] Erich A. Helfert, *Techniques of Financial Analysis,* 3rd ed. (Homewood, Ill.: Richard D. Irwin, Inc., 1972), p. 71.

[30] *Ibid.,* p. 53.

[31] For an insightful analysis, see Eugene M. Lerner, *Managerial Finance* (New York: Harcourt Brace Jovanovich, Inc., 1971), p. 46ff.

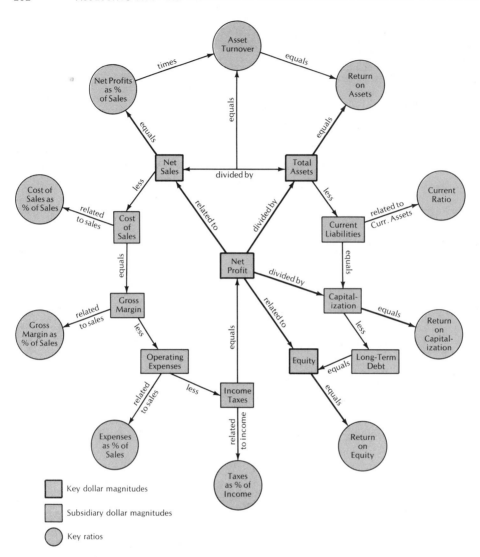

FIGURE 6-2   An Example of a DuPont Chart Showing Key Ratios as a System

SOURCE: Erich A. Helfert, *Techniques of Financial Analysis,* 3rd ed. (Homewood, Ill.: Richard D. Irwin, Inc., 1972), p. 71.

may be insufficient in relation to capacity, i.e., the amount of capital invested in assets used in obtaining sales.[32]

In addition, the ratio of net profits to net sales should also be consid-

[32] Ralph D. Kennedy and Stewart Y. McMullen, *Financial Statements* (Homewood, Ill.: Richard D. Irwin, Inc., 1973), p. 390.

ered in connection with the turnover of inventory and accounts receivable. Rapid turnovers of inventory and receivables may be a result of reduced sales prices and relatively high rates of cash discounts. When not accompanied by reduced costs and operating expenses, the smaller sales income would result in a lower net profit. A low net profit may be a result of excessive selling and general administrative expenses.[33]

Net Sales/Total Assets (Asset Turnover).   The ratio of net sales to total assets is a measure of the effectiveness of management's employment of capital and may show whether there is a tendency toward overinvestment in assets, especially in inventory and receivables in the case of wholesalers and retailers. This ratio (sometimes referred to as the "turnover" ratio) provides a clue as to the size of asset commitment required for a given level of sales or, conversely, the sales dollars generated for each dollar of investment.[34]

Net Profits/Total Assets (Return on Assets).   Neither the net profit margin (net profits/net sales) nor the turnover ratio (net sales/total assets) by itself provides an adequate measure of operating efficiency. The net profit margin ignores the utilization of assets, whereas the turnover ratio ignores profitability on sales. The return on assets ratio (ROA), or earning power, resolves these shortcomings. As pointed out by Van Horne, an improvement in the earning power of a firm will result if there is an increase in turnover on existing assets, an increase in the net profit margin, or both.[35] The interrelation of these ratios is shown in the SPM (Fig. 6–1). Two firms with different asset turnovers and net profit margins may have the same earning power. For example, if wholesaler A has an asset turnover of 4:1 and a net profit margin of 3 percent and wholesaler B has an asset turnover of 1.5:1 and a net profit margin of 8 percent, both have the same earning power—12 percent—despite the vast differences in operating modes. Thus, earning power can be improved by increasing sales revenue through higher prices (and probably lower volume) or higher volume (at probably lower prices). This may increase both profit margin and turnover. Costs can be reduced up to the point where they do not affect quality, and profit margin can be widened through improved control. The amount of capital employed can be reduced by increasing the

[33] *Ibid.*, p. 390.

[34] It should be noted that, while simple to calculate, the overall asset turnover is a crude measure at best, since the balance sheets of most well-established companies contain a variety of assets recorded at widely different cost levels of past periods. Helfert, *op. cit.*, p. 55.

[35] James C. Van Horne, *Fundamentals of Financial Management*, 2nd ed. (Englewood Cliffs, N.J.: Prentice-Hall, Inc., 1974), p. 39.

turnover of inventory and accounts receivable, and by utilizing the fixed assets more efficiently.[36]

Total Assets/Net Worth (Leverage Ratio). The ratio of total assets to net worth provides an indication of how reliant a firm is on borrowed funds for both short- and long-term purposes. The lower the ratio, the more the firm is being financially supported by owners' equity as opposed to debt capital. Although a low ratio indicates a high degree of solvency as well as a desire on the part of management to rely on ownership or equity capital for financing purposes, it also indicates that management is probably highly conservative and risk-averse. Debt capital requires fixed interest payments on specific dates and eventual repayment, as well as the threat of legal action by creditors relative to overdue payments. On the other hand, dividends on ownership capital are paid at the discretion of the directors, and there is no provision for repayment of capital to stockholders.

Furthermore, equity capital is typically more costly than debt capital. Thus, by retaining an excessive amount of ownership capital relative to debt capital, the company may be foregoing opportunities to trade on its equity (so-called *leveraging operations*) by refusing to borrow funds at relatively low interest rates and using these funds to earn greater rates of returns. Consequently, aggressive management will often rely heavily on debt capital, because if there is a difference between these two rates on a large investment base, management can increase earnings per share without having to increase the number of common shares outstanding.

Net Profits/Net Worth (Return on Investment). The main interest of the owners of an enterprise will be the returns achieved by management effort on their share of the invested funds. An effective measure of the return on owners' investment (ROI) is the relationship of net profit to net worth (equity). The ratio reflects the extent to which the objective of realizing a satisfactory net income is being achieved. A low ratio of net profits to net worth may indicate that the business is not very successful because of several possible reasons: inefficient and ineffective production, distribution, financial, or general management; unfavorable general business conditions; or over-investment in assets. A high ratio may be a result of efficient management throughout the company's organization, favorable general business conditions, and trading on the equity (effective leveraging).[37]

[36]Donald H. Schuckett and Edward J. Mock, *Decision Strategies in Financial Management* (New York: AMACOM, 1973), p. 122.

[37]Kennedy and McMullen, *op. cit.,* pp. 353–354.

As McCammon has explained, the SPM has four important managerial purposes:

1. The model specifies that a firm's principal financial objective is to earn an adequate or target rate of return on net worth.

2. The model identifies the three "profit paths" available to an enterprise. That is, a firm with an inadequate rate of return on net worth can improve its performance by accelerating its rate of asset turnover, by increasing its profit margin, or by leveraging its operations more highly.

3. The model dramatizes the principal areas of decisionmaking within the firm, namely, capital management, margin management, and financial management. Furthermore, firms interrelating their capital, margin, and financial plans may be described effectively as engaged in the practice of high-yield management.

4. The model provides a useful perspective for appraising the financial strategies used by different organizations to achieve target rates of return on net worth.[38]

We shall return in later chapters to some of these points. Here, we are concerned with the past performance of wholesalers and retailers (the distribution system, narrowly defined) in terms of high-yield management. The answer is provided in Fig. 6–3. Retailers and wholesalers experienced difficulty in improving their capital productivity ratios over the 1968–1972 time period. Given the previous discussion regarding costs, productivity, and profit margins, it is not surprising that the resulting ROI for both sectors of distributive trade is well below the minimum acceptable level of 10.0 to 15.0 percent recommended by Dun and Bradstreet and security analysts. Furthermore, the gap between the norm set by the analysts and the performance achieved by distributive institutions appears to be widening.[39]

In addition, McCammon and his associates have used the SPM to study retailing and wholesaling performance data spanning twenty years. For retailing, their conclusions were as follows:

1. A secular decline in retailing profit margins was due, primarily, to declining gross margin percentages, rising payroll expense ratios, and increased occupancy costs.

[38]Bert C. McCammon, Jr., "Perspectives for Distribution Programming," in Louis P. Bucklin (ed.), *Vertical Marketing Systems, op. cit.,* p. 38.

[39]Part of the reason for the poor return on investment (ROI) performance of retailers in 1972 can be attributed to developments in the food retailing industry. In this industry, the ROI generated by large food chains dropped from approximately 10 percent in 1971 to 5.8 percent in 1972 primarily because of A & P's "WEO" discount pricing program and competitors' responses to it. However, in 1974, after-tax ROI for the large chains averaged 8.9 percent, or about 50 percent higher than the 6 percent average for other retail industries. On the other hand, the chains' profit margin of about 1 percent has remained relatively constant over time. The more recent ROI figure merely indicates that the chains are beginning to regain their former levels of returns. There is some evidence, how-

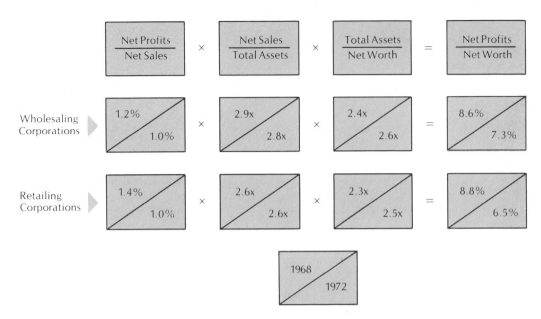

FIGURE 6-3   Composite Strategic Profit Model (SPM) for Retailing and Wholesaling Corporations (1968-1972)

Note: The above calculations may not equal the results indicated because of rounding.

SOURCE: Bert C. McCammon, Jr. and William L. Hammer, "A Frame of Reference for Improving Productivity in Distribution," *Atlanta Economic Review,* Vol. 24 (September–October, 1974), p. 11.

Other factors influencing the decline were increased taxes, liberalized depreciation allowances, and escalating media costs.

2. The rate of asset turnover and the ratio of total assets to net worth for all retail corporations have risen over the past several decades, offsetting, to some extent, the decline in profit margins. Converting to high turnover operations (supermarketing, discounting, etc.) and engaging in a considerable amount of leveraging were, however, not enough to counterbalance the decline in profit margins. As a result, the after-tax rate of return on net worth for all retailing corporations declined from 11.82 percent in 1950 to 6.5 percent in 1972.[40]

---

ever that the large food chains are beginning to utilize their assets more effectively and are engaging in aggressive leveraging operations. Ellen Soeteber, "Grocery Chain Profits Tops Among Retailers, U.S. Says," *Chicago Tribune,* July 12, 1975, Section 1, p. 3; and "FTC Staff Report on Food Chain Profits is Published," *Federal Trade Commission News,* July 11, 1975.

[40] *Ibid.,* p. 41 and McCammon and Hammer, *op. cit.,* p. 11. Data covering retailing and wholesaling performance in 1974 show basically the same results, but were obviously affected by the 1973-1974 recession, which was particularly hard on the distributive trades. See Albert D. Bates and Bert C. McCammon, Jr., "Reseller Strategies and the Financial Performance of the Firm," a paper presented at the Structure, Strategy, and Performance Conference of the Graduate School of Business, Indiana University, November 1975, p. 3.

Furthermore, retailers expanded their operations at an unprecedented rate during the 1950's and 1960's. New and significantly larger stores were opened in outlying areas, smaller facilities were abandoned, existing outlets were simultaneously remodeled and expanded, and inventory assortments were increased dramatically. As McCammon has pointed out:

> A rising proportion of the capital required to finance this expansion has been obtained from outside sources of funds with trade creditors being particularly important sources of short- and long-term capital. As a result, suppliers have become major financial institutions—the implications of which deserve careful study.[41]

The interorganization management consequences of such a development are explored in later chapters.

For wholesaling, some of McCammon's conclusions were very similar to those he found for retailing:

1. A decline in profit margins for wholesaling establishments was due, primarily, to rising payroll expenses, higher real estate costs, and declining gross margin percentages.

2. Contrary to retailing, rates of asset turnover declined over the period studied, which indicates that assets have been employed less productively over time. On the other hand, wholesaling corporations strongly pursued a strategy of leveraging their operations more highly, and the ratio of total assets to net worth climbed significantly. By 1970, creditors had more dollars invested in wholesaling than did the wholesalers themselves.

3. The increase in leverage ratios did not fully offset either the decline in profit margins or the deterioration in rates of asset turnover. As a result, wholesalers experienced a sharp contraction in their rates of return on net worth during the period studied. The composite ROI for all wholesaling corporations declined from 13.1 percent in 1950 to 7.8 percent in 1970.[42]

Thus, many retailers and wholesalers generated rates of return on net worth that were substantially below their effective cost of capital. If such a situation continues, it is likely that these organizations will find it increasingly difficult to raise equity capital; if inflationary pressures persist, the problem of capital attraction will become even more severe. In order to improve their profitability, the distributive trades *must* concentrate on improving rates of return on assets via increases in space productivity (sales per square foot of

---

[41] *Ibid.,* p. 41.

[42] Bert C. McCammon, Jr., "The Changing Economics of Wholesaling: A Strategic Analysis," in Barnett A. Greenberg (ed.) *Proceedings of the 1974 Marketing Association* (Atlantic, Ga.: Georgia State University, 1975), p. 91.

selling area), inventory productivity, scale of operation, and management of accounts receivable.[43]

From a microperspective, then, it is difficult to be laudatory about the aggregate performance of retailing and wholesaling institutions. There is, however, a curious contradiction in this area between macro- and microviewpoints. While businessmen view low profits as evidence of weak performance, economists and antitrust enforcement agencies often take an opposite position.[44] The latter would tend to attribute low profits to a high degree of competition in the marketplace which has served to force prices down to levels close to average and marginal costs. Although there is some evidence that competition has had some real effect on profits, as pointed out in previous chapters, it would be wrong to make the global assumption that the financial conditions in the distributive trades are solely or even primarily the result of competitive forces. In fact, it would be more logical to assume, given McCammon's data, that lack of innovative, effective, and aggressive management has been as much the cause as any other factor. Organizations such as Sears, J. C. Penney, Familian (plumbing wholesalers), W. W. Grainger (electrical distributors), Federated (department store chain), and McDonald's (fast-food restaurants) are uniquely and skillfully managed from an *inter-* as well as an *intra*organizational perspective, and, therefore, their profitability reflects this. But such organizations are obviously the exception, not the rule, in distribution.[45]

EQUITY IN SERVING VARIOUS MARKETS

Given the profusion of wholesaling and retailing institutions in the United States, it is difficult to imagine pockets of the population that are not adequately served by the distributive trades, at least in terms of the availability of goods and services at fairly reasonable prices. Yet it has been carefully documented by a number of scholars that the poor in the United States, especially those individuals living in ghetto areas of major cities and in rural communities, are disadvantaged by the distributive system as well as by other aspects of our economy and society.[46] While there is some evidence of out-

---

[43] Bates and McCammon, *op. cit.*, pp. 8–10.

[44] For a discussion of these points, see Louis W. Stern and John R. Grabner, Jr., *Competition in the Marketplace* (Glenview, Ill.: Scott, Foresman and Co., 1970).

[45] For a financial analysis of some highly successful retailers and wholesalers, see Bates and McCammon, *op. cit.*, pp. 27ff; and Bert C. McCammon, Jr., and James M. Kenderdine, "High Performance Wholesaling," *Hardlines Wholesaling* (September 1975), pp. 17–51.

[46] See, for example, David Caplovitz, *The Poor Pay More* (New York: The Free Press, 1963); Louise G. Richards, "Consumer Practices of the Poor," in Lola M. Irelan (ed.), *Low-Income Life Styles* (Washington, D.C.: U.S. Department of Health, Education, and Welfare, Welfare Administration,

right discrimination against minority groups by merchants in their pricing and credit practices,[47] the primary reasons for the absence of broad assortments of reasonably priced merchandise and services seem to be related more to the structure of trade in these areas than to any purposive strategy of racial or socioeconomic bias. For example, it has been shown that food chain prices do not vary significantly between ghetto and suburban locations within a given trading area, although there is still some controversy as to whether quality differs among outlets of a given chain organization.[48] Rather, it is the absence of food chain and major department store operations in the ghetto and rural areas that prohibits the residents of these areas from obtaining the benefits available to their suburban counterparts. The mobility of the poor is limited, so they must rely on the stores within their communities. While these stores have been known to charge high prices and to extend credit at usurious rates, their profitability is very low, which indicates that their costs of doing business are extremely high.[49]

A partial explanation of this inequity in distribution is the fact that ghetto retailers in particular are offering "services" of some importance to their constituents, most of whom, according to Goodman, are aware of the high prices being paid. Among these services are high-risk credit, small-lot transactions, convenient purchasing, and a persuasive (often deceptive) rationale to buy goods poor consumers would like to have but cannot really afford.[50]

From a competitive perspective, the structure of retailing in ghettos is highly atomistic. There are many small stores offering similar merchandise. Barriers to entry, as Sturdivant points out, are also quite low.[51] Therefore, on the basis of economic theory,[52] one would predict that performance,

---

Publication No. 14), pp. 67–86; Frederick D. Sturdivant and Walter T. Wilhelm, "Poverty, Minorities, and Consumer Exploitation," *Social Science Quarterly*, Vol. 49 (December, 1968), pp. 643–650; and Frederick D. Sturdivant (ed.), *The Ghetto Marketplace* (New York: Free Press, 1969).

[47] See Sturdivant and Wilhelm, *op. cit.*

[48] Donald E. Sexton, Jr., "Do Blacks Pay More?" *Journal of Marketing Research*, Vol. 8 (November, 1971), pp. 420–426; Charles S. Goodman, "Do the Poor Pay More?" *Journal of Marketing*, Vol. 32 (January, 1968), pp. 18–24; Donald F. Dixon and Daniel J. McLaughlin, Jr., "Low-Income Consumers and the Issue of Exploitation: A Study of Chain Supermarkets," *Social Science Quarterly*, Vol. 51 (September, 1970), pp. 320–328; and Louis W. Stern and William S. Sargent, "Comparative Prices and Pedagogy: Towards Relevance in Marketing Education," *Journal of Business Research*, Vol. 2 (October, 1974), pp. 435–46.

[49] *Economic Report on Installment Credit and Retail Sales Practices of District of Columbia Retailers* (Washington, D.C.: Federal Trade Commission, 1968), p. 18.

[50] Charles S. Goodman, "Whither the Marketing System in Low-Income Areas," *Wharton Quarterly* (Spring, 1970).

[51] Sturdivant, "Distribution in American Society . . . ," *op. cit.*, pp. 102–103.

[52] See the arguments presented by Joe S. Bain, *Industrial Organization*, 2nd ed. (New York: John Wiley & Sons, 1968) and Richard Caves, *American Industry: Structure, Conduct and Performance*, 2nd ed. (Englewood Cliffs, N.J.: Prentice-Hall, Inc., 1967). These positions have been summarized in Stern and Grabner, *op. cit.*

from a macroperspective, would be higher in ghetto areas than in the suburbs, where there are generally fewer outlets of larger size. The fact that marketing practices and performance are generally unbearably bad in the ghetto calls into question the assumptions of industrial organization economists about the benefits that derive from atomistic competition.[53] In fact, this questioning is supported by the findings of scholars who have studied less highly developed economies where similar structural conditions appear to hold. For example, in their critique of distributive systems for eggs, milk, and produce in sections of South America, Riley, Harrison, Slater, *et al.*, concluded that

> ... excessive atomistic competition hampers productivity improvements by stifling technological innovations and inhibits the agricultural and marketing development process by fostering market uncertainty, high transaction costs and excessive market wastes and by preventing the effective transmission of incentives to firms in the production-marketing system.[54]

While it is no doubt the case that the reluctance of food chains, department stores, and regional shopping centers, among others, to enter the ghetto and poor rural areas can be traced to high occupancy costs, crime rates, and/ or lack of discretionary income to support new, large-scale ventures, the fact remains that these areas are truly disadvantaged relative to other shopping areas and that, as long as they remain so, there will exist a high degree of inequity in the distributive system.[55] In this situation, only the institutionalization of a significant amount of interorganizational coordination between government agencies, chain organizations, wholesalers, manufacturers, and various facilitating agencies (such as insurance companies) will bring about needed change. Many suggestions relative to solutions on the supply side have been forthcoming, such as tax incentives for chain organizations entering the ghetto, investment credits, and the like,[56] but few have

[53]See Stern and Grabner, *op. cit.,* pp. 36–40 for a summary of the assumed benefits. Bucklin and Carman have, implicitly at least, raised similar questions regarding the performance of the present "atomistic" health care delivery system in the United States. See Louis P. Bucklin and James M. Carman, "Vertical Market Structure Theory and the Health Care Delivery System," in Jagdish N. Sheth and Peter L. Wright (eds.), *Marketing Analysis for Societal Problems* (Urbana-Champaign, Ill.: University of Illinois, Bureau of Economic and Business Research, 1974), pp. 7–39, and Chapter 14 of this book.

[54]Harold Riley, Kelly Harrison, Charles C. Slater, *et al.*, *Market Coordination in the Development of the Cauca Valley Region—Colombia* (East Lansing, Michigan: Michigan State University, Latin American Studies Center, 1970), p. 189.

[55]It is possible that shopping areas adjacent to many university campuses are subject to many of the same problems as those found in ghetto communities. See, for example, Stern and Sargent, *op. cit.*

[56]See Frederick D. Sturdivant, "Better Deal for Ghetto Shoppers," *Harvard Business Review,* Vol. 46 (March–April, 1968), pp. 130–139.

been enacted on a sufficiently large scale to have any major impact. On the demand side, it will obviously be necessary to elevate the incomes and increase the mobility of ghetto and rural residents so that they can have a modicum of bargaining power to use in their dealings with merchants located in their communities.

OTHER PERFORMANCE VARIABLES

There are a host of other variables that would be meaningful to evaluate in order to arrive at an overall judgment about performance in distribution.[57] From a macroperspective, it would be useful to know whether channels and channel institutions have been progressive over time, that is, whether they have been innovative and adaptive, especially with regard to changes in technology. From a social perspective, the effect of various distributive practices on energy consumption, hard-core unemployment, and the quality of the environment should be assessed. On the "micro" side, an evaluation of the number of stockouts, obsolete inventories, damaged shipments, and markdowns over time, among other operating variables, would provide a closer approximation to actual performance.

Unfortunately, aggregate measures for these macro and micro performance variables are generally unavailable or are restricted to narrow lines of trade. It is necessary, therefore, at this time to rely basically upon the information pertaining to system output, cost, efficiency, profitability, and equity provided above in arriving at a judgment about the performance of the distributive trades.

SUMMARY AND CONCLUSION

The focus of this chapter has been on assessing the performance of the distributive trades—particularly retailing and wholesaling—in terms of system output, costs, efficiency, profitability, and equity.

System output was evaluated in terms of the services (lot size, delivery time, market decentralization, and assortment breadth) that the commercial channel provides to ultimate household consumers and to business and in-

---

[57]For a discussion of a number of performance variables, see Robert D. Buzzell, "Marketing and Economic Performance: Meaning and Measurement," and John R. Grabner, Jr. and Roger A. Layton, "Problems and Challenges in Market Performance Measurement," in Fred C. Allvine (ed.), *Public Policy and Marketing Practices* (Chicago, Ill.: American Marketing Association, 1973), pp. 143–182. See also Steven H. Sosnick, "A Critique of the Concepts of Workable Competition," *Quarterly Journal of Economics,* Vol. 72 (August, 1958).

dustrial users. Historically, there has been an increase in the size of retail transactions, which has generated more direct buying on the part of retailing institutions. As a result, the need for wholesalers' services in the form of large-lot buying has been reduced. On the other hand, there appears to be no slackening in the desire of customers for rapid delivery, although it is possible that such demands may soften somewhat as periods of shortages are experienced both in the United States and abroad.

Market decentralization requirements have been reduced relative to convenience goods due to the development of greater mobility in personal transportation. But decentralization has been increased relative to shopping goods with the emergence of planned regional shopping centers. In addition, the requirements on the part of customers for broader assortments have spurred the movement toward larger retail stores and have, concomitantly, created an increased need for wholesaler services in gathering together diverse merchandise for retail display. A similar development has been witnessed in certain industrial goods markets (e.g., machinery, equipment, and supplies) that have sustained relatively rapid growth and have traditionally relied on a full range of services from wholesalers. On the other hand, the incidence of "double wholesaling" has been declining as manufacturers have become more sophisticated in managing promotional flows for their industrial products.

The costs of distribution—measured in terms of gross margins and "value added"—have remained high. These costs have, to a large degree, resulted from the process of industrialization and economic growth. If economic growth slows down, it can be expected that more emphasis will be placed, by both management and government, on reducing these costs. In order to do this, however, productivity will have to be increased. Productivity in the distributive trades—measured in terms of output per man-hour and output per employee—has historically been quite low relative to the manufacturing and agricultural sectors of the economy. The result has been that wage rates in distribution are below those in many other sectors, and, therefore, the ability of retailing and wholesaling institutions to attract skilled and competent labor has been poor. This factor, in turn, has bred further reductions in productivity levels.

The strategic profit model (SPM) has been employed in this chapter to assess financial productivity and profitability in the distributive trades. Profit margins (net profits/net sales) have declined for both retailing and wholesaling over time. Asset turnover (net sales/total assets) has increased in retailing but declined in wholesaling, while leveraging operations (measured in terms of total assets/net worth) have increased for both sectors. Overall, the decline in profit margins has not been offset by improvements in asset turnover or in leveraging, with the result that return on investment (net profits/ net worth) is relatively poor for both retailing and wholesaling institutions, in the aggregate. These findings, based on an application of the SPM, indicate that, in general, management in the distributive trades has not been highly innovative or effective.

While there is undoubtedly a great deal of flexibility and choice provided by the variety of available retailing and wholesaling institutions, from both a macro- and a microperspective, inequities in distribution do, in fact, exist, particularly with regard to the servicing of ghetto and rural communities. Although racial, economic, and social discrimination accounts for some of the inequity, the predominant reason for the problem appears to be structural inadequacies, especially in the ghetto marketplace. The atomistic retail market structures present there are not performing as well as industrial organization economists would lead us to expect they should. Incentives on the supply side and improvements on the demand side are required if the inequity is ever to be eliminated.

In general, there is a lack of data available to assess other key performance variables, such as progressiveness, ecological and environmental considerations, and operational efficiencies. Thus, it is necessary to rely on the present data in evaluating aggregate performance. On this basis alone, the conclusion must be that the overall picture is not very impressive, although it must be recognized that the standards applied are very high relative to those that might be employed in other parts of the world.

From both a macro and micro viewpoint, what appears to be needed is more coordination in distributive systems. Suboptimization is likely to occur in the absence of effective coordination.[58] From a management perspective, improved results for retailers and wholesalers are most likely to be achieved when, working in concert with other commercial channel members, profit margins *and* rates of asset turnover can simultaneously be increased, especially in light of the fact that retailing and wholesaling organizations are already highly leveraged.[59] On the macro side, it is likely that increased intra-channel coordination will lead to less duplication of efforts within the system and thus greater output at lower or at least stable costs. Furthermore, a resolution of inequities in distribution will, obviously, demand a synergistic effort on the part of government and commercial channel members.

The coordination required can be accomplished through effective inter-organization management combined with enlightened government policies

[58]See Helmy H. Baligh and Leon E. Richartz, *Vertical Market Structures* (Boston, Mass.: Allyn and Bacon, Inc., 1967) for an analytical proof of this assertion.

[59]McCammon and Hammer, *op. cit.,* p. 10.

and actions. In order fully to comprehend the variables involved in achieving such management within distribution systems, it is necessary to understand and analyze the behavioral dimensions of channel relationships. Through the judicious use of socioeconomic power and the employment of functional conflict management strategies, more efficient and potent distribution systems can be and, to some extent, are currently being structured.

DISCUSSION QUESTIONS

1. What criteria should be used to evaluate the performance of the distributive trades, other than those addressed directly in this chapter, from a macro (societal) perspective? From a micro (firm) perspective? How would the distributive trades rate on the additional criteria relative to manufacturing?

2. What criteria of performance should be used to assess the work of logistical institutions, from both a macro- and a microperspective? How would logistical institutions rate relative to the distributive trades on the criteria specified?

3. Should different criteria of performance be applied to channels comprised of nonprofit or publicly financed organizations? If yes, what criteria would you suggest? If no, explain how the various criteria would have to be modified to fit nonprofit situations.

4. What steps might be taken to increase productivity (output per manhour) in wholesaling? In retailing?

5. Debate the pros and cons of using value added as a measure of performance of marketing channels.

6. Explain how capital, margin, and financial management are interrelated. What problems pose the largest hurdles to the practice of high yield management within marketing channels?

7. Describe what you perceive to be the strategic profit models (or the strategies for achieving a high return on investment) for such firms as Neiman-Marcus (a department store catering to middle class and above consumers), A & P, Levitz (a furniture warehouse-showroom chain), Graybar Electric (a wholesaler of major appliances), and McKesson (a drug wholesaling firm).

8. What alternatives are open to retailers who face declining gross margin percentages, rising payroll expense ratios, and increased occupancy costs?

9. According to industrial organization economists, one would predict that when low seller and buyer concentration, little product differentation, and easy entry exist simultaneously in a market, the chances for good economic performance, from a social welfare perspective, are higher than in a reversed situation. How, then, could they (or you) explain the performance of the ghetto marketplace?

10. What are some likely solutions to the distribution problems in the ghetto marketplace?

11. Overall, how would you characterize the performance of the distributive trades? Is it poor, improving, or strong from a macroperspective? From a microperspective? If poor, what needs to be done in order to improve it?

SEVEN

THE INTERORGANIZATION MANAGEMENT OF MARKETING CHANNELS: AN OVERVIEW

In order to improve or maintain the competitive viability of any given channel of distribution, it is essential that the activities and flows within it be coordinated in an effective and efficient manner. It is only through purposive interorganizational coordination that channels can obtain their full potential as systems involved in producing satisfactory outputs for ultimate, business, and industrial consumers. Although it is possible that uncontrolled or free market forces could provide considerable benefits for these consumers, it is also likely that permitting such an atomistic, and potentially chaotic, functioning of markets would involve considerable waste in terms of resources and a minimal impact in terms of business policy. Therefore, it would seem that the individual organization could improve its market performance, from both a managerial and social welfare viewpoint, by recognizing its vertical interdependence with other organizations in achieving its market objectives and by coordinating its actions with them accordingly.

Interestingly enough, it should be noted that the coordinative approach advocated here and in later chapters is heresy when viewed from a classical economics perspective. This is so because the classical model implicitly denounces collective action and concentration of resources. The classical model suggests that ideal socioeconomic performance will be derived from a market comprised of a large number of competing firms, each of which holds a nonsignificant portion of the market and acts in a truly independent fashion in its policy formulation.[1] However, in the United States and around the world, it has been shown, consistently and over time, that those entities that are capable of organizing collective and consistent approaches to their respective markets have been most successful in garnering the rewards of "free" enterprise. On the other hand, those units that have permitted themselves to be buffeted by the whims of the marketplace without making concerted efforts to satisfy those whims through coordinated activities with other channel members or through vertical integration of one form or another have been left at the starting gate.[2]

The above realization is not to deny the significance of antitrust activities in a society where size can get out of hand and where dominance over the nation's vital resources can be achieved by a small number of firms. The legal framework within which channels of distribution operate is the subject of the next chapter; it is this framework that provides, for the most part, an effective constraint on the extent of vertical "collusion." However, a high degree of coordination is crucial if a channel is to survive and, hopefully, flourish.

In this chapter, an analytical framework for achieving effective coordination is discussed. Emphasis is placed on understanding the relevant behavioral dimensions of interorganizational relations, because it is through such an understanding that the manager can learn how to organize, manipulate, and exploit the resources available to him in the commercial channel system of which his firm is a part.[3] While attention is primarily focused on channels comprised of independently owned institutions and agencies, the same principles and premises apply directly to situations typified by vertical integration, where ownership arrangements among channel members are prevalent. However, in vertically integrated systems, the managerial technique and dimensions are more of an intra- than an *inter*organizational nature. This chapter is an elaboration and extension of the basic concepts developed in Chapter 1; it is, therefore, useful to review, very briefly, the underlying perspective developed in Chapter 1 before we expand on the concepts mentioned there. The approach taken is prescriptive rather than

[1]See Joe S. Bain, *Industrial Organization* (New York: John Wiley & Sons, Inc., 1968), Chapter 10, pp. 372–429. For a critique of Bain's discussion, see Louis W. Stern and John R. Grabner, Jr., *Competition in the Marketplace* (Glenview, Ill.: Scott, Foresman and Co., 1970), Chapter 4, pp. 48–68.

[2]One need only study the history of agricultural production and marketing in the United States to understand that farmers have slowly come to understand this basic premise regarding competition in an economy where oligopolistic patterns are the rule rather than the exception.

[3]The fields of organizational behavior and sociology are giving increased attention to the subject of interorganization relations. For some relevant reading, see Merlin B. Brinkerhoff and Philip R. Kunz (eds.), *Complex Organizations and Their Environments* (Dubuque, Iowa: Wm. C. Brown Co., 1972); and John G. Maurer (ed.), *Readings in Organization Theory* (New York: Random House, 1971).

descriptive; the focus is on how channels should be organized in order to remain viable.

THE CHANNEL AS AN INTERORGANIZATIONAL SYSTEM

In Chapter 1, it was postulated that a channel of distribution might be viewed as an interorganizational system comprised of interdependent and interrelated institutions and agencies involved in the task of moving goods and services from points of production to points of consumption. The commercial channel of distribution is the subset of the entire channel that excludes the consumer. The institutions and agencies within that subset can be manipulated and organized in such a way as to enhance competitive abilities, that is, to satisfy consumer needs and wants in a more complete way than other less organized systems might.

From a normative perspective, the allocation and exchange of resources in commercial channels first require a specification of role relationships for each of the channel members who will or do already act within a given interorganizational system. In order to accomplish such a specification in a reasonably efficient and rapid manner, either a formal or informal chain of command must be established within the channel. However, because of the interdependency that exists among channel members, conflict is inevitable. In other words, the dependency relationship will lead, at varying times, to frustration of individual members' goals. Furthermore, the use of power in role specification may generate additional conflict. It is, therefore, necessary to develop responses to conflict so that the frustration that is bound to arise within the system does not become dysfunctional. Thus, despite some possible negative side effects, economic and social power must be used to further rearrange the marketing flows and to alter roles, if need be, in order to arrive at a channel condition where only functional conflict exists—that is, a condition where solutions to conflict situations provide for more effective commercial channel performance than previously existed.

The interrelation among role specification, conflict, power usage, conflict management strategies, and commercial channel performance is depicted, in a simplified manner, in Fig. 7–1. It should be noted that feedback loops reconnect performance to conflict and to power usage. Thus, if performance is unsatisfactory, it is likely that a heightened sense of frustration will develop leading to increased levels of conflict, that power and its use may shift within the system, and that, as a result, roles will be further re-

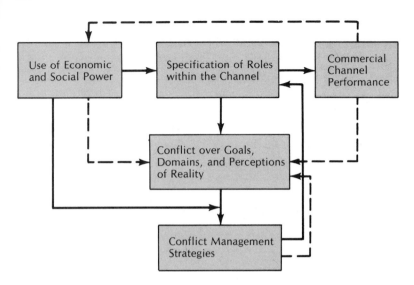

FIGURE 7-1　Interrelations among Role Specification, Power Usage, Conflict, Conflict Management Strategies, and Commercial Channel Performance

specified and realigned. In the discussion that follows, each of the behavioral dimensions of channel relationships is explained in some detail.

ROLE SPECIFICATION

The concepts of positions and their associated roles are basic to understanding the relationship of members in a socioeconomic system.[4] A *position* pertains, in general, to the location of a person or class of persons in a network of social relationships. *Roles* are the unifying factors relating persons or groups of persons to positions in that they define appropriate behavior for the occupant of each position.[5]

Positions connect the individual to the system and link each system, in turn, to the larger system of which it is a part. For example, an individual may occupy a position in a sales department. The sales department in turn occupies a position in a distribution channel system. Basically, each channel

---

[4]Much of the discussion in this section is based on Lynn E. Gill and Louis W. Stern, "Roles and Role Theory in Distribution Channel Systems," in Louis W. Stern (ed.), *Distribution Channels: Behavioral Dimensions* (Boston: Houghton Mifflin Company, 1969), pp. 22–47.

[5]Bruce J. Biddle and Edwin J. Thomas (eds.), *Role Theory, Concepts and Research* (New York: John Wiley & Sons, 1966), p. 29.

member selects a channel position. The channel position decision is a function of the channel member's goals, expectations, values, and frame of reference.[6] For example, if the member's goal is to realize a 15 percent return on investment and if such a return cannot be realized in retailing and wholesaling, then manufacturing may be a more attractive position for the member to assume.

As mentioned above, the roles associated with a position define the behavior of the position resident. On the basis of their knowledge of the roles assumed by a given channel member, occupants of counterpart positions are able to anticipate his behavior. In fact, the status associated with certain positions defines a series of rights or prerogatives as well as a series of obligations for a position-occupant. As pointed out by Gill and Stern:

> . . . a wholesaler and retailer in a distribution channel are aware of each other's role and are able to anticipate behavior. The retailer knows that salesmen will call at specific times, that goods will be delivered when needed and in good condition, and that special deliveries can be counted on to meet unexpected shortages. The wholesaler expects payment for the merchandise after a certain time period, knows the retailer will carry out promotional plans, and that a helper will be provided to unload delivered merchandise. Marketing channels cannot function without such sustained cooperation, in which each party knows what to expect from his opposite number.[7]

In fact, in specifying role relationships among channel members, prescriptions for role behavior evolve. Basically, *role prescriptions* are determined by the norms or behavioral standards (values and commonly shared ideals) of channel members for each other. Role prescriptions implicitly define certain levels of cooperation and coordination in the performance of marketing tasks. For example, a wholesaler has a set of role prescriptions for his position as well as for the positions of his suppliers and customers. The wholesaler may expect the manufacturers who supply him to stimulate ultimate consumer demand, to provide consistent levels of product quality, to consider the impact that major product additions and deletions would have upon his business, and to furnish up-to-date information about inventory conditions. By the same token, the wholesaler may expect the retailers to whom he sells to adequately forecast their needs, to cooperate with manufacturer-sponsored cooperative advertising programs, and to participate in wholesaler-sponsored training programs. In actuality, role prescriptions in-

[6]See Gill and Stern, *op. cit.*, p. 23.
[7]*Ibid.*, pp. 23-24.

dicate what each member desires from all channel members, including himself, relative to their respective degree of participation in the various marketing flows of physical possession, ownership, promotion, negotiation, financing, risking, ordering, and payment.

Obviously role behavior or performance frequently deviates from the prescriptions established by various channel members. While this deviation occurs for many reasons, the most likely causes of the deviation are specific situational factors (e.g., a price war in a retailer's trading area), incompatible organizational objectives, lack of clear and open communication flows between channel members, and differences between the deviating channel member's personal expectations and other members' expectations.[8] Furthermore, if adherence to the norms associated with a particular role behavior is not especially crucial to the survival of the channel system, then deviation from the established prescriptions by a channel member is not only more likely to occur, but should also be more tolerable to other channel participants. However, if the norms are "central" to system survival, then just the opposite will likely be true. Thus, role behavior is only partially a function of role prescriptions; each channel member brings to a channel position role behavior or performance unique to himself that is based on his own view of the marketplace and his status. The likelihood is high that a channel member will define his own domain—the population to be served, the territory to be covered, and the functions or duties to be performed—in a way which is, at least in part, incongruent with those with whom he deals.

In summary, attendant to each channel position is a set of role prescriptions. Each channel position-occupant brings to his chosen position different role behavior or performance that is determined by role prescriptions as well as by situational variables, organizational objectives, personal expectations, and channel communications. To the extent that different organizations in the channel have the same prescription for a role, that their prescriptions are the same as the channel member's conception of his own role, and that the channel member's performance is consistent with the prescriptions, *consensus* exists in the system. Consensus enables the members of the channel system to anticipate each other's behaviors, and therefore to operate collectively in a relatively unified manner. Functional role (domain) specification is, therefore, a key determinant of the effectiveness and efficiency of channel performance. Clearly, it should not be left to chance, for if it is, dysfunctional conflict is likely to erupt among channel members.

[8]See Warren J. Wittreich, "Misunderstanding the Retailer," *Harvard Business Review*, Vol. 40 (May–June, 1962), pp. 147–152.

THE EMERGENCE OF CONFLICT

As indicated in previous chapters, channel members tend to specialize in performing certain functions; that is, they have, at least in part, unique roles. Thus, manufacturers specialize in production and national promotions while retailers specialize in merchandising, distribution, and promotions on the local level. This specialization results in the creation of a significant amount of operational interdependence among channel members. Each channel member becomes dependent on the other members to realize his organizational objectives. For example, both the manufacturer and the retailer are dependent on each other to reach the final consumer. Members are "pushed" into such interdependencies because of their need for resources—not only money, but specialized skills, access to particular kinds of markets, and the like. Thus, functional interdependence requires a certain minimum level of cooperation in order to accomplish the channel task. Without this minimum cooperation, the channel ceases to exist. Such cooperation allows channel members to find means to coordinate their planning, information, and decision-making and so to arrange the payoff structure so that each member can justify joint goals on independent criteria.[9]

There is, however, as Gouldner asserts,[10] a strain toward organizations maximizing their autonomy; therefore, the establishment of mutual interdependencies creates conflicts of interest. In channels comprised of independently owned institutions and agencies, the strain toward autonomy will be juxtaposed to the desire to cooperate; that is, a mixture of motives will be present. It is, therefore, possible to predict with certainty that distribution channels will exhibit evidence of conflict. The relationship between interdependence and conflict has been documented in the social science literature;[11] Fig. 7-2 depicts this relationship. The greater the level of interdependence, the greater will be the opportunity for interference of goal attainment,[12] and hence the greater the potential for conflict among organizations. However, cognitive and affective states generally precede the taking of overt opponent-

---

[9]Matthew Tuite, Roger Chisholm, and Michael Radnor (eds.), *Interorganizational Decision Making* (Chicago: Aldine Publishing Co., 1972), p. vi.

[10]Alvin Gouldner, "Reciprocity and Autonomy in Functional Theory," in L. Gross (eds.), *Symposium on Sociological Theory* (New York: Harper and Row, 1959), pp. 241–270.

[11]See, for example, Henry Assael, "Constructive Role of Interorganizational Conflict," *Administrative Science Quarterly*, Vol. 14 (1969), pp. 573–582; John M. Dutton and Richard E. Walton, "Interdepartmental Conflict and Cooperation: Two Contrasting Studies," *Human Organization*, Vol. 25 (1966), pp. 207–220; Stuart M. Schmidt and Thomas A. Kochan, "Conflict: Toward Conceptual Clarity," *Administrative Science Quarterly*, Vol. 17 (1972), pp. 359–370; and James D. Thompson, *Organizations in Action* (New York: McGraw-Hill, 1967).

[12]Schmidt and Kochan, *op. cit.*, pp. 361–363.

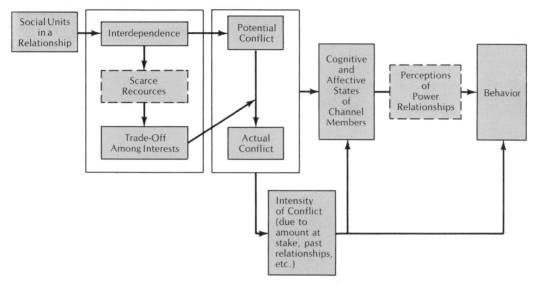

FIGURE 7-2 The Conflict Field

SOURCE: Reprinted from Fuat A. Firat, Allice M. Tybout, and Louis W. Stern, "A Perspective on Conflict and Power in Distribution," in *1974 Combined Proceedings of the AMA Fall and Spring Conferences,* ed. Ronald C. Curhan (Chicago: American Marketing Association, 1975), p. 436.

centered actions on the part of either party to a conflict situation. That is, the parties must usually first become aware or cognizant of the conflict situation as well as personalize the conflict so that hostile feelings develop.[13]

Channel conflict is a situation in which one channel member perceives another channel member(s) to be engaged in behavior that is preventing or impeding him from achieving his goals.[14] It is, in essence, a state of frustration brought about by a restriction of role performance.[15] The degree to which the behavior of one channel member could potentially destroy, thwart, or hinder the goal attainment of another is a function of goal incompatibility, domain dissensus, and differences in perceptions of reality between them[16] as well as the extent of their interdependence.

[13] Louis R. Pondy, "Organizational Conflict: Concepts and Models," *Administrative Science Quarterly,* Vol. 12 (September, 1967), pp. 296-320.

[14] Raymond W. Mack and Richard C. Snyder, "The Analysis of Social Conflict—Toward an Overview and Synthesis," *Journal of Conflict Resolution,* Vol. 1 (June, 1957), pp. 212-248.

[15] Louis W. Stern and Ronald H. Gorman, "Conflict in Distribution Channels: An Exploration," in Louis W. Stern (ed.), *Distribution Channels: Behavioral Dimensions, op. cit.,* p. 156.

[16] See Louis W. Stern and J. L. Heskett, "Conflict Management in Interorganization Relations: A Conceptual Framework," in Louis W. Stern (ed.), *op. cit.,* pp. 293-294; and Larry J. Rosenberg and Louis W. Stern, "Conflict Measurement in the Distribution Channel," *Journal of Marketing Research,* Vol. 8 (November, 1971), pp. 437-442.

Each channel member has a set of goals and objectives that are very often incompatible with those of other channel members. For example, large manufacturers tend to be growth-oriented, whereas small retailers are more interested in maintaining the status quo.[17] The likelihood of conflict is high in such a situation, because, in their pursuit of policies that are congruent with "dynamic" goals (e.g., increased market share and higher investment returns), the former will likely adopt innovative programs that contradict the more static orientation of the latter.

In addition, conflict arises over role performance (the defining of domains), via the process depicted in Fig. 7–3. Role conflict is often present in so-called dual distribution situations when, for example, a manufacturer competes directly with his own wholesalers by selling to some of the wholesalers' customers on a direct basis. Conflict may also occur when a channel member is assigned a role that he does not have the capacity to fulfill, when demands are made upon the channel member that are more than can be expected from the position within the channel that the member holds, and when a channel member feels he must relate to two reference groups and cannot decide which role is dominant.[18]

Differing perceptions of reality are important sources of conflict, because they indicate that there will be differing bases of action in response to the same situation. As a result, behaviors stemming from these perceptions are likely to frustrate and produce conflict. Incongruent perceptions of reality can be attributed to technical problems of communication,[19] as shown later in this chapter, as well as to differences in goals and orientations.[20]

A commercial channel system continues to function as long as the subsystems are willing to remain in the system. Each unit is induced to participate in a channel of distribution by the offering of certain rewards for its supposed unique potential contributions. The basic problem, then, is to

---

[17]Wittreich, op. cit. See Chapter 12 in this text for a fuller discussion of the communication problems encountered between large manufacturers and small retailers.

[18]Alvin L. Bertrand, Social Organizations: A General Systems and Role Theory Perspective (Philadelphia: F. A. Davis, 1972), pp. 173–177.

[19]See, for example, James G. March, "The Power of Power," in David Easton (ed.), Varieties of Political Theory (Englewood Cliffs, N.J.: Prentice-Hall, Inc., 1966), pp. 39–70; Clagett G. Smith, "A Comparative Analysis of Some Conditions and Consequences of Intra-Organizational Conflict," Administrative Science Quarterly, Vol. 11 (1966), pp. 504–529; and Kenneth W. Thomas, Richard E. Walton, and John M. Dutton, "Determinants of Interdepartmental Conflict," in Tuite, Chisholm, and Radnor (eds.), op. cit., pp. 45–69.

[20]See, for example, Assael, op. cit.; Dutton and Walton, op. cit.; Bert C. McCammon, Jr. and Robert W. Little, "Marketing Channels: Analytical Systems and Approaches," in George Schwartz (ed.), Science in Marketing (New York: Wiley & Sons, 1965), p. 322; Joseph C. Palamountain, The Politics of Distribution (Cambridge: Harvard University Press, 1955); C. G. Smith, op. cit.; Stern and Gorman, op. cit.; and Wittreich, op. cit.

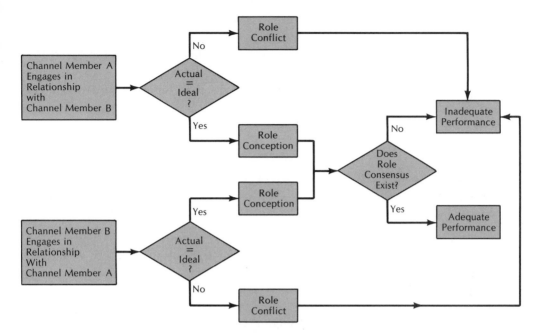

FIGURE 7-3   The Process of Conflict over Roles (Domains)

SOURCE: John R. Walton, Assistant Professor of Marketing, University of Minnesota.

achieve an inducements-contributions balance for each of the channel members—that is, a channel condition where the rewards offered by the channel system to a channel member are commensurate with the efforts expended by that member. Theoretically, this is accomplished when a channel member is successfully utilizing the distribution system of which he is a part for the achievement of his own organizational objectives, while at the same time the distribution system is effectively employing this individual channel member to attain its superorganizational or system objectives. If either of these conditions is not fulfilled, a satisfactory inducement-contributions balance cannot be affected, since dissatisfaction will flow from such a disparate channel system-channel member relationship. Thus, conflict will inevitably result when there is an imbalance between inducements and contributions.

If the conflict becomes dysfunctional or destructive (in which "pathological" moves are made that ultimately impede the performance of the conflicting parties *and* the system itself),[21] the channel system will move toward

---

[21]See Kenneth E. Boulding, "A Pure Theory of Conflict Applied to Organizations," in Robert L. Kahn and Elise Boulding (eds.), *Power and Conflict in Organizations* (New York: Basic Books, 1964), pp. 136–145.

eventual demise, even though organizational objectives may be satisfied in the short run. On the other hand, as pointed out in Chapter 1, channel conflict is a highly positive and necessary social phenomenon so long as it does not go above the threshhold where it becomes "malign" and impairs the output of the system.[22] As conflict approaches the functional or constructive end of the continuum, there is a strengthening of the system, because there is a receptivity to change within it.[23]

USING POWER TO SPECIFY ROLES AND RESPOND TO CONFLICT

If roles within a distribution channel were perfectly congruent, if role performance were maximal, and if conflict were minimal, there would, on the surface at least, be no need to induce changes in it. It is unlikely, however, that roles will be congruent, especially in newly formed channels, and even if they were, it is possible that economic, social, and political forces external to the channel would demand a realignment. It is obvious that role performance will probably never be maximal and that, as pointed out above, very low levels of conflict are unlikely over the long run (even in vertically integrated channels) because of the interdependency that exists in interorganizational systems. In order to achieve effective role congruence and performance and to keep conflict within its functional range, it is necessary to employ economic and social power.[24]

Simply put, *power* is the ability of one channel member to get another channel member to do what the latter would not otherwise have done.[25] More rigorously stated, one channel member's (A's) power over another (B)

---

[22]Kenneth E. Boulding, "The Economics of Human Conflict," in Elton B. McNeil (ed.), *The Nature of Human Conflict* (Englewood Cliffs, N.J.: Prentice-Hall, Inc., 1965), pp. 174–175.

[23]Lewis A. Coser, *The Functions of Social Conflict* (Glencoe, Ill.: The Free Press, 1956).

[24]Much of the following discussion on power is developed from Frederick J. Beier and Louis W. Stern, "Power in the Channel of Distribution," in Louis W. Stern (ed.), *Distribution Channels: Behavioral Dimensions, op. cit.*, pp. 92–116.

[25]For a more complete discussion, see Ernest R. Cadotte and Louis W. Stern, "A Process Model of Dyadic Interorganizational Relations," Working Paper Series of the Division of Research, College of Administrative Science, The Ohio State University; Ian Wilkinson, "Power in Distribution Channels," Cranfield (England) Research Papers in Marketing and Logistics, Session 1973–1974; Donald F. Dixon and Roger A. Layton, "Initiating Change in Channel Systems," in George Fisk (ed.), *New Essays in Marketing Theory* (New York: Allyn and Bacon, 1971), pp. 315–332; and Beier and Stern, *op. cit.*, pp. 92–116.

can be defined as the net increase in the probability of B's enacting a behavior after A has made an intervention, compared to the probability of B's
enacting the behavior in the absence of A's intervention.[26] There are several
implications of this formal definition that should be noted:

> 1. In stating a power relationship, it is not sufficient to say, "A is powerful";
> rather, A must be powerful over someone else (e.g., B). (Think of Sears relative to
> Tinkertoy versus Sears relative to Goodyear.)

> 2. The definition makes no distinction as to the means of getting B to do what he
> would not otherwise have done. The range of available means—coercion, rewards,
> expertise, identification, and legitimacy—are discussed below.

> 3. The definition does not require each application of power by A to result in overt
> reactions by B in order to be considered successful. Power attempts may only in-
> crease the probability of desired overt action on the part of B. Additional efforts
> may be required to achieve the actual movement of B.[27]

In addition, power can be viewed in terms of the extent to which one channel
member depends upon another. The more highly dependent B is on A, the
more power A has over B. For example, a small neighborhood retail druggist
may be much more dependent upon his wholesaler than the wholesaler is on
the druggist. According to Emerson, the dependence of B on A is (1) directly
proportional to B's motivational investment in goals mediated by A, and (2)
inversely proportional to the availability of those goals to B outside of the
A-B relation.[28] That is, the more A can directly affect B's goal attainment
and the fewer the number of alternatives there are open to B to obtain what
he needs in order to function properly, the greater the power A has over B.[29]

The use of power by individual channel members to affect the decision-
making or the behavior of others is the mechanism by which congruent and
effective roles become specified, roles become realigned, when necessary,
and appropriate role performance is enforced. As indicated above, there are a

[26]John Schopler, "Social Power," in Leonard Berkowitz (ed.), *Advances in Experimental Social
Psychology*, Vol. 2 (New York: Academic Press, 1965), p. 187. See also Robert A. Dahl, *Modern
Political Analysis* (Englewood Cliffs, N.J.: Prentice-Hall, Inc., 1964), p. 40; and Abraham Kaplan,
"Consequences and Prospects," in Kahn and Boulding, *op. cit.*, p. 12.

[27]J. L. Heskett, Louis W. Stern, and Frederick J. Beier, "Bases and Uses of Power in Interorganization
Relations," in Louis P. Bucklin (ed.), *Vertical Marketing Systems* (Glenview, Ill.: Scott, Foresman
& Co., 1970), p. 76.

[28]Richard M. Emerson, "Power-Dependence Relations," *American Sociological Review*, Vol. 27
(February, 1962), pp. 32–33.

[29]See, for further discussion, Adel I. El-Ansary and Louis W. Stern, "Power Measurement in the
Distribution Channel," *Journal of Marketing Research*, Vol. 9 (February, 1972), pp. 47–52.

number of bases of power that may be available to one channel member in his attempts to influence another and vice versa. These involve using:[30]

Rewards.   Reward power is based on the belief by B that A has the ability to mediate rewards for him. The effective use of reward power rests on A's possession of some resource that B values and which B believes he can obtain by conforming to A's request. Specific rewards that may be used by individual channel members may include the granting of wider margins and the allocation of various types of promotional allowances.

Coercion.   Coercive power stems from the expectation on the part of B that he will be punished by A if he fails to conform to A's influence attempt. Coercion involves any negative sanction or punishment that a firm is perceived to be capable of. Examples would be reductions in margins, the withdrawal of rewards previously granted (e.g., an exclusive territorial right), the slowing down of shipments, and the like. In fact, coercive power can be viewed as the "other side of the coin" relative to reward power. It should be noted, however, that the threat and use of negative sanctions can often be viewed as "pathological" moves and may be less functional over the long run than other power bases that may produce more positive side effects.[31] Therefore, coercion should be employed only when all other avenues to evoke change have been travelled.

Expertness.   Expert power is based on B's perception that A has special knowledge. Examples of channel members assuming expert roles are widespread. It has become rather common, for example, for small retailers to rely heavily on their wholesale suppliers for expert advice. For example, in the drug, grocery, and hardware trades, merchant wholesalers generally provide retailers with sales promotion counsel and aids, sales training for store employees, information about other retailers' promotions, advice on getting special displays, advice on store layout and arrangement, information on sources of items not stocked by the wholesaler, and managerial counselling. Such services may also be provided by manufacturers in the form of management training for marketing intermediaries.[32]

---

[30] John R. P. French and Bertram Raven, "The Bases of Social Power," in Dorwin Cartwright (ed.), *Studies in Social Power* (Ann Arbor, Mich.: University of Michigan Press, 1959), pp. 150-167.

[31] Louis W. Stern, Robert A. Schulz, Jr. and John R. Grabner, Jr., "The Power Base-Conflict Relationship: Preliminary Findings," *Social Science Quarterly*, Vol. 54 (September, 1973), pp. 412-419; and David A. Baldwin, "The Power of Positive Sanctions," *World Politics*, Vol. 24 (October, 1971), pp. 19-38.

[32] John Howard, *Marketing Management*, rev. ed. (Homewood, Ill.: Richard D. Irwin, 1963), p. 336.

However, the durability of expert power presents a problem in channel management. If expert advice, once given, provides the receiver with the ability to operate without such assistance in the future, then the expertise has been transferred and the power of the original expert in the relationship is reduced considerably. The receiver's dependence on his tutor is lessened or eliminated. In order for a firm to retain, over the long run, expert power over other firms in a given channel, any training or advice offered would have to be of a specialized nature so that the subject could not apply it to any other relationship except the one with which he is presently involved. For example, a manufacturer might retain his expert power by periodically offering to middlemen unique, well-planned, multifaceted promotional programs each time he introduces a new product.

Crucial to the retention of expert power is the ability of a channel member to position himself well with respect to the flow of communication and information within a channel system. For example, manufacturers may be highly dependent on the balance of the channel for information concerning consumer demand. Retailers and industrial distributors occupy preferred positions in this regard because of their close contacts with consumers of the manufacturers' products.[33] By gathering, interpreting, and transmitting valuable market information, a channel member can absorb uncertainty for other channel members. Through the process of uncertainty absorption,[34] the latter become more dependent upon the former relative to obtaining inferences about market developments.

Identification. Identification and referent power are, according to French and Raven, linked in a cause and effect sense.

> The referent power of A over B has its basis in the identification of B with A. By identification, we mean a feeling of oneness of B to A, or a desire for such an identity. . . . If A is an attractive group, B will have a feeling of membership or a

---

[33] Robert W. Little, "The Marketing Channel: Who Should Lead this Extracorporate Organization," *Journal of Marketing,* Vol. 34 (January, 1970), pp. 31–38.

[34] The concept and process of *uncertainty absorption* is discussed in more detail later in this chapter. Also see James G. March and Herbert A. Simon, *Organizations* (New York: John Wiley, 1958), p. 165. The implementation of uncertainty absorbing techniques could also be viewed more broadly as the use of *information power* rather than the enhancement of *expert power.* Informational influence or persuasion is involved when A provides information not previously available to B or when A points out contingencies of which B had not been aware. B may do what he might not otherwise have done, because, with the new information, he may view the specific action suggested by A to be in his best personal interest, aside from any consideration for A or possible rewards and punishments that A might mete out. Thus, information power is based on the acceptance by B of the logic of A's arguments rather than on A's perceived expertise. See Bertram H. Raven and Arie W. Kruglanski, "Conflict and Power," in Paul Swingle (ed.), *The Structure of Conflict* (New York: Academic Press, 1970), p. 73.

desire to join. If B is already closely associated with A, he will want to maintain this relationship.[35]

As an illustration, picture the situation where an individual is simultaneously offered a Mercedes Benz dealership and a Simca dealership. If he discovers, through careful analysis, that both dealerships will yield him the same rate of return on his investment and that the management of both companies will give him comparable support in promotion, training servicemen, finding a location, and the like, it is possible to conjecture that the individual will choose the Mercedes Benz dealership and that, in turn, the Mercedes Benz organization will be able to exercise referent power relative to its new dealership. The existence of referent power within many channels is undeniable, especially in situations where wholesalers or retailers pride themselves on carrying certain brands (e.g., Schwinn bicycles and Estee Lauder's perfumes) and where manufacturers pride themselves on having their brands carried in certain outlets (e.g., Marshall Field and Saks Fifth Avenue).

Legitimacy. Legitimate power stems from the values internalized by B which give him a feeling that A "should" or "has a right" to exert influence and that he (B) has an obligation to accept it. The appearance of legitimate power is most obvious in intraorganizational relations. That is, when a supervisor gives a directive to a subordinate, the latter feels that the former has a right to direct him in a certain manner, and therefore, he will generally conform to the superior's desires. Such legitimized power is synonymous with authority.

Within a nonintegrated marketing channel, there is no formal hierarchy of authority. However, individual firms may perceive that such a hierarchy exists. For example, the largest firm could be considered the leader by other channel members. If this is the case, then legitimate power may be available to that firm. It is highly likely that the scope of legitimate power may be limited; that is, the number of marketing flows over which a given firm may be thought to have a right to exert influence may be quite small (e.g., wholesalers may have legitimate power relative to elements of physical possession, retailers relative to the flow of local promotion and pricing, and the like).

Obviously, the system of laws allows firms to maintain agreements, such as franchises and other contracts, that confer legitimate power. In addition, patent and trademark laws give the owner a certain amount of freedom and justification in supervising the distribution of his products. Another example of this type of legitimate power is the protection afforded a manufac-

---

[35] French and Raven, *op. cit.*, p. 161.

turer and his dealers when the former adopts an exclusive distribution policy.[36]

The above discussion of power bases has treated each separately. In reality, however, the power bases are used in combination. Certain synergistic effects may be operative, e.g., legitimacy may enhance expertise and vice versa, identification may increase with the use of rewards, and coercion may sometimes be necessary to reinforce legitimacy. On the other hand, there may be conflict between certain bases; for example, the use of coercion by a channel member may destroy any referent power that member might have been able to accumulate.

In addition, it should be understood that there are economic, social, and political costs associated with the use of the various power bases which must be taken into account prior to the implementation of programs in which they are incorporated. Influence attempts are also constrained by norms that exist within channel systems. These norms, which are, in fact, "rules" of the competitive "game," aid in defining appropriate industrial behavior and can be even more restrictive than public laws in certain types of situations. For example, during periods of short supply in the steel industry, many buyers are willing to pay above "normal" prices for steel. This alternative is less expensive than shutting down production. Because of short supply, steel distributors in the established marketing channels can command higher prices; however, they frequently refrain from doing so, because they feel that their customers expect certain restraints from them, even though some of their customers go outside the legitimate, established channel structure and purchase higher-priced steel from so-called gray market sources.[37] The established distributors also refrain from using coercive power, such as boycotts, relative to the latter customers, because the norms of market behavior among them do not sanction such actions.

The bases of power can be used to shift the marketing flows and thus are central in fostering a more efficient and effective allocation of resources within a channel. On the other hand, power use is also extremely important in developing functional reactions to conflict situations. When conflict occurs, the various responses to the conflict on the part of channel members may be conceptualized as: (1) withdrawal, which occurs when a social unit addresses conflict by disengaging itself from the conflict relationship; (2) repression or concealment, which occurs when an involved party ignores or

---

[36]Exclusive distribution and other policies involving legal issues are discussed in Chapter 8.

[37]Louis Kriesberg, "Occupational Controls Among Steel Distributors," in Stern (ed.), *Distribution Channels: Behavioral Dimensions, op. cit.,* pp. 48–62.

refuses to acknowledge the conflict situation; (3) intraorganizational change; (4) the exercise of power.[38] Within the realm of the exercise of power are a number of conflict management strategies that may be invoked in an attempt to discourage "pathological" moves and to move the conflict situation towards useful settlement. The first two responses to conflict—withdrawal and repression or concealment—can, however, frequently be viewed as dysfunctional, especially if considerable effort has not been expended to seek out and remedy the cause of the conflict. Organizational selection of a specific response to a particular conflict state is largely determined by the organization's perception of its own power over others, its perception of the power of others over it, and its perception of others' perceptions of its own power over these others.[39]

The relationship between conflict and the power response to conflict is depicted in Fig. 7-4, which includes the notion of dependence as well as recognition of costs and benefits secured in a channel relationship. The conflict aftermath noted in Fig. 7-4 can result in changes in goals, domain definitions, and perceptions of reality, as well as in the benefits and costs mediated by the relationship between A and B. It is to be hoped that the end result of the use of power would be improved channel performance (that is, greater output at constant costs or the same output at declining costs).

CONFLICT MANAGEMENT STRATEGIES

If conflict within marketing channels is to be managed, it will eventually be essential for the members involved to come to grips with the underlying causes of the conflict issues that arise among them. The specific strategy employed will depend not only on the cause of the conflict but also on the weight of power of the channel member seeking to manage the conflict.[40] Several strategies for use in channel relations are suggested below, each of

---

[38]See Fuat A. Firat, Alice M. Tybout, and Louis W. Stern, "A Perspective on Conflict and Power in Distribution," in Ronald C. Curhan, *1974 Combined Proceedings of the AMA Fall and Spring Conferences* (Chicago: American Marketing Association, 1975), p. 436; and Louis W. Stern and Ronald H. Gorman, *op. cit.*, pp. 161-164.

[39]For a more detailed discussion of this point, see Firat, Tybout and Stern, *op. cit.*, pp. 437-438.

[40]The "weight" of power is a specification of how much A influences B. When the weight of A's power over B is at the maximum, it may be referred to as control, according to Kaplan. At this point, A can predict with certainty that B will respond in the desired manner. Abraham Kaplan, "Power in Perspective," in Kahn and Boulding (eds.), *op. cit.*, p. 14.

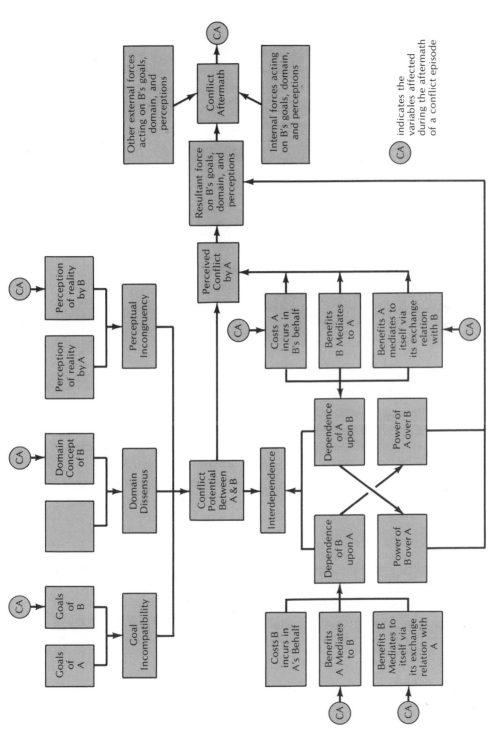

FIGURE 7-4   The Dynamic Process of a Conflict Episode in Dyadic Interorganizational Relations[a]

[a]The conflict episode portrayed here is taken from organization A's perspective.

SOURCE: Ernest R. Cadotte and Louis W. Stern, "A Process Model of Dyadic Interorganizational Relations," Working Paper, p. 2.

which can be modified depending upon the situational variables present in and the structural dimensions of a specific channel.[41]

Bargaining Strategies

No matter what conflict management strategy is adopted by policy-makers within a channel, resolution is always the result of bargaining—the making of commitments, offering of rewards, or threatening of punishments or deprivation—between and among the members.[42] In developing a bargaining strategy, two questions appear central: (1) How much is it necessary to concede? (2) How can the other side be induced to accept less favorable terms than it wants?[43]

A stable bargaining situation depends on the development and mainte-nance of trust and mutual respect between bargainers. One means for estab-lishing trust in channel relations is the taking of unilateral steps to reduce tension (e.g., a manufacturer lowering prices to intermediaries during a period of slack demand). For a unilateral act to be effective in inducing another channel member to reciprocate, however, it should

1. Be clearly disadvantageous to the member making it, yet not cripplingly so.

2. Be such as to be clearly perceived by the other member as reducing his external threat.

3. Be such that reciprocal action by the other member is available and clearly indicated (e.g., ordering in larger quantities).

4. Be announced in advance and widely publicized to all channel members (its nature, its purpose as part of a consistent policy, and the expected reciprocation).

---

[41] For a more detailed discussion of each of the conflict management strategies listed here, see Louis W. Stern, "Potential Conflict Management Mechanisms in Distribution Channels: An Interorganiza-tional Analysis"; in Donald N. Thompson (ed.), *Contractual Marketing Systems* (Boston: Heath-Lex-ington Books, 1971), pp. 111–146. For empirical research results relating to superordinate goals and exchange-of-persons as conflict management strategies, see Louis W. Stern, Brian Sternthal, and C. Samuel Craig, "Managing Conflict in Distribution Channels: A Laboratory Study," *Journal of Marketing Research*, Vol. 10 (May, 1973) pp. 169–179; and J. David Hunger and Louis W. Stern, "An Assessment of the Functionality of Superordinate Goals in Reducing Intergroup Conflict," Northwestern University Graduate School of Management Working Paper, #74-25. For additional ideas, see Larry J. Rosenberg, "A New Approach to Distribution Conflict Management," *Business Horizons* (October, 1974), pp. 67–74.

[42] For an empirical study of bargaining behavior in a marketing channel context, see Orville C. Walker, Jr., *An Experimental Investigation of Conflict and Power in Marketing Channels*, an un-published Ph.D. dissertation, University of Wisconsin, 1970.

[43] Thomas C. Schelling, *The Strategy of Conflict* (Cambridge, Mass.: Harvard University Press, 1960), p. 28. See also R. E. Walton and R. B. McKersie, *A Behavioral Theory of Labor Negotiations* (New York: McGraw-Hill Book Company, 1965).

5. Not demand prior commitment to reciprocation by the other member as a condition of its commission.[44]

Compromise, like trust, is a prerequisite in successful bargaining. Negotiations are possible only if each side is prepared to give up something in order to gain some of its objectives. In other words, the contending parties must be ready to accept a compromise rather than to seek a final solution to all of their differences. The difficulty with compromise outcomes is that the basic problem may not be solved and may continue to be a source of tension.[45] For example, steel manufacturers and distributors have reached, on many separate occasions, compromise solutions over the size of functional discounts to be given to distributors in the channels for stainless steel. And yet the basic problem—achieving more effective market resistance with regard to the threat posed by imported steel—still provides the foundation for continuing disagreements over pricing policies in the channel. Neither side to the bargain has been satisfied with the outcome.

The willingness to negotiate a compromise depends, of course, on correct assessment of the conflict situation; such assessment and the following accommodation are possible only if each party is aware of the relative strength of the others.[46] If implicit assessment is difficult, mediation, as discussed later, may be helpful.[47]

Within channels of distribution, it is likely that there will be considerable problems in selecting the appropriate negotiators for any given conflict issue. The obvious answer would seem to be that, if the issue is of major importance, the chief executive officer or, at least, the vice-president in charge of marketing (in the case of large organizations) should act as negotiator. Although such individuals have the unique advantage of being best able to commit their companies, they often suffer from lack of time, lack of specific experience, and undue pressures to produce results.[48] It may, therefore, be best to send to the channel bargaining "table" pragmatic, task-oriented men (rather than ideologues, as some top corporate executives must be) with at least some system perspective and an intimate understanding of the nature of the channel structure.

[44]C. E. Osgood, "Suggestion for Winning the Real War with Communism," *Journal of Conflict Resolution*, Vol. 3 (December, 1959), pp. 295–325.

[45]Daniel Katz, "Nationalism and Strategies of International Conflict Resolution," in Herbert C. Kelman (ed.), *International Behavior* (New York: Holt, Rinehart and Winston, 1965), p. 385.

[46]Lewis A. Coser, "The Termination of Conflict," *Journal of Conflict Resolution*, Vol. 5 (December, 1961), p. 352; and Coser, *The Functions . . .*, *op. cit.*, p. 137.

[47]Coser, "The Termination ...," *op. cit.*, p. 352.

[48]Jack Sawyer and Harold Guetzkow, "Bargaining and Negotiation in International Relations," in Kelman, *op. cit.*, p. 508.

One major limitation on the scope of negotiation in channel relation-ships is the difficulty of settling ideological differences through bargaining. For example, the desire to preserve small business is, in the United States at least, an ideological issue. While subject to debate, bargaining is not likely to resolve conflicts that arise when this "ethic" is juxtaposed to the desire to attain efficiencies through scale economies. Another limitation is the fact that, often, the purpose of one or more of the parties is not an agreement on the conflict issue but rather the pursuit of a side effect. Such side effects can be positive or negative, e.g., to maintain contact (to keep channels of communication open), to gain more knowledge of the other party's true position, to reveal the intentions of the other side, to deceive (to buy time, for example), to permit a forum for propaganda, or to affect a third party (the government, consumers, suppliers, middlemen outside the negotiation, etc.).[49]

Furthermore, public debate among channel members will also limit the chances of achieving an effective accommodation through negotiation. Taking a public position intensifies the problems faced by a negotiator, for when he deviates from a fixed public position (as he must, if a compromise is to be struck), it means that he is openly going against the publicized desires of his firm. It may, therefore, be impossible to negotiate successfully in channel situations if one side takes a specific and adamant public stand.

Boundary Strategies

A *boundary* position within a particular organization can be defined as one for which some role prescriptions are generated by individuals in an or-ganization's task environment.[50] The personnel of an organization who are concerned primarily with "external affairs" are called, in this context, "boundary persons." Within a channel of distribution, two key classes of boundary personnel are, obviously, salesmen and purchasing agents.

Diplomacy. In an analogy from international relations, channel *diplomacy* is the method by which interorganizational relations are conducted, adjusted, and managed by "ambassadors," "envoys," or other persons operating at the boundaries of member organizations. Channel members must engage in, cul-tivate, and rely upon diplomatic procedures, especially in nonintegrated

[49]Vernon Van Dyke, *International Politics,* 2nd ed. (New York: Appleton-Century-Crofts, 1966), p. 255.

[50]Robert L. Kahn, Donald M. Wolfe, Robert P. Quinn, and J. Diedrick Snoek, *Organizational Stress: Studies in Role Conflict and Ambiguity* (New York: John Wiley & Sons, Inc., 1964), p. 101.

systems. The functions of a channel "diplomat" should, in the widest inter-pretation, be to help shape the policies he is to follow, to conduct negotia-tions with channel members to whom he is assigned, to observe and report on everything that may be of interest to the firm employing him, and to provide information concerning his firm to the operatives in counterpart channel organizations.[51]

The presence of individual diplomats or of diplomatic committees is frequent in distribution channels, e.g., the use of business management specialists in the automobile industry and of factory specialists in the U.S. electrical equipment industry.[52] Perhaps the best example of channel diplo-macy can be found, however, in the U.S. food industry. Manufacturers appoint "liaison men" who represent and interpret company policy to wholesalers and retailers. According to an official of one major grocery manufacturer, the use of liaison executives in this industry has resulted in a resolution of many conflicts before they have matured.[53]

Because of some well-documented strains on boundary personnel,[54] it would probably be best to place the diplomat position at an executive level within organizations. It is essential that the status of the diplomat be high enough so that the power that the diplomat holds is at least relatively ob-vious to the parties with whom the diplomat interacts. This caveat would probably exclude salesmen or purchasing agents in most companies as candidates. The suggestion of Kahn, *et al.*, is highly pertinent:

> With respect to the liaison of the organization with the outside world, create specialized positions for which liaison is the major and continuing function. Pro-vide strong support for such positions, in terms of power, ancillary services, and organizational recognition.[55]

A channel diplomat should be thoroughly indoctrinated in and knowl-edgeable about organizational procedures and operations if he is to resolve

---

[51] Van Dyke, *op. cit.*, p. 252.

[52] Apparently, some of the "diplomats" in the automobile industry have used their positions for personal gain by helping dealers to falsify warranty claims and then blackmailing the dealers in return. Clearly, then, effective monitoring is required when this strategy is used, particularly when the diplo-mats are given considerable power by their firms. See "General Motors is Countersued by Ex-Dealer," *Wall Street Journal*, July 10, 1975, p. 4.

[53] Albert Adler, Herbert Johnson, Jr., and William Meschio, "The Food Industry," in Henry Assael (ed.), *The Politics of Distributive Trade Associations: A Study in Conflict Resolution* (Hempstead, N.Y.: Hofstra University, 1967), p. 195.

[54] Kahn, *et al., op. cit.*, pp. 123–124. See also Louis W. Stern, "Potential Conflict Management Mecha-nisms in Distribution Channels: An Interorganizational Analysis," *op. cit.*, p. 131; and Mahmoud Triki and Louis W. Stern, "Role Strain in Personal Selling," Northwestern University Graduate School of Management Working Paper #74-35.

[55] *Ibid.*, p. 393.

the uncertainty that his role often prescribes. In addition, to prevent occupants of these positions from developing too strong an identification with
specific channel members, diplomats should be periodically reassigned to
cover different members of the channel.

Interpenetration Strategies

Organizations with frequent interactions may be more likely to develop
patterns of conflict management in their interrelationships than those whose
relationship consists of only occasional events.[56] *Interpenetration* strategies
provide direct means for increasing the number of meaningful interactions.
Here, two primary approaches to interpenetration—membership and ideological—are suggested.

Membership. According to Lasswell and Kaplan, conflict among groups
varies inversely with their mutual permeability. "The permeability of a group
is the ease with which a person can become a participant."[57] Thus, in a specific channel context, the U.S. television receiver industry provides an explicit example of membership penetration:

> ... the lack of communications in the channel of distribution was one of the major
> dealer complaints. Another was the lack of product knowledge and the lack of un-
> derstanding of the dealers' problems on the part of the distributor salesmen. The
> approach used to correct the lack of communications was to invite the manufac-
> turers to become members of the National Appliance and Radio TV Dealers Asso-
> ciation (NARDA). Twelve of the major manufacturers are now members, and
> representatives of these and other companies now attend NARDA conventions.
> Manufacturers' relations meetings are a regular convention feature. Executives of
> manufacturing organizations are regular speakers at NARDA training seminars
> and at the regular convention.[58]

Interaction among the various representatives in trade association-
sponsored events is, however, infrequent. What is more desirable is the
creation of a network of primary relations among channel members. But
even on a relatively infrequent basis, the arranging of interorganizational

[56]Harold Guetzkow, "Relations Among Organizations," in Raymond V. Bowers (ed.), *Studies on Behavior in Organizations* (Athens, Georgia: University of Georgia Press, 1966), p. 14.

[57]Harold D. Lasswell and Abraham Kaplan, *Power and Society* (New Haven: Yale University Press, 1950), p. 35.

[58]Robert G. Biedermann and Richard L. Tabak, "The Television Receiver Industry," in Assael, *op. cit.,* p. 287.

collaboration on a common task jointly accepted as worthwhile and involving personal association of individuals as operating equals should result in lessened hostility among organizations.[59] Perhaps one of the most meaningful interpenetration mechanisms, in this respect, might be an "exchange of persons" program among channel members, similar to those implemented in international relations.

Exchange-of-persons involves a bilateral trade of personnel for a specified time period. The technique involved in such programs is essentially the same as role reversal, a procedure where one or both of the participants in a discussion present the viewpoint of the other. Conflict theorists have long suggested that role reversal would create a greater understanding of the other party's position than merely presenting one's own side of the issue.[60]

In distribution channels, exchange-of-persons could take place on several different levels of an organization or at all levels. Thus, as part of the initial executive training program, the recruit (perhaps fresh from college) could spend a prescribed period of time working in the organization of suppliers, middlemen, and/or customers. A salesman employed by a manufacturer could, on a periodic basis, spend a specified time as an employee of a wholesaling or retailing firm selling the latter's assortment of products of which the original manufacturer's product may be only one of several. In like fashion, traffic and inventory personnel could be exchanged, as well as other line and staff personnel. For certain types of employees, such as relatively prominent executives, it might even be possible to work out a sabbatical system similar to that at universities, so that these individuals could replenish themselves by taking positions either closer to or farther away from the ultimate market in which the product of the particular channel is sold.

Persons participating in such exchanges would no doubt take back to their "home" organizations a view of their job in an interorganizational context and a personal and professional involvement in the channel network, as well as added training. In addition to learning something of the complexities of another channel member's organization and mission, participants in such programs would have the opportunity of coming together with channel counterparts who share specific tasks, professions, and interests. These shared tasks could form the basis of continuing relationships that are extraorganizational in content and perhaps interorganizational in commitment.[61] It is

[59] Robin M. Williams, Jr., *The Reduction of Intergroup Tensions* (New York: Social Science Research Council, Bulletin No. 57, 1947), p. 69.

[60] For relevant citations, see Louis W. Stern, C. Samuel Craig, and Brian Sternthal, "Conflict Management in Interorganizational Relations," *Journal of Applied Psychology*, Vol. 60 (August, 1975).

[61] Anita L. Mishler, "Personal Contact in International Exchanges," in Kelman, *op. cit.*, p. 552.

highly likely that positive changes in attitudes toward other channel members would occur.[62]

An exchange-of-persons program in a distribution channel would be of little significance, however, if the only individuals with whom the "exchangee" comes into contact are no potential threat to channel cooperation or are already "converted" to an interorganizational view of channel relations. Furthermore, the "best" type of exchange might involve not merely a transfer of persons but common enterprises, jointly initiated and carried out on a relatively large scale. That is, optimally, the individuals participating in the exchange should participate in major projects concerned with policy-making within the channel.

Ideological.   Basically, ideological penetration refers to informational, propaganda, and educational activities aimed at managing conflict. Some of the aims of such activities may be

1. Simply to enhance knowledge and understanding.
2. To cultivate goodwill among channel members, gain prestige, and perhaps to undermine the goodwill and prestige of a competitor or competitive channel.
3. To shape attitudes among the personnel of another firm so as to influence its management to follow or not to follow a certain course of action.

What the channel propagandist (or educator) may be seeking is some sort of ideological "conversion." The effort by many manufacturers and wholesalers to influence certain retailers to think in terms of return-on-investment criteria rather than in terms of gross profit margins, for example, would, if accomplished, represent an ideological conversion, as well as result in changes in retail operating methods.

All other things being equal, educational programs will have maximum effects when information is presented as part of the ordinary action of a group or organization carrying out its usual socioeconomic function.[63] Thus, it would appear that ideological "conversion," if that is the aim, would be accomplished more quickly in on-the-job training situations where channel members interact directly with one another in the performance of a common task than through trade publications or other general information programs. A unique approach, which is somewhat in between the on-the-job and the general information approaches, might be the establishment of either libraries or training schools or both by channel members, either individually or collectively.

---

[62] See Jeanne Watson and Ronald Lippitt, "Cross-cultural Experience as a Source of Attitude Change," *Journal of Conflict Resolution,* Vol. 2 (March, 1958), pp. 61–66.

[63] Williams, *op. cit.,* p. 65.

Perhaps ideological penetration can be best accomplished through the process of *uncertainty absorption* by one channel member for others in the system.[64] This process was referred to briefly earlier in discussing expert power. Uncertainty absorption takes place when inferences are drawn from a body of evidence and the inferences, instead of the evidence itself, are then communicated.[65] The problem is to reduce uncertainty to the point where meaningful predictions are possible, and, as a result, to achieve at least a relatively uniform perception of the environment in which channel members operate. Once perceptual consensus is established, one can expect at least some reduction in conflict that was based on incongruent views.

The McKinsey study commissioned by General Foods provides an excellent illustration of an uncertainty absorption mechanism. McKinsey's recommendations on cost allocation and prices, shelf space, and inventories in supermarkets have been communicated to wholesalers and retailers with, reportedly, good results in helping the parties involved in the distribution of food to resolve conflict on these issues.[66] Another example is found in the automobile industry, which has experienced considerable intrachannel conflict in the past. Both Ford and General Motors develop statistical averages on sales volume, profit margins, and operating data useful for comparisons by dealers and area sales managers. The data provide the dealers with norms to strive for in altering their sales policies. Through their actions based on a more complete understanding of their markets, the dealers, with the support of the area sales managers, may thereby "negotiate" their "environment" in a more realistic and calculated manner.

Combinations of Membership and Ideological Penetration.

Perhaps the most effective type of interpenetration in terms of changing the goals, attitudes, or behavior of another organization occurs when the penetration involves both membership and ideology.[67] An important strategy in this respect is *cooptation*.

> Cooptation is the process of absorbing new elements into the leadership or policy-determining structure of an organization as a means of averting threats to its stability or existence.[68]

---

[64]Louis W. Stern and J. L. Heskett, "Conflict Management in Interorganizational Relations: A Conceptual Framework," in Louis W. Stern (ed.), *Distribution Channels: Behavioral Dimensions* (Boston: Houghton Mifflin Co., 1969), pp. 288–305.

[65]Simon, *op. cit.*, p. 166.

[66]Adler, Johnson, and Meschio, "The Food Industry," in Assael, *op. cit.*, p. 194.

[67]Guetzkow, *op. cit.*, p. 17.

[68]Philip Selznick, *TVA and the Grass Roots* (Berkeley, Calif.: University of California Press, 1949), p. 13.

The positive attributes of cooptation as a conflict resolution strategy are many. Cooptation may permit the achievement of ready accessibility among channel members in that it requires the establishment of routine and reliable channels through which information, aid, and requests may be brought. Administration of the channel may become more centralized so that the execution of a broad policy is adapted to local market conditions by utilizing the special knowledge of individuals attached to distributive organizations located in diverse markets. Cooptation also permits the sharing of responsibility so that a variety of channel members may become identified with and committed to the programs developed for a particular product or service.

A channel member, once afforded responsibility with regard to the generation of policy decisions throughout the channel, should gain increased awareness and understanding of the problems which the channel as a whole faces. As Thompson and McEwen observe, "By providing overlapping memberships, cooptation is an important social device for increasing the likelihood that organizations related to one another in complicated ways will in fact find compatible goals."[69] It might also be said that cooptation of channel members encourages their ideological transformation, so that they subsequently tend to carry the ideology of the coopting unit into their other membership groups.[70]

There are, however, some real dangers in implementing this device, especially for the coopting organization. Selznick states:

> The significance of cooptation for organizational analysis is not simply that there is a change in or a broadening of leadership, and that this is an adaptive response, but also *that this change is consequential for the character and role of the organization or governing body*. Cooptation results in some constriction of the field of choice available to the organization or leadership in question. The character of the coopted elements will necessarily shape the modes of action available to the group which has won adaptation at the price of commitment to outside elements.[71]

Thus cooptation makes inroads on the process of deciding goals and means. Not only must the final choice be acceptable to the coopted channel member(s), but to the extent that cooptation is effective, it places an "outsider" in a position to determine the occasion for a goal decision, to partic-

---

[69] James D. Thompson and William J. McEwen, "Organizational Goals and Environment," in Amitai Etzioni (ed.), *Complex Organizations: A Sociological Reader*, 2nd ed. (New York: Holt, Rinehart and Winston, Inc., 1969), p. 195.

[70] Guetzkow, *op. cit.*, p. 18.

[71] Selznick, *op. cit.*, pp. 15–16.

ipate in analyzing the existing situation, to suggest alternatives, and to take part in the deliberation of consequences.[72] Furthermore, as Etzioni warns, cooptation may be used to create a semblance of communication from others to those in control without effective communications really existing. Manipulated or fictitious cooptation only conceals the need for real communication and influence.[73] Establishing dealer and distributor advisory councils, for example, is merely patronizing if the firms convening such councils pay only lip service to what the participants say. In many cases, however, especially for such firms as Prudential Insurance and Belden, these councils or advisory boards have represented the use of cooptation in its most effective sense.

Supraorganizational Strategies

In channels of distribution characterized by a high degree of interdependence and interaction among members, fertile ground is found for the institutionalization of supraorganizational conflict resolution strategies. The supraorganizational strategies discussed below are (1) employing conciliation, mediation, and arbitration and (2) adopting superordinate goals. A significant level of unification within the channel would likely be necessary for the permanent establishment of these types of strategies. That is, channel members would have to view themselves as part of a channel *system* and thereby recognize, overtly, their functional interdependence. Even in these situations, however, the members will generally have different sets of active goals (or at least different preference orderings for the same set of goals), and thus the conditions for conflict will continue to exist among them.

Employing Conciliation, Mediation, and Arbitration. The process of reconciliation presumably leads to the convergence of opposing images held by the conflicting parties. In theory, *conciliation* is the passive role of attempting to bring harmony and a spirit of cooperation to a negotiation over conflicting issues and primarily involves adjustment of the dispute by the parties themselves.[74] In the U.S. pesticide industry, where both manufacturers and distributors belong to the National Agricultural Chemicals Association, the association frequently assumes a conciliator's role, often passively, with re-

[72]Thompson and McEwen, in Etzioni, *op. cit.,* p. 194.

[73]Amitai Etzioni, "Administration and the Consumer," *Administration Science Quarterly,* Vol. 3 (September, 1958), p. 261.

[74]Charles M. Rehmus, "The Mediation of Industrial Conflict: A Note on the Literature," *Journal of Conflict Resolution,* Vol. 9 (March, 1965), p. 119.

gard to distributive issues within the industry.[75] It is likely that, in many distribution channels, independent wholesalers also serve as conciliators between their suppliers and their customers and may occasionally serve as mediators. Here, the term "intermediary" has a double meaning, pertaining to marketing tasks assumed as well as to conciliatory functions performed.[76]

Mediation implies more active intervention by the third party. Mediation is the process whereby the third party attempts to secure settlement of a dispute by persuading the parties either to continue their negotiations or to consider procedural or substantive recommendations that the mediator may make.[77] Mediation essentially involves operating on the field of the conflicting parties in such a way that opportunities or trading moves are perceived that otherwise might not have been perceived. Solutions might be given an acceptability simply by being suggested by the mediator and hence acquire a degree of saliency that is important in making them mutually acceptable.[78] Effective mediation succeeds in clarifying facts and issues, in keeping parties in contact with each other, in exploring possible bases of agreement, in encouraging parties to agree to specific proposals, and in supervising the implementation of agreements.[79]

A prime function of a mediator is to restructure conflict situations so that the contenders can deal rationally with the divergent claims at issue. Once he has discerned what the realistic positions of the contending parties are (relative to their stated positions on an issue), he can then suggest proposals in the intermediate area of realistic demands or leak information to the various sides about what each side will settle for.[80] Through control of the communications structure, the mediator can reinforce or minimize the intensity of the position of one party as it is transmitted to the other.

A contemporary example of this form of conflict resolution, although not in a marketing channels context, was the establishment of a Board of Mediation in New York City. Financed by the Ford Foundation at a cost of $1.1 million, the Board acted as an agent for solving disputes among New Yorkers. In supporting the establishment of the Board, Mayor John Lindsay stated, "Men and women of the community will find new avenues for resolu-

---

[75] Robert W. Wesson, "The Pesticide Industry," in Assael, *The Politics of Distributive . . . , op. cit.,* p. 79.

[76] Rehmus, *op. cit.,* p. 119.

[77] Vernon H. Jensen, "Bibliography on Dispute Settlement by Third Parties," *Labor Law Journal,* Vol. 6 (August, 1955), p. 572.

[78] Kenneth E. Boulding, "A Pure Theory of Conflict Applied to Organizations," in Elise Boulding, *Conflict Management in Organizations* (Ann Arbor, Mich.: Foundation for Research on Human Behavior, 1961), p. 50.

[79] Robert H. Cory, Jr., "Conflict Resolution in the United Nations: A Review of Three Studies by the Brookings Institution," *Journal of Conflict Resolution,* Vol. 2 (June, 1958), p. 615.

[80] Katz in Kelman, *op. cit.,* p. 384.

tion of conflicts."[81] Similarly, a worthwhile investment in industries with a record of distribution conflicts might be the establishment of such boards, whereby respected individuals (e.g., retired judges, professors, and consultants) are held on retainer to aid in mediation with the consent of the parties. Many trade associations attempt to play the role of mediator, but their usually slanted interest makes them inappropriate for the task (aside from the possible antitrust implications of their actions).

Arbitration is another supraorganizational conflict management strategy that can be applied to channel situations.[82] Arbitration can be compulsory or voluntary. Compulsory arbitration is a process wherein the parties are required by law to submit their dispute to a third party whose decision is final and binding.[83] In a channel context, the government (or the courts) have served to settle disputes, as was the case when the automobile dealers and manufacturers clashed publicly over certain distribution policies and when fair trade pricing was a conflict issue between resellers and drug manufacturers. Voluntary arbitration is a process wherein parties voluntarily submit their dispute to a third party whose decision will be considered final and binding.[84] Examples of such arbitration are found by reviewing the Trade Practice Conferences of the Federal Trade Commission. One case is the television receiver industry. In 1955, the Federal Trade Commission, in concert with television set manufacturers, distributors, and dealers, set up 32 industry rules to protect the consumer and to reduce distributive conflicts. Five distribution conflict areas were arbitrated: (1) tie-in sales, (2) price-fixing, (3) mass shipments used to clog outlets and foreclose competitors, (4) discriminatory billing, and (5) special rebates, bribes, refunds, and discounts.[85]

Conflict management through voluntary arbitration requires at least three prior commitments among the disputants:

1. They have to agree that some form of settlement—even one involving the loss of a position—is preferable to continued conflict.

2. They have to agree to resolve the conflict on the basis of legal standards rather than according to political, economic, or social criteria.

3. They have to agree to the jurisdiction of a specific court, commission, or committee.[86]

---

[81] "$1 Million for 'Persuaders,'" *San Francisco Chronicle* (January 7, 1970), p. 9.

[82] Robert E. Weigand and Hilda C. Wasson, "Arbitration in the Marketing Channel," *Business Horizons* (October, 1974), pp. 39–47.

[83] Jensen, *op. cit.*, p. 573.

[84] *Ibid.*

[85] Biedermann and Tabak, *op. cit.*, pp. 280–282.

[86] K. J. Holsti, "Resolving International Conflicts: A Taxonomy of Behavior and Some Figures on Procedures," in Louis Kriesberg (ed.), *Social Processes in International Relations* (New York: John Wiley, 1968), p. 550.

Thus, in arbitration, a preliminary bargain must be struck, in the sense that the parties have to agree to submit to arbitration.

It should be noted, though, that the whole question of relying on law and law enforcement to manage conflicts in distribution is suspect, because it is doubtful whether permanently legislated solutions can be equitably applied to future conflicts in different channel contexts. As Assael has found, "internal" (intrachannel) conflict resolution has proven, historically, to be more satisfactory, from both a micro and a macro viewpoint, than "external" or legally imposed resolution.[87]

Adopting Superordinate Goals

> *Superordinate goals* are those ends greatly desired by all those caught in dispute or conflict, which cannot be attained by the resources and energies of each of the parties separately, but which require the concerted efforts of all parties involved.[88]

Conflict resolution of a relatively permanent nature requires an integration of the needs of both sides to the dispute so that they find a common goal without sacrificing their basic economic and ethical principles. The difficult task is, obviously, to articulate a goal or common interest on which all parties can agree.

If we disregard the social merits of certain goals for now, it is possible to provide two pertinent examples. In the U.S. television receiver industry, the desire for stabilized prices has served as a superordinate goal for certain manufacturers, distributors, and most retailers.[89] Similarly, in the U.S. liquor industry, distillers and small retailers have established the superordinate goal of preventing large, discounting retailers from gaining a significant market share. In carrying out this objective, small retailers have endorsed price controls in their attempts to prevent price competition, while distillers have provided continued small-retailer support in order to insure their leadership and thus resist the power of larger retailers.[90] It is doubtful, however, whether a defensive goal would be as effective, over the long run, in maintaining a viable channel system as one that would, say, emphasize the neces-

---

[87]Henry Assael, "The Political Role of Trade Associations in Distributive Conflict Resolution," *Journal of Marketing,* Vol. 32 (April, 1968), pp. 21–28.

[88]Muzafer Sherif, *Social Interaction* (Chicago, Ill.: Aldine Publishing Company, 1967), p. 457; see also Muzafer Sherif, O. J. Harvey, B. Jack White, William R. Hood, and Carolyn W. Sherif, *Intergroup Conflict and Cooperation: The Robbers Cave Experiment* (Norman, Okla.: The University of Oklahoma, 1961), p. 202.

[89]Biedermann and Tabak, "The Television Receiver Industry," in Assael, *The Politics of Distributive . . . , op. cit.,* p. 278.

[90]John Mingst and Robert A. Soriano, "The Liquor Industry," in *ibid.,* p. 369.

sity of increasing the efficiency of moving a product through the channel, with the result that greater sales volume would be obtained at lower, or at least stable, distribution costs.

The establishment of a superordinate goal requires equitable participation and contribution from all parties as well as mutual identification in interdependent activities.[91] In his experiment utilizing such goals, Sherif found that "ways of doing things, of meeting problems, of behaving under certain conditions were standardized, permitting variation only within limits."[92] Such standardization or routinization of behavior within channel systems is a prerequisite to effective channel performance.[93]

As indicated above, a superordinate goal can be an explicit desire by channel members to resist a threat to the channel's survival or growth from some outside pressure (e.g., competitive, legal). In such situations, the channel members may set aside their differences for the sake of defense. The process of meeting a threat external to the system will serve to displace or transfer hostility between and among channel members to the "common enemy."[94] However, a major question remains: When the outside threat is removed, will the internal conflicts return? In other words, is the cohesion ephemeral and is the prior conflict among channel members merely postponed?

The unified reaction on the part of channel members to an outside threat can be viewed as a behavior change, and as behavior changes, attitudes are usually altered to become more consistent with the new behavior. These new attitudes may remain once the threat is removed. In addition, during the process of countering the threat, information will be exchanged, some of which may have a bearing on sources of conflict beyond that posed by the threat. Because of the information exchanged and because of the monetary and psychological costs jointly borne by the parties during the time of combating the threat, future relationships between the parties may be significantly different than they were during previous interactions.[95] Channel members may gain empathy by seeing, perhaps for the first time, other channel members' points of view, even though these viewpoints are presented in a different context than under "normal" circumstances. Finally, the original conflict

---

[91]Sherif, *et al., op. cit.*, p. 212.

[92]*Ibid.*, p. 206.

[93]Wroe Alderson, *Marketing Behavior and Executive Action* (Homewood, Ill.: Richard D. Irwin, Inc., 1957).

[94]Amitai Etzioni, "The Kennedy Experiment," in Louis Kriesberg (ed.), *Social Processes in International Relations, op. cit.*, p. 431.

[95]George C. Homans, *Social Behavior: Its Elementary Forms* (New York: Harcourt, Brace and World, 1961).

issues—prior to the threat occurrence—may decay over time as energies are directed at the outside threat.[96]

On the other hand, there is a strong possibility that the prior conflict will reemerge, unaffected by the temporary unity of the parties. Blake, Shepard, and Mouton have observed that:

> The condition under which superordinate goals will produce cooperative effort, *without resolving the intergroup relations* problem, is when the assumed *superordinate goal is really a superordinate threat.* . . . In this circumstance, the groups put aside their own conflict until the greater enemy has been annihilated. But the differences that were set aside earlier return once the threat or superordinate need has been removed. In truth, then, the problem has not been solved. It has only been deferred under conditions of more pressing need for cooperative effort.[97]

In addition, while channel members are coalescing to combat the threat, it is unlikely that they will tolerate more than limited departures from the unity that they establish. Needed innovation and change, apart from that used in combating the threat, may be stultified during the time of unified action; the only way the channel members can solve the problem of dissent within their "ranks" at this time is, presumably, through the dissenter's voluntary or forced withdrawal.[98]

Thus, establishing superordinate goals on the basis of threats from the outside, whether conjured up or real, can be a double-edged sword. Extended periods of integrated effort may be achieved only when the institutions and agencies within a given channel come to grips with the underlying causes for their conflict and attempt to resolve them. The strategies previously discussed, if employed wisely, could lead channel members to the eventual adoption of *positive* superordinate goals.

The most significant output of effective conflict management is improved performance of the interorganizational system. Indeed, a concomitant result is likely to be increased satisfaction of the individual members of the system with their roles within it. Studies of distribution channels have found owner-manager satisfaction to be highly correlated with high levels of organizational performance.[99] Although it is difficult to specify causal relationships between performance and satisfaction (it is not known whether high

---

[96] For additional discussion on superordinate goals, see Stern, Sternthal, and Craig, *op. cit.*, and Hunger and Stern, *op. cit.*

[97] Robert R. Blake, H. A. Shepard and Jane S. Mouton, *Managing Intergroup Conflict in Industry* (Houston, Texas: Gulf Publishing Co., 1964), p. 89.

[98] Coser, *The Functions . . . , op. cit.*, p. 103.

[99] Hal B. Pickle and Brian S. Rungeling, "Empirical Investigation of Entrepreneurial Goals and Customer Satisfaction," *Journal of Business*, Vol. 46 (April, 1973), pp. 268–273.

satisfaction causes high performance or vice versa), it is possible to assert that effective conflict management strategies should produce benefits relative to both variables and thus, in the long run, be a key determinant in assuring the survival and growth of any given channel system.

THE NEED FOR CHANNEL LEADERSHIP

In order to achieve effective conflict management and thus improved coordination and performance within a channel system, it may be necessary to locate an institution or agency within the system that is willing to assume a leadership role, that is, an organization that will use its power bases to aid in overcoming the spontaneous variability of individual channel member behavior and to allocate the resources within the system so as to enhance the system's viability. Thus, channel leadership can be viewed as the use of power to intentionally affect the behavior of other channel members in order to cause them to act in a manner that contributes to the maintenance or achievement of a desired level of channel performance. In fact, the system may have to gravitate to one where control is required.

Channel control is the ability of a channel member to predict events and achieve desired outcomes in his relations with other channel members.[100] Channel control can result from channel leadership. Furthermore, like channel power, the level of channel control achieved by one firm over others in a channel may be issue specific. For example, while the manufacturer may have control over pricing, retailers may have control over inventory levels in the channel. Whether or not control can be exerted depends, of course, on the power at the command of the channel leader, on the drive for autonomy on the part of the members over whom control is being exerted, and on the latter's tolerance for control. Clearly, numerous intra- and extrachannel factors will determine how successful leadership attempts can be. Some of these factors include the demand and supply conditions pertaining to each source of power held by the potential channel leader, his efficiency in controlling his resources, the attractiveness of alternatives, the activities of other competitive channels, and developments in the socio-political-economic environment of which the channel in question is a part.[101]

The primary function of a channel leader will be to engage in channel management, using his power to further coordinative efforts and to dampen

---

[100] Adel I. El-Ansary and Robert A. Robicheaux, "A Theory of Channel Control: Revisited," *Journal of Marketing,* Vol. 38 (January, 1974), pp. 2–7.

[101] See Wilkinson, *op. cit.,* pp. 16–18.

dysfunctional conflict. The conflict management strategies suggested above will undoubtedly have a major effect in determining the character of the conflict aftermath. In fact, the end result of their successful implementation should be, as indicated above, channel member agreement on positive superordinate goals.

COMMUNICATION PROCESSES

As indicated earlier, communication is the vehicle through which channel systems are likely to be effectively organized. In fact, the development of a routinized channel communication system is necessary for the resolution of dysfunctional conflict, the development of channel coordination, and thus successful channel management.

Communication between channel members as senders and receivers of information is subject to "noise" in the form of omission and distortion of message contents. Omission occurs when a complete message is transmitted but not received, or when symbols are technically received but their meaning is ignored. Distortion occurs when the message is received but some change has taken place in the signal between the transmitter and the receiver, or a change in content meaning occurs between what the sender intended and that which the destination attaches to it.[102] Problems with regard to communication in distribution channels may result because of the overload of communication network capacity, the secrecy of information, the timing of message flows, or the perceptual differences between senders and receivers.[103]

Developments in the distribution channels for prescription drugs provide an excellent example of the overload problem.

> Doctors, faced by increasingly heavy patient loads, have less time available to spend with detail men from pharmaceutical companies. At the same time, the detail men have an increasing number of drugs to present to doctors. These overload factors may force the detail men to omit certain drugs from their presentations; moreover, the doctors may forget some significant portion of the variety of presentations to which they are exposed; and/or doctors may simply refuse, on either a random or purposive basis, to see all of the detail men calling on them. Doctors may tend to rely more and more heavily on the information supplied them by their peers in the profession, rather than that supplied by the detail men. This has been shown to occur especially in the adoption of new drugs.[104]

[102] John R. Grabner, Jr. and Larry J. Rosenberg, "Communication in Distribution Channel Systems," in Stern (ed.), op. cit., p. 239.

[103] Ibid., pp. 240–242.

[104] Ibid., p. 240.

The problem of secrecy in communication within channels is relatively clear; because certain channel members assume roles in more than one system at any given time, the willingness to divulge operating information will be, of necessity, stilted. Furthermore, as McVey has observed:

> . . . it is seldom practical (for a manufacturer) to disclose a forthcoming promotional plan in all its details and to ask the middlemen whether the plan will be timely, acceptable, and supportable by their efforts. To do so would jeopardize the advantage of surprise, usually a significant competitive strategem. Yet the value of synchronized, coordinated action on any new plan by all firms in the channel is obvious.[105]

The timing problem occurs frequently because information will often arrive at a particular point in the channel either too early or too late to be of maximum value for decision and control purposes. Finally, as indicated earlier, it is likely that channel members will often attach different meanings to the same symbols and assign different weights to the value of information, which leads to perceptual differences within the system.

In response to the abovementioned problems, several "noise"-reducing techniques have been suggested.[106] These include:

1. *Queuing.* The placing of messages in a line and delaying their receipt until adequate receiving and decoding capacity is available (i.e., "backlogging" messages).

2. *Sequencing.* Assigning specific times for each member of the channel to transmit specific pieces of information, such as orders, merchandising plans, and pricing schedules.

3. *Bypassing.* Avoiding one or more links in the normal communication network to eliminate bottleneck situations, especially during periods of crisis within the system.

4. *Specialized languages.* Systematically omitting some details or elements of a message by attaching a common, yet unique, meaning to a specific set of symbols to be shared by all senders and receivers in a channel system (e.g., uniform product codes).

5. *Altering technology.* Changing the form in which messages are transmitted and received by substituting machines for people, adding both machines and people to the system, or turning over a portion of the communications task to units or agencies specializing in some part of the communication process.

6. *Instituting feedback.* Providing a mechanism by which the sender can verify that the intended receiver has received and understood a message.

[105] Philip McVey, "Are Channels of Distribution What the Textbooks Say?" *Journal of Marketing*, Vol. 24 (January, 1960), p. 64. This problem is even more acute in certain international markets as discussed in Chapter 13.

[106] Grabner and Rosenberg, *op. cit.*, pp. 242–246.

7. *Repetition.* Transmitting the same message to the intended destination several times in identical or different forms and/or sending the same message through several different communication networks.

It should be recognized, however, that these means of noise reduction may, in turn, produce other kinds of omissions and distortions within the channel. For example, the fewer the number of sources from which information is received by channel members, the less likely will be differentiation of perceptions of reality among the members. Use of a number of different communication networks (i.e., repetition) to reduce omission may, therefore, serve to increase the likelihood of perceptual differences. It is one of the primary tasks of channel management to develop "noise"-free data systems that cross company boundaries; the selection of the appropriate communication vehicles will be a crucial determinant of channel success.[107] The subject of communications and information systems in channels is, therefore, discussed in some detail in a later chapter.[108]

SUMMARY AND CONCLUSIONS

The central theme of this chapter is that a high degree of interorganizational coordination is required within a marketing channel if that channel is going to have a long-run impact on the markets that it serves. Such coordination is achieved via concerted efforts at interorganizational management. Emphasis has been placed on a normative rather than a descriptive treatment. In essence, this chapter contains a prescriptive model for channel relations and management.

The basic model may be summarized as follows: Functional role specification among channel members is a prerequisite to achieving effective and efficient channel performance and is accomplished through the judicious use of social and economic power. However, conflict arises within channels due to (1) the interdependency of channel members relative to goal attainment and (2) the use of power in specifying roles. Thus, power must be reemployed in order to evoke conflict management strategies. These strategies will be significant in bringing about a realignment of channel roles and reallocation of resources within the channel system. The level of channel performance

---

[107] For illustrations of interorganizational computerized data systems, read Felix Kaufman, "Data Systems that Cross Company Boundaries," *Harvard Business Review,* Vol. 44 (January–February, 1966), pp. 141–155; and Louis W. Stern and C. Samuel Craig, "Interorganizational Data Systems: The Computer and Distribution," *Journal of Retailing,* Vol. 47 (Summer, 1971), pp. 73–86ff.

[108] See Chapter 12.

attained via this dynamic process will, in turn, affect the level of conflict in the system as well as the extent, use, and bases of power of the channel members. Each component of the model is briefly reviewed below.

Positions link channel members to each other, while roles define appropriate behavior for the occupant of each position. In the process of specifying role relationships, a series of prescriptions for role behavior evolves. The prescriptions are determined by the norms or behavioral standards of channel members for each other. Role prescriptions indicate what each member desires from all channel members relative to their respective degree of participation in the various marketing flows. There is, however, a strong likelihood that role performance will deviate, at least occasionally, from prescriptions because of situational factors, differing objectives, communication problems, and differing personal expectations among channel members. Thus, the process of role specification is likely to generate conflict within the system.

More generally, conflict is brought about because of the operational interdependence of channel members. The need to cooperate is juxtaposed to the desire to retain autonomy, and thus channels can be characterized as systems encompassing mixed motives. Channel conflict can be defined as a state in which one channel member perceives another channel member to be engaged in behavior that is impeding or preventing him from achieving his goals. Conflict is caused by goal incompatibility, domain dissensus, and differences in perceptions of reality as well as by the level of interdependence in the system. It results when there is an imbalance between the rewards a member receives from and the contribution he makes to the channel. While conflict is a positive social force which breeds adaptation and innovation, efforts are required to manage it, because it has the potential of preventing a system from achieving effectiveness and efficiency in providing outputs.

Viewed from a normative perspective, social and economic power must be employed in a marketing channel to assure role congruence, induce satisfactory role performance, and manage conflict. Power is the ability of one channel member to get another member to do what the latter would not otherwise have done. Power is synonymous with dependence; the more highly dependent one channel member is on another, the more power the latter has relative to the former. Available to channel members are several power bases that they may use to evoke change; these include rewards, coercion, expertness, identification, and legitimacy. They are most potent when used in combination. There is a cost associated with their use, however, which must be included as an integral part of the analysis in the development of interorganization management programs.

Perhaps one of the most significant functions of interorganization management is the generation of conflict management strategies, given the fact that conflict is an inherent phenomenon in interorganizational systems. Bargaining and negotiation strategy—which involves the making of commitments, the development of trust, and the willingness to compromise—appears to underlie the institutionalization of channel diplomacy, the effective use of exchange-of-persons programs, cooptation, conciliation, mediation, arbitration, and the establishment of superordinate goals. Perhaps even more important, the implementation of these latter strategies is likely to bring forth more rational and functional collective decision-making within the channel.

In order to activate the model of interorganization management, it is likely that channel leadership will be a prerequisite. It is even possible that control will need to be exercised within the system. The only means remaining for achieving control in certain situations will be vertical integration. There are, however, a number of interorganizational programs that can be enacted prior to actually acquiring a variety of channel institutions and agencies. Such programs (such as franchising and programmed merchandising) are discussed in Chapter 10.

Communication is the vehicle through which channel systems are likely to be effectively organized. There are, however, problems of "noise" in communication created by omission and distortion of message contents. Some of the primary causes of "noise" are overloaded communication network capacity, the secrecy of information, the timing of message flows, and perceptual differences between channel members. Several "noise"-reducing techniques are queuing, sequencing, bypassing, developing specialized languages, altering technology, instituting feedback, and repetition. From an interorganization management perspective, there is a strong need to develop "noise"-free data systems that cross company boundaries.

As indicated at the very outset of this chapter, the approach to the marketplace advocated here is very different from one that might be put forth by a welfare economist who believes that pure or perfect competition among and within the various levels of distribution will produce the greatest good for the greatest number. Although the latter argument may be valid, it would be foolish for the manager to ignore reality. Reality is that organized approaches to the marketplace have historically been permitted to exist, that such approaches have been commercially successful, and that it is unlikely, even in the very long run, that anything approximating pure or perfect competition will exist in industrialized societies. Thus, in order to insure long-term viability, interorganization management appears to be important for marketing channels. There are, however, constraints on the extent of vertical "collusion" that is possible; myriad laws restrict certain channel activities. Before we turn to specific interorganizational policies and strategies, we next address the scope and specifics of the legal constraints to interorganization management.

DISCUSSION QUESTIONS

1. What is the value of a prescriptive model for the interorganization management of distribution channel systems?

2. Distinguish between the terms "position," "role," "role behavior," "role prescription," "role conflict," and "role consensus." Develop a diagram of a wholesaler-retailer relationship that highlights the interrelationships between these terms. What other variables must be included in such a diagram in order to make it a complete pictorial description of the relationship?

3. Generate a list of potential sources of conflict in distribution channel relations. Give examples of each of these potential sources by relating them to any channel situation with which you are familiar.

4. "All conflict in channel relations is undesirable." Critically evaluate this statement.

5. Why is the use of power double-edged? Does conflict provoke the use of power, or does the use of power provoke conflict? Of the various bases of power, which would tend to produce less (more) conflict? Why?

6. Describe what you believe should be the executive background requirements and task obligations for the hypothetical corporate position of Vice-President—Interorganizational Relations. For what types of industries, as well as for what types of channel organization, would such a position seem necessary? How might the position's requirements and obligations change as channel structure changes?

7. Develop a list of likely role conflicts within channels of distribution. Discuss how such conflicts are or might be resolved.

8. How is the process of uncertainty absorption related to the amassing of power? When can the process of uncertainty absorption lead to less rather than more power for the absorber?

9. Describe the manufacturer-dealer system in automobiles in terms of power and role relationships. What are the dominant bases of power that are likely to be employed by either party in this particular channel system?

10. With recent deteriorations in consumer disposable income, more and more buyers are placing emphasis on product warranties and product service in their purchasing decisions. However, warranty programs have long been a source of conflict in marketing channels for consumer durables, especially in the appliance, automobile, and television industries,

with the ultimate result often being poor warranty program performance. Typically, conflict arises from dealer dissatisfaction with the warranty programs, stemming from such issues as increased dealer parts-inventory costs, the overloading of dealer-service capabilities, and the attendant substandard service levels these problems cause at the consumer level.

Select any of the above mentioned industries, and develop at least *five* specific and realistic manufacturer-dealer conflict issues involving a warranty service program. Then describe what you believe to be the most effective conflict management strategies that might be employed in dealing with each issue. Justify your selection.

EIGHT

LEGAL CONSTRAINTS
ON THE INTERORGANIZATION
MANAGEMENT
OF MARKETING CHANNELS

In order to institute effective interorganization management, the use of power is, as pointed out in the preceding chapter, a necessary predicate. There are, however, significant legal constraints on the manner in which power may be employed in the marketing channel. Prior to developing and implementing interorganizational strategies and programs, it is imperative that marketing managers at all levels of distribution comprehend the intention and the scope of these constraints so that any strategy or program that is promulgated will not meet with a negative reaction from the various anti-trust enforcement agencies.

The focus in this chapter is on federal legislation, even though it is recognized that there are a myriad of international, state, and local laws that directly affect distribution practices. In addition, attention is given here only to legislation directly affecting relations among commercial channel members. Excluded from the discussion is mention of consumer-oriented legislation, even though such legislation obviously tempers certain kinds of activities among and between commercial channel members.[1]

[1] The Federal Trade Commission has attacked thousands of devious schemes in distribution that directly affect the consumer. The largest categories have been fictitious pricing, wherein goods are falsely advertised as bargains; "bait and switch" advertising, by which customers, lured into a store by a spectacular bargain not intended to be sold, are "switched" to other more expensive purchases; exaggerated claims for the efficacy of drugs and cosmetics; the selling of used products as new; failure to disclose the limitations of guarantees; and misrepresentations of the quality of products. In addition, the FTC polices the labeling of furs and textiles so that a buyer can be sure the product is made

Although all legislation may be said to affect the legitimate power of channel members, the legal constraints examined below basically confine the use of coercive and reward power in channel management. In situations where vertical integration is employed to achieve the goals of a given distribution system, there are additional laws that inhibit the means by which such integration is accomplished and practiced. Therefore, the following discussion centers on legal limitations to the use of coercive and reward power *and* to vertical integration. The principal laws constraining interorganization management in marketing are listed in Table 8-1.

LEGAL LIMITATIONS ON THE USE
OF COERCIVE POWER

If a firm desires intensive distribution for its product, it will try to put it into as many channels as possible. This leads to relatively few legal problems in the area of customer selection, since *intrabrand* competition, or competition among resellers of the same brand, is usually unrestricted under these conditions. If, however, a firm wishes to limit the distribution of its product to certain outlets or to limit the freedom of its outlets in their methods of doing business, legal problems are more likely to arise. In such situations, a firm's refusal to sell or its adherence to distribution control policies may ultimately restrict intrabrand competition and lead to conflict with the antitrust laws. Each of the distribution policies and practices discussed below involves the use of coercive power in its implementation and enforcement, and each is circumscribed by law.

Exclusive Dealing

Exclusive dealing is the requirement by a seller or lessor that its customers sell or lease only its products, or at least no products in direct competition with the seller's products. If the buyer does not comply, the seller may invoke negative sanctions by refusing to deal with the buyer. Thus, such

---

of the material claimed on the label, the Flammable Fabrics Act to protect consumers from dangerously flammable clothing, the Fair Packaging and Labeling Act to inform the consumer as to the net contents of a package, the Truth in Lending Act, which enables consumers to shop for credit by comparing the finance charges and the annual percentage rates of creditors, the Fair Credit Reporting Act, which seeks to protect consumers from the reporting of erroneous personal information by credit bureaus, and the Consumer Product Safety Act, which attempts to minimize the number of physical injuries to consumers caused by dangerous or defective products. Major federal consumer legislation is reviewed in Burton Marcus, et al., *Modern Marketing* (New York: Random House, 1975), pp. 680-683.

TABLE 8-1   Principal Laws Affecting the Interorganization Management of Marketing Channels

Act	Key Provisions
Sherman Antitrust Act, 1890	1. Prohibits contracts or combinations in restraint of interstate and foreign commerce. 2. Makes monopoly or attempt at monopoly a crime in interstate or foreign commerce.
Clayton Antitrust Act, 1914	Where competition is substantially lessened it prohibits: 1. Price discrimination in sales or leasing 2. Exclusive dealing 3. Tying contracts 4. Interlocking directorates among competitors 5. Intercorporate stockholding
Celler-Kefauver Act, 1950	Prohibits purchase of assets of another firm if competition is lessened.
FTC Act, 1914	1. Prohibits unfair trade practices injurious to competition or a competitor. 2. Sets up FTC to determine unfairness.
Robinson-Patman Act, 1936	1. Discriminatory prices are prohibited if they reduce competition at any point in the channel. 2. Discriminatory prices can be given in good faith to meet competition. 3. Brokerage allowances are allowed only if earned by an independent broker. 4. Sellers must give all services and promotional allowances to all buyers equally if the buyers are in competition. Alternatives must be offered. 5. Buyers are prohibited from knowingly inducing price discrimination. 6. Price discrimination can be legal if it results from real cost differences in serving different customers. 7. Prohibits agreement with competitors to charge unreasonably low prices to destroy competition.
State Sales Below Cost	Prohibits selling below cost or without minimum markup.
FTC Trade Practice Rules	1. Enforced by FTC. Define unfair competition for individual industries. These practices are prohibited by FTC. 2. Define rules of sound practice. These rules are not enforced by the FTC, but are recommended.

arrangements clearly reduce the freedom of choice of the buyer. In establishing exclusive dealing provisions, the seller gains a market protected from competition within the buyer's outlets. The buyer, however, will generally receive some benefits from the arrangement, such as promotional support. He also avoids the added inventory costs that go with carrying multiple brands.[2]

Exclusive dealing contracts are legal under some circumstances and il-

[2]W. F. Brown, "The Effect of Federal Legislation upon Marketing Channels," in R. M. Clewett (ed.), *Marketing Channels for Manufactured Products* (Homewood, Ill.: R. D. Irwin, Inc., 1954), pp. 485–486.

legal in others. Section 3 of the Clayton Antitrust Act provides that this kind of restriction on wholesalers or retailers is unlawful if the effect of the contract may be substantially to lessen competition or to tend to create a monopoly in any line of commerce. These contracts have also been attacked under Section 5 of the Federal Trade Commission Act.

Exclusive dealerships do tend to lessen competition and create monopoly, since other sellers are excluded from the particular outlet. Whether this is considered substantial by the courts depends on two major factors:

1. Whether the volume of the product in question is a substantial part of the total volume for the product type.

2. Whether the exclusive dealership excludes competitive products from a substantial share of the market.

When either of these conditions obtains, the agreement is subject to attack as a restraint of competition. Both of these conditions depend on the relative size of the firms in their respective markets.

In the Brown Shoe case,[3] the Supreme Court decided that Brown Shoe Company, one of the world's largest shoe manufacturers, could be prohibited by the FTC from using exclusive dealerships as an unfair trade practice under the FTC Act. According to the Court, the contracts were in conflict with the spirit of the Sherman and Clayton Acts; therefore, the FTC was not required to prove actual or potential injury to competition as required by the Clayton Act.[4] This finding means that exclusive dealerships or franchises will be more vulnerable in the future to prosecution under Section 5 of the FTC Act than under provisions of the other antitrust laws.[5]

In the Standard Oil of California case, exclusive dealership arrangements between the company and its independent stations were declared illegal by the Supreme Court under Section 3 of the Clayton Act on grounds that competitors had been foreclosed from a substantial share of the line of commerce affected.[6] At the time, these exclusive dealerships accounted for only 6.8 percent of the total sales of petroleum products in the area.[7] The use of exclusive dealing contracts by Standard and other companies had, however, foreclosed over 50 percent of the market to independent oil refiners and

[3] *Brown Shoe Co., Inc. v. Federal Trade Commission*, 384 U.S. 316 (1966).

[4] T. N. Beckman, W. R. Davidson, and J. F. Engel, *Marketing*, 8th ed. (New York: Ronald Press Co., 1967), p. 407.

[5] R. O. Werner, "Marketing and the United States Supreme Court, 1965–1968," *Journal of Marketing*, Vol. 33 (January, 1969), pp. 18–19.

[6] *Standard Oil Company of California and Standard Stations Inc. v. U.S.*, 337 U.S. 293 (1949).

[7] Beckman, et al., *op. cit.*, p. 406.

wholesalers. The court declared "that exclusive dealing contracts as such are not illegal and that they might be a useful competitive device when employed by smaller firms, particularly when entering the market, but that their use by large, established firms might constitute an unwarranted restriction with consequent 'substantial lessening of competition.'"[8] Therefore, it becomes apparent that the use of exclusive dealerships by several firms in a market may be relevant to the legality of their use by one firm.[9]

Exclusive dealing can be imposed by the use of coercive power even in the absence of an explicit agreement. For example, tires, batteries, and accessories have been sold in gasoline stations of major oil companies in two different ways:

1. Purchase-Resale Agreements. Under this plan, the products are purchased from the manufacturer by the oil company and resold to the gasoline wholesalers and retailers.

2. Sales Commission Plans. Under these plans, the products are sold directly to the gasoline wholesalers and retailers by the manufacturer. The oil company receives a commission on all sales, and in return it assists with promotion.

In three cases ending in 1968, the courts held that the sales commission plan is inherently coercive because of the control that the oil company has over its dealers.[10] Market exclusion of other brands will result, and thus the plans are an unfair practice whether illegal intent is shown or not. In the Atlantic Refining case the Supreme Court confirmed this view.[11] The merits of purchase-resale agreements were not ruled upon by the courts.

A seller has the right to choose his own customers, but no coercion or intimidation can be used against the dealer to insure exclusive dealing.[12] Exclusive dealing arrangements are legal when they are entered into for reasons not connected directly with lessening competition. In the Sinclair case, the Supreme Court held that oil companies could forbid the sale of competing brands of gasoline from equipment supplied to the dealers by the companies.[13] The purpose of the plan was to prevent the dealers from switching brands without the knowledge of the consumers.[14] In addition, the dealers

[8]*Standard Oil Company of California, loc. cit.*

[9]Brown in Clewett, *op. cit.*, p. 489.

[10]D. F. Dixon, "Market Exclusion and Dealer Coercion in Sponsored TBA Sales," *Journal of Marketing*, Vol. 35 (January, 1971), pp. 62–63.

[11]*Atlantic Refining Co.* v. *Federal Trade Commission*, 381 U.S. 357.

[12]M. C. Howard, *Legal Aspects of Marketing* (New York: McGraw-Hill Book Company, 1964), p. 98.

[13]*Federal Trade Commission* v. *Sinclair Refining Co., et al.*, 261 U.S. 463 (1923).

[14]Beckman, et al., *op. cit.*, pp. 406–407.

were not prohibited by the agreement from having other pumps devoted to competing brands, so competition was not foreclosed.[15]

The Federal Trade Commission is also using Section 5 of the FTC Act to challenge retailers to stop making, carrying out, or enforcing anti-competitive leasing agreements. Similar to exclusive dealing arrangements, such agreements have given a retailer the right to be the only retailer of its kind (e.g., drugstore) in a shopping center, the right to reject or accept the opportunity to operate an additional outlet in a shopping center where it already has one ("rights of first refusal"), the right to prohibit or control the entrance of tenants into shopping centers, and the right to restrict the business operations of other tenants in shopping centers.[16]

In addition, requirements contracts are a variant of exclusive dealing contracts. They are agreements that a purchaser will buy all or a specified portion of his requirements for a good from a specified seller for a stipulated time period.[17] They may violate either the Sherman Act or Section 3 of the Clayton Act if it can be shown that the seller has some kind of coercive power over the buyer.[18]

Tying Contracts

Tying contracts are often found in exclusive dealing and franchising arrangements. These contracts require a buyer to take other products in order to obtain a product which he desires. These contracts can be held to be illegal under Section 3 of the Clayton Act when it can be shown that the seller has so much coercive power with respect to the tying product that he can restrain competition relative to the tied product *and* that a substantial portion of interstate commerce is affected.[19] The classic case in this area was *Thomson Manufacturing Co.* v. *Federal Trade Commission.* Thomson leased rivet setting machines at a low rental, but required its customers to purchase all rivets from the company at a price higher than that in the open market. Rivet makers that did not provide machines were excluded from the market. The court ruled that "the practical effect is to preclude the use of supplies of a competitor and thus substantially lessen competition."[20]

[15] Brown in Clewett, *op. cit.*, p. 476.

[16] "Order Against Drug Chain Bans Shopping Center Lease Restrictions," *FTC News Summary* (October 10, 1975), p. 1. See also "Antitrust Action in the Shopping Malls," *Business Week*, December 8, 1975, p. 51.

[17] L. W. Stern and J. R. Grabner, Jr., *Competition in the Marketplace* (Glenview, Ill.: Scott, Foresman and Co., 1970), pp. 133–134.

[18] Howard, *op. cit.*, p. 99.
[19] Stern and Grabner, *op. cit.*, p. 132.

[20] Beckman, et al., *op. cit.*, p. 406.

Certain types of tying contracts are legal. If two products are made to be used jointly and one will not function properly without the other, the courts have ruled that the agreement is within the law.[21] In other cases, if a company's goodwill depends on proper operation of equipment, a service contract may be tied to the sale or lease of the machine. The practicality of alternatives to the tying arrangement appears to be crucial. If a firm will suffer injury unless it can protect its product, and there is no feasible alternative, the courts go along with tying agreements.[22]

Serious legal questions regarding tying agreements have been raised in recent years relative to the franchising of restaurants and other eating places, motels, and movie theatres, among others. Under franchise agreements, an individual or group of individuals (the franchisee) is usually permitted to set up an outlet of a national chain in return for a capital investment and a periodic fee to the parent company (the franchisor).[23] In some cases, the parent company also requires the franchise holders to buy various supplies, such as meat, baked goods, and paper cups in the case of restaurants, either from the corporation or an approved supplier. In franchising, the tying product is the franchise itself and the tied products are the supplies that the franchisee must purchase to operate his business. Companies with such requirements have argued that they are necessary in order to maintain the quality of their services and reputation. However, critics of such agreements assert that franchisors often require franchisees to purchase supplies and raw materials at prices far above those of the competitive market.[24] The potential for a conflict of interest on the part of franchisors is high, especially when the volume of revenue generated by sales of supplies is taken into account, as shown in Table 8–2.

Such tying agreements have been sustained by the courts and the antitrust enforcement agencies only when franchisors have been able to prove that the tied product is, in fact, essential to the maintenance of quality control. For example, in a lawsuit against Carvel (a soft ice cream franchise), the court concluded that Carvel's ingredient-supply restrictions were justified by the need for quality control connected with the problem of ingredient secrecy.[25]

---

[21] Stern and Grabner, *op. cit.*, p. 132.

[22] *Ibid.*

[23] Franchising as a form of channel organization is described in some detail in Chapter 10 of this text.

[24] *The Impact of Franchising on Small Buisness*, Hearings Before the Subcommittee on Urban and Rural Economic Development (Washington, D.C.: U.S. Government Printing Office, 1970), p. 5.

[25] *Susser v. Carvel*, 332F. 2d 505 (1964).

TABLE 8-2 Sales of Supplies by Franchisors to Franchisees, 1974

Franchisees by Industry		Amount Spent with Franchisors (millions of dollars)
Shoe stores, apparel shops, florists, photo stores		$2200
Auto accessory stores, repair services, car washes, tire stores		1500
Convenience stores		330
Fast-food restaurants (hamburgers, chicken, pizza, ice cream, donuts)		325
Includes:		
Food ingredients	$206	
Supplies (paper)	81	
Equipment (nonfood)	38	
Do-it-yourself stores, cleaning services, repair shops		109
Travel facilities (hotels, motels, etc.)		50
Copying services, income tax preparation, employment services		33

SOURCE: U.S. Department of Commerce, *Franchising in the Economy, 1972–1974* (Washington, D.C.: U.S. Government Printing Office, 1974).

Likewise, in a decision involving the Chock Full O'Nuts Corporation, it was held that the franchisor "successfully proved its affirmative defense (to tying charges) of maintaining quality control with regard to its coffee and baked goods."[26] On the other hand, Chock Full O' Nuts was unsuccessful in defending its tying practices with respect to a number of other products (e.g., french fries, soft drink syrups, napkins, and glasses). The latter adverse finding paralleled that in an antitrust case involving Chicken Delight.[27] The parent company's contract requiring Chicken Delight franchisees to purchase paper items, cookers, fryers, and mix preparations from the franchisor was declared to be a tying contract in violation of Section 1 of the Sherman Act. Chicken Delight failed in its attempt to convince the court that its system should be considered a single product. The paper products were viewed as illegally tied to the franchise because they were easily reproducible. The issue of the cookers, fryers, and spice items was less clearcut, and the court left it to a jury to decide whether they were justifiably tied on the basis of quality control of the finished product. The jury eventually determined that quality control could have been effected by means other than a tie-in and thus rejected the franchisor's claims.

A survey conducted by Hunt and Nevin indicated that about 70 percent

[26]*In re* Chock Full O'Nuts Corp. Inc., 3 Trade Reg. Rep. 20, 441 (October, 1973).

[27]*H. Siegal, et al. v. Chicken Delight, et al.*, 448 F. 2d 43 (1971).

of over 600 fast-food franchisee respondents were required to purchase at least some of their operating supplies from their franchisors and that the supplies so obtained represented 50 percent of the franchisees' total purchases.[28] Furthermore, almost half of those respondents who purchase supplies from their franchisors believed that they were paying higher prices for the supplies than they would have had to pay in the open market.[29] There is, no doubt, a very great need for conflict management within a number of fast-food franchising systems with regard to this issue.

Tying agreements were also involved in the previously mentioned Brown Shoe Company Case.[30] Under Brown's franchise plan, held to be unfair and illegal by the FTC, independent dealers were given what was admittedly a valuable package of services—architectural plans, merchandising records, the help of a Brown field representative, and an option to participate in inexpensive group insurance—in return for a simple promise of the dealer-franchisee to concentrate on the Brown Shoe line and not to handle competing lines. Justice Hugo Black, in writing the Supreme Court's decision, stated that the records showed "beyond doubt" that Brown's program required shoe retailers, "unless faithless to their contractual obligations with Brown, substantially to limit their trade with Brown's competitors."[31] The conclusion in this case was that franchising poses a restraint to trade if the parent company places unreasonable limitations on the right of the franchisee to make his own business decisions.

Full-line Forcing

Full-line forcing is a requirement that a middleman carry a full line of a manufacturer's product if he is to carry any single items in the line. Contracts of this kind are not illegal unless the dealer is prevented from handling competitors' products. In the case of a farm machinery manufacturer, a court held that the practice was within the law, but inferred that full-line forcing which caused the exclusion of competitors from this part of the market might be illegal if a substantial share of business were affected.[32] This might be termed *de facto* exclusive dealing.

[28]S. D. Hunt and J. R. Nevin, "Tying Agreements in Franchising," *Journal of Marketing,* Vol. 39 (July, 1975), pp. 24–25.

[29]*Ibid.*

[30]*Brown Shoe Co., Inc. v. Federal Trade Commission,* 384 U.S. 316 (1966). For critical discussion of the Court's ruling in this case, see John L. Peterman, "The Brown Shoe Case," *Journal of Law and Economics,* Vol. 18 (April, 1975), pp. 81–146.

[31]S. D. Hunt, *op. cit.,* p. 35.

[32]Beckman, et al., *op. cit.,* p. 409.

Resale Restrictions

The right of a supplier to impose restrictions on where or to whom a wholesaler or retailer may resell his goods and services has been narrowed in recent years. These arrangements may be very desirable for manufacturers or distributors in the marketing of some goods, since they can reserve certain large customers to themselves for direct sales and also control the reselling of their goods through the channel. Such restrictions may be beneficial to the reseller also, since intrabrand competition at his distributive level will be lessened accordingly. There are times when this restriction of intrabrand competition may act to enhance the competition existing between resellers of different brands, usually referred to as *interbrand* competition.

Contracts of this type become illegal when it can be shown that their effects tend to reduce competition. Since the antitrust enforcement agencies feel that effective competition is necessary on both the inter- and intrabrand levels, they have attacked resale restrictions in many cases. They tend to permit them in cases where a new firm or a new product is entering the market, or where a firm is failing and must retain such restrictions in order to survive.[33]

The legal limits relative to resale restrictions were defined in the General Motors[34] and Schwinn[35] cases. Each presents slightly different issues; thus, they will be discussed separately.

General Motors used location restrictions to prevent dealers in the Los Angeles area from selling spare parts through discount houses. The Chevrolet franchise agreement provided that dealers could not change the location of their businesses or open at new locations without permission by the company. When several dealers started to sell spare parts through discount houses, the company found them in violation of the location clause and forced them to suspend the practice.[36] A key element in the case was that other Chevrolet dealers in the area helped G.M. to police the ban and, indeed, complaints from them had been a primary motive of General Motors' enforcement actions. The court ruled that the cooperation between G.M. and the other dealers was a conspiracy to eliminate a class of competitors and was, therefore, illegal. This decision indicates that enforcement of resale restrictions must be absolutely unilateral if they are to be legal. However, in the Schwinn

[33]Betty Bock, *Antitrust Issues in Restricting Sales Territories and Outlets*, Studies in Business Economics No. 98 (New York: National Industrial Conference Board, 1967), pp. 19–24.

[34]*U.S. v. General Motors Corp., et al.*, 384 U.S. 127 (1966).

[35]*U.S. v. Arnold Schwinn and Co., et al.*, 388 U.S. 365 (1967).

[36]Stern and Grabner, *op. cit.*, p. 135.

decision, use of these restrictions, even on a unilateral basis, was further circumscribed.

The Schwinn Company had a policy of selling its bicycles in several different ways. Under the "Schwinn Plan" the company shipped and extended credit directly to its retail outlets, and paid commissions on the sales to the distributors who took the orders. The company also sold to the distributors, who could then resell only to franchised Schwinn dealers. In addition, sales were made through some distributors on a consignment basis. The franchised retail dealers were permitted to sell only to consumers and not to resellers, such as discount houses.[37] The dealers were allowed to handle other brands of bicycles. Therefore, there was no restraint of interbrand competition through exclusive dealing.

In the district court, the government charged, among other things, that this system was an unlawful restriction of distributor sales. In its decision, the district court did not prohibit the restriction of sales by distributors to franchised dealers only, nor the restriction that franchised dealers could sell only to consumers.[38] However, the Supreme Court rejected this decision. It held that "once the manufacturer had parted with title and risk, he has parted with dominion over the product, and his effort thereafter to restrict . . . persons to whom the product may be transferred—whether by explicit agreement or by silent combination or understanding with his vendee—is a *per se* violation of Section 1 of the Sherman Act."[39]

The result is that resale restrictions seem to be legal only if imposed unilaterally from above *and* if the party imposing the restriction retains the ownership of the goods and the risk. This converts the dealerships into agents rather than independent resellers. No condition, agreement, or understanding can be imposed that limits the freedom of resellers as to whom they can resell unless the seller retains title, risk, and dominion.[40]

Reciprocity

Reciprocity is the practice of making purchasing decisions at least partly on the basis of whether the vendor is also a customer. In some cases the relationship may be more complex, involving three or more customer-vendors in a circular arrangement. Reciprocity comes down to doing business with your

[37] S. P. Bridges, "The Schwinn Case: A Landmark Decision," *Business Horizons* (August, 1968), pp. 78–79.

[38] *U.S. v. Arnold Schwinn and Company, et al.*, 388 U.S. 365–368 (1967).

[39] *Ibid.*, 388 U.S. 365 (1967). See also Betty Bock, *op. cit.*, pp. 26–27.

[40] R. O. Werner, "Marketing and the United States Supreme Court, 1965–1968," *Journal of Marketing*, Vol. 33 (January, 1969), p. 20.

friends.[41] Business reciprocity has come under antitrust scrutiny, especially if there is an inequality of bargaining power in the relationship. This may arise from differences in the relative sizes of the firms.[42] The antitrust laws regulate reciprocity, because sellers influence their customers to buy not only on the basis of marketing competition but also because the buyer wishes to sell his own products to the seller.

There is a body of cases that determines the division between illegal and legal reciprocity. In general, reciprocity is illegal under two circumstances.[43]

1. Coercive reciprocity involving the use of pressure may be illegal as an unfair trade practice.

2. A merger that may cause a reciprocity program to be formed will violate Section 7 of the Clayton Act if the reciprocity may reduce competition.[44]

This latter circumstance can come about when a firm that operates a reciprocity program merges with another firm and one of the two has a customer that sells to the other. In some cases a corporate policy against reciprocity will shield a merger from Section 7.[45] We will return later in this chapter to the issue of reciprocity stemming from mergers when vertical integration is discussed.

Noncoercive reciprocity is legal so long as the policy is not aggressive, is outside of a merger context, and is not supported with elaborate records of purchases and sales from and to other firms. The Federal Trade Commission has held that where reciprocity is prevalent and systematized and where a substantial amount of commerce is involved, there is a violation of Section 5 of the Federal Trade Commission Act.[46] A recent case in which a major tire manufacturer and its three subsidiaries were barred from any reciprocity purchases from their suppliers has confirmed this view.[47]

Price Maintenance

Resale price maintenance was one of the few channel policy areas where the use of coercive power was sanctioned, in a positive manner, by federal

[41] R. Moyer, "Reciprocity: Retrospect and Prospect," *Journal of Marketing*, Vol. 34 (October, 1970), p. 47.

[42] Howard, *op. cit.*, p. 93.

[43] Moyer, *op. cit.*, p. 48.

[44] See *FTC v. Consolidated Foods Corp.*, 380 U.S. 592.

[45] Moyer, *loc. cit.*

[46] "Federal Trade Commission Statement on Reciprocity," *Journal of Marketing*, Vol. 35 (April, 1971), pp. 76-77.

[47] "United States v. General Tire and Rubber Co., Aerojet-General Corp., A. M. Byers Co., and RKO General Inc.," *Journal of Marketing*, Vol. 35 (April, 1971), p. 71.

laws. State resale price maintenance (fair trade) laws were set up to enable manufacturers to fix resale prices for their goods if they chose to do so. Although on the surface such laws seemed to support a manufacturer's desire to influence prices at the retail level, their initial development was due to the coercive power of coalitions of small, independent retailers who wished to be protected from the direct price competition of mass merchandisers and discounters.[48]

As of December 1, 1975, fair trade laws were in effect in 21 states. These laws permitted, but did not require, a producer or distributor of a good bearing his trademark to determine a minimum resale price for the good. In a few states, the price could be stipulated. The price was controlled by contract with the resellers.[49] In 13 of these states, a nonsigner's clause was in effect which bound all resellers of the good to the contract if one reseller signed it. Up until the end of 1975, price maintenance was still being used for certain brands of high-fidelity equipment and television sets, jewelry, bicycles, clothing, cosmetics, and kitchenware.[50]

Fair trade laws now represent an historical curiosity, because, early in 1976, a bill went into effect that repealed the Miller-Tydings Act and the McGuire Act, laws that Congress had passed in 1937 and 1952 exempting retail price-fixing by manufacturers from the federal antitrust laws in states which permitted such vertical pricing arrangements.[51] If manufacturers are to have any influence on the prices of resellers, they now have to use power bases other than coercion and will, clearly, have to be extremely cautious in doing so. Maintaining prices, in the absence of fair trade laws, may prove very difficult indeed, given the growing significance of mass merchandisers in retailing. Emphasis will have to be placed on "moral suasion" relating to the consequences of widespread price-cutting on both the wholesale and retail level, segmenting markets into those typified by inelastic and elastic demands, or keeping gross margins so low that room for price-cutting does not exist.[52]

On the other hand, still in effect in a number of states are unfair practices acts which regulate the right of sellers to sell below costs or below

[48]J. C. Palamountain, Jr., *The Politics of Distribution* (Cambridge, Mass.: Harvard University Press, 1955), pp. 235–253.

[49]Howard, *op. cit.,* p. 39.

[50]L. Wiener, "Depression's Fair Trade Laws May be Retired by Congress," *Chicago Tribune* (February 10, 1975), Section 6, p. 9. For a summary of the issues surrounding the controversy over fair trade, see Louis E. Boone and Robert Stevens, "Resale Price Maintenance in Theory and Practice," in Louis E. Boone and James C. Johnson (eds.), *Marketing Channels* (Morristown, N.J.: General Learning Press, 1973), pp. 340–352.

[51]"Measure to End State 'Fair-Trade' Laws Is Sent to Ford, with Approval Certain," *Wall Street Journal* (December 3, 1975), p. 2.

[52]See Louis W. Stern, "Approaches to Achieving Retail Price Stability," *Business Horizons*, Vol. 7 (Fall 1964), pp. 82–84.

specified markups on some or all products. These laws are designed to prevent deep and predatory price cuts or "loss leader" selling.[53] Marketing managers whose firms operate in states having such laws must be familiar with the provisions of the laws of each state, since they vary. Sales made for charitable purposes, to relief agencies, for clearance, closeout, liquidation of business, or sales of goods whose marketability is declining are usually exempted from these laws.[54]

Price Discrimination by Buyers

When a seller discriminates in his pricing between two customers, such an action can be viewed as an attempt to exercise reward power relative to the customer receiving the lower price. However, when one of the customers uses his power to force a discriminatory price from the seller, then such an action may be viewed as coercion on the part of the customer. The latter situation is addressed here; the former is left to the next part of the chapter, which deals with limitations on the use of reward power.

Section 2(f) of the Robinson-Patman Act makes it unlawful for a person in commerce knowingly to induce or receive a discrimination in price. To violate this section, a buyer must be reasonably aware of the illegality of the price he has received. This section prevents large, powerful buyers from compelling sellers to give them discriminatory lower prices.[55] It is often enforced by means of Section 5 of the Federal Trade Commission Act on grounds that this use of coercive power is an unfair method of competition. Likewise, it is illegal for buyers to coerce favors from suppliers in the form of special promotional allowances and services.[56]

In addition, large buyers (like A & P) have been known to set up "dummy" brokerage firms as part of their businesses in order to obtain a brokerage allowance from sellers which, in effect, permits them to receive lower prices than their competitors. This form of coercive power is deemed illegal under Section 2(c) of the Robinson-Patman Act, which makes it unlawful to pay brokerage fees or discounts or to accept them except for services rendered in connection with sales or purchases. It also prohibits

---

[53]Beckman, et al., *op. cit.,* pp. 529–531.

[54]Howard, *op. cit.,* p. 45.

[55]*Ibid.,* pp. 73–75.

[56]See "Order Against Retail Chain Bans Inducement of Preferential Treatment," *FTC News Summary* (February 6, 1976), p. 1; "Thrifty Drug Accepts FTC Ban on Inducing Favors From Suppliers," *Wall Street Journal,* February 2, 1976, p. 9; and "Fred Meyer Inc. Pays $200,000 Fine to Settle an FTC Complaint," *Wall Street Journal,* January 30, 1976, p. 2.

brokerage fees or discounts paid to any broker who is not independent of both buyer and seller.[57]

Refusals To Deal

A seller can select his own dealers according to his own criteria and judgment. He may also announce in advance the circumstances under which he would refuse to sell to dealers. These two commercial "freedoms" were granted in *U.S. v. Colgate & Co.* in 1919 and referred to as the "Colgate Doctrine."[58] The doctrine was formally recognized by Congress in Section 2(a) of the Robinson-Patman Act, which reads that ". . . nothing herein contained shall prevent persons engaged in selling goods, wares, or merchandise in commerce from selecting their own customers in *bona fide* transactions and not in restraint of trade." Although the selection of dealers poses little problem from a legal perspective, the cutting off or termination of a dealership does. The use of such coercive power is possible only when the refusal to sell involves no joint action or conspiracy in the channel (as discussed in the General Motors case earlier under "Resale Restrictions") or when the end sought by the refusal is not itself illegal.[59]

Clearly, refusal to deal is a major "punishment" underlying a channel member's coercive power. It is, however, heavily circumscribed, as the following quotation indicates:

> . . . (Sellers') right to terminate dealerships is somewhat qualified. In general, sellers can drop dealers "for cause." But they cannot drop dealers, for example, if the latter refuse to cooperate in a dubious legal arrangement, such as exclusive-dealing or tying arrangements. The acuteness of this problem in the automobile industry led to the passage of the Automobile Dealers Franchise Act in 1956, which established the rights of automobile dealers to secure a judicial determination whenever they feel a manufacturer has not acted toward them in good faith.[60]

Despite the numerous limitations discussed above on the use of coercive power in channel relations, it should be emphasized that it is still feasible for both sellers and buyers to employ negative sanctions in interorganizational management. The use of such sanctions has not been outlawed, except in highly extreme forms. For example, exclusive dealing and tying

[57]Stern and Grabner, *op. cit.,* p. 119.

[58]*U.S. v. Colgate & Co.,* 250 U.S. 300 (1919).

[59]Stern and Grabner, *op. cit.,* p. 131.

[60]Philip Kotler, *Marketing Management: Analysis, Planning and Control,* 2nd ed. (Englewood Cliffs, N.J.: Prentice-Hall, Inc., 1972), p. 834.

agreements are illegal only if it can be shown that through their implementation, competition is substantially lessened, and proving *substantial* lessening is a difficult task, indeed. As pointed out in Chapter 7, it is, however, generally more functional, from a long-run interorganization management perspective, to mediate rewards rather than punishments in attempting to influence a channel member to do something he would not otherwise have done. Whereas fear, anxiety, and resistance are typical responses to negative sanctions, the typical responses to positive sanctions are hope, reassurance, and attraction.[61] Furthermore, if a channel member uses negative sanctions in the present, it is likely that the member being influenced will be less willing to cooperate in the future, whereas the opposite is true when positive sanctions are employed.[62]

LEGAL LIMITATIONS
ON THE USE OF REWARD POWER

In this section, we consider those situations in which the use of reward power is limited by law. As was the case with coercive power, the laws do not prevent a channel member from employing rewards as a central component of his interorganizational strategy; rather, they place restrictions around how certain enticements or incentives might be used.

Exclusive Territories

In order to influence a wholesaler or retailer to handle a particular product or brand, the manufacturer of that item may offer these middlemen an exclusive territorial arrangement. In effect, the manufacturer is providing the wholesaler or the retailer with a monopoly relative to the sales of his brand within a defined geographic area. Under such an exclusive arrangement, no other middleman will be granted the right to sell the brand within the area. These arrangements are intended to make the manufacturer's line so attractive to individual resellers that they will concentrate their efforts on his brands and not concern themselves unduly with competition from other dealers selling the same brands.

The attempt to dampen *intrabrand* competition in order to strengthen *interbrand* competition makes sense from an interorganization manage-

[61] David A. Baldwin, "The Power of Positive Sanctions," *World Politics*, Vol. 24 (October, 1971), p. 32.
[62] *Ibid.*, p. 33.

ment perspective. The antitrust enforcement agencies' attitude is, however, that effective competition invoves *both* intrabrand and interbrand competition. Consequently, they view attempts to confine distributors' or dealers' selling activities to one area as illegal restraints on competition under the Sherman Act and Section 5 of the FTC Act.

For example, in 1958, the Justice Department brought suit against the White Motor Company, charging, among other things, that its franchises, which limited the area in which its dealers could sell or solicit customers, constituted an agreement to restrain trade. The decision by the lower courts concurred with the Justice Department's argument and held that such exclusive territorial arrangements were illegal *per se*, regardless of their competitive effects.[63] The Supreme Court demurred and suggested a retrial.[64] Before a retrial could be held in the lower courts, White accepted a consent decree to drop the exclusive territorial provisions in its franchise agreements.[65]

Another court case involving this issue concerned Sealy, Inc., a company which licensed other firms to manufacture and sell its products (mattresses) under the Sealy trademark at uniform prices and in specified areas.[66] However, the Sealy licensees were in reality the owners of Sealy, Inc. The courts held that the exclusive territorial restraints were simply a collusive means of horizontal price-fixing and policing, in *per se* violation of Section 1 of the Sherman Act.

The most definitive ruling on the status of territorial arrangements was handed down in the Schwinn case,[67] which was referred to earlier under "Resale Restrictions." The same line of reasoning that was applied against Schwinn's restrictions on to whom its wholesalers and retailers could sell its bicycles was used relative to its territorial restrictions. The latter were found to be a *per se* violation of the Sherman Act (as were the former) unless Schwinn was willing to retain title, risk, and dominion over its products—that is, to sell them on a consignment basis or vertically integrate.[68]

It is obvious that such decisions against exclusive territorial arrangements will undoubtedly have far-reaching effects on the channels in which they are used. Such arrangements are widespread in certain food and beverage industries (e.g., soft drinks, bread, beer), and there has been considerable

---

[63] *White Motor Co. v. U.S.,* 194 F. Supp. 562 (1961).

[64] *White Motor Co. v. U.S.,* 372 U.S. 253 (1963).

[65] Stern and Grabner, *op. cit.,* p. 135.

[66] *U.S. v. Sealy, Inc.,* 388 U.S. 350 (1967).

[67] *U.S. v. Arnold Schwinn and Co., et al.,* 388 U.S. 365 (1967).

[68] See Betty Bock, *op. cit.,* for a complete discussion of the case.

pressure brought to bear by these industries to encourage Congress to pass a law that would, in effect, overturn the Schwinn decision.[69]

It should be noted, however, that when the actual remedy was imposed by the District Court, Schwinn was not prohibited from designating areas of prime responsibility for its distributors nor from designating the location of the place of business in its franchise agreements. Schwinn also retained the right to select its distributors and franchised dealers and to terminate dealerships for cause so long as such arrangements do not involve exclusive dealing clauses.[70] Furthermore, the legality of limiting the territories of manufacturers' agents (who do not hold title to goods) has been confirmed by a federal court decision in Pennsylvania, which held that a producer has the right to establish exclusive territories for its agents who solicit business for it. This was not considered to be unreasonable restraint of trade.[71]

Incentives for Resellers' Employees

The Federal Trade Commission originally took the position that one firm could not reward (via the use of "push" money[72] or similar incentives) the employees of their commercial customers for reselling its product. The Commission considered these incentives a violation of Section 5 of the FTC Act, alleging that competing products suffered a disadvantage under such schemes. In 1921, the courts declared that the practice was legal if the employer consented to it, because, it was curiously reasoned, if a seller sold his goods outright to a reseller, the relevant competitive market was now the reseller's. Thus, the original seller was no longer in the competition under consideration once title passed to the reseller.[73]

The Federal Trade Commission has issued trade practice rules that forbid push money if the employer does not consent, if the payment involves a lottery, where competitive products are affected severely, where competition is lessened, or where the inducements are not available to salesmen of all competing resellers.

---

[69] See U.S. Senate Subcommittee on Antitrust and Monopoly, *Hearings on Exclusive Territorial Allocation Legislation*, August 8, 9, and 10, and September 12 and 14, 1972, Parts 1 and 2 and also U.S. House of Representatives Subcommittee on Commerce and Finance, *Hearings on the Exclusive Territorial Franchise Act*, June 27 and 28 and July 1 and 2, 1974. For contrasting views on the proposed legislation, see the testimony of Lee E. Preston and William S. Comanor in the Senate *Hearings* and Louis W. Stern in the House *Hearings*.

[70] "U.S. v. Arnold Schwinn and Co., et al.," *Journal of Marketing*, Vol. 33 (January, 1969), p. 107.

[71] "Clommer Moving and Storage v. North American Van Lines and Louderback Transportation Co.," *Journal of Marketing*, Vol. 34 (April, 1970), p. 84.

[72] "Push money" is extra monetary payment from a manufacturer to a customer's salesman for "pushing" the manufacturer's brand.

[73] Howard, *op. cit.*, pp. 135–136.

Push money payments transferred to the employers are subject to restrictions under the price discrimination articles of the Robinson-Patman Act, discussed below.

Commercial Bribery

Commercial bribery is the practice of paying the employees of customers to purchase from the payer. The Federal Trade Commission considers this practice unfair, but enforcement has been limited by the courts, because gratuities and entertainment have historically been used to promote sales. The Federal Trade Commission was successful in barring payola to disc jockeys as an unfair trade practice unless the listening public is informed of the payment.[74] In addition to the FTC, the Securities and Exchange Commission (SEC) is concerned about commercial bribery in distribution, especially after it was discovered in 1975 that several major United States corporations had been involved in making illegal or questionable payoffs to foreign nationals in order to obtain business abroad. The SEC has applied the techniques it used to uncover foreign payoffs in examining domestic situations.[75] Under investigation are payments from beer and liquor companies (brewers, distillers, and distributors) to retailers, especially restaurant owners, which were supposedly given to induce retailers to exclude competitors' products. The SEC's interest is not in violations of antibribery laws themselves, but rather with the possibility that publicly owned companies engaged in illegal activities may be violating the securities laws if they do not disclose that fact to the investing public.

Price Discrimination by Sellers

Section 2(a) of the Robinson-Patman Act states,

It shall be unlawful for any person engaged in commerce, . . . either directly or indirectly, to discriminate in price between different purchasers of commodities of like grade and quality, where either or any of the purchases involved in such discrimination are in commerce, where such commodities are sold for use, consumption, or resale within . . . (any area) . . . under the jursidiction of the United States, and where the effect of such discrimination may be to substantially lessen competition or tend to create a monopoly in any line of commerce, or to injure, destroy or prevent competition with any person who either grants or knowingly receives the benefit of such discrimination, or with customers of either of them.

[74] *Ibid.*, pp. 137–138.

[75] Carol H. Falk, "SEC May Uncover More Domestic Bribes using Foreign-Payoff Detection Methods," *Wall Street Journal,* March 10, 1976, p. 4.

It goes on to allow price differentials due to differences in the cost of serving different customers, up to the amounts justified by the cost savings, but cost-justified quantity discounts can be limited by the Federal Trade Commission. Other provisions are that sellers can select their own customers unless in restraint of trade, and that price changes due to market value, marketability of goods, distress sales, or discontinuance of business are allowed.

What does Section 2(a) really mean? It is obvious that discriminating in selling price among customers can be illegal, but there are several other key areas to consider.

1. Like Grade and Quality. Where products are of different materials or workmanship level, they are not ordinarily considered to be of "like grade and quality," but where differences are small and do not affect the basic use of the goods, then selling at price differentials has been attacked.[76]

In cases where competition between two buyers from a single seller is under consideration, products of the same composition have been declared of like grade and quality even if the brand preference shown to one of them in the market is significant. In the Borden Case,[77] the Supreme Court held that evaporated milk sold under the Borden label and evaporated milk manufactured by Borden and sold under "private" labels were of like grade and quality, illustrating the point that "perceived" product differentiation fails to constitute an "actual" difference in grade and quality under the law's interpretation.

In cases where two sellers are in competition for the same buyer, the Federal Trade Commission has held that brand identification by the public is a difference in grade and quality, so that cutting the price on a product labeled as "premium" to the same level as others charge for a standard (non-premium) product is actually undercutting the competitor's price. Price discrimination to do this, then, is not protected by the "meeting competition" defense.[78]

2. To Substantially Lessen Competition. There is an important difference between injury to competitors and injury to competition. A loss of sales by one firm and their gain by another is the essence of competition, and the object of each competitor is to outsell his rivals. Evidence of predatory intent to destroy a competitor may indicate an injury to competition. Other factors to consider are the number of firms in the market and the market share of the discriminating seller.[79]

[76]Stern and Grabner, *op. cit.,* pp. 112–113.

[77]*U.S. v. Borden Co.,* 383 U.S. 637 (1966).

[78]Stern and Grabner, *op. cit.,* pp. 113–114.

[79]Howard, *op. cit.,* pp. 54–55.

In the Anheuser-Busch case, the Court of Appeals ruled that injury to competition and not injury to competitors was a critical factor in determining the legality or illegality of price discrimination.[80] The injury to competition need not be actual to be unlawful, but a remote possibility of injury is not sufficient for illegality.[81]

Because of the requirement of injury to competition, a time and space dimension must be applied in price discrimination cases. In one recent case, for example, a sulphur producer had a ten-year contract with a fertilizer manufacturer to supply a fixed quantity of sulphur every year at a specified price, or at the price charged to the fertilizer firm's competitors, whichever was lower. In times of high prices, the stipulated price was lower than that charged to other customers. Therefore, the sulphur firm attempted to have the contract declared illegal as unlawful price discrimination. The court ruled that the lower price was legal so long as the other firms were offered the same prices and terms at the time the contract was made.[82]

Price discrimination among customers who are not in competition is not illegal. The Federal Trade Commission has issued an advisory opinion that an apparel manufacturer may grant extended credit terms to new stores in ghetto areas, even though other classes of customers would be excluded from the plan. The FTC justified its decision on grounds that there should be little competition between favored and nonfavored stores in this case.[83]

Injury to any of three levels of competition may bring price discrimination under the prohibition of the Robinson-Patman Act.

    a. *Primary Level.* Competition between two sellers may be injured when one of them gives discriminatory prices to some customers. This was the situation in the Utah Pie Case.[84] The Utah Pie Company was a local concern that sold its frozen pies in the Salt Lake City market at low prices due to its low costs. It had 66 percent of the market. Several national concerns competed with Utah Pie in that market. They cut their prices in Salt Lake City below those that they charged in other markets. In some cases these prices were below full cost.[85] The Supreme Court ruled that the evidence in the case was sufficient for a jury to decide whether the defendants had engaged in predatory tactics and whether competition had been lessened, even though Utah's market share had declined

[80] *Anheuser-Busch, Inc. v. Federal Trade Commission,* 265 F. 2d 677 (7th Cir. 1959), 363 U.S. 536 (1960), 289 F. 2d 835 (7th Cir. 1961).

[81] Howard, *op. cit.,* p. 55.

[82] "Texas Gulf Sulphur Co., v. J. R. Simplot Co.," *Journal of Marketing,* Vol. 34 (April, 1970), p. 82.

[83] "Federal Trade Commission Advisory Opinion No. 253," *Journal of Marketing,* Vol. 33 (January, 1969), p. 105.

[84] *Utah Pie Co. v. Continental Baking Co., et al.,* 386 U.S. 685 (1967).

[85] R. O. Werner, "Marketing and the United States Supreme Court 1965–1968," *Journal of Marketing,* Vol. 33 (January, 1969), p. 17.

only to 45 percent and its sales had expanded.[86] In this case the dominant local firm was protected from discriminatory price cutting by national firms.[87]

b. *Secondary Level.* Competition between two customers of a seller may be affected if the seller differentiates between them in price. In effect the seller is aiding one customer and harming the other in their mutual competition, and this is sufficient to cause substantial lessening of competition.[88]

c. *Tertiary Level.* If a manufacturer discriminates in prices between two wholesalers such that the customers of one wholesaler are favored over those of the other, the competition is being injured by the price discrimination.[89]

3. In Commerce.   Price discrimination is illegal only if the discriminatory sales are in commerce. In one recent case, a court held that National Food Stores could advertise and sell certain items at one store at lower prices than they charge at others. The court ruled that the sales were not in commerce, since they were to anyone who came in and were completed on the premises.[90] Furthermore, discrimination in pricing can be lawful when the products involved are not identical, when a product is sold for different uses, when separate markets are involved, when sales of the product(s) take place at different times, and when sales are made to government agencies[91] as well as in the situations where the cost justification or the good faith defense can be applied, as described below.

4. Cost Justification Defense.   Price differences between customers are permitted if they can be justified by differences in the costs of sale or delivery to the different customers. The burden of proof of cost differences is on the seller. However, the courts have been reluctant to accept the cost figures as valid.[92] As one author puts it, "The record shows that few firms have been able, in litigation, to justify price differences on the basis of cost."[93] The difficulties lie in ascertaining exactly what costs are to be included in the calculation and how overhead and joint costs are to be allocated.[94]

[86] *Utah Pie Co. v. Continental Baking Co., et al.,* 386 U.S. 685 (1967).

[87] Werner, *loc. cit.*

[88] Howard, *op. cit.,* pp. 53–54.

[89] *Ibid.*

[90] "Plotken's West Inc. v. National Food Stores, Inc.," *Journal of Marketing,* Vol. 35 (January, 1971), pp. 79–80.

[91] Donald V. Harper, *Price Policy and Procedure* (New York: Harcourt, Brace & World, Inc., 1966), pp. 105–106.

[92] Stern and Grabner, *op. cit.,* p. 114.

[93] Howard, *op. cit.,* p. 62.

[94] *Ibid.*

5. Quantity Discounts.   Are permitted under Section 2(a) to the extent that they are justified by cost savings. The Supreme Court has ruled that quantity discounts must reflect cost savings in deliveries made to one place at one time.[95] This places limitations on the use of cumulative quantity discounts. Furthermore, quantity limits may be placed on discounts on some commodities by the Federal Trade Commission, if it can be determined that only a few very large buyers can qualify for the largest discount category in a seller's pricing schedule.[96]

6. Good Faith Defense.   Section 2(b) of the Robinson-Patman Act allows a firm to charge lower prices to some of its customers than others, if it is done "in good faith to meet an equally low price of a competitor." This defense is valid even if there is substantial injury to competition, but the burden of proving good faith falls on the defendant.[97]

  a. The price being met must be lawful and not a price produced by collusion. A seller does not have to prove the price that he is meeting is lawful, but he must make some effort to find out if it is.[98]

  b. The price being met must really exist,[99] and the price must be met and not undercut.[100] As mentioned previously, price reductions on a "premium" product to the level of "standard" products can be a form of illegal price discrimination. If the public is willing to pay a higher price for the "premium" product, the equal prices may be considered beating and not meeting competition.[101]

  c. The competition being met must be at the primary level. Granting a discriminatory price to some customers to enable them to meet their own competition is not protected.[102]

The question of whether the good faith defense is applicable to gaining new customers as well as to retaining old customers is basically unsettled. The Federal Trade Commission has argued that a company is only allowed to

[95] Stern and Grabner, *op. cit.*, p. 121.

[96] *Federal Trade Commission v. Morton Salt Company*, 334 U.S. 37 (1948). Although the FTC may establish maximum discounts or quantity limits, its only attempt to use this power was unsuccessful because of a basic discrepancy between the FTC's order and the evidence on which it was based. See *Federal Trade Commission v. B. F. Goodrich et al.*, 242 F (2d) 31 (1957).

[97] Howard, *op. cit.*, p. 56.

[98] *Ibid.*, pp. 60–61.

[99] *Standard Oil Co. v. FTC*, 340 U.S. 231 (1951).

[100] Howard, *op. cit.*, pp. 56–59.

[101] Stern and Grabner, *op. cit.*, p. 116.

[102] *Federal Trade Commission v. Sun Oil Co.*, 371 U.S. 505 (1963).

grant price discriminations "in good faith" to retain old customers.[103] However, the 7th Circuit Court overruled this view in holding that the law does not distinguish old and new customers.[104]

A controversy similar to that associated with the resale price maintenance (fair trade) laws surrounds the Robinson-Patman Act. Because of the difficulty encountered by companies in trying to apply the abovementioned defenses and the likelihood that, in certain instances, the Act merely protects competitors from competition, there is considerable question about its ultimate value and equity. In fact, like the fair trade laws, there have been efforts made, especially by President Gerald Ford, to gain a repeal of the Act.[105]

Promotional Allowances and Services

Section 2(d) of the Robinson-Patman Act prohibits the payment of any special allowances to customers for their services in connection with the processing, handling, selling, or offering for sale of any products sold by them, unless the allowances are available to all other competing customers on proportionately equal terms. Section 2(e) makes the same prohibition of discrimination among purchasers in the giving of services or facilities to aid them in reselling the goods.

These sections forbid the creation of price discrimination among customers indirectly by the granting of special promotional allowances to some but not all customers. It is not illegal to give promotional allowances or services, but the seller must grant them to all competing customers on "proportionately equal terms." Both of these prohibitions are absolute and are not dependent on injury to competition, and cost justification of the discrimination is not a defense.[106]

There are several points to be considered before allowances and services are judged illegal.[107]

    a. The customers among whom the discrimination has taken place must be in competition with each other; thus, the markets in which the customer-resellers sell are a consideration. These markets may be local, regional, or national, depending upon the particular customer involved. A time dimension is also involved.

---

[103]Stern and Grabner, *op. cit.,* p. 115.

[104]Howard, *op cit.,* p. 57.

[105]Stanley Cohen, "Bigger 'n' Better Doesn't Always Mean Cheaper," *Advertising Age,* July 28, 1975, p. 54.

[106]Howard, *op. cit.,* pp. 69–73.

[107]*Ibid.*

b. The type of customer is a consideration. For the purposes of the law, a wholesaler whose customers compete with retailers buying direct from the manufacturer is entitled to promotional allowances if the retailers are granted them.

The Fred Meyer case illustrates the difficulties involved in avoiding discrimination when dual distribution is used. The Supreme Court ruled that if Fred Meyer was granted promotional fees and allowances as a direct buying retailer, then its retail competitors who purchased through wholesalers were entitled to them also; and it was the duty of the supplier to see that the competing retailers actually received them.[108] The Federal Trade Commission has issued a new set of guidelines for advertising and other allowances and services that implement the key elements of the decision. The seller may enter into agreements with distributors or other third parties to guarantee the performance of the seller's obligations to the customers of wholesalers, but the legal responsibility is on the seller.[109]

c. The law requires allowances to be granted to all on proportionately equal terms. The Federal Trade Commission guidelines indicate that the allowances should be based on the quantity of goods purchased or on the dollar volume of sales in a given time. In some cases, promotional services such as demonstrators in stores are not practical for all customers. When this happens, a substitute for this service must be made available to those unable to use the demonstrators, and the availability of the alternative must be made known.[110]

Functional Discounts

Discounts given to resellers on the basis of their position in the channel and the nature and scope of their marketing functions are regarded as the margin a manufacturer or wholesaler must give to resellers in order for them to handle their products. Although the Robinson-Patman Act does not explicitly mention functional discounts, a seller may be charged with price discrimination when discounts are made available to one reseller but not to the reseller's competition.[111] Furthermore, if a retailer has integrated the wholesaling function (as most chains and department stores have), the FTC and the courts have ruled that the retailer cannot be given a wholesaler's discount by a seller on the goods that the former sells at retail.[112] In this sense, the legal limitations placed on the use of functional discounts seem to be aimed at preserving the viability of independent wholesalers and/or discouraging vertical integration.

[108] *Federal Trade Commission v. Fred Meyer et al.,* 390 U.S. 341 (1968). Also see "Fred Meyer Inc. Pays $200,000 Fine to Settle An FTC Complaint," *op. cit.*

[109] "FTC Guides for Advertising and Other Merchandise Payments and Services," *Journal of Marketing,* Vol. 33 (October, 1969), p. 81.

[110] Howard, *op. cit.,* pp. 69–73.

[111] Stern and Grabner, *op. cit.,* p. 120.

[112] *Federal Trade Commission v. The Mennen Co.,* 288 F. 2d 774 (1923), *certiorari denied* 262 U.S. 759 (1923).

Delivered Pricing

Delivered prices are the quotation of prices so that all customers within a given area pay the same price for a product regardless of differences in shipping costs from the seller to the buyer. These systems have been popular over the years and have been used to promote price stability in some industries. On some occasions, they have been attacked successfully by the Federal Trade Commission in the courts.[113]

Delivered pricing systems are legal under some circumstances.[114]

> *When a seller acts independently and not in collusion with competitors, provided that individual actions of a variety of competitors do not result in a systematic matching of delivered prices*, a delivered pricing plan or policy of freight absorption is legal under any of the following qualifying conditions:
>
> 1. If the seller is willing to sell on an f.o.b. basis when a purchaser so requests.
>
> 2. If the seller maintains a uniform delivered price at all points of delivery . . . as when he charges nationwide uniform delivered prices.
>
> 3. If the seller absorbs freight costs, or some portion of them, in order to meet competition, as when his factory price plus actual freight to destination is higher than the amount a customer would have to pay when procuring the goods from a competitor.
>
> 4. If the buyers and/or their customers are noncompetitive.

LEGAL LIMITATIONS REGARDING VERTICAL INTEGRATION

The marketing manager is faced with another set of legal constraints when considering vertical integration. Vertical integration in the channel may come about through forward integration by a producer, backward integration by a retailer, or integration in either direction by a wholesaler or other intermediate level of distribution. Integration may be brought about by the creation of a new business function by existing firms (internal expansion) or by acquisition of the stock or the assets of other firms (mergers).

The two methods of creating integration are fundamentally different in their relationship to the law. Internal expansion is regulated by Section 2 of

---

[113]Stern and Grabner, *op. cit.*, p. 117.

[114]Beckman, et al., *op. cit.*, pp. 518-519.

the Sherman Act, which prohibits monopoly or attempts to monopolize any part of the interstate or foreign commerce of the United States. External expansion is regulated by Section 7 of the Clayton Act and its amendment, the Celler-Kefauver Act, which prohibits the purchase of stock or assets of other firms, if the effects may be to substantially lessen competition or tend to create a monopoly in any line of commerce in any part of the country. Internal expansion is given favored treatment under the law. The theory seems to be that internal expansion expands investment and production, and thus increases competition, whereas growth by merger removes an entity from the market.[115]

Integration, whether by merger or internal expansion, may result in the lowering of costs and make possible more effective interorganizational management of the channel. It may also be a means of avoiding many of the legal problems previously discussed, because an integrated firm is free to control prices and allocate products to its integrated outlets without conflict with the laws governing restrictive distribution policies.

Vertical Integration by Merger

The major legal consideration in a vertical merger is the effect the merger will have on competition among firms at the various distributive levels involved in the merger. That is to say, if the merger will tend to foreclose a source of supply to independent firms at the buyer's level or to foreclose a market to other firms at the seller's level, the merger can be questioned. This kind of situation comes about when either level contains only a few firms, so that the merger of one in each level can make it difficult for third parties to obtain suppliers or outlets that are not competitors as well.[116] The merger of the Brown Shoe Company and the G. R. Kinney Company, the largest independent chain of shoe stores, was declared illegal by the Supreme Court because it was believed that the merger would foreclose other manufacturers from selling through Kinney.[117]

In determining whether a merger will reduce competition, the two critical variables involved are the definition of the line of commerce and the market involved. If either is defined narrowly enough, almost any merger can be questioned.

[115] E. T. Grether, *Marketing and Public Policy* (Englewood Cliffs, N.J.: Prentice-Hall, Inc., 1966), p. 104. In order to show their goodwill relative to preserving competition, some companies relinquish their voting privileges on the stock they acquire in merger activities.

[116] Stern and Grabner, *op. cit.*, p. 95.

[117] *Brown Shoe Co. v. U.S.*, 370 U.S. 294, Vertical Aspects, 370 U.S. 323 (1962).

The Federal Trade Commission has long been interested in the trend of vertical mergers in the cement industry, and has required firms to give notice to the Commission before the consummation of any merger involving a ready-mixed-concrete producer. The Commission will attempt to block the merger if it feels that the merger has anticompetitive features.[118] A recent case illustrates the critical nature of the relevant market to be considered in this industry. The OKG Corporation acquired 88 percent of Jahnke Service Inc. Jahnke produces building materials, including ready-mixed cement, while OKG is a producer of cement and other products. Jahnke's purchases of cement were about 27 percent of the total in the New Orleans metropolitan area and about 4 percent of the total in the Southern Louisiana, Mississippi, and Pensacola areas combined. The Federal Trade Commission decided, first, that the relevant market was the smaller one, and second, that even if it had accepted the larger market as the relevant one, the extent of market foreclosure would violate the Clayton Act. It then ordered OKG to divest itself of Jahnke.[119]

As indicated earlier, vertical mergers creating the opportunity for forcing reciprocal buying agreements upon suppliers or buyers are subject to attack under the Clayton Act.[120] For example, Consolidated Foods, a large processor and distributor of food products, purchased Gentry, Inc., a processor of dehydrated onion and garlic, putting Consolidated in a position to require its suppliers to obtain onion and garlic from Gentry as a condition of doing business with Consolidated. The FTC objected to such uses of reciprocity, and filed suit to force Consolidated to divest itself of Gentry. The court found that the particular practice in this situation was moving in the direction of coercion and "foreclosure" as well as possible "price squeezing," and stated, ". . . the establishment of the power to exert pressure on customers because those customers are also suppliers, when such power was acquired by merger, is in violation of Section 7 of the Clayton Act."[121]

Vertical Integration by Internal Expansion

This form of integration is limited only by the laws preventing monopoly or attempts to monopolize. A firm is ordinarily free to set up its own distribution and retailing system unless this would overconcentrate the market

---

[118]Stern and Grabner, *op. cit.,* pp. 95–96.

[119]"In re OKG Corporation, et al.," *Journal of Marketing,* Vol. 35 (April, 1971), pp. 69–70.

[120]Stern and Grabner, *op. cit.,* p. 96.

[121]*Federal Trade Commission v. Consolidated Foods Corp.,* 380 U.S. 592 (1965).

for its product.[122] Section 7 of the Clayton Act specifically permits a firm to set up subsidiary corporations to carry on business or extensions thereof if competition is not substantially reduced.

Problems Created by Dual Distribution

The term "dual distribution" describes a wide variety of marketing arrangements by which a manufacturer or a wholesaler reaches its final markets by employing two or more different types of channels for the same basic product. However, a dual arrangement that often creates controversy is the one that involves marketing through competing vertically integrated *and* independent outlets on either the wholesale or the retail level.[123] This kind of practice is customary in some lines of trade, such as the automotive passenger tire, paint, and petroleum industries. Dual distribution also takes place when a producer sells similar products under different brand names for distribution through different channels.[124] This latter kind of dual distribution comes about because of market segmentation, or because of sales to distributors under "private" labels. In all dual distribution situations, conflict among channel members is likely to be relatively high.

Dual distribution may have undesirable effects on independent distributors, and in turn on competitors, as the independent channels are replaced by integrated channels, and the competitor's markets are dried up. A second possible negative effect is the creation of a price squeeze on the independent distributors by the primary supplier. He can charge a high price to the resellers and a relatively low price as a competitor to the reseller. If alternative sources of supply are not reasonably available, the real profits of the distributor can be taken by the integrated firm. This can be called a quasi-monopoly. A committee of the United States House of Representatives has investigated dual distribution, and has recommended that firms in dual distribution should maintain sufficient price differentials to prevent substantial injury to competition.[125]

Dual distribution in itself is not illegal under the antitrust laws, but the courts have begun to draw lines between illegal and legal practices in this area. In a recent case the court of appeals reversed a district court and held

[122]"Industrial Buildings Materials v. Interchemical Corp.," *Journal of Marketing,* Vol. 35 (July, 1971), p. 76.

[123]Grether, *op. cit.,* p. 84.

[124]L. E. Preston and A. E. Schramm, Jr., "Dual Distribution and Its Impact on Marketing Organization," *California Management Review,* Vol. 8 (Winter, 1965), p. 61.

[125]*Ibid.,* pp. 66–67.

that, where a manufacturer has dominant or monopoly power over a given product, it must preserve the independent distributor of its products. According to the court of appeals, the public benefits by being able to buy from a distributor who may handle competing products. A dominant manufacturer may replace a distributor, but he may not enter into competition with him and destroy him.[126]

SUMMARY AND CONCLUSIONS

In order to institute effective interorganizational management programs that will not conflict with antitrust enforcement agency programs, the marketing manager must become intimately familiar with the various legal constraints on the manner in which power may be employed in the marketing channel. It is also imperative that he have a clear understanding of the restrictions imposed on vertical integration, should he decide that interorganization management is best accomplished through ownership rather than persuasion. The focus in this chapter has been on federal legislation that directly affects relations among commercial channel members.

Legal limitations on the use of coercive power are addressed primarily to the following distribution policy areas.

1. Exclusive dealing. The requirement by a seller or lessor that its customers sell or lease only its products or at least no products in direct competition with the seller's products. Such a policy is illegal if the requirement substantially lessens competition and is circumscribed by the Clayton and FTC Acts.

2. Tying contracts. The requirement by a seller or lessor that its customers take other products in order to obtain a product that they desire. As with exclusive dealing, such a requirement is illegal when it substantially lessens competition. The policy is directly limited by Section 3 of the Clayton Act.

3. Full-line forcing. The requirement by a seller that its customers carry a full line of its products if they are to carry any of them. Such a policy is a variant of tying agreements and is, therefore, subject to similar scrutiny.

4. Resale restrictions. The requirement by a seller that its customers can resell its products only to specified clientele. Such a policy is illegal when competition is substantially lessened and has recently been viewed by the courts as a *per se* violation of the Sherman Act.

5. Reciprocity. The requirement by a buyer that those from whom he purchases must also be buyers of his products. Such a policy is prohibited by Section 5 of

[126]"Industrial Building Materials Inc., v. Interchemical Corp.," *Journal of Marketing*, Vol. 35 (July, 1971), p. 76.

the FTC Act when a substantial amount of commerce is involved and where reciprocity is prevalent and systematized.

6. Price maintenance. The requirement by a seller that a buyer can resell his products only above a specific price or at a stipulated price. Price maintenance (fair trade) laws have been nullified by the repeal of the Miller-Tydings and the McGuire Acts. Similar in intent to now obsolete state fair trade laws are unfair practices acts, which regulate the right of resellers to sell below costs or below specified margins.

7. Price discrimination by buyers. The requirement by a buyer that a seller offer him a price lower than that offered or available to his competitors. Such a policy, as well as one involving the establishment of "dummy" brokerage firms, are covered under the Robinson-Patman Act if they substantially lessen competition and under the FTC Act as unfair methods of competition.

8. Refusals to deal. The right of the seller to choose his own customers or to stop serving a given customer. This threat obviously underlies the enforcement of the abovementioned policies. Although its use is permitted under Section 2a of the Robinson-Patman Act, it is strictly forbidden if it fosters restraint of trade or is employed so as to substantially lessen competition.

Reward power is employed in establishing the specific distribution policies listed below, each of which is limited by federal law.

1. Exclusive territories. The granting by a seller of a geographical monopoly to a buyer relative to the resale of his product or brand. Such a policy is circumscribed by the Sherman Act and Section 5 of the FTC Act. Like resale restrictions, exclusive territorial arrangements are increasingly being viewed as *per se* or outright violations of the law, irrespective of their competitive effects.

2. Incentives for resellers' employees. The offering of special incentives (e.g., push money) by a seller to buyers' employees. While generally permitted, the providing of such incentives is limited by Federal Trade Commission Trade Practice Rules and by the Robinson-Patman Act if they can be shown to injure competition substantially.

3. Commercial bribery. The offering of bribes by a seller to a buyer in order to induce the buyer to purchase his products. Although such bribery is viewed as an unfair trade practice under the FTC Act, it is difficult to enforce because of the liberal use of gratuities and entertainment to promote sales.

4. Price discrimination. The offering of different prices by a seller to two competing resellers on merchandise of like grade and quality. Such a policy is illegal when it substantially lessens competition, but is legal when it can be justified on the basis of cost differentials or as being adopted in "good faith" to meet competition. It is directly circumscribed by the Robinson-Patman Act.

5. Promotional allowances and services. The granting by a seller of payments to resellers for services rendered in connection with processing, handling, selling, or the offering for sale of any of his products sold by them. In order to be

legal, such payments must be offered on proportionately equal terms to all resellers and must be used for the purpose for which they were intended (e.g., advertising allowances must be used for advertising). Again, the Robinson-Patman Act directly limits the way in which such allowances may be employed.

6. Functional discounts. The granting by a seller of price reductions to resellers on the basis of their positions in the channel and the nature and scope of their marketing functions. Although no law directly deals with such discounts, they are circumscribed indirectly by the Robinson-Patman Act and the FTC Act in circumstances where they are allocated unfairly in such a way as to substantially lessen competition.

7. Delivered pricing. The quotation of prices by a seller so that all customers within a given area pay the same price for his product regardless of differences in shipping costs from the seller to the customers. Delivered pricing policies are viewed as restraining trade and lessening competition if their effect is similar to that of price collusion among sellers. Such pricing policies have been attacked under the Federal Trade Commission Act and under the Sherman Act.

Vertical integration via internal expansion seems to be positively sanctioned by the antitrust enforcement agencies so long as it does not lead to monopolization in restraint of trade, a Sherman Act offense. On the other hand, vertical integration by merger is much more heavily scrutinized and may be viewed rather negatively by the agencies and the courts. In the case of such mergers, Section 7 (the Celler-Kefauver Amendment) of the Clayton Act comes into play and can be used if the agencies believe that there may be a tendency for the merger, once consummated, to substantially lessen competition. Thus, the agencies can challenge such mergers in their incipiency.

The policy of vertically integrating often leads to dual distribution conflicts when sellers become competitors of some of their independently owned resellers. Although there are no additional laws beyond those mentioned earlier circumscribing the practice of dual distribution, this phenomenon has undergone considerable scrutiny in Congress, and it is not at all unlikely that legislation may be forthcoming to limit its practice, especially if it can be shown that small independent middlemen are being severely hurt by it.

With regard to most of the legal limitations referred to above, it should be noted that the antitrust enforcement agencies have been highly successful in terms of the number of court cases they have won when they have brought suit against alleged offenders. Furthermore, in order for a firm to defend itself adequately once charged with a violation, it would doubtless have to spend a large sum of money preparing its case, given the complexity of the defenses available. The costs involved may, in fact, exceed the benefits of winning. Therefore, marketing managers might spare themselves considerable difficulties by devoting energies to avoid being in conflict with the antitrust laws or with the edicts of the antitrust enforcement agencies.

DISCUSSION QUESTIONS

1. What laws affecting distribution are more likely to be protecting competitors rather than competition? Is the distinction important? Why?

2. Why might manufacturers wish to engage in resale price maintenance practices? What tactics could they employ to maintain prices, other than invoking the fair trade laws?

3. Which is preferable—intrabrand or interbrand competition? Can there be one without the other? Where do you stand on the issue of intrabrand competition—is it necessary in order for there to be viable general competition from a macroperspective? Discuss these questions in the context of resale restrictions and the granting of exclusive territories.

4. Explain the relationship between vertical "arrangements" and horizontal competition.

5. How does the Celler-Kefauver Amendment (Section 7) to the Clayton Act relate to vertical mergers? What are the key issues involved in these situations?

6. Do you believe that the Robinson-Patman Act should be stricken from the laws of this country? Debate the pros and cons of this question and come out with a position on it.

7. The president of an automobile accessory manufacturing business wants to purchase a chain of automotive retail stores. What legal issues might this raise?

8. Discuss the similarities and differences between a tying contract and the business practice of reciprocity. Do the practices, on balance, appear to be significantly different?

9. Name five uses of coercive power that would be legal in interorganization management. Name five uses of reward power that would be legal.

10. Can you think of any instances where the use of expert or referent power in interorganization management might be illegal?

11. Which conflict management strategies that were suggested in Chapter 7 might be questionable from a legal perspective? Why?

12. Opposition to dual distribution is another example of entrenched institutions trying to protect themselves against competition by resort to law. Is this true in whole or in part?

NINE

MARKETING CHANNEL ORGANIZATION AND DESIGN: POLICIES

Organizing and designing the distribution channel for a good or service is but one aspect of the marketing strategy of an organization. The set of decisions surrounding channel organization hinges on other decisions relating to product, price, promotion, and physical distribution.[1] For example, the adoption of an exclusive dealing policy may result in the elimination of certain merchandisers as potential channel participants. On the other hand, heavy brand advertising for convenience-type products (e.g., cigarettes) may necessitate, because of the large promotional investment undertaken by the manufacturer, wide distribution through numerous retail outlets in order to secure adequate sales and profits to cover the investment. In the case of perishable products, such as fruits and vegetables, any wholesaling intermediaries employed must be chosen so as to facilitate the rapid turnover of the products to prevent spoilage. The physical characteristics of products often dictate physical distribution requirements, which, in turn, influence channel strategy.

The starting point in designing the marketing channel is the ultimate consumer. Knowledge about what consumers need, where consumers buy, why they buy from certain outlets, when they buy, and how they buy is critical. The task of organizing and designing a marketing channel involves

---

[1]William R. Davidson, "Channels of Distribution—One Aspect of Marketing Strategy," *Business Horizons* (February, 1961), pp. 84-90.

the seller in determining the most profitable and effective ways to reach the markets that he wants to serve, and such a determination is only possible from an understanding of consumer behavior, both for industrial and household goods and services.[2]

In this chapter, attention is focused on the various means by which a seller (manufacturer, wholesaler, or retailer) can influence the organization and design of the channels in which he participates through the selection or acceptance of a number of distribution policies and practices. A large number of these policies were enumerated and discussed in the previous chapter dealing with legal limitations to the use of coercive and reward power. Here, basic issues related to the selection of various policies are dealt with, under the assumption that implementation of them is accomplished within the legal boundaries specified in Chapter 8.

BASIC CRITERIA IN CHANNEL DESIGN

Aside from the strong stipulation that channel design must start from an understanding of consumer purchasing patterns, there are several additional factors that provide constraints on channel organization that are important in structuring an interorganizational distribution system. These factors are discussed in some detail in basic marketing and marketing management texts and, therefore, will be reviewed only briefly here.[3]

First, it is important to realize at the outset that the choice of outlets, in the case of manufacturers, and of suppliers, in the case of middlemen, is frequently highly restricted. For example, in the automotive passenger tire industry, a new manufacturer would find it extremely difficult to find retail outlets for his replacement tires, because most of the suitable outlets have already been secured by the existing manufacturers (e.g., Goodyear, Firestone, Goodrich, General, and Uniroyal). In order to generate sales volume and thus achieve scale economies in production, a new tire manufacturer would probably have to vie for private label business. The manufacturer would likely be forced into an unequal bargaining position relative to his

---

[2]See, for in-depth analyses of consumer behavior, John A. Howard and Jagdish N. Sheth, *The Theory of Buyer Behavior* (New York: John Wiley & Sons, Inc., 1969); and James F. Engel, David T. Kollat, and Roger D. Blackwell, *Consumer Behavior*, 2nd ed. (New York: Holt, Rinehart and Winston, 1973).

[3]See, for example, Philip Kotler, *Marketing Management: Analysis, Planning and Control*, 2nd ed. (Englewood Cliffs, N.J.: Prentice-Hall, Inc., 1972), pp. 565-569; Burton Marcus, et al., *Modern Marketing* (New York: Random House, 1975), pp. 546-555; Charles F. Phillips and Delbert J. Duncan, *Marketing: Principles and Methods*, 6th ed. (Homewood, Ill.: Richard D. Irwin, 1968), pp. 620-640; and David J. Schwartz, *Marketing Today: A Basic Approach* (New York: Harcourt Brace Jovanovich, 1973), pp. 279-284.

prospective customers, because in such situations, middlemen can usually play suppliers off against one another and thereby are able to establish highly favorable terms of trade on private label arrangements.[4] On the other hand, wholesalers are obviously foreclosed from many channels in which direct distribution is practiced (e.g., automobiles, computers), and specific retailers may find themselves similarly foreclosed because of the policies of suppliers to deal with only certain types of outlets (e.g., Schwinn bicycles and Stiffel lamps are not sold through discount houses). While the problem associated with channel choice is particularly vexing for new, unestablished organizations, it is also worrisome for units wishing to diversify or to broaden their distribution. Certainly, the extent of financial and other sources of power held by a channel member seeking to enter or enlarge a distribution network will have a strong effect on the amount of freedom of choice available to him.

Second, the number, size, and geographic concentration of customers will have a direct effect on channel design. Thus, if customers are few in number, large in size, and geographically concentrated, direct channels of distribution are likely to be feasible. If the opposite conditions hold, the mechanics of distribution become more cumbersome; the employment of a large number of intermediaries on the part of a seller will probably be required. In the latter situation, intermediaries serving a large number of small, widely dispersed customers will probably find it necessary to invest in branch operations.

Third, as mentioned above, product characteristics will directly influence channel design. Perishable products require direct marketing or at least the use of middlemen who can assure rapid turnover of merchandise. Bulky products require channels that minimize shipping distance and excessive handling. Unstandardized products that call for technical expertise in their sale may require direct selling because of the need for specialized attention. Nonperishable, nonbulky, standardized products can be handled more readily by indirect channels.

Fourth, middleman, competitive, company, and environmental characteristics also influence channel design.[5] Thus, in certain lines of trade (e.g., furniture), manufacturers' representatives are particularly well adapted to serve producers and customers because of their ability to carry full lines of complementary products assembled from a variety of manufacturers. For shopping goods, comparisons as to style, price, and suitability are significant

---

[4]Federal Trade Commission, *Economic Report on the Manufacture and Distribution of Automotive Tires* (Washington, D.C.: U.S. Government Printing Office, 1966).

[5]For a complete discussion of each of these constraints, see Kotler, *op. cit.*, pp 567–568.

to consumers, and, therefore, the selection of appropriate channels is dictated, to a large degree, by the need to provide such comparisons. Furthermore, companies obviously vary in their financial strength, the breadth of their product mix and assortments, the orientation of their marketing policies, and their experience with certain types of outlets or suppliers. All of these latter factors constrain channel design. Finally, economic conditions and legal restrictions are influential in determining the amount of channel strategy discretion an organization will have.

The above constraints clearly limit the distribution strategy to be employed in any specific situation and thus place boundaries around interorganization management. Once the constraints are assessed, two crucial decisions must be made. First, the way in which an organization will try to make its products available to designated end markets must be determined. Second, the number of outlets or suppliers with which a channel member wishes to work must be arrived at. Once these decisions are made, the manager can then turn his attention to the means by which he can allocate resources within the system efficiently and effectively via role specification and conflict management.

For the most part, the discussion in the remainder of this chapter focuses on channel decision problems from the manufacturer's perspective. Although it is recognized that interorganization management can be practiced by middlemen as well as manufacturers (as explored in Chapter 11), the focus on the manufacturer has been chosen for ease of exposition. It is believed that the analysis and techniques presented below can and should apply in reverse. Thus, middlemen can use similar logic when choosing suppliers and, in the case of wholesalers of consumer goods particularly, when lining up retail distribution outlets.

Determining Types of Middlemen

Every organization faces a series of alternatives relative to how it is going to make its product or service available and accessible to consumers. While obviously constrained by the factors listed briefly above, there is little doubt that firms are rarely restricted to one means of reaching their markets. The question then becomes: How can firms arrive at a rational choice in the most efficient manner? In an excellent treatment, Philip Kotler has laid out the mechanics of this decision process.[6] His explanation is summarized here.

Assume that an old-line manufacturer of chemicals facing declining

---

[6]Philip Kotler, *Marketing Decision Making: A Model Building Approach* (New York: Holt, Rinehart and Winston, 1971), pp. 290–298.

profits is considering marketing a product that can be used to kill germs in swimming pools. Assume further that the product is a significant departure from the company's present line—that the company has never done any previous consumer marketing and that its present channels of distribution are far from ideal for tapping the swimming pool market.

The first step in determining the type of middlemen to use in reaching this market would be to itemize alternative ways in which swimming pool owners could purchase this product. In other words, as emphasized earlier, the consumer represents the starting point in channel design. For example, the swimming pool owner may obtain the product from at least the five sources listed below:

1. Conventional retail outlets, such as hardware stores and drug stores.
2. Specialized swimming pool supply and equipment retailers.
3. Swimming pool service companies.
4. Mass retailer outlets such as supermarkets, department stores, and discount houses.
5. Direct mail supply companies.

Management will want to assess the relative volumes of swimming pool germicides that move through each of these types of outlets, their relative rates of growth, and their relative profitability as channels. It will also want to find out from swimming pool owners the value they place on price, convenience, packaging, germicide effectiveness, etc., in order further to assess the relative standing of the various outlets in facilitating the delivery of these features. For this example, it is assumed that management has the option of using one or more of these sets of outlets. (As indicated previously and examined later, this assumption is often erroneous.)

The next step in the analysis of alternatives is to specify the primary channel paths the company might follow in reaching these various outlets or in tapping the various markets. Five radically different paths the company might take to market the new product are:

1. Market through the present distributors of its industrial chemicals (*present distributors alternative*).
2. Marketing through new distributors already selling to the swimming pool trade (*new distributors alternative*).
3. Buying a small company already in this market to utilize its distributors (*acquisition alternative*).

4. Selling the chemical in bulk to companies already in this market (*private brand alternative*).

5. Packaging and selling the chemical through mail campaigns directed at swimming pool owners (*direct mail alternative*).

Each of these alternatives has, obviously, drawbacks as well as strengths. In order to assess these in an analytical manner, however, it is useful to go beyond qualitative debate as to their merits and demerits. Thus, the third step in the channel alternative assessment process is to attempt to quantify the relevant factors in the consideration of each.

Three different decision techniques can be fruitfully applied to this problem: the weighted factor score method, the hierarchical preference method, and the simulation method. In addition, it should be noted that the multiattribute choice strategies specified in Chapter 2 are also directly applicable to the problem of channel design.

Weighted Factor Score Method.   This method calls upon management to list the major factors that the company should consider, to assign weights to reflect their relative importance, to rate each distribution alternative on each factor, and to determine the overall weighted factor score for each alternative. In this way, the five distribution alternatives can at least be ranked and the lowest ranked ones can be dropped.

An example of this method is shown in Table 9–1 relative to the "present distributors alternative." Clearly, different factors might be selected and different weights applied to each factor. It has been assumed here that the relevant factors involve an alternative's likely effectiveness in reaching the target market, its profitability, the experience that the company will gain in consumer marketing, the level of investment required to implement the alternative, and its ability to aid the company in cutting short its losses on other operations. It should be noted that the factor weights sum to 1.00; thus, they reflect the *relative* importance of each factor to management.

Although this method represents an improvement over simply listing the pros and cons of each alternative and is particularly useful in the early stage of evaluation when little data are available, it is subject to a number of statistical limitations, the major one of which is that the method misleadingly uses an interval scale for data that are properly only ordinal.[7] The hierarchical preference ordering method avoids this criticism.

---

[7] See, for this and additional limitations, Wroe Alderson and Paul E. Green, *Planning and Problem Solving in Marketing* (Homewood, Ill.: Richard D. Irwin, 1964), p. 206.

TABLE 9-1 Weighted Factor Score Method Applied to Distribution of Swimming Pool Germicide: Present Distributors Alternative

Factor	(A) Factor Weight	(B) Factor Score											Rating (A × B)
		.0	.1	.2	.3	.4	.5	.6	.7	.8	.9	1.0	
1. Effectiveness in reaching swimming pool owners	.15				√								.045
2. Amount of profit if this alternative works well	.25						√						.125
3. Experience company will gain in consumer marketing	.10			√									.020
4. Amount of investment involved (high score for low investment)	.30									√			.240
5. Ability of company to cut short its losses	.20								√				.140
	Σ 1.00								Total score				.570

SOURCE: Philip Kotler, *Marketing Decision Making: A Model Building Approach* (New York: Holt, Rinehart and Winston, 1971), p. 293.

Hierarchical Preference Ordering Method. This method calls for management (1) to rank, not rate, the five factors in order of importance, (2) to set a minimum level from 0.00 to 1.00 for each factor that a distribution alternative must satisfy, in order to be considered, and (3) to examine all distribution alternatives against the first important factor, then the second, etc., eliminating those strategies at each stage that fail to satisfy that factor. The method is essentially the same as the sequential elimination choice strategy procedure referred to in Chapter 2.

An example is presented in Table 9-2 using the swimming pool germicide example. Note that the factors have been reordered according to the factor weights shown in Table 9-1. For each factor, a minimum pass level is established by management. In this example, all but one distribution alternative scored at or above the pass level. Thus, alternative 3 is eliminated from further consideration, because it requires too much investment. Alternative 5 is eliminated when the second most important factor is considered, because it fails to promise enough profits. The procedure is continued by bringing in successively less important factors until, as Table 9-2 indicates, only alternative 2 remains. The relative standings of the five alternatives are shown in the bottom row.

Although this method probably comes close to reflecting how many

TABLE 9-2 Hierarchical Preference Ordering Method Applied to Five Distribution Alternatives

Factors in Order of Importance	Minimum Pass Level	Alternative 1	Alternative 2	Alternative 3	Alternative 4	Alternative 5
1. Amount of investment involved	.3	.8 = P	.6 = P	.2 = F	.9 = P	.9 = P
2. Amount of profit if this alternative works well	.5	.5 = P	.8 = P	.6 = —	.5 = P	.4 = F
3. Ability of company to cut short its losses	.5	.7 = P	.6 = P	.1 = —	.8 = P	.8 = —
4. Effectiveness in reaching swimming pool owners	.3	.3 = P	.7 = P	.8 = —	.6 = P	.3 = —
5. Experience company will gain in consumer marketing	.4	.2 = F	.5 = P	.6 = —	.2 = F	.4 = —
Ranking		3rd	1st	5th	2nd	4th

Note: P = Pass
F = Fail

SOURCE: Philip Kotler, *Marketing Decision Making: A Model Building Approach* (New York: Holt, Rinehart and Winston, 1971), p. 295.

managers tend to think about choosing among alternatives, it gives no credit to how well a particular distribution alternative exceeds a minimum level required by some factor. A particular strategy may be almost perfect on the most important criterion and slightly below the minimum level on a minor criterion and as a result be eliminated. In these situations, it may be necessary for management to adopt another choice strategy, such as one of those suggested in Chapter 2, which would more equitably discriminate between the options under consideration.

Both the weighted factor score and the hierarchical preference ordering methods fail to produce an actual estimate of profit and risk for each alternative. To accomplish this, it would be desirable to create a simulation model for examining the estimated monetary consequences of each alternative under different assumptions and sets of data.

Simulation Method. Plausible data were developed by Kotler and Vialle relative to the problem specified above.[8] These data are shown in Table 9-3. For example, the acquisition alternative was considered to require the high-

[8]Kotler, *Marketing Decision Making . . . , op. cit.*, p. 296.

TABLE 9-3   Example of Data Input for Simulation of Alternative
Distribution Strategies

| | Distribution Strategies | | | |
| | *(1)* | *(2)* | *(3)* | *(4)* |
Variables	*Present Distributors Alternative*	*New Distributors Alternative*	*Acquisition Alternative*	*Private Brand Alternative*
Investment	$300,000	$500,000	$2,500,000	$100,000
Price per bag	$2.70	$2.50	$2.70	$2.20
Contribution margin per bag	$1.20	$1.00	$1.20	$0.70
Mean monthly advertising budget	$5,000	$50,000	$10,000	$5,000
Advertising effectiveness coefficient	1/2	1/1.8	1/1.9	1/2
Initial number of distributors	80	20	60	60
Growth rate per month in number of distributors	0.02	0.04	0.01	0.02
Maximum number of distributors permitted	150	150	150	150
Distribution effectiveness coefficient	1/2.5	1/2.0	1/2.2	1/2.2

SOURCE: Philip Kotler, *Marketing Decision Making: A Model Building Approach* (New York: Holt, Rinehart and Winston, 1971), p. 296.

est investment, while the private brand alternative required the lowest level of investment. Furthermore, each distribution alternative involves a somewhat different pricing policy and contribution margin as well as different levels of advertising expenditures and effectiveness. Thus, under the new distributors alternative, the initial number of distributors would be low but the growth rate would be high, because it is assumed that potential distributors would react favorably to the large advertising budget and the higher margin given to them under this alternative.

Other inputs used by Kotler and Vialle, but not shown in Table 9-3, were (1) the rate of growth in demand expected under the different distribution alternatives, (2) a provision for substantial competitive reaction if the company's market share starts to exceed a certain figure, and (3) a provision for the effect of test marketing before making a decision. The particular distribution alternatives were simulated for a 48-month period; the results, in terms of three different measures of performance, are shown in Table 9-4. "Pay-back period" refers to how many months will pass before the accumulated revenue covers the accumulated cost to the company. The "share of potential" refers to the percentage of the company's potential share of the market that is realized by the particular distribution alternative. "Accumulated discounted profit" refers to the present value of 48-month earnings

TABLE 9–4   Results of Simulation of Alternative Distribution Strategies

Criterion	(1) Present distributors alternative		(2) New distributors alternative		(3) Acquisition alternative		(4) Private brand alternative	
	Value	Rank	Value	Rank	Value	Rank	Value	Rank
Pay-back period (months)	14	3	8	1	25	4	9	2
Share of potential	44%	4	100%	1	62%	2	43%	3
Accumulated discounted profit (millions)	3.25	3	6.10	1	5.60	2	1.99	4

SOURCE: Philip Kotler, *Marketing Decision Making: A Model Building Approach* (New York: Holt, Rinehart and Winston, 1971), p. 297.

stream discounted at 10 percent. Clearly, the new distributors alternative is superior relative to the performance criteria.

Although it should be clear that the three methods described above are useful means for determining the most effective channel alternative, other considerations of a more qualitative nature must enter into the analysis as well.[9] Simplistically put, the choice among channel alternatives in the latter example comes down to judgments on the basis of economic criteria. Thus, if it were possible to assume that two alternative channels (for example, employing one's own sales force versus using manufacturers' representatives or developing a wholly owned system of warehouses versus renting space in public warehouses) produce the same sales, a straightforward breakeven analysis could be developed to aid in making the decision between the two.[10] Figure 9-1 portrays the average costs associated with these alternatives. The average cost of using manufacturers' representatives (or public warehouses) is constant over the range of sales, while the per unit cost of employing one's own sales force (or owning one's own warehouses) declines as the level of sales increases (if it is assumed that the salesmen are paid on a straight salary basis or that the warehouses are bought outright and not leased back).

[9]A theoretical treatment of this subject matter is found in Frederick E. Balderston, "Design of Marketing Channels," in Reavis Cox, Wroe Alderson and Stanley Shapiro (eds.), *Theory in Marketing* (Homewood, Ill.: Richard D. Irwin, 1964), pp. 176–189. See also Ronald Artle and Sture Berlund, "A Note on Manufacturers' Choice of Distribution Channels," *Management Science* (July, 1959), pp. 460–471; and Helmy H. Baligh, "A Theoretical Framework for Channel Choice," in P. D. Bennett (ed.), *Economic Growth, Competition, and World Markets* (Chicago: American Marketing Association, 1965), pp. 631–654.

[10]A similar approach can be found in Kotler, *Marketing Management . . .*, *op. cit.*, pp. 575–578.

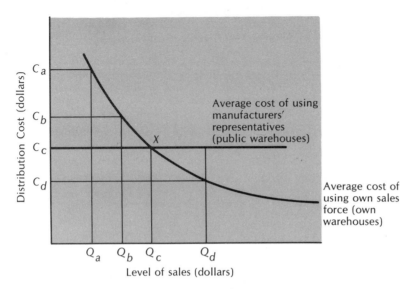

FIGURE 9-1 Breakeven Cost Chart: Manufacturers' Representatives versus Own Sales Force and Public Warehouses versus Own Warehouses

In this highly simplified example, the breakeven point between the various alternatives is at X. Thus, at sales levels less than Q_c, the decision maker should employ manufacturers' representatives (or use public warehouses) and at sales levels greater than Q_c, he should hire his own sales force (or purchase his own warehouses).

There is, however, a constraint present in the marketplace that is not readily apparent when one is considering economic variables alone. As indicated in Chapter 5 and also earlier in this chapter, it is likely that channel alternatives will be limited for new entrants to a market. Thus, when sales are at level Q_a, the manufacturer (or middleman, in the case of alternatives available to intermediaries) may be forced to integrate the personal selling or the warehousing function even though the breakeven analysis indicates otherwise, because the volume that he can generate is not sufficiently attractive to independent intermediaries. The missionary effort that the latter would have to expend on the new entrant's product or service might not, in their eyes, be justified by the returns they would receive. Therefore, the shifting of marketing flows within the channel may be restricted until the market becomes larger—when the sales level reaches Q_b. The division of labor in channels may be limited by the extent of the market.[11]

Management's desire to exert sufficient control over channel members'

[11] For a discussion of this point, see George J. Stigler, "The Division of Labor is Limited by the Extent of the Market," *Journal of Political Economy*, Vol. 59 (June, 1951), pp. 185–193. For an

activities so as to assure adequate performance throughout the channel system frequently modifies decisions based on economic criteria alone. Management may be willing to trade off short-term economic benefits in order to gain a long-term ability to manipulate the channel. In conventional channels of distribution, the members are independent businessmen. Therefore, each is primarily interested in maximizing his own profits, which can sometimes lead to suboptimization within the system, as pointed out in Chapter 1. Suboptimization refers to the fact that each channel member may make a set of decisions on the various elements of marketing strategy (e.g., price, advertising, and physical distribution) which maximizes his profits but which conflicts with the ability of the entire system to perform most efficiently or effectively. As Stasch has observed, the remedy to this problem is to seek an adjustment of the strategy decisions of each member so that total channel performance (measured in terms of profits, market share, or some other commonly shared goal) will be higher.[12] The greater the difference between present channel performance and projected channel performance under the systems approach, the greater will be the incentive of channel members to pursue joint planning or to vertically integrate.

The accomplishment of some semblance of channel control requires, as indicated in Chapter 7, the use of power in order to generate appropriate role specifications for each channel member in the system. A channel can be viewed as being in equilibrium when there is no structural or functional change that would lead to increased channel performance.[13] A structural change involves the addition or elimination of some level in the channel, whereas a functional change calls for a reallocation of one or more of the marketing flows among the channel members. Maximum control can be achieved through vertical integration; however, the investment required may be beyond the reach of certain firms. Furthermore, there are benefits available in operating nonintegrated systems that may be desired by the channel members.

There are numerous means by which an organization can use its power to secure effective control within a system comprised of independently owned units. One of these means is the establishment of a franchise system whereby legitimate power is combined with reward and expert power in developing a programmed network.[14] An example where franchising is used

---

application to distribution problems in developing economies, see Reed Moyer, "The Structure of Markets in Developing Economies," *MSU Business Topics*, Vol. 12 (Autumn, 1964), pp. 43–60.

[12] Stanley F. Stasch, *A Method of Dynamically Analyzing the Stability of the Economic Structure of Channels of Distribution*, an unpublished doctoral dissertation, School of Business, Northwestern University, 1964, p. 63ff.

[13] *Ibid.*, pp. 19–28.

[14] Franchising and other forms of vertical marketing systems are described in considerable detail in Chapter 10.

to influence the policies, operations, and activities of franchisees is found in Exhibit 9–1, where the language used by the 7-Eleven Store System, a division of the Southland Corporation, to describe briefly its franchising arrangement in answer to inquiries concerning a 7-Eleven Store franchise has been reproduced. The reader should carefully note that Southland provides training, store and location, a system of operation and bookkeeping, and arranges for an inventory of fast-moving items. In the 7-Eleven system, Southland leaves very little to chance, which explains why the organization is one of the most profitable in the food retailing industry.

Also significant in organizing and designing a marketing channel is a qualitative assessment of the ability of the various potential channel members to adapt to changing conditions. Problems of adaptability are most evident during times of economic downturn or when a channel is being threatened by intertype competition of an innovative nature. The example used in the examination of the crisis-change model in Chapter 5 showed that independent retailers and wholesalers have not always been highly adaptable, as when the chain store organizations invaded their respective fields. The willingness of channel members to accept new or different role specifications in such circumstances is crucial to a channel's long-term viability.

Determining the Degree of Market Exposure

Among the various channel policies referred to in the preceding chapter, perhaps one of the most crucial, from a producer's perspective, relates to how many sales outlets should be established and, from a middleman's perspective, how many suppliers should be used within a given product category.[15] As stated above, the decision will be determined primarily through studying consumers' purchasing habits relative to product or brand in question. Three basic choices appear to be available. A producer could decide on a policy of *intensive* distribution in which he will place his product or brand in every available outlet. Likewise, a middleman could decide to purchase all available brands within a product class in order to offer the broadest possible assortments to his customers. *Or* a producer could use *selective* distribution, whereby he will place his product or brand in a more limited number of outlets within a defined geographic area. A middleman may use concomitant selectivity in his purchasing patterns. *Or* a producer could decide on a policy of *exclusive* distribution, in which he will place his product or brand in the hands of only one outlet in a specified geographic area. In similar fashion, a middleman may decide to concentrate his efforts on one manufacturer's brand(s) within a given product category.

[15] For a theoretical discussion of this subject, see Balderston, *op. cit.*

EXHIBIT 9–1   Initial Information to Inquiries for a 7-Eleven Store Franchise

7-Eleven . . . A Way of Life

7-Eleven is, to busy people of all ages, the friendly little store that's "just around the corner". It's the convenient place to stop for a loaf of bread, quart of milk, package of cigarettes, groceries, beverages, picnic supplies, candy, "hot to go" foods, or everyone's favorite ice drink . . . Slurpee. 7-Eleven Stores are small, compact, easily accessible, and usually open for business 24 hours a day, 7 days a week. Their convenient locations, fast service, and friendly image have combined to make 7-Eleven shopping a familiar part of the American lifestyle.

7-Eleven is a division of The Southland Corporation, pioneer of the convenience store and a recognized leader in the food and dairy industries. More than 5,000 7-Eleven Stores are located virtually throughout the nation and, in some areas, stores are available for franchise to qualified applicants.

7-Eleven offers a business system in a ready-to-operate store on a carefully selected site. It includes training, counseling, bookkeeping, financing, and merchandising assistance. This brochure, which briefly introduces the 7-Eleven System, is your invitation to meet with a company representative to discuss in detail how you and your family can become a part of 7-Eleven.

Real Estate

7-Eleven's real estate representatives research an area and select the sites which, based upon population, traffic flow, convenience to homes, and competition, are most likely to produce sales. 7-Eleven buys or leases these sites, and leases the completed 7-Eleven Stores to franchisees.

Equipment

All equipment in the stores, including heating and air conditioning, vaults, shelving, cash registers, and refrigerated cases, are included in the lease to the franchisee, who is responsible for maintenance of the equipment.

Merchandise

7-Eleven arranges for the initial inventory of merchandise in the store. Thereafter, the franchisee orders and stocks his own merchandise. 7-Eleven recommends vendors who, we believe, offer the best service and the highest quality merchandise at the lowest costs. Franchisees are, however, free to purchase from any vendors they choose. The franchisee receives credit for all discounts on merchandise purchased.

In addition, 7-Eleven prepares for the franchisees lists of recommended merchandise and suggested retail selling prices. These lists are based upon the

EXHIBIT 9–1 continued

company's many years of experience in convenience store merchandising and appear to afford the greatest potential for profit. Some recommended vendors may be affiliated with 7-Eleven, and some suggested merchandise may be produced by divisions of The Southland Corporation. However, franchisees are free to purchase the merchandise they choose and establish the retail prices they prefer.

Advertising

Advertising plays a significant role in assisting franchisees in building the sales and profits of their 7-Eleven Stores. For many years, 7-Eleven advertising has received widespread recognition.

> "OH, THANK HEAVEN FOR 7-ELEVEN"
> "IT'S ABOUT TIME"
> "IF IT'S NOT AROUND THE HOUSE,
> "IT'S JUST AROUND THE CORNER"

Franchisees are, of course, free to further advertise at their own expense.

Training

Prior to opening the stores, applicants for 7-Eleven Franchise are required to attend a 7-Eleven training school to learn the mechanics of the day-to-day 7-Eleven Store operations. Following the one-week classroom training program, the franchisee is trained on-the-job for one week in a training store under 7-Eleven's supervision. Successful completion of the training programs is a prerequisite for final acceptance by 7-Eleven of an applicant. Additional in-store training is also provided the franchisee from time to time as deemed necessary by local management. An initial training fee and (in addition) a store set-up fee are required.

Employees

Although most franchised 7-Eleven Stores are family operated, it is usually necessary for the franchisee to employ additional part-time and full-time help.

It is the franchisee's responsibility to hire and train his employees. The franchisee is responsible for all payroll expenses, including employee taxes. Based on the franchisee's authorization and his employees' time cards, 7-Eleven prepares his payroll checks.

Personal Insurance

7-Eleven franchisees, their families and employees are eligible to participate in the 7-Eleven Franchise Trust which provides financial relief in the event of sickness, disability, or death. An H.R.10 Retirement Plan is also available in most areas at the option of the franchisee.

EXHIBIT 9–1 continued

Bookkeeping

7-Eleven keeps bookkeeping records on the franchisee's operation of the 7-Eleven Store. Franchisees make their own daily cash deposits of sales receipts. From these, 7-Eleven pays all expenses approved by the franchisee in connection with operations of the stores. The franchisee purchases his merchandise and, upon his approval of the invoices, 7-Eleven will make payment on their behalf.

Investment

The investment requirements for a 7-Eleven Store Franchise include the cost of the inventory and the cash register fund. The exact amounts vary depending upon the location of the store and the inventory requirements. Average investments range from $17,000 to $25,000, a portion of which 7-Eleven will finance for qualified applicants.

Franchisees Can Most Affect Profits By:

- General Management Aptitude
- Ability to hire and train competent employees
- Control of employee and customer pilferage
- Creative Salesmanship
- Sincere Customer relations
- Ability to create a friendly store atmosphere
- Keep a clean and orderly store profile

Profits

A local 7-Eleven representative will discuss the financial history of the store being considered and other stores in the nearby area.

The GROSS PROFIT of the store is shared by the franchisee and 7-Eleven.

The percentage of GROSS PROFIT paid by the franchisee to 7-Eleven is a continuing charge for the rental of the store building and equipment, utilities, advertising, bookkeeping and merchandising and general management assistance.

From the remainder of the GROSS PROFIT split the franchisee pays all other operating expenses such as:

- Payroll
- Payroll Taxes

EXHIBIT 9-1 continued

- Supplies

- Laundry

- Telephone

- Interest

- Business Taxes and Licenses

- In-store maintenance

- Landscaping maintenance

- Bad checks

- Cash Variation

- Inventory Variation

The NET PROFIT after payment of the operating expenses is the franchisee's net income.

SOURCE: The Southland Corporation, *The 7-Eleven Franchise*, promotional brochure (Reprinted with the permission of the Southland Corporation.)

Intensive distribution appears to be a rational policy for goods that people wish to purchase frequently and with minimum effort; examples are tobacco products, soap, newspapers, chewing gum, gasoline, candy bars, and aspirin. Selective distribution can be used for goods that buyers seek out and can range from almost intensive to almost exclusive; examples are certain brands of television sets (e.g., Zenith, RCA), mattresses (e.g., Simmons), cosmetics (e.g., Revlon, Estee Lauder), industrial supplies (e.g., Norton abrasives), and clothing (e.g., Arrow shirts). Exclusive distribution is used to bring about a greater partnership between seller and reseller and is commonly found in the marketing channels for new automobiles, some major appliances, commercial air-conditioning equipment, some brands of apparel, and high-priced furniture. In addition, channel structure tends to interact with the degree of market exposure. For example, the use of numerous wholesale intermediaries (i.e., "long" or indirect channel structures) often permits greater market decentralization and thus intensive distribution, while the opposite tends to hold for shorter, more direct channels, as indicated in Chapters 5 and 6.

It could be argued that the more intensive a product's distribution, the greater the sales that product will achieve in the short run. In fact, one could call this statement a "law" of marketing. Thus, if Magnavox, a producer of high-quality stereophonic phonograph consoles, decided to disband its present system of selective distribution in favor of a more intensive arrangement, one could predict, with certainty, that its sales would increase in the short run. But, as Magnavox expanded the number of its outlets to include drugstores (picture Walgreen's selling major stereo consoles, if you will), supermarkets, discount stores, and other outlets, it is highly likely that adverse consequences would take place over the long term. First, because some of the new outlets would undoubtedly begin to use the Magnavox brand as a leader item to attract traffic, retail prices on Magnavox equipment would begin to drop, and valued dealers such as Lazarus in Columbus, Ohio, might have second thoughts about selling a product on which profit margins were becoming slimmer and slimmer.[16] Second, service would deteriorate. Drugstores, supermarkets, and discount stores might not be willing to install service facilities, and repair work under warranty arrangements with consumers would have to be assumed by those stores with such facilities or by the manufacturer. Often, warranty business is not the most lucrative element of a service department's repair work, and leading stores offering such service would become increasingly disaffected at having to handle problems on equipment sold by other concerns. When General Electric decided to adopt a more intensive distribution policy for its small electrical appliances some years ago, it found that it could not obtain adequate service from its expanded retail network. The company had to institute a nationwide, company-owned chain of service centers in order to solve this significant marketing problem.

Third, it is likely that, because of its intensive distribution policy, Magnavox would find itself assuming a greater participation in a number of the marketing flows. Thus, promotion by the company would probably have to be increased, because dealers who once were willing to promote the product (through advertising and especially through in-store personal selling and display) might find their margins reduced to the point where such efforts on their part were no longer warranted, relative to other brands of stereo equipment that they might have in stock. In addition, more of the burden of holding inventory would undoubtedly have to be assumed by Magnavox as smaller outlets were added. In fact, it is possible to conceive of Magnavox's having to

---

[16] It is interesting to note that when W. T. Grant, a major retail chain, was attempting to avoid bankruptcy in 1975, it decided to drop the lines of major appliances that it was carrying because margins had been competed away on them. While this move did not save Grant's, it did at least permit the chain to concentrate on more profitable lines. Other retailers are having similar problems in selling major appliances at a profit, given the extent of discounting on these items.

sell stereo equipment on a consignment basis in order to secure distribution in outlets where cash flow is a considerable problem.

The example could go on, but the point should now be evident. The type of distribution policy employed clearly interacts with the product itself and with other marketing policies. Gaining sales volume in the short run is not an appropriate goal for numerous companies, and uncontrolled distribution is likely to bring with it some serious long-term problems.

This is not to say that intensive distribution policies are inappropriate for certain types of goods and services. Quite the contrary. To aid in the selection of a distribution policy, it is best to consider the relationship between store and product types. Bucklin has combined the traditional threefold classification of consumer goods (convenience, shopping, and specialty goods) with a threefold classification of outlets according to patronage motives (convenience, shopping, and specialty stores) in order to facilitate decision-making in this area.[17] As can be seen in Table 9–5, knowledge of consumer behavior is again the key in unlocking the problem of distribution policy.

The selection of a distribution policy involves a consideration of relevant tradeoffs. As indicated above, when a channel member decides to adopt an intensive policy, he generally relinquishes a significant amount of control over the marketing of his products within the channel. The only way he can reestablish such control in these cases is to assume greater participation in each of the marketing flows. For example, O. M. Scott & Sons Company, a prominent manufacturer of lawn products, decided to adopt a less selective distribution policy, because it wanted to obtain more exposure for its product line among a large percentage of medium- to upper-income home-owning families who were, according to marketing research study conducted in the 1960's, not users of lawn fertilizers.[18] In order to obtain the proper merchandising support and control throughout its expanded reseller base, Scott found it necessary to develop special detailed programs for each retail account. Monthly sales plans were formulated by Scott account executives in terms of the retailers' requirements, and promotional plans were defined for each store. Many of these programs involved more than fifty pages of plans developed for an individual account. As a result of this programmed merchandising,[19] retail store executives rarely had to make a decision that was not covered in detail in the individual account prospectus. Scott's pro-

---

[17]Louis P. Bucklin, "Retail Strategy and the Classification of Consumer Goods," *Journal of Marketing*, Vol. 23 (January, 1963), pp. 50–55.

[18]Ronald D. Michman, *Marketing Channels* (Columbus, Ohio: Grid, Inc., 1974), pp. 152–153.

[19]Programmed merchandising is discussed again in the next chapter, when attention is given to administered vertical marketing systems.

TABLE 9-5 Selection of Suitable Distribution Policies Based on the Relationship between Type of Product and Type of Store

Classification	Consumer Behavior	Most Likely Form of Distribution
Convenience store/convenience good	The consumer prefers to buy the most readily available brand of product at the most accessible store	Intensive
Convenience store/shopping good	The consumer selects his purchase from among the assortment carried by the most accessible store	Intensive
Convenience store/specialty good	The consumer purchases his favorite brand from the most accessible store carrying the item in stock.	Selective/exclusive
Shopping store/convenience good	The consumer is indifferent to the brand of product he buys but shops different stores to secure better retail service and/or retail price.	Intensive
Shopping store/shopping good	The consumer makes comparisons among both retail-controlled factors and factors associated with the product (brand).	Intensive
Shopping store/specialty good	The consumer has a strong preference as to product brand but shops a number of stores to secure the best retail service and/or price for this brand.	Selective/exclusive
Specialty store/convenience good	The consumer prefers to trade at a specific store but is indifferent to the brand of product purchased.	Selective/exclusive
Specialty store/shopping good	The consumer prefers to trade at a certain store but is uncertain as to which product he wishes to buy and examines the store's assortment for the best purchase.	Selective/exclusive
Specialty store/specialty good	The consumer has both a preference for a particular store and for a specific brand.	Selective /exclusive

SOURCE: Louis P. Bucklin, "Retail Strategy and the Classification of Consumer Goods," *Journal of Marketing*, Vol. 23 (January, 1963), pp. 50–55. The specific table was developed by and appears in Burton Marcus, et al., *Modern Marketing* (New York: Random House, 1975), p. 550.

grams were first instituted in department stores and subsequently were developed for supermarkets and other types of mass merchandisers. Therefore, not only did Scott assume the investment burden involved in formulating marketing plans for each channel member, but it was also able, through its store-by-store programmed merchandising efforts, to retain many of the policies it had adopted when its distribution was more selective (e.g., price maintenance, advertising incentives, and the like). Scott relied heavily on its expert power base relative to the marketing of lawn products, as well as the promise of significant rewards in terms of profits, to convince resellers to participate in programs that they would not otherwise have adopted.

On the other hand, as channel members move towards exclusive distribution, role expectations become more sharply delineated. Specific agreements are possible with respect to degrees of participation in the marketing flows. But each of these agreements demands careful bargaining over rights and obligations. For an exclusive distribution policy, the bargaining points (and relevant tradeoffs) generally concern the following:

1. *Products covered.* The specific items in the line that are to be handled by the exclusive wholesaler or retailer must be clearly delineated. For example, there may be certain products, especially those of a highly technical nature, that a supplier will wish to sell through his own sales force direct to ultimate customers. Other products will be made available for sale through exclusive distributors. To avoid future conflict over the division of product line responsibilities, a clear understanding must be forged among the channel members as to the relevant domains of each with regard to the items in the line. In the cases where an item has been assigned to a distributor, any sales of that item by the supplier in the distributor's territory should be credited to the distributor. Otherwise, a domain violation is obvious.

2. *Classes or types of customers.* Agreement over who is responsible for various types of customers must be arrived at to prevent future dysfunctional conflict. Thus, as in the case of products covered, the supplier may wish to retain the right to sell directly to specific classes of customers, such as the military or to very large commercial accounts (e.g., General Motors). Any sales to customers allocated to distributors or dealers must be credited to the latter if domains are not to be violated. The expectations with regard to who is to serve whom must be clearly understood and/or resolved through bargaining at the outset of the exclusive arrangement.

3. *Territory covered.* Clearly, this is another crucial element in establishing relevant domains. In many cases, agreement on territories can prevent future jurisdictional disputes among the distributors handling the supplier's products. However, tight restrictions here are circumscribed by federal law, as indicated in the chapter dealing with legal limitations.

4. *Inventories.* The questions to be resolved here are who is going to bear the burden of holding inventories and how much and where is the inventory to be held? In situations of fluctuating price levels, these questions become particularly acute. Suppliers may have to enter into price guarantees or may have to consign merchandise when economic conditions are turbulent.

5. *Installation and repair services.* This bargaining issue is obviously relevant for durable goods both in the industrial and consumer goods sectors. Here, ques-

tions relative to the handling of warranties are crucial, and the rights and obligations of suppliers and distributors must be clearly specified. Distributors may be asked to commit resources to the training of servicemen, while suppliers may have to assure distributors that service "troubleshooters" will be available on an on-call basis in situations that are beyond the distributors' service capabilities. Considerable conflict among middlemen and manufacturers has been evidenced in the automobile, home appliance, and capital equipment industries due to misunderstandings over inadequate specification of roles relative to installation and repair.

6. *Prices.* Under exclusive distribution policies, it is likely that the parties involved can come to an agreement over prices to be charged to customers. The distributor may agree to maintain "reasonable margins," while the supplier is likely to agree to some form of price or margin guarantees in times of declining market prices.

7. *Sales quotas.* The establishment of unrealistic sales quotas has brought about considerable friction in channel relations. In agreeing to an exclusive distribution arrangement, the parties involved should arrive at a consensus relative to the way in which the quotas are to be calculated. They should also agree on the rewards to be received or punishments to be levied for performance that is above or below the quotas arrived at.

8. *Advertising and sales promotional obligations.* Responsibilities for the development of catalogs, sales aids, display work, local advertising and promotion, etc., must be specified in the agreement. The basis for calculating cooperative advertising allowances should be spelled out in detail so that each party realizes its obligation to the other.

9. *Exclusive dealing.* In some situations, suppliers prefer that their distributors handle no products that will compete directly with their own. If this is the case, then these suppliers will often be called upon to give added promotional support to their distributors in order to assure that the latter will be able to achieve a satisfactory sales volume in the product category affected. As with territorial restrictions, exclusive dealing is also circumscribed by federal law, as was noted in the immediately preceding chapter.

10. *Duration, provision for renewal, and termination.* If exclusive distribution arrangements are desired, then it is important that the specifics of each of the previous nine points be agreed upon in writing. The contract established should, however, permit for enough flexibility to meet extraneous events and contingencies, should they arise. In addition, it is important for the parties to agree on the length of time that the agreement is to be in effect and on renewal provisions. Especially important, given the legal implications involved, are specifics regarding when and how the arrangement can be terminated by either of the parties.

The list above is not exhaustive; it merely serves to indicate the detail required in formulating distribution policy as one moves toward the exclusive end of the spectrum.[20] The reader is encouraged to read the "Distributor Sales Agreement" and the statement of "Distribution Policy and Practices" of Rex Chainbelt, Inc., which have been reproduced in the appendix to this chapter, to obtain a more complete perspective of the specifics involved in establishing such a policy. It is very important to note, however, that the establishment of such policies is not a "one-way street." In other words, explicit in such agreements is a tone of mutual support—each of the parties gains something by the agreement from the other under each and every point. Thus, benefits and costs are, or should be, divided equitably.[21]

The selection of the specific wholesalers and retailers to participate in selective or exclusive policies is crucial to the long-term effectiveness of a channel system. To aid a supplier in the selection process, Mauser has developed a checklist of 21 questions,[22] each of which must be assessed carefully by the supplier prior to making a final decision (see Exhibit 9-2). The reader is encouraged to develop a comparable checklist taking the perspective of middlemen selecting suppliers with whom they might deal. Indeed, with slight modification, the reader can apply the checklist in Exhibit 9-2 to the problem of deciding which *specific* outlets or suppliers are most appropriate, among all of those available, in any given distribution situation. Underlying each of the various points in the checklist is the concept of role specification and the securing of appropriate domain definitions so that dysfunctional conflict within the channel can be avoided and adequate channel performance can be secured. The type of distribution policy adopted and the specific routes to markets selected will influence all elements of each channel member's marketing mix decisions as well as the extent of participation of each in the various marketing flows. As indicated in Chapter 1, the latter

[20] It is important, however, to recall the legal limitations on exclusive distribution which were enumerated in Chapter 8. In fact, the Federal Trade Commission is becoming increasingly concerned about the use of exclusive distribution policies, even when such policies do not exclude intra-brand competition, but merely limit it. For example, the FTC has issued a complaint against General Motors Corporation alleging that GM sells crash parts (fenders, doors, bumpers, grills, and related items) *exclusively* through its 12,000 franchised dealers, many of whom both wholesale and install the parts. The complaint charges that, as a result of GM's policy, independent body shops must obtain parts from GM dealers and in so doing have frequently paid more than their GM-dealer competitors. Thus, even though there is likely to be competition among the franchised dealers on GM parts, the fact that independent body shops are disadvantaged in their ability to compete has raised a strong legal question regarding exclusive distribution policies, beyond the question raised in the *Schwinn case.* See "GM Distribution of 'Crash Parts' Spurs FTC Move," *Wall Street Journal,* March 23, 1976, p. 3; and "FTC Challenges GM's System of Distributing Crash Parts," *FTC News Summary,* March 26, 1976, p. 1.

[21] For specific examples, especially in industrial goods marketing, see National Industrial Conference Board, *Building a Sound Distributor Organization* (New York: National Industrial Conference Board Experiences in Marketing Management, No. 6, 1964). See also, "Their Cup Runneth Over," *Forbes,* October 1, 1975, p. 30 for a negative example of how Gallo Winery used its coercive power over exclusive distributors to increase its benefits at the distributors' cost.

[22] Ferdinand F. Mauser, *Modern Marketing Management* (New York: McGraw-Hill, 1961), p. 338.

EXHIBIT 9-2   A Checklist of 21 Questions for Rating Prospective Applicants for a Distributorship (Dealership)

1. What is the caliber of the man who is the head of the distributor's (dealer's) organization? Does the firm have the respect and confidence of the community?

2. Do they have conflicting lines or products?

3. Do they have a well-trained, smoothly running organization?

4. Are they adequately financed?

5. Are they making money?

6. Do they have plant, equipment, and facilities for handling the line?

7. Do they have an adequate and well-informed sales team?

8. Do they have other products that fit in and harmonize with our line?

9. Do they have a sales training program? Do they allow suppliers to participate in their training program?

10. What is the average educational background of their personnel?

11. Are they marketing-minded? Do they have the interest and ability to promote our product?

12. Are they willing to appoint one executive to concentrate on our lines and be responsible for it? Who would he be and what are his qualifications?

13. Do they cover their territory thoroughly?

14. Do they penetrate through to customers, executives, engineers, and operating people, or do they cover only the purchasing agents?

15. Will they accept a quota and make a reasonable effort to meet it?

16. Will they accept and use our promotional materials in accordance with our marketing program?

17. Do they have the courage to maintain reasonable margins when times are tough?

18. Do they have a good setup for giving continuing service to customers in order to maintain customer goodwill for our product?

19. Will they welcome our executives for conferences and sales meetings?

20. Will they give us the names and home addresses of their inside and outside salesmen, so we can quickly send information to them?

21. If our line is small, are they willing to feature it and push it?

SOURCE: Ferdinand F. Mauser, *Modern Marketing Management* (New York: McGraw-Hill, 1961), p. 338.

factor is (or should be) the basis for compensating the various channel members.

THE MIDDLEMAN'S PERSPECTIVE

The pros and cons of particular distribution policies from a middleman's point of view may differ radically from those of manufacturers. Wittreich has presented examples of the brewing, appliance, and building products industries to show that small retailers speak a different language from and are not as growth-oriented as the large manufacturers whose products they sell.[23] In fact, it is likely that the perceptions and outlook of wholesalers are more congruent with retailers and vice versa than are the manufacturers' with either.

Marketing programs can fail because managers at the manufacturer's level do not tailor their programs to the capabilities and orientations of their middlemen. For example, a promotion campaign may be too complicated for middlemen to understand or implement properly. The number of calls per customer required by a manufacturer from his wholesalers may exceed the wholesalers' capacity, or the minimum orders specified by the manufacturer may be beyond the inventory handling and storage facilities of a middleman.

In general, and in the absence of effective interorganization management, the "independence" of independent middlemen can work at cross-purposes to the desires of manufacturers. First of all, the middleman is in business to satisfy his customers.[24] In consumer goods marketing, there are relatively few exceptions to the statement that consumers buy products from retailers, not from manufacturers. Thus, retailers possess "veto power" over virtually all marketing programs.[25] (An analogous situation holds when manufacturers of industrial goods employ industrial distributors or manufacturers' representatives.) Although the manufacturer could theoretically market his products directly to consumers, consumer buying behavior and distribution economics often preclude this possibility. As Star observes:

---

[23]Warren J. Wittreich, "Misunderstanding the Retailer," *Harvard Business Review,* Vol. 40 (May-June, 1962), pp. 147–159. This communication problem among others is examined in detail in Chapter 12.

[24]For an interesting discussion of the weaknesses inherent in assuming too much about middlemen's orientations, see Philip McVey, "Are Channels of Distribution What Textbooks Say?" *Journal of Marketing,* Vol. 24 (January, 1960), pp. 61–65.

[25]Steven H. Star, "Obtaining Retailer Support for Marketing Programs," Project Description P-82 (Cambridge, Mass.: Marketing Science Institute, August, 1973), p. 1.

While retailers *can* influence brand sales significantly in most product categories, such influence is clearly a more decisive factor in some product categories than in others. Conceptually, we would expect such influence to be most important in product categories (1) where the buying process is very unimportant to the consumer (e.g., frequently purchased, low-priced staple commodities), and (2) where the buying process is extremely important to the consumer (e.g., infrequently purchased, high-priced products perceived to be differentiated along complex dimensions). In the first case, the consumer's need for information is so low that manufacturers are generally unable to create strong brand preference. As a result, retailers are free to carry any brand(s) they wish without fear of lost sales or lessened consumer goodwill. In the second case, the consumer's need for information is so great that manufacturers can directly satisfy the need only partially. Under these circumstances, the retailer must provide additional information in order to "close" a sale. In the process of providing this information, the retailer has considerable opportunity to influence the consumer's ultimate brand choice.[26]

Thus, the manufacturer is continuously engaged in seeking support from middlemen, especially for the kinds of products mentioned by Star (and their analogues in the industrial market). Such support is not, by any means, automatically available; receiving it depends, to a great extent, on the ways in which power of all types (coercive, reward, expert, referent, and legitimate) is employed within the channel.[27]

Second, independent middlemen are in business for themselves, not for manufacturers.[28] For example, retailers resort to selling private brands to increase their independence from manufacturers of branded merchandise and to guarantee a continuous source of supply of products they desire to provide for their customers. Third, middlemen generally have existing lines of products. The manufacturer seeking to "employ" a specific middleman must develop a product that closely fits the line that the middleman handles. Finally, in the case of retailers, the middleman allocates display space, which is, indeed, a scarce resource, given the number of items desiring placement.[29] Although some manufacturers have gained considerable control over the display space allocation process in the grocery trade (e.g., Kraft relative to certain dairy products, Campbell relative to soup, and Nabisco relative to crackers and cookies), and in the sale of cosmetics through department

[26]*Ibid.*, pp. 4–5.

[27]Selected methods of gaining reseller support are listed in Chapter 10, Exhibit 10–1.

[28]McVey, *op. cit.*

[29]For some interesting and useful empirical work on this subject, particularly relating to shelf space in supermarkets, see Ronald C. Curhan, "The Relationship Between Shelf Space and Unit Sales in Supermarkets," *Journal of Marketing Research*, Vol. 9 (November, 1972), pp. 406–412; and Robert D. Buzzell, Walter J. Salmon, and Richard F. Vancil, *Product Profitability Measurement and Merchandising Decisions* (Boston: Harvard University Graduate School of Business Administration, Division of Research, 1965).

stores, the majority of manufacturers must vie for this space by granting significant concessions or by investing heavily in consumer promotions of various kinds.

In addition, a manufacturer seeking to market through middlemen must recognize and sell to three publics. The first are the middlemen's customers. The second are the managements of the various intermediary organizations. The third are the salesmen employed by the latter. Successful wooing of management does not automatically mean that market penetration will be forthcoming. A middleman's salesmen have to be convinced of the merits of the product, and thus manufacturers must engage themselves in selling to the salesmen via sales training programs, sales contests, special promotions, and other incentives.

On the other hand, a manufacturer may have considerable power in his attempt to recruit and influence channel intermediaries. Instead of trying to *push* his brand through a channel and pursuing a hard-sell policy with regard to middlemen, he has the option of trying to *pull* his brand through the channel by advertising heavily to gain consumer preference. If the latter strategy works, middlemen may actually solicit the manufacturer to carry his brand, and reseller support is likely to be available to him. However, the alternative costs must be carefully assessed in a manner similar to that specified earlier. The different strategies require varying amounts of capital investment. The key problem is to determine whether greater channel performance can be generated by manufacturers assuming more participation in the marketing flows *or* by shifting more of the work of the channel to middlemen or consumers.[30]

SUMMARY AND CONCLUSIONS

Channel organization and design is only one aspect of marketing strategy. At the outset of the channel planning process, managers must acknowledge the important interrelationship between channel design *and* all other elements of the marketing mix. The starting point in designing and organizing a channel is, however, at the consumer level, irrespective of the type of goods and services involved. Furthermore, channel design is always conditioned by the particular characteristics of products, middlemen, competitors, company, and environment.

---

[30] For a discussion of the financial considerations involved in this decision, see Eugene W. Lambert, Jr., "Financial Considerations in Choosing a Marketing Channel," *MSU Business Topics*, Vol. 14 (Winter, 1966), pp. 17–26.

The choice of outlets or suppliers may be highly restricted. Not every wholesaling and retailing establishment is available to every supplier, and vice versa. Achieving distribution through Sears, Roebuck is not a foregone conclusion for manufacturers, just as obtaining clothing supplies from Hart, Schaffner, and Marx is not a certainty for channel middlemen. If, however, there is some freedom of choice available to a manager in designing an appropriate channel for his products or brands, there are four basic steps involved in determining the types of middlemen to use. These include:

1. Itemizing the alternative ways in which ultimate (household or industrial) consumers can purchase the product in question and assessing the relative volume of the product class moving through the purchase outlets, their relative rates of growth, and their relative profitability. Underlying this step is a thorough evaluation of consumer preferences.

2. Specifying the primary channel paths that can be used in reaching these various outlets or in tapping the relevant markets for the product.

3. Quantifying the relevant factors in the consideration of each channel path by employing the weighted factor score method, the hierarchical preference method, and/or the simulation method.

4. Evaluating qualitative criteria relative to the amount of control and adaptability desired.

Having determined the type of middlemen, managers can then turn their attention to deciding on the degree of market exposure their products should have. From a wholesaler's perspective, this decision can involve a determination of both the number of suppliers *and* the number of retailers with whom to deal. As we look down the channel (from manufacturer to wholesaler to retailer), the three basic policy choices seem to be intensive, selective, or exclusive distribution. It is likely that the more intensive the distribution of a product or brand, the greater its sales will be in the short run. However, there is an important tradeoff between sales and control over the channel, which must be taken into consideration by the manager. Loss of control can result in lower long-term profits.

Development of an appropriate distribution policy for consumer goods requires consideration of the relationship between type of good and type of store. Again, as in choosing the relevant middlemen, knowledge of consumer purchasing behavior is critical.

If channel strategy dictates a more exclusive type of distribution policy, specific agreements are possible with regard to the allocation of marketing effort among channel members. An appropriate allocation is arrived at through bargaining over products covered, class or types of customers, territory covered, inventories, installation and repair services, prices, sales quotas, advertising and sales promotional obligations, and exclusive dealing. These agreements should be put in writing, reviewed on a yearly basis, be reasonably flexible, and contain information on the duration, renewal, and termination of the agreement. The forging of such an agreement, if it is to be functional over the long term, must reflect mutual support and an equitable division of benefits and costs in carrying forward distribution. It involves the specification of the rights and obligations of each of the parties.

Despite efforts on the part of managers to organize an efficient and effective channel system, such efforts are sometimes futile, because they do not fully account for the differences in perspective and orientation of independent middlemen. The latter are in business to satisfy their customers and are not in business to satisfy the desires of other channel members. In addition, middlemen generally have existing product lines from which they frequently do not wish to deviate. Finally, middlemen, especially retailers, control display space and the process by which it is allocated. Therefore, gaining reseller support is often not a simple matter, to say the least. Various approaches have been employed to gain such support and have evolved into modes of channel organization called vertical marketing systems. The next chapter is devoted to a discussion of these systems.

DISCUSSION QUESTIONS

1. Explain how the characteristics of the following consumer and industrial goods affect the channels for them:

Consumer Goods	Industrial Goods
Bread	Typewriter ribbons
Breakfast cereal	Uranium (for nuclear power plants)
Women's hats	Cement
Refrigerators	Data processing equipment

2. Use the weighted factor score method to evaluate the acquisition alternative in the swimming pool germicide example, using the factors and weights suggested in Table 9-1. Suppose the acquisition alternative receives the following ratings on the five factors: 0.8, 0.6, 0.7, 0.2, and 0.5. What is the total score for this alternative?

3. A prestigious designer of men's fashions (suits, pants, shirts, ties, etc.) has just decided to manufacture his own designs, but has no experience in distribution methods. (a) Conceive of four alternative retail outlets for his line of merchandise. (b) Conceive of four major alternative distribution strategies for his line.

4. A weakness of the hierarchical preference ordering method is that a particular strategy may be almost perfect on the most important criterion and slightly below the minimum level on a minor criterion and as a result be eliminated. Which of the choice strategies outlined in Chapter 2 would eliminate this problem? How would it eliminate the problem?

5. What additional variables should have been included in the simulation of alternative distribution strategies shown in Table 9–3? How would you obtain relevant input data on these variables in order to use them in the simulation?

6. Under the new distributors alternative in Table 9–4, the share of potential is said to be equal to 100 percent. Is this realistic, given that there are likely to be competitive products available on the market?

7. In Table 9–3, tell the meaning of the data associated with the variables "Advertising effectiveness coefficient" and "Distribution effectiveness coefficient."

8. Name and discuss four different variables that might prohibit a manufacturer from gaining distribution through a prestige department store. Name and discuss four different variables that might prohibit a discount department store chain from obtaining a manufacturer's product line. Finally, name and discuss four different variables that might prohibit a manufacturer from gaining distribution through an industrial wholesaler.

9. Debate the pros and cons of intensive versus selective versus exclusive distribution for the following product classes: (a) panty hose; (b) drill presses; (c) tractors; (d) toasters.

10. Develop a checklist, comparable to that shown in Exhibit 9–2, taking the perspective of middlemen selecting suppliers with whom they might deal.

11. Develop a checklist, comparable to that shown in Exhibit 9–2, that would apply to the problem of deciding which specific outlet (Store A versus Store B) a manufacturer might select to market his product.

Appendix

Rex Chainbelt's
Distributor Sales Agreement
for the Bearing Division

REX CHAINBELT INC., a Wisconsin Corporation (herein called REX CHAINBELT), having its principal place of business in Milwaukee, Wisconsin, is pleased to submit this Agreement to

_____

of

_____

(herein called DISTRIBUTOR). Under this Agreement, DISTRIBUTOR will act as an authorized stock-carrying distributor for the products listed in this Agreement for the purpose of actively soliciting and serving users of REX CHAINBELT products in DISTRIBUTOR'S territory to secure satisfactory sales of these products from each type of industry.

The purpose of this Agreement is to set forth the basis on which DISTRIBUTOR and REX CHAINBELT INC. agree to do business together, and to insure understanding and cooperation between both parties.

Appointment and Territory

1. REX CHAINBELT hereby appoints

_____

Source: National Industrial Conference Board, _Building a Sound Distributor Organization_ (New York: National Industrial Conference Board Experiences in Marketing Management, No. 6, 1964), pp. 20-31.

its distributor in

_____

_____

(a) While DISTRIBUTOR may sell outside of the above area, REX CHAINBELT will furnish sales promotion and field selling assistance only in the area described in this Agreement. Since this area is not exclusive, REX CHAINBELT will not pay commissions or other compensation for sales or shipments made into the DISTRIBUTOR'S area except by specific arrangements in connection with individual orders.

(b) REX CHAINBELT will follow the general policy of not appointing additional stock-carrying distributors other than such as we already have in the described area for those products listed in attached Supplement A provided the volume of business developed by DISTRIBUTOR is satisfactory and reasonable, taking into consideration prevailing business conditions. DISTRIBUTOR will be consulted whenever changes in distribution in his trading area seem necessary.

Products

2. The products covered in this Agreement are listed in attached Supplement A. Any new or different products which REX CHAINBELT may from time to time manufacture or sell are expressly excluded except by REX CHAINBELT'S specific consent.

Sales Coverage

3. The area of DISTRIBUTOR'S primary sales responsibility will be the Industrial Consumer and reselling accounts. REX CHAINBELT will sell directly to Original Equipment Manufacturers and Contract Engineers. While it will be REX CHAINBELT'S policy to direct sales from consumer accounts to the distributor best able to handle the sale, REX CHAINBELT reserves the right to make sales direct to any consumer when this seems necessary in the best interests of customer service.

Prices and Terms

4. REX CHAINBELT shall sell to DISTRIBUTOR the products listed in Supplement A at prices set forth in the schedule of published net distributor prices then prevailing, or according to discounts applicable to the prevailing REX CHAINBELT price lists. Terms and conditions of sale are set forth in the section entitled, "Conditions of Sales" for the Industrial Equipment Section in the prevailing REX CHAINBELT price lists.

Changes in Prices,
or Terms, etc., of Sale

> 5. REX CHAINBELT will endeavor to give DISTRIBUTOR advance notice of changes in price, discounts, and terms and conditions of sale, but reserves the right to make such changes without prior notice if circumstances necessitate it.

Quality

> 6. The DISTRIBUTOR is authorized to extend to his customers on the resale of REX CHAINBELT products the same warranty then being made by REX CHAINBELT in prevailing price lists (see paragraph on Quality in Standard Conditions of Sale). DISTRIBUTOR is not authorized to make any other warranty.

Stock Requirement

> 7. To perform the proper distribution function, DISTRIBUTOR will carry an adequate inventory of REX CHAINBELT products as outlined in Paragraph 10 of the Statement of Policy attached.

Return of Stock

> 8. DISTRIBUTOR may, during the term of this sales Agreement, return any standard REX CHAINBELT products purchased under this Agreement according to the provisions of Paragraph 11 of the Statement of Policy attached.

Sales Promotion
and Sales Coverage

> 9. Distributor shall at all times vigorously promote the sale of REX CHAINBELT products by means of:
>
> (a) an adequate number of qualified salesmen for good market coverage.
> (b) an adequate stock and warehouse services.
> (c) sales promotion activity including effective use of catalogs and advertising.
>
> REX CHAINBELT will cooperate with DISTRIBUTOR in promoting the sale of REX CHAINBELT products, and will supply DISTRIBUTOR with catalogs, product bulletins, and other sales promotion aids. REX CHAINBELT District Sales Engineers and Representatives will provide the DISTRIBUTOR with field sales assistance in the promotion of

REX CHAINBELT products, but will be free to contact directly all customers to demonstrate, promote and otherwise advertise REX CHAINBELT products.

Acceptance of Orders

10. All orders placed by DISTRIBUTOR are subject to acceptance or refusal by REX CHAINBELT, at its originating plants, and delivery is F.O.B. the originating plant.

Adherence to Manufacturer's Policy

11. Distributor agrees to follow the policies of REX CHAINBELT as announced in the Policy Statement attached herein as well as subsequent changes in such policies.

Construction of Agreement

12. This Agreement does not constitute DISTRIBUTOR as the legal representative or agent of REX CHAINBELT for any purpose, nor authorize DISTRIBUTOR to transact business in REX CHAINBELT'S name. The rights and privileges of DISTRIBUTOR under this Agreement are personal, cannot be assigned and will not inure to the benefit of any receiver, trustee in bankruptcy or any other legal representative, unless consented to by REX CHAINBELT INC. This Agreement supercedes all previous agreements and constitutes the entire Agreement between the parties.

Effective Date, Term and Termination

13. This Agreement shall become effective when formally signed and accepted by DISTRIBUTOR and REX CHAINBELT and shall continue until_____. Execution of orders after said date shall not constitute a renewal of this Agreement.

(a) Termination of this sales agreement can be made by either party. Notice of intent to terminate shall be made by letter by either party to the other's headquarters. The mailing date of such letter shall be considered the date of said notice. Termination shall become effective thirty (30) days after date of notice.

(b) In the event of termination by REX CHAINBELT, DISTRIBUTOR may within thirty (30) day termination period, return for credit all standard stock items. Credit will be issued at current prices for all such returned items which are current, unused and salable, less any cost of reconditioning.

(c) In the event of termination by DISTRIBUTOR, REX CHAINBELT will have the option of purchasing within thirty (30) days at current prices any or all of REX CHAINBELT products in DISTRIBUTOR'S inventory at the time of termination. Reshipment transportation charges shall be paid by the party terminating the Agreement, and shall not exceed those for transportation back to **REX CHAINBELT'S** originating plant.

_____

(Distributor's Corporate or Firm Name)

By_____

Date of Distributor's Signature _____ 19 __

REX CHAINBELT INC.

By _____

(Authorized Official)

Date of Acceptance by
REX CHAINBELT INC._____ 19 __

REX CHAINBELT'S DISTRIBUTION POLICY
AND PRACTICES FOR THE BEARING DIVISION

Objectives

1.   Our primary objective in the distribution of REX CHAINBELT products is to provide:
   a. Prompt availability to all customers.
   b. Assistance to distributors in carrying out their part of our marketing program.

In order to -

   c. Sell the largest possible share of the market at the lowest possible cost.
   d. Provide a fair return to REX CHAINBELT and its Distributors.

2.   Our Sales Agreement covers our fundamental sales relationship. The following paragraphs are intended to explain recommended procedures and to serve as a guide in directing our mutual selling efforts.

REX CHAINBELT Indirect Sales Through Distributors

3.   The purpose of our Distributor Policy is to provide the most effective sales coverage to produce the largest share of available business in each trading area and to permit distributors to obtain maximum sales volume. To accomplish this purpose, REX CHAINBELT'S Standard Industrial Products as shown in the current merchandise catalog are sold to all consumer accounts and to all resale or jobber accounts through the following Distribution channels:
   a. Industrial Supply and Power Transmission Distributors
   b. Bearing Specialist Distributors
   c. Special Industry Distributors in markets not satisfactorily covered by 3-a

REX CHAINBELT Direct Sales

4.   To accomplish the sales objectives previously mentioned, REX CHAINBELT sells directly as follows:
   a. Original Equipment Manufacturers and Contract Engineers
   b. Agencies and offices of the U.S. Government or subcontracts for such agencies and offices.

Definition of Territory

5.   The basic territory definition is given in Article 1 of our Distributor Agreement.
6.   Distributors may sell REX Standard Products to all Consumer and Resale or Jobber

accounts in their regularly traveled area. Any questions concerning area assignment should be cleared through the REX District Office.

7. When two or more REX Distributors in the same trading area solicit the same account, the REX District Office will provide product application assistance as required but will maintain impartiality in respect to each distributor's position with such accounts.

Selective Distribution

8. REX CHAINBELT'S objective is to appoint the minimum number of Distributors necessary to obtain satisfactory market penetration in each trading area. Generally only one Bearing Specialist distributor will be appointed in a small size trading area. Where heavy industry concentration or unusual market conditions make additions or changes in distribution seem necessary, the Distributor affected will be consulted before any action is taken.

Handling of Inquiries and Orders

9. a. REX CHAINBELT, where practical, will refer orders and inquiries from consumer accounts to the Distributor best equipped to service the account. However, inquiries and orders received directly will be handled directly where such handling seems necessary in the best interests of customer service.

b. When such inquiries are handled directly by REX CHAINBELT INC., whenever possible, copies of the inquiry and reply will be furnished to the Distributor, and the customer will be advised of the services available from the Distributor.

c. In the case of orders received and shipped directly to such consumer accounts, we will advise the consumer account of the service available from the Distributor and recommend that their future orders be placed with the distributor.

d. All orders and inquiries received from resale or jobber accounts will be referred to the local Distributor on an impartial basis.

e. Customer preferences will be major influencing factors in all inquiry or order referrals.

Distributor's Inventory of REX CHAINBELT Products

10. The Distributor will be required to carry an adequate stock of REX products to perform the proper distribution function in his trading area. The stock should amount to *not less* than (__%) of the Distributor's current annual purchases. This percentage is based on the relation between a Distributor's out-of-stock and direct sales. The out-of-stock sales should account for a minimum of (__%) of the Distributor's volume resulting in an inventory of no less than (__%) of annual purchases to achieve a desirable inventory turnover of four times. In no case should the Distributor's inventory be less than ($____) to adequately service the industries in Distributor's Marketing area.

The (__%) or ($____) minimum Distributor inventory will apply to each branch warehouse location of the Distributor's operation.

Review and Return of Distributor Stock

11. Periodically, at least every twelve (12) months, the Distributor stock should be reviewed and a list of slow moving, unaltered stock items submitted to the REX District Office or Representative. Credit for return stock will be allowed in accordance with the following provisions:

    a. Written approval has been obtained from REX CHAINBELT INC.

    b. Full credit at current prices less any original transportation allowance will be allowed on current standard catalog items in good salable condition. Credit on this basis will be issued upon receipt of an order for stock material equal to the dollar value of the credit.

    c. Where returned stock as outlined in 11-b is not to be accompanied by an order of equal dollar value, credit will be allowed as under 11-b except that a 10% handling charge will be deducted from the value of the credit.

    d. The credit on returned stock in any one year should not exceed 3% of the average of the Distributor's annual purchases for the preceding three years.

    e. If it is necessary for REX CHAINBELT to recondition any stock returned under 11-b or 11-c, all reconditioning costs will be deducted from any credit issued.

    f. The Distributor will prepay return transportation charges on all returned material.

    g. Each request for return of slow moving stock must be accompanied by a completed stock analysis sheet.

    h. In event of termination of our Agreement with a distributor, return of stock will be in accordance with Article 13 of REX CHAINBELT Distributor Agreement.

Sales Coverage

12. The Distributor will provide sufficient qualified salesmen properly trained to sell REX BEARING Division products, covered in Supplement A of this REX CHAINBELT Distributor Sales Agreement, to consumer and reselling accounts in his trading area.

REX CHAINBELT will cooperate with the Distributor in training Distributor's organization in the sales and application of BEARING Division products.

The Distributor is expected to cooperate in reporting sales volume to selected accounts in order to help in evaluation of account coverage.

The Distributor is also expected to cooperate in reporting sales activities of Bearing Division products from each individual branch warehouse to assist in the evaluation and increased effectiveness of territory coverage.

Sales Training

13. a. Each Distributor should hold a minimum of two sales meetings annually in cooperation with the REX District Sales Engineer or Representative. It is strongly recommended that the sales meetings be held more frequently in the more active marketing areas. The meetings will be held to instruct the Distributor personnel in the selling and

application of Bearing Division products, and the meetings will be so conducted as to be closely related to each Distributor's marketing problem.

b. The Distributor will be asked to hold sales meetings wherever necessary to tie in with REX's sales promotion plans on any product line. Meetings should be arranged at least two weeks in advance and generally will be approximately one and a half hours in length.

Field Sales Assistance

14. The REX District Sales Engineer or Representative will provide field sales assistance to the Distributor through cooperation on local sales meetings and through field sales calls with Distributor salesmen.

All field sales call schedules should be carefully planned in advance. Distributor management should cooperate with the REX District Sales Manager or BEARING Representative in setting up agendas for such calls. The agenda should show, insofar as possible, the problems and subjects which the Distributor salesman intends to cover with the customer.

REX CHAINBELT and the Distributor must recognize the continued need for application selling and the creation of brand preference, and the responsibility of the REX Field Sales organization in this regard. Therefore, our sales organization shall be free to contact all customers in a Distributor's territory to demonstrate, promote and apply REX products. Where practical, calls on the Distributor customers will be made with the Distributor salesman. In the case where such calls are made without Distributor salesmen, the Distributor involved will be informed of the results of such calls and suggestions will be made by our sales organization for follow-up action required by the Distributor to gain the maximum benefits from such REX CHAINBELT direct contacts.

Pricing

15. Individual net price schedules are furnished for each trade classification.

Occasionally, the Distributor may submit inquiries or orders for special products, repair parts, or requirements for major modifications to existing products. In such cases, the prices and discounts will be determined from manufacturing and engineering costs and current market conditions. The Distributor margin on such products may not be the same as the discount on standard products in the same product class.

Price Protection

16. REX CHAINBELT'S standard practice is to hold prices firm for orders that are on our books on the effective date of a price increase, provided shipment is requested, scheduled and made within sixty (60) days from date of price change. However, we reserve the

right to make price changes without advance notice; in such cases, Distributors will be notified not later than effective date.

Resale Prices

17. REX CHAINBELT strongly recommends the maintenance of suggested resale prices. Such prices are based on providing Distributors with a gross margin adequate for maintaining a reasonable operating profit based on current average Distributor operating costs.

Advertising and Sales Promotion

18. a. Distributors will be furnished regularly with information about REX promotion plans and lists of available literature and bulletins and necessary requisition blanks. The Distributor should maintain a stock of sales literature applicable to his marketing area. The REX District Sales Engineer or Representative will assist the Distributor wherever possible in selecting the literature to be requisitioned.

b. REX CHAINBELT will assist the Distributor in preparing the material for use in Distributor Catalogs but will not pay any of the cost incurred for the actual publication of this Distributor Catalog. Available inserts for catalog use will be furnished at no charge.

c. REX CHAINBELT will furnish suitable displays for Distributor Open Houses and Exhibits. REX personnel will cooperate in manning the displays wherever possible, but will not share the cost of exhibition space. The displays will be shipped by REX CHAINBELT prepaid to the Distributor and the Distributor will prepay the freight in return shipment of display.

d. REX CHAINBELT will cooperate with the Distributor in furnishing visual aids and other program material for product clinics which the Distributor conducts before special groups such as Plant operating and engineering personnel or technical societies.

The REX World

19. The REX World is a REX CHAINBELT publication providing customers with information on the use of REX products. It includes good reference material and is also a valuable advertising piece. The use of the REX World is beneficial to the Distributor. REX World issues are available to the distributor in bulk quantities for him to distribute through his own mailing facilities.

Customer Service

20. In addition to supplying product information and carrying adequate stocks of REX BEARING Division products, the Distributor should render any other service which the customer may expect or require.

REX CHAINBELT Warehousing

21. REX District Warehouses are strategically located so that there is a warehouse stock available to practically all REX Distributors. Warehouse stock lists are printed to show the range of stocks available for any one or more of the warehouses which can be drawn on by each Distributor to serve his trading area. It is important each Distributor Salesman be familiar with the warehouse stocks available, and that his name be placed on the warehouse stock mailing list.

REX CHAINBELT Distributor Advisory Board

22. The REX CHAINBELT Distributor Advisory Board consists of one management representative from twelve REX Distributors selected from varied geographical areas. Membership is composed of individuals from power transmission, bearing specialist, and general line houses. One third of the Board is succeeded each year by new members. The function is advisory in relation to current and contemplated REX Distributor programs and policies.

DISTRIBUTOR Personnel Mailing List

23. REX CHAINBELT will maintain a mailing list of all Distributor personnel to insure prompt receipt of product and pricing information, stock lists, and other important releases by proper parties. The Distributor should cooperate with the Rex District Sales Engineer or Representative in periodically furnishing an up-to-date list of personnel.

Financial Responsibility

24. The Distributor will be expected to furnish REX CHAINBELT, upon request, any financial information having a direct bearing on our mutual relationship. In turn, the REX CHAINBELT Credit Department will be happy to confer with the Distributor at any time on matters of finance.

The Distributor should immediately refer any questions of policy or procedure not covered by this Statement or our Agreement to the REX District Office. A clear understanding of mutual objectives is imperative.

TEN

CHANNEL ORGANIZATION AND DESIGN: VERTICAL MARKETING SYSTEMS

A traditional or conventional marketing channel can frequently be described as a piecemeal coalition of independently owned and managed institutions, each of which is prompted by the profit motive with little concern about what goes on before or after it in the distributive sequence. As McCammon notes:

> Goods and services in the American economy have historically been distributed through highly fragmented networks in which *loosely* aligned manufacturers, wholesalers, and retailers have bargained with each other at arm's length, negotiated aggressively over terms of sale, and otherwise behaved autonomously. For the most part, the firms participating in these provisional coalitions have traditionally operated on a relatively small scale and performed a conventionally defined set of marketing functions.[1]

From an interorganization management perspective, such coalitions have no inclusive goals. The locus of decision-making and authority is exclusively at the unit or individual channel member level. There is no formally structured division of labor, and commitment is only to one's own organization. In fact,

---

[1] Bert C. McCammon, Jr., "Perspectives for Distribution Programming," in Louis P. Bucklin (ed.), *Vertical Marketing Systems* (Glenview, Illinois: Scott, Foresman and Company, 1970), p. 43.

there is little or no prescribed systemwide orientation of the members.[2] The members are almost totally self-oriented as they pursue their goals.

In contrast with the conventional channel, vertical marketing systems can be described as:

> ... professionally managed and centrally programmed networks (that are) pre-engineered to achieve operating economies and maximum market impact. Stated alternatively ... vertical marketing systems are rationalized and capital intensive networks designed to achieve technological, managerial, and promotional economies through the integration, coordination, and synchronization of marketing flows from points of production to points of ultimate use.[3]

Thus, the emergence of vertical marketing systems implies the existence of a power locus in the system that provides for channel leadership, role specification, coordination, conflict management, and control.

In this chapter, the organization and design of such systems are explained in some detail. Comparisons and contrasts between conventional marketing channels and the various types of vertical systems (administered, contractual, and corporate) are enumerated. In order to provide a basis for comparison, it is first necessary briefly to elaborate on the opening paragraphs of this chapter, which discussed the organization of conventional channels.

CONVENTIONAL MARKETING CHANNELS[4]

As mentioned above, conventional marketing channel networks are generally comprised of isolated and autonomous units, each of which performs a traditionally defined set of marketing functions. Coordination among channel members is primarily achieved through bargaining and negotiation. The operating units within such channels are frequently unable to achieve systemic economies. Furthermore, there is usually a low index of member loyalty and relatively easy entry to the channel. The network, then, tends to be relatively unstable. As Etgar points out:

> ... each stage of production and marketing is entrusted to independent decision

---

[2]The basis for this perspective can be found in Roland L. Warren, "The Interorganizational Field as a Focus for Investigation," in M. B. Brinkerhoff and P. R. Kunz, *Complex Organizations and Their Environments* (Dubuque, Iowa: Wm. C. Brown Company, 1972), p. 316.

[3]McCammon, *op. cit.,* p. 43.

[4]With the exception of the motion picture example, this section is based largely on McCammon, *loc. cit.,* p. 44.

making managerial units; products and services are transferred from one stage of production or marketing to another through intermediary markets using pricing and related operational modes of the market mechanism.[5]

Within conventional channels, there are a large number of decision makers who tend to be preoccupied with cost, volume, and investment relationships at a *single* stage of the marketing process. Decisions are often tradition-oriented, and decision makers are frequently emotionally committed to established patterns of operation and interaction.

The distribution channel for motion pictures provides an excellent example of the dysfunctional consequences of conventional channel organization.[6] The commercial channel for movies is comprised of companies that make movies (producers), independent distributors, and theatre owners. Prior to 1948, the channel was almost totally integrated—the companies that made the movies also owned the theatres that played them. In 1948, the United States Supreme Court ordered the five major film production-distribution companies to divest themselves of their movie theatres.[7] During the years since 1948, the locus of power in the channel has shifted from the distributor to the theatre owner and back to the distributor. As described by Siskel:

> At first, the new, independent theatre chains were able to bully producers and distributors suddenly bedeviled by television. In recent years, however, the distributors have gained the upper hand. With fewer and fewer pictures being made, the movie world has become a seller's market. The distributors have a limited number of films to rent, and the theatre owners are competing furiously with each other to land the few prize attractions.[8]

Siskel reports, ". . . there has never been any love lost between the major distributors (companies like Universal, Twentieth Century-Fox, and United Artists) and theatre owners. For example, one Chicago representative of a distribution company has been quoted as telling a theatre owner, 'If you make any money on this deal, I'm not doing my job right.'"[9]

While the remark by the representative is obviously facetious, the ac-

---

[5]Michael Etgar, "Structure and Performance of Distributive Systems: A Case Study," a paper presented to the American Marketing Association's Fall Educators' Conference, Rochester, N.Y., August, 1975, p. 2.

[6]Gene Siskel, "Five Powerful Pieces Set into Place," *Chicago Tribune*, Section 6 (February 23, 1975), pp. 2, 3, and 8.

[7]*United States v. Paramount Pictures, Inc.* 334 U.S. 131 (1948); also see *Theatre Enterprises, Inc. v. Paramount Film Distributing Corp.* 346 U.S. 537 (1954).

[8]Siskel, *op. cit.*, p. 2.

[9]*Ibid.*

tions taken by distributors show that there is considerable truth behind it. Apparently, the drive for a good cash flow position is stimulating distributors to ask theatre owners to give them advances or guaranteed money *before* a picture even opens. As a consequence, the public suffers, because only the large downtown movie houses and a few shopping center theatres are able to afford the large, first-run, advance guarantee costs. Smaller theatres are squeezed. Particularly disadvantaged are people who live near the small theatres typically located between downtown and the suburbs.

Thus, the suboptimization within the marketing channel for movies has severely impaired the output of the channel from the consumer's perspective. Certainly, distributors could use their power in more constructive ways to provide for more effective competition vis-a-vis television, but rather than practice interorganization management, distributors are obviously maximizing their own interests and thereby engendering a high degree of conflict within the channel. In his excellent article, Siskel describes additional evidence of myopic behavior on the part of distributors, the existence of which has placed both the consuming public and the theatre owners in somewhat untenable positions.[10] As a reaction, a countervailing force has emerged within the channel in the form of the recently organized Association of Specialized Film Exhibitors. The association is comprised of 34 members who run art theatres all over the United States. While still in its formative stages, the association hopes to improve the availability of films for its membership. However, until it can amass enough power to specify roles and manage conflict, the channel for motion pictures will retain all of the negative attributes of many other conventional marketing channels.

In an effort to eliminate or penalize the suboptimization that frequently exists in conventional channels and thus improve channel performance, several significant modes of channel organization have emerged. We discuss each of these modes in turn, starting with the least integrated (in a formal, ownership sense) and moving, by steps, to the most highly integrated form. It should be noted at the outset, however, that as one moves closer to formal vertical integration, there are powerful tradeoffs between the control achieved *and* the investment and bureaucracy required to maintain the system.

ADMINISTERED SYSTEMS

Administered vertical marketing systems are one step removed, in an analytical sense, from conventional marketing channels. In an administered system, coordination of marketing activities is achieved through the use of

[10] *Ibid.,* pp. 2, 3, and 8.

programs developed by one or a limited number of firms. In such systems, administrative strategies combined with the exercise of power are relied on to obtain systemic economies. Successful administered systems are conventional channels in which the principles of effective interorganization management have been correctly applied.

In administered systems, units can exist with disparate goals, but a mechanism exists for informal collaboration on inclusive goals. Decision-making takes place by virtue of the effective interaction of channel members in the absence of a formal inclusive structure. The locus of authority still remains with the individual channel members. The latter are structured autonomously but are willing to agree to an *ad hoc* division of labor without restructuring. As in conventional channels, commitment is self-oriented, but there is at least a minimum amount of systemwide orientation among the members.[11]

As McCammon has observed:

> Manufacturing organizations . . . have historically relied on administrative expertise to coordinate reseller marketing efforts. Suppliers with dominant brands have predictably experienced the least difficulty in securing strong trade support, but many manufacturers with "fringe" items have been able to elicit reseller cooperation through the use of liberal distribution policies that take the form of attractive discounts (or discount substitutes), financial assistance, and various types of concessions that protect resellers from one or more of the risks of doing business.[12]

A number of concessions available to suppliers were discussed in the preceding two chapters; a listing of them, as well as some additional ones, is provided in Exhibit 10–1.

While administration of the channel can flow backwards from retailer to manufacturer (e.g., Sears, Montgomery Ward, and J. C. Penney administer many of the channels in which they are engaged without committing themselves totally to a program of vertically integrating manufacturing facilities), the application of the concept has, as indicated above, been most frequently undertaken by suppliers. For example, Kraftco has developed facilities management programs to administer the allocation of space in supermarket dairy cases. Kraft's power stems from the fact that the company accounts for 60 percent of dairy case volume, exclusive of milk, eggs, and butter. In addition to facilities management programs, some manufacturers and wholesalers have developed modular merchandising programs, coordinated display programs, and automatic replenishment programs. The latter have been used with a high degree of success by Corning Glass and Genuine Parts, a major

[11]See Warren, *op. cit.,* p. 316.
[12]McCammon, *op. cit.,* p. 45.

EXHIBIT 10-1 Selected Concessions Available to Suppliers When Seeking To Gain Reseller Support of their Marketing Programs

I. "Price" Concessions

A. Discount Structure:
   trade (functional) discounts
   quantity discounts
   cash discounts
   anticipation allowances
   free goods
   prepaid freight
   new product, display, and advertising allowances (without performance
      requirements)
   seasonal discounts
   mixed carload privilege
   drop shipping privilege
   trade deals

B. Discount Substitutes:
   display materials
   premarked merchandise
   inventory control programs
   catalogs and sales promotion literature
   training programs
   shelf-stocking programs
   advertising matrices
   management consulting services
   merchandising programs
   sales "spiffs"
   technical assistance
   payment of sales personnel and demonstrator salaries
   promotional and advertising allowances (with performance requirements)

II. Financial Assistance

A. Conventional Lending Arrangements:
   term loans
   inventory floor plans
   notes payable financing
   accounts payable financing
   installment financing of fixtures and equipment
   lease and note guarantee programs
   accounts receivable financing

EXHIBIT 10-1 continued

  B. Extended Dating:
    E.O.M. dating
    seasonal dating
    R.O.G. dating
    "extra" dating
    post dating

III. Protective Provisions

  A. Price Protection:
    premarked merchandise
    "franchise" pricing
    agency agreements

  B. Inventory Protection:
    consignment selling
    memorandum selling
    liberal returns allowances
    rebate programs
    reorder guarantees
    guaranteed support of sales events
    maintenance of "spot" stocks and fast delivery

  C. Territorial Protection:
    selective distribution
    exclusive distribution

SOURCE: Bert C. McCammon, Jr., "Perspectives for Distribution Programming," in Louis P. Bucklin (ed.), *Vertical Marketing Systems* (Glenview, III.: Scott, Foresman and Company, 1970), pp. 36–37.

auto parts wholesaler. In fact, the long-term viability of many wholesaling firms is dependent upon their administration of such programs for the small retailers, other wholesalers, jobbers, and industrial customers with whom they deal. Wholesalers in the drug, hardware, sporting goods, and phonograph records industries have been particularly successful in this respect. Many industrial distributors have also committed themselves to program management, as shown in Table 10-1.

One of the most innovative approaches to developing administered systems has been the emergence of programmed merchandising agreements. Under this concept, manufacturers formulate specialized merchandising

TABLE 10-1   Percentage of Industrial Distributors Providing Various Programs and Services to Their Customers, 1973

Stockless purchasing programs	64%
Systems engineering programs	38%
OSHA, pollution control consulting services	37%
Fabrication	31%
Consignment buying programs	23%
Preventive maintenance programs	21%
Operator training programs	15%
Equipment leasing programs	8%
Scrap reclamation programs	5%

SOURCE: Bert C. McCammon, Jr. and James W. Kenderine, "Mainstream Developments in Wholesaling," a paper presented at the 1975 Conference of the Southwestern Marketing Association, p. 6.

plans for each type of outlet they serve. (The reader may wish to refer back to the O. M. Scott example that was provided in the preceding chapter.)

> Programmed merchandising is a "joint venture" in which a specific retail account and a supplier develop a comprehensive merchandising plan to market the supplier's product line. These plans normally cover a six-month period but some are of longer duration.[13]

Such programming generally involves the activities listed in Exhibit 10-2 for each brand and for each store included in the agreement. Manufacturing organizations currently engaged in programmed merchandising activities include: General Electric (on major and traffic appliances), Baumritter (on its *Ethan Allen* furniture line in nonfranchised outlets), Sealy (on its *Posturepedic* line of mattresses), and Villager (on its dress and sportswear lines), as well as Scott (on its lawn care products).

The concept of channel administration through instituting systemic programs is also being applied in the logistics field. For example, Ryder System, Inc., inaugurated a program recently that eliminates several intermediate warehousing operations for its truck-leasing customers. Ryder has begun offering its trucks as rolling warehouses. Newly manufactured goods usually go first into the manufacturer's warehouse, next are shipped to a retailer's warehouse, and then are shipped once again either to the store or to the retailer's customer. This process often leads to a minimum of six loadings and unloadings into warehouses before the goods get to their final destina-

[13] *Ibid.*, p. 48.

EXHIBIT 10–2 Plans and Activities Covered in Programmed Merchandising Agreements

1. Merchandising Goals
   a. Planned sales
   b. Planned initial markup percentage
   c. Planned reductions, including planned markdowns, shortages, and discounts
   d. Planned gross margin
   e. Planned expense ratio (optional)
   f. Planned profit margin (optional)
2. Inventory Plan
   a. Planned rate of inventory turnover
   b. Planned merchandise assortments, including basic or model stock plans
   c. Formalized "never out" lists
   d. Desired mix of promotional versus regular merchandise
3. Merchandise Presentation Plan
   a. Recommended store fixtures
   b. Space allocation plan
   c. Visual merchandising plan
   d. Needed promotional materials, including point-of-purchase displays, consumer literature, and price signs
4. Personal Selling Plan
   a. Recommended sales presentations
   b. Sales training plan
   c. Special incentive arrangements, including "spiffs," salesmen's contests, and related activities
5. Advertising and Sales Promotion Plan
   a. Advertising and sales promotion budget
   b. Media schedule
   c. Copy themes for major campaigns and promotions
   d. Special sales events
6. Responsibilities and Due Dates
   a. Supplier's responsibilities in connection with the plan
   b. Retailer's responsibilities in connection with the plan

SOURCE: Bert C. McCammon, Jr., "Perspectives for Distribution Programming," in Louis P. Bucklin (ed.), *Vertical Marketing Systems* (Glenview, Ill.: Scott, Foresman and Company, 1970), pp. 48–49.

tion. By using trucks as warehouses, and thereby minimizing loadings and unloadings while speeding up the shipment cycle, Ryder claims it can reduce a customer's trucking needs by 20 percent.[14]

CONTRACTUAL SYSTEMS

Often organizations desire to formalize role obligations within their channel networks by employing legitimate power as a means of achieving control. In these situations, vertical coordination is frequently accomplished through the use of contractual agreements. According to Thompson:

> Independent firms at different levels can integrate their programs on a contractual basis to achieve systemic economies and an increased market impact . . . Contractual integration occurs where the various stages of production and distribution are independently owned, but the relationships between vertically adjacent firms are covered in a contractual arrangement . . .[15]

Contractual integration takes a variety of forms, as shown in Exhibit 10–3. However, the three principal forms of contractual integration are wholesaler-sponsored voluntary groups, retailer-sponsored cooperative groups, and franchise systems. The focus here is primarily on these three forms.

From an interorganization management perspective, contractual vertical marketing systems can be viewed as networks in which the members have disparate goals but where there exists some formal organization for inclusive goals. Decision-making is generally made at the top of the inclusive structure but is subject to the ratification of the members. The locus of authority in such networks resides primarily (but not exclusively) with the individual members. The latter are structured autonomously, but will generally agree to a division of labor that may, in turn, affect the basic structure of the channel. In such networks, norms of moderate commitment to the channel system exist, and there is at least a moderate amount of systemwide orientation among the members.[16] Clearly, along each of the above mentioned dimensions, contractual systems are more tightly knit than administered systems.

---

[14]"Marketing When the Growth Slows," *Business Week* (April 14, 1975), p. 50.

[15]Donald N. Thompson, "Contractual Marketing Systems: An Overview," in D. N. Thompson (ed.), *Contractual Marketing Systems* (Lexington, Mass.: Heath Lexington Books, 1971), p. 5.

[16]Warren, *op. cit.*, p. 316.

EXHIBIT 10-3 Principal Types of Contractual Vertical Marketing Systems

---

Contractual Systems Involving Forward Integration

Wholesaler-sponsored voluntary groups
Wholesaler-sponsored programmed groups
Supplier franchise programs for individual brands and specific departments
Supplier franchise program covering all phases of the licensee's operation
Nonprofit shipping associations
Leased department arrangements
Producer marketing cooperatives

Contractual Systems Involving Backward Integration

Retailer-sponsored cooperative groups
Retailer/wholesaler-sponsored buying groups
Retailer-sponsored promotional groups
Nonprofit shipping associations
Retailer/wholesaler resident buying offices
Industrial, wholesale, and retail procurement contracts
Producer buying cooperatives

To a significant extent, channel members are willing to trade some degree of autonomy in order to gain scale economies and market impact.[17]

Voluntary and Cooperative Groups

A wholesaler, by banding together a number of independently owned retailers in a voluntary group, can provide goods and support services far more economically than these same retailers could secure acting solely as individuals. Perhaps the most well-known wholesaler-sponsored voluntary is the Independent Grocers Alliance (IGA). In the hardware field, Pro, Liberty, and Sentry are examples of wholesalers who provide retail establishments with services similar to those found in the IGA system. Other examples of voluntary groups are found in the automobile accessory market (Western

---

[17]William R. Davidson, "Changes in Distributive Institutions," in W. G. Moller, Jr. and D. L. Wilemon (eds.), *Marketing Channels: A Systems Viewpoint* (Homewood, Ill.: Richard D. Irwin, Inc., 1971), p. 389.

Auto) and in the notions and general merchandise market (Ben Franklin). Some of the largest voluntary groups in the drug and hardware industries are listed in Table 10-2.

Automatic Service, Genuine Parts, Fleming, Malone & Hyde, and Canadian Tire are also leading proponents of the voluntary group concept.[18] Automatic Service sponsors a voluntary group program for vending machine operators. Genuine Parts is the largest member of the NAPA (auto parts) network, and Fleming and Malone & Hyde are leading voluntary group wholesalers in the food field. Canadian Tire is a large voluntary group wholesaler that supplies affiliated stores with a variety of lines, including automotive parts and accessories, hardware, housewares, small appliances, and sporting goods. A typical Canadian Tire outlet contains approximately 25,000 square feet of space and carries over 20,000 items in inventory.[19] The performance of these organizations is shown, in strategic profit model terms, in Table 10-3.

The retailer-sponsored cooperative is also a voluntary association, but the impetus for the cooperative comes from the retailers rather than from a wholesaler. The retailers organize and democratically operate their own wholesale company, which then performs services for the member retailers. Seen chiefly in the food line (for example, Associated Grocers and Certified Grocers), this cooperative operates where it is feasible for small member retail establishments to obtain their products from a central source.

These contractual systems are not new forms of channel organization. Voluntary and cooperative groups emerged in the 1930's as a response to the appearance of chain stores. However, the scope of the cooperative effort has expanded from concentrated buying power to the development of a vast number of programs involving centralized consumer advertising and promotion, store location and layout, training, financing, accounting, and, in some cases, a total package of support services. For example, Malone & Hyde serves 1600 stores in 15 southern states, and is the nation's fifth largest food wholesaler, outranked by two voluntaries, Super Valu Stores, Inc. and Fleming Companies, and by two retailer-sponsored cooperatives, Certified of California and Wakefern Foods. It has achieved its strong position by instituting efficient, innovative procedures which enable it to serve its customers better. Some of these procedures include the following:

> When Malone & Hyde's customers place an order, it is accompanied by a signed blank check, virtually eliminating the wholesaler's collection problems and giving

[18] Bert C. McCammon, Jr., "The Changing Economics of Wholesaling: A Strategic Analysis," a paper presented at the 1974 Annual Conference of the Southern Marketing Association, p. 6.

[19] Bert C. McCammon, Jr., and William L. Hammer, "A Frame of Reference for Improving Productivity in Distribution," *Atlanta Economic Review*, Vol. 24 (September–October, 1974), p. 12.

TABLE 10-2   Selected Voluntary Groups in the Drug and Hardware Fields, 1974

Voluntary Group	Number of Affiliated Stores
Drug Field	
Economost	5,000
Good Neighbor Pharmacies	1,400
Associated Druggists	1,132
United Systems Stores	744
Family Service Drug Stores	350
Triple A	300
Velocity	250
Community Shield Pharmacies	200
FIP	200
Sell-Thru Guild	200
Total	9,776
Hardware Field	
Western Auto	4,230
Sentry	4,200
Pro	2,650
Ace	2,500
Gamble-Skogmo	1,200
Coast-to-Coast	1,040
Trustworthy	800
Stratton & Terstegge	550
Farwell, Ozman, Kirk & Co.	495
American Wholesale Hardware	175
Total	17,840

SOURCE: Bert C. McCammon, Jr. and James W. Kenderine, "Mainstream Developments in Wholesaling," a paper presented at the 1975 Conference of the Southwestern Marketing Association, p. 6; and Albert D. Bates and Bert C. McCammon, Jr., "Reseller Strategies and the Financial Performance of the Firm," a paper presented at the Structure, Strategy, and Performance Conference, Indiana University Graduate School of Business, November 1975, p. 21.

it the use of cash for several extra days. This procedure allows Malone & Hyde to pay cash for whatever it buys.

Using electronic inventory devices, supermarket operators can place an entire week's order directly with the Malone & Hyde computer in minutes by telephone instead of waiting for a salesman to visit. Groceries in all but one of the firm's nine warehouses are stacked according to family groups, just like the groceries in supermarket aisles. This means that orders can be filled without backtracking by warehouse workers.

The company has developed a labor-saving system whereby cases in the warehouse are stacked on a cart that can be rolled directly onto a truck, into the supermarket, and down the aisles.

TABLE 10-3   Strategic Profit Model Profiles for Leading Wholesalers Engaged in Voluntary Group Programs

Company	Strategic Profit Model Ratios, 1973[a]					Compound Annual Growth Rates, 1968–1973	
	Net Profits to Net Sales (percent)	Net Sales to Total Assets (times)	Net Profits to Total Assets (percent)	Total Assets to Net Worth (times)	Net Profits to Net Worth (percent)	Net Sales	Net Profits
Automatic Service Company	1.4	3.8	5.1	2.6	13.1	51.4	19.8
Genuine Parts Company	4.1	2.8	11.5	1.4	16.3	12.7	16.6
Fleming Companies, Inc.	0.8	9.6	7.5	2.0	15.0	8.8	9.8
Malone & Hyde, Inc.[b]	1.3	6.5	8.4	1.9	16.2	11.0	11.0
Canadian Tire Company	5.2	1.9	9.9	1.6	16.2	19.5	27.4

[a]The strategic profit model ratios may not multiply to the totals indicated because of rounding.
[b]Malone & Hyde has pursued a vigorous diversification policy in recent years and currently obtains 34 percent of its earnings from company-owned stores and related ventures.

SOURCES: Bert C. McCammon, Jr., "The Changing Economics of Wholesaling: A Strategic Analysis," a paper presented at the 1974 Annual Conference of the Southern Marketing Association, p. 9; and Bert C. McCammon and William L. Hammer, "A Frame of Reference for Improving Productivity in Distribution," *Atlanta Economic Review,* Vol. 24 (September–October, 1974), p. 12.

In addition to distributing food and other items to the retailer, the company provides the retailer with such services as store design, site location, insurance, inventory and accounting controls, and group advertising.

The company will lease a site location and turn it over to an independent operator. It will also sell the operator equipment and initial inventory on credit and may also inject a sizable amount of operating cash into the store. In return, the new owner-operator completely commits to the store whatever assets he has.[20]

Contractual systems have experienced phenomenal growth. For example, IGA now operates more stores than A & P, and Super Valu outlets' annual sales are higher than Kroger's. In fact, nationally, the share of grocery store sales enjoyed by voluntary and cooperative groups combined is almost equal to that held by corporate chains.[21] One of the reasons for this successful growth is the "clarity of total offer" made possible by the implementation of systemwide programs. Once the customer sees the store sign, there is

[20]Richard A. Shaffer, "Why Farm-Price Dips Don't Help You Much at the Grocery Store," *Wall Street Journal,* May 8, 1975, pp. 1 and 17.

[21]National Commission on Food Marketing, *Organization and Competition in Food Retailing,* Technical Study No. 7 (Washington, D.C.: U.S. Government Printing Office, 1966), p. 33.

a clear understanding of the outlet's marketing orientation, including the product, service, and atmosphere.[22]

Generally, wholesaler-sponsored voluntary groups have been more effective competitors than retailer-sponsored cooperatives, primarily because of the difference in channel organization between the two. In the former, a wholesaler can provide strong leadership, because he represents the locus of power within the voluntary system. In a retailer-sponsored cooperative, power is diffused throughout the retail membership, and therefore role specification and concomitant allocation of resources are more difficult to accomplish. In the voluntary groups, the retail members have relinquished some of their autonomy by making themselves highly dependent on specific wholesalers for expertise. (It should be recalled from an earlier chapter that the more one party depends upon another, the more power the latter has relative to the former.) In retailer cooperatives, individual members tend to retain more autonomy and thus tend to depend much less strongly on the supply unit for assistance and direction.

Franchise Systems

Franchise systems comprise major components of the distribution structure of the United States. Because of their growing importance, their makeup, design, and orientation are examined in considerable detail in this section.[23]

Franchising as it is generally known today is a form of marketing and distribution in which a parent company customarily grants an individual or a relatively small company the right, or privilege, to do business in a prescribed manner over a certain period of time in a specified place.[24]

> The parent company is termed the *franchisor*; the receiver of the privilege the *franchisee*; and the right, or privilege itself, the *franchise*. The privilege may be quite varied. It may be the right to sell the parent company's products, to use its name, to adopt its methods, and to copy its symbols, trademarks, or architecture, or the franchise may include all of these rights. The time period and the size of the area of business operations, which are specified, may also vary greatly. The rights

---

[22] Bert C. McCammon, Jr., Alton F. Doody, and William R. Davidson, *Emerging Patterns of Distribution* (Columbus, Ohio: Management Horizons, Inc., 1969), pp. 5–6.

[23] For additional detail, see Urban B. Ozanne and Shelby D. Hunt, *The Economic Effects of Franchising* (Washington, D.C.: U.S. Government Printing Office, 1971); Donald N. Thompson, *Franchise Operation and Antitrust* (Lexington, Mass.: Heath Lexington Books, 1971); Donald N. Thompson, *Contractual Marketing Systems, op. cit.;* and Charles L. Vaughn, *Franchising* (Lexington, Mass.: Heath Lexington Books, 1974).

[24] Vaughn, *op. cit.*, pp. 1–2.

that are granted and the duties and obligations of the respective parties, the franchisor and the franchisee, are usually, but not always, spelled out in a written contract.[25]

The franchisor may occupy any position within the channel. For example, the franchisor may be: (a) the manufacturer, as in the case of Midas Mufflers; (b) a service specialist, as in the case of Kelly Girl; or (c) a retailer franchising other retailers, as in the case of Howard Johnson's during its early years of operation.

There appear to be four basic types of franchise systems:[26]

1. *The manufacturer-retailer franchise* is exemplified by franchised automobile dealers and franchised service stations.

2. *The manufacturer-wholesaler franchise* is exemplified by Coca-Cola, Pepsi-Cola, Royal Crown Cola, and Seven-Up, who sell the soft drink syrups they manufacture to franchised wholesalers who, in turn, bottle and distribute soft drinks to retailers.

3. *The wholesaler-retailer franchise* is exemplified by Rexall Drug Stores and Sentry Drug Centers.

4. *The service sponsor-retailer franchise* is exemplified by Avis, Hertz, and National in the car rental business; McDonald's, Chicken Delight, Kentucky Fried Chicken, and Taco-Tio in the prepared foods industry; Howard Johnson's and Holiday Inn in the lodging and food industry; Midas and AAMCO in the auto repair business; and Kelly Girl and Manpower in the employment service business.

There is no general agreement as to which channel arrangements should be included as franchise systems. For example, some classification schemes include wholesaler-sponsored voluntary chains as franchise systems. Others include channels in which a retailer or a wholesaler is franchised to sell a product in a specified territory along with other products obtained from other sources. The latter interpretation more accurately describes the franchise method of distribution rather than franchise *systems*. This confusion leads to inaccurate statistics on the number of franchisors and franchisees as well as the sales volume of franchise systems. One of the major sources of confusion is the variety of franchise agreements, which take many forms, as shown in Exhibit 10-4.

A *franchise system* is defined for our purposes here to denote the licensing of an *entire* business format where one firm (the franchisor) licenses a number of outlets (franchisees) to market a product or service and engage in a business developed by the franchisor using the latter's trade names,

---

[25]*Ibid.*, p. 2.

[26]William P. Hall, "Franchising: New Scope for an Old Technique," *Harvard Business Review*, Vol. 42 (January–February, 1964), pp. 60–72.

EXHIBIT 10-4 Types of Franchise Systems

Type	Explanation
Territorial franchise	The franchise granted encompasses several counties or states. The holder of the franchise assumes the responsibility for setting up and training individual franchisees within his territory and obtains an "override" on all sales in his territory.
Operating franchise	The individual independent franchisee who runs his own franchise. He deals either directly with the parent organization or with the territorial franchise holder.
Mobile franchise	A franchise that dispenses its product from a moving vehicle, which is either owned by the franchisee or leased from the franchisor. Examples include Tastee Freeze and Snap-On Tools.
Distributorship	The franchisee takes title to various types of goods and further distributes them to subfranchisees. The distributor has exclusive coverage of a wide geographical area and acts as a supply house for the franchisees who carry the product.
Co-ownership	The franchisor and franchisee share the investment and profits. Examples include Aunt Jemima's Pancake Houses and Denny's Restaurants.
Co-management	The franchisor controls the major part of the investment. The partner-manager shares profits proportionately. Examples include Travelodge and Holiday Inn in the motel business.
Leasing	The franchisor leases the land, buildings, and equipment to franchisees. This is used in conjunction with other provisions.
Licensing	The franchisor licenses the franchisee to use his trademarks and business techniques. The franchisor either supplies the product or provides franchisees with a list of approved suppliers.
Manufacturing	The franchisor grants a franchise to manufacture its product through the use of specified materials and techniques. The franchisee distributes the product, utilizing the franchisor's techniques. This method enables a national manufacturer to distribute regionally when distribution costs from central manufacturing facilities are prohibitive. One example is Sealy.
Service	The franchisor prescribes patterns by which a franchisee supplies a professional service, as exemplified by employment agencies.

SOURCE: Based on Gerald Pintel and Jay Diamond, *Retailing* (Englewood Cliffs, N.J.: Prentice-Hall, Inc., 1971), pp. 23–26.

trademarks, service marks, know-how, and methods of doing business. While heavily circumscribed by law, as pointed out in Chapter 8, the franchisor may sell the products, sell or lease the equipment, and/or sell or lease the premises necessary to the operation.[27] For example, McDonald's insists that all of its units purchase from approved suppliers, provides building and design specifications, provides or helps locate financing for its franchisees, and issues quality standards that each unit must abide by in order to hold its franchise. However, the following warning of James T. Halverson, former Director of the Federal Trade Commission's Bureau of Competition, should be carefully heeded by all those seeking to understand the future of channel arrangements, in general, and franchise relationships, in particular.

> (Antitrust) is moving in the direction of ensuring larger numbers of independent decision-makers at all levels of distribution, and this means greater freedom of choice and action by customers and franchisees. . . . manufacturers and franchisors will find it becoming increasingly difficult, absent vital business justifications, to exert an influence on the businessmen who deal in their products and on the markets in which their products are sold. The law is making it easier for customers to choose alternative suppliers and for distributors to establish their own geographic markets, to do business with whom they choose, and to establish their own prices. And the more a supplier or franchisor attempts to resist these trends by making it difficult for franchisees to exert their independence in legally permissible ways, the harder it becomes to terminate the franchise relationship without inviting a lawsuit.[28]

The franchise system is present in almost all business fields, as indicated in Exhibit 10-5. It can be readily seen that the franchise system covers a wide variety of goods and services—accounting service, auto accessories, auto rentals, campgrounds, child care, computer services, dance studios, dry cleaning, employment agencies, fast foods, convenience food markets, sewer cleaning, home care, movie theatres, book stores, construction, industrial and commercial chemical products, and vending machine operations. Despite this diversity, automotive and petroleum franchise systems dominate the franchise industry. As reflected in Table 10-4, they account for about 54 percent of all franchised outlets and 81 percent of sales.

---

[27] In addition to reviewing Chapter 8, the reader interested in the extent of restrictions on tying agreements should see Shelby D. Hunt and John R. Nevin, "Tying Agreements in Franchising," *Journal of Marketing*, Vol. 39, (July, 1975), pp. 20-26.

[28] James T. Halverson, "What's in Store at the Federal Trade Commission," *Franchising and Antitrust* (Washington, D.C.: International Franchise Association, 1975), p. 25.

EXHIBIT 10-5   Business Classification of Franchise Organizations and Representative Examples in Each Classification

Accounting and Tax Services
  Business Management Systems
  Edwin K. Williams & Co.
  H & R Block, Inc.

Agricultural
  Harvestall Industries
  Harvestore Products, Inc.

Art Galleries
  Continental Art Galleries, Ltd.
  Heritage Galleries International, Ltd.
  Original Oils, Ltd.

Automotive Accessories and Parts
  Firestone Tire & Rubber Co.
  Goodyear Tire & Rubber Co.
  Western Auto Supply Co.
  White Stores

Automotive Repair and Service
  Brake-O International, Inc.
  AAMCO Transmission, Inc.
  Midas Muffler

Auto Wash, Products and Equipment
  Johnson Waxway Centers
  Robo Wash, Inc.

Auto Rental
  Airways Rent-A-Car System, Inc.
  Budget Rent-A-Car Corp.

Building Construction
  Structural Concepts, Inc.
  Pieper Electric, Inc.

Campgrounds
  Holiday Camps, U.S.A.
  Kampgrounds of America, Inc.

Child Day Care Centers
  Mary Moppet's Day Care Schools, Inc.
  Pied Piper Schools, Inc.

Coffee Service
  Coffee Clubs of America, Inc.
  International Coffee Service, Inc.

Computer Services
  Automated Management Systems
  Binex Data Centers

Convenience Food Markets
  E/Z Food Shops

Collection and Credit
  Action Credit Bureau
    International, Inc.
  Credit Service Co.
  Check and Balance, Inc.

Dance Studios
  Fred Astaire Studios

Drug Stores
  Rexall Drug Co.
  Sentry Drug Centers

Dry Cleaning and Laundry Services
  Maytag Co.

Employment Agencies
  Manpower, Inc.
  Snelling & Snelling, Inc.
  Tempositions, Inc.

Food Operations
  Kentucky Fried Chicken
  Korn Kettle, Inc.
  Mr. Donut of America
  Burger King
  McDonald's
  Baskin Robbins 31 Flavors Stores
  Orange Julius of America
  International Pancake House
  Bonanza International, Inc.

EXHIBIT 10–5 continued

Gas Stations
  Shell Oil
  Mobil Oil

Health Aids and Services
  Unihealth

Industrial and Chemical Products
  Tuff-kote International, Inc.

Industrial Supplies
  Vulcan Tools, Inc.

Motels and Hotels
  Alamo Plaza Hotel Courts
  Holiday Inns, Inc.
  Quality Court Motels, Inc.

Ramada Inns, Inc.
Rodeway Inns of America
Travelodge International, Inc.

Pest Control
  Redd Man Services

Printing & Duplicating
  Kopy Kat, Inc.
  Kwik-Kopy, Inc.

Theatres
  Jerry Lewis Cinemas

Vending Operations
  Vend Marketing, Inc.

SOURCE: *National Franchise Directory*, 1972 (Denver, Colorado: Continental Reports, Inc., 1972).

Modes of Operation.[29]   All franchisees are expected to provide a continuing market for a franchisor's product or service. The product or service offering is, in theory, differentiated from those offered by conventional outlets by their *consistent* quantity and quality and strong promotion. Through his market- and image-building promotional strategy, which is instituted at an early stage of a franchise system's development, a franchisor hopes to gain automatic and immediate acceptance on the part of prospective franchisees and the public.

Franchisors provide both *initial* and *continuous* services to their franchisees.[30] *Initial* services include:

Market survey and site selection

Facility design and layout

Lease negotiation advice

[29]This section is based largely on National Industrial Conference Board, *Franchised Distribution* (New York: National Industrial Conference Board, 1971).

[30]For a specific example, see the 7-Eleven Food Store information in the preceding chapter.

TABLE 10–4   Number and Sales of Franchised Outlets by Type
of Franchised System, 1973

	Number of Units (thousands)	Percentage of Total	Sales (billions)	Percentage of Total
Manufacturer-Retailer	209	54.1%	$108	81.0%
Automobile and truck dealers	33	8.5	82	61.3
Gasoline service stations	176	45.7	26	19.6
Manufacturer-Wholesaler	3	0.7	5	4.0
Soft drink bottlers	3	0.7	5	4.0
Wholesaler-Retailer	78	20.2	9	6.3
Automotive products and services	34	8.8	3	1.9
Retailing (including drugs, hardware, paints, etc.)	44	11.4	6	4.3
Service-Sponsor Retailer	95	24.7	12	8.7
Business aids and services	15	4.0	1	0.5
Construction, and remodeling, home cleaning, etc.	11	2.8	1	0.4
Convenience grocery	5	1.3	1	0.9
Educational products and services	2	0.5	0.2	0.1
Fast food restaurants	28	7.3	5	4.0
Food retailing (other than fast food and convenience grocery)	11	2.9	1	0.4
Hotels and motels	4	1.0	2	2.0
Laundry and drycleaning	4	1.0	0.2	0.1
Recreation, entertainment and travel (including campgrounds)	5	1.2	0.2	0.1
Rental services	8	2.1	0.5	0.3
Miscellaneous (beauty salons, carpet cleaning, etc.)	2	0.6	0.2	0.1
Other				
Vending	1	0.3	0.03	0.02
Total:				
All franchising	385	100.0%	$134	100.0%

SOURCE: Charles L. Vaughn, *Franchising* (Lexington, Mass.: Heath-Lexington Books, 1974), pp. 5 and 6.

Financing advice

Operating manuals

Management training programs

Franchise employee training

The extent to which these initial services are provided is shown in Table 10–5. *Continuous services* include:

Field supervision

Merchandising and promotional materials

Management and employee retraining

Quality inspection

National Advertising

Centralized purchasing

Market data and guidance

Auditing and record keeping

Management reports

Group insurance plans

Table 10-6 presents data on the extent to which continuing services are provided by franchisors. Almost all franchisors have a continuous program of field services. Field representatives visit the franchise outlet to aid the franchisee in everyday operation, check the quality of product and service, and monitor performance.

All franchisees are usually required to report monthly or semi-monthly on key elements of their operations, e.g., weekly sales, local advertising, employee turnover, profits, and other financial and marketing information. The regular reporting is intended to facilitate the various financial, operating, and marketing control procedures.

As might be expected, the reaction of franchisees to field services and operating controls is not always positive. Franchisees are independent businessmen, even though they have signed contractual agreements with franchisors. When conflict over supervision exists within their systems, franchisors have tended to rely on their field representatives to act as channel diplomats. However, these representatives not only are responsible for field service and liaison with franchisees but also must recruit additional franchisees. Complaints are often heard that the franchisor is providing too little attention to

TABLE 10-5   Initial Services to Franchisees, as Reported by Franchisors

Type of Service Provided	Franchisors Reporting				
	Total, All Companies	Fast-food & Beverage	Nonfood Retailing	Personal Services	Business Products & Services
Operating manuals	100.0%	100.0%	100.0%	100.0%	100.0%
Management training	100.0	100.0	100.0	100.0	100.0
Franchisee employee training	88.3	83.9	83.7	90.9	100.0
Market/surveys and site selection	84.4	98.2	93.0	83.6	42.3
Facility design and layout	80.0	100.0	83.7	81.8	26.9
Lease negotiation	62.7	78.5	72.0	58.1	23.0
Franchisee fee financing	37.7	25.0	37.2	47.2	46.1
All other services	21.1	21.4	25.5	20.0	15.3

Note: Based on information reported by 180 franchise companies. Includes 56 franchisors of fast-foods and beverages, 43 of nonfood consumer products, 55 of personal services, and 26 of business (or industrial) products and services.

SOURCE: National Industrial Conference Board, *Franchised Distribution* (New York: National Industrial Conference Board, 1971), p. 23.

franchisees' management problems, especially when the field representatives have too many conflicting responsibilities.[31]

Another source of conflict is the fact that many franchisors own a number of their outlets and some of these outlets compete with those owned by franchisees. In managing a franchise system, however, efforts are made to avoid the problems generally associated with dual distribution. Besides the necessity of owning certain outlets because of bankruptcy problems on the part of some franchisees (franchisors may be the only available source of funds for ownership in these cases), there are a number of other reasons why a franchisor might wish to vertically integrate. First, franchisor-owned and -operated units serve as models for the rest of the system and can be used for research and training purposes. Second, such units may facilitate accelerated network growth, especially during the initial development period. Third, wholly owned units may be profitable. They will also permit the franchisor first-hand insight into day-to-day operating problems. Finally, court decisions and legislation, such as that regarding exclusive territorial restrictions, may force franchisors to own more and more of their outlets if they wish to main-

[31] For documentation of conflict issues in franchising, see Shelby D. Hunt and John R. Nevin, "Power in a Channel of Distribution: Sources and Consequences," *Journal of Marketing Research*, Vol. 11 (May, 1974), pp. 186-193.

TABLE 10-6 Continuing Services to Franchisees, as Reported by Franchisors

Type of Service Provided	Total, All Companies	Fast-food & Beverage	Nonfood Retailing	Personal Services	Business Products & Services
	Franchisors Reporting				
Field supervision	96.1%	92.8%	100.0%	100.0%	89.6%
Merchandising and promotion materials	94.5	94.6	100.0	96.3	79.3
Franchisee employee retraining	85.1	78.5	83.3	94.5	82.7
Quality inspections	79.6	98.2	80.9	69.0	62.0
Advertising	66.4	62.5	61.9	83.6	48.2
Centralized purchasing	65.3	64.2	73.8	61.8	62.0
Market data and guidance	62.6	48.2	69.0	67.2	72.4
Auditing and recordkeeping	51.0	48.2	57.1	52.7	44.8
Group insurance plans	48.9	50.0	47.6	58.1	31.0
All other continuing services	13.1	8.9	21.4	12.7	10.3

Note: Based on information reported by 182 franchise companies. Includes 56 franchisors of fast-foods and beverages, 42 of nonfood consumer products, 55 of personal services, and 29 of business (or industrial) products and services.

SOURCE: National Industrial Conference Board, *Franchised Distribution* (New York: National Industrial Conference Board, 1971), p. 24.

tain strong control over the operations of the system as a whole. The incidence of company-operated units is increasing. One study reported that the ratio of franchisee-owned to franchisor-owned units went from 81 to 1 in 1960 to 10 to 1 in 1970, despite the accelerated growth of franchising during this period.[32] On the other hand, McDonald's, for example, plans to maintain a 30–70 split between company-owned and independently owned outlets over the long term. This means that, as the company expands, the number of units that it owns will increase, but the proportion of owned outlets will remain the same.

Sources of Franchisor Revenue. Sources of franchisor revenue and their relative importance are illustrated in Fig. 10–1. The various sources include:

1. Initial franchise fees. Many franchisors charge an initial fee to new franchisees. The fee ranges from $1000 to $100,000, with the mode falling between $10,000 and $25,000. The fee is charged to cover the franchisor's expenses for site locations, training, setting operating controls, and other initial services as well as developmental costs in building the system. Initial fees tend to rise as a franchise becomes more successful.

[32] National Industrial Conference Board, *op. cit.*, p. 24.

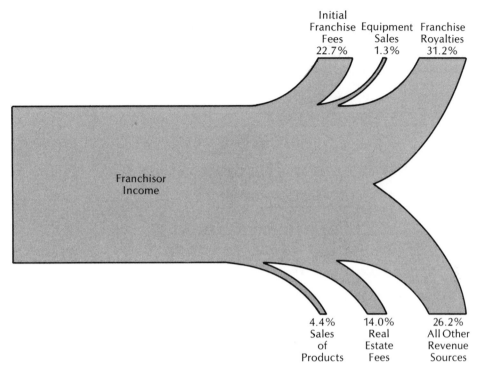

FIGURE 10-1   Principal Sources of Franchise Company Revenue

SOURCE: E. Patrick McGuire, *Franchised Distribution,* (New York: The Conference Board, 1971), p. 20.

2. Royalty fees. Many franchisors charge a royalty fee or commission based on the gross value of a franchisee's sales volume. Five percent of gross sales is the most common royalty agreement in franchising. Some franchisors require a minimum payment of $150 to $200 per month. In certain cases, the royalty rate decreases as sales volume increases while in others, the royalty fee is a flat rate regardless of the sales volume. Some franchisors collect a royalty on a unit-of-sale basis. For example, motel franchisors charge a fee per room; soft ice cream franchisors charge a fee for each gallon of mix sold to the franchisee; car wash equipment franchisors charge a fee per car washed. Figure 10-2 presents survey results regarding franchise royalty practices.

3. Sales of products. Some franchisors function as wholesalers in that they supply franchisees with raw materials and finished products. Other franchisors manufacture their products; for example, as mentioned earlier, Holiday Inns owns furniture and carpeting manufacturing facilities, and a significant amount of Coca Cola's revenue is derived from the sale of its soft drink syrups to its franchised bottlers. In some cases, the franchise company sells the equipment needed

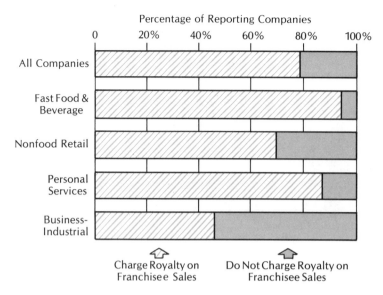

FIGURE 10-2   Franchise Company Royalty Practices

Note: Survey of 185 franchise companies, including 56 fast-foods and beverages, 45 nonfood retail, 56 personal services, and 28 business/industrial franchisers.

SOURCE: E. Patrick McGuire, *Franchised Distribution,* The Conference Board (New York: National Industrial Conference Board, 1971), p. 21.

by the franchisee. These practices are circumscribed by recent court decisions, however, as was pointed out in the chapter on legal limitations.

4. Rental and lease fees. The franchise company often leases the building, equipment, and fixtures used in its outlets. Some franchise contracts involve an escalator clause that requires the franchisee to increase his lease payment as sales volume increases.

5. License fees. The franchisee sometimes is required to pay for the use and display of the franchisor's trademark. The license fee is used more in conjunction with industrial franchises, where a local manufacturer is licensed to use a particular patent or process.

6. Management fees. In a few cases, franchisees are charged fees for consulting services received from the franchisor such as management reports and training.

Sambo's Restaurants, Inc., and Koffler Stores, Limited (a Canadian-based corporation, which is the largest franchisor of drugstores in North America) have both relied on creative management of their revenue sources in order to generate high profit yields from their franchise operations. Both franchise companies offer owner-managers a wide range of financial incentives and a comprehensive array of supporting services. In 1970, Sambo's generated a return on investment of 34.3 percent (with a profit ratio of 30.3 percent and a return on assets of 16.6 percent). Koffler earned a return on investment of 14.3 percent in 1973 (with a profit ratio of 2.1 percent and a return on assets close to 13 percent).

The Social View of Franchising.   A number of arguments have been raised, pro and con, relative to the socioeconomic and legal consequences of franchising.[33] On the pro side, for example, it has been contended that franchising greatly increases the opportunity for individuals to become independent businessmen, even though it is becoming more difficult to qualify for a franchise.[34] Hunt estimates that if franchising did not exist, approximately 52 percent of the owner-managers he surveyed would not be self-employed.[35] It has also been argued, without support one way or the other, that franchised businesses have lower failure rates than other businesses. Furthermore, to various observers, franchising seems to decrease economic concentration by providing a viable alternative to completely integrated corporate vertical marketing systems.

On the con side, some claim that: (1) franchise agreements are one-sided in favor of protecting the franchisor; (2) franchisors employ unethical techniques in selling franchises, including "pyramid" distribution schemes,[36] celebrity promotion of franchises, and misrepresentation of the potential profitability of the franchise; and (3) franchising is an anticompetitive system of distribution. Most of these contentions, especially the last one, involve legal as well as socioeconomic factors.

The bulk of evidence seems to be in support of the contention that franchise agreements favor the franchisor. Franchise contracts involve termination clauses, provisions on operating manual changes at the prerogative of the franchisor, and "covenants not to compete" clauses that prohibit a franchisee from practicing his trade for a specified time period within a specific geographic area after franchise termination. Sixty percent of sample con-

---

[33] See Shelby D. Hunt, "The Socioeconomic Consequences of the Franchised System of Distribution," *Journal of Marketing,* Vol. 36 (July, 1972), pp. 32–38.

[34] See Gary Washburn, "Franchising Good but Hard to Enter," *Chicago Tribune,* Section 2, September 21, 1975, p. 13.

[35] Hunt, "The Socioeconomic Consequences. . . ," *op. cit.,* p. 33.

[36] A pyramid distribution scheme is one in which a parent company sells the right to a territory to an individual, who in turn has the right ("franchise") to sell the right to operate under him or her. The procedure may be repeated in turn at several descending levels and has been used to amass fortunes in the cosmetics field, and especially by Glenn W. Turner with firms he named "Koscot Interplanetary" and "Dare-to-Be-Great," Vaughn, *op. cit.,* p. 23.

tracts examined by Hunt included such clauses.[37] Observed in these contracts were also clauses requiring the franchisee to buy supplies and equipment from the franchisor, restricting the franchisee's right to sell, and prohibiting the franchisee from joining any union of franchisees. Lack of arbitration clauses was evident in 77 percent of the contracts examined. It is interesting to note, however, that 40 percent of the sample of franchisees responding to Hunt's survey did not consult a lawyer prior to signing a contract.[38]

Partly as a result of some of the above-mentioned practices on the part of franchisors, ten states (as of 1975) have passed legislation designed to protect franchisees from misrepresentations by franchisors.[39] These so-called "full disclosure" laws require franchisors to provide potential franchisees with sufficient unbiased information to enable them to make sound investment decisions. On the federal level, two full disclosure measures were pending in the United States Senate as of 1975, and the Federal Trade Commission has contemplated issuing a trade regulation rule on the subject.[40]

The use of unethical techniques in selling is, obviously, not restricted to franchising. The FTC is, however, cracking down on pyramid schemes, and several states have declared such schemes to be an unfair trade practice. Relative to inflated estimates of profitability, Hunt's study showed that 73 percent of the franchisees had incomes below the minimum projected by the pro-forma income statement; 92 percent had incomes below the average projected figures; and 99 percent had incomes below the maximum projected incomes.[41]

Franchising generally involves tying agreements, territorial restrictions, and uniform pricing policies. These legal issues and related case rulings were discussed in detail in the chapter on legal limitations to interorganization management. Hunt's study reported that 50 percent of the fast-food franchisors responding to his survey specified prices for the franchisee's products, 28 percent required the franchisee to buy paper goods from the franchisor, and 85 percent assigned an exclusive territory.[42] All of these practices may be viewed by antitrust enforcement agencies as restricting competition.

[37] Hunt, *op. cit.*, p. 37.

[38] *Ibid.*

[39] The ten states are California, Hawaii, Illinois, Michigan, Minnesota, Oregon, Rhode Island, South Dakota, Washington, and Wisconsin.

[40] See Shelby D. Hunt and John R. Nevin, "Full Disclosure Laws in Franchising: An Empirical Evaluation," *Journal of Marketing*, Vol. 40 (April, 1976), pp. 53–62.

[41] Hunt, *op. cit.*, p. 38.

[42] *Ibid.*, p. 36.

CORPORATE SYSTEMS

Corporate vertical marketing systems exist when channel members on different levels of distribution for a particular product are owned and operated by one organization. Corporate forward integration occurs frequently when a manufacturing firm decides to establish its own sales branches and wholesale outlets, as when Evans Products Company (a manufacturer of plywood) purchased wholesale lumber distributors in order more aggressively to promote its products through retail lumber establishments. As pointed out in earlier chapters, it may also occur when a manufacturer takes over both the wholesale and retail functions by establishing its own system of retail outlets. Although integration of wholesaling functions alone is more common, evidence of complete forward vertical integration is found in such diverse companies as Singer, Sherwin-Williams (which owns and operates over 2000 retail outlets),[43] Hart, Schaffner, and Marx (which operates over 200 stores), Eagle (which generates 30 percent of its volume from captive locations), International Harvester, Goodyear, and Sohio.[44] In fact, complete forward vertical integration by manufacturers seems to be on the increase. Among the largest producers to develop corporate systems through to the retail level of distribution in recent years are Edmos (yarns and knits), Pepperidge Farms (baked goods), Eaton (auto parts), Dannon (yogurt), Texas Instruments and Hewlett-Packard (calculators), and GAF (duplicating supplies and services) plus hundreds of manufacturers who are quietly opening retail warehouse outlets.[45] One of the latter is Keller Industries, Inc., of Miami, which makes carpeting, tubular furniture, and aluminum doors, windows, and other products for residential construction. Managers

---

[43]For an interesting discussion of some of Sherwin-Williams' problems and opportunities in maintaining a corporate vertical marketing system, see "A Paintmaker Puts a Fresh Coat on its Marketing," *Business Week*, February 23, 1976, pp. 95-96.

[44]While the extent of vertical integration in the petroleum industry is great (including crude oil production, refinery operations, and wholesaling), most major oil companies moved away from direct service station operation by the mid-1930's. Chain store taxes, the threat of unionization, and the chance to shift the burden of low returns from retailing to others were important factors in this decision. Sohio is an exception to the rule, owning approximately 30 percent of its stations. The other majors operate fewer than one percent of their outlets with company employees. For example, in 1973, Gulf operated only 32 stations out of 29,540 and Shell only 171 out of 20,464 stations. Fred C. Allvine and James M. Patterson, *Highway Robbery* (Bloomington, Indiana: Indiana University Press, 1974), p. 25.

[45]"Marketing When the Growth Slows," *Business Week, op. cit.,* p. 48.

of such newly formed corporate systems see forward integration as a good way to increase sales volume in a slow growth economy while also letting the consuming public know about all of the various products they offer.

Corporate backward integration occurs in distribution when either a retailer or a wholesaler assumes ownership of institutions that normally precede them in the marketing flow of goods and services. To many, corporate systems are regarded as roughly synonymous with integrated chain store systems.[46] While all chain store organizations have integrated wholesaling functions, many of them also own some manufacturing facilities. For example many food chains obtain 15 to 20 percent of their requirements from company-owned processing facilities.[47] Sears and Safeway are important examples of backward vertical integration. Both organizations offer unusually good values in the product categories in which they elect to compete, with value being defined to include all dimensions of the product and service offer. Both companies have created vertical systems to coordinate the procurement and redistribution process.

For example, in 1974, Sears had a financial interest in 31 of its 12,000 suppliers.[48] The companies ranged from small companies with less than 100 employees to large corporations listed on the New York Stock Exchange, including Armstrong Rubber Co., Whirlpool Corp., and De Soto, Inc. The 31 "affiliated manufacturing sources," as Sears refers to them, had combined sales of $4.2 billion and supplied about 28 percent of Sears' purchases.[49] Examples of its affiliated manufacturing sources are shown in Fig. 10-3. In most cases, Sears has a minority interest in terms of common stock ownership, but may account for a large percentage of their sales, as indicated in Table 10-7. According to company executives, Sears' interest in maintaining factory ownership, a practice which dates back to 1906, is to provide its retail and catalog outlets with "a reliable and continuous supply of merchandise, built to our specifications, delivered in the right quantities at the right time and at the lowest possible cost."[50] However, Sears will become interested in a manufacturing investment only when it "insures continuity of sound management, quality, service, price and design obtainable in no other

[46]See, for example, Davidson, *op. cit.*, p. 388.

[47]McCammon, "Perspections for Distribution Programming," *op. cit.*, p. 45.

[48]William Gruber, "Sears' Success Affects Many," *Chicago Tribune*, Section 2, September 2, 1975, p. 7.

[49]*Ibid.*

[50]*Ibid.*

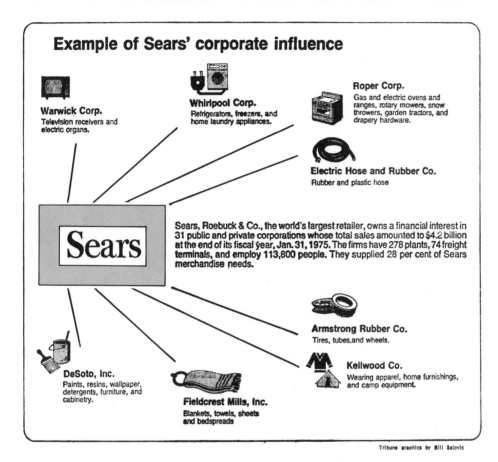

Example of Sears' corporate influence

Warwick Corp.
Television receivers and electric organs.

Whirlpool Corp.
Refrigerators, freezers, and home laundry appliances.

Roper Corp.
Gas and electric ovens and ranges, rotary mowers, snow throwers, garden tractors, and drapery hardware.

Electric Hose and Rubber Co.
Rubber and plastic hose

Sears, Roebuck & Co., the world's largest retailer, owns a financial interest in 31 public and private corporations whose total sales amounted to $4.2 billion at the end of its fiscal year, Jan. 31, 1975. The firms have 278 plants, 74 freight terminals, and employ 113,800 people. They supplied 28 per cent of Sears merchandise needs.

Armstrong Rubber Co.
Tires, tubes, and wheels.

Kellwood Co.
Wearing apparel, home furnishings, and camp equipment.

DeSoto, Inc.
Paints, resins, wallpaper, detergents, furniture, and cabinetry.

Fieldcrest Mills, Inc.
Blankets, towels, sheets and bedspreads

Tribune graphics by Bill Salovic

FIGURE 10-3   Examples of Sears' Affiliated Manufacturing Sources

SOURCE: William Gruber, "Sears' Success Affects Many," *Chicago Tribune,* Section 2, September 7, 1975, p. 7. Reprinted, courtesy of the Chicago Tribune.

way."[51] In fact, there are nine criteria that Sears uses to determine whether to establish an investor relationship with a supplier. They include:

> ... a competent management, adequate facilities, an accurate cost accounting system that permits both management and Sears buyers to know the actual cost of each product, effective production and budget controls, enlightened personnel policies, a sound sales policy, creative research and development programs, profitable factory operations, and "acceptance by the merchandising departments of their full merchandising responsibility."[52]

[51] *Ibid.*
[52] *Ibid.*

TABLE 10-7   Sears' Ownership of and Extent of Purchases From Selected Affiliated Manufacturing Sources in 1974

Affiliated Manufacturing Source	Sears' Ownership of Stock (percent)	Total Sales of Source (millions)	Sears' Share of Total Sales (percent)
DeSoto, Inc.	32.0%	$271	64%
Roper Corp.	41.4	366	71
Whirlpool Corp.[a]			
Parent company	4.7 ⎱		
Heil-Quaker subsidiary	20.0 ⎰	1260	62
Warwick Electronics subsidiary	25.5		
Kellwood Co.	23.0	400	79
Armstrong Rubber Co.	10.0	259	36
Globe-Union Co.[b]	2.6	276	33
Fieldcrest Mills	4.2	NA[c]	NA
Electric Hose and Rubber Co.	5.6	NA	NA

[a]Includes trash compactors, vacuum cleaners, home heating equipment, and home entertainment units, in addition to the products listed in Fig. 10–3.
[b]Globe-Union supplies Sears with automobile batteries and other electronic components.
[c]NA = not available

SOURCE: William Gruber, "Sears' Success Affects Many," *Chicago Tribune*, Section 2, September 7, 1975, p. 7.

According to a famous study by Kaplan, Dirlam, and Lanzillotti, Sears' method of operation at one time produced selling prices ranging from about 15 percent to 30 percent below the retail list prices of less integrated competitors in such product lines as water heaters, refrigerators, men's shoes, house paint, garden hoses, shotguns, and girdles.[53]

Some major wholesalers are engaged in successful backward vertical integration as well. For example, W. W. Grainger, Inc., an electrical distributor with sales of $315 million and a return on net worth of 17 percent in 1974, operates seven manufacturing facilities and has an aggressive private brand program. American Hospital Supply Corporation is both a major distributor and a manufacturer of health care products and services; its sales amounted to $982 million in 1974, and its return on net worth was 11 percent. In addition, a number of steel wholesalers (e.g., Joseph T. Ryerson & Son, Inc., A. M. Castle & Co., and Earle M. Jorgenson Co.) have become metal service centers, offering a wide variety of preprocessing services, including slitting, welding, and forming. These service centers now dominate the wholesale segment of the steel market.

[53]A. D. H. Kaplan, Joel B. Dirlam, and Robert F. Lanzillotti, *Pricing Big Business* (Washington, D.C.: The Brookings Institution, 1958), pp. 194–195.

By virtue of ownership, a channel member can achieve operating economies and *absolute* control over the marketing activities of other channel members. From the perspective of organization behavior, corporate systems are those in which units are organized for the achievement of inclusive goals where the locus of both inclusive decision-making and authority is clearly delineated within the structure. Thus, decision-making is *not* subject to unit ratification as it is in contractual systems. Wholly owned channel members are structured for a division of labor within the inclusive organization. Norms of commitment are high. Most important, perhaps, the systemwide orientation of the members is greater than in other vertical marketing systems.[54]

The development of corporate systems assures a channel member strong and long-term contact with customers and/or suppliers. Through this form of channel organization, the member may secure adequate representation in a market, reduce the cost of goods purchased, secure relatively scarce supplies, reduce production costs, gain greater inventory control and more pertinent market information, and employ excess funds that have been generated in effective ways.[55]   Vertical integration may permit a manufacturer, for example, to set and maintain the price at which his goods are sold at wholesale or retail. In addition, the vertically integrated firm may find it easier to control the quality of the product, engage in selective store promotions, or sell to its various retail outlets at different prices for the purpose of achieving greater market penetration in selected geographic areas. The integrated firm may also find it easier to protect its goodwill and trademarks than otherwise might be the case if it were to depend on a large number of independently owned middlemen who simply use its name.

The advantages of corporate marketing systems have been explored by a number of economists and marketing scholars.[56] The major emphasis of most of the studies on the subject is placed on the ability of such systems to

---

[54]Warren, *op. cit.*, p. 316.

[55] Frederick D. Sturdivant, et al., *Managerial Analysis in Marketing* (Glenview, Ill.: Scott, Foresman and Company, 1970), pp. 649–653.

[56]See, for example, R. H. Coase, "The Nature of the Firm," in G. J. Stigler and K. Boulding (eds.), *Readings in Price Theory* (Homewood, Ill.: Richard D. Irwin, Inc., 1952), p. 331; Arthur R. Burns, *The Decline of Competition* (New York: McGraw Hill Book Company, 1936); Melvin G. de Chazeau and Alfred Kahn, *Integration and Competition in the Petroleum Industry* (New Haven, Conn.: Yale University Press, 1959); Nugent Wedding, *Vertical Integration in Marketing* (Urbana, Ill.: University of Illinois Bureau of Economic and Business Research, 1952); Oliver E. Williamson, "The Vertical Integration of Production: Market Failure Considerations," *American Economic Review*, Vol. 61 (May, 1971), pp. 112–123; Lars Mattson, *Integration and Efficiency in Marketing Systems* (Stockholm, Sweden: Stockholm School of Economics, 1969); Louis P. Bucklin, "The Economic Base of Franchising," in Donald N. Thompson (ed.), *op. cit.*, pp. 33–62; Samuel H. Logan, "A Conceptual Framework for Analyzing Economies of Vertical Integration," *American Journal of Agricultural Economics*, Vol. 51 (November, 1969), pp. 836–848; and Michael Etgar, "Determinants of Structural Changes in Vertical Marketing Systems," Working Paper No. 201, School of Management, State University of New York at Buffalo, December, 1974.

achieve economies of scale through standardization, automation, and better streamlining of channel operations.[57] It has been argued, though, that, in order to achieve scale economies, there must also be a concomitant reduction in the level of services provided to consumers. For example,

> ... standardization implies a decline in the product variety offered as retailers reduce breadth of their product line. Similarly, automation and the introduction of self-service reduces personal selling service; while the quest for economies of scale implies that retail outlets have to be larger, and have to draw their buyers from larger trade areas reducing the location convenience of the consumers.[58]

Interestingly, though, a recent study testing the hypothesis that service levels are lower in corporate systems versus more conventionally organized channels showed the reverse to be the case.[59] Even though this study was restricted to the channels for property and casualty insurance, it is possible that the higher efficiencies generated in corporate systems, combined with more sophisticated, marketing concept-oriented approaches to markets, generate higher service levels than are forthcoming in less efficient and less well-organized systems.

Although corporate integration has, on paper at least, many advantages, a number of reasons can be advanced that specify why a firm might want to avoid taking such a significant step. Besides the large monetary investment that is often required to vertically integrate, there are managerial drawbacks as well. In such systems, the various levels of distribution are tied to one another, and thus their ability to take advantage of market opportunities elsewhere is limited.[60] Furthermore,

> Integrated operators may find that the hoped for advantages of better control prove illusory. The product mix and the marketing style of firms on different levels of the channel are, of necessity, quite different. To alter strategy in one level to meet the needs of another level may result in disaster simply because survival on the annexed level cannot be maintained in this manner.[61]

Other managerial problems include the likelihood that more employees may be needed to serve the various levels of distribution, and this can mean higher

---

[57]Etgar, "Structure and Performance of Distributive Systems," *op. cit.*, p. 3.

[58]*Ibid.*

[59]*Ibid.*, pp. 7–8.

[60]A recent example has been provided by Sears. The company's profits dropped 25 percent between 1973 and 1974, and the main reason appears to be Sears' ponderous size and growing unwieldiness, especially when it comes to inventory management. See "Why Sears' Profits Tumbled," *Business Week*, April 21, 1975, pp. 32–33 and "Sears' Identity Crisis," *Business Week*, December 8, 1975, pp. 52–58. See also Sturdivant, et al., *op. cit.*, p. 652.

[61]Sturdivant, et al., *op. cit.*, p. 653.

payroll, more insurance, and perhaps involvement with different unions. The firm must also consider the possible diseconomies of inventory control and, in the case of manufacturers, whether the product is marketed more efficiently by more diversified wholesale and retail outlets. Integration may also require increased warehousing and storage capacities and showrooms with adequate floor and shelf space to achieve reasonable product exposure. Furthermore, as corporate systems grow in size, diseconomies set in, especially with regard to the ability of management to absorb and process information. Finally, as was pointed out in the chapter on legal limitations, there are certain restrictions on corporate integration, particularly when such integration is accomplished via merger or acquisition.

SOURCES OF DIFFERENTIAL ADVANTAGES TO VERTICAL MARKETING SYSTEMS

As contrasted with conventional channels, vertical marketing systems are networks comprised of interconnected units, each of which, in theory, participates in an optimum combination of the marketing flows. Coordination is achieved through the use of detailed plans and comprehensive programs; channel members are, in fact, programmed to achieve systemwide economies. Entry is rigorously controlled by the system's requirements and by market conditions. In the case of contractual and corporate systems, membership loyalty is assured through the use of specific agreements or ownership. As a result, the network tends to be relatively stable. The limited number of strategists in such systems are preoccupied with cost, volume, and investment relationships at *all stages* of the marketing process. There is likely to be a heavy reliance on relatively "scientific" decisions, and the decision makers are generally committed, in a philosophical and analytical sense, to sophisticated marketing concepts and the formation of viable systems rather than emotionally committed to established business methods and traditional approaches.[62]

Unlike many conventional channels, the tasks of vertical marketing systems are routinized. As Bucklin has observed:

Of the many dimensions that form the relationship between agencies on different levels of a distribution channel, perhaps the most important is the extent of the role of day-to-day market pressure. Day-to-day market forces comprise the panoply of

[62]This paragraph is based on McCammon, "Perspectives for Distribution Programming," *op. cit.,* p. 44.

shifting prices, deals, allowances, promotions, and minor competitive crises that constitute the most visible strains of a market agency's work. Their presence in the interfirm relationship is manifested by detailed negotiations for each contract for the sale of goods to provide continuous adjustment to these prices. They disappear when goods are transferred as part of long-range plans where the issue is not optimal profit on each sale, but the means of better exploiting the market for mutual advantage of both parties.

If the importance of day-to-day forces is defined as a continuum ranging from one pole, where each transaction is negotiated separately in the light of market conditions, to the other, where the movement of goods is an automatic element part of a long-range marketing plan, then franchising as a mode of distribution may be said to occupy the middle ground. At the planned end of the continuum is to be found the integrated system (corporate vertical system); at the day-to-day pole is the independent (conventional) system.[63]

Vertical marketing systems seem to capitalize on programmed organization, economies of scale, and economies of standardization that exist within activities at the various levels of distribution. On the other hand, although the absence of long-term planning in independent channels results in higher distribution cost, it must be recognized that the independent retailer is free to tap supplies from a number of manufacturers and wholesalers in order to better adapt to his market. Thus, as pointed out above, although distribution cost is lower for corporate chains, for example, chain store managers are heavily circumscribed when it comes to adaptation to their markets. The franchise operator seems to occupy the middle ground on both the cost and adaptation fronts. While cost advantages work in the favor of vertical marketing systems, independent operators seem to have a differential advantage when it comes to ability to adapt to heterogeneous market opportunity.[64] The standardized level of performance achieved within vertical marketing systems is, though, rarely attained in conventional channels. Both industrial and household consumers prefer uniformity in the quality of goods and services they purchase, which gives systems capable of delivering such uniformity a strong differential advantage.

From a managerial perspective, vertical marketing systems are developed in order to achieve a degree of control over the cost and quality of the functions performed by various channel members. The strength of such systems lies in their capitalization on role specification through shifting and allocating the marketing flows. In theory, the performance of a vertical marketing system can approximate the performance of Bucklin's "norm-

[63] Louis P. Bucklin, "The Economic Base of Franchising," in Donald N. Thompson (ed.), *Contractual Marketing Systems* (Lexington, Mass.: Heath Lexington Books, 1971), p. 33. (Parentheses supplied.)
[64] *Ibid.*, pp. 33–62.

ative channel"[65] in that institutions can be grouped and organized in such a way so that no other type of grouping could create greater profits or more consumer satisfaction per dollar of product cost.

In conventional channels, power is often diffused among channel members.[66] In corporate systems, power is concentrated at one channel level through ownership. At least a moderate degree of expert and reward power must exist at the administrator's level in administered systems, whereas legitimate power obviously resides with the initiator of the legal agreements in contractual systems.[67] All in all, unlike conventional marketing channels, vertical marketing systems contain a locus of power, and as was pointed out in earlier chapters, such a locus is a prerequisite for channel leadership.[68] Because power is centralized, role specification and conflict management are more likely to be accomplished, and thus greater channel performance can be expected.

Implicit within the concept of a vertical marketing system is the fact that management recognizes the entire channel to be the relevant unit of competition. In conventional channels, independent members tend to believe that competitive viability is the result solely of actions taken on their specific levels of distribution.

THE MARKET IMPACT
OF VERTICAL MARKETING SYSTEMS

As McCammon observes:

> The autonomy of operating units in conventional marketing channels frequently results in duplicative programming, scheduling inefficiencies, and high selling costs. Similarly, the persistence of small units results in the sacrifice of scale economies ... And, perhaps most importantly, the functional rigidity characteristic of most conventional marketing channels ignores the economies that can be achieved by

[65] Louis P. Bucklin, *A Theory of Distribution Channel Structure* (Berkeley, California: Institute of Business and Economic Research, University of California, 1966), p. 5; Louis P. Bucklin, "A Normative Approach to the Economics of Channel Structure," in Louis P. Bucklin (ed.), *Vertical Marketing Systems, op. cit.,* pp. 164–173; and discussions of Bucklin's theory earlier in this book.

[66] For an example, see Adel I. El-Ansary and Louis W. Stern, "Power Measurement in the Distribution Channel," *Journal of Marketing Research,* Vol. 9 (February, 1972), pp. 47–52.

[67] Other bases of power are also in evidence in contractual systems as shown in Hunt and Nevin, *op. cit.*

[68] See also Louis W. Stern, "The Interorganizational Management of Distribution Channels: Prerequisites and Prescriptions," in George Fisk (ed.), *New Essays in Marketing Theory* (Boston, Mass.: Allyn and Bacon, Inc., 1971), pp. 301–314.

realigning activities within the network . . . Consequently, it is not surprising to observe that planned vertical marketing systems are rapidly displacing conventional marketing channels as the dominant mode of distribution in the American economy.[69]

As evidence of the market impact of vertical marketing systems, it is known that retailers affiliated with contractual systems (wholesaler-sponsored voluntary groups, retailer-sponsored cooperatives, and franchise networks) account for over 40 percent of retail sales and that corporate chains represent another 32 percent of the market.[70] Although no figures are available for administered systems, other forms of corporate systems, or for the industrial market, it is obvious that a vast preponderance of trade is enjoyed by vertical marketing systems of all types. In fact, McCammon and Hammer predict that, if present trends continue, contractual and corporate systems could account for 85 percent of total retail sales by 1980.[71]

Given the competitive advances made by vertical marketing systems, it is blatantly obvious that members of conventional channels will be forced to evoke fresh strategies if they are going to survive. A few suggested strategies are advanced below. The first three can be implemented in the short term, but the fourth requires long-run adjustments.[72] In fact, an implementation of the latter would begin to position the channel within the set of vertical marketing systems.

1. Develop programs to strengthen customers' competitive capabilities. This alternative would involve manufacturers and wholesalers in such activities as sponsoring centralized accounting and management reporting services, formulating cooperative promotional programs, and co-signing shopping center leases.

2. Enter new markets. For example, building supply distributors have initiated cash-and-carry outlets. Steel warehouses have added glass and plastic product lines to their traditional product lines. Industrial distributors have initiated stockless buying plans and blanket order contracts so that they may compete effectively for customers who buy on a direct basis.

3. Effect economies of operation by developing management information systems. For example, some middlemen in conventional channels have installed the IBM IMPACT program to improve their control over inventory.

4. Determine, through research, the locus of power in the channel and urge the channel member designated to undertake a reorganization of the marketing

[69] McCammon, "Perspectives for Distribution Programming," *op. cit.*, p. 43.

[70] McCammon and Hammer, *op. cit.*, p. 13.

[71] *Ibid.*

[72] The first three suggestions were adapted from McCammon, Doody, and Davidson, *op. cit.*, pp. 9–10.

flows. The potential channel leader may be located on any level of the channel, as is discussed in the following chapter.

SUMMARY AND CONCLUSIONS

Conventional marketing channels comprised of independently owned institutions and agencies frequently suffer from several weaknesses, the foremost among them being the absence of a systemwide orientation and inclusive goals. If a locus of power is also absent, the specification of roles and the management of conflict in conventional channels are likely to be difficult, at best. Even when a locus of power is present (as in the marketing channel for motion pictures), there is no guarantee that the performance of the channel will be any better than when power is diffused.

Vertical marketing systems have emerged as significant forms of channel organization and represent, for the most part, sophisticated attempts on the part of management to overcome the inherent weaknesses of conventional channels. Administered vertical marketing systems are those in which coordination of marketing activities is achieved through the use of programs developed by one or a limited number of firms. Administrative strategies combined with the exercise of power are relied on to obtain systemic economies. Such strategies have been most frequently adopted by suppliers and by carriers. They have involved the use of facilities management, modular merchandising, coordinated display, and automatic replenishment programs as well as programmed merchandising agreements.

Contractual vertical marketing systems are those in which independent firms at different channel levels integrate their programs on a contractual basis to achieve systemic economies and increased market impact. They include, among other forms of organization, wholesaler-sponsored voluntary groups, retailer-sponsored cooperative groups, and franchise systems. By virtue of the use of legitimate power in their formulation, contractual systems tend to be more tightly knit than administered systems.

Corporate vertical marketing systems are those in which channel members on different levels of distribution are owned and operated by one organization. In fact, such systems are synonymous with both forward and backward vertical integration. Forward integration is on the increase, even within franchise systems. Backward integration has long been typified by corporate chain store systems. The key tradeoffs in instituting any corporate vertical marketing system are the investment required plus the flexibility lost, on the one hand, versus the control secured over marketing activities of channel members plus the operating economies gained, on the other.

Vertical marketing systems appear to offer a series of differential advantages over conventional channels. The former employ a systemic approach and are committed to scientific decision-making while engendering channel member loyalty and network stability. Tasks are routinized, and economies of standardization are likely within them. Because a locus of power is available and utilized in a positive manner, it is possible to gain at least some control over the cost and quality of the functions performed by various channel members. Furthermore, inherent within systems management is the notion that the channel itself is the relevant unit of competition.

DISCUSSION QUESTIONS

1. According to Bucklin, the issue of channel performance focuses on the major conflict that exists between two major dimensions of channel performance. On the one hand, consumers and users are primarily concerned with lowering costs of the goods and services sold and therefore on reducing the costs of distribution. On the other hand, consumers want to benefit from and receive some marketing services in conjunction with the good or service they purchase. However, provision of these services increases the costs of distribution.

Evaluate conventional, administered, contractual, and corporate systems relative to the performance dimensions mentioned by Bucklin. Which, if any, would tend to be superior on an overall basis?

2. It has been argued that the price mechanism is the formal means through which vertical coordination is achieved in conventional or fragmented channels. What does this mean and what are its consequences for channel performance, both from a macro- and microperspective?

3. Suggest three ways in which the marketing channel for motion pictures might be improved.

4. What are the advantages of administered systems versus contractual systems? What are the disadvantages of administered systems that might be overcome by forming contractual systems?

5. Classify the selected concessions available to suppliers when seeking to gain reseller support of their marketing programs (Exhibit 10-1) by the various bases of power (coercive, reward, expert, referent, and legitimate).

6. Which of the various concessions listed in Exhibit 10-1 are likely to be useful in marketing through supermarkets? Through department stores? Through catalog showrooms? Through warehouse showrooms? Through industrial (full-function) distributors?

7. Which type of cooperative—wholesaler-sponsored, retailer-sponsored, or consumer-

sponsored—would you expect to be more successful? Why have consumer cooperatives never enjoyed widespread popularity in the United States?

8. After studying Table 10-3, can you pinpoint any factors which seem to differentiate the operating styles of the five leading wholesalers, simply on the basis of the financial data presented in the table?

9. Write a plan for starting your own franchising operation. What would be the essential ingredients of the plan? What specific points would you include in the contractual arrangement you establish with your franchisees?

10. From 1973 to 1975, Sears experienced lower-than-normal returns. What factors accounted for these low returns? What changes would you suggest to Sears to improve its returns from its merchandising operations? (Do you feel, for example, that the company has too many affiliated manufacturing sources?)

11. Assume that you are the manufacturer of a broad line of moderately priced furniture. When would you seriously consider forming a corporate vertical marketing system for your line? What factors would you take into account in making your decision?

12. Montgomery Ward describes its supplier investments as "very minimal" and says it will consider such relationships "only as a last resort in order to meet the company's requirements for satisfying its customer needs." According to a Ward's executive, the firm's only major supplier investment is in the Standard T Chemical Co., which manufactures paint. (William Gruber, "Sears' Success Affects Many," *Chicago Tribune*, Section 2, September 7, 1975, p. 7)

Compare and contrast Ward's philosophy with that of Sears. Which would you endorse as an overall corporate policy, if you were running a comparable retailing organization (e.g., Penney's)?

13. Name two additional survival (or growth) strategies that you might suggest to members of conventional channels, beyond those mentioned at the end of Chapter 10.

ELEVEN

CHANNEL MANAGEMENT
BY
CHANNEL PARTICIPANTS

At this point in this text, it should be clear to the reader that some form of interorganization management is necessary and desirable if a channel is to maintain or achieve satisfactory performance as a competitive entity. Thus, the discussion here focuses not on the need for management but rather on which institutions are capable of assuming managerial roles within commercial channel systems. In this chapter, consideration is given to the leadership potential of manufacturers, wholesalers, retailers, and common carriers. Clearly, the question of leadership hinges, to a large degree, on the locus of power within various systems, and, therefore, considerable attention is devoted to this subject. The reader should be forewarned, however, that attempts to generalize are often misleading, since each system will, in reality, vary widely in its composition and orientation. Only through an in-depth empirical analysis is one likely to discover the best answer to the question, "Who should lead the channel?"

Too often it is automatically assumed that the manufacturer or producer will be the channel leader and that middlemen will be the channel followers. As Mallen points out, manufacturers have not always been the channel leaders.

> The growth of mass retailers is increasingly challenging the manufacturer for channel leadership, as the manufacturer challenged the wholesaler in the early part of this century.[1]

[1] Bruce Mallen, "Conflict and Cooperation in Marketing Channels," in Bruce Mallen (ed.), *The Marketing Channel: A Conceptual Viewpoint* (New York: John Wiley & Sons, Inc., 1967), p. 127.

Underlying Mallen's statement, however, is the assumption (or belief) that either manufacturers or mass retailers will manage the interorganizational relations within channels. Although this assumption has a great deal of appeal, as will be shown below, it is not necessarily valid in all cases and need not be valid in the future. Furthermore, the answer to the question, "Who does lead?" may vary greatly from the answer to the question, "Who should lead?"

CHANNEL MANAGEMENT BY MANUFACTURERS

Large manufacturers can always be considered potential leaders of channels because, by definition, they have amassed a significant amount of reward and coercive power, given their size and dominance in the markets in which they compete. Their power emanates from their considerable financial resources, which enable them to maintain superior product research and development, cultivate consumer franchises through promotion, maintain continuous flows of market information, offer high margins and support to middlemen, and retain control over their products until they reach the point in the channel where ultimate consumers or industrial buyers can purchase them.

However, small manufacturers may, as Little observes, also serve as potential sources of control and direction of an interorganizational channel network.[2] Limited economic resources hamper their opportunity, but a good product offers control possibilities.[3] Such possibilities are manifestations of their legitimate, referent, and, to some extent, expert power. The manufacturer with an outstanding product may have, from the perspective of those purchasing it, a "right" to dictate how it should be sold and consumed, an image with which others seek to identify, and probably a greater assumed knowledge about the market for his product than anyone else. Furthermore, those in the position of controlling a new product that is desired by many consumers—irrespective of whether they are large or small—can elect to offer or withhold their product from various middlemen and therefore exercise reward or coercive power.

In general, the traditional viewpoint of manufacturer dominance in the marketing channel flows from an emphasis on production economies that

---

[2] Robert W. Little, "The Marketing Channel: Who Should Lead This Extracorporate Organization," *Journal of Marketing*, Vol. 34 (January, 1970), p. 34.

[3] Neil H. Borden, *Acceptance of New Products by Supermarkets* (Boston, Mass.: Division of Research, Graduate School of Business Administration, Harvard University, 1968), p. 13.

can be achieved only by increases in sales. As sales grow, a manufacturer realizes the benefits of large-scale operations and is able to spread his overhead costs over a large number of units. In fact, Mallen argues that the manufacturer must control the channel in order to assure himself of adequate sales volume and thereby justify the investment risk he alone must take relative to development and production.[4] In addition, it has also been asserted that as long as a manufacturer has the legal right to select the middlemen with whom he will deal, then he should be able to specify roles and allocate resources within the system that he selects for the marketing of his product.[5] Thus, the manufacturer-directed channel concept is based primarily on the belief that because the manufacturer creates and produces the product and designs the network through which it passes on its way to consumers, he is entitled, on the basis of legitimacy if nothing else, to impose his marketing policies on other channel members and to direct the activities of the channel.

Although it is the case that a number of channels are manufacturer-dominated for just these reasons (especially when the manufacturers in question have considerable economic power), the question of channel leadership is not as easy to answer as the above discussion would imply. There are many other factors that must be considered before manufacturers are deemed the logical channel managers. First, the manufacturer is not always eager to concern himself with the matters of channel management. His sole concern may simply be with the firms above and below him in the channel. After all, the manufacturer's dealings are usually with his immediate suppliers and customers and not with any of the other resellers of his products. The manufacturer may not care at all about the problems of other channel members as long as his own needs are satisfied. Similar assertions could be applied to middlemen as well. A manufacturer, it must be noted, is not unique in this respect. Furthermore, the manufacturer may prefer to concentrate his efforts on product research and development because of limited marketing management capacity or capability. As was shown in an earlier chapter, this latter factor accounts for the heavy reliance on wholesalers in a number of industrial goods industries.

Second, as pointed out later in this chapter, the manufacturer may simply not be powerful enough, in relation to other channel members, to impose his marketing policies on them. This is particularly true if the manufacturer is interested in employing large wholesaling and retailing institutions.

[4] Mallen, *op. cit.,* p. 129.

[5] Eli P. Cox, *Federal Quantity Discount Limitations and Its Possible Effects on Distribution Channel Dynamics* (unpublished doctoral dissertation, University of Texas, 1956), p. 12.

In general, middlemen have as much, if not more, freedom of choice as the manufacturer. They do not have to handle the manufacturer's product if they do not desire to do so, especially if substitutes are readily available. Given limited display and warehouse space as well as the need for immediate cash flow on the part of many resellers, manufacturers must often curry the favor of middlemen in order to assure that adequate inventories of their products are maintained, not to say promoted. In addition, middlemen frequently can develop a great deal of local strength in their particular markets so that customers become more loyal to them than to the various brands they carry.

In summary, manufacturer dominance of the marketing channel is not an absolute certainty for several reasons. Among these are the manufacturer's own reluctance to lead and the relative strength of middlemen in the channel. On the other hand, *if* the manufacturer possesses a relatively unique product with a strong consumer demand (or can provide unique services that enhance the use of his products) and *if* middlemen are relatively weak (e.g., if they have limited options and limited resources), then it is likely that the manufacturer could assume the channel management role quite easily.

Methods of Manufacturer Dominance

Of the many methods that the manufacturer can use to dominate the channel, perhaps the most common is, as indicated above, the development of strong consumer attraction or loyalty to his products. This factor is particularly important in the case of products sold through convenience retail outlets, where little or no sales assistance in the form of salesperson interaction is provided with the sale and where the locational density of outlets is high. Porter has explained how manufacturers amass power in these situations:

> For products sold through convenience outlets, low unit price and frequent purchase of the product reduce the desire of the consumer to expend effort on search. The consumer demands a nearby retail outlet, is unwilling to shop around, and needs no sales help, thus the consumer considers the purchase relatively unimportant. Since the purchase is not perceived to be important, the consumer is willing to rely on less objective criteria (attributes) accordingly . . .

> In view of these characteristics, the manufacturer's prime strategy for differentiating his product is to develop a strong brand image through advertising. If the manufacturer can develop a brand image, the retailer has very little power because (1) the retailer is little able to influence the buying decision of the consumer in the store; (2) a strong manufacturer's brand image creates consumer demand for the product, which assures profits to the retailer from stocking the product and at the

same time denies him the credible bargaining counter of refusing to deal in the manufacturer's goods.[6]

A manufacturer may also use coercive methods or policies, such as refusing to deal with particular middlemen or limiting sales to them unless they conform to his desires. He can also employ resale restrictions, exclusive dealing, and tying contracts. When legal, these latter methods work only when middlemen strongly desire to carry a manufacturer's product line, and therefore they must generally be coupled with significant brand identification, the availability of few comparable product sources, and the opportunity for sizeable rewards. In addition, other methods of manufacturer dominance are forward vertical integration and/or the use of contractual agreements, as discussed in Chapter 10.

If a manufacturer can amass sufficient expert, referent, and/or legitimate power, it is possible that he will be able to assume a position of channel leadership. In such cases, he must have made a long-term commitment to gathering and disseminating crucial market information (i.e., to absorbing uncertainty for other channel members) as well as to continual innovation in products and managerial practice so that other channel members seek to identify with him and come to believe that he has a right to direct their activities. It should be obvious, though, that such efforts, with the exception of new-product development, are not necessarily unique to manufacturers. If channel members at other levels choose to undertake them, the mantle of leadership (or the rights of dominance) may fall to them. Thus, it should not be surprising that, in at least some industries, channel management is practiced by wholesalers and retailers and not by manufacturers, because the former have done a more effective job of accumulating a significant amount of power within their channel networks than have the manufacturers supplying them.

CHANNEL MANAGEMENT BY WHOLESALERS

The wholesaler's management role in the modern marketing channel is greatly reduced from what it once was. During the early stages of economic development in the United States (prior to the mid-1800's), the merchant wholesaler was in a natural position to assume leadership, because he was

---

[6]Michael E. Porter, "Consumer Behavior, Retailer Power and Market Performance in Consumer Goods Industries," *The Review of Economics and Statistics*, Vol. 56 (November, 1974), p. 423.

generally flanked by small manufacturers and small retailers who had little interest in delineating the various actors in their respective channel networks, let alone engaging in interorganization management. However, by the late 1800's, the country was caught up in a period of rapid industrial growth, and large manufacturers and retailers were beginning to develop. Increased pressure was placed on wholesalers. Manufacturers often felt that, given their increased production capacities, they could more effectively market their own goods without using wholesalers. And retailers, as their size increased, were more capable of buying direct from manufacturers, obtaining discounts and allowances that normally went to wholesalers.

From a historical and comparative perspective, the wholesaler has been able to remain in a dominant channel position only in those industries where the buyers and producers are small in size, large in number, relatively scattered geographically, and where manufacturers are financially weak and lack marketing expertise.[7] Except in a limited number of fields, these conditions no longer exist in the United States. The fact that wholesalers are still a significant factor in distribution, as was shown in detail in an earlier chapter, attests to their success in readjusting to their changing environment, at least to some degree.

Despite this rather gloomy description of the wholesaler's opportunity for channel leadership, it is shown below that there are certain circumstances in which wholesalers do, in fact, engage in strong and effective interorganization management. However, it is equally important to observe that not every institution can or should assume a leadership position within a channel and that efficient followership is as essential to a channel's long-term viability as the existence of a centralizing force.

Methods of Wholesaler Dominance

One form of channel organization that has been particularly successful for wholesalers in strengthening their positions has been the voluntary chain, especially in the marketing of grocery products. As noted in the preceding chapter, wholesalers are clearly the leaders of these contractual vertical marketing systems. Retailers obtain the benefits of centralized buying, private brands, the identity of the group, large-scale promotion, and other management aids, while the wholesalers allocate the resources of their respective voluntary systems in such a way as to enhance their overall performance rel-

---

[7]Edwin H. Lewis, "Channel Management by Wholesalers," in Robert L. King (ed.), *Marketing and the New Science of Planning* (Chicago, Ill.: American Marketing Association, 1968), p. 138.

ative to competitive systems. However, there is evidence that wholesaler-sponsored voluntary chains have not been uniformly successful. According to Lewis:

> Voluntary chains in hardware have been rather loosely knit, compared with those in groceries, and the sponsoring wholesalers frequently continue to service nonaffiliated stores. Furthermore, some of these organizations also operate centrally-owned chains. In these cases, the voluntary-group stores tend to be located in communities where it would not be profitable to establish chain stores.
>
> The hardware trade has experienced a greater amount of inter-type competition than the grocery field. Mail order houses with their retail chains, and more recently, discount houses have been major competitors of independent hardware merchants and wholesalers. Also, the wide range of lines carried in the hardware trade places wholesalers and retailers alike in a position of competing with several types of stores.[8]

Besides voluntary groups, wholesalers have also been active in franchising, as indicated in Chapter 10. The wholesaler-franchisor clearly dominates his channel by exercising strict control over and surveillance of operations at the retail level. Also, because he is rarely tied to brand names, a wholesaler-franchisor's purchasing power combined with the maintenance of alternative sources of supply enable him to influence the marketing activities of his suppliers and thus to specify roles throughout the entire franchise system.

Another method used by wholesalers to achieve dominance has been the development of their own private brands.[9] The promotion of private brands by wholesalers appears to be successful mainly in fields where the products are relatively undifferentiated, frequently purchased, and where demand for the product has already been established. However, the fact that the products are relatively undifferentiated forces the wholesaler to use price as the primary appeal in order to sell his brand. In addition, unless the wholesaler can develop a private brand in each of his key lines, the control he may enjoy will be slight. The development of private brands also requires considerable capital and substantial promotion as well as products of relatively high quality. Therefore, the use of private brands to secure dominance is obviously far from an easy task. Perhaps the most successful wholesalers, in this respect, have been those who have established multiunit operations, such as McKesson in the drug field. Multiunit organizations, like their chain counterparts in the

[8] *Ibid.,* p. 139.
[9] *Ibid.,* p. 140.

retail field, can secure buying leverage both with respect to manufacturer's brands and private labels. When the convenience and quick delivery attributes of multiple locations are combined with a strong private label program, it is likely that wholesalers can play a leadership role in their various channels.

It is important to note, however, that the majority of wholesalers actually do not attempt to gain significant control in their channels but instead seek merely to maintain the foothold that they already have. Significant means of maintaining their present positions include selective distribution, reduction of competing product lines, reduction of some service, the development of new and improved services, and improved operating procedures.[10] First, the use of selective distribution practices assures closer ties between wholesalers and their suppliers or their retail customers. The acceptance or adoption of an exclusive or selective distribution policy results in stronger support for the wholesaler than would ordinarily be the case. Second, a reduction in the number of competing product lines encourages remaining suppliers to provide greater all-around support to the wholesaler. Such a step should, however, be undertaken only after careful consideration of potential long-term consequences, because, clearly, one result will be that the wholesaler's dependence on his suppliers will increase markedly. Third, there has been a trend in wholesaling towards limited-line operations, especially in such fields as frozen foods, floor covering, and stationery. Instead of reducing the number of competing lines carried, the limited-line wholesaler develops a broad and deep assortment within a product category. Thus, so long as the product category remains strong, suppliers and customers may find themselves more dependent on the wholesaler as the wholesaler specializes and thereby becomes more adept at merchandising his limited line.

Finally, another promising means by which wholesalers are able to maintain their positions is by improving, modifying, or even eliminating some of the services that they offer to both suppliers and customers. Although the elimination of certain services may bring a negative reaction from other channel members, such service "pruning" should enable wholesalers to do better jobs on the remaining ones. Relative to improvement or modification, one of the most fertile areas for wholesaler attack is the development of information systems. In fact, some wholesalers in the hardware and drug fields have begun absorbing uncertainty within their channels by establishing on-line computer networks between themselves and their suppliers and customers. Through such a network, wholesalers are able to control inventories at various levels in their channels and to realize economies in the physical

[10] *Ibid.*

and information flows. In fact, the development of computerized interorganizational data systems (IDS) is seen by some as a means that wholesalers could use to recapture positions of dominance in specific channels. For example:

> ... in a channel characterized by a loose coalition of independent retailers and wholesalers, where no middleman is particularly dominant, one of the wholesalers may take the lead in developing IDS, thereby "tying" a number of the retailers to him. As a consequence, it is likely that the market will sustain a "shakeout" with a few large wholesalers emerging and displacing the smaller ones. Those wholesalers who do not establish a clientele large enough to support an IDS will probably fail. In a channel situation similar to that posed above, the member(s) best able to establish strong dependency bonds and limit alternatives for those with whom they deal will dominate, and IDS is seen as a means to this end.
>
> Positionally, wholesalers are probably best able to assume leadership in the development of IDS in such channels. It would not be feasible, from an economic perspective, to maintain a great number of parallel (communication) flows, since each data link represents a cost. In any channel with more than two retailers and more than two manufacturers, the number of links can be minimized by employing a wholesaler. With a large number of possible links, the saving can be substantial. The emergence of wholesalers as power loci is an example of technological determinism. Ipso facto their position in distribution channels bestows power on them in this regard.
>
> Interorganizational data systems portend great promise for wholesalers in another area—computer services. A wholesaler is in an ideal position to help smaller retailers with inventory management, accounts receivable, payroll, and other applications beyond the capabilities of the latter's own equipment. ... Moreover, with the wholesaler-retailer links established, the wholesaler can readily build on the wholesaler-manufacturer links. With a large exclusive domain of retailers, a wholesaler will be able to exert power over manufacturers. By controlling inventories, maintaining receivables, and helping to prepare the payroll, the wholesaler will further entrench himself in the retailer's operation.[11]

Overall, though, it would seem that wholesalers are not qualified to lead channels in many of today's highly developed markets. The methods they use have enabled them to dominate channels in only a few industries (e.g., hardware, drugs, motion pictures, liquor, auto accessories and parts, and industrial supplies). It seems that the strength of wholesalers lies in their role as builders of assortments, integrators of product lines, and reliable sources of merchandise for their customers. In order simply to hold their present positions, they must maintain their differential advantage in performing this

---

[11] Louis W. Stern and C. Samuel Craig, "Interorganizational Data Systems: The Computer and Distribution," *Journal of Retailing,* Vol. 47 (Summer, 1971), pp. 83–85.

role. Otherwise, they will become increasingly vulnerable and will eventually be bypassed.

CHANNEL MANAGEMENT BY RETAILERS

A significant number of retailers have grown in size to a point where they rival or even dwarf many large manufacturers. It is likely, therefore, that these retailers may want to exert some control over the channels in which they are members.

The large retailer is, in reality, a multilevel merchandiser (MLM).[12] That is, such retailers have integrated the wholesaling functions within their channels and a number of them have, as was pointed out in the preceding chapter, integrated backwards to the manufacturing level.[13] Similar to large manufacturers, MLM's have considerable coercive, reward, and expert power that can be employed in an effort to control channels. As Little observes:

> They can control resources, "buy" time by utilizing staff specialists, and employ their resources in a manner to help the channel reduce conflict arising from any of the basic sources of organizational conflict. For example, (they) can employ research personnel to learn more about customers and markets and therefore reduce uncertainty and improve communications throughout the channel. They have the economic power to communicate and enforce a greater recognition of the system's common goals which are congruent with some goals in each member firm. They have the ability to enforce, through economic sanction, a reward and penalty system within the interorganizational structure. They are thus able to design and administer joint-decision efforts and responsibilities in a manner that can lead to less conflict than would likely be the case without their intervention.[14]

Large retailers have unique overlapping attributes that may give them an edge in the struggle (if there is one) for channel control. First, by virtue of their close proximity to local markets, they have an opportunity to accumulate expert power by continuously assessing the needs of consumers within their communities. While other members of the channel could perform the same information-generating and uncertainty-absorbing tasks, they would undoubtedly have to expend more effort in data collection than large re-

---

[12]See Little, *op. cit.,* p. 33.

[13]Wholesalers can also be characterized as multilevel merchandisers when they sponsor voluntary groups.

[14]Little, *op. cit.,* p. 34.

tailers, simply because of the latter's locational advantage. Second, retail-directed MLM's have ready access to large markets that manufacturers are desirous of reaching. In effect, they are gatekeepers. The larger the markets that they serve, the more important they become to manufacturers, and thus the stronger their potential leadership becomes. Third, so long as MLM's can maintain alternative sources of supply, manufacturers will tend to be more dependent on them, especially in cases where a generic demand for a given product class has been established. Dickinson has observed that it is reasonable to assume that, under most conditions, the supplier has more to gain by selling to the retailer than the retailer has to gain by buying from the supplier.

> ... the manufacturers usually have (or think they will have) excess capacity ... , and when they operate at full capacity it is only for a small part of the year. This is even truer of wholesalers. For manufacturers and wholesalers, then, no sale nearly always means no profit. Retailers, on the other hand, are sitting on a scarce resource whether they make a particular purchase or not. That resource is shelf space, the battle for which is so fierce that some suppliers even pay to have space reserved for them. Moreover, if a particular supplier does not sell to a particular retailer, the loss to the retailer is only relative, since there is always another supplier with other goods for a particular unit of space. In fact, it may be no loss at all, since in retailing most products can be replaced without great loss of profit by the retailer.[15]

Interestingly, channel management is not always practiced by large retailers, even though they often have the necessary power to do so. Instead, they frequently seem more concerned with obtaining specific types of concessions than they do in exerting a strong influence over aspects of new product development, promotional and inventory policies of the entire channel, and the like.[16] As a result of their self-selected task of serving wide markets, the managers of MLM's concentrate the majority of their efforts on selecting and maintaining stocks and providing and merchandising the services that accompany them.[17] Therefore, two very important functions that might be considered within the domain of channel leaders—product development and demand stimulation—are, to a large extent, left unattended by large retailers. Even though the latter are, by dint of their closeness to and contact with ultimate consumers, in the best position of any channel members to discover exactly what the preferences of consumers are, they are

---

[15] Roger A. Dickinson, *Retail Management: A Channels Approach* (Belmont, California: Wadsworth Publishing Company, Inc. 1974), p. 37.

[16] Roger A. Dickinson, "Channel Management by Large Retailers," in Robert L. King, *op. cit.*, p. 128.

[17] Little, *op. cit.*, p. 35.

much too engrossed with the details of their own operations to consider performing these functions on a channelwide basis. Thus, by default, they frequently leave channel leadership to manufacturers.

Methods of Retailer Dominance

The large retailers or MLM's have at their disposal a variety of means by which they could secure dominance in their channels. As with manufacturers, the most prominent means is the building of a consumer franchise through advertising, sales promotion, and branding.[18] The strong patronage motives relative to shopping at stores like Dayton-Hudson, Filene's, Bullock's, Sears, Gold Circle, I. Magnin, and Safeway have been established as the result of the assembling of an assortment of merchandise appropriate to each store's target market, the adequate promotion of that assortment, and the provision of ancillary services. In other words, the successful retail operations have achieved positions of power within their markets through effective programming of the retailing mix elements, just as manufacturers have achieved success by combining the various elements of the marketing mix in unique ways.

In addition, many MLM's have generated private-label programs that reinforce or further the establishment of strong patronage motives. Although it is possible that some MLM's have probably overemphasized their private-label programs,[19] there can be little doubt that such programs can be a means for securing channel control.[20] However, as in wholesaling, retailers' brands are economically feasible only after widespread market acceptance of the product has been established.[21] On the other hand, if generic product acceptance exists, then the MLM not only can decide to enter the market with its own

---

[18]Mallen, *op. cit.*, p. 131.

[19]A & P distributes no fewer than 1500 varieties of private label grocery, dairy, bakery, and fish products that account for 15 percent of the chain's total sales. Its overemphasis on private labels has been one of the factors responsible for its decline over the past 25 years. See "Can Jonathan Scott Save A & P?" *Business Week* (May 19, 1975), p. 133. It is also likely that both Sears and Wards will be carrying more manufacturers' brands in the future in order to increase the potency of their assortments and to provide on-the-spot price comparisons for consumers between their privately branded products and manufacturers' brands.

[20]See Louis W. Stern, "The New World of Private Brands," *California Management Review*, Vol. 8 (Spring, 1966), pp. 43–50; Victor J. Cook and Thomas F. Schutte, *Brand Policy Determination* (Boston: Allyn and Bacon, 1967); Ray A. Goldberg, *Agribusiness Coordination* (Boston: Division of Research, Graduate School of Business Administration, Harvard University, 1968), pp. 181–184; and Victor J. Cook, "Private Brand Mismanagement by Misconception," *Business Horizons*, Vol. 11 (December, 1968), pp. 63–74. Weiss has argued that private brands will increase in importance over the next decade due to the growth of "giant" retailing and the advertising support that such retailers give to their private-label programs. See E. B. Weiss, "Advice to Suppliers: Private Labels Will Loom Large; Don't Hold Back," *Advertising Age*, August 4, 1975, p. 10.

[21]Little, *op. cit.*, p. 35.

brand, but it can decide which of the leading brands it will stock and thus be able to play off one supplier against another in order to achieve various concessions.[22]

In the absence of the development of a strong consumer franchise for their brands on the part of manufacturers, power is clearly weighted in favor of large-scale retailers in many of the channels where they are strong participants. As pointed out above, however, these retailers are not always willing to assume leadership roles, and therefore the task of marshalling the resources of the various channel systems falls to other parties. Given the prerequisites to the application of interorganization management that were specified earlier in this book, channelwide organization may be very difficult under these circumstances, because the units with the most power are often simply not willing to take an active part in specifying roles and managing conflict. It is likely, though, because of the power that they hold, that they retain veto power over attempts to reallocate resources throughout the channel.

Small Retailers as Channel Leaders

Even though small retailers, on an individual basis, generally lack sufficient power to assume leadership roles within their channels, dominance may accrue to them, as well as to larger retailers, because of the nature of the buying process itself. For example, the retailer becomes very powerful when a manufacturer selling through convenience outlets is unable to develop a brand image through advertising. In such situations, the manufacturer's ability to achieve product differentiation in the eyes of the consumer is severely limited. The manufacturer becomes highly dependent on retailers, because many outlets must stock the product in order for the former to achieve an efficient density of market coverage.[23] Furthermore, in situations where retail outlets provide significant sales assistance and the outlets are selectively rather than densely located, it is also possible to hypothesize that retailers, irrespective of size, will be dominant. As Porter points out:

> For products sold through nonconvenience outlets, the consumer considers the purchase relatively important and is willing to expend effort in shopping and comparing products.
>
> For products sold through nonconvenience outlets, the retailer is influential in the consumer's purchase decision. Although advertising can lead the consumer to consider a particular brand, it will not prevent him from considering other brands and

---

[22]*Ibid.*, p. 36.

[23]Porter, *op. cit.*, p. 423.

shopping several outlets. The retailer can negate the effect of advertising by changing the consumer's mind in the store.[24]

Thus, in the case of shopping goods, the retailer exerts considerable influence on the purchase decision of the consumer in several ways. First, the retailer controls or is a proxy for some of the attributes that the consumer may desire. The reputation, image, physical amenities, and attendant services (e.g., credit, billing, delivery, warranty, repair) of a retail store can sway consumer purchase decisions. Second, the retailer can influence the sale of products sold through nonconvenience outlets through the provision of information via a selling presentation, advice solicited by the consumer, the perceived expertise of the salesperson with respect to the product, or any combination of all of these.[25] In fact, as the retailer's influence on product differentiation increases, the bargaining power of the retail stage vis-à-vis the manufacturer or the wholesale supplier increases.

Collectively, small retailers have been known to exert considerable pressure on channel activities. They have been instrumental in gaining particularistic legislation on the local, state, and national levels that has had the effect of restraining competition or of providing impediments to change.[26] They have colluded to prevent marketing activities that they have perceived to be threatening to their survival. Through their legislative and collusive actions, they have sometimes been able to influence marketing strategy throughout the channel. Thus, there exist state and local restrictions on entry, licensing requirements, antipeddler and anti-itinerant vendor ordinances, chain store taxes, evening and Sunday closing laws, advertising restrictions (particularly price-posting regulations), as well as a whole host of other small retailer-inspired and -promoted laws that are designed to soften or curb competitive impacts.[27] Clearly, this form of negative leadership is not laudatory. It is fortunate that the effect of these impediments has been short-lived, in many situations, and that they have been unable to effectively restrain many innovations in distribution.

On the other hand, small retailers have attempted to exert positive channel leadership through the development of retailer-sponsored cooperatives. The retailer cooperative is an obvious effort to overcome the size and thus the buying disadvantages faced by individual small retailers. However, as in-

---

[24]*Ibid.*, p. 424.

[25]*Ibid.*, pp. 420–421.

[26]Stanley C. Hollander, *Restraints upon Retail Competition* (East Lansing, Michigan: Bureau of Business and Economic Research, Michigan State University) and Stanley C. Hollander, "Channel Management by Small Retailers," in Robert L. King (ed.), *op. cit.*, pp. 132–134.

[27]Hollander, "Channel Management by Small Retailers," *op. cit.*, p. 133.

dicated in the preceding chapter, retailer-sponsored cooperatives face some very serious problems. Within them, power is diffused, and therefore, there is considerable doubt whether they can provide the tightly knit control needed to compete successfully with corporate and voluntary chains. As Hollander points out,

> Membership turnover can be high. Coordination is difficult. Investment in manufacturing or processing facilities may be hazardous and inadvisable, since acceptance of the output may not be assured. Financing problems may inhibit growth, since the members may have little interest in financing newcomers, and particularly in helping potential competitors. Risk allocation difficulties tend to deter experimentation. Personality conflicts can exacerbate many of the cooperative's problems. None of these difficulties is entirely absent from the corporate chain sector, but quite obviously, their impact is substantially reduced when ownership, risk, and control are centralized.[28]

Evidence of the need for greater control is found in the fact that a significant number of the member supermarkets in the successful Wakefern-Shop Rite retail food cooperative located in New Jersey are owned by internal corporate chains, for example.

CHANNEL MANAGEMENT BY CARRIERS

Although not normally considered as potential managers of channel relations, common carriers could possibly assume such roles if they were to utilize more effectively the power bases at their disposal. In fact, logistical institutions of all types occupy unique positions in this respect, because they have the advantage of being *neutral* relative to many of the channel policies and activities of major concern to manufacturers, wholesalers, and retailers.[29] While the latter channel members may have difficulty in looking beyond their immediate suppliers and customers, logistical institutions can take a broader perspective of channel problems.

Consideration of common carriers as channel leaders serves to focus attention on a salient characteristic of all channel relations. That is, leadership is possible with regard to each of the marketing flows taken separately or to all of the flows. Thus, it is clear that common carriers can assume an interorganizational management stance relative to the flow of physical posses-

[28] *Ibid.*, p. 135.

[29] J. L. Heskett, "Costing and Coordinating External and Internal Logistics Activities," in Donald J. Bowersox, Bernard J. LaLonde, and Edward W. Smykay (eds.), *Readings in Physical Distribution Management* (New York: The Macmillan Company, 1969), pp. 81–83.

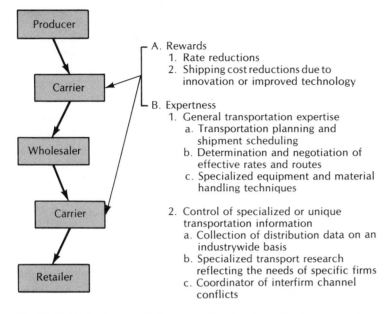

A. Rewards
   1. Rate reductions
   2. Shipping cost reductions due to innovation or improved technology

B. Expertness
   1. General transportation expertise
      a. Transportation planning and shipment scheduling
      b. Determination and negotiation of effective rates and routes
      c. Specialized equipment and material handling techniques

   2. Control of specialized or unique transportation information
      a. Collection of distribution data on an industrywide basis
      b. Specialized transport research reflecting the needs of specific firms
      c. Coordinator of interfirm channel conflicts

FIGURE 11-1   Range of Common Carrier Contributions to Other Channel Members

SOURCE: Frederick J. Beier, "The Role of the Common Carrier in the Channel of Distribution," *Transportation Journal*, Vol. 9 (Winter, 1969), p. 19.

sion, but their influence relative to the remaining flows is likely to be minimal. In other words, the scope of a common carrier's power is limited to those activities with which it is directly concerned.

Figure 11-1 illustrates the position occupied by common carriers within a generalized channel arrangement and some of the power bases that are available to them.[30] Some specific examples of the reward and expert power bases that could be, and sometimes are, used by common carriers have been enumerated by Beier.[31] These include:

> Reductions in rates charged to shippers. (However, because of competitive reaction, such reductions are likely to have limited impact over the long run.)

[30] For an extended example, see J. L. Heskett, "Interorganizational Problem Solving in a Channel of Distribution," in Matthew Tuite, Roger Chisholm, and Michael Radnor (eds.) *Interorganizational Decision Making* (Chicago: Aldine Publishing Co., 1972), pp. 152–161. See also J. L. Heskett and Ronald H. Ballou, "Logistical Planning in Inter-Organization Systems," in M. P. Hottenstein and R. W. Millman (eds.), *Research Toward the Development of Management Thought*, Papers and Proceedings of the 26th Annual Meeting of the Academy of Management, San Francisco, December 27–29, 1966, pp. 124–136.

[31] Frederick J. Beier, "The Role of the Common Carrier in the Channel of Distribution," *Transportation Journal*, Vol. 9 (Winter, 1969), pp. 12–21.

Reductions in the overall cost of transportation by eliminating loss and damage claims, special schedules, and/or minimum weight requirements.

Providing special arrangements such as rent-a-train services whereby carriers rent specialized equipment designed to serve particular clients. The provision of specialized equipment increases the dependence of shippers on carriers.

Providing consulting services to shippers whereby staff specialists assigned to a particular industry advise shippers in that industry about rates, routing, and LTL and LCL loading-in-transit privileges. Traditionally, carriers have acted as advisors relative to plant locations in their operating areas.

Making available part of a carrier's large computing facilities in order to institute a channelwide communication system relative to information about shipments. (Carriers are in a position to draw sample data with regard to product movements from a broader population than is generally available to individual shippers. Thus, they could operate as uncertainty absorbers within the channel).

Providing information with regard to the transportation and material-handling requirements of other channel members. (Carriers can thereby suggest compatible handling systems that would lead to more efficient coordination of the physical and information interface between channel members).

WHO SHOULD LEAD THE CHANNEL?

Although the question as to which institution or agency should lead the channel has been debated in the literature for many years and by a variety of scholars,[32] there exists no single satisfactory answer. The fact is that the answer demands empirical evidence from *specific* settings. It is necessary to look closely at the issues involved in each industrial setting and to define the scope of power of each commercial channel member with respect to each of the marketing flows. It may even be necessary to break the flows down into component parts in order to perform an adequate analysis. For example, the flow of physical possession incorporates both transportation and storage of merchandise. One channel member may be able to exert more influence with regard to the first component, while another may have more power with respect to the second. Clearly, the analysis—based on empirical findings—must

[32]For a variety of different arguments and perspectives, see the following: David Craig and Werner Gabler, "The Competitive Struggle for Market Control," *The Annals of the American Academy of Political and Social Science* (May, 1940), pp. 84 ff. (reprinted in Howard J. Westing, ed., *Readings in Marketing* (Englewood Cliffs, N.J.: Prentice-Hall, Inc., 1953, pp. 84–107); John K. Galbraith, *American Capitalism*, rev. ed. (Boston: Houghton Mifflin Co., 1956), pp. 110–114, 117–123; Bruce Mallen, *op. cit.*, pp. 127–134; Robert W. Little, *op. cit.*, pp. 31–38; Richard B. Heflebower, "Mass Distribution: A Phase of Bilateral Oligopoly or of Competition?" *American Economic Review,* Vol. 47 (May, 1957), pp. 274–285; Valentine F. Ridgway, "Administration of Manufacturer-Dealer Systems," *Administrative Science Quarterly,* Vol. 1 (March, 1957), pp. 464–483; and Louis P. Bucklin, "A Theory of Channel Control," *Journal of Marketing*, Vol. 37 (January, 1973), pp. 39–47. These authors present various anecdotal evidence and/or analytical models for arrving at particular choices.

account for the tolerance levels in the channel for control by each of the members as well as the payoffs that accrue to each as a result of control.[33] Anecdoctal evidence can be accumulated that leads an individual to suspect that one particular institution is the most logical leader in a particular situation, but such evidence rarely permits the generation of counter-intuitive findings. In such an important area as this—where concern is over the allocation of resources throughout an entire distributive system—opinions and hearsay are not satisfactory in making the appropriate selection. Furthermore, allowance must be made for the influence of elements in a commercial channel's task environment (e.g., consumers and government) in determining or constraining the leadership question. With the emergence of consumerism as a vital force in marketing relations and with the increased interest in distribution matters on the part of government, it would be foolhardy to think that the decision on leadership (or even the use of interorganization management techniques generally) will be free from scrutiny or limitations. It should, however, be clear from the discussion in this chapter that each commercial channel member has at least the potential for leadership with regard to one or more of the marketing flows, because each has amassed or is capable of amassing power of one form or another relative to other channel members. The ultimate answer as to who should lead must, however, be left to an empirical analysis of power and the relevant payoffs from its use on a case-by-case basis.

A Methodology for Determining the Locus of Channel Power

Some tentative steps have been taken towards developing a methodology that permits a determination of the locus of power within specific marketing channels. The approach reported below was first employed by the authors of this text[34] and has been subsequently applied, in modified forms, by Hunt and Nevin,[35] by Etgar, and by Wilkinson.[36]

[33] Adel I. El-Ansary and Robert A. Robicheaux, "A Theory of Channel Control: Revisited," *Journal of Marketing,* Vol. 38 (January, 1974), pp. 4–7.

[34] Adel I. El-Ansary and Louis W. Stern, "Power Measurement in the Distribution Channel," *Journal of Marketing Research,* Vol. 9 (February, 1972), pp. 47–52.

[35] Shelby D. Hunt and John R. Nevin, "Power in a Channel of Distribution: Sources and Consequences," *Journal of Marketing Research,* Vol. 11 (May, 1974), pp. 186–193.

[36] Michael Etgar, *An Empirical Analysis of the Motivations for the Development of Centrally Coordinated Vertical Marketing Systems: The Case of the Property and Casualty Insurance Company,* an unpublished Ph.D. dissertation, University of California at Berkeley, 1974. See also Ian Wilkinson, "Power in Distribution Channels," Cranfield [England] Research Papers in Marketing and Logistics, Session 1973–1974.

For purposes of research on isolating potential or actual leaders of channels, the power of a channel member can be operationally defined as the
member's ability to control the decision variables in the marketing strategy
of another member in a given channel at a different level of distribution. For
this control to qualify as a power, it should be different from the influenced
member's original level of control over his own marketing strategy.

As indicated in Chapter 7, power can be viewed as a function of dependence. The power of a wholesaler over a retailer, for example, is related to
the dependence of the retailer on the wholesaler. In addition, the magnitude
of a power source can be employed as an index of influence. For example, a
manufacturer who advertises directly to consumers maintains an influence
base or power source relative to retailers who distribute his brand. A measure
of the magnitude of advertising and the resulting consumer preference might
be used as an index of the manufacturer's power over his retailers. Thus, the
power of any given channel member is a function of the sources of power
available to him at any given time. As explained previously, the sources or
bases of power can be classified as reward, coercive, expert, referent, and
legitimate. Based on this reasoning, a fundamental model underlying research
into power relationships within a given marketing channel may be depicted
by the equations listed in Table 11–1.

Measures of power, dependence, and sources of power can be developed
from gauging the self-perceptions of various channel members and attributions about them by other channel members.[37] A questionnaire can be
constructed that probes self-perceptions and attributions of each channel
member with respect to (1) control over marketing strategy variables, (2)
the relative importance of each of the various marketing strategy variables,
(3) the extent of dependency, and (4) sources of power.[38] For example, the
marketing strategy variables can relate to such elements as inventory policy,
order size, pricing, sales promotion, cooperative advertising, distribution
policies (e.g., selective versus intensive), delivery, credit, quality of installation work, salesmen's training, sales meetings, service schools, and participation in the activities of professional associations. A raw power score can be
obtained by summing the power scores of the strategy variables for each
channel member. Next, each channel member can be asked to specify the
relative importance of each marketing strategy variable in his total marketing

[37]Support for such an approach can be found in El-Ansary and Stern, *op. cit.*, p. 48. For an extension of the self-perception, attribution approach, see Fuat A. Firat, Alice M. Tybout, and Louis W.
Stern, "A Perspective on Conflict and Power in Distribution," in Ronald C. Curhan (ed.), *1974 Combined Proceedings* (Chicago, III.: American Marketing Association, 1975), pp. 436–438.

[38]A five-point Likert-type scale can be used as a measuring tool. The five points of the scale could
be "nonexistent or of no importance," "of insignificant importance," "of some importance," "of
significant importance," and "of very significant importance." See El-Ansary and Stern, *op. cit.*,
p. 49.

TABLE 11-1   A Model of Power Relationships in Marketing Channels[a]

Power of channel member i over member j	Power of channel member i over all other members, n
(1) $P_{ij} = C_{ij}$	$P_i = \sum_{j=1}^{n} C_{ij}$
(2) $P_{ij} = f(D_{ij})$	$P_i = f\left(\sum_{j=1}^{n} D_{ij}\right)$
$P_{ij} = \alpha D_{ij}$	$P_i = \sum_{j=1}^{n} \alpha D_{ij}$
(3) $P_{ij} = f(S_{ij})$	$P_i = f\left(\sum_{j=1}^{n} S_{ij}\right)$
$P_{ij} = \beta S_{ij}$	$P_i = \sum_{j=1}^{n} \beta S_{ij}$
(4) $P_{ij} = f(D_{ij}, S_{ij})$	$P_i = f\left(\sum_{j=1}^{n} D_{ij}, \sum_{j=1}^{n} S_{ij}\right)$
$P_{ij} = \alpha D_{ij} + \beta S_{ij}$	$P_i = \sum_{j=1}^{n} \alpha D_{ij} + \sum_{j=1}^{n} \beta S_{ij}$

where:

P_{ij} = power of channel member i over member j.

C_{ij} = control of i over the decision variables in the marketing strategy of j.

P_i = power of i over all other members with whom i is vertically linked.

D_{ij} = dependence of i on j.

α = direction coefficient of dependence[b]: if $D_{ij} > 0, \alpha = -1$; if $D_{ij} < 0, \alpha = +1$.

S_{ij} = sources of power held by i relative to j.

β = direction coefficient of power sources: if $S_{ij} > 0, \beta = +1$; if $S_{ij} < 0, \beta = -1$.

[a]Although the model is stated in static terms, some implicit notion of history (past relations) should be read into it.
[b]D_{ij} is undefined at zero; if $D_{ij} = 0$, no channel relationship exists.

SOURCE: Adel I. El-Ansary and Louis W. Stern, "Power Measurement in the Distribution Channel," *Journal of Marketing Research*, Vol. 9 (February, 1972), p. 48.

strategy. A weighted power score can be generated by multiplying the basic information on control over marketing strategy variables (the raw power score) by the weight of relative importance given to each variable and then summing the weighted power scores for each channel member.

Dependency can be viewed as a function of (1) the percentage of a channel member's business which he contracts with another member and the size of the contribution which that business makes to his profits; (2) the commitment of a channel member to another member in terms of the relative importance of the latter's marketing policies to him; and (3) the difficulty in effort and cost faced by a channel member in attempting to replace another member as a source of supply or as a customer. A dependence score can be obtained by summing the scores of the various dependency issues for each member.

Finally, sources of power could include such factors as customer preference, completeness of line, financial and business advice, sharing advertising expenditures, product sales meetings, service schools, salesmen's training, image and reputation in the community, prompt delivery and service, access to market information, selective distribution, promotion programs, large lot buying, ability to buy directly, ability to control customer's brand choice, middleman brand support, and competitive pricing. A sources-of-power score can then be obtained by summing the scores of the various sources for each channel member.

In sum, for every channel member four basic scores can be obtained: (1) a (raw) power score, (2) a weighted power score, (3) a dependence score, and (4) a sources-of-power score. If a power structure exists within a channel, there should be a significant, *positive* correlation between self-perceptions of power (i.e., control over marketing strategy variables) and attributions of power. Likewise, the means of perceptions and attributions should be highly similar. There should also be a significant, *negative* correlation between a channel member's self-perceived power over another member and the latter's perception of the former's dependence on him as well as between attributed power and self-perceived dependence. Finally, if a well-defined power structure exists, there should be a significant *positive* relationship between a channel member's self-perceived power over another channel member and the sources of power attributed to the former by the latter. In addition, a similar relationship should be found between the power that one member attributes to another and the sources of power that the latter perceives himself as possessing.

SUMMARY AND CONCLUSIONS

This chapter has focused on the potential of manufacturers, wholesalers, retailers, and common carriers to assume the role of channel managers or leaders. In coming to grips with this issue, a crucial consideration is the amount and kinds of power available to each institution.

The potential channel management role of manufacturers appears to hinge on the strength of their products, brands, and services as viewed by ultimate consumers, both on the household and industrial levels. In other words, their power relative to other channel members is derived primarily from the final marketplace. The traditional manufacturer-directed channel concept is based on the belief that because the manufacturer creates and produces the product and designs the network through which it passes on its way to consumers, he is entitled to impose his marketing policies on other channel members and to direct the activities of the channel.

From a historical perspective, wholesalers have been able to remain in dominant positions only in those industries where the buyers and producers are small in size, large in number, relatively scattered geographically, and where manufacturers are financially weak and lack marketing expertise. Wholesalers have, however, been particularly successful in strengthening their positions by organizing voluntary groups and franchising systems as well as by developing private label programs and interorganizational data systems.

The potential of large (multilevel) retailers as channel leaders appears to stem from their close physical proximity to consumers, their roles as gatekeepers relative to market access, and their maintenance of alternative sources of supply. Their continuous control over display space within their outlets, the development of strong patronage motives, and their use of private-label programs have enhanced their power considerably.

Small retailers have, collectively, been able to assume leadership in the channel—but primarily from a negative perspective. Through collusion, they have been able to secure particularistic legislation, which has restrained competition and impeded change. The most positive step they have taken has been the formation of cooperatives.

Common carriers could possibly assume a greater role in channel leadership if they were to utilize more effectively the reward and expert power at their disposal. Their influence would, however, generally be limited to activities involved in the flow of physical possession, even if they were to become more aggressive within the channels in which they participate.

The question as to who should lead the channel cannot be answered without an in-depth empirical analysis of channels on a case-by-case basis. Because each and every institution has at least some power relative to the various marketing flows, leadership may take the form of control over or management of only one or a few of the flows, depending of course on the scope of power enjoyed by the various institutions comprising a given system. Furthermore, leadership will clearly be constrained by consumerism issues and by the increased interest of antitrust enforcement and regulatory agencies (particularly the Consumer Protection Agency and the Federal Trade Commission) in distribution practices.

Power relationships within the channel can be measured by gauging the perceptions and attributions of individual channel members through the use of survey research techniques. Such measurements might focus on the relationship between perceptions and attributions of power (i.e., control over marketing strategy variables), the relationship between power and dependence, and the relationship between power and sources of power.

If channel management is going to be instituted, it will be necessary for appropriate information and communication systems to be established. Such systems are particularly crucial if a variety of institutions take a role in channel leadership. The dovetailing of decision-making must form an essential part of the overall channel management job; otherwise, suboptimization of the marketing flows can be expected. The marketing flows, taken as a whole, comprise a system; they must be combined in such a way as to permit strong impact of the channel on its environment. This combination can only be achieved through the sharing of relevant data among channel members. Therefore, the next chapter is concerned with the development of effective communication within channels.

DISCUSSION QUESTIONS

1. How do you account for the persistence and survival of some distribution channels without a channel leader, captain, or manager? Does a channel have to have a leader in order to survive over the long term?

2. What are the consequences of increased "scrambled merchandising" for power and leadership in the channel? How will such product line diversification on the retail level affect the positions of manufacturers, wholesalers, and retailers relative to their potential for channel leadership?

3. If, within the channels in which it participates, a major department store chain is the most powerful member, what might the chain do to gain increased coordination and cooperation throughout each of the channels serving it?

4. It has been stated by one writer, "The more a retailer can concentrate his purchasing, the more dominating he can become; the more he spreads his purchasing, the more dominated he becomes." Do you agree?

5. Do private brands come into being as a result of a conflict situation between manufacturers and middlemen? Describe the issues and factors surrounding a decision to market private brands on the part of both manufacturers and middlemen.

6. In those cases where the absolute number of retail buyers for a manufacturing industry's product are small and the size of these retailers is large, it has been argued that

retailer power flows conventionally from buyer concentration. Explain what this statement means, from the perspective of power, dependence, and sources of power.

7. An important structural characteristic of retailing is the presence or absence of multiple forms of retailers selling a given industry's product (e.g., drugstores and supermarkets). Explain the consequences of this structural characteristic for channel management.

8. It has been stated that "as the retail outlet (establishment) becomes more specialized and carries fewer product categories, its power to influence the sale will generally increase." Give examples that support this statement. Then give examples that would support the reverse of this statement.

9. In general, which type of institution—manufacturer, wholesaler, or retailer—should lead the channel of distribution for the following products:

Toys

Automobiles

Stainless steel

Health and beauty aids

What assumptions did you have to make in order to arrive at an answer for each product category? What were the relevant variables you considered in each case?

10. In view of the emphasis on consumerism issues, do you think that the consumer will eventually be the channel leader in many consumer goods industries? If yes, which industries? How will the leadership be made manifest?

TWELVE

CHANNEL COMMUNICATIONS AND INFORMATION SYSTEMS

Irrespective of whether particular institutions or agencies assume leadership roles with respect to specific marketing flows within distribution channels, communication of one form or another provides the means by which the work of channels is coordinated. However, as indicated briefly at the close of Chapter 7, omission and distortion of message contents are frequent occurrences within channels. In fact, inadequate communication or miscommunication is often a major stimulator as well as an outcome of deep-rooted and dysfunctional channel conflict.

In this chapter, attention is focused directly on problems arising from lack of effective communication within channels and on suggestions for developing and improving information systems. At the outset, however, it should be understood that the operation of a channel communication system is frequently limited by the legality, availability, cost, and confidentiality of the information flow. Furthermore, any attempt to achieve a distortion-free communication system is doomed to failure, because manufacturing, wholesaling, retailing, and logistical firms are obviously comprised of individual human beings who will always continue to perceive situations in different ways. Nevertheless, construction even of a moderately successful system seems mandatory, because, as Gross points out:

> Cross-purpose activities, redundant operations, blunted impact of uncoordinated promotional activities, (reseller) resentment when not invited to participate in

available promotional allowances and aids, unbalanced inventories, and other difficulties that are the outcome of poor communication procedures are burdensome and expensive.[1]

The difficulty in securing adequate communication in channels generally centers around a wide variety of structural and activity issues. In the first section of this chapter, we shall deal with problems arising because of the length of channels as well as with difficulties associated with determining inventory levels, transportation modes and storage facilities, promotional programs, product designs, and prices. In the second section, discussion focuses on a specific accounting method that permits a significant start towards developing interorganizational information systems—distribution cost analysis.

COMMUNICATIONS PROBLEMS AND POSSIBLE SOLUTIONS

The Length of Channels

Clearly, the longer a channel—the more middlemen involved in the distribution of a given product, brand, or service—the more likelihood there is for omission and distortion of message contents to take place, all other things being equal. The number of links in a communication network is inversely related to accurate reception.[2] Perceptual and secrecy problems are compounded as more and more channel members become involved in the uncertainty absorption process. Consider, for example, the case of a pharmacist for a large public hospital who complained to the president of a drug wholesaling firm that manufacturers did not keep him well informed about their new products. He wanted to know why he was not detailed regularly and promptly on new ethicals (prescription drugs) as they were developed and why the manufacturers did not provide him with printed materials. As explained by Cox, Schutte, and Few:

The wholesaler agreed that the manufacturers were "falling down on their job," but when he interviewed detail men for several manufacturers, he found that they, too,

---

[1] Walter Gross, "Profitable Listening for Manufacturers and Dealers: How to Use a Communication System," in William G. Moller, Jr. and David L. Wilemon (eds.), *Marketing Channels: A Systems Viewpoint* (Homewood, Ill.: Richard D. Irwin, Inc., 1971), p. 351.

[2] See, for example, Alex Bavelas, "Communication Patterns in Task-oriented Groups," *Journal of the Acoustical Society of America*, Vol. 22 (1950), pp. 725-730; and Harold Guetzkow and Herbert Simon, "The Impact of Certain Communication Nets upon Organization and Performance in Task-oriented Groups," *Management Science*, Vol. 1 (April-July, 1955), pp. 233-250.

were frustrated. They had more than adequate information to give out—written and oral. To them, the pharmacist himself was the villain. They were fed up with waiting as much as four hours to conduct a detail call. "That pharmacist thinks he is God," one salesman said. "He couldn't care less about how long he makes the salesman wait." The wholesaler took the initiative, told the pharmacist what the real problem was, and made appointments for him to see the detail men at given hours.

But note that it is the manufacturer's communication line that has broken down, not the wholesaler's. The manufacturer has depended upon detail men to tell the potential pharmacist buyer about his products, which could then be sold and delivered by wholesalers to the buyer. The wholesaler's responsibility in communication was only to tell prospective buyers that they had the manufacturer's products available. Obviously, the manufacturer's feedback was inadequate in that it took a wholesaler to straighten out the manufacturer's communication problem.[3]

Thus, as Cox, Schutte, and Few imply, the longer the channel, the more highly developed the feedback system available to each channel member and especially to the channel leader must be. Furthermore, in such situations, there is obviously a need for a mechanism permitting the bypassing of messages. That is, a working information system should have been established that permitted the directly affected and conflicting parties to avoid one or more links in the normal communication network so that such a bottleneck situation could have been eliminated, especially during the period of crisis within the system.[4]

Reliance on indirect communication links frequently multiplies chances for distortion.[5] This problem is exemplified by the case of a leading manufacturer of electronic products who had received *indirect* complaints about his order-filling service. From these complaints, certain key executives con-

---

[3]Reavis Cox, Thomas F. Schutte, and Kendrick S. Few, "Towards the Measurement of Trade Channel Perception," in Fred C. Allvine (ed.), *Combined Proceedings 1971 Spring and Fall Conferences* (Chicago: American Marketing Association, 1972), pp. 190–191.

[4]Discussion of the various communication noise-reduction mechanisms throughout this chapter and in Chapter 7 is largely based on John R. Grabner, Jr. and L. J. Rosenberg, "Communication in Distribution Channel Systems," in Louis W. Stern (ed.), *Distribution Channels: Behavioral Dimensions* (Boston, Mass.: Houghton Mifflin Co., 1969), pp. 238–249.

[5]Technological advances are significant in reducing the need for indirect communication. The development of electronic funds transfer systems (EFTS) in the banking industry is an example of the substitution of direct for indirect communication links. Banks and savings and loan associations are placing electronic terminals in supermarkets, making it possible for customers to pay for their groceries via a transfer of funds from their accounts to that of the store. In these situations, the supermarket becomes the financial and operational medium between the customer and the bank. The supermarket does not, however, become a financial institution, according to some, because the terminal is only a means of communication; the actual transfer of funds takes place inside the bank's computer, which is, of course, located inside the bank and not at the supermarket. The consequences of such a development could be profound, especially for the banking industry. See "Bank Cards Take Over the Country," *Business Week*, August 4, 1975, pp. 44–54. See also Robert M. Lilienfeld and Diane Wolgemuth, *Consumer Reactions Toward an Electronic Funds Transfer System in Supermarkets* (Chicago: Super Market Institute, Inc., 1975).

cluded that most of the customers were dissatisfied because of the length of time elapsing between the sending of an order and the receipt of goods. The executives laid detailed plans to remedy this "perceived" problem, and included among them was a plan to establish an elaborate system of regional warehouses. Shortly before instituting these plans, the president of the company suggested gathering some additional information directly from customers. The results of a preliminary field survey that was conducted at his request indicated that the original information was completely erroneous— that most of the company's customers were highly satisfied with the service they were receiving. While the customers indicated that shorter turnaround time would be welcomed, they were impressed with the consistency of the manufacturer's service. That is, they said they could count on the receipt of goods from the company a specified number of days after orders had been placed and that such consistency was extremely important to them.[6] Thus, in this situation, the company in question was saved from making a considerable investment in both time and money. Future problems of this sort, however, could be eliminated or mitigated only by assuring adequate feedback from the field, by instituting bypassing mechanisms (in the form of manufacturer-directed periodic field surveys), and by assuring repetition of messages that bear such heavy consequences for the firm's operations.

Inventory Problems

As was clearly witnessed during the recession of 1974-1976, problems with inventory can pose tremendous difficulties for all members of a marketing channel. In fact, the poor profit performance of both Sears and Penney's during the recession can be directly traced to problems of inventory management and control, which led to the steep markdowns that were taken by both firms to reduce excessive stocks of merchandise.[7] Inventory management is a channelwide problem and demands channelwide communication. As Gross has observed:

> ... the manufacturers, wholesalers, and retailers can control physical stock problems better when each knows about changes in the quantity and the location of the others' inventory. To be complete, ... physical inventory should cover more than the number of units located at premises owned by manufacturers or resellers. It is equally important to know how much merchandise is stored in public warehouses,

[6] This example was drawn from Cox, Schutte, and Few, *op. cit.,* p. 191.

[7] The consequences of Sears' and Penney's 1974 inventory problems are documented in Alvin Nagelberg, "Retailers Eye Very Merry Christmas," *Chicago Tribune,* Section 2 (May 25, 1975), p. 11 and in "Why Sears' Profits Tumbled," *Business Week,* April 21, 1975, pp. 32-33.

how much is in transit, and what is on display in wholesale showrooms and on retail sales floors.[8]

Not only will such information aid the manufacturer's production scheduling, but it will also have a direct impact on a retailer's or wholesaler's buying plans, because the latter will be able to anticipate the length of order lead times. For example, one furniture manufacturer's study revealed that his shipments were uncoordinated with dealers' needs—some merchandise was shipped out too late to prevent out-of-stock situations, and other items were delivered before the dealers expected them, causing unanticipated handling problems. The situation came to a head when one retailer dropped the manufacturer's line after concluding that the inventory and warehousing problems associated with it generated costs that more than offset the advantages of the line.[9]

As the example above indicates, inventory problems are intimately tied to ordering, shipping, and delivery difficulties. The first step in eradicating the problems causing inventory mismanagement is the development of an *intra*organizational information system. Without doubt, the greatest aid to the management of inventories has been the introduction and adaptation of programs associated with the use of high-speed electronic data processing equipment. By utilizing such programs, manufacturers can systematize their production, shipping, and delivery operations, and middlemen can maintain up-to-date inventory records. Computerized inventory information systems can lead to greater inventory turnover, reduction in freight costs, better buying decisions, rapid assessment of physical inventory, availability of disaggregated sales data, and reduction in clerical costs.

As indicated in Chapter 4 in the discussion of inventory policy, International Business Machines Corporation has been at the forefront in the development of inventory management and control techniques tailored to each level in the marketing channel. Through its IMPACT system,[10] the company has been able to formulate advanced methodologies to solve basic inventory problems.

In IMPACT, two types of models are of major concern: a forecast model and an order model.[11] As discussed in Chapter 4, the *forecast* model identifies the essential and underlying pattern of demand for an item. The IM-

---

[8]Gross, *op. cit.*, p. 344.

[9]This example was drawn from Gross, *op. cit.*, p. 341.

[10]IMPACT stands for Inventory Management Program and Control Techniques.

[11]These models are described in detail in *Wholesale IMPACT—Advanced Principles and Implementation Reference Manual*, 2nd ed. (White Plains, N.Y.: IBM Corporation Technical Publications Department, May, 1969).

PACT Computer Program Library classifies demand patterns in terms of three models: horizontal (which represents demand as centering around an average value, with variations which can be attributed only to random causes and which cannot be expected to occur in any consistent pattern), trend (which represents demand as consistently increasing or decreasing with the passage of time), and seasonal (which represents demand as having high and low periods that recur as a function of time). The program recommends whichever model yields the minimum forecast error. However, the IMPACT forecast model suffers from the same problems as many other forecasting models in that it cannot anticipate the effect of short-term influences on demand, such as the promotion of an item through additional, short-run sales effort, advertising, or special prices. Furthermore, it does not solve the difficult problems associated with forecasting the demand for new items, fads, style goods, etc.

To overcome some of these limitations, IBM has developed the Retail IMPACT fashion system.[12] Retail IMPACT detects fast- or slow-moving styles rapidly and recommends to the retail buyer that they be reordered, returned, marked down, or, in the case of chain operations, transferred to another store. The criteria upon which Retail IMPACT bases its selection are designed to yield maximum return per dollar invested in inventory by providing (1) the maximum oportunity for reordering profitable styles and (2) the ability to eliminate unprofitable merchandise rapidly.[13] It should be remembered from the discussion in Chapter 4, however, that in inventory management and control, the sales forecast is crucial in providing the basis for future order quantities. With fashion goods, where styles change rapidly, the forecast depends greatly on subjective human judgment. Thus, even with compensating features programmed into the model, it is still possible for a retailer's inventory to become quickly out of line, requiring manual readjustment, revised forecasting, and reprogramming. Also, unexpected longer or shorter seasons, fads on which individual initiative must be taken, and fluctuations in the large number of other variables a retail manager must "manage" relegate fashion models to the category of decision aids. They are certainly not a panacea to achieving optimum turnover with minimum stock-outs.

The *order* models used in IMPACT are concerned mainly with identify-

[12]For a complete description of the Retail IMPACT fashion system, as well as an IMPACT system for stable merchandise, see *Retail IMPACT—Inventory Management Program and Control Techniques Application Description*, 6th ed. (White Plains, N.Y.: IBM Technical Publications Department, March, 1970).

[13]Sears has recently installed in its larger stores a computerized inventory system (called RIM—Retail Inventory Management) which is similar to the Retail IMPACT fashion system, but which also includes features found in the order model.

ing the relevant costs incurred by ordering decisions so that management can determine when to buy (using the forecasts developed by IBM's forecasting system referred to above) and how much to buy. The IMPACT Computer Program Library provides the means of analyzing, for each vendor, various alternative order models that take all pertinent factors into account [e.g., economic lot size (EOQ) adjusted for the availability of quantity discounts and desired safety stock], and of selecting the best of the alternatives based on the criterion of lowest total cost.[14] An example of the application of the IMPACT information system is provided in Exhibit 12-1.

Many retailing organizations use computerized inventory control and management systems to establish automatic reorder procedures. Although originally developed by manufacturers, such procedures are increasingly being employed by retailers to control their basic stocks. Some shoe chains, for example, have set up carefully determined basic stocks for each store and control each store's inventory on a central basis. A card placed in each shoe box is removed when a sale is made, and the cards representing a day's sales are returned to the main office. Each store's stock is then automatically replenished on the basis of the store's sales and the individual item's reorder point. Similar procedures are used by variety stores. Department stores also use automatic replenishment procedures for such merchandise as men's shirts, sheets and pillow cases, women's hosiery, etc. Both the shipping of merchandise from the warehouse and the reordering of merchandise are controlled automatically. By maintaining a vendor name and address card file, the store can use the system to generate purchase orders automatically.

As reported by manufacturers, wholesalers, and retailers, computerized automatic reorder systems have resulted in the following benefits:[15]

1. Retailers' sales have increased as a result of having the right quantities of the right stock on their shelves, fewer stockouts, faster turnover, and rapid service from the manufacturer or wholesaler.

2. Simplified reordering saves time and work for retail store personnel.

3. Errors in orders and shipments are greatly reduced.

4. Changes in colors, styles, and models can be handled quickly, with minimum confusion to the retailer.

5. Production planning and control, billing, shipping, and accounts receivable are simplified and stabilized for the manufacturer.

6. Periodic order analyses are easily obtained.

[14]See *Wholesale IMPACT . . . , op. cit.,* pp. 64–75.

[15]*Guide to Inventory and Material Accounting* (White Plains, N.Y.: IBM Technical Publications Department, September, 1969), p. 31.

**EXHIBIT 12-1   The Application of IMPACT
to Ralphs Grocery Company**

INTRODUCTION

Ralphs Grocery Company is a prominent chain grocery with 47 stores serving the Los Angeles area. Facilities include grocery, frozen food, produce, and meat warehouses, in addition to private creamery, bakery, and delicatessen kitchen operations. The stores are within a 30-mile radius of these facilities and are serviced five days a week. All stores operate seven days a week.

The scope of the IMPACT project at Ralphs is the control of the approximately 8000 items carried by the grocery and frozen food warehouses. The operational descriptions in the paragraphs below pertain to the handling of these lines.

Store stock is surveyed daily (Saturday through Thursday), and orders are written for those items requiring replenishment. Orders are submitted on mark-sense cards, using specially prepared order books to facilitate the ordering process. Order books are organized basically by location of the items in the store; therefore, each book contains a portion of the line. Stores follow a prescribed order book schedule so that all stores do the bulk of their ordering from the same book on any particular day. This procedure simplifies ordering and warehouse picking. However, the stores are allowed to deviate from this procedure as required.

Orders are picked up by messenger service and are delivered to the main office for data processing, which updates inventory balances and prepares shipping manifests for the warehouse and invoices for the stores (copies of same form). Order quantities not available in stock are accumulated by item, extended by unit cost, and summarized by buyer in a Daily Unfilled Order report.

The shipping manifests are sent to the warehouse for selection and shipment to the stores. Whenever the quantity of an item available in the warehouse is less than is shown on the manifest, the smaller quantity is shipped and an adjustment is processed to correct the billing to the store and adjust the inventory file.

The entire cycle—comprised of ordering, updating of file, and shipment—covers a time span of less than a day. Orders submitted on a given day are delivered the morning of the following day.

Replenishment orders for warehouse stock are placed by a group of eight buyers located at the main office. Each buyer is responsible for the selection, sales, evaluation, and maintenance of a specific portion of the line. The line is divided categorically by type of product—for example, grocery, nonfood, frozen food, etc. Consequently, each buyer deals primarily with a "type-of-product" line. In general, buyer reviews are cycled on a two-week schedule, with the buyer reviewing approximately 10% of his line daily. Order quantities are marked on punched cards which accompany the buyer report. The specified quantities are keypunched and are processed through the IBM 1401 system which prepares the purchase orders.

EXHIBIT 12-1 continued

OBJECTIVES OF IMPACT

The role of the IMPACT system varies with the desires and needs of each company. Great flexibility is possible in the functions of the operational system, as well as in the responsibilities of the staff that controls and maintains the IMPACT system. Some very important questions must be answered as early as possible. For example:

- For what functions of the overall inventory-control and order-placing processes should the IMPACT system be responsible?

- Where in the company organization will IMPACT (and primarily the IMPACT staff) be positioned?

Once these basic management decisions are made, the objectives of the inventory system can be defined.

The early definition of objectives at Ralphs was complicated by uncertainty about what IMPACT would do. The primary purpose was to find a generalized approach to a computer-controlled inventory system. Only when this approach had been determined was it possible to set proper objectives for the second phase of the project, installation of IMPACT at Ralphs.

The IMPACT system at Ralphs is expected to:

- Control inventory at an economical level

- Maintain a specified high degree of service

- Act as a tool to help the buyers make most effective utilization of their time and experience

- Provide management with timely information needed to assess performance and to assist in evaluation of decisions that affect the future of the business

- Reduce operating costs

How these objectives are being met, the methods used to accomplish goals, and the extent of success realized to date, will be discussed in considerable detail throughout this manual.

ADVANTAGES OF IMPACT

Among the advantages of IMPACT are the following:

Better service. At Ralphs, the buyers have consistently maintained an excellent warehouse service level. Control has been maintained through diligent review of a Daily Unfilled Order report. A 98.5% service objective was specified for the

EXHIBIT 12-1 continued

IMPACT system. The last review of performance showed a combined service level for the lines on IMPACT to be 98.4% and a combined service level for the lines not on the system to be 97.0%.

Lower inventory. The behavior of Ralphs' inventory under IMPACT was difficult to evaluate because of the existence of promotional and speculative stock. A comparison of the inventory level for this year with the level for last year proved unsatisfactory because each contained unknown components of "promotion" and "special buy" merchandise. Buyers' assistance was needed to extract as much of the noncomparable stock as possible before a meaningful comparison could be made. To eliminate the need for the manual extraction process in the future, the system is now maintaining records of all "out-of-system" buys. The last analysis revealed that the inventory level for the items on IMPACT (80% of total line) was down 15% from the level of last year.

Advantages to the Buyer

The buyer now receives from the IMPACT system a convenient combined Stock Status-Buyer Guide report. This one-sheet report combines the information that was previously contained in three separate reports. The system suggests to the buyer what items need replenishment and how much of each to order. The routine computations required to answer these two questions are easily handled by the computer; only the abnormal situations require the buyer's time and effort.

The allocation or mixing required to make up a carload or truckload shipment also is handled by the system. The proper balance of the vendor's line, in terms of time supply and the meeting of order size requirements, is assured.

The scheduling of vendor shipments in order to meet service objectives requires complex analysis provided by the system. Normally the buyer does not have the time to consider all of the factors involved. The IMPACT system handles this chore with ease.

Actually, Ralphs buyers are buyer-merchandisers. They are responsible for the complete performance of the product line they control, such as the introduction, the sales performance, the inventory level, the profit, and the discontinuance of items when warranted. IMPACT is charged with freeing as much of the buyer's time as possible from the clerical phases of the buying job.

Value as a Management Aid

IMPACT proved valuable to Ralphs' management from the beginning. The study phase uncovered conditions that warranted improvement. For example, vendors were not meeting quoted lead times; time lags were noticed between receipt of a shipment and notification of the Data Processing department; and variations

EXHIBIT 12-1 continued

between actual inventory and book inventory were found. Corrected and tighter control procedures were instituted, since all of the conditions described tended to build up inventory in order to compensate for the inaccuracies.

By maintaining a tighter control on inventory, IMPACT is permitting management to scrutinize more closely this phase of the company's operation. Inadequacies are recognized and corrected earlier than was previously possible.

SOURCE: *Wholesale IMPACT—Advanced Principles and Implementation Reference Manual,* 2nd ed. (White Plains, N.Y.: IBM Technical Publications Department, May, 1969).

7. Because of systematic and frequent reordering, fewer customers are lost to competitors, and sales and deliveries tend to be constant rather than having infrequent peaks.

It should be noted, however, that, on the retail level, automatic reorder systems are especially applicable to grocery retailing, where there is generally a continual demand for relatively staple items with a steady turnover. Automatic reordering applied to all but the most staple items in a department store would be limited, because of the many variables that the manager must balance. In addition, for general merchandise operations, the on-hand quantities with which the computer works may be inaccurate because of clerical error at the point of purchase, marking room errors, shoplifting, spoilage or deterioration, and errors in entering merchandise as it is received. Also, although speed may be increased if orders are processed automatically, the goal of speedier arrival of the merchandise is still constrained by the speed of the transportation mode used for delivery of the merchandise from the manufacturer to the retailer.

Of all the remarkable advances in the field of electronic data processing related to *intra*organizational inventory management and control, none has the potential impact of those information systems that permit data retrieval at the point-of-sale at the retail store level. These computerized cash register systems provide data processing, merchandise-processing, and point-of-sale functions at both chain headquarters and at individual stores in the chain. At the store level, a variety of terminals is used for sales and checkout and for the accounting functions associated with the processing of merchandise and the management of the store.[16]

---

[16]Here, attention is focused on electronic systems with laser scanners. There have been a number of technical breakthroughs in recent years involving cash registers prior to the use of scanners. These

While performing these functions, the terminals record comprehensive data on their activity. A store controller (minicomputer) coordinates the activity of the terminals, collects data from the terminals, and performs additional specific store-level functions. It also communicates with a computer at area headquarters (the host), providing it with data collected from the terminals, receiving store-level system support and other communication from it, and communicating interactively with it when required.[17]

In supermarkets, a significant benefit available from such point-of-sale or "front-end" systems, beyond those directly related to the production of up-to-the-minute inventory and store management data, is that of checker productivity. As indicated in earlier chapters, the trend in food retailing over the past several decades has been toward increased operating expense, which has been caused primarily by the rise of labor cost relative to productivity. Technology has recently provided an adequate device to address the productivity requirement of the supermarket checkstand—the *laser checkout scanner*. The scanner contains a light source to illuminate and automatically identify each premarked item as it passes across the checkstand. In April, 1973, the supermarket industry established a novel identifier for all supermarket items made in the United States and Canada: the *Universal Product Code* (UPC) symbol that enabled economic use of scanners for checkout.

The UPC symbol is, typically, a unique, 12-digit item identification number, marked both in decimal characters and in bar-coded form that can be read by an optical scanner (see Fig. 12-1). When front-end systems are installed, all the codes in a supermarket's inventory can be maintained at the store controller in a file of price description records that contain both the prices and alphabetic descriptions of the items. The code item is invariant, even though its price may vary among stores. Prices are marked on the shelf but not necessarily on the merchandise, since the system reads the code of an item at the checkstand, retrieves its price and description, and displays that information to the shopper, while also printing it on his receipt tape. At headquarters, the front-end system provides item-movement data so that management can implement optimal inventory policies and shelf allocation procedures, which, in turn, should lead to a reduction of both backroom inventory and stockouts, increased turnover because of more efficient shelf

include "stand alone" electronic cash registers and electronic registers with some information processing capabilities. For a discussion of these, see Gordon F. Bloom and Ronald C. Curhan, "Technological Change in the Food Industry," Marketing Science Institute Working Paper P-63 (Cambridge, Mass.: Marketing Science Institute, December, 1974), pp. 29-34.

[17] P. V. McEnroe, H. T. Huth, E. A. Moore, and W. W. Morris III, "Overview of the Supermarket System and the Retail Store System," *IBM Systems Journal*, Vol. 14 (1975), pp. 3-4. Much of the discussion regarding the supermarket and general merchandise systems in this chapter is based on information supplied in this article.

FIGURE 12-1 A sample of the Universal Product Code, found on the side of a food package, which will be read by the scanner of a computerized register at the checkout counter

allocation, and a reduction in ordering cost as a consequence of the adoption of automatic reordering procedures. Furthermore, management can analyze the effectiveness of advertising, the performance of new items, and the performance of similar items by different vendors as well as study store needs as a function of the store location within the chain and the overall effect of price management programs.[18] Some of the potential benefits of the system are listed in Exhibit 12-2.

Widespread adoption of UPC-oriented systems at the retail level is, however, largely dependent on the capital position of food retailers. Equipment manufacturers are quoting a cost of $90,000 to $120,000 per supermarket for an 8-store chain installation—including scanners, computers, and cash registers. The capital requirement for equipment alone for a regional chain or division of a national chain with 150 large stores has been estimated to be $21 million, or $140,000 per store.[19] And, as Bloom and Curhan point out, not only are there important one-time equipment and software installation costs, but the cost in management time is so substantial that it too must be explicitly recognized.[20]

While effective use of the UPC seems to have its greatest potential benefits at the retail level via more accurate and rapid checkout, better inventory records, improved reordering procedures, and the like, it also has the potential for improving the performance of food processors as well. In fact, certain

[18] For further details, see *ibid.,* pp. 5-6.

[19] The $140,000 figure includes installation costs for new cableways, etc., in existing stores and costs for in-store symbol marking equipment. Bloom and Curhan, *op. cit.,* p. 37.

[20] *Ibid.,* p. 28.

EXHIBIT 12–2   Potential Benefits to Food Retailers from Adoption of UPC-Oriented Systems

Front-end Benefits	*Merchandising Benefits*
Improved throughput	Point-of-sale item movement data
Checker productivity	Advertising analysis
Reduced misrings	Vendor analysis
Tender reconciliation	New item performance analysis
Cash reporting	Location analysis (for items within
Store funds control	stores and between stores)
Check authorization	Price management

Store Operations Benefits	*Inventory Management Benefits*
Eliminates price marking and	Shelf-space allocation
remarking	Reduced out-of-stock
Permits routine ordering	Reduced backroom inventory
Reduce shrinkage	

Warehouse and Transportation Workload Balancing

SOURCE: IBM Corporation, November, 1975.

food processors believe that the next logical application of the UPC beyond the retail level is to employ it for production, distribution, and inventory applications at the manufacturing level.[21] For example, Pillsbury foresees receiving retail UPC-coded sales from a large number of strategic metropolitan areas and using the data to generate better short-range product forecasts. The company feels that monitoring retail activity in this way will permit early warning relative to the reordering of fast-moving items as well as provide information about local shifts in product movement. The major gain from such monitoring will be a substantial lowering of on-hand inventory levels and stockouts, as well as higher product movement velocity throughout the entire distribution system. Recognizing that several years will be needed to develop all segments of a retail-physical distribution-production-purchasing communication network, Pillsbury has already adopted UPC for internal use so that it will be ready to reap the potential interorganizational benefits as UPC is implemented more widely at the retail level.[22]

[21] See James R. Carman, "Stretching Your Food Dollar," *Handling and Shipping,* June, 1975, p. 47.
[22] *Ibid.*

Similar advances have been made relative to the management of general merchandise items sold through department, variety, and discount stores. The development of a Standard Merchandise Classification (SMC) by the Controllers Congress of the National Retail Merchants Association, as discussed in Chapter 2, permits benefits similar to those available to supermarkets via UPC. However, even with SMC, each general merchandise retailer usually tickets merchandise in a manner that best suits his own environment. The retail sales ticket contains a great deal more information (e.g., stockkeeping unit number, buying division, selling division, class, size, and price) than that required in a supermarket identification system. There is also much variability both in size and content of such tickets. The front-end information systems developed for general merchandise retailers contain the capability of making and reading a variety of tickets, because they often include point-of-sale terminals with magnetic wands and magnetic ticket units.[23] It is possible, though, that, in general merchandise retailing, the utilization of product codes and more routinized operations will not lead to a more streamlined operation and greater clerk productivity due to the relatively complicated nature of general merchandise transactions compared with the normal "cash and carry" transactions in supermarkets. Because there are many more information bits that must be entered for a transaction, including the salesperson number, specific credit plan, additional services attending the sale (e.g., delivery, warehouse pickup, layaway, etc.), return adjustments, allowances for defective merchandise, and the like, implementing the laser scanner reduces the time associated with information input only by a small amount.

These truly innovative *intra*organizational systems have the potential of alleviating much of the "noise" present in *inter*organizational communication dealing with stock levels and shipments. They should permit more effective queuing and sequencing of messages among channel members as well as nearly instantaneous feedback relative to item movement. Most significantly, these innovations indicate the potential for more functional communication via the development of specialized languages (e.g., UPC and SMC) and the altering of technology. Machines are substituted for people, and a portion of the communications task is delegated to units specializing in a crucial aspect of the communication process.

There are also numerous economic, social, and political consequences of such innovations. First, if retailers' willingness to purchase and perfect front-end systems is assumed,[24] market data critical to the functioning of

---

[23] A magnetic hand-held scanner, or wand, is normally a more accurate and faster data entry device than the cash register keyboard when many characteristics of data are to be entered.

[24] Clearly, adoption will be relatively slow, given the investment required. Furthermore, the systems, especially those designed for supermarkets, are likely to be most feasible when installed in large stores, irrespective of the total number of stores in a chain. See Bloom and Curhan, *op. cit.*, pp. 35–38 for estimates of the rate of diffusion of these systems.

channels of distribution will be instantaneously retrievable by retailers. Thus, unless manufacturers, wholesalers, carriers, and warehousing firms can somehow tie into the retail systems, they will become highly dependent on retailers for updated information. The uncertainty absorbing attributes of the retail store information systems are profound, and thus, the opportunity for retailers to assume channel leadership roles will undoubtedly be greatly magnified.

Second, it is likely that manufacturers, wholesalers, and logistical institutions will recognize the potential economic benefits as well as the above-mentioned political consequences of these *intra*organizational devices and will, therefore, begin to accelerate efforts to develop *inter*organizational data systems. Evidence of computerized interorganizational data connections was present even before front-end systems became a reality. Electronic linkages such as data phones have emerged as significant communication media for the transmission of ordering, billing, and inventory data among channel members. Order cycles can be reduced markedly when orders are transmitted instantly under real-time information system conditions. Inventory costs can be lowered for all members because less inventory is needed throughout the channel. As Gross has observed:

> Manufacturers, wholesalers, and retailers are moving toward lower and lower stock ratios as almost immediate transmittal of financial and inventory data becomes feasible. A hardware wholesaler in Texas has established a Data-phone connection with certain customers; Kellogg's warehouses are linked directly with warehouses of Safeway Stores and of the Wakefern Food chain; the Pillsbury Company has electronic hookups with Spartan Stores.[25]

Once interorganizational data systems are instituted within a distribution channel, the most immediate and obvious change will be an increase in the speed with which communication takes place.[26] When a retail stockout occurs, or an order point is reached, it will not be days or hours before the appropriate supplier knows about it, but seconds. This linkage brings each level of the channel temporarily closer together. It is not only the retailer who will be able to perceive shifts in ultimate consumer markets as they happen, but all key members of the channel. In addition to the greater speed with which data will be sent through the channel, greater accuracy of data transmittal can be effected.

Channel management would be enhanced if all *intra*organizational data

---

[25] *Gross, op. cit.*, pp. 350–351.

[26] The discussion here is based on Louis W. Stern and C. Samuel Craig, "Interorganizational Data Systems: The Computer and Distribution," *Journal of Retailing*, Vol. 47 (Summer, 1971), pp. 81–82. See also Felix Kaufman, "Data Systems That Cross Company Boundaries," *Harvard Business Review*, Vol. 44 (January–February, 1966), pp. 141–155.

systems were compatible and able to communicate freely with one another. However, social orientations (e.g., the desire for privacy, the maintenance of trade secrets) and technical requirements (e.g., computer hardware and software) vary from firm to firm. If patterns of data processing development continue such as they have in the past (i.e., most systems are tailored to the individual firm's specifications), computers and programs will continue to be unique. Also, computer manufacturers have a vested interest in maintaining unique systems. This problem was evident in the early development of supermarket checkout systems. According to Bloom and Curhan:

> . . . during the mid-1960's, various companies, including RCA, Zellweger, IMS Marketron, and others, had begun to develop automated checkout systems incorporating scanning technologies, using their own proprietary symbols. For the most part, these various symbols were incompatible in that they could not be read by devices of other equipment manufacturers.[27]

Unless trade associations and computer manufacturers exert considerable pressure for a high degree of standardization, members in the same channel will not be able to interact freely and speedily. Firms will not be able to switch to competitive systems without substantial changes.

From an interorganizational management perspective, it is, however, encouraging to note that the development of the new codes and classification schemes (UPC and SMC) was the result of interorganization cooperation in the marketing channels for both food and general merchandise. In fact, the Grocery Manufacturers of America *pioneered* the UPC and the computerized checkout.[28] In 1970, food processors, wholesalers, and retailers established the Grocery Industry Ad Hoc Committee to determine the design and feasibility of a code, and more than $1 million was obtained from various members of the food industry to support the work of the committee.[29] Thus, it appears that the desire for systemwide inventory management and control— and for increased productivity at the point-of-sale—is nearly universal among commercial channel members in these industries.

Third, there are a number of economic, ethical, and legal issues that will have to be assessed relative to the further development of both *intra*- and *inter*organizational information systems of the nature described above. On one hand, the antitrust enforcement agencies will, quite naturally, be concerned about the potential anticompetitive effects generated by closer and

---

[27] Bloom and Curhan, *op. cit.,* p. 21.

[28] "Electronic Pricing Faces an Uphill Fight," *Business Week,* March 31, 1975, p. 23.

[29] Bloom and Curhan, *op. cit.,* p. 20. Also, see Willard R. Bishop, Jr., "New Approaches to Improving Social Productivity in Food Distribution," in Ronald C. Curhan (ed.), *1974 Combined Proceedings* (Chicago: American Marketing Association, (1975), pp. 299–303.

closer ties between channel members, by an increase in the power of large retailers through the installation of such systems, and by the fact that numerous firms may be placed at a severe competitive disadvantage if they do not adopt or tie into these systems. Consumers, on the other hand, have already and will continue to resist supermarket front-end systems, particularly if implementation means the elimination of price-marking on individual items. Negative reaction to the new supermarket system, for example, has been voiced by consumers at the federal, state, and local governmental levels.[30] Three states—California, Rhode Island, and Connecticut—have passed legislation requiring price marking for shelf goods in addition to UPC marking.[31] Serious charges of deceptive pricing practices have been directed at chains that have adopted the system. In addition, there is some question in the minds of many consumers as to whether the savings in labor costs, made possible by the higher productivity mentioned earlier, will be passed along to them. Also, there are the retail clerks unions, which wish to protect the jobs of their members being threatened by the innovation. The consumer and union reaction has been so strong that legislation has been introduced at all governmental levels to limit full use of the system. Thus, one of the most significant innovations in distribution in the last half-century is already in jeopardy before it has even become widely diffused.

Aside from the innovations in electronic data processing and the consequences of their use, some retailers have limited their stocks in order to secure higher stockturns. Manufacturers have been critical of retailers for taking such actions, because they believe that, by limiting stocks, retailers are failing to provide adequate amounts of their products to meet customer demand. Manufacturers are also increasingly concerned about retailers' hesitancy to stock new items until demand has been stimulated at the consumers' level. On the other hand, retailers must constantly be aware of the need to "tailor" their lines to promote profitable turnover for their generally limited market areas. Instituting informational assistance appears to be one means by which dysfunctional conflict has been avoided over this issue in certain channels. As reported by Duncan, Phillips, and Hollander:

> . . . some manufacturers, aware of the retailer's need for strict inventory control,

[30]See "Electronic Pricing Faces an Uphill Fight," *Business Week, op. cit.,* p. 21; "Grocery Pricing Plan: Will It Hurt or Protect Consumers?" *Chicago Tribune,* Section 1 (June 1, 1975), p. 14; "Computerized Register Here, Rings Up Opposition," *Chicago Sun-Times,* February 23, 1975, p. 64. The Chicago city council has, as a reaction to the UPC system, already approved strict consumer amendments to the city code that require virtually every item in supermarkets to be individually price-marked. Items sold through vending machines are exempted. For items that are not prepackaged, the store must show the price on a sign next to the merchandise displayed. See Edward Schreiber, "Council Votes Stiffer Food Pricing Controls," *Chicago Tribune,* July 17, 1975, p. 1.

[31]"Food Brokers Told Most Products Have UPC, 50 Stores Have Scanners, and 3 States Require Prices on Products," *Marketing News,* January 30, 1976, p. 6.

have developed stock-control plans providing a reasonable display of their products and also yielding a good turnover figure to the retailer. One skirt manufacturer, for instance, helps the retailer set up a model stock, has his salesmen take a weekly inventory, and offers to replace slow-selling items with fast-selling ones. Such assistance is of particular value to smaller retailers who often lack the stock-control programs of larger firms.[32]

Such interorganizational arrangements are essential if perceptual differences and their accompanying "noise" are going to be reduced relative to inventory problems.

Transportation and Storage Problems

Communication with regard to transportation and storage is clearly a critical feature of interorganizational relations in marketing. Inadequate communications between shippers and their selected transportation modes or storage facilities can lead to excessive inventories, poor customer service, erratic production scheduling, poor material handling, and costly transportation expenditures.

Transportation information systems should concentrate on appropriate queuing and sequencing of messages. To a large extent, specialized languages, especially via advanced technology, are the major means by which communication noise can be reduced and coordinative mechanisms established between shippers and their respective transport modes. For example, General Mills has developed a "Shipment Status System" (called S-3 by the company), which was established to eliminate certain problems it was having in moving its products via its major transport mode, the railroad.[33] Specifically, in order to assure on-time delivery from the railroad, General Mills, in consultation with railroad management, established standard times along every route relative to the number of days or hours required for a shipment from a company plant or distribution center to reach various checkpoints. Under S-3, General Mills' computer communicates with railroad computer terminals on a daily basis to determine if particular freight cars have arrived at designated checkpoints. Electronic scanners positioned at railroad stations are used to examine reflective identification tape on the cars and report the status and location of the cars to the railroad computer terminal, which, in turn, reports to General Mills' computer. If a car fails to arrive at a designated

[32] Delbert J. Duncan, Charles F. Phillips, and Stanley C. Hollander, *Modern Retailing Management*, 8th ed. (Homewood, Ill.: Richard D. Irwin, Inc., 1972), p. 326.

[33] Information concerning S-3 was received from James C. Johnson, Associate Professor of Transportation and Traffic at the University of Tulsa, via personal correspondence.

checkpoint within a one-day grace period, General Mills reports this fact on computer "exception" sheets to railroad management personnel who then track down the car and correct the situation. As a result of the S-3 system, General Mills has achieved the highest rate of on-time delivery service (76 percent) in the company's history.

Similar types of coordinative communication systems have also been established with motor carriers. For example, General Electric's Insulating Materials Product Section has developed a "Ship-By-Number" system.[34] Under this sytem, each GE shipment container is marked with a large, highly visible bill-of-lading number (as opposed to plain tab-on stenciled addresses with no bill of lading). The presence of this "specialized language" enables truckers to better match freight with the proper bill-of-lading form, thus minimizing the confusion on shipping docks and in carrier terminals. The result for General Electric has been improved customer service, both from the point of view of misdirected shipments as well as speed of receipt of merchandise.

Transportation companies themselves are instituting communication-enhancing systems, which frequently involve shared services. Such efforts are exemplified by the National Association of Freight Payment Banks whose service simplifies the clerical and accounting tasks asociated with freight payment.[35] In addition, TransporData Corps., Inc., has initiated a nonprofit shipper-oriented freight-bill payment service in the Northwest region of the United States that not only aids in solving payment problems but also performs data collection operations as well. The services of TransporData may eventually be expanded to include freight consolidation in the region.[36]

The idea of shared services has been extended beyond transportation-oriented problems to other areas in physical distribution. As Friedman observes:

> In the past few years, shared data-processing services for all distribution functions have come into common use. These services offer expensive computer hardware and sophisticated software systems to individual warehouses and other users who would not be able to afford the same kind of information on a private basis. A service of this type usually includes invoicing, billing, credit checking, accounting, inventory control, storage and retrieval, and other scheduling.[37]

[34] See Jim Dixon, "Streamlining Distribution and Storage," *Distribution Worldwide*, May, 1975, pp. 30–31.

[35] Walter F. Friedman, "Physical Distribution: The Concept of Shared Services," *Harvard Business Review*, Vol. 53 (March–April, 1975), p. 26.

[36] *Ibid.*

[37] *Ibid.*

For example, a communication system called STORE (an acronym for Storage, Transmission, Order-Entry, Receiving, and Enquiry) has been developed by USCO, a large public warehousing company, which permits customers to have a direct computer link-up to USCO's warehouses.[38] Through this linkup, customers can obtain prompt and complete reports relative to billing, inventory control, and customer service. Customers tie into the communications network via teletypewriter, phone, or mail. The system is particularly adaptable to shippers who have limited but nationwide physical distribution requirements, fluctuating physical distribution needs, or commitments to rapid service.[39] STORE is programmed to generate weekly inventory summaries, shipments-by-suppliers reports, and monthly unit movement reports and can, if used effectively, result in reduced order preparation and shipment times, lowered accounts receivable, and improved cash flow.

The potential for shared services in physical distribution is enormous. Clearly, they can increase the effectiveness of communication markedly through the reduction of communication overload. The feedback systems that are fostered by such services can lead to better control, and, thus, lower cost distribution or, at least, improved customer service at the same cost. It is, however, the efficiency of such services that provides the greatest benefits. Through them, duplication of effort is circumscribed, thereby permitting each firm in the interorganizational network to concentrate more heavily on those marketing activities for which it has a comparative advantage.[40]

Promotional Problems

Communication failures weaken or nullify promotional efforts of both manufacturers and resellers. For example, a well-known tire manufacturing company, which prided itself on its dealer point-of-purchase promotional pieces, learned, after conducting a research study on the subject, that its promotional programs were largely wasted; dealers did not want the promotional materials and discarded them almost immediately upon receipt. The tire company found that dealers were primarily concerned with getting customers into their stores and not with selling the consumers once they entered the stores.[41]

[38]"Meeting Those Distribution Center Needs," *Handling and Shipping,* July 1975, pp. 37–38.

[39]*Ibid.*

[40]For an interesting example of the shared services concept in the fast-food industry, where merchant wholesalers have provided so-called "third party physical distribution," see "Fast Food," *Distribution Worldwide,* May, 1975, pp. 29–33.

[41]This example was drawn from Cox, Schutte, and Few, *op. cit.,* p. 191.

The communication problem in this case was clearly one of omission—the manufacturer really did not know what it was the dealers needed and had not taken the trouble to find out until he had spent considerable resources on the wrong kind of materials. The remedy for the problem may be the instituting of appropriate feedback mechanisms. The manufacturer's sales force should be tapped for information on this subject on a regular basis.[42] The problem could have been compounded as a result of communication overload, which occurs when one channel member supplies more material than another can effectively assimilate. The remedy here would be appropriate sequencing of communications.

The problem could also have arisen because the dealers and the manufacturer were operating at crossed purposes and using confused languages. In this respect, corporate management's point of view is generally characterized by a growth psychology, whereas the typical small retail dealer is more concerned with maintenance of the status quo than he is with growth.[43] The executives in a major corporation constantly strive for more income, status, power, security, fame, or self-satisfaction; small retailers may have similar goals, but each goal has a relatively easily defined end point. Furthermore, the language of modern industry often revolves around words like profit, profit margin, profitability, merchandising, marketing, promoting, and the like. Small retailers talk in terms of "making money" and of "giving their customers what they ask for." Some of the problems faced by the tire manufacturer with his dealers are no doubt similar to those described by Wittreich relative to brewers in their interaction with tavern owners:

> ... a situation of conflicting interests and misunderstanding exists between the brewer and the tavern owner. The latter generally does not feel that brewers are genuinely interested in his problems. He sees industry "take-home" advertising as undermining his business. He sees the individual brewer as primarily interested in pushing his own brand—something in which the tavern operator is not interested because pushing one brand over another does not really add to *his* over-all business.[44]

Integral to solving the communication problems in these cases would be a willingness on the part of the "sender" (1) to deal with the "receiver" on the latter's own level, within the framework of the latter's value system, and (2)

---

[42] For a detailed discussion of the potential feedback roles of salesmen, see Louis W. Stern and J. L. Heskett, "Grass Roots Market Research," *Harvard Business Review*, Vol. 43 (March–April, 1965), pp. 83–96.

[43] Warren J. Wittreich, "Misunderstanding the Retailer," in Louis W. Stern (ed.), *Distribution Channels: Behavioral Dimensions, op. cit.*, pp. 254–255.

[44] *Ibid.*, p. 258.

to discuss promotional strategy in down-to-earth, concrete language that the latter understands.[45] The role of the salesman is critical in these situations.

Clearly, poor communication with regard to promotion results in duplication of effort and dilution of promotional impact. For example, all channel members advertise, but frequently retailers are not fully informed about the assistance that they can obtain from manufacturers in the planning and implementation of campaigns. Also, both the manufacturer and the retailer may be advertising at the same time in the same market with no benefit to either in media purchases or unified campaign themes for maximum impact. Institutional advertising directed at retailers may not be coordinated with wholesalers' personal selling efforts directed at the same retailers. By the same token, manufacturers need information about intermediaries' promotional needs. For example, manufacturers can help in planning anniversary and other special sales by providing specially designed displays and even products. Manufacturers and wholesalers may combine efforts with retailers to push their particular brands during such occasions.

Communication "noise" can lead to serious conflicts regarding other promotional areas as well, such as packaging, sales incentives, and merchandising aids. Consider the following examples:

> A manufacturer's research indicated that consumers wanted a package that would be easier to open. Accordingly the product (bubble gum balls) was packaged in a redesigned box with a simple tear-open feature. Retailers became highly upset with the new package because it led to free sampling by children as well as display floor clean-up problems.[46]

> An appliance manufacturer provided his distributor and dealers with promotional incentives including travel prizes and free merchandise for their outstanding salesmen. Difficulties ensued when the travel prizes aggravated the middlemen's personnel shortages during peak sales periods and when the middlemen learned that their salesmen were selling the free merchandise to customers on company time.[47]

> An advertising agency recommended that one of its clients—a national food manufacturer—use odd-shaped cents-off coupons (e.g., poodle-shaped for dog food). The manufacturer enthusiastically endorsed the recommendation, but found his retailers up-in-arms about the promotional scheme. If enacted, retailers would have found it extremely difficult to stack, sort, and store the coupons.[48]

---

[45]*Ibid.*, p. 260.

[46]This example was drawn from Gross, *op. cit.*, p. 341.

[47]This example was drawn from Gross, *op. cit.*, p. 342.

[48]This example was drawn from Stephen Baker, "Wild Shapes, Sizes Are Today's Look in Coupons," *Advertising Age*, August 4, 1969 and was paraphrased in Reavis Cox and Thomas F. Schutte, "A Look at Channel Management," in Philip R. McDonald (ed.), *1969 Fall Conference on Proceedings* (Chicago, Ill.: American Marketing Association, 1970), p. 102.

It is reasonably safe to assume that, in each case cited above, problems could have been alleviated or perhaps would not even have arisen if there had been adequate and continuous (or at least periodic) feedback throughout the system.[49]

Besides judiciously using salesmen for this purpose (which involves developing a sales-force compensation system that would motivate salesmen to perform such a crucial function), a number of interpenetration conflict management strategies might also be employed. These strategies include the formation of dealer and distributor advisory councils, exchanging personnel, purposive uncertainty absorption techniques, and cooptation.[50] In addition, certain middlemen, such as merchant wholesalers, manufacturers' representatives, and brokers, could perform mediating roles with respect to such problems. However, it would probably be better, over the long term, for retailers, wholesalers, and manufacturers alike to establish channel diplomat positions within their firms in the form of trade relations departments or distribution specialists in order to avoid the conflicts of interest that often plague salesmen and independent middlemen when they seek to perform conflict management functions.[51]

Product Problems

Many of the same problems that exist in the transmittal of promotional information are found for product information as well. For example, appliance retailers and manufacturers do not often mean the same thing when they discuss product quality. The former are concerned with the consequences of product quality; they want an item that results in a high level of consumer satisfaction and that minimizes consumer complaints and servicing problems. The latter are concerned with technical features. Thus, refrigerator manufacturers see quality as reflected in such things as maintenance of constant temperature and avoidance of excessive "frosting," while television set manufacturers measure quality in terms of picture clarity, pulling power, and tonal effect.[52] This problem of confused languages can be remedied only by the similar kinds of feedback and interpenetration mechanisms suggested above for promotional problems.

Typical of some of the recurring problems faced by channel members

---

[49] It should also be understood, however, that too much feedback can create as much "noise" as too little feedback. See Grabner and Rosenberg, *op. cit.,* pp. 247–248.

[50] See Chapter 7 for a discussion of each of these interpenetration strategies.

[51] See Chapter 7 for additional discussion of this point.

[52] Wittreich, *op. cit.,* pp. 261–262.

when they fail to communicate effectively about product policy are the following examples:

> A well-known manufacturer of consumer paper products decided to introduce a giant economy size box of one product in its line. Although consumers desired the box—especially after the manufacturer had engaged in heavy promotion of it —retailers stocked it reluctantly because it did not fit existing shelf space, and thus they were forced to place it on the floor.[53]

> A manufacturer of outdoor braziers introduced a high-priced and high-quality line into a certain market area. After an introductory sales increase, sales volume started dwindling, even though the product was of superior quality. A special study revealed that newly hired sales personnel in retail outlets were not informed about the distinctive features of the line, let alone that these features needed to be demonstrated to prospective buyers. Although brochures and other training materials were available for retailers, they were not read. The sales personnel simply used the high-priced superior line to promote other, less expensive lines.[54]

> A major producer of electric appliances hired a well-known actress to present new items on a television program. When she announced a new electric frankfurter cooker, it was not only news to the consumer; it was also news to retailers and even to the manager of a wholesale subsidiary owned by this manufacturer.[55]

Obviously, retailers and wholesalers need advance notice of forthcoming model and style changes and new-product introductions. A whole series of steps necessarily precedes successful introduction at the local level, not the least of which is adequate training of sales personnel. For example, it would be useful, from a training perspective, if distinctions could be drawn between "features" and "benefits" of products. A feature is a technical attribute (31-100 wide-ratio derailer on bicycles), whereas a benefit is a feature translated into everyday salable terms (wide-range gears for easier peddling). Although it is standard practice for many manufacturers to keep channel members abreast of developments by sending out a stream of newsletters and other information-giving mail pieces, the problem of communication overload quickly becomes evident, especially if many suppliers are following the same course and if new product introductions are relatively frequent. As with promotion, the salesman must play a key role in carrying salient information. Otherwise, the messages are likely to become damped by the noise surrounding middlemen, which often reaches uncomfortable decibel levels.

On the other hand, it is incumbent on middlemen to communicate local environmental nuances to their suppliers so that products can be adapted to

---

[53]This example was drawn from Cox and Schutte, *op. cit.,* p. 100.

[54]This example was drawn from Gross, *op. cit.,* p. 341.

[55]This example was drawn from Gross, *op. cit.,* p. 348.

fit the needs of specific markets. The dealer and distributor advisory notion appears to be ideally suited to such interchanges with respect to both industrial and consumer goods.[56] Wholesalers and retailers are in a position to provide suppliers with information about demographic changes, competitive activities, and changes in consumer preferences and shopping habits in local market areas. For their part, manufacturers who have developed quotas for their own salesmen can readily supply middlemen with estimates of what they should be able to sell.[57] In fact, the process of uncertainty absorption is a mutual one, especially as it relates to product problems.

Another area where communication in marketing channels has tended to be weak has to do with new product warranties. Retailers, wholesalers, and even manufacturers themselves have been confused as to role relationships here, and "noise" within channels regarding the issue of warranties has sometimes been deafening. Problems with warranty arrangements have surfaced in almost all consumer durable goods industries,[58] but perhaps the automobile industry has been the one most frequently plagued with difficulties. In an effort to eliminate warranty-claim discrepancies on the part of its dealers, which came glaringly to the surface during 1975 when certain dealers were found to be charging General Motors for service under warranties which they never performed, GM instituted a new franchise agreement with its dealers that was much more stringent in specifying dealer obligations.[59] Clearly, the problems GM faced with respect to warranties made the company rethink its means of communicating with and gathering intelligence at the retail level. While the problems that have occurred in automobile marketing may be extreme, there are similar problems in other industries, although they do not necessarily revolve around false claims. In the long run (and perhaps even in the short run), consumers are the ones who are injured, because the lack of domain consensus over warranty arrangements places them squarely in the middle. Although the Warranties Improvement Act of 1975 may help to alleviate these problems somewhat by giving consumers more power to deal with inadequate warranty service and unclear warranty

[56] For examples of the effective use of dealer and distributor councils, see Chapter 7; H. Thomas Douglas, "I-E and its Distributors Communicate for Profit," *Industrial Marketing* (February, 1970), pp. 51–53; "Belden Co. Airs its Distributors' Views," *Industrial Marketing* (November, 1969), pp. 56–58; and R. D. Brown, "Selling Through—Not to—Retailers," in Malcolm P. McNair and Mira Berman (eds.), *Marketing Through Retailers* (New York: American Management Association, 1967), p. 60.

[57] Gross, *op. cit*, p. 349.

[58] *Product Warranties*, Report of the Sub-Council on Warranties and Guarantees of the National Business Council for Consumer Affairs (Washington, D.C.: U.S. Government Printing Office, 1972).

[59] Terry P. Brown, "GM's Relations with Dealers Are Roiled as Some Dealers Call New Pack Unfair," *Wall Street Journal*, October 30, 1975, p. 34. See also Terry P. Brown, "GM Offers Dealers Special Explanation of Controversial Franchise Agreement," *Wall Street Journal*, February 10, 1976, p. 2.

claims, it is obvious that commercial channel members must involve themselves more deeply with this issue.[60] Unfortunately, the mechanisms for effective bargaining over it often seem to be lacking, with the result that the courts are called upon too frequently to arbitrate matters which would be better handled by a well-functioning intrachannel conflict management system.

Pricing Problems

Effective communication between channel members on pricing policy matters is of vital importance to channel operations. Problems relative to this element of the marketing mix are especially acute in periods of inflation and recession, as evidenced during the 1974–1976 stagflation.[61] Prices have a direct effect on the ability of firms within the channel to successfully manage their inventories and maintain adequate assortments; considerable "hedging" is necessary if firms are going to avoid often catastrophic results relative to profits.

Typically, a manufacturer's price list is an inaccurate and misleading communication medium. The net price available to middlemen includes a host of additional factors, some of which are only vaguely transmitted to existing and potential buyers. As Gross points out,[62] allowances may be made to defray advertising and/or to cover shipping, warehousing, internal chain-unit distributing, merchandise defects, and other middleman costs. Special pricing may be available for quantity purchases, for preferred shelf and floor positions, and for trade show market specials. Dating plans, price adjustment guarantees, and other incentives to early ordering are frequently available, but are often not explicitly included in sales presentations or, if presented, are cumbersome and confusing in many cases. In actuality, pricing traditions have given rise to specialized languages (e.g., credit terms, chain discounts), which may lead to more efficient communication but are sometimes subject to considerable interpretation.[63]

Wholesalers and retailers need such information to help them plan their

[60]C. L. Kendall and Frederick A. Russ, "Warranty and Complaint Policies: An Opportunity for Marketing Management," *Journal of Marketing*, Vol. 39 (April, 1975), pp. 36–43. See also Stanley E. Cohen, "FTC Gears Up for Rule-Making Task; Engman Cities Public's Frustrations," *Advertising Age*, July 16, 1973, p. 1.

[61]See, for some excellent examples, "Marketing When the Growth Slows," *Business Week*, April 14, 1975, pp. 44–50 and "Pricing Strategy in an Inflation Economy," *Business Week*, April 6, 1974, pp. 43–48.

[62]Gross, *op. cit.*, p. 349.

[63]Frederick E. Balderston, "Communication Networks in Intermediate Markets," *Management Science*, Vol. 4 (January, 1958), pp. 167–168.

buying effectively. For example, middlemen may decide to place preseason orders, thereby financing manufacturing operations, if they can be convinced that the discount savings available are greater than inventory carrying costs and if manufacturers are willing to guarantee price levels, especially in times of unstable economic conditions. Clearly, manufacturers need information about the price structure at retail and wholesale levels in order to be assured that their pricing is in line with competition, that they are receiving their fair share of price specials at local levels, and that realistic margins are being maintained on their lines so as to avoid price "footballing" situations and thus the possible disaffection of valued distributors and dealers.

Evidence of ineffectiveness in pricing communication and execution is found with regard to the thousands of "trade deals" or temporary price reductions that are offered to retailers by manufacturers. Manufacturers, especially in the food industry, employ a number of different types of short-term inducements in order to encourage increased purchases and/or promotional support by retailers. The most common trade deals in the food industry are "off-invoice" and "bill-back" allowances; the former are applied directly to reduce billed costs, while the latter are paid retroactively for all purchases within a specified period. The hope of the manufacturers granting these allowances is that retailers will pass along at least part of their savings to consumers and/or that they will erect special displays for and advertise the brands on which prices have been reduced. However, Chevalier and Curhan found, after monitoring a total of 1043 trade deals offered to one supermarket chain over a 24-week period, that only 33 percent of those manufacturer-brand items for which deals were recorded received significant advertising mention by the retailers, only 37 percent received an important price cut (only 17 percent excluding in-ad coupons redeemed at the retail store), and only 22 percent were given special displays.[64] In fact, for over 50 percent of the deals that were recorded, the brands involved received *no* price reductions at the retail level.[65] Similar negative results were found with regard to advertising mention and displays. In a considerable understatement of their findings, Chevalier and Curhan concluded that:

> In this particular situation, the retailer promoted only a limited number of items for which he accepted deals. It is unlikely that manufacturers realized the support to which they probably considered themselves entitled.[66]

[64]Michel Chevalier and Ronald C. Curhan, "Temporary Promotions as a Function of Trade Deals: A Descriptive Analysis," Marketing Science Institute Report No. 75–109 (Cambridge, Mass.: Marketing Science Institute, May, 1975), p. 13.

[65]*Ibid.*, p. 12.

[66]*Ibid.*, p. 28.

While such actions (or lack of them) relative to trade deals provide some evidence of where power resides in this channel as well as the potential for conflict, it is also clear that manufacturers are experiencing considerable communication problems, caused, to some extent, by their tendency to overload retailers with deals. However, it should be pointed out that the retailer in the study referred to here promoted only a *very* few items for which no manufacturer deal was offered.

The pricing area is one that is often shrouded in secrecy. The bargaining that usually ensues with respect to final price makes communications about prices subject to a wide variety of omissions and distortions. To some extent, these problems are alleviated by the kind of information exchange that takes place among channel members at trade shows and trade association meetings as well as through trade journals and trade association publications. There are, however, immense legal obstacles to such exchanges, because they can be viewed by antitrust enforcement agencies as efforts to conspire to fix prices. In fact, there has recently been a renewed, concerted effort by the Justice Department, with full support of the President's office, to "crack down" on price conspiracies.[67] The latter tend to become more prevalent and more overt in a period of recession coupled with inflation when profits are squeezed hardest. The cause for concern by the Justice Department seems warranted, especially if the following examples are typical of practices in other areas and industries.[68]

> According to a key government witness in a recent price-fixing case against five Phoenix-based bakeries, the price of a loaf of bread went from 35¢ up to 69¢ between 1969 and 1973. The witness further indicated that 15 percent of this increase is the result of the conspiracy.

> For allegedly conspiring with other large retailers to fix prices paid for wholesale beef, A & P, in 1974, was fined $32.7 million for damages.

> The members of the National Broiler Marketing Association have been charged with fixing prices on chickens in a suit still pending. Private damage claims from 15 states, plus additional claims from hotel, restaurant, and supermarket chains, are being made against Pillsbury, Heublein, Cargill, and 35 other producers.

> Fines in the amount of $360,500, which have already been paid, and additional private damage claims on charges of rigging prices are being brought against DuPont's Organic Chemicals Department and eight other large dyemakers.

> A number of suits by building owners and stage governments were set off when a terminated distributor sued his supplier and other members of an alleged conspir-

[67]"Price-Fixing: Crackdown Under Way," *Business Week*, June 2, 1975, p. 42. See also Bill Neikirk, "Probers Find Price Fixing is Pervasive in America," *Chicago Tribune*, Section 2, March 7, 1976, p. 9.

[68]These examples were drawn from "Price-Fixing: Crackdown Under Way," *op. cit.*, pp. 42–48.

acy and settled out of court for $300,000. The franchised distributor was terminated by his supplier because he refused to go along with anticompetitive bidding practices instituted by other distributors in the building materials market.

While the guilt or innocence of a number of the above-mentioned companies charged with price conspiring remains to be determined in the courts, it is clear that channel members on all levels of distribution must be very cautious when discussing pricing arrangements of any type, including those dealing with credit and discount terms. In addition, it is likely that any vertical price maintenance arrangements will come under deep scrutiny, as a result of the repeal of Fair Trade.[69]

Nevertheless, meaningful communication relative to all marketing flows is essential if the practice of interorganization management is to be successful. To facilitate the development of information systems, the variety of direct and indirect media listed in Fig. 12-2 is available to merchandise sources (factories and/or wholesalers) and resellers (wholesalers and/or retailers). However, as Gross has observed:

> The adequacy of the vertical channel communication systems that have evolved within various firms and industries varies considerably. Two reasons appear fundamentally to account for a weak system: (1) the profitability potential of providing certain data to associated firms in the channel may not have been analyzed, or (2) if the profitability is recognized, a *standard* procedure for such data communication has not been established.[70]

The development of an effective information system will probably result in a higher degree of loyalty and commitment on the part of the channel members to a particular channel arrangement. Furthermore, the firm that is instrumental in originating and maintaining the system may acquire more power within the channel as the other members become more dependent on the data transmitted. In essence, such a system represents for its developer a basis for exerting power throughout the channel, and thus can have profound long-term effects on the channel's organization, design, and competitive viability.

The starting point in initiating an interorganizational information system must come from an analysis of a channel's performance and profitability. One type of analysis that would be extremely beneficial, in this respect, is a channel audit of marketing flows, as suggested in Chapter 1. In addition, perceptual data should be gathered that would show how each channel member

---

[69] See discussion of price maintenance in Chapter 8.

[70] Gross, *op. cit.,* p. 352.

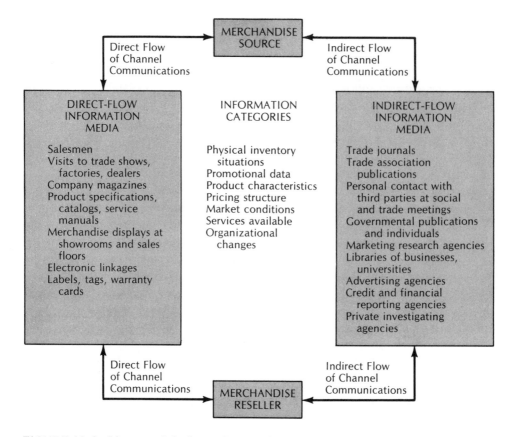

FIGURE 12-2 Direct and Indirect Communications Media Available to Merchandise Sources and Resellers

SOURCE: Walter Gross, "Profitable Listening for Manufacturers and Dealers: How To Use a Communication System," in *Marketing Channels: A Systems Viewpoint,* eds. William G. Moller, Jr. and David L. Wilemon (Homewood, Ill.: Richard D. Irwin, Inc., 1971), p. 346.

perceives existing marketing programs and the roles of each member in carrying forward the programs.[71] Strategic profit models of the type suggested in Chapter 6 should also be developed. Of equal importance would be some form of distribution cost analysis. Below, the basic rudiments of such an analysis are explained.

[71] See Cox, Schutte, and Few, *op. cit.,* pp. 192–193. Also, for an example, see J. Robert Foster and F. Kelly Shuptrine, "Using Retailers' Perceptions of Channel Performance to Detect Potential Conflict," in Thomas V. Greer (ed.), *1973 Combined Proceedings* (Chicago: American Marketing Association, 1974), pp. 118–123.

DISTRIBUTION COST ANALYSIS

Distribution cost analysis is a tool which, when properly employed, can aid channel members in determining whether the channels in which they participate are profitable or whether alterations and modifications in existing channels are needed based on a knowledge of the revenues and costs associated with serving them. Generally, a distribution cost analysis would be undertaken by a manufacturer or the original supplier of a particular good or service, because these channel members tend to have the greatest vested interest with respect to the performance of the good or service throughout the channel.

The use of the method rests on the adequacy of accounting data which can be manipulated to provide an assessment of various channels. The benefits of distribution cost analysis can be far-reaching. For example,

> One manufacturer allocated marketing costs to his four different channels of distribution, and on the basis of the results, one entire channel was eliminated and a number of small customers in another channel were discontinued. In addition, marketing efforts were increased on the remaining profitable channels. In one year, net profits doubled from approximately $150,000 to $300,000.

> Another manufacturer found through a distribution cost analysis that two-thirds of all customers sold direct were responsible for losses ranging from 26 to 86 percent of sales. By transferring unprofitable small accounts to wholesalers, the company has achieved a 40 to 50 percent net reduction in marketing costs and a 25 percent increase in the percentage of net profits.[72]

Thus, there appears to be considerable opportunity to reduce costs and increase profits through analyses of relative costs by channels.

In order to perform a distribution cost analysis, the accounting data typically available to a firm on its profit and loss statement must first be reorganized and reclassified into marketing function or flow categories.[73]

---

[72]These examples were drawn from Charles H. Sevin, *How Manufacturers Reduce Their Distribution Costs*, Economic Series No. 72, U.S. Department of Commerce (Washington, D.C.: U.S. Government Printing Office, 1948), p. 4.

[73]Complete and thorough explanations of distribution cost accounting methods and procedures can be found in J. Brooks Heckert and Robert B. Miner, *Distribution Costs*, 2nd ed. (New York: The Ronald Press Co., 1953) and Donald R. Longman and Michael Schiff, *Practical Distribution Cost Analysis* (Homewood, Ill.: Richard D. Irwin, Inc., 1955). The discussion of distribution cost analysis here is based largely on Martin Zober, *Marketing Management* (New York: John Wiley & Sons, Inc., 1964), pp. 241–267 and Philip Kotler, *Marketing Management: Analysis, Planning and Control*, 2nd ed. (Englewood Cliffs, N.J.: Prentice-Hall, Inc., 1972), pp. 790–797.

TABLE 12-1   Harrison Manufacturing Company Profit and Loss Statement (in thousands of dollars)

Sales		$35,000
Cost of goods sold		20,000
Gross margin		15,000
Expenses		
Salaries	$ 3,000	
Advertising	2,500	
Trucking	500	
Rent	3,500	
Insurance	1,400	
Supplies	1,000	
	11,900	
Net profit		$ 3,100

Assume, for example, that Table 12-1 is the profit and loss statement of Harrison Manufacturing Company, a hypothetical producer of plastic towel racks, dish drains, soap dishes, and other kitchen and bathroom accessories. Assume, also, that the expenses listed in Table 12-1 have been limited to those associated with the marketing flows of physical possession (storage and delivery), promotion (personal selling, advertising, sales promotion, and publicity), and ordering and payment (billing and collecting). The first step in distribution cost analysis is to show how each of the natural expense items shown in Table 12-1 were incurred through Harrison's participation in each of the flows. A hypothetical breakdown is presented in Table 12-2. For ex-

TABLE 12-2   Functional (Flow) Expense Breakdown (in thousands of dollars)

Natural Expenses	Total	Physical Possession		Promotion			Ordering and Payment
		Storage	Delivery	Personal Selling	Advertising	Sales Promotion	Billing and Collecting
Salaries	$ 3,000	$ 150	$ 100	$2,000	$ 500	$ 200	$ 50
Advertising	2,500				1,500	1,000	
Trucking	500		500				
Rent	3,500	2,500	50	500	200	100	150
Insurance	1,400	1,000	350				50
Supplies	1,000		500	100	150	150	100
Total	$11,900	$3,650	$1,500	$2,600	$2,350	$1,450	$350

ample, it has been determined that most of the salaries went to salesmen and the rest went to an advertising manager, a sales promotion manager, a traffic manager, and an accountant, along with various support personnel in each area.

The simplistic example used belies the difficulty involved in splitting natural expenses into functional cost groups. Generally, careful study is required, along with considerable research, before the costs can be allocated equitably. An example of the various means by which natural expense categories may be assigned to various functional categories is provided in Table 12-3. Also, it has been assumed that all of the natural expenses listed

TABLE 12-3   Classification of Natural Expense Items into Function—(Flow)—Cost Groups

Expense Items	Means by which Natural-expense Items Are Assigned to Functional-cost Groups	Function-cost Groups to which Natural-expense Items Are Assigned
Sales salaries and expense	Time study	Order routine and promotion
Truck expense	Direct (to cost group)	Handling (or delivery)
Truck wages	Direct (to cost group)	Handling (or delivery)
Truck depreciation	Direct (to cost group)	Handling (or delivery)
Outside trucking	Direct (to cost group)	Handling (or delivery)
Warehouse wages	Time study (or direct to cost group)	Handling, storage, and investment
Office wages	Time study (or direct to cost group)	Order routine, reimbursement, or other functions
Executive salaries	Managerial estimate	All functional groups
Rent	Space measurement	All functional groups
Storage (outside)	Direct (to cost group)	Storage
Warehouse repairs	Managerial estimate	Storage and handling
Warehouse supplies	Managerial estimate	Storage and handling
Insurance:		
Property and equipment	Managerial estimate	All functional groups
Inventory	Direct (to cost group)	Investment
Personnel	Wages	All functional groups
Office expense	Direct (to cost groups and managerial estimate)	Order routine, reimbursement, promotion, or other functions
Utilities	Some direct (to cost groups), others to cost groups via space measurement	All functional groups
Professional services	Managerial estimate	Functions benefited
Taxes, inventory	Direct (to cost group)	Investment
Social security	Add to wages	All functional groups
Bad debts	Direct (to cost group)	Reimbursement

SOURCE: U.S. Department of Commerce, *Distribution Cost Analysis*, Economic Series No. 50 (Washington, D. C.: U. S. Government Printing Office), p. 17.

in Table 12-1 were directly allocable to the functional (flow) groupings. Clearly, this is an oversimplification, because many of the expenses incurred by a firm do not relate directly to the performance of marketing functions.

The second step in distribution cost analysis as it applies directly to marketing channel decisions involves determining how much of each activity has gone into serving the various channels used by the firm. This step calls for allocating the various costs associated with each functional (flow) category to each channel. Some of the bases available for allocating selected costs associated with various functional categories to different channel or customer groupings are shown in Table 12-4.

Assume, in the case of Harrison Manufacturing Company, that the firm sells directly to department stores, discount houses, and supermarket chains. Using allocation bases similar to those shown in Table 12-4 and applying the results to the Harrison example give the data in Table 12-5. Thus, it costs Harrison $3.65 per cubic foot of warehouse space to store the merchandise it sells, $0.65 to deliver each case of its merchandise to its retail customers, $47.00 for every sales call made to each of the stores in the various retail chains, and $35.00 for billing and collecting per order. The advertising and sales promotion figures (1.57 X and 1.45 X) reflect the multipliers that must be applied to each advertising and sales promotion dollar expended by Harrison in each channel. These multipliers permit inclusion of the cost of the support (personnel, rent, and supplies) that has been given to each of these functional areas.

TABLE 12-4   Selected Bases of Manufacturer's Allocation of Functional—(Flow)—Cost Groups to Channels or Customer Groupings

Functional-Cost Groups	Bases of Allocation to Channels or Customer Groupings
Storage of finished goods	Floor space occupied
Order assembly (handling)	Number of invoice lines
Packing and shipping	Weight or number of shipping units
Transportation	Weight or number of shipping units
Selling	Number of sales calls
Advertising	Cost of space, etc., of specific customer advertising
Sales promotion	Cost of promotions
Order entry	Number of orders
Billing	Number of invoice lines
Credit extension	Average amount outstanding
Accounts receivable	Number of invoices posted

SOURCE: Adapted from Martin Zober, *Marketing Management* (New York: John Wiley & Sons, Inc., 1964), p. 246.

TABLE 12–5   Allocating Functional-group Costs to Marketing Channels

Function (Flow) Group	Physical Possession		Promotion			Ordering and Payment
	Storage	Delivery	Personal Selling	Advertising	Sales Promotion	Billing and Collecting
Allocation Bases	Floor space occupied in own warehouse (000 cu ft)	Number of shipping units (000 cases)	Number of sales calls (000)	Cost of advertising space (000)	Cost of Promotions (000)	Number of orders (000)
Channel Types						
Department stores	200	500	5	$ 150	$ 100	1
Discount houses	450	1000	20	700	400	5
Supermarket chains	350	800	30	650	500	4
Total	1000	2300	55	$1500	$1000	10
Functional-group Cost (000)	$3650	$1500	$2600	$2350	$1450	$350
Number of units	1000	2300	55	$1500	1000	10
Average cost	$3.65	$.65	$47	1.57 X	1.45 X	$35

The third step in distribution cost analysis is the preparation of a profit and loss statement for each channel. In Table 12-6, cost of goods sold has been allocated to each channel in proportion to the revenues that the channel delivers to Harrison. The expense figures are derived from the information in Table 12-5. Although it is clear from Harrison's distribution cost analysis that all channels are returning a net profit (in reality, a contribution to profit, since not all cost figures have been included in this hypothetical example), the return from serving supermarket chains is very low relative to the return from the other two channels. In addition, the return from the department store channel is surprisingly high. Thus, Harrison might consider increasing his business to department stores and/or deemphasizing sales to supermarket chains.

It must be understood that the results of a distribution cost analysis *do not* constitute an adequate informational basis for making explicit moves of the type suggested. Before a decision is made to emphasize or deemphasize a particular channel or to take *any* corrective action, answers to the following kinds of questions must be generated by management.[74]

[74] Kotler, *op. cit.*, p. 796.

TABLE 12-6   Profit and Loss Statement for Harrison's Channels (in thousands of dollars)

	Department Stores	Discount Houses	Supermarket Chains	Total
Sales	$7,500	$15,500	$12,000	$35,000
Cost of goods sold	4,400	8,800	6,800	20,000
Gross margin	3,100	6,700	5,200	15,000
Expenses				
Storage ($3.65 per cu ft)	$ 730	$ 1,643	$ 1,277	$ 3,650
Delivery ($0.65 per case)	325	650	525	1,500
Personal selling ($47 per call)	245	940	1,414	2,600
Advertising (1.57 ×)	235	1,095	1,020	2,350
Sales promotion (1.45 ×)	145	580	725	1,450
Billing and collecting ($35 per order)	35	175	140	350
Total expenses	$1,715	$ 5,083	$ 5,102	$11,900
Net profit (or loss)	$1,385	$ 1,617	$ 98	$ 3,100
Profit-to-sales ratio	18.5%	10.4%	0.8%	8.9%

To what extent do buyers buy on the basis of the type of retail outlet versus the brand? Would they seek out the brand in those channels that are to be emphasized?

What are the future market trends with respect to the importance of these three channels?

Have marketing efforts and policies directed at the three channels been optimal?

It would also be imperative to generate an analysis by product line and to study the interaction effects between channel and product profitability. In isolation, a distribution cost analysis can only indicate symptoms; coupled with a product line analysis, a channel audit, some knowledge of channel members' perceptions of marketing programs, and a strategic profit model analysis, it may lead directly to causes.

Furthermore, the decision to eliminate or deemphasize a channel is far-reaching, affecting every aspect of the business. For example, such a decision would need to be reviewed in light of the fact that smaller production runs and a reduced scale of production with the same amount of fixed costs might increase the unit manufacturing costs. In addition, a forecast of just what will happen to sales volume over a period of time is needed in order to assess the possible change in distribution policy.[75] It is also necessary to

[75] Sevin, *op. cit.*, p. 11.

estimate the decrease in total expense that would result from the action. In performing such an analysis, it is important to separate the nonsaveable (fixed) costs from the saveable costs, because, even when decisions to eliminate or deemphasize a channel are made, some of the costs associated with the deemphasized channel are likely to continue.

Besides the decision-making dilemma, there is considerable controversy surrounding the allocation methods to be used in distribution cost analysis. This controversy generally revolves around whether to allocate all costs or only direct and traceable costs. If the latter is the case, as it was in the hypothetical example presented above, then the analyst must be satisfied in dealing with a contribution-to-profit figure as his final output, rather than a net profit figure. For marketing channel problems, this approach is acceptable, because it is extremely difficult, if not impossible, to find reasonable ways of allocating indirect, nontraceable common costs (e.g., general management salaries, taxes, interest, and other types of overhead) to alternate channels.[76]

Even with these accounting questions, distribution cost analysis, performed in only a rudimentary fashion, can form the beginning step in the development of a channelwide information system, for in the process of going through the exercise, the manager is forced to consider all of the critical variables making for profitable channel relations. He will, in turn, begin to ask for appropriate information from other departments within his own firm and from other channel members. This process, in and of itself, should lead to more effective communication of common problems and, it is to be hoped, more successful interorganization management.[77]

SUMMARY AND CONCLUSIONS

Inadequate or inappropriate communication, or miscommunication can lead to wasted resources and stimulate interorganizational conflict. The development of a working information system is a prerequisite to securing efficient channel coordination. However, an information system will always be imperfect, because its construction will be impeded by legal, cost, and privacy constraints. Information systems, no matter how carefully developed,

---

[76]Those readers interested in pursuing this controversy, as well as a deeper understanding of the details and difficulties associated with distribution cost analysis, are urged to consult Sevin, *op. cit.*, Heckert and Miner, *op. cit.*, and Longman and Schiff, *op. cit.*

[77]In fact, Warshaw has argued that manufacturers *must* assume responsibility for introducing wholesalers to the use of distribution cost analysis if they wish to escape wholesalers' blanket condemnations for inadequate margins. See Martin R. Warshaw, "Pricing to Gain Wholesalers' Selling Support," in William G. Moller, Jr. and David L. Wilemon (eds.), *Marketing Channels: A Systems Viewpoint* (Homewood, Ill.: Richard D. Irwin, Inc., 1971), p. 247.

are also always subject to distortion, given the perceptual bias inherent in all individuals.

Problems in channel communications generally center around structural and activity issues having to do with the length of the channel, inventory levels, promotion, products, and prices.

The longer the channel, the more highly developed the feedback system available to each channel member must be. Also, there should be mechanisms permitting the bypassing of messages in the channel. There is also likely to be a need for the repetition of messages, given the number of links in the channel that can distort message contents.

Inventory management is a channelwide problem and demands channelwide communication. Inventory difficulties are intimately tied to problems associated with ordering, shipping, and delivery. To solve these problems, the first step must be the development of an effective *intra*organizational information system. Programs associated with the use of high-speed electronic data processing have revolutionized management's capability to deal with problems of inventory management and control. An especially significant innovation has been the introduction of computerized point-of-sale or front-end systems. These various systems have the potential for facilitating the queuing and sequencing of *inter*organizational messages relative to inventory management and control as well as providing instant feedback throughout a marketing channel. They represent communication breakthroughs whereby a significant amount of "noise" can be reduced via the formation of specialized languages and the alteration of technology. However, the economic, social, ethical, and political issues surrounding the widespread adoption of such systems are profound and must be carefully assessed and/or accounted for as the development of such systems progresses.

Beyond computerized systems, and perhaps in conjunction with them, there is a strong need for informational assistance programs, especially on the part of the larger firms in the channel for the smaller ones, who are less able to afford sophisticated inventory programs. Obviously, such assistance will be self-serving if it is successful.

Coordinated systems involving transportation modes and storage facilities demand appropriate queuing and sequencing of messages if communication noise attending timing problems is to be reduced in physical distribution. The development of specialized languages and the aid of computer technology have been significant in securing on-time delivery and adequate inventory, billing, and shipment information for a number of companies. The application of the concept of shared services also is likely to help reduce redundancy in physical distribution services and communication.

Adequate feedback is critical to the solution of promotion problems.

Here, the sales force of channel members—or other personnel operating at the boundary of channel organizations—are in key positions to observe difficulties associated with promotion and to enhance the communication process, except, of course, in situations where they themselves are involved in impeding the information flow. When conflicts of interest are suspected, use should be made of other interpenetration strategies, such as channel diplomacy. Clearly, poor communication with regard to promotion results in duplication of effort and dilution of promotional impact.

Difficulties associated with channel communication about product features are similar to those faced in reference to promotion, and therefore require similar types of attention and solution. However, understanding the significance of mutual uncertainty absorption may be even more crucial when one is dealing with product design changes and product innovation. In addition, a high degree of domain consensus appears to be a prerequisite to conflict management regarding warranty arrangements and can only be achieved through effective communication between channel members relative to rights and obligations with regard to the performance of in-warranty service.

Although pricing presents continual problems in channels, communication about prices is particularly cumbersome during stagflationary periods. Price lists are often inaccurate, misleading, and/or frequently out of date. However, sharing information in this area is dangerous, because the probability of being accused of conspiring to fix prices is increasing, even if conversations about pricing problems are informal and seemingly innocuous.

The starting point in initiating an *inter*organizational information system must come from analysis of a channel's performance and profitability. Four approaches should be taken in making this assessment: (1) developing a channel audit of marketing flows (as suggested in Chapter 1); (2) determining channel members' perceptions as to role behavior; (3) formulating strategic profit models (as suggested in Chapter 6); and (4) analyzing distribution costs. Distribution cost analysis, which has been focused on in this chapter, permits an evaluation of revenues and costs associated with the use of alternative existing channels.

The first step in distribution cost analysis is the reorganization and reclassification of accounting data found in a firm's profit and loss statement into marketing function (flow) categories or groupings. The second step calls for allocating the various costs associated with each functional (flow) category to each channel used by the firm. The third step is the preparation of a profit and loss statement for each channel.

The results of a distribution cost analysis *do not* constitute an adequate informational basis for taking corrective action. Such an analysis can only indicate symptoms. Despite controversies over the relevant costs to include, it can be a powerful diagnostic tool, especially when coupled with additional analyses.

DISCUSSION QUESTIONS

1. In long channels, it has been suggested that there is a need for mechanisms permitting the bypassing of messages. Suggest three possible mechanisms that might be used for "bypassing" purposes. Then discuss how, in such situations, conflict might be avoided relative to a "bypassed" channel member.

2. In what ways can the computer be used to make communication in marketing channels more efficient and effective? What effect will such data systems have on power relationships in channels? On the roles of channel members?

3. Compare and contrast the problems and opportunities of supermarkets and department stores in installing and utilizing front-end systems. What benefits will each receive from such systems? What difficulties will each face in fully utilizing them?

4. Debate the pros and cons of the adoption of UPC-code-oriented systems from a consumer's perspective and from society's perspective. Develop a position on such systems that you could present to the city council of your home town, assuming that the council is considering an ordinance banning such systems.

5. It has been argued by some that the major manufacturers of data processing equipment have embarked on different competitive strategies to further differentiate themselves, create "safe" market niches, lessen the chances for interorganizational hookups, and generally confuse users. IBM has even been accused of making word processing so complex that users think they need IBM to help them. Suggest some conflict management strategies that might be used by channel members to alleviate this situation.

6. What is the concept of "shared services"? In what ways might it be applied to transportation and storage problems, other than those directly mentioned in the text? What is the relationship between shared services and efficient intrachannel communications?

7. In dealing with false warranty claims on the part of its dealers, General Motors' new contract with its dealers requires dealers to keep two years of records available for inspection by GM instead of one, and it permits GM to provide copies to courts or governmental agencies whenever it decides the information is pertinent. According to the *Wall Street Journal* (October 30, 1975, p. 34), some dealers have complained that their business privacy is thus being eroded. As a result of these provisions, one dealer in the New York area has observed that GM has granted itself wider power to investigate its dealers, or to help others investigate them. What problems in communications within the channel is this situation evidence of? What solutions are there to these problems? Does the new contract provision seem equitable?

8. If you were a brand manager for a consumer goods manufacturer, what would you do in order to increase implementation of your trade deals at the retail level?

9. One author has observed that repositioning, scheduling/synchronization, simplification, access, and scale economies are the most important factors explaining the emergence and growth of vertical marketing systems. Explain what you believe is meant by each term, using examples to do so. Then explain what role information systems have had, relative to each factor.

10. Specify four separate distribution channels that might be used by a manufacturer of typewriters which are sold both for consumer and industrial use. Then, specify how each of the following costs might be allocated to the various channels: (1) billing, (2) district sales manager's expenses, (3) national magazine advertising, (4) marketing research, and (5) storage.

11. A wholesaler conducts a distribution cost study to determine the minimum-size order for breaking even. After finding this size, should the wholesaler refuse to accept orders below this size? What issues and alternatives should be considered.

THIRTEEN

INTERNATIONAL MARKETING CHANNELS

Except for the smallest marketers of goods and services, it is doubtful whether any commercial institution can avoid contact with the international marketplace in one form or another, even if such avoidance were somehow desirable. The opportunities to be gained from trading with foreign companies, serving foreign consumers, or offering assortments comprised of merchandise selected from the world's production are simply too great to pass by. In fact, a remarkable 30 percent of all U.S. corporate profits in 1974 was generated abroad.[1] An increasing number of American companies receive more than half of their net income from overseas operations. Table 13-1 provides data for a few of the numerous U.S. corporations that are finding foreign markets extremely attractive. In addition, foreign operations accounted for a very high proportion of the *growth* in net earnings of some of the corporations listed in Table 13-1. For example, 69.9 percent of Xerox's growth in net earnings between 1972 and 1974 could be traced to its foreign operations.[2] At Citicorp and at Pfizer, comparable figures for 1974 alone were 61.5 percent and over 100 percent, respectively.[3] This phenomenon is not limited to American multinationals. For example, some German companies, including Bayer and Volkswagen, generate over 60 per-

---

[1] "Those Overseas Earnings Can Turn Into an Albatross," *Business Week*, (May 12, 1975), p. 72.

[2] *Ibid.*

[3] *Ibid.*

TABLE 13-1 Foreign Earnings of Selected U.S. Companies, 1974

Company	(millions of dollars)		Foreign Share of Total Earnings
	Total Earnings	Foreign Earnings	
Black & Decker	$ 44.6	$ 23.5	53.6%
Citicorp	313.0	173.4	55.4
IBM	1,837.6	919.8	50.1
International Flavors & Fragrances	32.0	16.4	51.3
Pfizer	135.3	91.0	67.3
Xerox	331.1	171.0	51.6

Data: Drexel Burnham & Co.

SOURCE: "Those Overseas Earnings Can Turn into an Albatross," *Business Week*, May 12, 1975, p. 72.

cent of their sales from exports and overseas subsidiaries, as shown in Table 13-2.

Meanwhile, the volume of foreign goods carried by U.S. wholesaling and retailing firms has risen significantly over the past 25 years. Major retailing firms are expanding their operations abroad. Multinational retailers constitute a long list that includes Federated Department Stores in Madrid; Sears in Mexico, South America, and Spain; J. C. Penney in Belgium and

TABLE 13-2 The Importance of Exports and Sales of Overseas Subsidiaries for Selected German Companies

Company	Percentage of Total Sales					
	Exports		Sales of overseas subsidiaries		Exports plus sales of overseas subsidiaries	
	1965	1970	1965	1970	1965	1970
AEG	20%	21%	6%	8%	26%	29%
Bayer	39	42	18	22	57	64
BASF	36	30	9	17	45	47
Daimler-Benz	34	33	6	12	40	45
Farbwerke Hoechst	32	33	11	21	43	54
Siemens	20	21	16	18	36	39
Volkswagen	47	44	15	25	62	69

SOURCE: C. Hederer, C. D. Hoffmann, and B. Kumar, "The Internationalization of German Business," *Columbia Journal of World Business*, September–October, 1972, p. 42.

Italy; Kresge in Australia; Walgreen in Mexico; Safeway in Great Britain, Germany, and Australia; and Jewel in Belgium, Italy, and Spain.[4] These are joined by scores of multinational franchisors exemplified by McDonald's, Kentucky Fried Chicken, Weight Watchers, Avis, Hertz, and Holiday Inn, to name only a few.[5] The internationalization of retailing is not limited to U.S. retailers, however. For example, Prisunic, Monsprix, and SCOA Trading Company of France; Ahlen & Holm and EPA of Sweden; and Booker McConnell, John Holt & Company, and Hudson's Bay of Britain have tapped worldwide markets, as have certain European franchisors such as Wimpy and Carrier Cook Shops.[6]

It is possible to postulate that unless a firm is somehow actively participating in the international marketplace—either through support of buying offices in the case of retailers and wholesalers or through attempts to sell abroad in the case of manufacturers, it will suffer a severe competitive disadvantage to those that are.

The purpose of this chapter is to examine the channels of distribution available to organizations that wish to tap foreign markets and to enumerate some of the myriad interorganizational problems associated with trying to use them. Attention is also directed to describing institutional responses and possible alternatives for overcoming these problems. It is, however, very important to note at the outset that generalizations about international marketing channels are frequently deceptive because of the vast environmental differences from country to country. To a large extent, as was pointed out in Chapter 1, channels are shaped by their environments, and, therefore, to equate retailing in India, for example, with retailing in West Germany or to make inferences about retailing in the two countries combined would be misleading and erroneous. Although there exists in all countries some semblance of a wholesaling and a retailing structure, the variations within each structure are vast, indeed, as indicated in Figure 13–1. The appendix to this chapter includes a brief description of the major institutional forms and channel structures in each of six different countries representing the world's continents, geographic regions, and some of its market systems. It provides for the reader a small sampling of the diversity referred to above.

[4]Stanley C. Hollander, "The International Store-Keepers," *MSU Business Topics,* (Spring, 1969), pp. 13–22.

[5]Bruce Walker and Michael Etzel, "The Internationalization of U.S. Franchise Systems: Progress and Procedures," *Journal of Marketing,* Vol. 37 (April, 1973), pp. 38–46.

[6]Stanley C. Hollander, *Multinational Retailing* (East Lansing, Michigan: Michigan State University, 1970), pp. 27–41 and 62–70. See also "Inflation and Recession Dampen Profits Worldwide," *Business Week* (July 14, 1975), pp. 71–75.

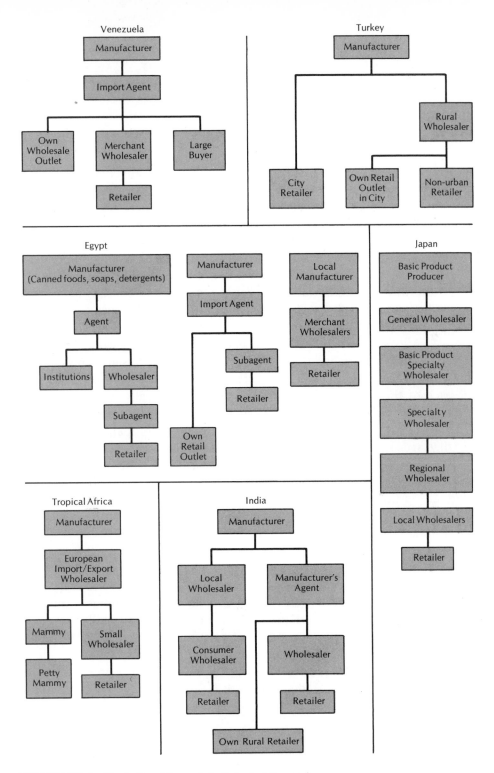

FIGURE 13-1 Marketing Channels in Selected Countries

SOURCE: George Wadinambiaratchi, "Channels of Distribution in Developing Economics," *The Business Quarterly,* Vol. 30 (Winter, 1965), pp. 74–82.

INTERORGANIZATIONAL PERSPECTIVE
OF ALTERNATIVE FORMS
OF INTERNATIONAL EXPANSION

The perspective taken in the chapter is basically that of a U.S. manufacturer considering expansion abroad. In this respect, there appear to be four basic routes to expansion, although clearly there are numerous possible variations. The simplest form of expansion is through the *exportation* of a company's products to other nations with a demand for the products. The advantage of this route to foreign markets is that it involves minimal investment, and thus, the risk of failure will not usually affect the overall activities of the firm. The disadvantage of relying mainly on export agencies, however, is that the company will usually have *little control* over the marketing of its products in foreign markets.

Another form of expansion is *licensing,* whereby the company forges a contractual agreement with a foreign organization to sell its products abroad with the understanding that a certain percentage of the profits will accrue to each of the parties.[7] The "home" company generally is expected to furnish technical assistance to the foreign firm. The main advantages of this route are the low investment required by the home company and the assurance that at least some form of purposive marketing strategy will be adopted for the firm's products. However, as in the case of simple exportation, there may be *little real control* over the licensee's operation. It is even possible that the licensee will eventually acquire the technical expertise of the home firm, thereby altering the dependency relationship. Thus, *power,* in such situations may *rapidly shift* to the foreign firm.

A third and more involved route to expansion is via the establishment of *joint ventures* whereby, through a collaborative arrangement, two or more firms share the investment and risk of the expansionary effort. If the joint venture is forged with a foreign firm, the home firm obviously gains the commitment of the foreign firm to share its skills and its market access. Again, there are problems of control, but they appear to be less than in situations where mutual investment is not involved.

If the home company wishes to achieve a high degree of control over the marketing of its products abroad, it will probably undertake to follow a fourth route—*direct investment.* If it does this, it must commit itself to

---

[7] In consumer goods marketing, soft drink companies (Pepsico, Coca-Cola) have long been engaged in international franchising. More recently, fast-food firms, such as McDonald's, have expanded, using licensing arrangements. See "Europe: A Wolfish Hunter for U.S. Fast Foods," *Business Week* (October 21, 1972), p. 34. Also, see Walker and Etzel, *op. cit.*

learning the mores and nuances of each foreign market that it enters. The dollar amount of the investment—both in terms of capital expenditure and management time—is likely to be substantial, and there is always the risk of expropriation and nationalization, particularly in politically unstable countries.[8] Much of the direct investment by U.S. firms abroad is accomplished by very large multinational corporations, and there are indications that the growth of their international operations, especially as they relate to direct investment, will be much slower than it was during the 1960's and early 1970's. Some of these indications are as follows:[9]

The United Nations and various national governments, including the United States, have begun studies aimed at controlling the future growth of the large multinational corporations. Because of their massive size (e.g., the 15 largest industrial companies in the world in 1975 were full-fledged multinationals), there is considerable attention being given to means by which their exercise of economic, social, and political power can be guided, especially through the introduction of some form of international accountability relative to their widespread activities.

The U.S. Congress has begun to question some of the alleged tax advantages of U.S. multinational firms. Key issues are the foreign-tax credit, which permits multinationals to use foreign-tax payments as a credit against U.S. taxes, and tax deferral, which delays U.S. taxes until earnings are brought back to the United States. Changes here would result in increasing the cost of foreign investment on the part of U.S. firms.

The worldwide recession of 1973–1975 reduced the profits of many multinational corporations and cast doubt on future growth prospects. In fact, the United States may become a better site for investment than many overseas markets, because U.S. economic recovery patterns appear to be stronger than those abroad.

Disclosure of bribery, "slush funds," and political manipulation have badly damaged the public image of multinational firms.[10]

United States labor unions are claiming that U.S.-based multinational corporations are exporting American jobs as a result of their direct investment programs.

[8]For a complete discussion of these and other expansionary routes, see Philip R. Cateora and John M. Hess, *International Marketing*, 3rd ed. (Homewood, Illinois: Richard D. Irwin, 1975), Chapter 17. For data on some of the political difficulties encountered in direct investment, see "Multinationals Find the Going Rougher," *Business Week* (July 14, 1975), pp. 64–69.

[9]Lindley H. Clark, Jr., "Global Crossroads: Multinational Firms, Under Fire All Over, Face a Changed Future," *Wall Street Journal*, December 3, 1975, p. 1.

[10]See Discussion Question 2 at the end of this chapter for an example. Also see Carol H. Falk, "No Company Has Proven Bribe Is Needed To Sell Its Products, SEC Chairman Says," *Wall Street Journal*, March 5, 1976, p. 5; and Jerry Landauer and Carol Falk, "Rollins Inc. Says It Will Continue Payoffs Abroad; Other Firm Tells of Resistance," *Wall Street Journal*, March 3, 1976, p. 3.

Direct investment has been encouraged by the fact that foreign trade restrictions have frequently made it difficult or impossible for a U.S. company to compete in a foreign market without having a plant or subsidiary located abroad. In addition, Robert Solomon, the Federal Reserve Board's chief adviser on international finance, has observed that:

> An overvalued dollar made it cheap to acquire assets abroad. It also made it unattractive to convert foreign earnings back into dollars and thus tended to encourage reinvestment of profits abroad. In the late 1950's and the early 1960's, the profitability of investment simply was higher abroad than in the U.S.[11]

Thus, by 1975, U.S. direct investment abroad was $110 billion compared with $22 billion of foreign direct investment in the United States.[12] However, the gap between the profitability of investment in the United States and the investment abroad has been narrowing ever since the early 1960's. Also, the reduction of trade barriers during the late 1960's and early 1970's has made such restrictions less of a problem for exports and thus less of an incentive for direct overseas investment. Finally, unit labor costs during the early 1970's rose more slowly in the United States than in other major industrial countries. This trend increased the competitiveness of U.S. exports and made production in the United States relatively more attractive, compared with production overseas.[13]

Regardless of the expansionary route followed, the international marketer will be faced with the problem of designing and implementing a distribution strategy. The channel system for international marketing, especially for those firms not undertaking direct investment, almost always involves two channel segments, one domestic and the other foreign. Compared to marketing within one's home country, the international marketing channel is, of necessity, longer, because it generally involves using a large number of intermediaries, which play a major role in facilitating the flow of products from domestic production to foreign consumption. Obviously, this results in increasing the complexity of managing the channel, from an interorganization perspective, because of the idiosyncracies of international intermediaries, the environments in which they operate, and the lack of effective and economically feasible control over their operations. The wholesaling and retailing institutions and agencies involved in the international distribution process are described briefly below.

[11] Clark, *op. cit.,* p. 21.
[12] *Ibid.*
[13] *Ibid.*

WHOLESALE LINKAGES
TO FOREIGN MARKETS[14]

Figure 13–2 provides some idea of the international channel alternatives available to a domestic producer. Domestic middlemen are located in the producer's home country and provide marketing services from the domestic base. As Cateora and Hess point out, they are convenient to use, but are removed from their foreign markets and, therefore, may not be able to provide the kind of market information and representation available from foreign-based middlemen.[15] Table 13–3 summarizes the primary functions performed by the major kinds of domestic middlemen selling to foreign markets. A brief description of a few of the various types of agents is given below, based on Cateora and Hess' classification scheme.[16]

> *CEM (combination export manager)*: An agent middleman who generally serves a number of principals, each of which has a relatively small international volume, and acts as the international marketing department for the firms he represents. He will usually do business under principal's name (e.g., using the principal's letterhead), and thus foreign customers seldom know that they are not dealing directly with the export department of the principal. He operates mainly on commission but may also receive fees.

> *MEA (manufacturer's export agent)*: An agent middleman similar to the CEM, except that the former does business in his own name rather than in the name of his principals.

> *Norazi*: An agent who specializes in shady or difficult transactions, such as those involving contraband materials (e.g., radioactive products, war materials), black market currency operations, untaxed liquor, and narcotics.

The "Merchants" category in Table 13–3 refers primarily to merchant wholesale operations. Their functions are almost identical to the merchant middlemen described in Chapter 3 except that they sell in foreign countries. In fact, most international merchant middlemen both import and export.[17] Rather than dealing with the domestic agents or merchant middlemen, a manufacturer may choose to deal directly with the middlemen located in

---

[14]The discussion in this section is based largely on the excellent descriptions provided in Cateora and Hess, *op. cit.*, Chapter 15.

[15]*Ibid.*, pp. 480–481.

[16]*Ibid.*, pp. 483–485 and 488–489.

[17]*Ibid.*, pp. 489–490.

TABLE 13-3   Characteristics of Domestic Middlemen Serving International Markets

	Agents				
Types of Duties	CEM	MEA	Broker	Buying[a] Offices	Other Manufacturers[b]
Take title	No	No	No	No	No
Take possession	Yes	Yes	No	Yes	Yes
Continuing relationship	Yes	Yes	No	Yes	Yes
Share of foreign output	All	All	Any	Small	All
Degree of control by principal	Fair	Fair	Nil	Nil	Good
Price authority	Advisory	Advisory	Yes (at market level)	Yes (to buy)	Advisory
Represent buyer or seller	Seller	Seller	Either	Buyer	Seller
Number of principals	Few—Many	Few—Many	Many	Small	Few
Arrange shipping	Yes	Yes	Not usually	Yes	Yes
Type of goods	Manufactured goods and commodities	Staples and commodities	Staples and commodities	Staples and commodities	Complementary to their own lines
Breadth of line	Specialty—wide	All types of staples	All types of staples	Retail goods	Narrow
Handle competitive lines	No	No	Yes	Yes—utilizes many sources	No
Extent of promotion and selling effort	Good	Good	One shot	N.A.	Good
Extends credit to principal	Occasionally	Occasionally	Seldom	Seldom	Seldom
Market information	Fair	Fair	Price and market conditions	For principal not for manufacturer	Good

[a]Commissionaire operates like a resident buyer but works on commission only.

[b]A manufacturer may take on complementary products to sell overseas. This spreads overhead and may strengthen the market position of both firms by providing a more complete line.

[c]Intermerchants are export brokers who arrange switch trades or triangular trading involving several principals from different countries who need to arrange trades in order to overcome soft currency or exchange restriction problems.

		Merchants				
Inter-merchant^c	Norazi	Export Merchant^d	Export Jobber^e	Buyers for Export	Importers and Trading Companies	Complementary Marketers
No	No	Yes	Yes	Yes	Yes	Yes
No	Yes	Yes	No	Yes	Yes	Yes
No	No	No	Yes	No	Yes	Yes
Small	Small	Any	Small	Small	Any	Most
Nil	Nil	None	None	None	Nil	Fair
Some	Yes	Yes	Yes	Yes	No	Some
Both at once	Both	Self	Self	Self	Self	Self
Several per transaction	Several per transaction	Many sources	Many sources	Many sources	Many sources	One per product
No	Yes	Yes	Yes	Yes	Yes	Yes
Any	Contraband	Manufactured goods	Bulky and raw materials	All types	Manufactured goods	Complementary to line
	N.A.	Broad	Broad	Broad	Broad	Narrow
Yes	Yes	Yes	Yes	Yes	Yes	No
Nil	Nil	Nil	Nil	Nil	Good	Good
No	No	Occasionally	Seldom	Seldom	Seldom	Seldom
No	No	Nil	Nil	Nil	Fair	Good

^d Also known as cable merchant.
^e Also known as export speculator.

SOURCE: Philip Cateora and John M. Hess, *International Marketing*, 3rd ed. (Homewood, Ill.: Richard D. Irwin, Inc., 1975), pp. 484–485.

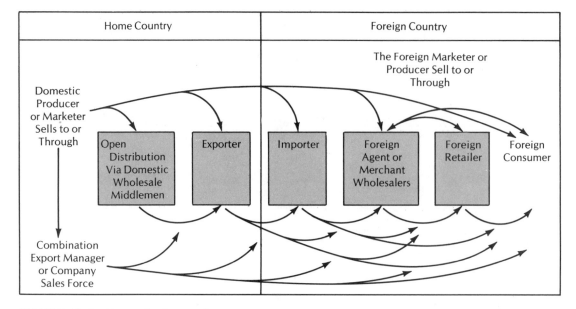

FIGURE 13-2   Alternative International Marketing Channels

SOURCE: Philip R. Cateora and John M. Hess, *International Marketing*, 3rd ed. (Homewood, Ill.: Richard D. Irwin, Inc., 1975), p. 461.

foreign markets. Although such a decision will bring the manufacturer closer to these markets and shorten his channel considerably, it will also involve him with problems of language, physical distribution, communications, and financing.[18] Table 13-4 summarizes the primary functions of foreign-based middlemen. While the functions of the various agent middlemen generally follow the description of U.S. agent middlemen found in the appendix to Chapter 3, it should be emphasized, once again, that in foreign commerce there seem to be very few "pure" types. In other words, the functions performed and marketing flows participated in may vary from situation to situation and are generally subject to negotiations. For example, one unique form of agent middleman is the *comprador* or *del credere* agent. According to Cateora and Hess:

> (The comprador) functions in Far Eastern countries and has historically been particularly important in trade with China. (He) is essentially a general manager who acts as the representative of a foreign merchant in his operations in a given Oriental country. A comprador is used because of his intimate knowledge of the obscure and enigmatic customs and languages of the importing country.[19]

[18] *Ibid.,* p. 481.
[19] *Ibid.,* pp. 495–496.

TABLE 13-4 Characteristics of Middlemen Located in Foreign Countries

Type of Duties	Agents						Merchant		
	Broker	Factor	Manufacturer's Representative[a]	Import Commission	Comprador	Distributor	Dealer	Import Jobber[b]	Retailer
Take title	No	No	No	No	No	Yes	Yes	Yes	Yes
Take possession	No	No	Seldom	Seldom	Yes	Yes	Yes	Yes	Yes
Continuing relationship	No	Sometimes	Often	With buyer, not seller	Yes	Yes	Yes	No	Usually not
Share of foreign output	Small	Small	All or part for one area	N.A.	All one area	All, for certain countries	Assignment area	Small	Very small
Degree of control by principal	Low	Low	Fair	None	Fair	High	High	Low	Nil
Price authority	Nil	Nil	Nil	Nil	Partial	Partial	Partial	Full	Full
Represent buyer or seller	Either	Either	Seller	Buyer	Seller	Seller	Seller	Self	Self
Number of principals	Many	Many	Few	Many	Few	Small	Few major	Many	Many
Arrange shipping	No	No	No	No	No	No	No	No	No
Type of goods	Commodity and food	Commodity and food	Manufactured goods	All types manufactured goods	Manufactured goods	Manufactured goods	Manufactured goods	Manufactured goods	Manufactured consumer
Breadth of line	Broad	Broad (often specialized)	Allied lines	Broad		Narrow to broad	Narrow	Narrow to broad	Narrow to broad
Handle competitive lines	Yes	Yes	No	Yes	No	No	No	Yes	Yes
Extent of promotion and selling effort	Nil	Nil	Fair	Nil	Fair	Fair	Good	Nil	Nil usually
Extends credit to principal	No	Yes	No	No	Sometimes	Sometimes	No	No	No
Market information	Nil	Fair	Good	Nil	Good	Fair	Good	Nil	Nil

[a]Also known as sales agent, residual agent, exclusive agent, commission agent, or indent agent. (The indent agent's title is derived from his use of indent orders—those which must be confirmed and accepted before they serve as contracts.)
[b]Also known as import house, import merchant.

SOURCE: Philip R. Cateora and John M. Hess, *International Marketing*, 3rd ed. (Homewood, Ill.: Richard D. Irwin, Inc., 1975), pp. 494–495.

In many respects, foreign merchant middlemen are also not signficantly different, in terms of functions performed, from the U.S. merchant middlemen described in Chapter 3. However, because of the absence of antitrust laws similar to those found in the United States, it is often possible for a U.S.-based producer to exercise greater coercive, reward, and legitimate power with regard to foreign intermediaries. Thus, many foreign distributors have been granted exclusive territorial rights by their suppliers, and relationships with suppliers are frequently formalized through tight franchise or ownership arrangements that might be challengeable in the United States.[20] Another difference is found in the fact that foreign retailers frequently engage directly in importing for both retailing *and* wholesaling purposes.

> The combination retailer-wholesaler is more important in foreign countries than in the United States. It is not at all uncommon to find most of the larger retailers in any city wholesaling their goods to local shops and dealers.[21]

From the perspective of interorganization management, control over the activities and operations of marketing channels is generally more difficult to accomplish than it is within the boundaries of the United States, even though antitrust laws may be more lenient in foreign countries. Despite the commonality in functions performed, wholesaling patterns are not as well developed as they are in the United States. It is not unusual to find that manufacturers based in such highly developed economies as Italy[22] are forced to undertake direct shipments to small retailing establishments on a daily or very frequent basis. This kind of distribution obviously eliminates any of the cost advantages of shipping merchandise in large lots as well as prohibits the obtaining of advantages accruing to an efficient division of labor within the channel. Furthermore, a recurring pattern in foreign countries is that huge middlemen and tiny middlemen predominate.[23] This means that the supplier seeking to tap international markets must either give over control to economically and often politically powerful distributors or must develop his own system. For example,

> In Malaya, . . . fewer than a dozen merchant houses (European) handle over half of the import trade, while hundreds of local trading companies handle the balance.

[20] See "Using Foreign Distributors Without Fearing Antitrust," *Business Abroad* (March 8, 1965), p. 28.

[21] Cateora and Hess, *op. cit.,* p. 497.

[22] Pietro Gennaro, "Wholesaling in Italy," in Robert Bartels (ed.), *Comparative Marketing: Wholesaling in Fifteen Countries* (Homewood, Illinois: Richard D. Irwin, Inc., 1963), pp. 37–46.

[23] For a thorough description of wholesaling in a variety of countries, see Robert Bartels (ed.), *op. cit.*

In Israel, there are some 1,500 wholesalers, most of whom are small. Contrast these with Hamashbir Hamerkazi, a giant wholesaler who handles all kinds of products and has full or partial ownership in 12 major industrial firms. In the early 1960's they reportedly handled approximately 1/5th of all the wholesaling volume of that country.... In India, ... outside companies may have a hard time gaining distribution because the large wholesalers have such an entrenched position that by providing the package of financial and marketing services, they are able to obtain monopsonistic power. Japan's zaibatsu (trading and financial combines) finance subwholesalers, retailers, and manufacturers as well, making a completely integrated link centering around the strongest middlemen.[24]

The emergence of huge wholesaling operations in foreign countries is due, in part, to the fact that foreign manufacturers have traditionally been production-oriented and, therefore, have avoided concerning themselves deeply with marketing and distribution problems. Such a situation may change somewhat as more and more U.S. fully integrated and semi-integrated marketers become involved in international marketing. However, any changes are likely to come slowly, because wholesalers, especially importers and exporters in developing nations,[25] have such a high degree of political influence. Through such influence, they can (and do) effectively forestall improvements in distribution methods. The polarity of wholesale trade is, therefore, likely to be an integral part of international business operations for some time to come.

Perhaps one of the most fascinating examples associated with the problems of achieving effective wholesale distribution abroad is the story of Levi Strauss' efforts to gain a large market share for its clothing products (jeans, pants, and shirts) in Europe in the late 1960's and early 1970's.[26] According to a *Fortune* report on its problems, the company made "a fast grab for the European market without sufficient control on inventory and distribution."[27] The upshot of its experience was that the debacle cost Levi Strauss at least $12 million and left the company with a deficit of over $7 million in the fourth quarter of 1973. Some of the relevant facts of the debacle are detailed below.[28]

Because demand in Europe was far outrunning supply, there seemed, from management's perspective, to be no pressing need for inventory con-

---

[24]Cateora and Hess, *op. cit.,* pp. 515–516 and previous revised edition (1971), p. 826.

[25]See Reed Moyer, "The Structure of Markets in Developing Countries," in William G. Moller, Jr. and David L. Wilemon (eds.), *Marketing Channels: A Systems Viewpoint* (Homewood, Illinois: Richard D. Irwin, Inc., 1971), pp. 76–78.

[26]Peter Vanderwicken, "When Levi Strauss Burst Its Britches," *Fortune* (April, 1974), pp. 131–138.

[27]*Ibid.,* p. 131.

[28]These details were reported in Vanderwicken, *op. cit.,* pp. 133–135.

trols. In 1970, Levi Strauss Europe (L. S. E.)'s inventory turned over seven times (about four is normal for apparel), and the main warehouse in Antwerp had to be fully replenished an incredible 19 times. Independent distributors were buying L. S. E.'s merchandise without any careful planning as to future demand. Learning that a shipment was arriving, distributors would send trucks to Antwerp and buy anything they saw.

To improve Levi's distribution within Europe as quickly as possible, L. S. E. acquired the firms that had been its national distributors in 10 countries and turned them into sales subsidiaries. This move was made rather than bringing in Levi Strauss salesmen, who were experienced in domestic apparel markets but unfamiliar with marketing in Europe. Close relationships between manufacturers and retailers are vital in the apparel business, and management believed that L. S. E.'s distributors and their salesmen would provide that tie, enabling the company to keep attuned to changes in each national market. However, meshing the acquired firms with L. S. E. proved to be unexpectedly difficult. Their presidents were long-established businessmen in their own countries, and they resisted changing their methods. In Britain, one former owner resisted proposals for warehouse consolidation and other managerial changes so strongly that the company shifted him into another job.

In keeping with well-established Levi Strauss policy, each national manager retained full autonomy and profit responsibility. At first, L. S. E. received only quarterly balance sheets—outdated information. Moreover, each new subsidiary operated differently, with its own accounting and inventory-control systems. Only in Switzerland was the operation computerized, but its system did not fit with L. S. E.'s. Furthermore, several of the firms did not have accurate information about their inventories. Their reports were often so lacking in details (about sizes and styles, for example) as to be meaningless.

Almost three-quarters of the pants the company sold in Europe were imported from plants located outside the continent. Once the goods did reach Europe, L. S. E. could not keep track of where they were. Moreover, the ever-increasing volume of pants overwhelmed the efforts of clerks to keep adequate records of the movements. As a result, warehouse workers often did not know where to find goods stacked in the bins. Incredible as it seems, if a retailer returned a shipment, L. S. E.'s warehouse had no means of reentering the goods into inventory.

On top of all this, fashion changes swept Europe and compounded what already was a major catastrophe in the making. Further evidence of L. S. E.'s lack of control was found when one distributor who had not been acquired requested a particular style, which L. S. E. declined to produce.

Rather than accepting L. S. E.'s decision, the distributor flew to Hong Kong and ordered two million pairs of the style he wanted directly from the Levi Strauss manufacturing subsidiary there.

Although one might argue that even with the lack of control, L. S. E. was able to accomplish its objective because it eventually captured the largest share of the European market for jeans,[29] there can be little doubt that the European experience was, for Levi Strauss, a traumatic experience that the corporation would not like to repeat. The fact remains that the European wholesalers were, to a very large extent, the root cause of L. S. E's major problems and that even vertical integration was ineffective in securing the needed control over their operations. One lesson is, therefore, abundantly clear—if adequate distribution and effective interorganization management were so difficult for a sophisticated U.S. manufacturer and marketer to secure in a developed, highly industrialized market like Europe, it is likely to be even more difficult to secure in less developed economies. In international marketing channels, nothing can be taken for granted.

As is so clearly evident in the Levi Strauss case, the need to develop functioning and meaningful information systems is absolutely crucial. Above anything else, this facet of international marketing may be the most arduous problem, given the current state of foreign distribution and the power held by the middlemen in those markets. As Fayerweather has observed:

> Secretiveness is one of the prominent characteristics of the independent trader in any society. The ability to outbargain and outmaneuver competitors in the marketplace often depends upon keeping your own counsel and playing a lone wolf game. So the . . . merchant . . . is thoroughly imbued with a philosophy quite at odds with the concept of transmitting information to producers. It is rank heresy by his standards, for example, to tell a manufacturer how much inventory he has, one of the key pieces of information that can help the producer. . . .
>
> Individualistic peoples are more inclined (than group-oriented societies) to look on others as antagonists and to think, especially in work relations, in terms of competing and outmaneuvering those around them rather than cooperating. The cultures of Latin America, the Middle East, and Far East generally lean in this direction. Clearly, group-oriented attitudes (such as exist in the U.S.) facilitate the transmission of information, while merchants in an individualistic culture find their natural disinclination to communicate reinforced.[30]

---

[29] It has been shown that companies that have achieved the highest market shares in various industries also have the highest returns on their investments. See Robert D. Buzzell, Bradley T. Gale, and Ralph G. M. Sultan, "Market Share—A Key to Profitability," *Harvard Business Review*, Vol. 53 (January–February, 1975), pp. 97–106.

[30] John Fayerweather, *International Marketing*, 2nd ed. (Englewood Cliffs, N. J.: Prentice-Hall, Inc., 1970), pp. 71–72.

RETAILING IN INTERNATIONAL MARKETS[31]

As frustrating as it must sound to someone looking for information about international distribution channels, the structure of retailing in foreign markets is even more diverse than the structure of wholesaling. It is possible to observe, however, that as industrial progress increases, retailing is, for the most part, performed by larger and larger units.[32] The retailing of food provides an example. As established in Chapter 2, food retailing in the United States is dominated by the larger supermarket. However, as Fayerweather points out:

> In Europe, supermarkets are progressing, but over 80 percent of the food trade is still in the hands of small merchants with modest stores. In India, food is still mainly sold through thousands of individual tradesmen squatting in open markets, hawking their goods from door to door, or selling from tiny hole-in-the-wall shops.[33]

The European experience appears to be paralleling the historical development of food distribution in the United States. Certain European marketers appear to have benefited markedly by the U.S. experience in the sense that as they develop new modes of food distribution, there is a high degree of concern with increased productivity. Thus, in West Germany and Switzerland, food discounting operations that provide limited assortments of merchandise have achieved remarkable performance records. These stores carry only dry groceries, are relatively small (compared to U.S. Standards), lack frills, rely on bulk merchandising (as contrasted with shelf display of individual items), use a minumum number of personnel, emphasize private label merchandise at remarkable values, and are located in densely populated areas.

The diversity between Europe and India in food retailing described above is found in diverse merchandise categories in other countries as well.

> In some countries, such as Italy and Morocco, retailing is composed largely of speciality houses carrying narrow lines. In other countries, such as Finland, most

---

[31]The discussion in this section is based largely on John Fayerweather, *op. cit.*, pp. 60–79. See also Vern Terpstra, *International Marketing* (New York: Holt, Rinehart and Winston, 1972), pp. 312–316.

[32]*Ibid.*, p. 61. See also Johan Arndt, "Temporal Lags in Comparative Retailing," *Journal of Marketing*, Vol. 36 (October, 1972), pp. 40–45.

[33]*Ibid.*, p. 62.

retailers carry a rather general line of merchandise. Retail size is represented at one end by Japan's giant Mitsukoshi Ltd., which today continues to set an unparalleled standard of excellence of goods, fair prices, and superior service, and enjoys the patronage of more than 100,000 customers every day. The other extreme is represented in the market of Ibadan, Nigeria, which has some 3,000 one- or two-man stalls.[34]

While the size of retail establishments appears to vary with economic development, so does the service and the assortment one gains with individual establishments. Thus, in developing nations there is emphasis on personal attention, and negotiation between retailer and consumer often takes on the character of a major social event. As one moves up the development ladder, self-service begins to become the predominant service mode. Specialization is greater in lower-income economies. But, as Fayerweather has observed, there is little difference in assortment breadth between low- and middle-income countries. For example, of the 650,000 retailers in France, most are small shops specializing in one class of products.[35] It is only when one reaches the higher-income economies that one finds a proliferation of lines carried by all sorts of retailers.

The reasons for these differences in service and specialization can be explained, in part, in terms of consumer behavior. The lack of mobility, refrigeration, and other amenities, combined with the desire for social interaction, support a maintenance of the present fragmented retailing systems in many low- and middle-income countries. On the other hand, the investment required in both facilities and education to enter retailing in developing nations is extremely low.[36] For some, retailing—of one form or another— represents the only avenue open to earn a living. Thus, from both a demand and a supply side, the existing system is reinforced.

Unfortunately for such nations the cost of such a system is extremely high, both for consumers and for retailers. From the standpoint of consumption, there are no opportunities to shop at outlets where distribution economies have been achieved, and lower prices can only be gained by effective bargaining and exhaustive search. On the supply side, tradesmen have an extremely low status in their societies; in fact, shopping expeditions represent for some consumers a way of being able to support their self-esteem,

[34]Cateora and Hess, op. cit., p. 517.

[35]Fayerweather, op. cit., p. 63.

[36]For an analytical discussion of some of these issues, with particular reference to Greece, see Lee E. Preston, "Marketing Organization and Economic Development: Structure, Products, and Management," in Louis P. Bucklin (ed.), Vertical Marketing Systems (Glenview, Ill.: Scott Foresman and Co., 1970), pp. 116-133, and Arieh Goldman, "Outreach of Consumers and the Modernization of Urban Food Retailing in Developing Countries," Journal of Marketing, Vol. 38 (October, 1974), pp. 8-16.

because during such expeditions, they can interact with someone of lower status than they. In fact, improvements in retail distribution have been seen by some as a primary means for elevating a developing country, because through lower prices, as gained through better distribution methods, the real income of the population will increase, and thus there is a greater likelihood for a long-term savings-investment cycle to commence.[37]

Retailing in many international markets has been slow to change, owing to cultural, economic, political, and managerial factors. For example, the reticence to share information and the low status accorded to merchants have had inhibiting effects. Also, in many countries, small retailers and wholesalers have, through political action, blocked distributive innovations.[38] Also, there appears to be a natural reluctance among numerous foreign middlemen to provide adequate after-sale service and to use modern promotional methods.[39] However, there are cases where consumers and merchants have combined forces to overcome stagnation. For instance, while consumer cooperatives have had a minimal impact in the United States, they are tremendously important in most European countries. They are strongest in the Scandinavian countries, accounting for a third of retail sales in Finland and comparable portions in Norway and Sweden.[40] In Switzerland, consumer cooperatives account for one-fifth of the retail food stores and over one-fourth of retail food sales.

> The Union of Swiss Cooperative Societies (U. S. K.) and the Federation of Migros Cooperatives (Migros) account for nearly ten percent of Switzerland's total (not only food) retail sales. Each of the two leading coops boasts memberships exceeding one-third of the households in Switzerland.[41]

The existence of these and other cooperatives throughout Europe can almost always be traced to a situation in which a group of consumers felt that the private distribution system was not providing goods at fair prices or of consistent quality.

There is evidence, however, that in France, Carrefour, an emerging supermarket chain, is slowly but surely winning a significant niche in its competitive arena even without enlisting the direct investment of consumers,

[37]This point has been developed by Charles C. Slater, "Market Channel Coordination and Economic Development," in Louis P. Bucklin (ed.), *op. cit.*, pp. 135–156.

[38]Cateora and Hess, *op. cit.*, p. 520. Also see J. J. Boddewyn and Stanley C. Hollander (eds.), *Public Policy Toward Retailing* (Lexington, Mass.: Lexington Books, 1973).

[39]See Fayerweather, *op. cit.*, pp. 69–70.

[40]A. J. Alton, "Marketing in Finland," *Journal of Marketing*, Vol. 27 (July, 1963), p. 49. For a detailed discussion of consumer cooperatives, see Hollander, *Multinational Retailing, op. cit.*, pp. 71–90.

[41]Cateora and Hess, *op. cit.*, p. 520.

though small food retailers and wholesalers in France appear to have a stranglehold on the issuance of supermarket licenses. Furthermore, superstores or hypermarches (hypermarkets) have made important inroads into French retailing, as indicated in the appendix to this chapter.[42] There are, indeed, innovations in European retailing from which U.S. marketers could learn much.[43] But the changeover to more efficient retailing methods in foreign markets is difficult, even in the absence of political resistance, because, as Fayerweather points out, critical risk-taking assignments such as buying and the whole sensitive area of relations with customers must be turned over to hired employees.

> Because hired employees lack the intimate motivations and controls that guide the owner-merchant, management must devise supervision methods, incentives, controls, and all the paraphernalia of business organization to achieve the same results. . . . (W)hen Weston Company of Canada started a supermarket chain in England in 1961, the company found it easier to move 500 managerial employees from its Canadian stores to England than to indoctrinate Englishmen used to small-store operations to run the organization.[44]

PROBLEMS IN ESTABLISHING INTERNATIONAL MARKETING CHANNELS

Although it may appear redundant to emphasize further problems in establishing foreign distribution since numerous difficulties have already been highlighted throughout this chapter, it is essential that the marketing manager be aware of most of the major obstacles in his way prior to initiating international trade. Careful planning is crucial if a company is to obtain

---

[42] In France, hypermarchés, on average, cover an area of 268,000 sq ft, have parking space for 3000 cars, include 49 checkouts up front and 11 department registers, cost approximately $11 million to construct, and generate $35 million in sales volume by retailing both general merchandise and food. Pricing averages 10 to 15 percent below normal retail, and annual sales run as high as $70 million per outlet (compared with only $20 to $30 million per outlet for major U.S. discount stores). Each store stocks from 20,000 to 50,000 brand name items and sells them at an average markup of 11 to 12 percent. Since their initial appearance in France in 1963, hypermarchés have spread rapidly; there are now more than 1000 such outlets throughout Europe. See E. B. Weiss, "The Hypermarché Marches into U.S. Mass Retailing," *Advertising Age*, December 30, 1974, p. 20. See also, Eric Langeard and Robert A. Peterson, "Diffusion of Large-Scale Food Retailing in France: Supermarché et Hypermarché," *Journal of Retailing*, Vol. 51 (Fall, 1975), pp. 43ff; and Douglas J. Tigert, "The Changing Structure of Retailing in Europe and North America: Challenges and Opportunities," University of Toronto Retailing and Institutional Research Program Working Paper 75-02 (January 1974), pp. 17-20.

[43] See Ralph Z. Sorenson, II, "U.S. Marketers Can Learn From European Innovations," *Harvard Business Review* (September–October, 1972), pp. 89-99 and Warren J. Keegan, *International Marketing Management* (Englewood Cliffs, N.J.: Prentice-Hall, Inc., 1974), pp. 302 and 311-314.

[44] Fayerweather, *op. cit.*, p. 68.

the lucrative benefits possible from serving foreign markets. Only through a knowledge of likely problem areas can such planning be undertaken.

First, it is not always an easy task to find out which middlemen may be available to handle a company's merchandise. Several directories have been published that may aid in this task.[45] Other sources suggested by Cateora and Hess include foreign consulates, Chamber of Commerce groups, middlemen associations, business publications, management consultants, and carriers.[46]

Second, it is likely that a relatively larger proportion of a company's advertising budget will have to be devoted to channel communications than in the United States, because there are so many small middlemen who must be reached.[47]

Third, access to markets may be blocked by existing financial and other tie-in arrangements with middlemen often not available to companies in the United States. In Japan, for example, manufacturers are one of the primary sources of financial assistance to the middlemen with whom they deal.[48] Such assistance solidifies trade relations in that country, and, given the emphasis on the accomplishments of the group rather than the individual (e.g., Japanese manufacturers are more likely to look upon their resellers as members of their "group" than are American executives), it may be extremely difficult for an "outsider" to break into an established channel system. This is true for other countries as well; for example, United Fruit Company found that the only way in which it could adequately gain satisfactory distribution in Europe was to purchase distributors.[49] The seriousness of this problem is reflected in the fact that some of the largest multinational corporations maintain 80 to 90 percent of their subsidiaries abroad solely for the purpose of distribution.[50]

In fact, difficulties encountered in establishing international marketing channels account for the worldwide trend toward increased backward vertical integration into manufacturing on the part of the middlemen and forward vertical integration into wholesaling and retailing on the part of

---

[45] See the U.S. Department of Commerce *Trade List* and *World Trade Directory Reports* as well as the commercially published *Trade Directories of the World* and a *Guide to Foreign Business Directories*, as suggested by Cateora and Hess, *op. cit.*, p. 524.

[46] Cateora and Hess, *op. cit.*, p. 524.

[47] *Ibid.*, p. 527.

[48] Robert E. Weigand, "Aspects of Retail Pricing in Japan," in Louis W. Boone and James C. Johnson (eds.), *Marketing Channels* (Morristown, N.J.: General Learning Press, 1973), p. 320.

[49] "United Fruit Purchases Distributors to Gain Common Market Entry," *Wall Street Journal* (November 2, 1962), p. 21.

[50] C. Hederer, C. D. Hoffman, and B. Kumar, "The Internationalization of German Business," *Columbia Journal of World Business* (September–October, 1972), p. 43.

manufacturers.[51] Such a trend may provide additional barriers to new entrants to foreign markets, given the capital requirements for integration. The situation is being further aggravated by the desire of large foreign wholesalers and retailers to develop their own private branding programs.[52] Evidence of such a movement is provided by the efforts of a large voluntary chain, Spar International, which is comprised of 200 wholesalers and 36,000 retailers in 12 Western European countries, to place greater and greater emphasis on its own labels.[53]

Fourth, because middlemen in less developed countries are distinctly less venturesome than those in more advanced ones and, therefore, are less willing to accept innovation risk, companies seeking to market to such countries must assume a greater burden of demand development than they must in the United States. This is particularly true of a country like India. Furthermore, as Fayerweather observes:

> . . . the small-merchant structure is very likely to result in gaps in market coverage. At the extreme, companies selling small expendable items—toothpaste, flashlight batteries, and razor blades—find in a country like India that only 10 percent or so of the thousands of little merchants are stocking their products. The cost of inventory is one deterrent, but even discounting that, the small operator wants to limit his line to keep it within the bounds of his personal control both physically and from a management point of view.[54]

Cateora and Hess underscore this problem by stating that:

> The high cost of credit, danger of loss through inflation, lack of capital, and other concerns cause foreign middlemen in many countries to carry inadequate inventories, causing out-of-stock conditions and loss of sales to competitors. Physical distribution lags intensify this problem so that, in many cases, the manufacturer must provide local warehousing or extend long credit to encourage middlemen to carry large inventories.[55]

Finally, the myriad of problems associated with maintaining adequate distribution can be summed up in the term "control." Securing some semblance of control may be absolutely necessary if the international marketer

---

[51] For examples of outright ownership of foreign wholesaling and retailing firms, see Vern Terpstra, *American Marketing in the Common Market* (New York: Frederic, A. Praeger, Inc., 1967), p. 98. See also Lars-Gunnar Mattsson, *Integration and Efficiency in Marketing Systems* (Stockholm, Sweden: Economic Research Institute, 1969).

[52] Cateora and Hess, *op. cit.*, p. 515, and Terpstra, *International Marketing, op. cit.*, p. 317.

[53] Terpstra, *ibid.*

[54] Fayerweather, *op. cit.*, pp. 68–69.

[55] Cateora and Hess, *op. cit.*, p. 527.

is going to achieve any success in foreign markets. Because power may reside in the hands of large wholesalers, it may be necessary to use some form of contractual arrangement (e.g., franchising) and make broad concessions in order to convince the wholesalers to monitor the marketplace and to engage in effective marketing practices. The control gained may come to the supplier via the process of osmosis, but at least there will be some assurance (although probably not a great deal) that one's product is receiving adequate care and attention throughout the channel. (It should be noted, however, that there are also considerable obstacles in establishing franchises in foreign countries, as summarized in Table 13–5.) The various types of channel arrangements are so diverse and the various features of different channels in different countries are so complex, as indicated in Table 13–6, that the difficulties associated with achieving such control can rarely be overstated.

SUMMARY AND CONCLUSIONS

International marketing can be very lucrative, as evidenced by the fact that an increasing number of American companies receive more than half of their net income from operations abroad. In addition, participation in the international marketplace may be a requirement if a company is to continue to survive and grow; effective distribution increasingly seems to demand a global view.

In seeking to describe channels serving foreign markets, it is essential to understand that generalizations must be treated cautiously and even with suspicion. The differences in the basic structures of distribution from country to country may not be vast, but the nuances and variations within the structures are significantly different.

The perspective taken in this chapter has basically been that of a U.S. manufacturer considering expansion abroad by either exporting, licensing, engaging in joint ventures, or direct investing. As a company moves from one expansion route to the next, the amount of control increases as does the amount of investment required on the part of the home company. In this respect, the choice and the consequences of the various routes are not far different, conceptually, from those associated with forming conventional, administered, contractual, and corporate channel systems on a domestic basis. Regardless of the expansionary route followed, the international marketer will be faced with the problem of designing and implementing a specific distribution strategy, and this problem generally involves assessing two channel segments—one domestic and the other foreign. Each seg-

TABLE 13-5 Major Problems Encountered in Establishing Franchises in Foreign Countries

Systems Encountering	Number of Responses	Percent
Governmental or legal restrictions[a]	31	60.8
Difficulty of recruiting enough qualified franchisees	23	45.1
Lack of sufficient local financing	19	37.3
Difficulty of controlling franchisees	19	37.3
Difficulty of redesigning the franchise package to make it saleable to franchisees in foreign countries	15	29.4
Trademark and/or copyright obstacles	15	29.4
Difficulty of making the products or services acceptable to foreign consumers	11	21.6
Oppressive tax structure	8	15.7
Insufficient suitable locations	6	11.8
Miscellaneous problems	10	19.6
Total	157	

[a]Read as follows: Of 31 systems specifying major problems, 60.8% designated governmental or legal restrictions as a major problem, etc.

SOURCE: Bruce Walker and Michael Etzel, "The Internationalization of U.S. Franchise Systems: Progress and Procedures," *Journal of Marketing*, Vol. 37 (April, 1973), p. 45.

ment is comprised of agent and merchant middlemen whose functions are not widely different from those performed by comparable middlemen in the United States. However, because of the mores and other environmental characteristics of international markets, the outcomes achieved by given channel arrangements may be far different from those predicted for U.S. channels. For example, control problems are more severe on an international basis because of the polarity of wholesale trade. This is true even though antitrust laws may not be as stringent as they are in the United States. Furthermore, all relationships are subject to intensive negotiations, and thus variations among and within channels abound.

In order to remain reasonably close to developments in international markets and to secure relevant and timely information, it is likely that firms seeking expansion abroad will have to rely heavily on foreign-based, as opposed to domestically-based, middlemen. Even with the market contact that such middlemen allow, difficulties can easily arise, as was evidenced in the case of Levi Strauss, which could not develop adequate distribution and inventory controls, even though it had vertically integrated a number of foreign wholesaling firms.

Retailing presents as much, if not more, diversity to the international

TABLE 13-6 Marketing Features in Channels of Selected Countries

	Japan	Brazil	Venezuela	Puerto Rico	Turkey	Egypt	India	Trop. Africa
A. Number of levels in channels	5		2		1	1 to 3	2	2
B. Influence of foreign import agent						Dying out		Very strong
C. Size of wholesalers	Very large		Small	Small	Small	Small	Small	Small
D. Wholesalers own retail outlets				No	Yes	Yes	Yes	
E. Background integration	Yes			No			Yes, some	
F. Wholesalers plan local distribution	Yes				Yes	Yes		
G. Wholesalers have active sales force	Yes		Yes		Yes	Yes	No	
H. Wholesalers provide warehousing field storage, delivery	Yes		Yes	Yes	Yes	Yes	Storage only	
I. Wholesalers order E.O.Q.	Yes		Yes	Yes	Yes	No	No	
J. Wholesaler lends marketing advice	Yes							
K. Wholesalers financing retailers	Important		Important	Important	Very important	Very important	Important	Very important
L. Wholesaler markups	Very high			Very high		5%	1.5 to 4%	Very high
M. Specialty stores and supermarkets		Yes, in cities	Yes					
N. Department stores		Yes, in cities	Yes, in cities			Yes, in cities	None	
O. Stores in rural areas		General store					Very large number	Very large number
P. Stores of small size							Small	Very small
Q. Size of retail store			Yes	Yes			Very important	Very important
R. Peddlars and itinerant traders		Yes				Yes	Yes	Yes
S. Open garden fairs		Yes						
T. Price competition		None	None	None		Little	Little	Little
U. Consumer credit			Very important	Very important		Little	Little	Little
V. Retail margins			25–50%	24%		35–40%	10%	

SOURCE: George Wadinambiaratchi, "Channels of Distribution in Developing Economies," *The Business Quarterly*, Vol. 30 (Winter, 1965), p. 77.

marketer as wholesaling—and many of the frustrations. The polarity of wholesale trade is mirrored by a similar polarity on the retail level. With economic development, there is increased evidence of larger retail units, but the small shop still predominates in lower- and middle-income countries and even throughout much of Europe. Consumer cooperatives have emerged in Europe to exert a countervailing pressure on some of the inefficiencies of traditional retail distribution. In developing nations, however, the retailing systems seem uniquely suited to consumer behavior and the level of affluence and mobility, but the cost to both consumers and traders is high, especially in terms of economics for the former and in terms of status for the latter. Improvements in distribution may produce far-reaching benefits for these countries, because such improvements will probably lead to increases in real income for individual consumers.

Several problems can be highlighted relative to the establishment of international marketing channels. First, it may be difficult to determine just which middlemen are available or willing to provide adequate distribution for a particular supplier. Second, considerable intrachannel promotion will be required in order to obtain adequate attention. Third, access to particular channels may be blocked because of existing arrangements, some of which would be illegal if practiced in the United States. Fourth, middlemen, especially in developing economies, may be less prone to accepting the risks of innovation that come with the marketing of new products. In addition, they may be less willing to assume inventory burdens (as compared with U.S. middlemen), and thus may force much of the effort associated with the flow of physical possession back onto suppliers. Finally, the securing of at least some semblance of control within an international channel is likely to be critical, and, in international marketing, reliance may have to be placed on foreign middlemen as the controlling agents or channel leaders.

The appendix to this chapter describes the commercial settings in six countries which represent reasonably strong potential markets for firms seeking expansion abroad.

DISCUSSION QUESTIONS

1. Compare and contrast the routes to expansion abroad—exportation, licensing, joint ventures, and direct investment—to the conceptual foundations, institutional arrangements, strengths, and weaknesses of conventional, administered, contractual, and corporate vertical marketing systems, respectively.

2. A number of U.S. companies have been questioned by the U.S. government about improper payments overseas. Cities Service Corporation was the first large corporation to admit voluntarily that it made such payments. Specifically, according to the *Wall*

Street Journal (September 14, 1975), Cities Service told the Securities and Exchange Commission that "subsidiaries abroad secretly funneled $30,000 through a Swiss Bank for 'political purposes,' paid $15,000 against a phony invoice to a foreign lobbyist and generated a $600,000 slush fund for overseas 'business purposes' funded by kickbacks from brokers and suppliers."

On the other hand, according to Adnan Khashoggi, a Saudi Arabian businessman, American companies risk losing huge sales in the Mideast unless the U.S. Government dispels the uncertainty over payments to sales agents abroad. Disclosures of large payments to foreign sales agents, as well as under-the-table payments to government officials, have made U.S. concerns wary of dealing with sales and marketing representatives. Mr. Khashoggi has been quoted as saying (*Wall Street Journal,* September 9, 1975), "If representatives can't sell American products, they'll sell someone else's," to oil-rich Mideast governments.

Do you suppose the same problem exists for foreign companies attempting to sell into the United States? Why do you suppose the problem is so acute abroad? What advice would you give to a company seeking foreign markets about such payments? What alternative does the company have, other than to make the payments?

3. In 1971, Congress, deeply concerned about the deterioration of the U.S. balance of trade, took a lesson from European competitors and established a tax incentive to increase American exports. Legislation enacted in 1971 provides that companies that form Domestic International Sales Corporations (commonly known as DISC's) may defer a portion of their income taxes on export profits, provided they plow such deferred taxes back into export development. According to Reginald H. Jones, chairman and chief executive officer of the General Electric Company, the DISC deferral of taxes is much less potent as an incentive than the tax rebates granted to exporters by the European Economic Community or the European border taxes on imports (*New York Times,* Section F, August 31, 1975). Nevertheless, the DISC tax deferrals have been remarkably successful. Since the DISC provisions were enacted, more than 7000 companies have organized DISC subsidiaries. There has, however, been a movement in Congress to repeal the DISC program. Debate the pros and cons of the DISC program and come out with a position of your own.

4. According to a *Business Week* article (July 14, 1975), governments all over the world are attempting to get for themselves a bigger share of the profits, jobs, markets, and technical and managerial skills that multinational companies create or control. To achieve this, governments are using the multinationals to promote a variety of their own objectives. For example:

> Mexico is pushing auto makers such as Ford and Volkswagenwerk to export more from their Mexican plants, requiring them eventually to sell as much abroad as in the local market.

> Colombia plans to put branches of foreign banks under majority Colombian control, thus shrinking the supply of local credit for subsidiaries of foreign companies and forcing them to bring more capital from abroad.

Saudi Arabia is asking oil companies to set up joint venture refineries and petro-chemical plants there in return for long-term supplies of crude oil.

France has insisted that Motorola, Inc.'s semiconductor division set up a research and development department to qualify for investment incentives.

Canada requires foreign companies to show that they will bring "significant bene-fits," ranging from jobs and increased productivity to manpower training and development of depressed areas, to get approval of corporate takeovers.

What do developments such as these portend for U.S. companies desirous of doing business abroad? What impact will such governmental activity have on channel strategy? Has the government formally entered the marketing channel in such instances, or is it still in the task environment to the channel?

5. It has been stated that "from an interorganization management perspective, control over the activities and operations of international marketing channels is generally more difficult to accomplish than it is within the boundaries of the U.S. . . ." Do you agree? Why?

6. Explain Levi Strauss' European problems in behavioral (e.g., power, conflict, conflict management, roles, etc.) terms. Applying an interorganizational analysis, what solutions can you suggest so that the company can avoid similar situations?

7. Chori Company, a large wholesale trading concern specializing in textiles, averted bankruptcy in 1975 through the conclusion of a comprehensive rescue agreement with its major creditors consisting of four banks and three synthetic fiber makers. According to the *Wall Street Journal* (September 8, 1975), the seven companies decided on the move because the Japanese textile industry would be thrown into confusion should the trading company collapse. Chori, one of the "Big Three" of Japan's domestic textile wholesale trade, has dealings with about 10,000 other companies, most of them rela-tively vulnerable small and medium-sized concerns.

Analyze this development from an interorganization management perspective. Is there any line of trade within the United States where wholesaling firms are likely to be accorded such support in times of crisis?

8. What obstacles are Sears or Jewel Tea Company likely to face as they seek to con-tinue their overseas expansion? Of the six countries described in the appendix, which two look like the best possibilities for Sears or for Jewel Tea? Which two look like poor choices? Explain your reasoning in full.

Appendix

Marketing Channels
in Selected Countries

This appendix is devoted to an examination of channel structures in selected host countries representing the world's continents, geographic regions, and some of its market systems. These include Australia, Brazil (South America), France (Europe), Israel (Middle East), Japan (Far East), and Nigeria (Africa).

CHANNELS OF DISTRIBUTION IN AUSTRALIA[1]

One of the most sparsely populated countries in the world, Australia has approximately four people per square mile. The east coast is the most densely populated area, with the heaviest concentration around Sydney, the leading commercial and industrial center, and Melbourne, which is also an important distribution center. On the other side of the continent, Perth, the capital of the state of Western Australia, is the primary center for commerce and industry. Since the six state capital cities and the East Coast encompass the large majority of the population, distribution channels are long and sometimes distorted, even though Australia has a highly urbanized and industrializing economy.

Import Channels. Participants in the import channels include sales agents, importer-distributors, and direct importer-users. For consumer products, sales agents are used to handle distribution to large wholesalers and retailers. Importer-distributors are used when keeping a stock and/or providing technical assistance and services are important factors. Typical goods handled by these representatives include foodstuffs, textiles, consumer durables, and heavy machinery for industry. In instances where the volume is substantial or a foreign company wants to control distribution, subsidiaries of foreign firms may import directly without utilizing the services of an agent. For new products seeking market penetration, there exist several companies in Australia who not only import but also provide many other services such as financing, transporting, packaging, and distributing.

---

[1]Based on U.S. Department of Commerce, Bureau of International Commerce, *Selling in Australia.* Overseas Business Reports: 73–43 (Washington, D.C.: U.S. Government Printing Office, 1973).

Physical Distribution. The railway system is the primary carrier of cargo in Australia. The lines radiate from the industrial centers and seaports, crisscrossing the entire continent. The flexivan system, in which loaded vans are transferred from trucks to railcars, and the new diesel-electric engines have made the railroads competitive with the trucking companies.

Highway transit complements rail carriage and is particularly effective for transporting commodities between the state capitals and for goods requiring refrigeration. Although no freeways have been constructed, the existing highways are well maintained. Coastal fleets operate between ports, providing a third alternative to meet the shippers' needs. Domestic air service is provided by ten airlines, which carry goods to the more distant inland points. Regardless of the mode employed, distribution in Australia is quite expensive because of the great distances usually involved.

Australia's ports are plentiful, with 66 regarded as commercially significant. Ports at Sydney and New Castle are the most modern, with handling and storage facilities for all types of commodities. Other major ports include Melbourne, Freemantle (port of Perth), Adelaide, Brisbane, and Hobart. Warehouses are maintained by a large number of firms, making finding space no difficulty.

Wholesale Channels. Wholesalers in Australia in the past have provided the traditional link between manufacturers and retailers. Now, however, with more retailers buying in bulk directly from the manufacturer, wholesalers have begun engaging in forward and backward vertical integration. According to the 1968-1969 economic census, there are over 34,000 wholesale establishments in Australia. More than 30 percent of these are located in New South Wales, the capital of which is Sydney. Most wholesalers operate on a nationwide basis, because certain industries cater to particular geographic regions (e.g., consumer durables in Adelaide and petrochemicals in Altona).

Retail Channels. As mentioned before, large retailers, such as department and chain stores, have developed in Australia to the point of purchasing merchandise in bulk from manufacturers. Additionally, smaller retailers and manufacturers have both formed their own associations in order to buy and sell in large quantities.

Sales in certain categories have catapulted in recent years. For example, furniture has increased 56.4 percent, motor vehicles, parts, and gasoline, 55.4 percent, pharmaceuticals, 54.9 percent, and hardware, 52.2 percent. Retail establishments licensed in 1968-1969 totaled almost 137,000, with the largest group being food stores. As with wholesaling, New South Wales has more retail outlets than any other state.

Advertising. The affluence and high degree of urbanization in Australia is reflected in the fact that the 1972 expenditures for advertising topped $495 million, which represents a doubling in ten years. Having one of the most vigorous and promotion-conscious public sectors in the world enables the advertising industry to be highly organized and national in scope.

The largest portion of the advertising (31 percent) is carried by the newspapers, with television, magazines, radio, cinema, and outdoor advertising comprising the balance. National public relations firms offer their services in all media, although movie advertising is usually limited to the promotion of consumer goods on a local level.

Market Research and Trade Organizations. Consumer goods industries are the primary users of market research agencies at the present, although capital and industrial commodities are also handled. Several institutes, firms, and professional individuals, the majority of which operate out of either Sydney or Melbourne, offer comprehensive market research services. Economic research organizations also provide data useful in market studies.

Practically every sector of the Australian economy is covered by a trade organization. Reference material is prepared for almost all commercial, industrial, and agricultural activity. There is also a National Chamber of Commerce located in the federal capital of Canberra as well as Chambers in all six of the state capitals. The American Chamber of Commerce has four offices in Australia to provide additional assistance.

Trade Customs. Probably the most noticeable difference between Australian and American business etiquette is in the emphasis placed on formality and personal titles by the Australians. Otherwise, business practices are quite similar. Correspondence is expected to be answered promptly and appointments kept punctually. Since English is the official language, no language barrier is present. Commercial enterprises usually operate between 9 a.m. and 5:30 p.m. Monday through Friday with a half a day on Saturday. Evening shopping is not as common as it is in the United States.

Exports to Australia from the United States have topped a billion dollars annually in recent years, making the United States the foremost supplier, with approximately 25 percent of the market. The young and growing population coupled with a high level of living makes Australia a very favorable area for further development. With only the east coast really commercialized, many more square miles await business ventures.

CHANNELS OF DISTRIBUTION IN BRAZIL[2]

The Brazilian economy has been expanding rapidly in recent years, as evidenced by a 10 percent annual increase in gross national product in 1970-1972. With development concentrated on the infrastructure (highways, communication, etc.), the largest country in South America is now integrating its heretofore fragmented economy. Income distribution is still a major problem, however. Less than one-third of the 100 million Brazilians are participants in the consumer economy.

[2]Based on U.S. Department of Commerce, Bureau of International Commerce, *Selling in Brazil.* Overseas Business Reports: 73-51 (Washington, D.C.: U.S. Government Printing Office, 1973).

The southeastern portion of the country is by far the richest geographical region. Commercial activity is centered around Rio De Janeiro and São Paulo, with these two urban areas handling roughly 75 percent of sales in Brazil. Recife and Salvador are also commercial and industrial centers.

Import Channels. Most imports are in capital good and raw material areas, because Brazil is practically self-sufficient in consumer goods. Agents, distributors, import houses, trading companies, and sales subsidiaries all function in Brazil. Most imports are arranged by an individual firm to meet its own needs.

Agents are used to a great extent. Because of the size of the country, one agent may not be able to adequately cover the entire market. This is dependent on the type of good being distributed. If it is a highly specialized item of interest to only a few buyers, one agent could probably handle it. If, however, it is a more widely used and demanded product with a high degree of service required, additional representatives may be needed. Agents still have a regional orientation and may not wish to cooperate with agents in other parts of the country. If a representative is appointed as the exclusive agent, he may expect a commission on all sales of that good regardless of whether he actually handles the sales or not.

Trading companies are also important in the import channels. Both Japanese and German firms have been operating in Brazil for a number of years. They usually market capital equipment in arrangements designed for a particular client. These trading houses are especially attractive to Brazilian companies that are short of capital, because they will engage in "switch trading." This is a type of barter agreement whereby the Brazilians pay the trading companies in goods, which are then sold in a third country. More recently Brazilian trading companies have been formed, primarily to increase the export capability of the small and medium-sized manufacturers. These export houses will no doubt eventually expand into the import business as well.

The Brazilian Government engages in both direct and indirect importing, particularly of machinery and equipment for telecommunications and electric power. Direct imports are authorized only for certain agencies, and even then only if no Brazilian-made substitute exists. Brazilian firms are usually utilized in indirect importing so that the Government will have a domestic supplier in case legal recourse is necessary.

Physical Distribution. The roads in Brazil are by far the best method for the internal transport of goods. In addition, the entire network is being expanded and improved. Railroads are used to some extent but are generally slower and not as extensive. Improvements in the system are planned, however. Domestic air cargo service is excellent and is used for the low-bulk high-value commodities.

Wholesale Channels. Domestic wholesalers are not a major part of the distribution channel in Brazil. Currently, a large percentage of the manufacturers are local, making selling directly to the retailer a relatively simple task. With further commercial expansion, however, wholesalers will grow in importance as the geographic area served by manufacturers expands. Food distributors are already becoming more important in the urban centers, where the greatest expansion in wholesale activity is expected.

Retail Channels. Modern retailing practices are becoming more popular in Brazil, particularly in the larger cities. Less than 10 percent of the commercial establishments in the country in 1969 had more than 20 employees, however. Outlets consist largely of general stores in the rural and smaller urban areas and specialty shops in the cities. The "company store" is still popular on the large farms and in the industrial complexes. Street vendors and open markets are still in operation, distributing fresh food and homemade goods. Department stores were established in the business centers over 20 years ago, and there were an estimated 3000 supermarkets in 1972.

Advertising. Although not as sophisticated as in the United States, Brazilian promotional practices are quite similar. All types of media are employed, but nationwide coverage is found only on a limited scale. Local advertising agencies are quite adept at gearing the available outlets to an individual firm's product. Consecutive billboards in close proximity carrying the same message are one departure from U.S. practices. This is done to enable the illiterate of the country to purchase consumer goods on the basis of brand recognition.

Market Research and Trade Organization. Because of the lack of centralization in wholesale and retail activity, market research services are rather limited. Companies wishing to sell their products in Brazil may have to carry out their own research or rely on government publications. Industry organizations called *sindicatos* facilitate trade relations. These organizations are grouped into federations of related industries in each state, which are represented by national confederations. Additionally, two American Chambers of Commerce operate in Brazil. The Rio de Janeiro Chamber represents about 800 firms and has a branch office in Recife. The larger São Paulo organization has a branch in Porto Alegre and has a membership of about 1600. Both provide information about Brazil and the American companies operating there.

Trade Customs. A slower pace of activity than is found in the United States is characteristic of the Brazilian business sector. Personal relationships extending over long periods of time are preferred. Rarely are important business negotiations concluded over the telephone. The majority of the commercial transactions occur between 10 a.m. and noon and 3 p.m. and 5 p.m. Lunch usually lasts two hours, and coffee is a frequently consumed beverage. Portuguese is the predominate language, although some English is spoken.

The potential market in Brazil is enormous. With a great deal of the land undeveloped, further expansion is assured. Although the channels of distribution are currently below the U.S. standard, rapid improvement can be expected as industrialization advances.

CHANNELS OF DISTRIBUTION IN FRANCE[3]

As the fourth leading importer in the world, importing half as much as the United States with only one-fourth the population, France is a highly industrialized country with sales opportunities for both capital goods and consumer items. Paris is by far the largest marketing distribution center, handling half of the total business in France. Approximately 20 percent of France's population lives in the Paris area and contributes nearly 40 percent of the individual income taxes. Lyon ranks second to Paris in importance as a commercial and industrial center. In the northern sector, Lille, Roubaix, and Tourcoing form another major business area.

Import Channels. Four major methods of importation-distribution are utilized in France: establishing a sales subsidiary, appointing an agent or distributor, selling through wholesalers or dealers, and direct selling to purchasing organizations. According to the characteristics of the commodity being imported and the magnitude of the market to be covered, different distribution channels are employed at different times.

Generally speaking, most Paris representatives do not cover the entire country, and the recruitment of additional agents in the provinces is required. Because of a lack of capital and facilities, these regional representatives cannot carry the stocks nor provide the services that their Parisian counterparts can and, therefore, require much more manufacturer support.

Direct selling to the large department and chain stores is a widely accepted method of introducing a new product. One advantage is in the fact that the middleman is eliminated, thus reducing the cumulative markup. Since small retailers will usually begin stocking products that prove successful in the larger outlets, a product that is successfully introduced in the larger store will catch the attention of the smaller retailer as well. One drawback is that department and chain stores are responsible for only about one-fifth of the retail sales in France. Hence, nationwide success is not assured because of a product's acceptance in one of the larger retail establishments.

Physical Distribution. A highly integrated network of railroad, road, and water systems makes France a transportation coordinator's delight. Goods can practically be guaranteed to be transported cross-country in less than five days from any import point. Freight forwarders are available to handle shipments from the port of disembarkation to the final destination.

The port at Marseille handles more merchandise than any other port in France and is the primary import point for tropical products and crude petroleum. Containerized shipments are handled there as well as at Le Havre, Bordeaux, and Dunkirk. Numerous

[3]Based on U.S. Department of Commerce, Bureau of International Commerce, *Selling in France.* Overseas Business Reports: 72–007 (Washington, D.C.: U.S. Government Printing Office, 1972).

departures from all major U.S. ports make trans-Atlantic shipping to France economical and relatively rapid. Shipping time varies from 10 days from the U.S. Atlantic coast to 22 days from the West coast.

Air freight, either in the form of combination cargo-passenger flights or all-cargo flights, is offered by many airlines to France. Excellent airport facilities include the new Paris Nord airport. Other principal airports are Le Bourget and Orly at Paris. Flying time between Paris and other major French cities is usually about one hour.

Wholesale Channels. Although a trend toward concentration in the wholesale sector has been noticed in recent years, the majority of wholesaling operations remain on a small or medium scale. Family-owned enterprises with little or no outside help are still by far the most numerous. As in other countries, larger retailers have begun bypassing the wholesaler and buying in large volume directly from the manufacturers.

Retail Channels. As in the wholesale channel, most retail channel participants fall into the small or at least the medium-size category. Concentration has increased in the retail outlets, however, and the percentage of total retail sales of the independent retailers has declined to 63.0 percent in 1970 from 81.1 percent in 1960. This is an indication of the growth of the *hypermarché* or superstore in recent years. These numbered 115 in 1971. Department and chain stores totaled $3.3 billion in sales in 1969.

Multibranch operations have become an integral part of the distribution of food products as well as clothing, hardware, furniture, construction materials, and jewelry. Also, over thirty cooperative organizations are in existence, pooling the orders of many smaller retailers in the same trade to obtain larger discounts. Self-service units are growing more slowly in France than in other Western European countries, but they account for about 35 percent of retail food sales.

Advertising. Many major advertising agencies are operating in France performing the standard promotional functions with most of the headquarters located in Paris. Media space can also be purchased, since one of the largest agencies controls newspapers, cinemas, and commercial radio time. Magazines and newspapers account for approximately one-third of advertising expenditures in France.

French newspapers generally do not have nationwide circulation. Thus, in order to reach the entire reading public, coverage may include over 20 provincial dailies and six Paris papers. This offers the advantage of geographic concentration, since there is very little overlap in regions. Magazines are circulated on a national as well as international basis and carry advertising similar to that found in U.S. periodicals.

Other advertising media are radio, television, direct mail, billboards, and the cinema. Commercial advertising is permitted on the state-controlled television networks. Radio stations located outside of France can be received across the country and may offer better market coverage than French stations. Movie theatres all show 50- to 100-foot advertising films before the feature, making cinema advertising within priorities set by the government. Cinema advertising can be quite profitable, since movie theatres are very popular in France.

Market Research and Trade Organizations. A number of market research firms and advertising agencies provide market information in France. Many employ psychologists for motivation research. Management consultants and public relations firms also enjoy a high degree of utilization in the "small-shop" French economy. French government statistical and economic publications contribute additional information. The Organization for Economic Cooperation and Development (OECD) and the European Economic Community (EEC) also make available market material.

Most French trade associations, which represent various manufacturing and service sectors, are members of the Counseil National de Patronat Francais (CNPF). The CNPF publications, as well as those of French banks, describe commercial and economic trends. Technical developments are usually given good coverage in the various trade journals.

Trade Customs. A knowledge of the French language is highly advisable for successfully doing business in France. Although it is true that many of the top French executives speak English very well and enjoy using it, many members of their staffs do not. Thus, correspondence should ordinarily be in French. Metric weights and measures are used almost exclusively. One peculiarity to note is that summer is an unusually bad time to conduct business in France. Frenchmen enjoy extended vacations, which frequently come in August. Therefore, a considerable number of firms close that entire month.

In considering the French distribution channels, the most vital thing to remember is the importance of having a resident representative who is familiar with the local business scene. This is considered a sound business practice in France, and, like marketing in any other country, being flexible enough to adjust to the French conduct can mean the difference between success or failure.

CHANNELS OF DISTRIBUTION IN ISRAEL[4]

Approximately one-fifth of Israel's population is concentrated in the Tel Aviv-Jaffa area on the Mediterranean Sea. This region is the center of commercial activity, making distribution a relatively simple task in Israel. The majority of heavy industry is located in Haifa, which is the second largest community. Hence, virtually all of the imported commodities and a major portion of those domestically produced are distributed through Tel Aviv or Haifa.

Import Channels. Local representatives, usually either a commission agent or a distributor, dominate import channels. Commission agents, who do not import on their own account, handle most of the heavy industrial equipment by approaching potential buyers

---

[4]Based on U.S. Department of Commerce, Bureau of International Commerce, *Selling in Israel*. Overseas Business Reports: 70–71 (Washington, D.C.: U.S. Government Printing Office, 1970).

and engaging in a nominal amount of promotional activity. For light industrial goods and consumer commodities, a distributor is ordinarily utilized. Not only does he import on his own account, but he also keeps an inventory of goods to fill rush orders, maintains a sales organization, and provides after-sales maintenance.

Regardless of the type of good handled or the type of representative handling it, exclusive agreements are almost always used. Israel is a small country geographically (about the size of New Jersey) with relatively few commercial centers. Therefore, one man can easily reach all potential customers for a given commodity within a week. Some representatives may even refuse to work on a nonexclusive basis.

Although not a major import channel as it is in some countries (e.g., Japan), there are over 100 Israeli trading companies handling goods coming into the country. They import both raw materials for manufacturers and finished goods for wholesalers and retailers.

Although having an Israeli representative is a rule in most cases, there are exceptions. Government agencies and affiliated organizations, purchasing agents for cooperative and collective settlements (called *moshavim* and *kibbutzim*), and very large firms frequently import directly. The prime example of this direct selling is found in the Histadrut, which is the General Federation of Labor. Having many industrial enterprises under its control, this organization purchases its major equipment and supplies directly from a company in New York.

Physical Distribution.   Israel has an extensive but crowded road network. Most inland transportation of goods is by truck, although the government-owned railroads do carry bulk cargos. Virtually no inland waterways exist. The imported commodities from Europe and the Americas dock at the deepwater ports of Haifa and Ashdod on the Mediterranean. The port of Eilat on the Gulf of Aqaba handles trade with Africa and Asia. Port facilities are modern, and handling is expeditious.

Wholesale Channels.   As stated before, importers prefer to act as exclusive agents and, therefore, few imported goods pass through wholesalers. In fact, for many goods such as furniture and textiles, no wholesale channel exists whatsoever. For agricultural and dairy products, the aforementioned cooperatives either retail the commodities themselves or act as suppliers for independent merchants.

Wholesalers find themselves serving primarily in a functional role serving smaller producers as well as retailers. Once again, we see the environmental influence on the channels of distribution in that the number of wholesalers is kept low by the small physical size of the country and the market concentration in a few urban centers. The short distances that exist encourage direct selling by the manufacturer, which does not create problems, since there are so few producers in each industry.

Retail Channels.   Retailing is in a period of rapid transformation from a "small shop economy" to a "superstore economy." With a current per capita income of $2200, more people are able to buy and maintain an automobile, thus reducing dependence on neighborhood facilities. At the present, however, the majority of the over 30,000 retail establishments are privately owned shops specializing in limited numbers of items. Food retailing is handled primarily by the agricultural cooperatives, which sell to middle- and lower-income consumers at prices below those found in the supermarkets.

Advertising. Advertising is a particularly promising industry in Israel, since the whole-salers and importers do little promotion for their clients. The over 100 advertising agencies are for the most part small operations, with fewer than 20 providing truly comprehensive service. Newspaper advertising is extremely profitable because of the high literacy rate of the country. Weekend supplements are popular substitutes for weekly magazines, and advertising covering shipping, medicine, and industry can be found in periodicals and trade magazines.

Other media are also employed. The movie theatre is the predominant source of entertainment and, therefore, theatre advertisements are extremely polished and heavily relied upon for promoting consumer products. Billboards can be seen along the highways in both Hebrew and English, and other outdoor advertising appears on wooden fences surrounding construction sites and in the form of neon signs. Point-of-sale and display advertising are almost totally ignored, however, because of the crowded stores and display windows. Radio advertising remains the most effective medium for consumer products promotion, although regular television broadcasts began in 1969.

Market Research and Trade Organizations. Market research is in the growth stage, being constrained by the production orientation of the market system. Nevertheless, the few firms that are in business are quite competent and receive competition from the market research departments of the larger advertising agencies. In addition, the Israel Institute of Applied Social Research, a government organization, cooperates with business in providing market information. Trade organizations such as the American-Israel Chamber of Commerce and Industry in New York, the Manufacturers' Association of Israel, and various businessman's clubs and organizations provide data.

Trade Customs. Israel has no strict "code of behavior" governing business transactions. Interactions tend to be informal and discussions open and straightforward. The Sabbath, which begins at sundown Friday and ends at sundown Saturday, is observed by most offices, which cease activity for the period. Otherwise, business establishments are open Sunday through Friday. Although Hebrew and Arabic are the official languages, English is spoken to a great extent in the business community. Foreign trade negotiation and correspondence can both be conducted in English.

Distribution channels in Israel, like the rest of the marketing systems, are progressing very rapidly. Characterized by few wholesalers and short distance, the channels handle goods efficiently within the country. Local representatives are the most recommended arrangement for exporters of consumer goods.

CHANNELS OF DISTRIBUTION IN JAPAN[5]

A revolution in distribution is taking place in Japan. Long characterized as fragmented and complex, the Japanese distribution system is attempting to correct its defi-

[5] Based on U.S. Department of Commerce, Bureau of International Commerce, *Selling in Japan.* Overseas Business Reports: 72–046 (Washington, D.C.: U.S. Government Printing Office, 1972).

ciencies through a program supported by the government, trading companies, research organizations, wholesalers, and retailers. Many factors contribute to the long channels of distribution, however, and thus the change will come slowly.

Urbanization has had considerable impact on distribution in Japan. Urban dwellers have increased from 25 percent of the total population in 1930 to over 70 percent in 1970. Tokyo, the second largest city in the world, accounts for over 10 percent of Japan's total population of 107 million, has 60 percent of Japan's annual industrial output, and produces 20 percent of the country's disposable income. The triangle formed by Kyoto, Kobe, and Osaka is also a major marketing area, with Osaka being the country's second largest wholesaling center.

Import Channels. The Japanese trading company is by the far the most widely used avenue of entry into the Japanese market. Found in all sizes, these firms can be diversified or specialized and operate either in close connection with a particular manufacturer or wholesaler or without allegiance. Trading companies can be categorized as general (handling a wide range of products and providing various services), specialized (handling fewer more sophisticated goods with greater attention paid to finding the best sale possible), and "captive," (dealing exclusively for particular manufacturers).

For those companies who prefer to have their own sales and service facilities in Japan, wholly foreign-owned subsidiaries are permitted to import and market all but a few products. Restricted commodities are computers, computer-related equipment, and petroleum. Disadvantages in such operations are the difficulties present in finding competent bilingual personnel and in obtaining adequate office space, particularly in the large urban commercial centers, where land and office space is at such a premium. Regardless, selling directly to Japanese consumers has not proved wise for foreign firms, and appointing a local representative who is familiar with the language and the market is a good investment.

Physical Distribution. The primary mode of transportation in Japan is via the Japan National Railways. In addition to the over 31,000 miles of track currently in use, a new high-speed rail network connecting the major cities is scheduled to go into operation in the mid-1980's with another 5400 miles of track. Although an extensive expressway system is being constructed, only about 11 percent of Japan's 617,900 miles of roads are paved.

Since Japan consists of four major islands, some 26 major ports handle the country's imports. Primary harbors on the largest island of Honshu are Yokohama and Nagoya on the Pacific side and Kobe and Osaka on the Bay of Osaka on the southern end of the island.

Wholesale Channels. As stated in the introduction, distribution channels in Japan have historically been very long. A large wholesaler located in one of the primary commercial centers would purchase goods from a manufacturer and transfer them to regional wholesalers. Several other wholesalers would handle the product before it finally reached the retailer on the neighborhood level.

With the advent of the self-service "superstores," however, wholesalers are being by-passed to a large extent, since the larger retailers can buy in quantities large enough to make it economical to deal directly with the manufacturer. Also, the existence of the secondary wholesaler is being threatened as more and more are being absorbed by the more powerful wholesalers and manufacturers. Nevertheless, some manufacturers, particularly those making consumer goods purchased primarily in the neighborhood, prefer to deal with wholesalers and will continue to do so.

Retail Channels.   As in most traditional economies, retail outlets in Japan tend to be small family-owned shops handling a limited assortment of commodities. Buyers visit many stores to purchase all that they need. Department stores have also been a part of Japan's retail history for a long time. Carrying goods of a higher price and quality than found in the neighborhood stores, these have primarily served the upper class in the larger cities. The new self-service stores are now challenging the dominant position of the department stores.

The key to the superstores' success is their large volume, which enables them to undersell the department stores by 10 to 20 percent. Because of the high cost of land and heavy traffic congestion in the cities, however, the further expansion of the self-service stores is uncertain, and the majority of the frequently purchased commodities will probably continue to be sold by the small retailers.

Advertising.   With a large population of literate and homogeneous people that is concentrated in a relatively small area, Japan is a near-perfect mass media market. This accounts for the huge increase in advertising expenditures in the last decade, which reached over $2.1 billion in 1970. Newspapers and television each accounted for over 30 percent of the total, with outdoor advertising, magazines, radio, and direct mail comprising the balance. Trade journals are widely used for specialized industrial products.

Language difficulties hinder media advertising because of the extreme sensitivity of the Japanese to linguistic nuances. In translating advertising campaigns that have been successful in other countries, particular care must be taken in order not to offend consumers. Major adjustments have to be made to fit the Japanese market, and an advertising agency should usually be consulted.

Market Research and Trade Organizations.   An effective sales program in Japan relies heavily on sound market research. Hence, in response to the demand, many market research firms are now in operation. The larger advertising agencies also have their own market research departments. Various Japanese government publications provide detailed economic data on many areas, including personal income and consumption patterns.

The Japan External Trade Organization (JETRO) has several offices in the United States to assist interested importers and investors. The American Chamber of Commerce has been in Japan for over 25 years, facilitating business transactions. The Keidanren (Federation of Economic Organizations) is an example of the federations of business associations that encompass almost every commercial and industrial sector. These publish much data in English and are excellent sources of information.

Trade Customs.   With all that has been written about the tremendous industrialization that has taken place in Japan in the past few decades, the fact that Japan is still a country relying heavily on tradition is sometimes forgotten. Employer-employee relations are still paternalistic, and promotion is based more on length of service than merit. Loyalty and discipline are highly regarded, and normally no attempt is made to lure an employee from one company to another.

Decisions usually are made after lengthy discussions with everyone involved to insure that all aspects have been considered. Personal relationships and the ensuing trust between business associates are also very important. Business hours are similar to those in the United States, with after-hours business entertainment quite popular. Such entertainment is customary and is used either to get acquainted or to return a favor.

Without a doubt, Japan is the foremost exception to the "poor Asian country" stereotype. A modern industrial and commercial sector has emerged from the valued Japanese customs. Foreign sellers in the Japanese market must recognize and accept these different values and methods of doing business if they are to be successful. High-quality products and sound business concepts will enable foreigners to adequately cope with the complicated channels of distribution in the Japanese marketing system.

CHANNELS OF DISTRIBUTION IN NIGERIA[6]

Nigeria has a population close to 70 million, which is the largest on the African continent and over half of the total in Western Africa. Only about one-sixth of Nigerians live in urban centers over 20,000, with the largest city of Ibadan having over one million inhabitants, thus serving as a major distribution center.

The capital of Lagos is the country's commercial and industrial center as well as the chief seaport and second largest city. Most major Nigerian businesses have offices here and, therefore, Lagos is the primary point of entry into the Nigerian market for foreigners. The densely populated eastern portion of the country receives most of its goods through Port Harcourt, the second largest seaport. Kano is the primary distribution center in the north.

Import Channels.   Three primary avenues are utilized for import purposes. These are appointing a local agent, selecting an established wholesaler, or establishing a sales subsidiary. European trading companies dominate import channels in Nigeria, making it difficult for new firms to find representatives who are not committed to the established British, French, German, and Dutch trading houses. Nigerian companies are increasing rapidly to fill this void, however. Under the Nigerian Indigenization Decree passed in 1972, foreign business enterprises, including those in the distribution channel, were restricted in their activities as of March, 1974. Therefore, a Nigerian agent or distributor may prove to be the wisest investment.

[6]Based on U.S. Department of Commerce, Bureau of International Commerce, *Selling in Nigeria.* Overseas Business Reports: 73–41 (Washington, D.C.: U.S. Government Printing Office, 1973).

For those firms with an established position in the Nigerian market, a sales subsidiary may prove beneficial. Because of the Nigerianization program, however, foreign offices may be limited in their activities.

Physical Distribution.   Nigeria is fortunate to have a natural inland transportation network provided by the rivers and waterways. The Niger River is the primary channel, allowing access to the majority of the western portion of the country. Railroads are state-owned and encompass 2200 miles of track. Main lines run from Lagos to Nguru and Port Harcourt to Maiduguri. Freight carried in 1966-1967 totaled 2.5 million tons. The roads closely parallel the rail system, though only approximately 20 percent are paved.

The only port actually on the seacoast is Lagos, which has facilities highly rated in both quantity and quality. Port Harcourt is located approximately 40 miles inland on the Bonny River. About 90 percent of Nigeria's imports are handled at Lagos and Port Harcourt combined.

Wholesale Channels.   Consumer commodities customarily pass through many hands before they reach the retail level. The aforementioned European trading companies are the major wholesalers as well as importers. Goods such as consumer products and industrial raw materials that require a local inventory may be kept within the trading firm's operation all the way to the retail level, since many of these companies have retail as well as wholesale outlets.

If goods are carried through the Nigerian channels, however, many layers of wholesalers may be involved. The national distributor operating out of Lagos, for instance, may ship goods to a territorial wholesaler in Kano, who passes it on to the regional distributor in Nguru and Kaduna for distribution to the local wholesaler, who eventually delivers it to the retailer.

Retail Channels.   There are two distinct retail markets in Nigeria. One is the urban retail outlets in the larger cities, whose composition much resembles similar commercial districts of other larger cities. This market is frequented primarily by the foreigners who are living in Nigeria. Only the wealthy Nigerians contribute to this sphere of retail operations, consisting of department stores, specialty shops, etc.

The other, much more popular retail center is the rotating collective market operating out of temporary facilities. Since the majority of Nigeria's population is rural and poor, this type of commercial activity is ideally suited for their needs. Products are fresh daily and can be purchased at varying prices in small quantities. These market stalls are usually set up around the larger cities and in the smaller urban areas, drawing people from miles around. Infrequently, some of the metropolitan areas have permanent structures for these traders, the majority of whom are women.

Advertising.   Because of Nigeria's high illiteracy rate (about 80 percent), advertising is hampered in its effectiveness in all but the highly urbanized areas. Informal communication by word of mouth reaches many more people than does a mass advertising campaign. Nevertheless, advertising in newspapers and magazines and on billboards is usually effective as well as inexpensive. It is estimated that these sources reach over six million inhabitants. Radio remains the principal instrument of communication, since illiteracy is not a hindrance. Television is gaining popularity, although only 75,000 sets are distributed across the country.

Market Research and Trade Organizations. Information sources vary in abundance and reliability, with only the commercial centers having adequate market research facilities. A limited number of Nigerian advertising agencies as well as banks will provide such services. American banks with either Nigerian branches or correspondent arrangements can also assist interested investors.

Many Nigerian business and government organizations can provide further market information. These include the Association of Chambers of Commerce, the Federal Ministry of Commerce and Industry, The Federal Institute of Industrial Research, and the Nigerian Produce Marketing Company, Ltd.

Trade Customs. Recognizing and respecting the African tribal customs and traditions that still influence Nigerian life is the primary rule of business etiquette, particularly when one is dealing with representatives from the outlying areas, where Westernization has not had as great an impact. Otherwise, business customs are much like those found in Western Europe and the United States, with English being the principal language. Personal contact between business acquaintances is highly valued, and formality is not stressed.

In summary, the market system in Nigeria is among the most advanced in developing Africa. The import channels are still dominated by the former colonial rulers, although this will change rapidly under the Nigerianization program. In fact, this increase in the Nigerian-owned business enterprises will provide an excellent market for expansion by foreign interests.

FOURTEEN

MARKETING CHANNELS FOR SERVICES

Effective application of marketing channel concepts to the distribution of tangible products sold by profit-oriented organizations is obviously a necessity if the organizations responsible for those products are to remain viable competitors in their respective markets. However, it is not always immediately clear how channel concepts can be applied to other contexts, such as those involving services generated by profit, nonprofit, and publicly financed organizations. In fact, some have argued that their application is exceedingly nebulous. For example, in a recent study covering a wide variety of service industries, George and Barksdale found it difficult to develop any meaningful conclusions concerning distribution activities.[1] They stated that:

> By their very nature, services do not involve tangible products that can be directed through specific channels and about which decisions can be made in the traditional sense.[2]

While it is no doubt the case that a one-to-one correspondence between the

---

[1] William R. George and Hiram C. Barksdale, "Marketing Activities in the Service Industries," *Journal of Marketing*, Vol. 38 (October, 1974), p. 67. Differing perspectives exist in the literature, however. See the interesting argument developed by James H. Donnelly, Jr., "Marketing Intermediaries in Channels of Distribution," *Journal of Marketing*, Vol. 40 (January 1976), pp. 55–70; and Seymour Baranoff and James H. Donnelly, Jr., "Selecting Channels of Distribution for Services," in Victor P. Buell (ed.), *Handbook of Modern Marketing* (New York: McGraw-Hill Book Co., 1970), Section 4, pp. 43–50.

[2] *Ibid.*

channels for services and the channels for tangible products is often lacking, there are enough points of overlap between the two areas that the subject is very much worth pursuing. Furthermore, it is believed that any insights generated in this pursuit should lead to more careful structuring of marketing programs in the service sector.

Therefore, this chapter focuses on applying marketing channel concepts to services of all types and, upon occasion, to tangible products distributed by nonprofit organizations. The first section of this chapter deals with a broadened view of the concept of marketing channels and explores a key dimension in service marketing as it relates to distribution—assuring availability. It also outlines some likely channel configurations in the marketing of services, discusses the need for and character of interorganizational coordination among service organizations, and isolates the dominant features of activities in the channels for services. The second section provides five specific examples—health care, educational innovations, accident prevention, population control and family planning, and recycling—where channel concepts have been or could be readily applied by nonprofit and publicly financed agencies. The final section describes the marketing channels used by two profit-oriented service industries—lodging and insurance.

MARKETING CHANNELS:
A BROADENED PERSPECTIVE

In a seminal article, Philip Kotler postulated that one of the major ways in which a marketer can seek to create value is by making the social object (product, service, idea, etc.) he is offering for consumption easier for the target market to obtain.[3] The process involved in gaining this end is the establishment of marketing channels or the securing of adequate distribution. *Broadly conceived*, distribution refers to the design, implementation, and control of institutional networks calculated to make social objects of all kinds readily *available* to the population to be served.

Achievement of availability often involves not only the reduction of the space, time, and economic cost separating consumers from the social object, but also may involve the reduction of psychic distances as well. For example, unless disadvantaged consumers feel personally at ease in using the facilities

---

[3]Philip Kotler, "A Generic Concept of Marketing," *Journal of Marketing,* Vol. 36 (April, 1972), p. 50. In fact, if a marketer is interested in dampening the demand or discouraging the use of a social object (demarketing), he may want to make the object difficult to obtain. See Philip Kotler and Sidney J. Levy, "Demarketing, Yes, Demarketing," *Harvard Business Review,* Vol. 49 (November-December, 1971), pp. 78-79.

of a free or low-cost neighborhood medical clinic or day care center, it will make little difference if medical or child care services are physically decentralized. While the services may be made more readily available, they may remain inaccessible in a psychological sense. In addition, many nonprofit organizations are in direct contact with their target populations, but in order to achieve a satisfactory usage level within their budget constraints, their managements must be continuously concerned with whether improvements could be made in service level or cost.[4] Furthermore, all organizations, irrespective of orientation, must be concerned to some extent with "after-sale" services, if their managers are going to maintain and monitor the organizations' ability to deliver what they have promised.[5]

All organizations must consider how to make their objects available, which involves decisions about the number and type of "retail" outlets to employ, the kinds of "middlemen" to use, and the extent of reliance placed on facilitating agencies. Even with regard to programs calculated to influence the acceptability of social ideas, a key element is the provision of "adequate distribution and response channels."[6] Once an individual has been motivated to adopt (or at least expose himself more fully to) an idea, he must be able to learn where the "product" can be obtained. In such situations, distribution planning means "arranging for accessible outlets which permit the translation of motivations into actions" and entails "selecting or developing appropriate outlets, deciding on their number, average size, and locations, and giving them proper motivations to perform their part of the job."[7]

From a managerial perspective, these channel decisions are often more complex for private nonprofit organizations than they are for firms in the business sector or for publicly financed agencies. The private nonprofit organization generally has two constituencies: clients to whom it provides goods and/or services, and donors from whom it receives resources.[8] Because there is frequently minimal overlap between the two groups (consider, for example, the users of and financial contributors to Father Flanagan's Boys Town), two separate distribution systems must be established, one dealing with resource *allocation* and the other with resource *attraction*. Clearly, dif-

[4]Philip Kotler, *Marketing For Nonprofit Organizations* (Englewood Clifts, N.J.: Prentice-Hall, Inc., 1975), p. 71.

[5]*Ibid.* For a cogent and provocative discussion about the consequences of not being able to deliver what has been promised, see Charles A. Reich, *The Greening of America* (New York: Random House, 1970). Particular attention should be given to Reich's description of Consciousness II.

[6]Philip Kotler and Gerald Zaltman, "Social Marketing: An Approach to Planned Social Change," *Journal of Marketing*, Vol. 35 (July, 1971), p. 8.

[7]*Ibid.*, p. 9.

[8]Benson P. Shapiro, "Marketing for Nonprofit Organizations," *Harvard Business Review*, Vol. 51 (September–October, 1973), p. 124.

ferent marketing approaches are required to satisfy the needs of these two "markets."

Location—A Key Element in the Marketing of Services

If, in fact, one of the main goals in constructing a distribution channel is the facilitation of resource availability and accessibility, then a crucial factor determining whether that basic goal will be achieved is the location(s) chosen or the modes selected by which various relevant exchanges will take place. The process involved in the creation of time and place utilities is even more important in the marketing of services, by both profit and nonprofit organizations, than it is for the marketing of tangible commodities. As Rathmell has observed, the inability to store or ship intangibles and the need to have service facilities in existence to meet intermittent or random demand over time suggest that the price paid for many services reflects a substantial portion of these utilities in the total value of the service product.[9] This observation is clearly borne out in the marketing of telephone, emergency medical care, electrical, automobile repair, motel, and airport services, to name only a few. Relative to the resource attraction functions of nonprofit organizations, location decisions are crucial, because selection of appropriate locations for both donations and services can (1) make donation easier (e.g., placement of collection tins in high-traffic outlets, use of direct collection by volunteers and direct mail), (2) provide a base for local fund-raising and operations, and (3) provide credibility and show an organization's interest in an area (e.g., the agency seeking a donation can point to a neighborhood facility—a health clinic, college branch campus, or a museum, for example—as evidence of the organization's commitment to a community).[10] In fact, for such organizations as well as for publicly financed agencies, location plays an even greater role in resource allocation, because location is an integral part of the service itself.[11] As Abler, Adams, and Gould have pointed out:

> Hospitals must be located in geographic space to serve the people with complete medical care, and we must build schools close to the children who have to learn. Fire stations must be located to give rapid access to potential conflagrations, and voting booths must be placed so that people can cast their ballots without expend-

[9] John M. Rathmell, *Marketing in the Service Sector* (Cambridge, Mass.: Winthrop Publishers, Inc., 1974), p. 104.

[10] Shapiro, *op. cit.*, p. 129.

[11] *Ibid.*

ing unreasonable amounts of time, effort, or money to reach polling stations. Many of our states face the problem of locating branch campuses to serve a burgeoning and increasingly well educated population. In the cities we must create and locate playgrounds for the children. Many overpopulated countries must assign birth control clinics to reach the people with contraceptive and family planning information.[12]

Several factors underlie the importance of location in the marketing of services. First, services that are not appropriately located may not be performed at all. Compared to tangible goods, it is easier, as Rathmell has observed, to postpone the purchase of a service, except in emergencies, or discard a planned purchase of services.[13] In addition, a poorly located service facility invites a "do-it-yourself" decision. Second, there are often a number of constraints on the marketing of services which make location the key element of the marketing mix. For example, competition through either price or promotion is considered unethical in a number of service areas (e.g., medical and legal assistance). For other services, regulated monopolies or oligopolies are the dominant institutional arrangements (e.g., utilities); in such cases, the regulated service agency must concern itself with making its service available to the maximum number of potential customers.[14] With few exceptions, publicly funded or protected organizations are typically expected to serve the entire community.[15]

Although these constraints obviously force certain agencies into locations that they might not otherwise choose, the locational decision-making process for most services should not be altogether unlike that described in Chapter 2 relative to the demarcation of trading areas and the selection of specific sites by profit-oriented retailing organizations. What is most important in this decision process, irrespective of organizational orientation, is the seller's or agent's location relative to the potential market. In fact, for all services, there has been a marked trend toward the dispersion of service locations,[16] with the increased use of consumer analysis leading to the relocation of sources of services closer to users' locations.[17]

[12]Ronald Abler, John S. Adams, and Peter Gould, *Spatial Organization* (Englewood Cliffs, N.J.: Prentice-Hall, Inc., 1971), pp. 531–532.

[13]Rathmell, *op. cit.,* p. 108.

[14]*Ibid.*

[15]Christopher H. Lovelock and Charles B. Weinberg, "Contrasting Private and Public Sector Marketing," in Ronald C. Curhan (ed.), *1974 Combined Proceedings* (Chicago, Ill.: American Marketing Association, 1975), p. 246.

[16]Rathmell, *op. cit.,* p. 108.

[17]Lovelock and Weinberg, *op. cit.,* p. 243.

Channel Configurations

Marketing channels for services are generally far shorter than those used in the marketing of tangible commodities. This is because there is frequently little need for reliance on physical distribution and the maintenance of inventories at various points along the channel. The dominant channel configurations in the service sector, as isolated by Rathmell, are depicted in Fig. 14–1. Direct marketing (i.e., between service creator or performer and end users) is much more common than it is in the marketing of goods. However, intermediaries in the form of agents or brokers do appear in particular service industries.

> Their essential function is to bring performer and consumer or user together. They represent either of the primary channel components, and the longest service channel results where agents and brokers representing both seller and buyer intervene. Examples include the following. Rental agents represent the owners of rental housing and office space. Travel agents represent all types of travel services: surface and air transportation, hotels and motels, and packaged tours. Insurance agents and brokers are probably the most widely known service intermediaries. . . . Artistic performers and entertainers are represented by agents.[18]

It is difficult to typify the functions performed by the various agents and brokers who appear in service channels, because the duties performed vary so widely from channel to channel. Thus, agents who represent entertainers are similar to sales agents, while rental agents are mainly processors of transactions rather than decision-makers. Clearly, however, service agents and brokers are, like their counterparts in other fields, involved primarily with the flows of promotion and negotiation. For some services, such as automobile repair and restaurants, merchant wholesalers play an important role in providing the basic supplies needed in their performance. The actual service, however, originates at the retail level.

It should also be recalled from Chapter 10 that franchising is extremely important in the marketing of a wide variety of services. In actuality, franchising, as a mode of channel organization and design, has undoubtedly become the most significant competitive force in the channels for a number of services, such as automobile rentals, carpet cleaning, dry cleaning, temporary

---

[18] Rathmell, *op. cit.,* pp. 109–110. Donnelly has argued that "any extra-corporate entity between the producer of a service and prospective users that is utilized to make the service available and/or more convenient is a marketing intermediary for that service." Thus, under this definition, when an employer is authorized by his employees to deposit their pay directly into their checking accounts and when the employer agrees to participate in a bank's "direct pay deposit" plan, the employer becomes an intermediary in the distribution of the bank's service. See James H. Donnelly, Jr., *op. cit.*

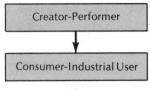

a.

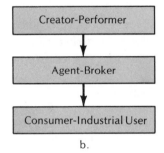

b.

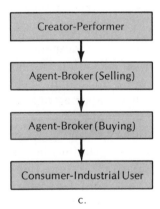

c.

FIGURE 14–1 Dominant Channel Configurations in the Service Sector

SOURCE: John M. Rathmell, *Marketing in the Service Sector* (Cambridge, Mass.: Winthrop Publishers, Inc., 1974), p. 110. Reprinted by permission of the publisher.

547

office help, motels, and the like. In fact, any *standardized* service is an appropriate candidate for franchising.[19]

The Need for Interorganizational Cooperation

Throughout this book, stress has been placed on the need for the interorganizational management of channel systems. The same stress is appropriate here, especially as services become more dispersed and decentralized. Perhaps the greatest evidence of decentralization is found in the public service area. Federal, state, and local governmental agencies are increasingly contracting with private firms to facilitate or even execute public services. In addition, as Rathmell observes:

> . . . through the revenue-sharing mechanism, the national government is turning over more and more public services to state and local government agencies. In essence, the national government *develops the social product* through legislation and compensates decentralized governmental bodies for performing the *other elements* in the social marketing mix.[20]

Furthermore, there seems to be a desperate need for interorganizational cooperation in such fields as education and health care, where redundancies, inequities, and inefficiencies exist that might be eliminated by fostering a more appropriate division of labor among the various units seeking to provide these services in a community.

Considerable attention has been given, especially by sociologists, to the subject of interorganizational relations in a wide variety of service-oriented fields.[21] However, it is important to note that most of the attention has been focused on the need for horizontal or lateral cooperation among agencies. That is, the focus has been similar to one that would urge greater collusion among manufacturers, or among wholesalers, or among retailers. Very little

---

[19]*Ibid.*, p. 111.

[20]*Ibid.*

[21]See, for example, with regard to health care, Sol Levine and Paul E. White, "Exchange as a Conceptual Framework for the Study of Interorganizational Relationships," *Administrative Science Quarterly*, Vol. 5 (March, 1961), pp. 583–601; with regard to rehabilitation and mental health, Bertram J. Black and Harold M. Kase, "Inter-Agency Cooperation in Rehabilitation and Mental Health," *Social Science Review*, Vol. 37 (March, 1963), pp. 26–32; with regard to delinquency prevention and control, William Reid, "Interagency Coordination in Delinquency Prevention and Control," *Social Science Review*, Vol. 38 (December, 1964), pp. 418–428; with regard to services for the elderly, Robert Morris and Ollie A. Randall, "Planning and Organization of Community Services for the Elderly," *Social Work*, Vol. 10 (January, 1965), pp. 96–102; with regard to community action, Roland L. Warren, "The Interorganizational Field as a Focus for Investigation," in Merlin B. Brinkerhoff and Phillip R. Kunz (eds.), *Complex Organizations and Their Environments* (Dubuque, Iowa: Wm. C. Brown Publishers, 1972), pp. 307–325; and with regard to government-business relations, William M. Evan, "An Organization-Set Model of Interorganizational Relations," in Matthew Tuite, Roger Chisholm, and Michael Radnor (eds.), *Interorganizational Decision Making* (Chicago, Ill.: Aldine Publishing Co., 1972), pp. 181–200.

interorganizational research has been performed relative to vertical relationships (i.e., those among units on different distribution levels, the ultimate consumer or user being excluded.)[22] The reason for this is relatively clear. Marketing channels for services are short—so short, in fact, that such channels are primarily comprised of the creator of the service and the consumer, as mentioned above. The existence of intermediaries, while evident in some service channels, is generally not required, and, therefore, a "commercial channel" of distribution, as defined in Chapter 1, is often absent. There are certainly a large number of wholesalers with whom service organizations interact, but the primary role of the wholesalers in these situations would be to supply tangible products (e.g., auto parts, food, movies) that facilitate the performance of the basic services (e.g., auto repairs, restaurant services, screenings).[23] The service itself does not generally pass through the hands of a number of intermediaries; that is, intermediaries do not generally participate in the marketing flows that must be performed in making the service available to client groups. Health care, rehabilitation, and community action agencies, for example, deal directly with their constituencies. Although resources, in the form of consultation, funds, and program ideas, may come from other organizations (e.g., the federal government), the services provided are usually produced and consumed at the "retail" level.

Therefore, problems of managing *vertical* interorganizational relations are not as acute in the marketing of services as they are in the marketing of tangible commodities. There is, however, a much greater opportunity to concentrate on problems related to *horizontal* interorganizational relations, particularly in the absence of antitrust constraints with regard to the provision of social welfare services and concepts by nonprofit and publicly financed organizations.[24] In fact, horizontal coordination is necessary with regard to

[22]The reader should recall the discussion in Chapter 1, where the focus of attention in this text was placed on the relationships within the commercial channel of distribution. The commercial channel is that subset of the total channel which excludes end users or ultimate consumers.

[23]Some producers of tangible goods and the merchant wholesalers with whom they deal are taking a more active role in facilitating the service functions of their customers. For example, in the channel for food services, increasing attention is being given to providing preportioned frozen items, broader assortments, and food portion control services to volume feeding establishments, such as airlines, cafeterias, hospitals, and government facilities and even to fine restaurants. In this case, the original suppliers and the wholesalers are, indeed, participating directly in the provision of services at the retail level. In addition, the Federal Reserve System as well as major city banks can be viewed as wholesalers in the channels for commercial banking services.

[24]Horizontal collusion is illegal, under the Sherman Act, in profit-oriented service industries. Yet, collusion does take place, some of which is highly questionable from a free enterprise perspective. Fees set by lawyers, doctors, and appliance and auto repairmen are remarkably similar for certain services. The reasons for this similarity are currently under investigation by the U.S. Justice Department and the Federal Trade Commission. In addition, professional ethics apparently dictate that certain marketing practices, such as advertising of services, are not to be practiced by lawyers and doctors. The enforcement of these ethics by professional associations can also be viewed as anticompetitive.

almost all social welfare concerns, and the same interorganizational principles apply to achieving such coordination as they do to situations involving vertical relations.

These observations about the character of the distribution of services is not meant, in any way, to minimize the importance of distribution questions in the service sector. Questions of availability and accessibility are absolutely crucial to the viability of any service organization. Nowhere are such questions more evident than in the marketing of public services. For example,

> A city's public library has to consider the best means of making its books available to the public. Should it establish one large library with an extensive collection of books, or several neighborhood branch libraries with duplication of books? Should it use bookmobiles that bring the books to the customers instead of relying exclusively on the customers coming to the books? Should it distribute through school libraries? Similarly the police department of a city must think through the problem of distributing its protective services efficiently through the community. It has to determine how much protective service to allocate to different neighborhoods; the respective merits of squad cars, motorcycles, and foot patrolmen; and the positioning of emergency phones.[25]

Similar questions exist with regard to the availability of fire and ambulance services,[26] the distribution of public welfare checks, the sale of government bonds, the provision of postal services, the establishment of public parks, and the placement of automobile license bureaus.[27] In fact, these questions are unavoidable for *every* kind of service, but are particularly important for public services. In each and every case, the dominant questions seem to relate directly to the functions and location of "retail" outlets. That is, the primary focus is on the best means available, subject to budget constraints, for permitting ultimate consumers access to specific services. Clearly, then, an appropriate combination of retailing marketing mix elements (hours of operations, facilitating services, assortments, location and facilities, expense management, promotion, etc.)[28] is critical in the service sector of the economy, irrespective of the profit orientation of the organizations providing the services or the basic nature of the service offered.

The remainder of this chapter concentrates on examples where channel concepts have been or could be applied to specific service situations. Although

---

[25] Philip Kotler and Sidney J. Levy, "Broadening the Concept of Marketing," *Journal of Marketing*, Vol. 33 (January, 1969), p. 13.

[26] See Frederick E. Webster, Jr., *Social Aspects of Marketing* (Englewood Cliffs, N.J.: Prentice-Hall, Inc., 1974), p. 87.

[27] See Kotler, *Marketing For Nonprofit Organizations, op. cit.,* pp. 336–337.

[28] See Chapter 2 for a discussion of significant aspects of the retailing marketing mix.

some attention is given to channels for commercial services (e.g., lodging and insurance), most attention is focused on services provided by nonprofit and publicly financed organizations, because the problems associated with channel organization and design in the former are very similar to those found in the marketing of commercial products, while the latter represent unique cases which demand concentrated examination.

THE APPLICATION OF CHANNEL CONCEPTS
TO THE MARKETING OF SERVICES
PROVIDED BY NONPROFIT
AND PUBLICLY FINANCED ORGANIZATIONS

Health Care Services[29]

Four different market structures for the delivery of health care services may be isolated, although a number of others also exist. The first, called the flat nonintegrated structure (see Fig. 14–2), is the archetype of the present private practice, fee-for-service system in which every hospital, each physician, and all other health care providers sell directly to consumers. The organizations involved in this system undertake no effort to coordinate their activities; any coordination that does take place comes from market pressures emanating from consumers.[30]

The second is a vertically integrated structure where coordination of the activities of all providers is shifted to a comprehensive health care institution, such as the Kaiser Health Care Foundation, which provides for all potential patient health needs within a single establishment.[31] Although there are a number of variations in existence, Fig. 14–3 is representative of a major form of these so-called health maintenance organizations (HMO's). Coordination among activities is achieved through an internal control mechanism. Payments are received from consumers on a capitation basis, and each consumer belongs to only one group.

In the third structure, coordination is achieved by means of the control exerted by one health provider or by a middleman (see Fig. 14–4). In this

[29]The discussion of health care services is drawn from the excellent and innovative essay by Louis P. Bucklin and James M. Carman, "Vertical Market Structure Theory and the Health Care Delivery System," in Jagdish N. Sheth and Peter L. Wright (eds.), *Marketing Analysis for Societal Problems* (Urbana, Ill.: University of Illinois Bureau of Economic and Business Research, 1974), pp. 7–39.

[30]*Ibid.*, p. 23.

[31]*Ibid.*, p. 24. See also Patrick E. Murphy and William A. Staples, "Health Maintenance Organizations: A Marketing Perspective," a paper presented to the 1975 American Marketing Association Educators' Conference, Rochester, N.Y., August 17–20, 1975.

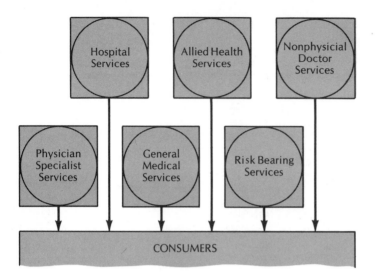

FIGURE 14-2   The Flat Nonintegrated Structure for the Delivery
of Health Care Services

SOURCE: Louis P. Bucklin and James M. Carman, "Vertical Market Structure Theory and the Health Care Delivery System," in *Marketing Analysis
for Societal Problems*, eds. Jagdish N. Sheth and Peter L. Wright (Urbana,
Ill.: University of Illinois Bureau of Economic and Business Research,
1974), p. 23.

nonintegrated arrangement, consumers make annual capitation payments to
the coordinator of their choice. It is then the responsibility of the central
coordinator—a pure middleman, a general practitioner individual or group, a
pediatric individual or group, or a general practice community clinic or hospital—to buy specialized services from other types of providers or to undertake to perform these internally.

The fourth type of arrangement is called the long, vertical nonintegrated
structure (see Fig. 14-5) and is characterized by the presence of multiple
modes of coordination. According to Bucklin and Carman:

> General financial support and insurance services are provided through a nonprofit
> foundation for a complete health package. Individual providers would similarly
> belong to the foundation which would reimburse the former on a fee-for-service
> basis. The foundation would develop its own techniques, such as peer review, to
> control the use of providers and their charges for service. All consumers within a
> given area, such as a county, would be members of the foundation.[32]

[32]*Ibid.*, pp. 26–27.

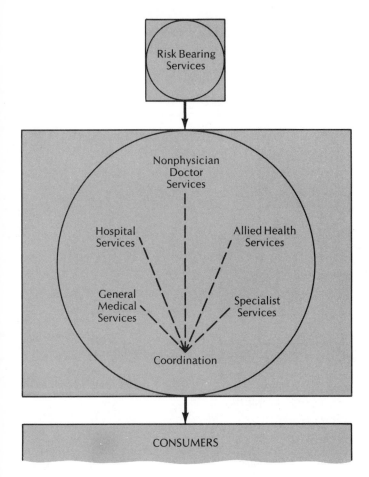

FIGURE 14-3 The Vertically Integrated Structure for the
Delivery of Health Care Services

SOURCE: Louis P. Bucklin and James M. Carman, "Vertical Market
Structure Theory and the Health Care Delivery System," in *Marketing
Analysis for Societal Problems*, eds. Jagdish N. Sheth and Peter L. Wright
(Urbana, Ill.: University of Illinois Bureau of Economic and Business
Research, 1974), p. 25.

Under this system, as in the previous two, consumers would make an annual
capitation payment, but in this case, their payment would go to the foundation.

In their analysis of these four arrangements, Bucklin and Carman have
relied heavily on Bucklin's theory of channel structure, which was discussed
in Chapter 5 of this book. Thus, their basic conclusions about the arrange-

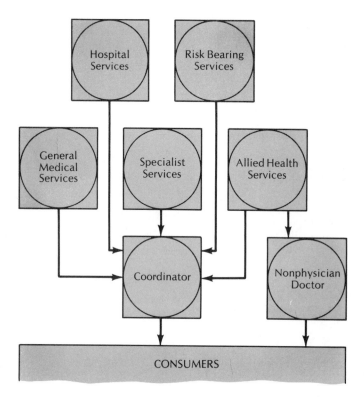

FIGURE 14-4   The Vertical, Nonintegrated Structure for the
Delivery of Health Care Services

SOURCE: Louis P. Bucklin and James M. Carman, "Vertical Market
Structure Theory and the Health Care Delivery System," in *Marketing
Analysis for Societal Problems*, eds. Jagdish N. Sheth and Peter L. Wright
(Urbana, Ill.: University of Illinois Bureau of Economic and Business
Research, 1974), p. 27.

ments are couched in terms of service outputs and costs. Some of their conclusions are as follows:[33]

1. Consumer search for information and the need for seller promotion appears to
   be greatest in the flat, nonintegrated structure. The least seller promotion and
   consumer search cost is provided by the vertically integrated structure.

2. The flat, nonintegrated structure is the one that is likely to adapt best to consumer needs in terms of providing facilitating outputs. It is also the one that
   enables the consumer to have the greatest opportunity to select that particular
   health service which he perceives as best suiting his needs.

3. The flat, nonintegrated structure is likely to be the one that incurs the greatest

[33]*Ibid.*, pp. 29 and 35.

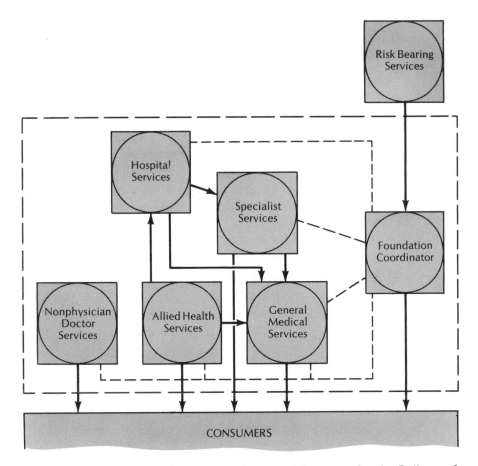

FIGURE 14-5 The Long, Vertical, Nonintegrated Structure for the Delivery of
Health Care Services

SOURCE: Louis P. Bucklin and James M. Carman, "Vertical Market Structure Theory and the
Health Care Delivery System," in *Marketing Analysis for Societal Problems*, eds. Jagdish N. Sheth
and Peter L. Wright (Urbana, Ill.: University of Illinois Bureau of Economic and Business Research, 1974), p. 28.

waste of resources, is least efficient, and provides the greatest degree of discrimination among consumer groups. Wealthy consumers may be able to cope
handily with the system. Impoverished consumers may literally fail to survive.

4. The vertically integrated system (HMO) is likely to result in better use of existing health supply resources and to be more efficient. It also provides the basis
   for evenhanded care for all people. On the other hand, there is likely to be minimal adjustment of facilitating outputs to consumer needs, problems in effecting
   community control in the absence of competition, and a tendency over time for
   bureaucratic rigidities to accrue. Consumers have the least choice of specific
   providers.

5. The vertically nonintegrated structures provide a middle ground, involving characteristics of both ends of the spectrum. Consumer choice opportunities are improved, but the possibilities for some discrimination in resource use also appears likely. Both vertically nonintegrated systems also provide maximum opportunity for the entry of new types of structures and hence incentive for innovation.

Any analysis of health care services must recognize, implicitly or explicitly, the significance of effective interorganization management in the organization of health care delivery systems. Each structure enumerated above varies in terms of the extent of role specification, centralization of power, and potential for conflict management that might be expected. In fact, the typology here is very similar to that developed throughout this book for conventional, administered, contractual, and corporate channels. The application of the concepts from vertical market structure theory (see Chapter 5) and from interorganization management theory (see Chapter 7) can, therefore, be combined to provide prescriptions for improving health care systems.[34]

It is important, however, to repeat the cautionary note that was inserted previously regarding what is meant by interorganizational coordination within this and many other service fields. That is, there is some real question as to whether a "commercial" marketing channel (comprised of producers and middlemen) exists in the health care field. In fact, it could be argued that the focus in each of the above-mentioned structures is really on the potential for *horizontal* coordination among institutions and agencies dealing primarily on the same level of distribution and not with vertical coordination. The "product" (health care) does not move through the system, but rather is the output of the interaction of a number of organizations, each of which interfaces in some way with ultimate consumers. Thus, basically, the concern is with the retailing of medical services, even though there are instances (e.g., between physician's offices and medical laboratories) where vertical kinds of interactions may take place.

Educational Services[35]

Distribution channel concepts may be applied to the problem of disseminating educational innovations. A key agency responsible for speeding up the diffusion of worthwhile educational innovations among the nation's

---

[34] For further discussion of this point, see Louis W. Stern and Frederick D. Sturdivant, "Discussion," in Jagdish N. Sheth and Peter L. Wright, *op. cit.*, pp. 39–41.

[35] The discussion of educational services is drawn from Kotler, *Marketing For Nonprofit Organizations, op. cit.*, pp. 192–194 and Burton R. Clark, "Interorganizational Patterns in Education," in Merlin B. Brinkerhoff and Philip R. Kunz, *op. cit.*, pp. 360–362.

locally controlled 18,000 school districts is the National Institute of Education (NIE).[36] Figure 14-6 illustrates four different distribution models that might be used by NIE to achieve its ends. According to Kotler:[37]

> The first model calls for direct distribution of innovations from NIE to each of the 18,000 school districts. This is clearly an inefficient system of distribution, involving too many first-hand contacts and the absence of an appreciation of local conditions.
>
> The second model calls for NIE to present the innovations to *regional dissemination centers* (RDC's—perhaps major universities) which in turn would disseminate them to all the local schools in their area.
>
> The third model is similar to the second, with the modification that the RDCs would not deal with all the school districts in their region but mainly with those schools designated as innovator schools which are looked up to by other schools in the region. These innovator schools will "retail" the innovations and presumably be more effective because of the high esteem in which they are held by other schools.
>
> The fourth model adds still one more channel link to the market, in the form of designated school district change agents. Each school district would designate one person to be the school district's change agent. This person would be responsible to the school district for (1) searching for new ideas and solutions to local school district problems by going to the local RDC, the NIE, or elsewhere, and (2) bringing innovations to the right parties within their school district. The establishment of this formal position within all school districts would make it easier for NIE and RDC to determine who to contact for information and communication.

Similar diffusion problems are faced continuously within commercial channels of distribution. Perhaps an interesting parallel to educational innovations will be found in the dissemination of information and the adoption processes among retail chains attending the diffusion of the various front-end data systems discussed in Chapter 12. While change agents have not generally been formally institutionalized within business firms, it would seem that, if the position of channel diplomat were to be established—as suggested in Chapters 7 and 12 of this book—then these individuals could perform functions similar to those described in the fourth model above relative to inter-organizational communication of innovative processes and concepts.

While the above example is primarily normative in nature, there are instances where marketing channels have emerged in education under circumstances not unlike the ones described by Kotler. The curriculum reform movement of the late 1950's provides an actual illustration.[38] The Physical Science Study Committee, a group of professors and secondary school

---

[36] Kotler, *ibid.*, p. 192.

[37] *Ibid.*, pp. 192 and 194.

[38] Clark, *op. cit.*, p. 360.

1. Direct Marketing Model
   (Zero-level marketing channel)

   0. NIE → all school districts

2. Regional Dissemination Center Model
   (One-level marketing channel)

   0. NIE → RDC
   1. RDC → school districts

3. RDC and Innovator School Model
   (Two-level marketing channel)

   0. NIE → RDC
   1. RDC → innovator schools
   2. Innovator schools → other schools

4. RDC, Innovator School, and Local
      Change Agent Model

   (Three-level marketing channel)

   0. NIE → RDC
   1. RDC → innovator schools
   2. Innovator schools → school district
         change agents
   3. Change agents → other schools

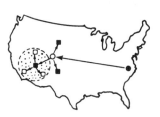

Symbols: ● NIE-National Institute of Education
          ○ RDC-Regional dissemination center
          ■ Innovator school
          □ School district change agents
          · School district

FIGURE 14-6 Four Distribution Models for Disseminating Educational Innovations

SOURCE: Philip Kotler, *Marketing for Nonprofit Organizations* (Englewood Cliffs, N.J.: Prentice-Hall, Inc., 1975), p. 193. By permission.

teachers funded by the National Science Foundation, undertook to improve the teaching of physical sciences in the nation's secondary schools. Once it had developed suitable materials, the Committee then saw to it that the materials would be actively promoted and made widely available throughout the nation by putting them into the hands of profit-oriented organizations with preformed marketing channels. Thus, during the winter of 1959–1960, the Committee gave its printed materials to a schoolbook publisher, its new scientific equipment to a manufacturer of scientific apparatus, and its films to an educational film distributor. Concurrently, the National Science Foundation also initiated and supported a program of summer institutes that were voluntary throughout—for the colleges that offered them, the professors who directed and staffed them, and the teachers who came as students. The Physical Science Study Committee was, for the most part, successful in convincing institutes to use its materials.

Thus, in this channel example, a federal agency provided the funds; a private nonprofit group received the money and developed a new course; commercial organizations made the new materials available to all units of the decentralized educational system; dispersed universities and colleges used the new materials to train teachers in all regions of the country; and eventually, existing local authorities adopted the materials and allowed their teachers to reshape local courses.

Clearly, the effective dissemination of the innovation rested to a large extent on the expert power of the various actors. As Clark observes:

> The National Science Foundation was expert and prestigeful; so also were the Committee, the Institutes, the teachers trained in the new materials. The very materials themselves traveled under the same aura.[39]

In this instance, the expert power of each channel member was reinforcing and not conflictful. The absence of dysfunctional conflict can be attributed, in part, to the presence of a superordinate goal based on the recognition, at the time, that our secondary school system was far inferior to that of the Soviet Union in the teaching of the physical sciences. In reality, the launching of Sputnik, the first satellite to reach outer space and orbit the Earth, had made it possible for groups to cooperate in a way that had been unprecedented previously. Interorganization management could be practiced in a supportive atmosphere, indeed. The final outcome was that, as early as 1963, 40 to 50 percent of the students taking high school physics were studying the materials generated by the Committee, even though the materials did not become available until after 1958.

[39] *Ibid.,* p. 362.

Accident Prevention Services[40]

Several nonprofit organizations are involved with providing services that will serve to reduce the incidence of industrial and consumer accidents, but perhaps the most prominent of these is the National Safety Council. One of the Council's goals concerns the promotion of highway safety, and one of the services it offers to help cut down on the number of highway mishaps is a defensive driving course (DDC).

Figure 14–7 shows the various channels through which this course is marketed along with the promotional tools it uses. The National Safety Council reaches potential prospects through business firms, service organizations, schools, and the police and court system.[41] For the 1970's, the National Safety Council has adopted

> . . . a four-point marketing program . . . One of the first objectives is to increase the sales effectiveness of our existing 150 state and local safety council cooperating agencies . . . The second part of the program is to create 500 new training agencies in communities not now served by safety councils . . . The third part of the marketing program will be aimed at selling big industry on adopting DDC as a training course for all employees in plant-run training programs . . . The fourth part of the marketing plan deals with a nationwide promotional effort built around a series of community special-emphasis campaigns running from February 1 through Memorial Day each year of the decade.[42]

In order for the National Safety Council to achieve its goals, it will have to rely on its expert, referent, and legitimate power bases in convincing channel members to do what they might not otherwise do. And while its power may be great relative to the issue of highway safety, for example, the issue itself may not be salient enough to the other firms within its channels to induce them to action. In other words, the Council will probably have to provide some significant inducement in order to secure the contribution of the channel members depicted in Fig. 14–7. Unless it can somehow mediate rewards or punishments for compliance, its efforts may be in vain.

Because such efforts on the part of the Council really involve the marketing of an idea—the concept of defensive driving as a deterrent to highway accidents—it is clear that there must be an effective merging of distribution

---

[40]The discussion of accident prevention services is drawn from Kotler and Zaltman, *op. cit.*, p. 11.

[41]*Ibid.*

[42]Chris Imhoff, "DDC's Decisive Decade," *Traffic Safety Magazine*, Vol. 69 (December, 1969), pp. 20 and 26.

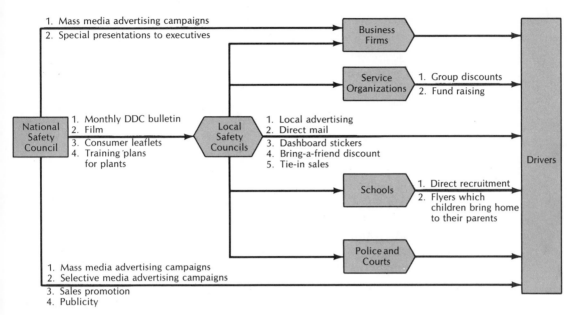

FIGURE 14-7   Marketing Channels and Promotional Tools Used by the National Safety Council: Defensive Driving Course

SOURCE: Philip Kotler, *Marketing for Nonprofit Organizations* (Englewood Cliffs, N.J.: Prentice-Hall, Inc., 1975), p. 299. By permission.

and promotion in its program. The use of specific agents who can carry out the idea and enforce it must be blended with such vehicles as advertising, press releases, and other promotional tools. Clearly, no marketing program can rely on any one element of the marketing mix; each must use all elements in combination in order to achieve its goals.

Population Control and Family Planning Services[43]

The topic of population control and family planning is highly controversial. Population control refers to the *control* of births, while family planning refers to the spacing of births and the limiting of family size to some number of children *desired* by the individual couple. Population control ad-

[43]The discussion of population control and family planning services is drawn from an unpublished term paper by Raymond Neil Maddox, "Distribution and Social Problems."

vocates are highly critical of the family planning approach to the world's population problem. For example, Kingsley Davis has stated:

> The things that make family planning acceptable are the very things that make it ineffective for population control. By stressing the right of parents to have the number of children they want, it evades the basic question of population policy, which is how to give societies the number of children they need. By offering only the means for *couples* to control fertility, it neglects the means for societies to do so.[44]

Without engaging in this debate, it is possible to observe that the present system in the United States for distributing birth control services to the population is quite fragmented and highly decentralized. Medical birth control services (e.g., abortion, the IUD, sterilization, and birth control pills) may be distributed through private or public health practice. In addition, they may be offered through clinics established solely for this purpose and staffed by personnel possessing the required level of medical expertise. The channels for nonmedical methods (e.g., condoms, chemical preparations, and information on so-called natural methods of contraception such as the rhythm system) are largely identical to those for the medically dependent techniques, except for one important exception—the addition of traditional commercial channels, including retail drug outlets and vending machines.

If one is interested in seeking improvements in the dissemination of birth control devices and information—either for population control or family planning purposes—attention must be focused on reducing the costs of the physical, temporal, and psychic distances separating individuals from the agencies providing the services or mechanisms. Private medical practitioners have, on the whole, historically been hesitant to *initiate* the subject of birth control with their established patients.[45] Presumably, they would be even more reluctant to become active agents in any channel whose sole function is the providing of such services. It is expected that if this group is to assume a more active role, two steps must be taken. First, the program must be remunerative to physicians. Second, the norms of the medical profession must be supportive of such activities.

Enrolling the physician as an active participant would definitely increase the availability of birth control services to the more affluent of the popula-

[44]Kingsley Davis, "Population Policy: Will Current Programs Succeed?" *Science*, Vol. 158 (November 10, 1967), p. 739.

[45]Sydney S. Spivack, "Family Planning in Medical Practice," in Clyde V. Kiser (ed.), *Research in Family Planning* (Princeton, N.J.: Princeton University Press, 1962), pp. 211-230.

tion. However, as pointed out earlier in the discussion of the present flat, nonintegrated structure in health care delivery, among the problems confronting the less fortunate is the limited availability of medical services of any type. Therefore, this suggestion would be, at best, of limited utility in raising the level of accessibility for these groups.

An innovative approach in solving the problem of accessibility has been that adopted in Louisiana. As reported by El-Ansary and Kramer, a major component of the so-called "Louisiana model" was an improvement in clinic site selection and service level determination.

> To reduce travel time, strategic locations were selected for the program's clinic satellites. Also, clinic layout was planned to reduce the time consumed in information and physical flows. The areas assigned for waiting rooms were limited to force faster customer flows. Bottlenecks in the system were identified and eliminated. It was realized that improving the service level would result not only in a higher percentage of kept appointments and active customers but also in better utilization of physical facilities and human resources.[46]

Although heavy reliance on clinics to provide birth control services may be functional in parts of the United States, it is not always the best distribution approach, especially in underdeveloped countries. As Farley and Leavitt point out,[47]

> ...a complete reliance upon clinics as outlets is questionable, especially when one considers their high cost per client visit and the relatively poor revisit rates they achieve. Several problems contribute to this situation:
>
> —Medical resources, especially personnel, are expensive and generally in short supply ...
>
> —Red tape may be substantial because of overly complex control systems ...
>
> —Clinical systems may bias a program's emphasis to the exclusion of (nonmedical types of contraception) ...
>
> —As a distribution network, clinics tend to be sparsely dispersed ... (Also,) a visit to a clinic may involve substantial waiting time ...
>
> —Clinics lack anonymity ...

However, in both developed and underdeveloped economies, the com-

---

[46] Adel I. El-Ansary and Oscar E. Kramer, Jr., "Social Marketing: The Family Planning Experience," *Journal of Marketing,* Vol. 37 (July, 1973), p. 3.

[47] John U. Farley and Harold J. Leavitt, "Marketing and Population Problems," *Journal of Marketing,* Vol. 35 (July, 1971), p. 31.

mercial distribution of nonmedical means seems to offer the greatest potential for rapidly expanding the number and availability of birth control mechanisms.

> ... most cultures have a functioning distribution structure which delivers basic commodities to even the most remote areas of the countryside. The network is intensive and provides relatively anonymous outlets which are physically close to the customer. Wholesalers and retailers know how to deliver goods to customers, and distributors know how to stimulate consumer demand. It is possible that the retail structure could be utilized to provide distribution outlets for contraceptive materials, thus helping resolve the logistical problems facing the clinic system ... Other channels, such as mail order, could be used in some nations to supplement the clinic system's distribution of certain items.[48]

Indeed, if food and variety stores, as well as pharmacies, were engaged as distributors of point-of-purchase information, contraceptive chemicals, and contraceptive devices, the increase in the number and accessibility of outlets would be tremendous. In India, for example, the government engaged the distribution services of some of the largest packaged-goods companies in the country, including Lever Brothers of India, because of their reach into the remotest areas.[49] In fact, the government eventually elected to work with the following retailers: (a) health clinics, (b) barbers, (c) field workers, (d) retail stores, and (e) vending machines.

A major advantage in using traditional commercial channels for the distribution of birth control services is that they tend to help reduce psychic distance, that is, the hesitancy to seek birth control services owing to the intimate nature of the product and the modesty or shyness associated with its use. Medical channels, including public agencies, no matter how available, are separated from certain segments of the population by major psychological barriers.[50] A consumer's basic familiarity with commercial retail outlets is an important means of reducing this distance factor.

There is a close correspondence between the marketing of birth control services and the marketing of "normal" products, because most contraceptive devices are tangible items. While there are numerous ancillary services (such as counseling) that attend population control and family planning, a major problem in this area is achieving the availability and accessibility of the devices themselves. Thus, thinking in terms of traditional marketing approaches seems to be a natural course. The principles of interorganization

---

[48] *Ibid.*

[49] Kotler, *Marketing for Nonprofit Organizations, op. cit.,* p. 196.

[50] See Gerald Zaltman and Ilan Vertinsky, "Health Service Marketing: A Suggested Model," *Journal of Marketing,* Vol. 35 (July, 1971), p. 26.

management seem as relevant here as they are to the marketing of all forms of packaged goods.

Recycling Services[51]

The recycling of waste products has become a subject of considerable notoriety over the past decade as increased concern has been voiced over environmental quality. In 1970, every American each day disposed of approximately 5½ pounds of solid waste (industrial, construction, commercial, and household). This daily disposal rate is predicted to increase to 8 pounds by 1980.[52] Although the problem is primarily commercial in nature and thus directly involves the activities of profit-oriented organizations, the major forces behind the movement to improve recycling services have been non-profit organizations (e.g., the Crusade for a Clean Environment), private citizens and legislators. For this latter reason, a discussion of the distribution issues involved in this service area has been included in this section.

Considering the low prices paid currently for waste materials (i.e., bottles, cans, paper, etc.) and the high costs involved in the collecting, sorting, and transportation of these objects to recycling plants, industry is relying heavily on civic and community groups, who use volunteer help primarily in the collection process. Normal business costs are usually absent when these groups handle the collection, because labor and vehicles are generally donated. However, one of the problems in relying on these groups is that their efforts are generally very sporadic, at best. Furthermore, the problem is growing faster than the membership of ecology-minded groups.

Traditional distribution channels have been used in some recycling efforts. During the immediate post-World War II years and before, distribution of soft drinks, for example, was specifically tied in to the use of the returnable bottle. From the bottler's point of view, the returnable bottle was desirable because its use reduced his production costs. He found it more economical to clean existing bottles and reuse them than to buy new bottles. Middlemen, such as retail food stores, cooperated because the system was the most convenient for the producer involved, and he could bring pressure to bear on the middlemen to secure their cooperation. Currently, however, returnable bottles account for less than 50 percent of the soft drink industry's business, because both retailers and consumers resisted the returning

---

[51]The discussion of recycling services is drawn primarily from an unpublished term paper by Sam B. Dunbar, Jr., "The Recycling of Waste Products: Effects on Distribution Channels and Marketing."

[52]"Cash in Trash? Maybe," *Forbes*, January 15, 1970, p. 20.

and handling of empty bottles.[53] Supermarkets directly influenced bottlers to introduce soft drinks in one-way bottles as early as 1948.[54] While one-way containers have increased the bottler's costs, these costs have been passed on to the consumer. The response of the consumers has been demonstrated by their willingness to pay higher prices for the convenience afforded by these containers. Thus, the recycling problem in this area has multiplied.

If recycling is to be a feasible solution to waste disposal, some means must be developed to channel these wastes back to firms for further use. But traditional channel concepts must be reversed because, in the case of soft drinks especially, the consumer is the *producer* of the waste materials that are to be recycled. Thus, the consumer becomes the first link in the recycling channel of distribution rather than the last. The recycling of waste materials is, therefore, essentially a "reverse-distribution" process.[55]

The contrast between forward and reverse channels is illustrated in Fig. 14-8 and in Table 14-1. The reverse direction channel returns the reusable waste products from consumer to producer.

[53]"Packaging Advances Promise Much But Environment Dampens Outlook," *Soft Drink Industry*, May 29, 1970, p. 1.

[54]William G. Zikmund and William J. Stanton, "Recycling Solid Wastes: A Channels-of-Distribution Problem," *Journal of Marketing*, Vol. 35 (July, 1971), p. 36.

[55]*Ibid.*, pp. 34–35.

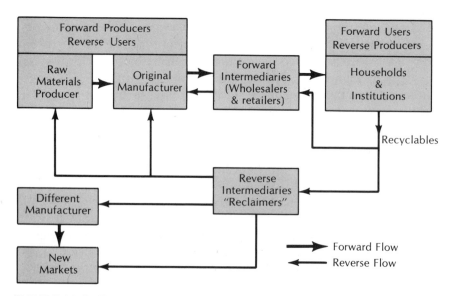

FIGURE 14-8   Forward and Reverse Channels of Distribution

SOURCE: Joseph Guiltinan and Nonyelu Nwokoye, "Reverse Channels for Recycling: An Analysis of Alternatives and Public Policy Implications," in *1974 Combined Proceedings*, ed. Ronald C. Curhan (Chicago: American Marketing Association, 1975), p. 341.

TABLE 14-1   Forward versus Reverse Channels: Some Key Distinctions

Forward Channels	Reverse Channels
Products:	
High unit value	Low unit value
Highly differentiated	Little or no differentiation
Much product innovation	Little or no innovation
Few producers	Many originators
Markets:	
Routinized transactions established	Routinized transactions not established
Many final users	Few final users
Varied customer demands	Standardized demands
Supply often less than or equal to demand	Supply typically greater than demand
Large assortment discrepancy	Small assortment discrepancy
Key Functions:	
Assorting	Sorting
Allocation	Accumulation
Heavy promotional effort	Low promotional effort
Speculative inventories	Few speculative inventories
Packaging	Collection

SOURCE: Joseph Guiltinan and Nonyelu Nwokoye, "Reverse Channels for Recycling: An Analysis of Alternatives and Public Policy Implications," in Ronald C. Curhan (ed.), *1974 Combined Proceedings* (Chicago, Ill.: American Marketing Association, 1975), p. 342.

> Conceptually, reverse distribution is identical to the traditional channel of distribution. The consumer has a product to sell, and in essence, he assumes the same position as a manufacturer selling a new product. The consumer's (seller's) role is to distribute his waste materials to the market that demands his product.[56]

However, the consumer, in most instances, does not consider himself to be the producer of waste materials. Therefore, he is not readily concerned with planning a marketing strategy for his product, which would be reusable wastes. When the producer is unaware of or indifferent to the fact that he is the producer, then the problem becomes acute.

So far, many recycling channels eliminate the middleman, unless that middleman is a voluntary group. The fact that there are generally no established middlemen in these backward channels between the producer and the consumer of waste products is unfortunate. It causes the producer (consumer) a number of inconveniences. Foremost is the accumulation of waste

[56]*Ibid.*, p. 35.

materials on his part, without adequate storage facilities, as well as an absence of transportation facilities when he does accumulate a mass of waste materials.

On the other hand, in the area of trash recycling, private and municipal trash collection systems provide the collection and storage functions. The buyer of the collected wastes may be a power plant, a metals company, a fertilizer company, etc. This channel is a convenient channel for the individual household. However, trash collection by basic trash collection agencies may not be the ultimate answer to the recycling problem. Trash needs to be sorted and then routed to storage centers for ultimate transportation to recycling centers, and most municipalities are unwilling to incur the costs associated with these tasks.

If an effective reverse channel of distribution is to become a reality, the ultimate consumer must first be motivated to start the reverse flow. In addition, a greater degree of cooperation has to be achieved among channel members than presently occurs relative to this problem area. A barrier to increased cooperation and coordination is the lack of profitability. In the absence of legislation mandating recycling efforts (or taxing noncompliers), improved recycling efforts may depend on a higher order of social responsibility on the part of middlemen, given the lack of profits.

It is possible, however, that several new types of intermediaries may emerge to facilitate recycling processes. One of these may be a reclamation or recycling center, a modernized "junk yard" placed in a convenient location for the customer, who would be paid an equitable amount for his waste goods. Initial processing of the waste materials, when they are collected, might be accomplished at these centers. In addition, central processing warehouses may be developed by existing middlemen in traditional channels, where trash can be stored and where limited processing operations on waste material may be performed.[57] Transportation costs would likely represent a major barrier to such recycling efforts, however. Other possibilities include such reverse channels as manufacturer-controlled recycling centers, joint-venture resource recovery centers, and secondary dealers.[58]

---

[57]"Tomorrow's Markets: Refuse Disposal, Trash Removal, Traffic Jam," *Sales Management*, November 10, 1969, pp. 24-26.

[58]For a discussion of these latter channels, see Joseph Guiltinan and Nonyelu Nwokoye, "Reverse Channels for Recycling: An Analysis of Alternatives and Public Policy Implications," in Ronald C. Curhan (ed.), *op. cit.*, pp. 343-344, and Zikmund and Stanton, *op. cit.*, p. 38.

THE APPLICATION OF CHANNEL CONCEPTS
TO THE MARKETING OF SERVICES
PROVIDED BY PROFIT-ORIENTED ORGANIZATIONS

Lodging Services[59]

Marketing channels associated with the lodging industry (hotels, motels, motor inns, tourist courts, etc.) are becoming increasingly complex and sophisticated, even in view of the fact that, in the United States, nearly 50 percent of the people have never stayed in a hotel, journeyed more than 200 miles from home, or travelled by plane or train.[60] While hotels throughout the world tend to be small (e.g., over 40 percent of U.S. hotels and motels are too small to have even one paid employee), there is an increasing amount of economic concentration in the lodging industry that has been due, in part, to the development of interorganizational communication systems, franchised networks, and corporate vertical marketing systems. The various channels of distribution in the lodging industry are shown in Fig. 14–9. Direct channels of distribution between hotels, motels, and other lodging operations and their customers are mainly concerned with the sales function. That is, an individual hotel's salesmen concentrate on:

1. Maintaining sales contact with channel intermediaries such as tour operators, travel agents, representatives and transportation companies.
2. Maintaining sales contact with community firms and organizations in an attempt to obtain lodging and function business.
3. Following the leads furnished by other sources.[61]

Indirect channels, however, are more significant to lodging providers than are direct channels. Intermediaries in these channels include travel agents, hotel representatives, tour operators, space brokers, airlines and the centralized reservation and sales operations of franchised or chain hotels.

---

[59]The discussion of lodging services is drawn from William H. Kaven, "Channels of Distribution in the Hotel Industry," in John M. Rathmell, *op. cit.*, pp. 114–121.

[60]*Ibid.*, p. 115.

[61]*Ibid.*, p. 116.

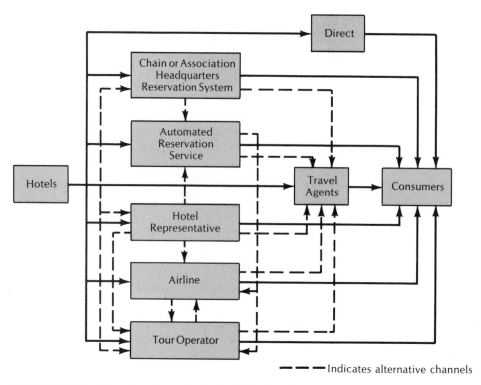

FIGURE 14-9   Marketing Channels for Lodging Services

SOURCE: William H. Kaven, "Channels of Distribution in the Hotel Industry," in *Marketing in the Service Sector*, ed. John M. Rathmell (Cambridge, Mass.: Winthrop Publishers, Inc., 1974), p. 118. Reprinted by permission of the publisher.

Travel agents may contract for rooms on a customer's behalf, but they more frequently deal through other intermediaries who hold blocks of rooms or otherwise act as agents for the hotels.

Hotel representatives act as sales and reservation agents for a number of noncompeting hotels, such as resorts.

Automated reservation services, such as American Express Space Bank, maintain for a fee in their computers an inventory of available hotel rooms from around the world so that travel agents can buy rooms for their customers.

Airlines, chiefly for overseas destinations, maintain an inventory of room availability to accommodate customers and travel agents who prefer to make complete arrangements with but one phone call for flight and room reservations.

Centralized reservation and sales operations of associated, franchised, or chain hotels/motels facilitate the flow of room availability information to potential consumers and promote, sell, and accept reservations for space.[62]

With the increased dependence of many hotel and motel operators on these intermediaries, power has shifted in the channels for lodging services. The intermediaries can maintain a wide number of alternatives and can mediate considerable rewards for lodging providers. Thus, in part as a reaction to the changing character of the power relationships, there has been a considerable movement within the industry to the formation of vertical marketing systems initiated not only by hotel and motel owners but by organizations closely connected to the industry, such as airlines. Either through contractual or ownership arrangements, these systems permit control over all channel flows, especially those associated with information processing.

Clearly, the move to vertical marketing arrangements, such as those forged by Holiday Inns and others, has been motivated by other reasons as well. As indicated in Chapter 10, such arrangements permit greater economies of scale in promotion, increased speed and economy in the flow of information, and an increased closeness to consumers when they are making their purchase decisions. The use of toll-free nationwide hotel reservation numbers, for example, has made the desired closeness to consumers a reality for many lodging organizations. In addition, these kinds of systems frequently lead to economies of scale in purchasing and operations. Most importantly, vertical systems that effectively employ interorganization management principles and techniques present to the public the image of a national or regional company of high standards with whom customers can deal with confidence.

Property and Casualty Insurance Services[63]

Although there are two main segments of the insurance industry—life and health insurance *and* property and casualty insurance—attention is focused here on the latter, because the channels are somewhat more complex

---

[62] *Ibid.*, pp. 116-117. Interorganizational linkages between airlines and travel agents are becoming highly sophisticated. TWA and American Airlines are offering their own automated reservations and ticketing equipment to travel agents with terminals linked to each airline's computerized reservations system. See "American Air, TWA To Offer Travel Agents Automated Systems," *Wall Street Journal,* February 2, 1976, p. 2.

[63] The discussion of property and casualty insurance services is drawn from Michael Etgar, *An Empirical Analysis of the Motivations for the Development of Centrally Controlled Vertical Marketing Systems: The Case of the Property and Casualty Insurance Industry,* unpublished PH.D. dissertation, University of California at Berkeley, 1974, pp. 17-20, and David L. Bickelhaupt, *General Insurance,* 9th ed. (Homewood, Ill.: Richard D. Irwin, Inc., 1974), pp. 128-130.

and dramatic changes are taking place within them. Over the past thirty years, the typical fragmented pattern of marketing property and casualty insurance—the so-called American agency system—has been consistently losing ground to centrally coordinated systems—so-called direct-writing or direct-selling systems, which now control more than a quarter of the overall property and casualty market and close to half of the automobile insurance market.[64]

Under the American agency system, insurance representatives operate under the authority given to them by insurers in forging legal transactions with the consumer of insurance. These representatives are commission-compensated "independent agents," who may and usually do represent several insurers. Independent agents sell only for insurers who are willing to permit them to retain ownership and control over policy and expiration records.[65] This means that, if an independent agent terminates his relationship with a particular insurance company, he customarily has the legal right to retain all agency records and to receive commissions on unexpired policies with the insurer in question. In such an event, the insurer does not have the right to communicate directly with the policyholder in an attempt to retain the coverage that may be expiring. Furthermore, the independent agent's accounts cannot be assigned to other agents, but he may sell to another agent his right to seek renewal of policies sold.

The historical roots of the American agency system go back to the second half of the nineteenth century. In order to serve a widely dispersed population and, at the same time, diversify their risk portfolios, insurance companies designed a distributive system that allowed them to have representatives in many population centers. The most efficient mode of distribution was through independent businessmen who represented several insurance companies. In this way, the specific risks of serving each community were spread among several insurers.[66]

The direct writing system, on the other hand, comprises a variety of different modes of distributing property and casualty insurance. In many cases, the distributor for a direct writing company has no ownership rights in renewals and represents only one company. Compensation for the representatives of a direct writing company may be in the form of commissions, salaries with bonuses, or a combination of these methods. When commissions are

---

[64] Etgar, *ibid.*, p. 17.

[65] Bickelhaupt, *op. cit.*, p. 128.

[66] James L. Athearn, *General Insurance Agency Management* (Homewood, Ill.: Richard D. Irwin, Inc., 1965), p. 10.

paid, the representatives are usually paid reduced commissions on renewed policies. The representatives are employees of the insurance company (e.g., Allstate) and not independent contractors.

Another form of the direct writing system is found in certain companies that typically develop out of an association with farm bureau organizations. These firms are represented by exclusive representatives who are independent contractors. The most prominent insurance companies that operate this way are those that belong to the State Farm Mutual Insurance Group and the Nationwide Mutual Insurance Group. The larger exclusive agency insurers have made tremendous increases in their sales of automobile insurance in the last decade and more recently are showing substantial gains in fire, homeowners, and even life and health insurance.[67]

A few insurers solicit business directly by mail. The most prominent insurance company that operates in this manner is Government Employees Insurance Company (GEICO). Although GEICO was initially established to sell insurance to employees of the Federal government, it now sells insurance to all. The applications that are received as a result of mail promotions are handled by company employees in headquarters and branch offices.

In a sense, the three modes of direct-writing distribution represent a continuum of centralized coordination and control. On one end of the spectrum is the channel that is closest in form to the independent agency —that is, distribution of property and casualty insurance by exclusive representatives who are independent contractors. In the middle, there is the commissioned employee system, and at the far end is the mail order system. The latter two are examples of corporate vertical marketing systems.

According to Bickelhaupt, the main advantage of the direct writing system is lower cost through reduced commissions or decreased expenses due to centralization of some functions, such as policy writing, records keeping, billing, training, advertising, and sales.[68] On the other hand, the American agency system offers the advantage of having a wide variety of independent entrepreneurs who provide an assortment of options, in the form of the companies they represent, to potential consumers.

Given the threat posed by the increasing trend toward contractual and corporate direct-writing marketing systems, there has been some evidence that the American agency system has begun to incorporate some features present in the former systems. Several of the largest insurance companies using independent agents (e.g., Insurance Company of North America,

[67]Bickelhaupt, op. cit., pp. 128-129.
[68]Ibid., p. 129.

Chubb Insurance Group, and Royal-Globe Group) began during the early 1970's to issue exclusive agency contracts for their regular clients.[69] In addition, billing arrangements have been routinized in a manner similar to that for direct-writing companies. On the other hand, some direct-writing insurers have granted their larger and more successful exclusive agents certain rights similar to the ownership rights that independent agents have to renewals and records. Under these agreements, the established exclusive agent, if he terminates his relationship with the insurer or retires from business, would be paid by the insurer for his book of business.[70]

In general, however, it is likely that the independent agency system is going to have to move closer to the direct-writing system (rather than vice versa) in order to remain competitive. The advantages that the latter are securing are similar to those that have been gained by vertical marketing systems in other fields.[71] There is, however, always the tradeoff between benefits of increased efficiencies in operation and the attractiveness to consumers of providing large assortments. In fact, direct-writing companies have begun to develop a wide line of "products," under different brand names, in order to serve the variety of segments in the market for insurance and thus are showing a willingness to sacrifice some of their efficiencies for even deeper market penetration.

SUMMARY AND CONCLUSIONS

In applying marketing channel concepts to the service sector, it is generally useful to adopt a broadened perspective of channel activities, because there is not always a one-to-one correspondence between the distribution of tangible products and the distribution of intangibles. Broadly conceived, distribution refers to the design, implementation, and control of institutional networks calculated to make social objects of all kinds readily *available* to the population to be served. It should be carefully noted, however, that there is often a difference between achieving availability and achieving accessibility. While certain services may be available, they may be inaccessible because of the economic and psychic costs associated with obtaining them. This latter observation is especially true for many disadvantaged consumers.

Critical decisions in assuring the availability and accessibility of services are those associated with location and determining the type of "retail" out-

---

[69] *Ibid.*, p. 130.

[70] *Ibid.*

[71] For an empirical study of the power relationships in the channel for property and casualty insurance, see Etgar, *op. cit.*

lets through which services are to be dispensed. The process involved in the creation of time and place utilities is even more important in the marketing of services than it is in the marketing of tangible products. In addition, problems in establishing marketing channels for certain services are often compounded by the need of some organizations to attract resources from groups that are different from those to whom their services are provided.

Marketing channels for services are generally very short; direct marketing (between service creator or performer and end users) is the norm. Franchising is, however, becoming an increasingly important form of channel organization in the profit-oriented service sector.

Services are also becoming more widely dispersed and decentralized, and thus the need for interorganizational cooperation and coordination has increased. In addition, redundancies, inequities, and inefficiencies are especially prevalent in the provision of many social welfare services. These deficiencies can be reduced considerably through the application of interorganization management principles. However, for the most part, the emphasis must be placed on interorganizational coordination at the "retail" level of distribution, because many services are both produced and distributed at the local level and do not involve the kind of extensive vertical networks that are found in the marketing of tangible commodities. Services do not generally pass through the hands of intermediaries. Concentrated attention must, then, be placed on developing effective combinations of the *retailing* marketing mix elements (e.g., hours of operations, facilitating services, assortments, location and facilities, expense management, promotion, and the like).

Although there are literally hundreds of service industries to which channel concepts have been or might be applied, the bulk of this chapter has been devoted to providing only seven examples. Five of the examples have been taken from the nonprofit and publicly financed service sectors; the specific illustrations include health care services, educational services, accident prevention services, population control and family planning services, and recycling services. The remaining two—lodging services and insurance services—come from the profit-oriented service sector. Similar examples could and should be developed for other service industries as well, because the process involves a rethinking of the roles of the agencies and institutions participating in the various channels and may thereby lead to a restructuring and reappraisal of the way in which a number of services are provided.[72]

---

[72] For very useful steps along this line, see Rathmell, *op. cit.*, for discussions and descriptions of air travel, regulated industries, spectator sports, commercial banking, medical care, and business services (e.g., consulting, public accounting) and Kotler, *Marketing For Nonprofit Organizations, op. cit.*, for discussions and descriptions of health services, public services, educational services, and political candidate marketing as well as case studies on planning commissions, art museums, the U.S. Army, colleges, recreation departments, mass transit, tourism, and the model cities program, among others.

DISCUSSION QUESTIONS

1. Is it appropriate to apply interorganization management concepts developed in connection with the marketing of tangible goods to the marketing of services? What are the basic differences between the marketing of goods and the marketing of services that make a transfer of concepts difficult? What concepts from interorganization management of channels appear to be most relevant to an analysis of services?

2. What is the difference between availability and accessibility? How might a health systems manager go about making health services more available? More accessible?

3. For a religious organization (church, crusade, etc.), isolate two separate distribution systems—one dealing with resource *allocation* and the other dealing with resource *attraction*. Which interorganization management concepts, if any, appear to apply to the two systems?

4. Why is it that "the process involved in the creation of time and place utilities is even more important in the marketing of services . . . than it is for the marketing of tangible commodities"?

5. Relate the discussion in Chapter 2 relative to location decisions to the marketing of services. Which aspects of the former discussion seem to be most pertinent to the marketing of services, and which appear to be least pertinent?

6. For health care delivery systems, explain the tradeoffs between the number of available product alternatives *and* search and information costs; between spatial convenience *and* seller costs.

7. Under which of the various health system structures outlined under "Health Care Services" is the consumer likely to be better off (if there is no government payment for health insurance)? Under which will the physician be better off? Which health system is likely to be most effective, over the long run? Which most efficient?

8. Explain how interorganization concepts were operating during the curriculum reform movement of the late 1950's.

9. If you were the marketing manager for the National Safety Council, what would you do to make the channel for its defensive driving concept more effective?

10. Does one set of institutions or agencies appear to be the logical locus of channel control in the distribution of population control and family planning services? If yes, what role should this set play in the channel—in other words, how could it manage the channel more effectively to achieve the goal(s) of the channel?

11. Portray, in diagram form, the specific flows (e.g., physical possession, ownership, etc.) involved in the channels for recycling services. Which institutions or agencies within these channels are likely to participate most heavily in each of the flows?

12. Analyze the role of travel agents in the marketing channels for lodging services. How much power do they have? What are the bases of their power? What types of conflicts are they likely to be involved in? Should they assume the role of channel managers?

13. According to a *Wall Street Journal* article of October 13, 1975, direct-writing agents of Sears Roebuck's Allstate Insurance Company have been attempting to form collective bargaining units. The movement to form such units resulted from what agents said was "an attempt by the company to alter its marketing strategy, bypassing the agent and, thereby, reducing the agent's income." Jim Barricks, an Allstate agent, has said that Allstate promised the agents that management would meet quarterly with agent representatives selected by the agents themselves to improve communications between the two groups. "Allstate had just lost sight of the fact that the agent is the mainstay of the company," according to Mr. Barricks.

Visit a number of Allstate agents in your local community and attempt to understand what the basic cause of the conflict seems to be. Then, develop a conflict management strategy for the Allstate system.

NAME INDEX

SUBJECT INDEX

582